THE HAGUE CHILD ABDUCTION CONVENTION

International child abduction is one of the most emotionally charged and fascinating areas of family law practice. The 1980 Hague Convention on the Civil Aspects of International Child Abduction was the response of the international community to the increase in the phenomenon of parental child abduction. However, behind the widely acclaimed success of this Convention – which has now been ratified by more than 90 states – lie personal tragedies, academic controversy and diplomatic tensions.

The continuing steady flow of case-law from the various Member-States has resulted in the emergence of different approaches to the interpretation of key concepts in the Convention. In addition, over the years other global and regional legal instruments and the recommendations of the Special Commissions have had an impact on the implementation of the Convention.

This book brings together all these strands and provides an up-to-date, clear and highly readable discussion of the international operation of the Abduction Convention together with in-depth critical academic analysis in light of the objectives of the Convention and other relevant legal norms, such as the 1989 UN Convention on the Rights of the Child. Throughout the book, examples are brought from case-law in many jurisdictions and reference is made to relevant legal and social science literature and empirical research.

Over the past decade, increasing focus has been placed on what might be seen as procedural issues, such as separate representation for children, undertakings, judicial liaison and mediation. The book analyses the significance of these developments and the extent to which they can help resolve the continuing tension between some of the objectives of the Convention and the interests of individual children.

This book will be essential reading for judges, practitioners, researchers, students, policy-makers and others who are seeking a critical and informed analysis of the latest developments in international abduction law and practice.

Volume 13 in the series Studies in Private International Law

Studies in Private International Law

Volume 1: Electronic Consumer Contracts in the Conflict of Laws
Sophia Tang

Volume 2: Foreign Currency Claims in the Conflict of Laws
Vaughan Black

Volume 3: Jurisdiction and Judgments in Relation to EU Competition Law Claims
Mihail Danov

Volume 4: Cases and Materials on EU Private International Law
Stefania Bariatti

Volume 5: International Commercial Disputes: Commercial Conflict of Laws in English Courts
Jonathan Hill and Adeline Chong

Volume 6: International Child Abduction: The Inadequacies of the Law
Thalia Kruger

Volume 7: Mediating International Child Abduction Cases
Sarah Vigers

Volume 8: International Antitrust Litigation: Conflict of Laws and Coordination
Edited by Jürgen Basedow, Stéphanie Francq and Laurence Idot

Volume 9: The Governing Law of Companies in EU Law
Justin Borg-Barthet

Volume 10: Intellectual Property and Private International Law: Comparative Perspectives
Edited by Toshiyuki Kono

Volume 11: Child Abduction within the European Union
Katarina Trimmings

Volume 12: International Surrogacy Arrangements: Legal Regulation at the International Level
Edited by Katarina Trimmings and Paul Beaumont

The Hague Child Abduction Convention

A Critical Analysis

Rhona Schuz

HART PUBLISHING

OXFORD AND PORTLAND, OREGON

2013

Published in the United Kingdom by Hart Publishing Ltd
16C Worcester Place, Oxford, OX1 2JW
Telephone: +44 (0)1865 517530
Fax: +44 (0)1865 510710
E-mail: mail@hartpub.co.uk
Website: http://www.hartpub.co.uk

Published in North America (US and Canada) by
Hart Publishing
c/o International Specialized Book Services
920 NE 58th Avenue, Suite 300
Portland, OR 97213-3786
USA
Tel: +1 503 287 3093 or toll-free: (1) 800 944 6190
Fax: +1 503 280 8832
E-mail: orders@isbs.com
Website: http://www.isbs.com

© Rhona Schuz 2013

Rhona Schuz has asserted her right under the Copyright, Designs and Patents Act 1988,
to be identified as the author of this work.

All rights reserved. No part of this publication may be reproduced, stored in a retrieval system, or transmitted,
in any form or by any means, without the prior permission of Hart Publishing, or as expressly permitted
by law or under the terms agreed with the appropriate reprographic rights organisation.
Enquiries concerning reproduction which may not be covered by the above should be addressed to
Hart Publishing Ltd at the address above.

British Library Cataloguing in Publication Data
Data Available

ISBN: 978-1-84946-017-0

Typeset by Hope Services, Abingdon
Printed and bound in Great Britain by
TJ International Ltd, Padstow, Cornwall

This book is dedicated to my parents, Sheila and Danny Levitt

SERIES EDITORS' PREFACE

This is the fourth volume in the Studies in Private International Law Series on the subject of child abduction. This reflects the profound importance of the subject. Each book offers a diverse approach and perspective on the subject. In this book, Rhona Schuz brings two decades of careful study of, and academic writings on the subject matter of child abduction to the table. This enables her to produce this mature and sophisticated overview of the current interpretation of the main provisions of the Hague Child Abduction Convention in a global context (Articles 3, 12, 13 and 20). This complements the other books on child abduction in the series, which focus on particular aspects of the Convention and its application: Thalia Kruger contributes to the sociological understanding of the phenomenon of child abduction by her careful empirical analysis of the stories of the people involved in international abductions to and from Belgium in a particular year; Sarah Vigers puts forward a coherent thesis as to why and how mediation should be available much more often in international child abduction cases; and Katarina Trimmings combines empirical research on the early operation of the EU Brussels IIa Regulation on intra-EU child abductions with analytical work on some of the key provisions of the Hague Convention as they are affected in intra-EU cases by the Brussels IIa Regulation (a subject that is complementary to, but largely not covered by, Schuz's book). Schuz is able to draw heavily on Vigers' book in her short chapter on mediation while indicating where she would take a different approach and to make full use of the book by Kruger in her chapter on inter-disciplinary aspects of international child abduction.

Schuz refers extensively throughout the book to the first monograph in English on the Hague Child Abduction Convention (P Beaumont and P McEleavy, *The Hague Convention on International Child Abduction* (Oxford University Press, 1999)). She relies on that book's detailed research into the history of the negotiations of the Convention and pays careful attention to many of the suggestions in that book as to how the Convention should be interpreted based on a critical analysis of the then existing case law in many of the leading countries that were then party to the Convention (Australia, Canada, France, Ireland, New Zealand, UK and USA). Schuz updates the analysis of the case law in all these countries (except France) on all the key provisions in the Convention (habitual residence, custody rights, wrongful removal and retention (Article 3), consent and acquiescence, grave risk of harm, child's objections to return (Article 13), human rights (Article 20) and settled in the new environment (Article 12)), making use of the International Child Abduction Database ('INCADAT') to cover some other countries and of her expertise in Israeli law to cover its case law in depth. Schuz does not attempt a comprehensive analysis of the case law: this is now an impossible task given the huge volume of case law on the Convention. Rather, she produces a well thought through distillation of many, if not all, of the key problems raised in the case law as to the correct interpretation of these core provisions of the Convention. The book also covers some subjects not treated at length in Beaumont and McEleavy, which reflect recent concerns of scholarship in this area. There are thoughtful chapters on: relocation; on how the child's views should be ascertained in Convention cases; on whether children should routinely be separately represented in child abduction cases; on mediation; and on compensating the left-behind parent.

The truly innovative part of the book is the attempt by the author to identify 'parameters for analysis' of the case law on the interpretation of the key provisions in the Convention and then to apply those parameters to the case law on those provisions and identify recommendations for the correct interpretation of the provisions. These parameters are: internal coherence of the Convention; consistency with the intention of the drafters; promotion of the objectives of the Convention; compatibility with the summary nature of Convention proceedings; consistency with the rights and interests of children; consistency with the rights of parents; private international law principles (eg comity) and certainty versus flexibility. The author adopts a balanced and pragmatic perspective and her recommendations are persuasive.

Schuz does not shy away from difficult legal and policy considerations. For instance, her strong defence of the rights of the child leads her to assert that 'returning children in situations where this will cause them real harm is also inconsistent with the purpose of the Convention and is in effect also non-compliance therewith'. (437). She is surely right to say that 'the policy of the Abduction Convention should be seen as including the policy behind the exceptions and not only that behind the return mechanism'. (438). It is highly likely that some harm will be done to a child by whichever decision the judge takes – to return or not to return. The exception in Article 13(1)(b) is designed to avoid a 'grave risk of harm' that equates to an 'intolerable situation'. Perhaps the true policy of the Convention for judges in an Article 13(1)(b) case is to uphold the return of the child to the country of his or her habitual residence for the purpose of deciding the custody dispute between the parents unless the return of the child is highly likely to cause him or her such harm that it would be equivalent to placing the child in an intolerable situation. Even this statement needs to be qualified because one of the key policies lying behind the Convention is for the administrative cooperation (led by the Central Authorities) to work in conjunction with the judicial authorities to reduce the risk of a return causing an intolerable situation for a child by a whole variety of processes. These processes include undertakings and mirror orders that are granted or supervised by the courts (which are carefully analysed in the book), as well as the very important (but often rather neglected or perfunctorily performed) duty on Central Authorities in both countries to 'take all appropriate measures to provide such administrative arrangements as may be necessary and appropriate to secure the safe return of the child' (Article 7(h)). The Convention is not just a Convention on international judicial co-operation but crucially it is also one on international administrative co-operation and much work still needs to be done to push the Governments of Contracting States to invest enough money in the Central Authorities and in the processes needed for the safe return of a child. The combination of best practice by the judicial and administrative bodies should, in the vast majority of cases, reduce to an acceptable level the risk of harm being caused to a child by being returned to the country of his or her habitual residence prior to the abduction. However, in the absence of such best practice being available or enforceable, judges may more often assess the risk of return of the child to the country of his or her habitual residence as being too likely to place the child in an intolerable situation, particularly in cases of domestic violence.

With the possibility of a Protocol to the Child Abduction Convention off the agenda for the foreseeable future, Rhona Schuz focuses on how improvements can be made to the operation of the Convention by good, consistent judicial interpretation of its key provisions.

She helpfully summarises all her recommendations in the final chapter, although we encourage readers to take the time to read the detailed analysis in each chapter that underpins these carefully compiled conclusions. The opportunity exists to influence the work in the Hague Conference to continue developing and refining their best practice guides for the Convention, particularly the current work on Article 13(1)(b) with particular reference to cases involving domestic violence.

The book is an extremely important contribution to the interpretation of one of the most successful private international law conventions in history. The author has already secured the endorsement in the foreword to this book of Baroness Hale, Deputy President of the UK Supreme Court and widely acknowledged academic expert in family law. Rhona Schuz's book should be read by all lawyers working in the field of child abduction. Practitioners will find it a rich source for arguments to be canvassed in cases, academics will enjoy the subtle and careful attempts at balancing the many parameters that the author identifies, and judges will be challenged to articulate their judgments with more thought to achieving nuanced policy objectives and consistent global interpretation of the Convention.

Paul Beaumont (University of Aberdeen)
Jonathan Harris (King's College, London)

FOREWORD

The 1980 Convention on the Civil Aspects of International Child Abduction is said to be the most successful of the family law products of the Hague Conference on Private International Law. The picture which emerges from this comprehensive and fascinating book is one of mixed success and disappointment.

Judged by the number of States party to it, currently 88, it can indeed be held a success. Judged by the number of applications made under it, reportedly 1961 (to 54 of the Member States) in 2008, success is harder to gauge. It is difficult to believe that this is anything other than a small proportion of the cases in which children have been taken from their home country to another, or kept away from their home country, without lawful authority. Judged by the success rate of those applications which are made, some 46 per cent overall, it also does not look so good, unless you deduct the 18 per cent which were withdrawn, the eight per cent still pending, and the five per cent rejected by the Central Authorities because they did not meet the criteria. Judged by the courts' refusal rate, then, which was only 15 per cent, the picture begins to look quite successful again. Judged by the speed of decision-making in what is meant to be a swift and summary procedure, however, a mean duration of 188 days (just over six months) does not look so good. More troubling still are the wide disparities between the Member States in both the rate of return and the speed of their decisions. Moreover, as Dr Schuz shows throughout the book, this suggests that there are real differences between the Member States in their interpretation and application of the Convention. One of her aims is to promote greater uniformity in the way in which the Convention is interpreted and applied.

This book is, as far as I am aware, the first scholarly monograph to study the interpretation and application of the Convention across the whole legal space which it occupies and critically to assess these in light of the object and purposes of the Convention and other relevant legal norms. Cases are drawn from many jurisdictions to discuss how different countries interpret the Convention and links are made with relevant statistical, social and psychological research in a thoughtful discussion of the significance of such material both to judicial decision-making and to policy development.

Crucially, of course, it is now well known that the paradigm has shifted. The framers of the Convention had in mind the parent who had either already lost custody or feared doing so and snatched the child away from her rightful home. Obviously, the right answer was to get her back home as quickly as possible. Gender did not come into it. But now 69 per cent of abductors are mothers and 73 per cent are sole or joint primary carers. In most cases, then, the child is not being separated from a parent who looks after her, although she will be separated from the other parent and from her home and familiar surroundings. There is also reason to believe, albeit from some smaller qualitative studies, that domestic violence and the abuse of children are among the most common reasons for abduction. In such cases, the right answer from the child's point of view does not look quite so obvious.

There is also a gender aspect to this new paradigm which was not there before. Only 13 per cent of mother abductors are non-primary carers, while 65 per cent of father abductors are non-primary carers and thus fit the original paradigm more closely. So there is room for arguments about gender bias on both sides. If a child who has been abducted by her primary carer (usually the mother) is sent back home, the mother may argue that the child's best interests are being sacrificed to the less powerful claims of the parent left behind, especially if there is a risk of domestic violence or abuse. But if the child is not sent home, the left-behind parent (usually the father) may argue that both his and the child's right to a continuing relationship are being sacrificed to the selfishness of the primary carer.

Legal developments since the Convention was drafted have sharpened this debate. The framers drew a clear distinction between rights of custody, which were to be protected by speedy return in all but exceptional cases, and rights of access, which were to be enforced by other arrangements between the States, if at all. However, in many Member States this distinction has been blurred, because the right to prohibit travel abroad, which may be possessed by a court as well as by a parent, is (quite understandably) interpreted as a right of custody. And in many Member States, no distinction is now drawn between the rights of married and unmarried fathers. This means that the Convention is often being used to enforce rights of access rather than rights of custody in the original sense. This may be a good thing, but it is not what the drafters had in mind.

Added to this is the increasing recognition of the prevalence and seriousness of domestic violence and the harm which this can do to the children who see or hear it. This poses very serious problems for decision-makers. It was not the object of the Convention to return children to a situation which would expose them to harm, but there are obviously questions of degree here. Worse still are the problems of proof. How is the court in the country to which the child has been taken to assess the truth of the allegations made, when the whole point of the process is that the left-behind parent should not have to travel from the home country in order to get his child back? Not surprisingly, some courts concentrate on how the child can be protected in the home country. Equally unsurprisingly, others are sceptical about how effective those protective measures can be.

Another shift which has taken place since the Convention was framed is the greater respect shown, not just for the best interests of the child, but also for her views. Since the 1989 United Nations Convention on the Rights of the Child, children have increasingly been seen, not as parcels to be posted about the world, but as actors in the drama of their own lives, with views which are also worthy of respect.

The author's main message is that the primary objective of the Convention was to protect both individual children and children in general from harm. The Convention should not be used as an instrument for doing harm to an individual child, even for the sake of setting a good example to other would-be child abductors. 'The notion that the interests of an individual child may be sacrificed on the altar of the collective benefit of the whole community of children is morally indefensible.'

That conclusion is only reached after detailed scholarly analysis of the Convention, its purposes, interpretation and application, in a study which deserves to be read by anyone with an interest in the modern phenomenon of international child abduction, whether judge, practitioner, policy-maker, parent, researcher or scholar. There is plenty for us all to think about.

Brenda Hale
Justice of the Supreme Court of the United Kingdom
27 March 2013

ACKNOWLEDGMENTS

Over the years, in the course of my research on various aspects of international child abduction, I have been provided with materials and insights by fellow academics, judges, practitioners and students. Although I cannot refer to all of them by name, I am grateful to each and every one. I would, however, like to make specific mention of some of those who have been of particular assistance to me in preparing this book.

Firstly, I am most grateful to colleagues who took the time to read and comment on draft chapters: Dr Ayelet Blecher-Prigat, Prof Ann Estin, Dr Ruth Lamont, Barrister Jacqueline Renton, Dr Yael Ronen, Dr. Sharon Shakargy, Dr Andrea Schulz (Director of the German Central Authority for International Custody Conflicts) and Prof Merle Weiner (listed in alphabetical order). Any errors in the text are of course my sole responsibility.

I would also like to express particular thanks to Justice Belinda Heerden of the South African Supreme Court, Chief Justice Peter Boshier of the New Zealand Family Court, and Anna Claudia Alfieri of the Private Law Division of the Swiss Department of Justice for sending me information and providing clarification about specific aspects of the operation of the Convention in their countries. In addition, I am grateful to Adv Leslie Kaufman and Adv Regina Tapuchi of the Israeli Central Authority for answering my questions over the years.

I thank the research assistants who have participated in my child abduction research at various times and in particular Gal Meshulam and Binyamin Arnowitz for their tireless work in editing the footnotes and checking the references in the book. I gratefully acknowledge the funding provided by the research funds of the Sha'arei Mishpat Law School and Bar Ilan University Law Faculty. I would also like to thank the librarians at these two law schools for their help in obtaining materials and the staff of the Permanent Bureau of the Hague Conference on Private International Law for sending me documents not available on their website.

I am most grateful to Lady Hale of the UK Supreme Court for kindly agreeing to write a foreword to the book. My thanks are also due to the staff at Hart Publishing for their helpfulness and efforts during the publication process.

On a personal note, I deeply appreciate the loving support and encouragement of my husband, children and parents.

Finally, I must express my gratitude to the Creator of the world for giving me the strength and ability to complete this project.

Rhona Schuz, 2013

CONTENTS

Series Editors' Preface   vii
Foreword   xi
Acknowledgements   xiii
Table of Cases   xxiii
Table of Legislation   xlv
Table of Conventions, Treaties, etc   li

Introduction   1

Part I – Overview   5

1. The Birth of the Abduction Convention and its Inter-Relationship with Other Legal Instruments   7
   I   The Birth of the Abduction Convention   7
      A Background   7
      B The Structure of the Abduction Convention   9
      C Ratification and Accessions   12
   II Inter-Relationship with Other Legal Instruments   14
      A National Legislation   14
      B The European Custody Convention   17
      C Brussels II bis Regulation   19
      D European Convention on Human Rights   25
      E The 1996 Hague Child Protection Convention   29
      F United Nations Convention on the Rights of the Child 1989   33

2. The Operation of the Abduction Convention   35
   I   Sources of Information and Statistics   35
      A Introduction   35
      B The Empirical Studies   35
      C Statistics   36
   II Institutions and other Actors Involved in the Operation of the Convention   38
      A Central Authorities   38
      B Judicial and Law Enforcement Authorities   39
      C Lawyers   39
      D The Permanent Bureau   40
   III The Abduction Convention Process   43
      A The Application   43
      B Locating the Child   43
      C Protecting the Child   44

		D	Voluntary Return	44
		E	Commencing Proceedings	45
		F	Conduct of the Proceedings	46
		G	Ensuring Safe Return	46
		H	Enforcement of Return Orders	47
	IV	After Return		50
		A	Obtaining Information	50
		B	The Surveys	51

3. Inter-Disciplinary Aspects of International Child Abduction — 54
  I Sociological Aspects — 54
     A Introduction — 54
     B Which Parents Abduct and Why — 55
     C Gender Issues — 58
  II Psychological Aspects of Abduction — 61
     A Introduction — 61
     B The Impact of Moving — 63
     C The Impact of Abduction — 64
     D The Impact of a Move Away from a Primary Carer — 65
     E The Impact of a Move Away from a Non-Primary Carer — 67
     F Parental Alienation — 69

4. International Relocation and its Inter-Relationship with Child Abduction — 71
  I   Introduction — 71
  II Relocation Law — 72
      A The Different Approaches — 72
      B Empirical Evidence — 77
      C Scholarly Analysis — 79
      D International Harmonisation Initiatives — 82
  III Inter-Relationship between Child Abduction and Relocation — 84
      A The Implications of Abduction Law for Relocation Law — 84
      B The Implications of Relocation Law and Research for Abduction Law — 86

Part II – Parameters for Analysis — 91

5. Parameters Relating to Text and Objectives — 93
  I   Introduction — 93
  II Explanation of the Parameters — 94
      A Internal Coherence — 94
      B Consistency with the Intention of the Drafters — 94
      C Promotion of the Objectives of the Convention — 96
      D Compatibility with the Summary Nature of Convention Proceedings — 106

6. Consistency with General Legal Doctrines — 108
  I   Introduction — 108
  II Rights and Interests of Children — 109

	A	Children's Rights and the Abduction Convention	109
	B	The Best Interests of the Child and Article 3 of the CRC	111
	C	The Child's Participation Rights and Article 12 of the CRC	113
	D	The Child's Right to Protection and to Survival and Development	118
	E	The Child's Right to Contact with his Parents	118
	F	The Child's Right to Identity	121
III	Rights of Parents		121
	A	Introduction	121
	B	The Status of Parental Rights	122
	C	The Scope of Parental Rights	123
	D	Conflicts between Children's Rights and Parental Rights	124
IV	Private International Law Principles		126
	A	The Abduction Convention and Private International Law	126
	B	Jurisdiction Rules	127
	C	Choice of Law Rules	128
	D	Rules for Recognition of Foreign Judgments	129
	E	Comity of Nations	132
V	Certainty versus Flexibility		136

Part III – Conditions for Application of Mandatory Return Mechanism   139

7. Wrongful Removal or Retention   141

I	Introduction		141
II	Removal or Retention		142
	A	Relationship between the Concepts	142
	B	Identifying the Date of the Wrongful Retention	142
	C	Analysis in Relation to the Concept of Retention	144
III	Rights of Custody		146
	A	Introduction	146
	B	Local Law versus Autonomous Definition	147
	C	*Ne Exeat* Rights	148
	D	Unmarried Fathers	151
	E	Article 15 Declarations	154
	F	Actual Exercise of Custody Rights	156
IV	Analysis in Relation to Breach and Exercise of Custody Rights		157
	A	Internal Coherence	157
	B	Intention of the Drafters	159
	C	Promotion of the Objectives of the Convention	161
	D	Compatibility with the Summary Nature of Convention Proceedings	165
	E	Consistency with Rights and Interests of Children	166
	F	Consistency with Rights of the Parents	167
	G	Consistency with Private International Law Principles	169
	H	Certainty versus Flexibility	173
V	Conclusions		173

8. Habitual Residence — 175

- I Introduction — 175
  - A Structure of the Chapter — 175
  - B Origin of the Concept of Habitual Residence — 175
  - C Use of Habitual Residence in Relation to Children — 176
  - D Does a Person have a Single Habitual Residence at all Times? — 178
  - E Nature of the Determination of Habitual Residence — 179
- II Role of Habitual Residence in the Abduction Convention — 180
  - A In Determining the Applicability of the Convention — 180
  - B In Determining Whether the Removal or Retention was Wrongful — 182
  - C As the Place to Where the Child is Returned — 182
- III The Different Models — 186
  - A The Parental Intention Model — 186
  - B The Independent/Child-Centred Model — 189
  - C The Combined/Hybrid Model — 192
- IV Illustrating the Different Models — 195
  - A Permanent Relocations — 195
  - B Fixed Term Relocations — 197
  - C Relocations for an Indefinite Period — 198
  - D Shuttle Custody Arrangements — 200
  - E Newborn Child — 201
  - F Re-Abduction — 203
- V Analysis — 204
  - A Internal Coherence — 204
  - B Consistency with the Intention of the Drafters — 206
  - C Promotion of the Objectives of the Convention — 207
  - D Compatibility with the Summary Nature of Convention Proceedings — 211
  - E Consistency with Rights and Interests of Children — 212
  - F Consistency with Rights of the Parents — 213
  - G Consistency with Matrimonial Law — 215
  - H Consistency with Contract Law — 216
  - I Certainty versus Flexibility — 218
- VI Conclusions — 220

Part IV – Defences to Mandatory Return — 223

9. Article 12(2) — 225

- I Introduction — 225
- II The Case Law — 226
  - A Expiration of the 12-Month Period — 226
  - B The Child is Settled in his New Environment — 228
  - C Discretion to Order Return — 233
- III Analysis — 236
  - A Internal Coherence — 236
  - B Consistency with the Intention of the Drafters — 237

		C Promotion of the Objectives of the Convention	237
		D Compatibility with the Summary Nature of Convention Proceedings	242
		E Consistency with Rights and Interests of Children	242
		F Consistency with Private International Law Principles	243
		G Certainty versus Flexibility	243
	IV	Conclusions	244

10. Consent and Acquiescence — 245

	I	Introduction	245
	II	Normative Framework	247
		A Content of Acquiescence or Consent	247
		B Subjective or Objective Test	248
		C Ignorance of Rights	249
		D Need for Reliance	250
		E Irrevocability	251
	III	Specific Situations	252
		A Vitiating Factors	252
		B Statements Made During Negotiations	252
		C Advance Consent	253
		D Statements Made in Immediate Aftermath of the Removal or Retention	254
		E Pursuance of Other Remedies	255
		F Actions for the Benefit of the Children	255
		G Inaction	256
		H Acquiescence Following Initiation of Proceedings	256
	IV	Exercise of Discretion	257
		A The Nature of the Discretion	257
		B The Relevant Factors	258
	V	Analysis	261
		A Internal Coherence	261
		B Consistency with the Intention of the Drafters	262
		C Promotion of the Objectives of the Convention	263
		D Compatibility with the Summary Nature of Convention Proceedings	265
		E Consistency with Rights and Interests of Children	265
		F Consistency with Principles of Private International Law	266
		G Consistency with Contract Law	267
		H Certainty versus Flexibility	268
	VI	Conclusions	268

11. Grave Risk of Harm — 270

	I	Introduction	270
		A The Dilemma	270
		B Scope of the Investigation	271
	II	Interpretation and Application of the Grave Risk Defence	273
		A General	273
		B Specific Situations	277

xx Contents

III Protective Measures	289
A Introduction	289
B Undertakings	291
C Ensuring Enforceability of Undertakings/Conditions	294
D Judicial Liaison	296
IV Analysis	298
A Internal Coherence	298
B Consistency with the Intention of the Drafters	300
C Promotion of the Objectives of the Convention	301
D Compatibility with the Summary Nature of Convention Proceedings	305
E Consistency with Rights and Interests of Children	306
F Consistency with Rights of the Parents	311
G Consistency with Private International Law Principles	312
H Consistency with Domestic Abuse Policy	314
I Certainty versus Flexibility	314
V Conclusions	315

12. Child's Objection — 317

I Introduction	317
A The Dilemma	317
B The Scope of the Court's Discretion	319
II Interpretation and Application of Article 13(2)	323
A Age and Maturity	323
B The Child's Objections	327
C Considerations Relevant to the Court's Exercise of its Discretion	336
III Analysis	343
A Internal Coherence	343
B Consistency with the Intention of the Drafters	344
C Promotion of the Objectives of the Convention	345
D Compatibility with the Summary Nature of Proceedings	348
E Consistency with Rights and Interests of Children	348
F Consistency with Private International Law Principles	349
G Certainty versus Flexibility	349
IV Conclusions	351

13. Violation of Fundamental Human Rights and Freedoms — 354

I Introduction	354
II The Case Law	355
A Claims Based on Inconsistency with the Best Interests of the Child	355
B Claims Based on Lack of Due Process in the Requesting State	358
C Claims Based on Right to Freedom of Movement	360
III Analysis	361
A Internal Coherence	361
B Consistency with the Intention of the Drafters	362
C Promotion of the Objectives of the Convention	363

		D Compatibility with the Summary Nature of Convention Proceedings	365
		E Consistency with Rights and Interests of Children	365
		F Consistency with Rights of the Parents	366
		G Consistency with Private International Law Principles	368
		H Certainty versus Flexibility	368
	IV	Conclusions	369

Part V: The Voice of the Child 371

14. Ascertaining the Child's Views 373

	I	Requirement to Ascertain the Child's Views	373
	II	Method of Ascertaining the Child's Views in Abduction Convention Cases	375
		A Introduction	375
		B Specific Jurisdictions	376
	III	Analysis	380
		A Arguments in Favour of Judges Hearing Children Directly	380
		B Arguments against Judges Hearing Children Directly	384
		C Making Participation Meaningful	386
	IV	Conclusions	387

15. Status of the Child in Abduction Convention Proceedings 389

	I	Introduction	389
	II	The Child's Right to Separate Representation	391
		A The Source of the Right	391
		B The Scope of the Right	392
	III	Separate Representation in Abduction Convention Cases	396
		A The Arguments Against	396
		B The Arguments in Favour	399
	IV	Application by the Child	403
		A The Legal Provisions	403
		B The Need for Provision for Application by Children	404
	V	Conclusions	405

Part VI: Related Proceedings and Processes 407

16. Mediation 409

	I	Introduction	409
	II	Advantages of Mediation	410
	III	Problems and Solutions	412
		A International Nature	412
		B Delay	412
		C Enforceability	413
		D The Voice of the Child	414
		E Domestic Violence	415
	IV	Conclusions	416

17. Compensating the Left-Behind Parent — 417
   I   Introduction — 417
   II   To What Extent is Compensation Appropriate? — 417
       A   Arguments in Favour of Compensation — 417
       B   Arguments against Compensation — 418
   III   Analysis of the Various Models — 419
       A   The Tort Model — 419
       B   The Criminal Model — 419
       C   The Abduction Convention Model — 420
   IV   Conclusions — 422

18. Enforcing Rights of Access — 423
   I   Introduction — 423
   II   Article 21 of the Abduction Convention — 424
       A   Interpretation and Application of Article 21 — 424
       B   Analysis — 426
   III   Other International Instruments — 430
       A   The 1980 European Custody Convention — 430
       B   The 1996 Hague Convention on the Protection of Children — 430
       C   The 2003 European Convention on Contact Concerning Children — 431
       D   The Brussels II bis Regulation — 431
   IV   Conclusions — 432

Part VII: The Way Ahead — 435

19. Conclusions and Recommendations — 437
   I   Introduction — 437
   II   Significance of the Developments Since 1980 — 437
       A   Children's Rights — 437
       B   Primary Carer Abductions — 439
       C   The Call for a Protocol — 441
   III   Conclusions — 442
       A   Hierarchy of Objectives — 442
       B   Recommendations in Relation to the Interpretation and Application of the Abduction Convention — 444
       C   Recommendations Concerning other Aspects of Implementation of the Abduction Convention — 447

Appendix – Hague Convention on the Civil Aspects of International Child Abduction — 451

Index — 461

TABLE OF CASES

Argentina

Altheim v Altheim (decision of 5 October 2011) 280

Australia

Central Authority v Maynard (Unreported, FamCA, Melbourne, 3 September 2003) 274
Commissioner, Western Australia Police v Dormann (1997) FLC 92–766 249
Cooper v Casey, No EA102 of 1994, slip op (FamCA, 5 May 1995), (1995)
    FLC 92–575 .... 179, 191, 202, 272
Craven v Craven (1976) FLC 90–049 74
D & SV (2003) FLC 93–137 74
D–G, Dept of Child Safety v Stratford [2005] CA 1115 246–247
D–G, Dept of Child Safety & Milson [2008] FamCA 872 .... 317, 327–328, 335, 337
D–G, Dept of Community Services v Apostolakis (1996) FLC 92–718 229
D–G, Dept of Community Services v De Lewinski (1996) FLC 674 327
D–G, Dept of Community Services v M and C and the Child Representative [1998]
    FLC 92–829 230
D–G, Dept of Community Services & Bindle [2009] FamCA 122 .... 252, 259, 265
D–G, Dept of Families & RSP [2003] FamCA 623 .... 273, 284
D–G Dept of Families, Youth and Community Care v Moore (1999) FLC 92–841 ...... 226, 238
D–G, Dept of Families, Youth and Community Care v Reissner [1999]
    FamCA 1238 425–426
D–G, Dept of Families, Youth and Community Care v Thorpe (1997)
    FLC 92–785 .... 228–229, 238
DG v Davis (1990) FLC 92–182 209
DP v Commonwealth Central Authority (2001) 180 ALR 402 .... 133, 273–274, 290, 298
DT v LBT [2010] EWHC 3177 (Fam) 272
DW & D–G, Dept of Child Safety [2006] FamCA 9 215
De L v D–G, NSW Dept of Community Service [1996] 20 Fam LR 390 288
De L v D–G, NSW Dept of Community Services (1996) FLC 92–674 322
De L v D–G, NSW Dept of Community Services (1996) FLC 92–706 .... 287, 397–398
De Lewinski [1997] 21 Fam LR 41 288
*De Lewinski and Legal Aid Commission of New South Wales v D–G, NSW Dept of
    Community Services* (1997) FLC 92–737 .... 191, 392
*Eldon Matthews (Barry)(Commissioner, Western Australia Police Service) v Ziba
    Sabaghian* (2001) PT 1767 249

Emmett and Perry and D–G Dept of Family Services and Aboriginal and Islander Affairs Central Authority and Attorney–General of the Commonwealth of Australia (Intervener) (1996) FLC 92–645 ....289, 356
Genish–Grant (Janine Claire) and D–G Dept of Community Services [2002] FamCA 346..279
Godfrey v Saunders [2007] FamCA 102 76
Graziano v Daniels (1991) 14 Fam LR 697...230, 232
Hanbury–Brown (Stephanie Selina) (Appellant/Wife) and Robert Hanbury–Brown (Respondent/Husband), In the Marriage of v D–G of Community Services (Central Authority) (1996) FLC 92–671 ....178, 181–183
Harries v Harries [2011] FamCAFC 113...284
Harris & Harris [2010] FamCAFC 22...303, 315
JLM v D–G, NSW Dept of Community Services [2001] HCA 39........................273, 284, 290, 293, 298–299, 343
Kilah v D–G, Dept of Community Services (2008) Fam CAFC 81..............251, 257, 259–260
L v D–G, NSW Dept of Community Services (1996) FLC 92–706....................................328
LK v D–G, Dept of Community Services [2009] HCA 9, (2009) 253 ALR 202 .... 178, 193, 262, 265
MRR v GR [2010] HCA 4 76
McCall and McCall: State Central Authority (1995) FLC 92–551 ....146, 306
McOwan and McOwan [1994] FLC 92–451 293
Murray v Director, Family Services (1993) FLC 92–416.. 135, 272, 283, 306–308, 312, 363
Patterson, DHCS v Casse (1995) FLC 92–629 ....191, 195
Police Commissioner of South Australia v Temple (1993) FLC 92–365...................156, 323
Police Commissioner of South Australia v Temple (No 2) (1993) FLRC 92–424 291
Resina, In the Marriage of [1991] FamCA 33.. 155–156
Richards & D–G, Dept of Child Safety [2007] FamCA 65 328
Secretary, Attorney–General's Dept v TS (2001) FLC 93–063 ....152, 232
Secretary, Attorney–General's Dept and TS [2000] FamCA 1692................................226, 232
Secretary, Dept of Human Services v Mander [2003] FamCA 1128........................272, 284
Secretary, Dept of Human Services State Central Authority v CR (2005) 34 Fam LR 354 ....226, 232
Sheldon & Weir (Stay Application) [2011] FamCAFC 5..86
State Central Authority v Ayob (1997) FLC 92–746 ....227, 234
State Central Authority v Best (No 2) [2012] FamCA 511 .... 391, 400, 402, 405
State Central Authority v CR [2005] FamCA 1050 ....227, 234
State Central Authority v McCall (1995) FLC 92–552 356
State Central Authority v Papastravrou [2008] FamCA 1120.................................299, 343
State Central Authority v Peddar [2008] FamCA 519.. 424–426
State Central Authority v Young [2012] FamCA 563..400
State Central Authority of Victoria v Ardito, 29 October 1997, FamCA (Unreported)...289, 358
Townsend v D–G Dept of Families, Youth and Community [1999] 24 Fam LR 495....230, 258
U v U (2002) 211 CLR 238 ....81, 85
Western Australian Police v Dorman (1997) FLC 92–766..328
Wolfe & D–G, Dept of Human Services [2011] FamCAFC 42 ....339, 342

Wood Russell v Wood- Hosig, Maya Aug. 24, 2006 44
Zotkiewicz & Commissioner of Police (No 2) [2011] FamCAFC 147..................211–212, 214

Austria

OGH (7 Ob 573/90), 17 May 1990...232
OGH (2 Ob 596.91), 2 May 2 1992 163
OGH (8 Ob 121/03g), 30 October 2003 ....156, 192

Canada

Droit de la Famille 2785, No 500–09–005532–973, Cour d'appel de Montréal,
   5 December 1997 242
Droit de la famille 3713, No 500–09–010031–003 196
FC v PA, Droit de la famille – 08728, No 150–04–004667–072, Cour Supérieure de
   Chicoutimi, 28 March 2008 246
Gordon v Goertz [1996] 2 SCR 27...75
Innes v Innes 2005 BCC LEXIS 1425 324
JEA v CLM (2002) 220 DLR (4th) 577 (NSCA) 230–231, 233, 240
Jabbaz v Mouammar (2003) 226 DLR (4th) 494 (Ont CA)..289
MBGA v RVM, No 500–09–014099–048 (500–04–034363–037), Cour d'appel du
   Québec, 8 June 2004 225
MG v RF [2002] RJQ 2132 (Quebec)..280
Medhurst v Markle (1995) 26 OR (3d) 178 (Gen Div)...292
NP v ABP [1999] RDF 38 (Que CA)..281
Parsons v Styger (1989) 67 OR (2d) 1 (LJSC), aff'd (1989) 67 OR (2d) 11 (CA) 360
SS–C v GC [2003] RDF 845 (SC)...178
Stav v Stav 2012 BCCA 154 (BCCA)..59, 75, 81
Suarez v Carranza (2008) 2008 CarswellBC 1829, 2008 BCSC 1187...........................292
Thomson v Thomson (1994) 3 SCR 551 .... 158, 168, 274, 276, 292, 300
Tolofson v Jensen (1992) 89 DLR (4th) 129...128
VBM v DLJ 2004 NLCA 56..228
Wilson v Huntley (2005) ACWSJ 7084, [2005] 138 ACWS (3d) 1107
   (Can Ont Sup CT J) 96, 98, 201, 210, 218
YD v JB [1996] RDF 753 (Que CA) 296, 360

Court of Justice of the European Union

A, In Proceedings brought by (Case C–523/07) [2009] ECR 1– 2805...........................194
McB v LE (Case C–400/10 PPU) [2010] ECR I–8965 ....150, 168, 173
Zarraga (Case C–491/10 PPU) [2010] ECR I–14247...387

Denmark

ØLK, 5 April 2002, 16. afdeling, B–409–02 198
VLK, 11 January 2002, 13. afdeling, B–2939–01 279

European Court of Human Rights

B v Belgium, App no 4320/11, 10 July 2012 27
Bianchi v Switzerland, App no 7548/04, 22 June 2006 47
Elsholz v Germany [2000] 2 FLR 486 124
Eskinazi & Chelouche v Turkey, App no 14600/05, 2005–XIII 357–358
Guichard v France, App No 56838/00, 2 September 2003 ....151, 168
Iglesias Gil and AUI v Spain, App no 56673/00, 2003–V 26
Ignaccolo–Zenide v Romania, App no 31679/96, 25 January 2000, 2000–I 26, 48–49
Iosub Caras v Romania, App no 7198/04, 27 July 2006 26
Johansen v Norway [1997] 23 EHRR 134 125
Maire v Portugal, App no 48206/99, 2003–VII 26
Maumousseau and Washington v France, App no 39388/05, 6 December 2007,
    2007–XIII 26, 47, 306
Monory v Romania and Hungary, App no 71099/01, 5 April 2005 261
Neulinger and Shuruk v Switzerland, App no 41615/07, 6 July 2010 ....27–28, 48, 112,
    124–125, 153, 281, 287–288, 292, 299,
    308–309, 311, 356, 360, 365–366, 439
Nielsen v Denmark (1988) 1 EHRR 175 122
Raban v Romania, App no 25437/08, 26 October 2010 ....26, 279, 287
Sahin v Germany, App no 30943/96, 2003–VIII 125
Šneersone and Kampanella v Italy, App no 14737/09, 12 July 2011 24
Sylvester v Austria, App nos 36812/97 and 40104/98, (2003) 37 EHRR 17 49
Van den Berg and Sarri v The Netherlands, App no 7239/08, 2 November 2010 287–288
X v Latvia, App no 27853/09, 13 December 2011 27

Finland

Supreme Court of Finland 1996:151, S96/2489 ....272, 278

France

CA Aix–en–Provence, 23 March 1989 360
CA Aix–en–Provence, L c Ministère Public, Mme B et Mesdemoiselles L (No de rôle
    02/14917), 8 October 2002 279
CA Aix–en–Provence, Zenou v Lebouef, 8th October 2002 279
CA Aix–en–Provence (No RG 06/03661), 30 November 2006 23
CA Paris, 1re Ch Section A, Époux H, 13 July 1993, JCP 1994, IV, No 224 228
CA Paris (05/15032), 27 October 2005 232

CA Paris, 15 February 2007 23
CA Paris (Nos 08/05791 & 08/07826), 8 August 2008.......................................242
CA Paris (No 06/12398), 19 October 2008 232
CA Rouen (No 05/04340), 9 March 2006 246
Cass civ 1ère, 12 July 1994 281
Cass civ 1ère (Arrêt no 1206, pourvoi no 98–17902)...281
Cass civ 1ère (No de pourvoi: 02–17411), 25 January 2005 281
Cass civ 1ère (No de pourvoi: 06–13177), 12 December 2006 242
TGI d'Abbeville, *W v G*, 10 June 1993..272
TGI Niort, *Procureur de la République c Y*, 9 January 1995..............................360

Germany

BVerfG (2 BvR 1206/98), 29 October 1998.............................192, 211, 352, 373, 377
OLG Dresden (10 UF 753/01) 280
OLG Hamm, *G and G v Decision of OLG Hamm*, 18 January 1995, 35 ILM 529
     (1996) 360
OLG Hamm (11 UF 121/03) 156
OLG Karlsruhe (2 UF 115/02)..192
OLG Stuttgart (Higher Regional Court) (UF 260/98), 25 November 1998......281

Hong Kong

AC v PC [2004] HKMP 1238...226–227, 231, 234
D v G [2001] 1179 HKCU 1..273, 278
S v S [1998] 2 HKC 316...323

Ireland

AS v PS (Child Abduction) [1998] 2 IR 244 278
B v B (Child Abduction) [1998] 1 IR 299 246
BB v JB [1998] 1 ILRM 136 246
CK v CK [1994] 1 IR 260 356
HI v MG [2000] 1 IR 110 ....151–152, 162–163, 167–168
P v B (Child Abduction: Undertakings) [1994] 3 IR 507 300
P v B (No 2) (Child Abduction: Delay) [1999] 2 ILRM 401 ....232, 241–242
RK v JK (Child Abduction: Acquiescence) [2000] 2 IR 416 ....135, 247, 255, 293, 312
WPP v SRW [2001] ILRM 371 150

Israel

ACH 10136/09, *Plonit v Ploni*, 21 December 2009, http://elyon1.court.gov.il/
     files/09/360/101/n01/09101360.n01.pdf..193, 210–211

ACH 9201/08, *Ploni v Plonit*, 05 April 2009, http://elyon1.court.gov.il/verdictssearch/HebrewVerdictsSearch.aspx 74, 82, 85
ACH 4117/11, *ShB–H v OB–H*, 12 July 2011, http://elyon1.court.gov.il/files/11/170/041/p05/11041170.p05.pdf 46, 253
CA 281/1990, *Re C*, Unreported 373
CA 2266/93, *Ploni (Child) v Ploni*, PD 49(1) 121 122
CA 165/60, *Union Insurance v Ezra*, PD 17(1) 646 364
CA 1/81, *Nagar v Nagar*, PD 38(1) 365 124
CA 5271/92, *Foxman v Foxman*, Nevo, 19 November 1992 148
CA 473/93, *Leibovitz v Leibvotiz*, PD 47(3) 63 .... 247–248, 250–251, 256–257
CA 5332/93, *Gunzburg*, PD 49(3) 282 306–308
CA 7206/93, *Gabbai v Gabbai*, PD 51(2) 241 .... 191, 193, 245, 249–250, 252, 255, 262, 265, 267
CA 870/94, *Barbie v Barbie*, Nevo, 22 June 1994 .... 156, 163
CA 6327/94, *Isik v Isik*, Nevo, 1 December 1994 .... 331, 399
CA 4391/96, *Ro v Ro*, PD 50(5) 338 .... 135, 280, 283, 290–292, 294, 306
CrA 5463/11, *RB v State of Israel*, 26 February 2013 http://elyon1.court.gov.il/files/11/280/063/a15/11063280.a15.htm 16
CrimC (BSH) 8150/08, *State of Israel v RB*, Nevo, 16 June 2011 133
FamA (BSH) 111/07, *Ploni v Almonit*, Nevo, 18 April 2007 .... 227, 232, 242
FamA (BSH) 121/07, *RB v VG*, Nevo, 18 June 2007 200
FamA (BSH) 121/07, *RB v VG*, Nevo, 21 October 2007 323
FamA (BSH) 104/08, *RB v VG*, Nevo, 20 February 2008 276
FamA (BSH) 130/08, *Plonit v Ploni*, Nevo, 31 August 2008 .... 189, 193, 196, 219
FamA (BSH) 3465–10–11, *DC v YAC*, Nevo, 2 November 2011 198
FamA (HA) 218/02, *Ploni v Plonit*, Nevo, 15 January 2003 .... 254, 261
FamA (HAI) 6591/97, *AB v YB*, Nevo, 31 December 1997 331
FamA (HAI) 128/99, *Shevach v Shevach*, Nevo, 30 April 1999 .... 327, 329–330, 336–338, 341–343, 346
FamA (HAI) 218/02, *Ploni v Plonit*, Tak–Mech 2003(1) 22302 .... 338, 346
FamA 393/06 (HAI), *Plonit v Ploni*, Unreported, 22 January 2007 379
FamA (HAI) 4646–11–08, *LM v MM*, Nevo, 13 January 2009 194
FamA (JLM) 34551–09–12, *GS v LS*, Nevo, 21 October 2012 86
FamA (JLM) 575/04, *YM v AM*, DM 34(7) 291 .... 197, 214, 218, 247, 250–251, 257
FamA (JLM) 584/04, *Plonit v Ploni*, Pador 63–1–683 228
FamA (JLM) 592/04, *RK v ChK*, Tak–Mech 04(4) 2608 257
FamA (JLM) 621/04, *DY v DR*, Nevo, 18 November 2004 256
FamA (JLM) 2059/07, *Ploni v Almonit*, Nevo, 1 July 2007 252
FamA (JLM) 132/08, *AS v MB*, Nevo, 5 May 2008 .... 198, 220
FamA (JLM) 34551–09–12, *GS v LS*, Dinim District 120 (114) 2012 200
FamA (JLM) 1109/06, *GH v GY*, Nevo, 24 December 2006 155
FamA (TA) 33/96, *Ploni v Plonit*, Nevo, 31 December 1996 .... 383, 385
FamA (TA) 28/97, *Plonit v Almonit*, Nevo, 19 April 1999 .... 69, 330, 379
FamA (TA) 70/97, *Dagan v Dagan*, Nevo, 13 December 1998 .... 113, 202, 211, 218, 358
FamA (TA) 90/97, *Moran v Moran*, Dinim District (2) 597 .... 216, 218
FamA (TA) 3/98, *Biton v Biton*, Nevo, 9 November 1998 .... 343, 351
FamA (TA) 1125/99, *DL v NCZ*, Nevo, 28 May 2000 124

FamA (TA) 1167/99, *R v L*, Unreported, 3 July 2000 ....69, 331–332, 348
RFamA (TA) 5253/00, *R v L*, Unreported 21 January 2001 274
FamA (TA) 1382/04, Nevo, 1 May 2006..136, 294
FamA (TA) 1026/05, *Ploni v Almoni*, Nevo, 17 March 2005 202
FamA (TA) 48471/05, *Ploni v Plonit*, Nevo, 11 September 2006 ....179, 219
FamA (TA) 1018/09, *Ploni v Plonit*, Tak–Mec 2009 (1) 12641 ....181, 183–185
FamA (TA) 1006/12, *ChSB v AAK*, Nevo, 24 December 2012 155
FamC (BSH) 14830/05, *PR v TAE*, Tak–mish 05(4) 266, Nevo, 8 December
    2005 .... 328, 331, 351, 379, 384, 388
FamC (BSH) 3450/07, *VG v RB*, Nevo, 9 January 2008 275
FamC (HAI) 44182/99, *KGL v YL*, Nevo, 11 September 2000 404
FamC (HAI) 15480/00, *D v D*, Unreported, 2 December 2000 421
FamC (HAI) 1515/06, *Ploni v Plonit*, Nevo, 28 August 2006 351
FamC (JLM) 430/01, *Ploni v Almonit*, Unreported 344, 351
FamC (JLM) 87403/07, *YDG v TG*, Nevo, 1 November 2007 295
FamC (JLM) 4810/05, *CA v CSh*, Nevo, 8 April 2005 ....252, 260
FamC (JLM) 18874/07, *BM v SA*, Nevo, 3 April 2008...219
FamC (JLM) 3140/01, *AB v Almoni*, Nevo, 13 June 2001 381
FamC (KS) 7400/08, *Z v RNS*, Nevo, 17 August 2008... 379
FamC (KS) 29189–12–09, *TsL v ATsM*, Nevo, 23 December 2009..............................156, 212
FamC (NAZ) 54043–08–10, *ShB–H v OB–H*, Nevo, 21 December 2010.............................252
FamC (RG) 74430/99, *P v P*, Unreported, 14 December 1999   13, 361
FamC (RLZ) 41179–08–11, *EA v SA*, Nevo, 11 December 2011 ....198, 254
FamC (TA) 2637/91, *Lukatz v Lukatz*, Tak–Mach 92(3) 1056 226
FamC (TA) 2860/96, *Ploni v Almonim*, Takdin Fam 2/97 (1987)................................393, 395
FamC (TA) 5063/97, *Pekan v Dolberg*, Nevo, 16 April 1999 421
FamC (TA) 89790/00, *MAB v ER*, Nevo, 8 February 2001.. 424, 426
FamC (TA) 42273/99, *Dr ZM v RMP*, *Nevo*, *9 August 2005*...*419*
FamC (TA) 107064/99, *KL v DSh*, Nevo, 30 December 2003 218
FamC (TA) 7300/01, *B v B*, Unreported 20 June 2001 ....420, 425
FamC (TA) 42721/06, *GK v YK*, Nevo, 18 March 2007..199
HCJ 243/88, *Consulos v Torjeman*, PD 56(2) 626 ....112, 123
HCJ 40/63, *Lawrence v The Head of the Enforcement Agency*, PD 17 1709 119
HCJ 4365/97, *Tur Sinai v The Minister of Foreign Affairs*, PD 53 (3) 673...........................357
HCJ 6056/93, *Eden v Eden*, PD 51(4) 197 323
Misc Application 2282/09, *DCM v PM*, Nevo, 7 October 2009 294
RCA 3052/99, *Shevach v Shevach*, 2 June 1999, http://elyon1.court.gov.il/files/
    99/520/030/L03/99030520.l03.pdf 325, 341
FamA 5253/00, *R v L*, Unreported, 21 January 2001..31
RFam 2270/13, *DZ v AMVD*, 30th May 2013 http://elyon1.court.gov.il/files/13/
    700/022/t04/13022700.t04.pdf 285–286
RFam 9441/12, *AAK v ChSB*, 17 February 2013, http://elyon1.court.gov.il/
    files/12/410/094/w02/12094410.w02.pdf 151
RFamA 4575/00, *Plonit v Plonit*, PD 56(2) 321 74
RFamA 672/06, *TAE v PR*, PD 61(3) 24 .... 318, 325, 328, 331–332, 334–335, 350–351, 384
RFamA 902/07, *Plonit v Plonim*, 26 April 2007, http://elyon1.court.gov.il/files/07/
    020/009/A06/07009020.a06.pdf 325, 328, 330, 335, 341, 379

RFamA 5579/07, *RB v VG*, 7 August 2007,
  http://elyon1.court.gov.il/files/07/790/055/B03/07055790.b03.pdf 183-4, 379,
    381–382, 386
RFamA 9114/07 *RB v VG*, 30 October 2007 http://elyon1.court.gov.il/files/07/140/091/
  B01/07091140.b01.pdf 330, 332, 345, 351
RFamA 1855/08, *RB v VG*, 8 April 2008 http://elyon1.court.gov.il/files/08/550/018/
  r03/08018550.r03.pdf 29, 47, 62, 67, 69–70, 97–98, 133, 273,
    275–276, 287, 290–292, 302-303, 305, 401–403, 448
RFamA 2338/09, *LM v MM*, 3 June 2009 http://elyon1.court.gov.il/files/09/380/023/
  h12/09023380.h12.pdf 211, 285–286
RFamA 8872/09, *Ploni v Plonim*, 1 December 2009, http://elyon1.court.gov.il/
  files/09/380/023/h12/09023380.h12.pdf 425
RFamA 672/06, *PR v TAE*, PD 61(3) 24 .... 134–135, 203, 320, 379, 385
RFamA 3241/09, *Plonit v Ploni*, 2 October 2009, http://elyon1.court.gov.il/files/09/
  410/032/b01/09032410.b01.pdf 419, 421
RFamA 9802/09, *Plonit v Ploni*, 17 December 2009, http://elyon1.court.gov.il/
  files/09/020/098/e03/09098020.e03.pdf 99, 197, 205, 214
RFamA 5072/10, *Ploni v Plonit*, 26 October 2010, http://elyon1.court.gov.il/
  files/09/020/098/e03/09098020.e03.pdf 74, 81, 85
RFamA 5690/10, *Plonit v Ploni*, 18 August 2010, http://elyon1.court.gov.il/
  files/10/900/056/z04/10056900.z04.pdf 227
RFamA 741/11, *OB–H v ShB–H*, 17 May 2011, http://elyon1.court.gov.il/files/
  11/410/007/b06/11007410.b06.pdf 245–246, 252–253, 259, 267
RFamA 8540/11, *DC v YAC*, 1 December 2011, http://elyon1.court.gov.il/files/
  11/400/085/z02/11085400.z02.pdf 256
RFamA 6039/12, *Ploni v Plonit*, 13 August 2012, http://elyon1.court.gov.il/
  files/12/390/060/w01/12060390.w01.pdf 271

Monaco

R 6136, *M. Le Procureur Général c MHK* *232*

Netherlands

246521/FA RK 12–2169 2 of 20 December 2012 155
*De Directie Preventie, optredend voor haarzelf en namens F (vader/father) en H
  (de moeder/mother)*, 14 juli 2000, ELRO–nummer: AA6532, Zaaknr R99/167HR 248

New Zealand

Anderson v Central Authority for New Zealand [1996] 2 NZFLR 517 278
Anderson v Paterson [2002] NZFLR 641 152
Armstrong v Evans [2000] NZFLR 984 284
B v B [1994] NZFLR 497 .... 280, 283

B v C [2002] NZFLR 433 .... 334, 353, 390
B v Secretary for Justice [2007] 3 NZLR 447 390
Chief Executive for Dept of Courts v Phelps [2000] 1 NZLR 168 .... 157–158, 164
Clarke v Carson [1995] NZFLR 926 326
Clarke v Carson [1996] 1 NZFLR 349 390
Collins v Lowndes, High Court, Auckland, Unreported, 6 March 2003 320
Damiano v Damiano [1993] NZFLR 548 291–292
Dellabarca v Christie [1999] 2 NZLR 548 151
El Sayed v Secretary for Justice [2003] 1 NZLR 349 .... 273, 280, 283, 307
Fairfax v Ireton [2009] NZFLR 433 (NZCA 100) 147, 151, 154–155, 162, 168
G v J [2001] NZFLR 593 425–426
Gross v Boda [1995] 1 NZLR 569 .... 150, 153–154, 158, 165
H v C, FC Lower Hutt, FP No 368/00, Unreported, 9 March 2001 273
H v H [1995] 13 FRNZ 498 .... 252, 276
Hollins v Crozier [2000] NZLR 775 .... 280, 334, 351
KS v LS [2003] NZLR 387 .... 273, 275, 281
KS v LS [2003] 3 NZLR 837 17
Kacem v Bashir [2010] NZSC 112 76
LJG v RTP (Child Abduction) [2006] NZFLR 589 .... 199, 322, 335, 337, 340, 342, 349
M v H (Custody) [2006] NZFLR 623 153–154
P v Secretary of State for Justice [2004] 2 NZLR 28 143
Punter v Secretary for Justice [2007] 1 NZLR 40 .... 192–193, 198, 201, 207–210, 217, 221
RCL v APBL [2012] NZHC 1292 144
Ryding v Turvey [1998] NZFLR 313 .... 303, 322, 328, 343, 345
S v M [1999] NZFLR 337 198
S v S [1999] NZFLR 625 333
S v S [1999] 3 NZLR 513 290
SK v KP [2005] 3 NZLR 590 .... 178, 180, 187, 193, 208
ST v MW, HC 7/10/2008 CIV 2008–404–4916 390
Secretary of Justice v Abrahams ex parte Brown [2001] FP 069/134/00 (Fam Ct)
  (Taupo NZ) 342
Secretary for Justice v HJ [2006] NZSC 97 .... 236, 239
Secretary of Justice v Penney [1995] NZFLR 827 319
Secretary for Justice (New Zealand Central Authority) v HJ [2007]
  2 NZLR 289 .... 99, 228, 238–242
TB v JPB HC [2011] NZHC 1135 421
U v D [2002] NZFLR 529 .... 259, 265–266
White v Northumberland [2006] NZFLR 1105 320–321
Winters v Cowen [2002] NZFLR 927 .... 329–330, 337, 346

Romania

Civil case No 3875, Bucharest Area Court VI, 15 April 2002 279
Raban v Raban 279

South Africa

B v G 2012 (2) SA 329 (GSJ) 395
Central Authority v H 2008(1) SA 49 (SCA) 247
Central Authority v Reynders [2011] 2 All SA 438 (GNP) 182, 184, 311, 422
Central Authority of the Republic of South Africa v B 2012 (2) SA 296 (GSJ) 331
Central Authority For The Republic Of South Africa v MA (Case No 11/39798),
    South Gauteng High Court, Johannesburg, Unreported, 20 March 2012 277
Family Advocate v Remy (Case No 2004/2012), Unreported, 15 February 2013 .... 281, 293
Family Advocate Cape Town v Chirume (6090/05) [2005] ZAWCHC 94,
    9 December 2005 .... 272, 283, 289, 305, 421
Jackson v Jackson 2002 (2) SA 303 (SCA) 74
KG v CB 2012 (4) SA 136 (SCA) 287, 294
Sonderup v Tondelli 2001 (1) SA 1171 (CC) 15, 283, 291–292, 294,
                                                                                                                    306, 309, 311, 356, 364
Smith v Smith 2001 (3) SA 845 (SCA) 181–182, 206, 249–250, 260

Spain

Menachem v Menachem, Ramirez–Ordina (Trial Court No 2 of L'Hospitalet de
    Llabregat, No 369/01), 27 January 2002 279
S, Re, Auto de 21 abril de 1997, Audiencia Provincial Barcelona,
    Sección 1a 357–358, 365, 367

Sweden

AFJ v TJ, RÅ 1996 ref 52, 9 May 1996, Supreme Administrative Court of Sweden 201

Switzerland

ATF 130 III 530 ss 48
ATF 131 III 334, consid 5 notamment 341
Beschluss und Urteil OGer ZH, 4 April 2011, NH110001–O/U 413
Decision of 29 May 2000, (2001) 42 ZfRV 30 309
Entscheid OGer BE vom 5 Mai 2010, consid. 7 notamment 362
Entscheid OGer BE vom 5 Juli 2011, ZK 10655, consid III 5 415
5P.1/1999 Bundesgericht (Tribunal Fédéral), 29 March 1999 360
5P.1/2005/bnm Bundesgericht, II Zivilabteilung (Tribunal Fédéral, 2ème
    Chambre Civile) 331
5P.254/2005/frs, Tribunal fédéral, IIè cour civile 226
5P.367/2005/ast Bundesgericht, II Zivilabteilung (Tribunal Fédéral, 2ème
    Chambre Civile) 192, 280
5P.1999/2006 /blb, Bundesgericht, II Zivilabteilung (Federal Court, Second
    Chamber) Decision of 13 July 2006 248

Table of Cases xxxiii

5A.582/2007 Bundesgericht, II Zivilabteilung (*Tribunal Fédéral, 2ème Chambre Civile*) 327
5P.3/2007/bnm Appellate Court (*Bundesgericht, II Zivilabteilung*) 350
Justice de Paix du cercle de Lausanne (Magistrates' Court) J 765 CIEV 112E 231
Obergericht des Kantons Zürich (Appellate Court of the Canton Zurich),
  28 January 1997, U/NL960145/II.ZK 278
Präsidium des Bezirksgerichts St Gallen (District Court of St Gallen), decision of
  8 September 1998, 4 PZ 98–0217/0532N 232
TC VD du 17.11.2010, 214, consid 3c, 15 ....277, 289
TF, 30.3.2012, 5A_764/2011, consid 3.3 324
Urteil AppGer BS vom 17 November 2011, consid 7.1 291

United Kingdom

A (A Child) (Wardship: Habitual Residence), Re [2006] EWHC 3338
  (Fam) 202, 204–205
A (A Minor) (Abduction), Re [1988] 1 FLR 365 ....275, 280, 291
A (Abduction: Habitual Residence), Re [1998] 1 FLR 497 187
A (Abduction: Habitual Residence), Re [2007] 2 FLR 129 195
A (Custody Decision after Maltese Non–Return Order), Re [2006] EWHC 3397
  (Fam) 24, 304
A (Foreign Access Order: Enforcement), Re [1996] 1 FLR 561 430
A (Minors) (Abduction) (No 2), Re [1993] 1 All ER 272 257
A (Minors) (Abduction: Acquiescence), Re [1992] 2 FLR 14 103
A (Minors) (Abduction: Custody Rights), Re [1992] Fam 106 ....248, 250–251
A (Minors) (Abduction: Custody Rights), Re [1992] 2 FLR 14 ....254, 259, 261
A (Minors) (Abduction: Custody Rights) (No 2), Re [1993] Fam 1 258–259
A (Minors) (Abduction) (Habitual Residence), Re [1996] 1 WLR 25 ....181, 197
A (Minors: Abduction), Re [1991] 2 FLR 241 251
A v A (Child Abduction) [1993] 2 FLR 225 ....187, 325
A v A (Children) (Abduction: Acquiescence) [2003] EWHC 3102 (Fam) 251, 254
A v B (Abduction: Declaration) [2008] EWHC 2524 (Fam) 152–153, 155, 173
A and D (Children), Re [2008] EWCA Civ 265 187
A, HA v MB (Brussels II Revised: Article (11)7 Application), Re [2007]
  EWHC 2016 (Fam) 20, 90, 304
AAA v ASH [2009] EWHC 636 ....127, 151–152, 168
AF v T [2011] EWHC 1315 (Fam) 24
AJ v FJ [2005] CSIH 36 156
AJJ v JJ [2011] EWCA Civ 1448 ....116, 377, 383, 388, 390, 396, 403
AQ v JQ, 12 December 2001, Outer House of the Court of Session 249, 256, 332, 336
AZ (A Minor)(Abduction: Acquiesence), Re [1993] 1 FLR 682 ....143, 247, 250, 258
Al Habtoor v Fotheringham [2001] EWCA Civ 186 ....135, 205
B (A Minor) (Abduction), Re [1994] 2 FLR 249 ....97, 151–152, 252
B (A Minor) (Respondent), Re [2001] UKHL 70 123
B (Abduction: Children's Objections), Re [1998] 1 FLR 667 ....203, 205, 337, 342
B (Child Abduction: Habitual Residence), In re [1994] 2 FLR 915 215

xxxiv Table of Cases

B (Child Abduction: Unmarried Father), Re [1998] 2 FLR 146 .... 151–152, 158, 167
B (Minors) (Abduction) (No 1), Re [1993] 1 FLR 988 .... 96, 179, 199, 211, 215
B (Minors) (Abduction) (No 2), Re [1993] 1 FLR 993 ....216, 219
B v B (Abduction: Custody Rights) [1993] 1 FLR 238 276
B v H (Habitual Residence: Wardship) [2002] 1 FLR 388..202
B v K (Child Abduction) [1993] 1 FCR 382.. 285, 327, 339
B v UK [2000] 1 FLR..168
B–G v B–G (Abduction: Acquiescence) [2008] EWHC 688 (Fam) 258–260
B–M (Wardship: Jurisdiction), Re [1993] 1 FLR 979 153
BD v AID and D (children) [2010] EWCA Civ 50 74
BT v JRT (Abduction: Conditional Acquiescence and Consent) [2008] EWHC 1169
    (Fam).. 245, 248, 252–254, 258–260, 266
Bates, Re (Unreported decision of 23 February 1989) 190
Boys v Chaplin [1971] AC 356..128
Bullock v IRC [1976] 3 All ER 353..207
C (A Minor) (Abduction), Re [1989] 1 FLR 403 146
C (Abduction) (Grave Risk of Psychological Harm), Re [1999]
    2 FCR 507 ....274, 285–286, 291
C (Abduction: Consent), Re [1996] 1 FLR 414 ....246, 259
C (Abduction: Interim Directions: Accommodation by Local Authority),
    Re [2004] 1 FLR 653 44
C (Abduction: Separate Representation of Children), Re [2008] EWHC 517
    (Fam)... 381, 390, 392, 397, 399, 405
C (Abduction: Settlement), Re [2004] EWHC 1245 (Fam)................ 229–231, 234, 236, 240
C (Abduction: Settlement) (No 2), Re [2005] 1 FLR 938.............................231, 238, 240–241
C (Child Abduction) (Unmarried Father: Rights of Custody), Re [2002]
    EWHC 2219 (Fam).. 152–153
C v C [2008] CSOH 42 231
C v C (Minor) (Abduction: Rights of Custody Abroad) [1989]
    2 All ER 465... 148, 150, 280, 291, 294, 300
C v C (Minors) (Child Abduction) [1992] 1 FLR 163 148
C v S (Minor: Abduction: Illegitimate Child) [1990] 2 All ER 449 .... 179, 188
C(B) (Child Abduction: Risk of Harm), Re [1999] 3 FCR 510...286
Cameron v Cameron [1996] SLT 306.. 195, 199, 208, 323
Canon v Canon [2004] EWCA CIV 1330............................ 227, 229–231, 233, 235, 237, 241
Corrie (A Minor), Re (Unreported, 14 October 1988) 306
Cruse v Chitum [1974] 2 All ER 940 187
D (A Child) (Abduction: Foreign Custody Rights), Re [2006]
    UKHL 51 ....21, 50, 98, 105, 147–149, 155, 165, 276,
                                            303, 376, 384–385, 390, 398, 401, 428–429
D (Abduction: Acquiescence), Re [1998] 2 FLR 335 ....257, 265
D (Abduction: Acquiescence), Re [1999] 1 FLR 36 .... 258, 260, 266, 373
D (Abduction: Discretionary Return), Re [2000] 1 FLR 24 .... 246, 259–261, 266, 373
D (Article 13B: Non–Return), Re [2006] EWCA Civ 146...274
D (Intractable Contact Dispute: Publicity), In the Matter of Re [2004] 1 FLR 1226............124
D v D [2001] ScotCS 103 ....187, 281
D v S (Abduction: Acquiescence) [2008] EWHC 363 (Fam) 196, 206, 208

Table of Cases xxxv

De L v H [2009] EWHC 3074 (Fam)..390, 401
Deak v Deak [2006] EWCA Civ 830 155
Donofrio v Burrell 2000 SLT 1051 ....424, 426
E, Re [2011] EWCA Civ 361 309
E (Abduction: Non–Convention Country), Re [1999] 3 FCR 497 14
E (Abduction: Non–Convention Country), Re [1999] 2 FLR 642........................361, 365, 367
E (Children), Re [2011] UKSC 27..............................27, 270, 272–274, 281, 286, 293, 295,
297, 305–306, 308–309, 312, 439
EC–L v DM (Child Abduction: Costs) [2005] EWHC 588 (Fam)................................418, 421
EM (Lebanon) v Secretary of State for the Home Dept [2008] UKHL 64 359
F, Re [1993] 2 FLR 830...119
F (A Child), Re [2007] EWCA Civ 393...397
F (A Child), Re [2009] EWCA Civ 416...166
F (A Child) (Abduction: Obligation to Hear Child), Re [2007] All ER (D) 452 376
F (A Minor) (Abduction: Custody Rights), Re [1991] Fam 25 310
F (A Minor) (Child Abduction), Re [1992] 1 FLR 548 .... 180, 195, 205–207, 215
F (Abduction: Joinder of Child as Party), Re [2007] EWCA Civ 393 ....24, 134
F (Abduction: Removal Outside Jurisdiction), Re [2008] EWCA Civ 842...........................390
F (Abduction: Unmarried Father: Sole Carer), Re [2003] 1 FLR 839..................................152
F (Children) (Abduction: Removal Outside Jurisdiction), Re [2008] EWCA Civ 854 310
F (Hague Convention: Child's Objections), Re [2006] Fam 685...47
F v F (Minors) (Custody: Foreign Order) [1989] Fam 1..18
F v M [2008] EWHC 1525 (Fam)...390
F v M and N (Abduction: Acquiescence: Settlement) [2008] EWHC 1525
(Fam).. 105, 228, 231, 239, 241, 443
Foster v Foster (decision of Family Division of 24 May 1993) 336
G (A Minor), Re, 3 October 1995 (UK Court of Appeal)...271
G (A Minor) (Abduction), Re [1989] 2 FLR 475 ....294, 300, 323
G (A Minor) (Enforcement of Access Abroad), Re [1993] Fam 216........................19, 424–426
G (Abduction) (Rights of Custody), Re [2002] 2 FLR 703 152
G (Abduction: Psychological Harm), Re [1995] 1 FLR 64..272, 284
*G (Abduction: Withdrawal of Proceedings, Acquiescence, Habitual Residence),
Re* [2007] EWHC 2807 (Fam)... 187, 202, 204, 249, 256
G (Children) [2010] EWCA Civ 1232 .... 71, 90, 329, 341, 383, 410
G (Children) (Foreign Contact Order: Enforcement), Re [2003] EWCA Civ 1607 430
G (Leave to Remove), Re [2007] EWCA Civ 1497 74
G v G (Minors) (Abduction) (1991) 2 FLR 506..510
G and A (Abduction: Consent), Re [2003] NIFam 16 ....245, 249
Gillick v West Norfolk and Wisbech Health Authority [1986] 1 AC 112....................... 122–123
Gsponer, In the Marriage of (1988) 94 FLR 164 ....306, 312
H (A Child: Child Abduction), Re [2006] EWCA Civ 1247 ....390, 396–398
H (A Minor) (Abduction: Rights of Custody), Re [2000] 2 AC 291............................ 152–153
H (Abduction: Acquiescence), Re [1998] 2 AC 72 .... 246, 249–250, 252–256, 265, 269
H (Abduction: Child of 16), Re [2000] 2 FLR 51 .... 227, 241, 251, 256
H (Abduction: Custody Rights), Re [1991] 2 AC 476.. 142, 145, 227
H (Abduction: Habitual Residence: Consent), Re [2000] 2 FLR 294...................................198
H (Child Abduction: Rights of Custody), Re [2000] 1 FLR 201 153

Table of Cases

H (Children) (Abduction), Re [2003] EWCA Civ 355 284
H (Children) (Abduction: Children's Objections), Re [2004] EWHC 211 327
H (Leave to Remove), Re [2010] 2 FLR 1875 74
H v H (Child Abduction: Stay of Domestic Proceedings) [1994] 1 FLR 530 105
H v H (Minors) (Forum Conveniens) (Nos 1 and 2) [1993] 1 FLR 958 .... 104, 209
H–K (Children) [2011] EWCA Civ 1100 .... 198, 221
HB, Re [1998] 1 FLR 392 47
HB, Re [1998] 1 FLR 422 .... 329, 344
HB (Abduction: Children's Objections), Re [1997] 1 FLR 392 .... 248, 307, 322, 329, 337, 341, 346
HB (Abduction: Children's Objections) (No 2), Re [1998] 1 FLR 564 .... 239, 339, 398
Habtoor v Fotheringham [2001] EWCA Civ 186 202
Hunter v Murrow [2005] EWCA Civ 976 .... 146–147, 151, 153, 156, 162
Hunter v Morrow [2005] 2 FLR 1119 424
Ikmi v Ikmi [2001] EWCA Civ 875 178
J (A Child) (Return to Foreign Jurisdiction: Convention Rights), Re [2005]
  UKHL 40 .... 89, 310, 359, 363, 365, 367
J (A Minor) (Abduction: Custody Rights), Re [1990] 2 AC 562 .... 151–152, 179, 195
J (Abduction: Declaration of Wrongful Removal), Re [1999] 2 FLR 653 152–153
J (Children) (Abduction: Child's Objections to Return), Re [2004] All ER (D) 72 ...... 327, 334
J v C [1970] AC 688 .... 66, 112, 123
J and K (Abduction: Objections of Child), Re [2004] EWHC 1985 335
JB (Child Abduction) (Rights of Custody: Spain), Re [2003] EWHC 2130 .... 146, 170
JMcB v LE [2011] 1 FLR 518 152
JPC v SMW [2007] EWHC 1349 (Fam) 105, 322, 341, 347, 382–383, 390, 443
JS (Private International Adoption), Re [2000] 2 FLR 638 141
Johnson v Coventry Churchill International Ltd [1992] 3 All ER 14 128
K (Abduction: Child's Objections), Re [1995] 1 FLR 977 .... 256, 274, 292
K (Abduction: Consent), Re [1997] 2 FLR 212 .... 246–249, 259, 261, 264
K (Abduction: Consent: Forum Conveniens), Re [1995] 2 FLR 211 .... 262, 265, 272
K (Abduction: Physical Harm), Re [1995] 2 FLR 550 .... 135, 293, 312
K v K [2009] EWCA Civ 986 .... 146, 152, 165, 168, 170
KD (A Minor) (Ward: Termination of Access), Re [1988] AC 806 123
Klentzeris v Klentzeris [2007] EWCA Civ 533 .... 21, 275, 313, 342
L (A Minor) (Abduction: Jurisdiction), Re [2002] 1 WLR 3208 258
L (Abduction: Pending Criminal Proceedings), Re [1999] 1 FLR 433 .... 99, 233–234, 307
L (Minors) (Wardship: Jurisdiction), Re [1974] 1 All ER 913 .... 7, 98
L (Minors) (Wardship: Jurisdiction), Re [1974] 1 WLR 250 310
Laing v Central Authority (1996) 21 Fam LR 24 216
M (A Child), In The Matter of [2010] EWCA 178 390
M (A Minor) (Abduction: Child's Objections), Re [1994] 2 FLR 126 344
M (A Minor) (Child Abduction), Re [1994] 1 FLR 390 .... 328, 374
M (Abduction: Acquiescence), Re [1996] 1 FLR 315 .... 228, 274
M (Abduction: Child Objections), Re [2007] EWCA Civ 260 .... 333, 352
M (Abduction: Habitual Residence), Re [1996] 1 FLR 887 .... 202, 205
M (Abduction: Intolerable Situation), Re [2000] 1 FLR 930 294
M (Abduction: Leave to Appeal), Re [1999] 2 FLR 550 .... 133, 272, 280

Table of Cases   xxxvii

M (Abduction: Non–Convention Country), Re [1995] 1 FLR 89 .... 135, 293, 312
M (Abduction: Psychological Harm), Re [1997] 2 FLR 573 272
M (Abduction: Psychological Harm), Re [1998] 1 FCR 488 .... 328, 341
M (Abduction: Undertakings), Re [1995] 1 FLR 1021 289
M (Abduction: Zimbabwe), Re [2007] UKHL 55 .... 135, 233–237, 239–240, 243, 246,
257–258, 260–261, 266–267, 321–322, 336–337,
341, 343, 347, 352, 390, 397, 399, 401–402, 405
M (Child Abduction) (European Convention), Re [1994] 1 FLR 551 171
M (Children), Re [2007] EWHC 1820 (Fam) 238
M (Children), Re [2007] EWCA Civ 992 .... 238, 401–402
M (Minors) (Residence Order: Jurisdiction), Re [1993] 1 FLR 495 195
M v M [1973] 2 All ER 81 119
M v M [2008] EWHC 2049 (Fam) 231
M v M (Abduction: England and Scotland) [1997] 2 FLR 263 178
MC v SC [2008] EWHC 517 (Fam) 393
MK v CK [2011] EWCA CIV 793 74
MM v AMR or M 2003 SCLR 71 256
MQ and A (By Her Next Friend) & Dept of Community Services [2005] FamCA 843 45
Mabon v Mabon [2005] 2 FLR 1011 399
MacMillan v MacMillan 1989 SLT 350 (Scot Ex Div 1989) 291
Mark v Mark (Divorce: Jurisdiction) [2004] EWCA Civ 168 231
Mark v Mark [2005] UKHL 42 231
Marshall v Marshall [1996] SLT 429 335
McB v LE [2011] Fam 364 152
McCarthy v McCarthy [1994] SLT 743 281
McKee v McKee [1951] AC 352 130
Mercredi v Chaffe [2011] EWCA Civ 272 .... 155, 173, 194, 196
Middleton v MacPherson (October 2000, Unreported) 47
Mohammed v Bank of Kuwait [1996] 1 WLR 1483 364
Moran v Moran 1997 SLT 541 197
N (Abduction: Habitual Residence), Re [2000] 2 FLR 899 187
N (Minors)(Abduction), Re [1991] 1 FLR 413 .... 225, 229
N v N (Abduction: Article 13 Defence) [1995] 1 FLR 107 .... 272, 275, 278, 328
NJC v NPC [2008] CSIH 34, 2008 SC 571 .... 231, 358
Nessa v Chief Adjudication Officer [1998] 2 All ER 728 207
Nessa v Chief Adjudication Officer [1999] 4 All ER 195
Norris, Re [1888] 4 TLR 452 176
Nyachowe v Fielder [2007] EWCA Civ 1129 341
O (Abduction: Consent and Acquiescence), Re [1997] 1 FLR 924 .... 262, 265
O (Child Abduction: Custody Rights), Re [1997] 2 FLR 702 152
O (Child Abduction: Undertakings), Re [1994] 2 FLR 349 .... 277, 289, 293
O (Contact: Imposition of Conditions), Re [1995] 2 FLR 124 123
O v O 2002 SC 430 .... 153, 285
Ontario Court, The v M and M (Abduction: Children's Objections) [1997]
    1 FLR 475 .... 285, 339
Osman v Elasha [2000] Fam 62 368
P (A Child) (Abduction: Acquiescence), Re [2004] EWCA Civ 971 ..... 246–247, 261–262, 265

P (A Minor) (Child Abduction: Non–Convention Country), Re [1997] Fam 45 310
P (Abduction: Declaration), Re [1995] 1 FLR 831..155
P (GE) (An Infant), Re [1965] Ch 568..186, 190
P v P [1998] 2 FLR 835 ....249, 252
P v P (Minors) (Child Abduction) [1992] 1 FLR 155 373
P v S [2002] Fam LR 2 ....229, 239
P v SA and West Lothian Council..44, 46
P–J (children), Re [2009] EWCA Civ 588.............. 198, 245–246, 251, 254, 261–262, 265, 267
PW v ALI, (Unreported, Outer House of the Court of Session, 25 February
    2003)...335, 337, 349
PW v ALI [2003] SCLR 478 ....285, 293
Payne v Payne [2001] EWCA Civ 166..74, 87
Perrin v Perrin 1994 SC 45 .... 216, 228, 230, 232
Q Petitioner [2001] SLT 243..278, 285
R (A Minor) (Contact), Re [1993] 2 FLR 762..119
R (A Minor: Abduction), Re [1992] 1 FLR 105.. 327–328
R (Abduction: Consent), Re [1999] 1 FLR 828 ....258, 261, 265–266
R (Abduction: Habitual Residence), Re [2003] EWHC 1968 (Fam)....187–188, 197, 208–209
R (Abduction: Hague and European Conventions), Re [1997] 1 FLR 663 18
R (Child Abduction: Acquiescence), Re [1995] 1 FLR 716..376
R (Minors), Re [1995] 1 FLR 716..320, 323, 341
R (Minors) (Wardship: Jurisdiction), Re [1981] 2 FLR 416 310
R (Wardship: Child Abduction) (No 2), Re [1993] 1 FLR 249 ....203, 211
R v Barnet London Borough Council, Ex p Nilish Shah [1983]
    2 AC 309 .... 177–178, 187–189, 198
R v R [2006] IESC 7 247
S, Re [2000] 1 FLR 454...359
S (A Child), Re [2002] EWCA Civ 1941 ....262, 264–266
S (A Child), Re [2012] UKSC 10 ....28, 88, 284
S (A Minor) (Abduction), Re [1991] 2 FLR 1 .... 135, 198, 201, 208,
                                                                                            229, 234, 238, 243, 292, 310
S (A Minor) (Abduction), Re [1998] AC 750..187
S (A Minor) (Abduction: Custody Rights), Re [1993] Fam 242............ 323, 327–328, 337, 376
S (A Minor) (Custody: Habitual Residence), Re [1998] AC 750 ....142, 145, 153
S (Abduction: Acquiescence), Re [1994] 1 FLR 819 325
S (Abduction: Acquiescence), Re [1998] 2 FLR 115 .... 89, 247, 250, 259–260
S (Abduction: Children: Separate Representation), Re [1997] 1 FLR 486...........................404
S (Abduction: Children's Representation), Re [2008] EWHC 1798 (Fam) 332–333
S (Abduction: Custody Rights), Re [1991] 2 AC 476..142, 145, 227
S (Abduction: Intolerable Situation: Beth Din), Re [2000] 1 FLR 454 13
S (Child Abduction) (Grave Risk of Harm), Re [2002] EWCA 908....... 272–274, 276, 279, 284
S (Minors) (Abduction: Acquiescence), Re [1994] 1 FLR 819..248, 256
S (Minors) (Child Abduction: Wrongful Retention), Re [1994] Fam 70 .... 143, 145, 198
S (Minors: Access), Re [1990] 2 FLR 166 119
S v B (Abduction: Human Rights) [2005] 2 FLR 878 389
S v B & Y (Abduction: Human Rights) [2005] EWHC 733 (Fam) 286, 301–302
S v H (Abduction: Access Rights) [1998] Fam 49 150

Table of Cases xxxix

S v S 2003 SLT 344 .... 156, 158–159, 163, 166
S v S (Child Abduction) (Child's Views) [1992] 2 FLR 492 .... 322, 329, 390
S v S & S [2009] EWHC 1494 (Fam) 232
S N and C (Non–Hague Convention Abduction: Habitual Residence: Child's Views),
    Re [2005] NI Fam 1 .... 338, 351
SC (A Child), Re [2005] EWHC 2205 241
SM v CM [2011] CSIH 65 75
Schisby v Westenholz (1870) LR 6 QB 155 131
Seroka v Bellah [1995] SLT 204 152
Singh v Singh 1998 SLT 1084 .... 322, 340
Soucie v Soucie 1995 SC 134 .... 226, 256
Spiliada Maritime Corporn v Cansulex Ltd [1987] AC 460 .... 103, 364
Starr v Starr 1999 SLT 335 281
T (Abduction: Child's Objections to Return), Re [2000] 2 FLR 192 .... 285–286, 318–320,
                                                                   325–326, 328, 331–335, 339, 343, 349
T (Minors) (Hague Convention: Access), Re [1993] 2 FLR 617 426
T v T (Abduction: Consent) [1999] 1 FLR 916 .... 251–252, 262, 265
TB v JB (Abduction: Grave Risk of Harm) [2001] 2 FLR 515 .... 47, 135, 273, 283,
                                                                                 336, 339, 344, 374
Tacanowska v Taczanowska [1957] P 301 129
Urness v Minto [1994] SC 249 .... 285, 327
V (Abduction: Habitual Residence), Re [1995] 2 FLR 992 178
V v B (A Minor)(Abduction) [1991] 1 FLR 266 195
V–B (Minors: Child Abduction: Custody Rights), Re [1999] 2 FLR 192 .... 147, 150, 152
Vigreux v Michel [2006] EWCA Civ 630 .... 21, 24, 134, 335, 337, 342, 347, 349
W (A Child), Re [2004] EWCA Civ 1366 .... 272, 283, 291, 294
W (Abduction: Domestic Violence), Re [2004] EWHC 1247 294
W (Abduction: Procedure), Re [1995] 1 FLR 878 156
W (Child Abduction: Unmarried Father), Re [1998] 2 FLR 146 .... 151–152, 158, 167
W (Children), Re [2011] EWCA Civ 345 74
W (Minors), Re [2010] EWCA Civ 520 .... 318, 320, 322–323, 337, 339, 345
W v H (Children) (Surrogacy: Habitual Residence) [2002] All ER (D) 222 126
W v W [2004] SC 63 .... 285–286, 335, 337, 339
W v W [2009] EWHC 3288 (Fam) 389, 400
W v W (Child Abduction: Acquiescence) [1993] 2 FLR 211 .... 89, 102, 156,
                                                                                      250, 256–260, 306
W and B v H (Child Abduction: Surrogacy) [2002] 1 FLR 1008 (HC) 186, 202
WF v RJ [2010] EWHC 2909 285
Watson v Jamieson [1998] SLT 180 201
Yousef v Netherlands [2003] 1 FLR 210 119
Z, Re [1999] 1 FLR 1270 310
Z (Children), In The Matter of [2008] EWCA Civ 1545 322
Z (Children), In The Matter of [2008] EWHC 3473 (Fam) 196–197, 214
Zaffino v Zaffino (Abduction: Children's Views) [2005] EWCA
    Civ 1012 .... 286, 320, 335–336, 339–340
Zenel v Hadow 1993 SC 612 .... 251, 254, 257

United States of America

AVPG and CCPG, Minor Children, In the Interest of SW3d 117 (Tex Ct. App2008) 225
Abbott v Abbott 176 L Ed 2d 789 (5th Cir Tex2008) 94–95, 147–150, 157–158, 160, 162, 164, 173, 221
Acosta v Acosta 2012 US Dist LEXIS 83063..283
Acosta Saldivar v Rodela 2012 US Dist LEXIS 141126..420–421
Altamiranda Vale v Avila 538 F3d 581 (7th Cir 2008)..278
Anderson v Acree 250 F Supp 2d 872 (SD Ohio 2002)..227
Antonio v Bello 2004 US Dist LEXIS 17254 (ND Ga June 2004) 283
Asvesta v Petrousas 580 F3d 1000 (2009) 133–134
Baby Jessica case. See *Clausen, Re* 502 NW 2d 649 (1993)
Baran v Beatty 526 F3d 1340 (US App 11th Cir 2008)..301
Barzilay v Barzilay 600 F3d 912 (8th Cir 2010)...192
Baxter v Baxter 423 F3d 363 (3rd Cir 2005) 248
Ben–Haim v Ben–Haim appeal Docketed No FD 02–906–11 (NJ Super Ct August 2011) 31, 134, 252–253, 267
Bickerton v Bickerton No 91–06694 (Cal Sup Ct 1991) 200, 324
Blondin v Dubois 189 F3d 240 (2nd Cir 1999) 133
Blondin v Dubois 238 F3d 153 (2d Cir 2001)............................... 275, 283, 287, 290, 323
Bose Corp v Consumers of Union of US Inc 466 US 485 (1984)...................................180
Burchard v Garay 724 P2d 486 (Cal 1986)..66
Marriage of Burgess, Re 913 P2d 473 (Cal 1996)...66, 74
Cantor v Cohen 442 F3d 196 (4th Cir 2006)...424
Caro v Sher 687 A2d 354 (NJ Super Ct Ch 1996)..89, 358, 368
Carrascosa v McGuire 520 F3d 249 (3rd Cir 2008)..134, 360
Castillo v Castillo 597 F Supp 2d 432 (D Del 2009)...334
Charalambous v Charalambous 627 F3d 462 (1st Cir 2010) 283
Ciotola v Fiocca 86 Ohio Misc 2d 24, 684 NE 2d 763 (Ohio Com Pl 1997)..........306, 356
Clausen, Re 502 NW 2d 649 (1993) 112, 123
Coffield, In re 96 Ohio App3d 52 (App Ct 1994) 232
Collopy v Christodoulou No 90 DR 1138 (D Colo May 1991).....................................232
Condon v Cooper 73 Cal Rptr 2d 33 (1998) 85
Croll v Croll 229 F 3d 133 (2d Cir 2000) 147–149, 168
Cuellar v Joyce 596 F3d 505 (9th Cir 2010)...288
Currier v Currier 845 F Supp 916 (DNH 1994)... 251–252
DD, Re 440 F Supp 2d 1283 (MD Fla 2006) 278
Dallemagne v Dallemagne 440 F Supp 2d 1283 (MD Fla 2006)...................................283
Danaipour v Mclarey 286 F3d 1 (1st Cir 2002)............................... 135, 271–272, 278, 290–295, 312–314, 396
Danaipour v McLarey 183 F Supp 2d 311 (D Mass 2002)...278
David S v Zamira S 151 Misc2d 630..232
de Silva v Pitts 481 F3d 1279 (10th Cir 2007) 323, 328, 331, 343, 351
Delvoye v Lee 329 F3d 330 (3rd Cir 2003)...178, 191, 202
Di Giuseppe v Di Giuseppe 2008 US Dist LEXIS 29785, 2008 WL 1743079 (ED Mich April 2008)..278
Dimer v Dimer No 99–2–03610–7 SEA (Wa Sup Ct July 1999).........................246, 249, 255

Diorinou v Mezitis 237 F 3d 133(2000) 134
Duran v Beaumont 534 F3d 142 (2nd Cir 2008) 133
England v England 234 F3d 268 (5th Cir 2000) 324
Escaf v Rodriguez 200 Supp 2d 603 (ED Va 2000) 324, 328–329, 358
Estrada v Salas–Perez 2012 US Dist LEXIS 139897, 28 September 2012..................312
FHU v ACU 427 NJ Super 354 (2012) 227, 235–236
Fabri v Pritikin–Fabri 221 F Supp 2d 859 (2001) 360
Falk v Sinclair 692 F Supp 2d 147 (D Maine 2010) 143
Falls v Downie 871 F Supp 100 (D Mass 1994)...196
Feder v Evans–Feder 63 F3d 217 (3rd Cir 1995) 179–180, 190–192, 197, 201, 215
Feder v Feder 922 So2d 213 (Fla 3d DCA 2006) 215
Freier v Freier 969 F Supp 436 (ED Mich 1996) 279, 360
Friedrich v Friedrich 983 F2d 1396 (6th Cir 1993) 178–179, 190
Friedrich v Friedrich 78 F3d 1060 (6th Cir 1996) 156–157, 166, 274, 279, 306, 312
Furnes v Reeves 362 F 3d 702 (11th Cir 2004) 147–148, 227
Giampaolo v Erneta 390 F Supp 2d 1269 (ND GA 2004)...................................330, 377
Gitter v Gitter 396 F3d 124 (2nd Cir 2005)..189, 199
Gonzalez v Gutierrez 311 F 3d 942 (9th Cir 2002)...148
Haimdas v Haimdas 720 F Supp 2d 183 (2010)...342
Harkness v Harkness 227 Mich App 581 (Mich App 1998).......................................188
Hilton v Guyot 159 US 113 (1895)..132–133
Holder v Holder 392 F3d 1009 (9th Cir 2004)..197
Hughes v Cornelius (1680) 2 Show 232 135
Isaacs v Rice 1998 US Dist Lexis 12602 ....203, 206, 211
Janakakis–Kostun v Janakakis 6 SW3d 843 (Ky Ct App 1999)..................................361
Jenkins v Jenkins 569 F3d 549 (6th Cir 2009)..190, 196
Johnson v Johnson 26 Va App 135, 493 SE2d 668 (1997) 201, 217
Kaiser v Kaiser 23 P3d 278 (Ordinary Court of Appeal 2001).....................................74
Karkkainen v Kovalchuk 445 F3d 280 (3d Cir 2006) 180, 191–192, 196, 213
Khan v Fatima 680 F3d 781 (7th Cir 2012) 272–273, 284, 299, 303
Koch v Koch 450 F3d 703 (7th Cir 2006) 189, 199
Kovacs v Kovacs (2002) 59 OR (3d) 671 (Ohio CA)...283
Krefter v Wills 623 F Supp 2d 12 (2009)..313
Kufner v Kufner 519 F3d 33 (1st Cir 2008)..278, 313, 356, 420
LL Children, In the Matter of (NY LJ May 2000) 314
LL Children, In the Matter of (Unpublished, 22 June 2000)......................................338
Lopez v Alcala 547 F Supp 2d 1255 (MD Fla 2008) 278
Lops v Lops 140 F3d 927 (11th Cir 1998) 231
Lozano v Alvarez 697 F3d 41 (US App (2nd Circ) 2012)....................................227, 230
Maynard v Maynard 2007 US Dist LEXIS 46838...422
McManus v McManus 354 F Supp 2d 62 (2005) 325, 331, 340, 351
Mendez Lynch v Mendez Lynch 220 F Supp 2d 1347 (MD Fla 2002)........................241
Meredith v Meredith 759 F Supp 1432 (D Ariz 1991)..211
Mikovic v Mikovic 541 F Supp 2d 1264 (MD Fl 2007) 196, 216
Miltiadous v Tetervak 686 F Supp 2d 544 (2010)...285
Maurizio R v LC 201 Cal App 4th 616 (2011)....................17, 280, 291, 301–302, 313
Morris, In the Matter of 55 FSupp 1156 (D Colo 1999)......................................198, 214

xlii *Table of Cases*

Mota v Rivera Castillo 692 F3d 108 (2d Cir 2012) 210
Mozes v Mozes 239 F3d 1067 (9th Cir 2001) 143, 177, 179, 181, 187–189,
                                                                  191–192, 195–196, 207, 219
Navarro v Bullock 15 Fam L Rep 1576 (Cal Sup Ct 1989) 324, 377
Neves v Neves 637 F Supp 2d 322 (WD North Carolina 2009) 422
Nicolson v Pappalardo 605 F3d 100 (1st Cir 2010) 249
Norden–Powers v Beveridge 125 F Supp 2d 634 (EDNY 2000) 327
Norinder v Fuentes 657 F3d 526 (2011) 312
Nunez–Escudero v Tice–Menley 58 F3d 374 (8th Cir 1995) 214
Ostevoll v Ostevoll 2000 WL 1611123 (SD Ohio) 284, 334
Otzalin v Otzalin (2d Cir 2013) 424
Panazatou v Pantazatos 1997 WL 614519 (Conn Super Ct 1997) 280
Papakosnias v Papakosinas 483 F3d 617 (9th Cir 2007) 196
Paz v Paz 169 FSupp2d 254 (SD New York 2001) 197
People v Neidinger 146 P3d 502 (Cal 2006) 16, 31
Philippopoulos v Philippopoulou 461 F Supp 2d 1321 (ND Georgia 2006) 143
Ponath, In re Application of 829 F Supp 363 (D Utah 1993) 179, 214
Prevot v Prevot 855 FSupp 915 (WD Tenn 1994) 191
Rajmakers–Eghage v Haro 131 F Supp 2d 953 (ED Mich 2001) 323, 338
Ramirez v Buyauskas 2012 US Dist LEXIS 24899 ....285, 377, 422
Robert v Tesson 507 F3d 981 (6th Cir 2008) 190–191, 196, 208
Roberts v Roberts 1998 US Dist LEXIS 4089 (D Mass February 1998) 293
Robinson v Robinson 983 F Supp 1339 (D Colo 1997) 237, 331–332, 336, 349
Ruiz v Tenorio 393 F3d 1247 (11th Cir 2004) 189, 199
Ryder v Ryder 49 F3d 369 (8th Cir 1973) 187
Santosky v Kramer 455 US (1982) 122
Sasson v Sasson 327 F Supp 2d 489 (D New Jersey 2004) 199
Shalit v Coppe 182 F3d 1124 (9th Cir 1999) 197
Silverman v Silverman 338 F3d 886 (8th Cir 2003) 192, 197, 219, 279, 422
Simcox v Simcox 511 F3d 594 (6th Cir 2007) 278, 293–294, 298
SJOBG, In The Interest of 292 SW3d 764 (Tex App 2009) 141, 191
Slagenweit v Slagenweit 841 FSupp 264 (ND Iowa 1993) 191
Slagenweit v Slagenweit 63 F3d 719 (8th Cir 1995) 199
State v Maidi 537 NW2d 280 (Minn 1995) 420
Steffen F v Severina P 966 FSupp2d 922 (E Ariz 1997) 67, 106, 281
Stern v Stern 132 SCt 1540 (2012) 186, 192, 208
Tabacchi v Harrison 2000 WL 190576 (ND Ill 2000) 291
Tahan v Duquette 600 A2d 472 (NJ Sup Ct 1991) 204
Tahan v Duquette 613 A2d 486 (NJ Sup Ct 1992) 323
Testerman v Testerman 193 P3d 1141 (2008) 74
Toren v Toren 191 F3d 23 (1st Cir 1999) 143
Trudrung v Trudrung 686 F Supp 2d 570 (MDNC 2010) 328
Tsai Yai Yang v Fu–Chang Tsui 499 F3d 279 (3d Cir 2007) 342
Tsarbopoulos v Tsarbopoulos 176 F Supp 2d 1045 (ED Wash 2001) 197, 214, 284
Tsimhoni v Eibschitz–Tsimhoni (Unreported, US District Court for Eastern
    District of Michigan March 2010) 156, 191, 196, 212
United States v Cummings 281 F3d 1046 (9th Cir 2002) 419–420, 422

Van de Sande v Van de Sande 431 F3d 567 (7th Cir 2005) 135, 283, 312
Viteri v Pflucker 550 F Supp 2d 829 (Nd Illinois 2008) 143
Walker v Kitt 2012 US Dist LEXIS 153611 359
Walker v Walker 2012 US App LEXIS 23505 (16 November 2012) 252
Walsh v Walsh 221 F3d 204 (1st Cir 2000) 287, 293
Wanninger v Wanninger 850 F Supp 78 (D Mass 1994) 252
Whiting v Krassner 391 F3d 540 (3rd Cir 2004) 189, 191, 196, 201
Wilchynski v Wilchynski 2010 US Dist LEXIS 25903 (18 March 2010) 313, 422
Wisconsin v Yoder 406 US 205 (1972) 122
Wojick v Wojick 959 F Supp 413 (ED Mich 1997) 228
Young v United States 535 US 43 (2002) 227
Zarate, In re Interest of No 96 C 50394 (ND Ill December 1996) 226, 229
Zuker v Andrews 2 F Supp 2d 134 (D Mass 1998) 143

TABLE OF LEGISLATION

Australia

Family Law Act 1975 15
   s 60B(2) 119
   s 64(1)(a) 355
   s 68L(3) 391
Family Law Amendment Act 2003 137

Statutory Instruments

Family Law (Child Abduction Convention) Regulations 1986 (Cth) 15, 134
   reg 1A(2)(c) 134
   reg 16(3)(c) 317
   reg 25 424
   reg 25(A) 426
   reg 30 421
Family Law (Child Abduction) Regulations 1989
   reg 16(3) 328

Canada

Charter of Rights and Freedoms
   s 6(1) 360
Children's Law Reform Act 1990, RSO Ch 12
   Pt II 8, 176
Civil Code of Québec
   Art 34 374
Criminal Code, RSC 1985, c C–46
   s 283 16
Divorce Act, RSC
   ss 9–10 215
Extra–Provincial Custody Orders Enforcement Act 1974 8

European Union

Charter of Fundamental Rights of the European Union
   Art 24 22
   Art 24(2) 119

xlvi   Table of Legislation

Regulations

Brussels I. *See* Council Regulation (EC) No 44/2001 of 22 December 2000
Brussels II. *See* Council Regulation (EC) No 1347/2000 of 30 June 2000
Brussels II bis. *See* Council Regulation (EC) No 2201/2003 of 27 November 2003
Council Regulation (EC) No 1347/2000 of 30 June 2000 on jurisdiction and the recognition and enforcement of judgments in matrimonial matters and in matters of parental responsibility for children of both spouses OJ L 160 (Brussels II) 19,
Council Regulation (EC) No 44/2001 of 22 December 2000 on jurisdiction and the recognition and enforcement of judgments in civil and commercial matters (Brussels I) 131
Council Regulation (EC) No 2201/2003 of 27 November 2003 concerning jurisdiction and the recognition and enforcement of judgments in matrimonial matters and the matters of parental responsibility (Brussels II bis) [2003] OJ L 338/1–29 .... 2, 12, 19, 21–24, 86, 103, 105, 131, 134, 148, 176, 187, 194, 239, 290, 304, 308, 347, 376, 381, 412, 415, 431, 443

    Preamble...19, 22
        para 5..19
        para 19..21
    Art 1...19
    Art 1(a)–(c)..19
    Art 2(3)..19
    Art 2(11)(b)..148
    Art 8(1)..20
    Art 10..20, 29, 194
    Art 10(b)...33
    Art 11..116
    Art 11(2)...21, 374
    Art 11(3)...21
    Art 11(4)..22, 284, 290
    Art 11(5)...22
    Art 11(6)...23, 105, 387
    Art 11(7)...20–21, 23–24, 105, 387
    Art 11(8)..23–24, 105, 134, 387
    Art 12..20
    Art 12(3)...413
    Arts 13–14 20
    Art 15..20, 103
    Art 19..376
    Art 21..21
    Art 23..21
    Art 23(b)...22
    Art 24..21
    Art 26..21
    Art 41(1)...431
    Art 42..23
    Art 42(2)...23

Art 46	431
Arts 59–60	19
Art 72	19
Regulation (EC) No 864/2007 of 11 July 2007 on the law applicable to non-contractual obligations (Rome II) [2007] OJ L199/40	176

Rome II. *See* Regulation (EC) No 864/2007 of 11 July 2007

Germany

Amending Act of 13 April 1999	39
International Family Law Procedure Act 2005	46

Hungary

Decree No 7 of 1988 of the Minister of Justice	46

Israel

Basic Law: Dignity and Freedom of Man	124, 343
Civil Wrongs Ordinance (New Version) 1972	
s 63	419
Family Court Law 1995	
s 3d	403
s 14	151
Hague Convention (Return of Abducted Children) Law 1991	14
s 2	15
Legal Capacity and Guardianship Law 1962	
s 14	151
s 15	148
Parents and Children Law 2012 (Draft)	137
Penal Law 1977	419
s 77	419
s 287	419
s 370	16
s 373	16, 419
Succession Law 1965	
s 142	129

Regulations

Civil Procedure Regulations 1984 (as amended)	
Ch 22(1)	46
reg 258(33) 2	380
reg 258(33)10	116

reg 258(33)12 414
reg 295(9) 374
reg 295(22) 155

Netherlands

Implementation Law 1980 on Child Abduction 46

New Zealand

Care of Children Act 2004 76
    s 6 378
    s 7(2) 390
    s 105(1)(d) 181
    s 106 321
    s 106(1)(a) 233, 378
    s 106(1)(c)–(d) 378
    s 106(2)(b) 358
Guardianship Amendment Act 1991 270
    s 4(a) 15, 154
    s 4(a)(1) 154
    s 4(a)(1)(a)–(b) 154
    s 12 15
    s 13 ....15, 321
    s 13(1)(c)(i)–(ii) 270

Norway

Child Abduction Act of 1988
    s 11 374
    s 17 374

Sharia Law

Majella
    s 1685 359

South Africa

Children's Act 38 of 2005
    s 55 390
    s 279 390
Constitution 310–311, 356

Art 28(2) 112
Legal Aid Act 22 of 1969
   s 3 390

Switzerland

Federal Act on International Child Abduction and The Hague Conventions on the
   Protection of Child and Adults 2007 315
   Art 4 409
   Art 5 .... 184, 277, 281, 315
   Art 5(a)–(c) 277
   Art 8 409
   Art 9(3) 389
   Art 11 48
   Art 12 49
   Art 13 48

United Kingdom

Adoption Act 1968 187
Child Abduction Act 1984
   s 1(1) 16
   s 1(2) 15
   s 2(1) 16
   s 4 16
Child Abduction and Custody Act 1985 14
   s 8 155
   s 9(b) 19
   s 16(4)(c) 19
Children Act 1989 233
   s 1 ....112, 355
   s 1(1)(a) 367
   s 1(2) 137
   s 8 403
   s 10(8) 403
   s 13(1)(b) 148
   s 31(2) 123
Domicile and Matrimonial Proceedings Act 1973
   s 9 104
Family Law Act 1986 15
   Pt I 176
Foreign Judgments Reciprocal Enforcement Act 1933 130
Human Rights Act 1998 ....359, 363
Law Reform (Miscellaneous Provisions Act) 1949 176
Matrimonial Causes Act 1973
   s 2 214

Table of Legislation

Statutory Instruments

Family Law (Child Abduction Convention) Regulations 1986
    reg 14 45
Family Proceedings Rules 1991
    r 6.5 389–390
Family Proceeding Rules 2010
    r 12.1(1)(e) 397
    r 12.6 397
    r 16.2 390
Rules of the Court of Session (Scotland) 424

United States of America

Cal Penal Code § 278.7(a) (West 2011) 16
51 Federal Regulation 10,494 (1986) 57, 277
Federal Rules of Civil Procedure 391
    r 17(c) 391
International Child Abduction Remedies Act, 42 USC § 1160 15
    § 11601(a)(4) 225
    § 11603 420
    § 11603(b) 424
    § 11603(e)(2)(A) 15, 273, 354
    § 11603(e)(2)(B) 317
    § 11607(b)(3) 420
    § 11611 133
International Parental Kidnapping Crime Act, 18 USC § 1204 .... 16, 420
    § 1204(C)(2) 314
La Rev Stat Ann § 9:355.13 75
New York Penal Law
    Art 135 16
Uniform Child Custody Jurisdiction Act 8–9, 15, 209
    § 3(a)(2) 104, 209
    § 8 9
    § 8(a) 8
Victim and Witness Protection Act, 8 USC § 3663(a)(1)(A) 419–420

TABLE OF CONVENTIONS, TREATIES ETC

Australia

Abduction Convention. *See* Hague Convention on the Civil Aspects of International Child Abduction 1980
Convention on Guardianship (1902) 175–176
Convention 80/934/ECC on the law applicable to contractual obligations 1980 [1980] OJ L266 (Rome I) 176
    Art 4(1) 128
Council of Europe Convention on the Recognition and Enforcement of Custody of Children and on Restoration of Custody of Children 1980 (European Custody Convention) 17–19, 430, 432
    Preamble 17
    Arts 7–8 18
    Art 9 .... 18, 430
    Art 9(3) 18, 430
    Art 10 .... 17, 430
    Art 10(1)(b) 18, 430
    Art 10(1)(d) 171
    Art 11(2)–(3) 430
    Art 12 18
    Art 17 18
EC Convention on the Law Applicable to Non-Contractual Obligations (Rome II)
    Art 4(3) 128
Europe Convention on Preventing and Combating Violence against Women and Domestic Violence 2011
    Art 3(b) 282
European Convention on Contact Concerning Children 2003 .... 119, 431
    Preamble 431
    Arts 6–7 431
    Art 10 431
    Arts 14–15 431
European Convention on the Exercise of Children's Rights
    Art 3(a) 116
    Art 6 375
    Art 6(b) 116
    Art 10 395
European Convention for the Protection of Human Rights and Fundamental Freedoms 1950 .... 2, 24–26, 28, 123–124, 168, 316, 355, 357, 359, 365, 368, 392, 439

Art 6 .... 359, 392
Art 6(1) 25
Art 8 .... 24, 26–28, 49, 112, 122, 124–125,
168, 308–309, 311, 355–357, 359, 392
Art 8(1) 25
Art 8(2) 25, 122, 125
Art 14 359
Art 30 25
Art 53 25
Fourth Protocol
Art 2 360
European Custody Convention. *See* Council of Europe Convention on the Recognition and Enforcement of Custody of Children and on Restoration of Custody of Children 1980
Hague Convention on Choice of Court Agreements 2005
Art 2 216
Art 6 216
Hague Convention on the Civil Aspects of International Child Abduction 1980
(Abduction Convention) .... i, v–vi, 1–3, 7, 9–24, 26–43, 46–47,
49–56, 58, 60–62, 64, 66–67, 69, 72, 75, 82, 84–90, 93–96, 98–100,
102, 104–114, 116–121, 124–128, 130–137, 141, 143, 146–147,
149, 154, 168–171, 173, 175–178, 180, 200, 204, 206, 211, 217–218,
221, 227, 233, 239, 242, 249–250, 253, 255–256, 270–272, 279,
282, 285, 288, 291, 296, 298, 301, 306–311, 317–318, 343, 351,
354, 355–356, 358, 360, 362–363, 367, 375, 377–380, 386, 388–391,
394, 396, 398–400, 402–403, 405, 410–424, 426, 428–430,
432–433, 437–444, 447, 449, 451
Ch I 451
Chs II–III 452
Ch IV 455
Ch V 10, 455
Ch VI 457
Preamble 1, 9, 11, 14, 66, 94, 96–97, 178, 181–182, 285, 356–357, 423, 428
Art 1 .... 10–11, 14, 96, 451
Art 1(a) 96, 423, 451
Art 1(b) 96–97, 169, 423, 428, 451
Art 2 .... 10–11, 14, 427, 451
Art 3 .... 10, 97, 126, 141, 147, 153–154, 157, 160, 169,
172–173, 204, 261–262, 265, 309, 451, 453–454, 456
Art 3(a) 141, 451
Art 3(b) 141, 156, 158–159, 161, 174, 245, 451
Art 4 .... 10, 425, 452
Art 5 .... 10, 15, 94, 149, 154, 429, 452
Art 5(a) 147, 452
Art 5(b) 452
Art 6 .... 10, 38, 452
Art 7 .... 10–11, 38, 423, 452, 455

Table of Conventions, Treaties etc liii

Art 7(a)	43, 452
Art 7(b)	44, 433, 452
Art 7(c)–(d)	44, 452
Art 7(e)	31, 452
Art 7(f)	45, 423, 428, 452
Art 7(g)	40, 452
Art 7(h)	46, 452
Art 7(i)	452
Art 8	452–453
Art 8(a)–(g)	453
Art 9	11, 453
Art 10	44, 453
Art 11	11, 39, 46, 106, 427–428, 453
Art 12	22, 39, 143, 182, 228, 234, 300, 327, 374, 429, 452, 453, 455
Art 12(1)	10–11, 145, 225–226, 228, 235, 321
Art 12(2)	11, 111, 143–145, 203, 225, 227, 229, 231, 233–237, 240–244, 262, 286, 299, 336, 341, 373, 390, 402, 439, 445
Art 13	11, 22–23, 234, 257, 271, 306, 308, 310–311, 317–319, 324, 344, 356, 374, 453
Art 13(a)	158–159, 453
Art 13(b)	71, 236, 272, 283, 315, 454
Art 13(c)	317
Art 13(1)(a)	11, 141, 158–159, 161–163, 174, 245–246, 251, 253–254, 261–263, 265–266, 268, 317, 405, 445
Art 13(1)(b)	11, 15, 22, 49, 60, 66, 69, 87–88, 133, 162, 267, 271–274, 276–278, 282–283, 285, 287–288, 300–301, 303, 306, 314, 317, 332, 339, 343, 354, 358–359, 362, 364–369, 404, 422, 440, 445–446
Art 13(1)(d)	352
Art 13(2)	11, 69, 115, 205, 234, 267, 282, 317–324, 327–328, 331–332, 334, 337, 340, 343–345, 348–349, 351–353, 373, 385, 438, 446
Art 13(3)	271
Art 14	10, 106, 165, 454
Art 15	11, 127, 147, 153–156, 165, 172, 212, 448, 454
Art 16	12, 15, 106, 126, 299, 428, 454
Art 17	12, 126, 171, 454
Art 18	12, 234–235, 237, 300, 454
Art 19	12, 454
Art 20	11, 13, 15, 234, 273, 282, 311, 354–369, 446, 455
Art 21	10, 30, 158, 301, 423–429, 432–433, 441, 455–456
Art 22	11, 453, 455
Art 23	12, 455
Art 24	12, 455, 458–459
Art 25	455
Art 26	11, 40, 291, 436, 456
Art 26(2)	418
Art 26(3)	458–459

Art 26(4)	11, 420–422, 447
Arts 27–28	456
Art 29	43, 155, 456
Arts 30–31	456
Art 31(a)–(b)	456
Arts 32–33	457
Art 34	300, 457
Art 35	457
Art 36	300, 457
Art 37	12, 457–459
Art 38	13, 40, 457–459
Arts 39–40	457–459
Art 41	458
Art 42	455–456, 458–459
Art 43	458–459
Art 43(1)–(2)	459
Arts 44–45	459
Art 45(1)–(7)	459

Hague Convention on Jurisdiction, Applicable Law and Recognition of Decrees relating to Adoptions 1965 176

Hague Convention on Jurisdiction, Applicable Law, Recognition, Enforcement and Co-operation in Respect of Parental Responsibility and Measures for the Protection of Children 1996 (Protection Convention) 29–32, 41–42, 82–83, 86, 105, 126, 131, 134, 170, 176, 203, 205, 295, 424, 430

Art 5(1)	29
Art 7	20, 29, 32–33, 413, 430
Arts 8–9	413
Art 10	32
Art 11	29–30, 413, 431
Art 12(2)	29
Art 13	32
Art 15	30, 126
Art 15(2)	170
Art 16	126
Art 16(1)	30
Art 16(3)	30, 170
Arts 17–20	126
Art 21	126
Art 21(1)–(2)	129
Art 22	126
Art 23	31
Art 23(1)	30
Art 23(2)	30, 430
Art 23(2)(a)	131
Art 24	430
Art 31(b)	430
Art 34	31

Art 35(1)–(2) 430
Art 50 30
Hague Convention on the Law Applicable to Maintenance Obligations towards
    Children 1956 176
Hague Convention concerning the Powers of Authorities and the Law Applicable in
    respect of the Protection of Infants 1961 .... 8, 29, 176–177
Hague Convention on Protection of Children and Co-Operation in Respect of
    Intercountry Adoption 1993 176
Hague Convention on the Recognition of Divorces and Legal Separations 1970 ...... 131, 176
Protection Convention. *See* Hague Convention on Jurisdiction, Applicable Law,
    Recognition, Enforcement and Co-operation in Respect of Parental Responsibility
    and Measures for the Protection of Children 1996
Rome I. *See* Convention 80/934/ECC on the law applicable to contractual obligations 1980
Rome II. *See* EC Convention on the Law Applicable to Non-Contractual Obligations
UN Convention on the Rights of the Child 1989 .... i, vi, 33–34, 93, 109–113, 115, 117,
                                                    119, 121, 307–308, 316–317, 319, 322, 326,
                                                    343, 351–352, 368, 381, 391, 438–439, 445
    Art 2 111
    Art 3 .... 111–113, 118, 306–308, 316, 355, 363, 439
    Art 3(1) 111
    Art 3(2) 118
    Art 5 .... 109, 115, 350
    Art 6 .... 111, 118
    Art 6(1)–(2) 118
    Art 7 119
    Art 9 .... 119, 438
    Art 10 438
    Art 10(2) 119
    Art 11 .... 110, 308
    Art 12 .... 22, 111–113, 115, 117, 213, 318, 328–329, 351, 379–380, 387
    Art 12(1) 113, 117, 404, 438
    Art 12(2) 113, 121, 391
    Art 35 308
UN International Covenants on Human Rights 358
Vienna Convention on the Law of Treaties 1969 (Vienna Convention) 94, 96
    Art 31 .... 93, 95
    Art 31(2) 93
    Art 31(3)(a)–(c) 93
    Art 32 95
Washington Declaration on International Family Relocation 2010 82–83
    para 4(i)–(xiii) 83

Introduction

I The Hague Convention on the Civil Aspects of International Child Abduction 1980

The phenomenon of international child abduction by parents has become significantly more widespread over the past half a century inter alia because of greater international mobility, increasing numbers of marriages between parties from different countries and soaring divorce rates.[1] The Hague Convention on the Civil Aspects of International Child Abduction 1980 ('the Abduction Convention') constitutes the response of the international community to this universally condoned phenomenon, which has been referred to as a 'human minefield'.[2] This Convention adopted a mechanism of automatic expedited return of abducted children, subject to a limited number of narrow exceptions. This remedy was designed to protect children from the harmful effects of the unilateral removal or retention, by returning them promptly to the State of their habitual residence.[3]

The Abduction Convention has been widely acclaimed as the most successful of the family law conventions drawn up under the auspices of the Hague Conference on Private International Law.[4] Indeed, it seems likely that the number of states which have acceded to this Convention[5] and the number of applications made thereunder[6] are way beyond the expectations of the drafters. Nonetheless, success cannot be measured solely on the basis of the extent to which the Abduction Convention is used, nor even by the percentage of cases in which the return of the abducted child is ordered.[7] Indeed, the very fact that the number of applications continues to rise[8] may be seen as casting doubt on the extent to which the Convention's professed objective of deterring abductions has been realised. Moreover, it is clear that the drafters of the Convention did not envisage that the typical abduction case

---

[1] For a sociological analysis of the reasons for the phenomenon, see ch three at I.
[2] M Freeman, 'Effects and Consequences of International Child Abduction' (1998) 32 *Family law Quarterly* 602, 607.
[3] Preamble to the Abduction Convention.
[4] eg P Beaumont and A McEleavy, *The Hague Convention on International Child Abduction* (Oxford, Oxford University Press, 1999) 4.
[5] According to the Status table, there were 89 Contracting States as at 12 December 2012: www.hcch.net/index_en.php?act=conventions.status&cid=24.
[6] In 2008, 1961 return applications and 360 applications for access were made under the Convention: N Lowe, 'A Statistical Analysis of Applications Made in 2008 under the Hague Convention of 25 October 1980 on the Civil Aspects of International Child Abduction, Part I Global Report, Prel Doc 8 (November 2011)', www.hcch.net/upload/wop/abduct2011pd08ae.pdf [2008 Statistical Survey] 4.
[7] R Schuz, 'The Hague Child Abduction Convention: Family Law and Private International Law' (1995) 44 *International and Comparative Law Quarterly* 771. A similar comment was made by Professor William Duncan, then Deputy Secretary-General of the Hague Conference at the opening session of the Sixth Special Commission in June 2011.
[8] A comparison of the data from the 2003 and 2008 Statistical Surveys (taking into account only data from those states which responded to both surveys) shows a 45% increase in the number of return applications, 2008 Statistical Survey (fn 5) 8.

would involve abduction by the primary carer mother, as is the case today.[9] Indeed, as will be seen, there is evidence to suggest that the return of the child in some such cases may cause him harm, or exacerbate the harm already caused, rather than protect him from harm.

Thus, in order to ascertain the real degree of success of the Abduction Convention, it is necessary to analyse in detail the way in which the Convention has been applied against parameters which test conformity with the objectives of Convention and other relevant norms. Moreover, such analysis must take place against the backdrop of the wider legal and sociological context in which the Convention operates and in which abduction cases arise and are adjudicated.

This book provides a wide-ranging in-depth analysis of the Abduction Convention and the way in which it has been applied. Conclusions are drawn from this analysis and recommendations are made as to how the objectives of the Convention might be better achieved in ways which are more consistent with general, widely accepted legal norms, with particular emphasis on the rights and interests of children.

II Structure of the Book and Methodology

Part I of the book provides a broad historical, international, practical, empirical and inter-disciplinary overview of the Abduction Convention and its operation. Chapter one considers the background to the Convention and its inter-relationship with other national, regional and global legal instruments. Particular emphasis is placed on the Council Regulation (EC) No 2201/2003 of 27 November 2003 concerning jurisdiction and the recognition and enforcement of judgments in matrimonial matters and the matters of parental responsibility ('Brussels II bis' or the 'Regulation')[10] and the European Convention on Human Rights which have had a significant impact on the application of the Abduction Convention in Europe in recent years. Chapter two explains the practical operation of the Convention. Chapter three considers relevant knowledge from the fields of sociology and psychology. Chapter four discusses the parallel phenomenon of relocation and its inter-relationship with child abduction.

Part II of the book develops two complementary sets of parameters for analysing the way in which the Abduction Convention has been interpreted and applied by the courts. The parameters in the first category are based on principles of treaty interpretation and are designed to test consistency with the text and objectives of the Convention. The purpose of the second set of parameters is to examine consistency with general legal doctrines, principles and policies that are relevant to the subject-matter of the Abduction Convention cases, taken mainly from the fields of family law and private international law. The most prominent of these is the doctrine of children's rights. Each of the parameters in the two categories is explained fully in chapters five and six respectively.

The six chapters in Parts III and IV of the book contain a detailed examination of how the main provisions of the Abduction Convention have been interpreted and applied by courts, followed by an analysis of the trends in the case law, in light of the parameters

---

[9] See detail in ch three at I B.
[10] [2003] OJ.L 338/1-29.

developed in Part II. Chapters seven and eight consider the two key threshold conditions which have to be established in order to trigger the mandatory return mechanism ('wrongful removal or retention' and 'habitual residence'). Chapters nine to 13 discuss the exceptions to mandatory return.

An important theme in modern child law is the need to give children a voice in relation to matters concerning them. Accordingly, Part V of the book considers to what extent children are, and should be, given a voice in child abduction disputes and the ways in which this can, and should, be done. Chapter 14 discusses methods of ascertaining children's views and chapter 15 examines the status of children in Abduction Convention proceedings.

The central remedy provided by the Abduction Convention is a court-ordered return of the abducted child. Part VI of the book briefly considers other remedies and procedures available in child abduction disputes: the use of mediation as an alternative to adjudication; methods of obtaining compensation for the left-behind parent and enforcement of access rights.

Finally, Part VII summarises the conclusions drawn from the analysis in the book and considers the way ahead. After a discussion of the significance of relevant legal and other developments which have taken place since 1980, recommendations are made as to ways in which the Abduction Convention might more successfully achieve its objectives and be more consistent with other important parameters.

III Sources and Notation

An analysis of the way in which the Abduction Convention has been applied must be based largely on case law. Over the nearly 30 years since the Abduction Convention came into force, it has been applied in thousands of cases. Whilst many of these were not available to the author because they are not reported at all or not in a source and language accessible to her, there were still large numbers of cases to which she did have access.[11] Clearly, it was only possible to refer to a relatively small proportion of these within the confines of a monograph. In selecting which cases to mention and discuss, the aim has been to provide examples of different approaches and to bring cases from a variety of jurisdictions. However, inevitably there is an emphasis on English and US cases and this can be justified both because of the large number of cases decided by these jurisdictions and because of the considerable influence which the case law from these countries has in other Contracting States. Similarly, whilst reference is made to recent case law (until the end of 2012), many older cases are also discussed, since these continue to be cited by the courts and still reflect the way in which the Convention is interpreted and applied.

Extensive reference is made throughout the book to the large body of academic literature which reviews and analyses the Convention case law and to other relevant legal and social science literature. In addition, use is made of a variety of other sources which cast

---

[11] The Hague Conference's database Incadat gave the author access to case reports, which would not have otherwise been available to her and she is grateful to the Hague Conference, Professor Peter McEleavy and others who have contributed over the years to this database. However, in order to avoid cumbersome references, the Incadat citation number is only given where the author only had access to the Incadat report and did not have access to the text of the decision itself in a language she could read. In addition, the Incadat citation is given for Israeli cases which are reported there, since most readers will not have access to or be able to read the full decision in Hebrew.

light on the operation of the Convention. These include documents produced by the Hague Conference on Private International law[12] and empirical research into child abduction and other related phenomena.

For the most part, for reasons of convenience, the masculine form is used in relation to both adults and children and this includes the feminine form. However, where the context is such that in practice most of the adults referred to are women (eg victims of domestic violence, primary carer abductors and relocation applicants), the feminine form is used.

Various terms are used interchangeably throughout the book. Abductors are sometimes referred to as taking parents and left-behind parents are also called applicants. The country to which the child has been abducted is referred to both as the State of refuge and the requested State. Conversely, the place where the child was habitually resident before the abduction is referred to as both the State of origin and as the requesting State. The exceptions to mandatory return are synonymously called defences. Finally, it will be more convenient to use the term 'abduction', as in the title of the Convention, rather than the more cumbersome phrase 'wrongful removal or retention', which appears in the text of the Convention. However, apart from where the context requires otherwise, the term 'abduction' refers to both removals and retentions.

---

[12] See detail in ch 2 at I A.

Part I

Overview

1

The Birth of the Abduction Convention and its Inter-Relationship with other Legal Instruments

I The Birth of the Abduction Convention

A Background

i *The Position before the Abduction Convention*

Prior to the Hague Convention on the Civil Aspects of International Child Abduction ('Abduction Convention'), many States did not have particular legal provisions for dealing with international child abduction. Thus, the best interests of the child standard was applied, as in all decisions concerning children. This situation provided an incentive to abductors who hoped that the law in the State of refuge would be favourable to them[1] or that they would be able to create a state of affairs in which the best interests of the child would require him to remain in that State of refuge.[2]

Nonetheless, attempts were made by some States to combat international child abduction. At a national level, some legal systems developed procedures which enabled abducted children to be returned to the country of origin without a full blown examination of the best interests of the child. For example, in England, the courts held that very often the best interests of an abducted child would require peremptory return to the country of origin and that the delay involved in conducting a welfare examination in the place of refuge would be harmful to the child.[3] In Israel, the High Court of Justice's habeas corpus jurisdiction was used to make orders 'releasing' children who were being held by an abductor in breach of the rights of the other parents, unless it was clearly against their best interests to do so.[4] Some US States used the 'clean-hands' doctrine as a basis to refuse to consider a request for custody modification where the applicant had violated that custody order.[5]

---

[1] Perez-Vera Report, Proceedings of the 14th Session of the Hague Conference Oct 1980, www.hcch.net/index_en.php?act=publications.details&pid=2779, para 116.
[2] ibid, 20.
[3] eg *Re L (Minors)(Wardship: Jurisdiction)* [1974] 1 All ER 913 (CA). For a detailed discussion, see N Lowe, M Everall and M Nicholls, *International Movement of Children: Law, Practice and Procedure* (Bristol, Family Law, 2004) 434–39.
[4] For detailed discussion of the exercise of this jurisdiction, see A Shapira, *Private International Law: Aspects of Child Custody and Child Kidnapping Cases* (Netherlands, Martinus Nijhoff, 1989) Recueil des Cours vol 214, 152–73.
[5] ibid 181–82.

The problem of child abduction was particularly acute in Federal States because of the ease of social mobility across state lines.[6] Thus, in both the US and Canada, Uniform Law Acts were promulgated which were designed to remove the incentive to abduct. The widely adopted US Uniform Child Custody Jurisdiction Act 1968 (UCCJA)[7] restricts jurisdiction to make and modify custody orders to the child's home State at the time of the commencement of the proceedings or the State which was the child's home State within the past six months, provided that one parent continues to live there. Moreover, Section 8(a) allows a competent court to decline to exercise jurisdiction where the petitioner 'has wrongfully taken the child from another state or has engaged in similar reprehensible conduct'. Similarly, in Canada, the Extra-Provincial Custody Orders Enforcement Act, approved by the Uniform Law Conference of Canada in 1974, was adopted by most of the Provinces.[8]

At an international level, there were bilateral and multilateral initiatives. Some countries made bilateral arrangements with other countries which provided for co-operation in cases concerning abduction of children or violation of custody or visitation rights at an international level.[9] The 1961 Hague Convention on the Protection of Infants also gave some degree of protection to abducted children by providing that the law of the child's habitual residence was to be applied. However, the usefulness of this Convention in combating international abduction was limited because it was only ratified by eight countries and because habitual residence was determined at the date of the proceedings.[10] This meant that where abducting parents were able to avoid being found or delay proceedings for sufficient time as to enable the child to acclimatise, the law of the State of refuge would be applicable and that law would inevitably conduct a full welfare examination.

ii The Drafting of the Convention

The Hague Conference first started to work on the subject of child abduction, then referred to as 'legal kidnapping', in 1976.[11] An analysis of the legal and social aspects of the phenomenon, carried out by the then First Secretary, Adair Dyer, was published in 1978.[12] This Report adopted the term 'child abduction' instead of the previously used 'kidnapping'[13] and took the view that cases of retention after visitation should be treated as cases of abduction.[14] The Report's analysis of the causes of the phenomenon makes clear that the typical abduction situation was envisaged as one in which the non-custodial parent abducted the child, either in order to pre-empt a non-favourable custody determination or out of frustration caused by the reduction in contact with the child as a result of losing custody.[15] The Report discussed a number of methods which might be adopted in order to reduce the

---

[6] ibid 157–81.

[7] By 1984, it was adopted by 50 states with some variations (ibid 179).

[8] A Dyer, *Report On International Child Abduction By One Parent Legal Kidnapping*, Preliminary Document No 1, Aug 1978, in *Hague Conference On Private International Law*, 3 Actes Et Documents De Laquatorzième Session (Child Abduction) (1980) 12, 17 (Dyer Report); see, eg, in Ontario, Children's Law Reform Act 1990, RSO ch 12 pt 2.

[9] Dyer Report ibid, 16.

[10] K Wahler, 'The Convention on the Protection of Infant and Judicial Practice in West German Courts' in F Bates (ed), *The Child and The Law (The Proceedings of the First World Conference of The International Society on Family Law, Held in Berlin, April 1975)* (New York, Ocean Publications, 1976) 510–12.

[11] P Beaumont and P McEleavy, *The Hague Convention on International Child Abduction* (Oxford, Oxford University Press, 1999) 16–17.

[12] Dyer Report (n 8) 12.

[13] ibid.

[14] ibid 14.

[15] ibid 19–20.

problems caused by international child abduction. These were divided into three categories: remedies through the courts; elimination of the abductor's access to the courts and international co-operation.[16] The first category included reciprocal enforcement of custody decisions; the creation of an international tribunal and expedited return of abducted children. The second category included creating a narrow jurisdictional rule,[17] which would usually confer exclusive jurisdiction on a single State; allowing a court to refuse jurisdiction due to the misconduct of the applicant parent[18] and providing courts with discretion to refuse jurisdiction on the basis of *forum non-conveniens*.

The Special Commission meeting in March 1979 discussed the options set out in the Dyer Report. The two options which were treated most seriously were a uniform jurisdiction rule and reciprocal recognition of foreign custody decrees. The former option was rejected because of the considerable differences between bases of jurisdiction where custody was sought within the framework of matrimonial proceedings.[19] In relation to the latter option, no consensus could be achieved as to the nature of the exceptions to automatic recognition and enforcement.[20] A further difficulty with this model was that it made it necessary for the left-behind parent to obtain a chasing order where there had been no custody order in force at the time of the abduction.

By the time of the Second Special Commission meeting in November 1979, the Permanent Bureau had developed a proposal based on a summary return mechanism, subject to limited exceptions.[21] The Special Commission accepted the Bureau's draft as the basis for negotiation and produced a Preliminary Draft Convention. At this stage, Professor Perez-Vera prepared her report on the Convention and governments were invited to comment.[22] The main area of concern was in relation to the exceptions to automatic return, with some States expressing the view that the exceptions were too wide and others that they did not allow sufficient weight to be given to the best interests of the child.[23] Finally, after a good deal of diplomatic manoeuvring, the Convention was adopted by the 14th Session of the Hague Conference in 1980.[24] The next section will explain the structure of the Convention and the main provisions therein.

B The Structure of the Abduction Convention

i *Purpose of the Convention*

The Preamble to the Convention sets out the motivation behind the adoption of the Convention. This recites the belief that the interests of children are of paramount importance in matters relating to their custody; the desire to protect children from the harmful effects of their wrongful removal or retention and to establish procedures to ensure their prompt return to the State of habitual residence and to secure protection for rights of access.

---

[16] ibid 46–49.
[17] As in the US by the Uniform Child Custody Jurisdiction Act (UCCJA).
[18] As under s 8 of the UCCJA.
[19] Beaumont and McEleavy (n 11) 18.
[20] ibid 19.
[21] ibid 21.
[22] ibid 22.
[23] ibid.
[24] ibid 23.

The text of the Convention itself opens with a statement of its objectives, which are

(a) to secure the prompt return of children wrongfully removed to or retained in any Contracting State; and
(b) to ensure that rights of custody and or access under the law of one Contracting State are effectively respected in other Contracting States.

In practice the first objective is the dominant objective and the second is subsidiary thereto. Indeed, the only method of respecting rights of custody is by ordering prompt return to the country of origin. Furthermore, it will be seen that due to a wide interpretation of custody rights, to include some access rights,[25] the latter will sometimes also be protected by return orders. In other cases, Article 21 may be used to secure respect for access rights. However, as will be seen in chapter 18, this provision is of limited value.

Article 2 can be seen as a continuation of Article 1. It provides that 'Contracting States shall take all appropriate measures to secure within their territories the implementation of the objects of the Convention'.

ii Central Authorities

Articles 6 and 7 of the Convention provide for the designation of Central Authorities and set out a non-exhaustive list of the tasks which they are expected to perform. These, together with other provisions relating to the work of the Central Authorities, contained in Chapter V of the Convention, will be discussed in chapter two of the book.

iii Trigger for the Summary Return Mechanism and Exceptions thereto

Article 12(1) embodies the summary return mechanism and so can be seen as the main operative provision of the Convention. This Article mandates the immediate return of a child to whom the Convention applies and who has been wrongfully removed or retained where, at the date of the commencement of the proceedings, less than one year has elapsed from the date of the wrongful removal or retention. The obligation to order return is imposed on the judicial or administrative authorities of the Contracting State to which the child has been removed or in which he has been retained (the 'requested State' or the 'State of refuge'). In practice, in most, if not in all Contracting States, judicial authorities are those empowered to make return orders and so for convenience, reference will be made to courts or judges throughout this book.

The conditions for application of the Convention and the definition of wrongful removal and retention are contained in Articles 3 to 5 of the Convention. These include the requirement that the child was habitually resident in a Contracting State (other than the requested State) immediately before any breach of custody rights and that the child has not yet attained the age of 16.[26] The way in which these conditions have been interpreted and applied is discussed in detail in Part III of the book.

In order to determine whether there has been a breach of custody rights under the law of the State of habitual residence, it is necessary to ascertain the relevant law of that state. This can be done in two ways. Article 14 allows courts to take direct notice of the law of the habitual residence of the child. Alternatively, the authorities of the State of habitual resid-

---

[25] See ch 7 at II C and D.
[26] Art 4 of the Abduction Convention.

ence may be asked to provide a determination that the removal or retention was wrongful under the law of that state, under Article 15.[27]

Articles 12(2), 13 and 20 set out the exceptions to the mandatory return mechanism. These are respectively passage of time together with settlement of the child;[28] consent or acquiescence by the applicant;[29] a grave risk that return will expose the child to harm or place him in an intolerable situation;[30] the objections of a mature child[31] and violation of fundamental human rights.[32] Where one of these defences is established, the Court has discretion as to whether to return the child.[33] The defences are discussed in detail in Part IV of the book.

iv Speed and Accessibility

The need for speed is reflected in the repeated use of the word prompt,[34] and synonyms thereof[35] in the provisions of the Convention.[36] Article 2 mandates Contracting States to use the most expeditious procedures available. Article 11 provides that judicial and administrative authorities shall act expeditiously in return proceedings and that where a decision has not been reached within six weeks from the commencement of the proceedings, the applicant or the Central Authority of the requested State have the right to request a statement of the reasons for the delay. In addition, some provisions of the Convention are clearly intended to promote speedy decision-making. For example, the provision allowing courts to take direct notice of the law of the habitual residence of the child is designed to save the delay which would be caused by the need to prove foreign law in the usual way through expert evidence.[37]

A number of the provisions are designed to maximise the accessibility of the Convention to left-behind parents by removing financial or other obstacles to submission of applications under the Convention. For example, Article 22 provides that no security bond or deposit can be required to guarantee the payment of costs of judicial or administrative proceedings under the Convention. Article 26 provides that Central Authorities and other public services of Contracting States may not impose any charges in relation to applications under the Convention. However, Contracting States who enter a reservation to this provision are not obliged to take upon themselves lawyers' fees or any other costs arising from court proceedings, except insofar as those costs are covered by that State's legal aid system.[38] Article 26(4) provides that courts, upon ordering the return of the child or making an order in relation to access, may direct the abducting parents to pay necessary

---

[27] Discussed in ch 7 at III E.
[28] Art 12(2).
[29] Art 13(1)(a).
[30] Art 13(1)(b).
[31] Art 13(2).
[32] Art 20.
[33] Conflicting views have been expressed as to whether there is discretion when the exception in Art 12(2) applies. See ch 9 at II C.
[34] eg, Preamble, Arts 1 and 7.
[35] eg 'expeditious' (Arts 2 and 11) 'forthwith' (Art 12(1)) and 'without delay' (Art 9).
[36] The Perez-Vera Report (n 1) para 104 points out that there are two aspects to the requirement of speed. Firstly that Contracting States should use the most expeditious procedures possible and secondly that they should give Abduction Convention applications priority treatment.
[37] Perez-Vera Report (n 1) para 119.
[38] 42 Contracting States have entered such reservations, according to the Status Table as at 14 December 2012: www.hcch.net/index_en.php?act=conventions.status&cid=24).

12 *Birth of the Convention and other Instruments*

expenses incurred by the applicant. This provision will be discussed in detail in chapter 17 of the book.

Other examples of provisions designed to reduce the burden on the applicant include Article 23, which provides that no legalisation or other formality can be required in the context of the Convention, and Article 24, which allows documents to be in French or English, where it is not feasible to translate into the language of the requested State, unless a reservation has been entered to this provision.[39]

v Inter-Relationship between the Abduction Convention and Domestic Proceedings

Article 16 provides that where the courts of the requested State have received notice of a wrongful removal or retention, no decision is to be made on the merits of the rights of the custody unless and until it has been determined that the child is not to be returned under the Convention or unless an application is not submitted under the Convention within a reasonable time. Article 17 effectively gives supremacy to the law of the State of habitual residence by providing that the fact that a custody decision has been given in or is entitled to recognition in the requested State is not a ground for refusing return, although the reasons for that decision may be taken into account in applying the Convention.

Article 18 makes clear that the Abduction Convention is not exhaustive and so courts may order the return of children under other legal provisions. However, there will be very few situations in which the Abduction Convention applies in which other means will be more favourable.[40] Article 19 provides that decisions under the Convention concerning the return of the child are not to be treated as determinations on the merits of any custody issue. This gives expression to one of the basic concepts which underlie the return mechanism; namely that return is ordered so that the merits of the custody dispute can be determined by the State of habitual residence.

C Ratifications and Accessions

As of 12 December 2012, there were 89 Contracting States to the Hague Child Abduction Convention.[41] States who were members of the Hague Conference on Private International Law at the time of its 14th session in 1980 could become parties to the Convention by signing and ratifying the Convention.[42] The Convention comes into force automatically between all such ratifying parties. Any other State may accede to the Convention by depositing an instrument of accession with the Ministry of Foreign Affairs of the Kingdom of the Netherlands, which will enter into force on the first day of the third calendar month after

---

[39] 23 States have entered such reservations, ibid.

[40] However, in some cases where there is already a custody order in force, it may be easier to apply for enforcement thereof where this can be done without the need for a cumbersome procedure, as under the Brussels II bis Regulation (see below at II C).

[41] See 'Status Table' (n 38). It should be noted that some Contracting States consist of more than one territorial unit. For example, the United Kingdom includes England and Wales, Scotland, Northern Ireland, The Isle of Man, The Cayman Islands and the Falkland Islands. However, in this book, in the context of the practical operation of the Convention reference to States should be seen as including reference to territorial units. This practice is also adopted by the Hague Conference. See, for example, fn 3 in their questionnaire on the operation of the Convention, Preliminary Document No 1 of 2010: www.hcch.net/upload/wop/sc2011pd01e.DOC.

[42] Art 37. There are 32 such States that have ratified the Convention (see table of ratifications and accessions): www.hcch.net/upload/abductoverview_e.pdf.

this deposit.[43] However, the accession only has effect in regards to the relations between the acceding State and other Contracting States who accept the accession. The Perez-Vera Report explains that the choice of a system based on express acceptance of accessions 'sought to maintain the requisite balance between a desire for universality and the belief that a system based on co-operation could work only if there existed amongst the Contracting Parties a sufficient degree of mutual confidence'.[44]

Indeed, the consequences of accepting another State's accession to the Hague Abduction are far-reaching. In particular, as seen above, once the Convention comes into force between two States, each one is obliged to return children who were habitually resident in the other State at the date of wrongful removal or retention. This requirement to return is mandatory, subject to a few narrowly drawn exceptions, and not subject to the discretion of the Court or to the examination of the best interests of the child in the particular case. Thus, Contracting States cannot question the legality or legitimacy of a decision of the requesting State or inquire into the standards of justice in that State's legal system.[45] Accordingly, acceptance of a State's accession to the Abduction Convention is effectively an 'implied acceptance of the social and legal regime prevailing in that State at that time'.[46] Thus, for example, it will be virtually impossible to prove that return will lead to a breach of fundamental principles relating to human rights, within the Article 20 exception, unless there has been a change of regime in the requesting State since it acceded to the Hague Abduction Convention.[47]

Therefore, the Member States should be careful to make sure that the standards of justice in a State which accedes to the Convention are acceptable to it before accepting that accession.[48] Indeed, the official Rapporteur of the Convention points out that the choice of a system based on express acceptance of accession by each Member State, rather than one which would assume acceptance in the absence of an objection, 'demonstrates the importance which the States attached to the selection of their co-signatories, in those questions which form the subject-matter of the Convention'.[49] However, the fact that most Contracting States have accepted most accessions[50] might suggest that States do not exercise great caution before accepting accessions or that States are concerned about the political and diplomatic ramifications of refusing to accept an accession.[51] Alternatively, States may believe that the advantages of accepting an accession outweigh any concerns about the legal system of the foreign country.[52] Indeed, Thorpe LJ has suggested that 'the

---

[43] Art 38.
[44] Perez-Vera Report (n 1) para 41.
[45] *Re S (Abduction: Intolerable Situation: Beth Din)* [2000] 1 FLR 454, 463.
[46] Beaumont and McEleavy (n 11) 174.
[47] FamC (RG) 74430/99 *P v P* (Unreported, 14 December 1999) (Isr); See generally, discussion of interpretation and application of Art 20 in ch 13.
[48] CS Bruch, 'Religious Law, Secular Practices, and Children's Human Rights in Child Abduction Cases Under the Hague Child Abduction Convention' (2000) 33 *New York University Journal of International Law and Politics* 49.
[49] Perez-Vera Report (n 1) para 41.
[50] See Status Table (n 38).
[51] Beaumont and McEleavy (n 11) 174.
[52] For example, Israel hurried to accept Russia's accession to the Abduction Convention in 2011, apparently because a number of children have been abducted from Israel to Russia and in the past it has not been possible to secure their return. This consideration seems to have outweighed concerns expressed in legal circles in Israel about the corruption in the Russian legal system and the evidence that Russian courts are likely to favour local nationals (personal communication to the author by a leading Israeli lawyer). For doubts about the likelihood of proper compliance with the Abduction Convention by Russia, see website surveying legal affairs in Russia: www.russianlawonline.com/content/children-abduction-no-more. It might be noted that nearly a year after Russia's accession came into force on 1 October 2011, there were few acceptances of her accession (see table of ratifications

number and the diversity of the states that have joined the Hague club have made it impossible to formulate minimum standard requirements of other family justice systems before recognising accession'.[53] Nevertheless, there are a few acceding States whose accessions have not been accepted by a substantial number of other Contracting States.[54] It is not possible to know whether the reason for this is concern about the justice system or other political considerations.

At first sight it might seem that the success of the Convention will be enhanced by maximising the number of signatories. However, this view is misconceived because accepting accession of States that are not committed to the best interests of the child or whose legal systems do not comply with basic standards of natural justice is liable to betray the objectives of the Convention. Accordingly, it may indeed be wise to recognise that some legal systems, at least in their current state, do not meet the requirements required to accede to the Convention. In relation to such States, other methods of developing co-operation should be sought, such as the Malta process which has promoted dialogue between Convention States and non-Convention, largely Muslim States, under the auspices of the Hague Conference on Private International Law.[55] In relation to these States, other methods of dispute resolution which do not require automatic mandatory return, such as mediation, may be helpful in resolving abduction cases.

II Inter-Relationship with Other Legal Instruments

A National Legislation

i Civil Law

In some Contracting States, international conventions are self-executing and thus there is no need to enact implementing legislation.[56] In those countries in which there is a need to pass domestic legislation in order to give effect to international treaties, two types of implementing legislation can be found. The first type of statute simply provides that the Abduction Convention has the force of law and attaches the Convention as a schedule,[57] translated into the local language where necessary.[58] The second type of legislation trans-

---

and accessions (n 38)), but this might simply be due to bureaucratic delays evidenced by the fact that there were also few acceptances of other recent accessions.

[53] *Re E (Abduction: Non-Convention Country)* [1999] 3 FCR 497, 506.

[54] eg, South Africa (Convention not in force with 45 States), Ukraine (Convention not in force with 27 States), and Zimbabwe (Convention not in force with 54 States), as per table of ratifications and accession (n 38). It should be borne in mind that where other States acceded after these States, the latter may have refused the accession of the newly acceding States. Some justification for States' hesitation to accept Zimbabwe's accession might be found in the concern expressed in Australia's response to the 2010 Questionnaire (n 41) at question 2 about Zimbabwe's ability to properly manage matters under the Abduction Convention.

[55] See Info Doc No 8 of 2012, 'Malta Declarations': www.hcch.net/upload/wop/abduct2012info08e.pdf.

[56] eg, France.

[57] eg, English Child Abduction and Custody Act 1985, but it should be noted that the Preamble and Articles 1 and 2 of the Abduction Convention are omitted.

[58] eg, Israeli Hague Convention (Return of Abducted Children) Law 1991, but it should be noted that the Preamble to the Convention is omitted.

poses the provisions of the Convention into a domestic statute.[59] In so doing, slight changes are sometimes made which may have an impact on the interpretation of the Convention. For example, the US legislation provides a heavier burden of proof in relation to the exceptions in Article 13(1)(b) and Article 20[60] and the New Zealand legislation substitutes the phrase 'the right to the possession and care of the child' in Article 5 of the Convention for the phrase 'rights relating to the care of the person of the child'.[61]

In some States, implementing legislation expressly provides that the Abduction Convention takes priority over other national laws.[62] However, even where this is not the case, Article 16 of the Abduction Convention obliges Contracting States to refrain from deciding on the merits of rights of custody, after it has received notice of a wrongful removal or retention. This effectively means that the Abduction Convention takes precedence over national legislation in relation to the determination of custody rights. Nonetheless, where application of the Abduction Convention is inconsistent with constitutional principles of the requested State, it may be possible to invoke the Article 20 defence which allows courts to refuse return where this 'would not be permitted by the fundamental principles of the requested State relating to the protection of human rights and fundamental freedoms'. However, even where there appears to be a clash with constitutional principles, the defence is rarely established in practice.[63]

Finally, it should be pointed out that the Abduction Convention does not apply to abductions between different territorial units within Contracting States. Such situations continue to be governed by national legislation.[64]

ii Criminal Law

a The Offence of Child Abduction

There is a considerable disparity between the approaches of criminal law in different countries to the phenomenon of parental child abduction. This difference relates not only to the question of whether and in what circumstances such behaviour is treated as criminal, but also in relation to whether parents are prosecuted in practice and to the level of punishments meted out. A few examples will illustrate some of the differences.

At one extreme, parental child abduction is not a criminal offence at all in Australia.[65] In Belgium, the offence of child abduction is only committed where there is a court judgment stipulating the residence and contact arrangements with the child.[66] In England, the offence of child abduction, which applies to children under the age of 16, is defined more narrowly where the abductor is the child's parent.[67] Thus, a parent will only commit the offence where he 'takes or sends the child out of the United Kingdom without the appropriate

---

[59] See eg, US International Child Abduction Remedies Act, 42 USC S 1160; New Zealand Guardianship Amendment Act 1991, ss 12 and 13; Australia Family Law (Child Abduction Convention) Regulations 1986 Statutory Rules 1986 No 85 as amended, made under the Family Law Act 1975.
[60] 42 USC S 11603 (e)(2)(A).
[61] New Zealand Guardianship Amendment Act 1991, s 4(a).
[62] eg, Israeli Hague Convention (Return of Abducted Children) Law 1991, s 2.
[63] eg, *Sonderup v Tondelli* 2001 (1) SA 1171 (CC) (S Afr), discussed in ch 13 at II A.
[64] eg UCCJA (US) and the Family Law Act 1986 (UK).
[65] Family Law Council, 'Parental Child Abduction' (1998): www.ag.gov.au/Documents/ParentalCHILDABduction.pdf.
[66] T Kruger, *International Child Abduction: The Inadequacies of the Law* (Oxford, Hart Publishing, 2011) 155.
[67] Or otherwise falls within the definition of a parent connected with the child. See Child Abduction Act 1984, s 1(2).

consent'.[68] In contrast, a person not connected with the child is guilty of the offence if he 'takes or detains' the child 'so as to remove him from the lawful control of any person having lawful control of the child or so as to keep him out of the lawful control of any person entitled to lawful control of the child'.[69] Moreover, prosecution against parents can only be instituted by or with the consent of the Director of Public Prosecutions. The maximum sentence is seven years imprisonment.[70]

In Israel, it is an offence to remove a minor under the age of 16 from the custody of his lawful guardian without the guardian's consent or to convey another beyond the borders of the State without the consent of a person legally authorised to consent on his behalf.[71] In relation to both offences, the penalty is up to 20 years in prison,[72] but the policy of the Prosecution Authorities is only to prosecute parents for child abduction where there are exceptional circumstances.[73] Recently, the Supreme Court held that the offence of removal from custody is committed where the child is removed from the legal framework in which he is meant to be and can be committed by an omission,[74] in this case failure to return the child to the other parent in accordance with a court order. In some countries, statute defines abduction in such a way that it clearly includes retention of a child. For example, in the US, a parent who wrongfully removes or retains his child outside the United States with intent to obstruct the lawful exercise of parental rights would be convicted of a federal crime.[75] Yet, the maximum penalty is only three years imprisonment.[76] In Canada, every parent, guardian or person having the lawful care or charge of a person under the age of 14 who takes, entices away, conceals, detains, receives or harbours that person with the intent to deprive a parent or guardian, or any other person who has the lawful care or charge of that person, of the possession of that person, is guilty of an indictable offence.[77] The maximum penalty is 10 years.[78]

b Inter-relationship between the Abduction Convention and Criminal Law

The Abduction Convention, of course, only regulates civil aspects of international child abduction. Thus, the question per se of whether a particular abduction constitutes a criminal offence in a particular country is not relevant to the operation of the Abduction Convention and equally the Abduction Convention does not have any impact on the criminal sanctions

---

[68] ibid, s 1(1).
[69] ibid, s 2(1).
[70] ibid, s 4.
[71] Penal Law 1977, ss 373 and 370 respectively.
[72] ibid.
[73] Guidelines of Israeli State Attorney referred to in Israeli response to 2006 questionnaire: www.hcch.net/upload/wop/abd_pd02efs2006.pdf, 259.
[74] CrA 5463/11 *RB v State of Israel*: http://elyon1.court.gov.il/files/11/280/063/a15/11063280.a15.htm (26 February 2013). The mother was sentenced to five years in prison (pending appeal).
[75] International Parental Kidnapping Crime Act 1993, 18 USC s 1204. In addition, child abduction is also an offence under State Law. See eg New York Penal Law, Art 135 (creating an offence of custodial interference), although some States provide specific defences for abducting parents, eg Cal Penal Code s 278.7(a) (West 2011) (defence to a custodial parent who abducts his child where he held 'a good faith and reasonable belief' that if the child was left with the other person the child would 'suffer immediate bodily injury or emotional harm, as in eg *People v Neidinger* 146 P3d 502 (Cal 2006)). See generally S Kreston, 'Prosecuting International Parental Kidnapping' (2001) 15 *Notre Dame Journal of Law & Public Policy* 533
[76] International Parental Kidnapping Crime Act ibid.
[77] Criminal Code (RSC 1985, c C-46) s 283, laws-lois.justice.gc.ca/eng/acts/C-46/page-144.html#docCont.
[78] ibid.

attaching to abduction.[79] Nonetheless, in practice there are a number of ways in which the two areas will impact on each other.

Firstly, the disparity between the criminal law and the civil law may cause confusion. Where a particular removal or retention is not a criminal offence, individuals may think that the act is lawful and so not be aware that the removal or retention is wrongful. Similarly, this may lead to left-behind parents being given wrong and misleading advice by law enforcement agencies, such as the police, when they report a removal or retention.[80]

Secondly, the fact that the abducting parent may be liable to criminal sanctions in the requesting State may be an impediment to that parent returning with the child.[81] As will be seen below, in such cases, at least where the abductor was the primary carer of the child, the return of the child may be made conditional on the left-behind parent retracting any complaint made to the police or obtaining an undertaking from the prosecution authorities that criminal proceedings will not be commenced or continued.[82] However, there have been cases where the risk of prosecution has resulted in a permanent separation between a child and his primary carer.[83]

B The European Custody Convention

The Council of Europe Convention on the Recognition and Enforcement of Custody of Children and on Restoration of Custody of Children (the 'European Custody Convention') was signed in 1980, the same year as the Hague Abduction Convention. Today, 37 States are signatories to the Convention.[84] Apart from Liechtenstein, all these States are also now parties to the Abduction Convention.

The aims of the European Custody Convention are remarkably similar to those of the Abduction Convention. In particular, the Preamble recites recognition that the 'welfare of the child is of overriding importance in reaching decisions concerning his custody' and expresses the view that 'the making of arrangements to ensure that decisions concerning custody of the child can be more widely recognised and enforced will provide greater protection for the welfare of children'. In addition, the Preamble notes the 'increasing number of cases where children have been improperly removed across an international frontier' and refers to the desirability of 'making suitable provision to enable the custody which has been arbitrarily interrupted to be restored'. Thus, it can be seen that the European Convention is also concerned to combat international child abduction. In addition, the

---

[79] *Maurizio R v LC* (2011) 201 Cal App 4th 616, 644. See generally, DN Leslie, 'A Difficult Situation Made Harder: A Parent's Choice between Civil Remedies and Criminal Charges in International Child Abduction' (2008) 36 *Georgia Journal of International & Comparative Law* 381.

[80] Kruger (n 66) 155.

[81] Kreston (n 75) 546-47.

[82] See ch 11 at III B and C. *cf* The California Court of Appeal's comment in *Maurizio R v LC* (n 79), 644 that the fact that the mother might be prosecuted in Italy is not a defence under the Hague Convention and the view expressed by the New Zealand High Court that 'there are strong policy reasons why Courts should not be influenced by the prospect of penalties imposed on an abducting parent unless perhaps there was evidence that a particular State was likely to impose Draconian punishments with scant regard to a child's interests', *KS v LS* [2003] 3 NZLR 837 [51]. With respect, this approach ignores the risk of harm which such a prosecution is likely to cause to the child.

[83] eg, case detailed in Netherlands Response to the 2010 Questionnaire, www.hcch.net/index_en.php?act=publications.details&pid=5291&dtid=33, para 6.6.

[84] See Status Chart at conventions.coe.int/Treaty/Commun/QueVoulezVous.asp?NT=005&CL=ENG.

European Convention forbids the reviewing of the substance of foreign custody decisions.[85] Furthermore, the European Convention provides for the designation of Central Authorities in Contracting States, which will be responsible for administrative aspects of the Convention and will co-operate with each other.

Nonetheless, the mechanism of the European Custody Convention is quite different from that of the Abduction Convention. The European Custody Convention is primarily a recognition and enforcement of judgments Convention, providing for reciprocal recognition between Contracting States,[86] subject to the exceptions in the Convention. Accordingly, it only applies where there has been a breach of a foreign custody order. However, an order obtained subsequent to the removal of the child, often referred to as a 'chasing order', will be sufficient for this purpose.[87]

Where there has been an improper removal, recognition of the foreign decision involves restoring custody, subject to the exceptions set out in the Convention. The latitude of the exceptions depends on whether a reservation is made to Article 8.[88] Where this Article applies,[89] the State addressed is obliged to '... cause steps to be taken forthwith to restore the custody of the child' provided that the

(1) request for restoration of custody is submitted within six months of the improper removal;
(2) the child is habitually resident in the State which gave the custody decision; and
(3) he and his parents have sole nationality of that State.

Where Article 8 applies and its conditions are satisfied, the only exceptions which may be invoked are the narrow procedural exceptions in Article 9. In contrast, in cases where these conditions do not apply or a reservation has been entered by one of the Contracting States, there is no obligation to restore the child forthwith and recognition may be refused not only on Article 9 grounds, but also on the wider grounds set out in Article 10. These include a finding that

> by reason of a change in circumstances including the passage of time but not including a mere change in the residence of the child after an improper removal, the effects of the original decision are manifestly no longer in accordance with the welfare of the child.[90]

It will be seen that the European Custody Convention has little to commend itself to a left-behind parent who can choose between using that Convention or the Abduction Convention. In particular, if he does not already have a custody order, he will now have to obtain one, whilst this is not necessary under the Abduction Convention. Furthermore, where a reservation has been made to Article 8, the welfare exception in Article 10 is considerably wider than the grave risk exception under the Abduction Convention.[91] Finally, recognition of the foreign order may well be dependent on registering the order, which is a

---

[85] Art 9(3).
[86] Art 7.
[87] Art 12.
[88] As permitted by Art 17; 26 States have entered a reservation, see Status Chart (n 84).
[89] ie both of the relevant Contracting States involved have not made a reservation thereto.
[90] Art 10(b).
[91] eg *F v F (Minors) (Custody: Foreign Order)* [1989] Fam 1; *Re R (Abduction: Hague and European Conventions)* [1997] 1 FLR 663.

relatively cumbersome procedure.[92] Thus, it is perhaps not surprising that comparatively little use has been made of the European Convention.[93]

Nonetheless, it should be emphasised that in relation to the enforcement of access orders, the European Convention has an important advantage over the Abduction Convention.[94] Access and contact orders are included within the definition of custody decisions[95] and thus are automatically recognisable unless one of the exceptions can be established. As will be seen in chapter 18, this is not so under the Abduction Convention.

Finally, it should be pointed out that neither the Abduction Convention nor the European Custody Convention provide for priority as between the two Conventions. However, in England and Wales, the legislation, which implements both the Conventions, provides that a custody decision may not be registered under the European Custody Convention where an application under the Abduction Convention is pending.[96]

C Brussels II bis Regulation

i General

Council Regulation (EC) No 2201/2003 of 27 November 2003 concerning jurisdiction and the recognition and enforcement of judgments in matrimonial matters and the matters of parental responsibility ('Brussels II bis' or the 'Regulation') makes changes to the way in which the Abduction Convention is applied between the Member States of the European Union.[97] This Regulation entered into force on 1st August 2004 and applies from 1st March 2005.[98]

The Regulation applies 'in civil matters relating to (a) divorce, legal separation or marriage annulment; (b) the attribution, exercise, delegation, restriction or termination of parental responsibility'.[99] The lengthy Preamble explains inter alia that the Regulation ensures equality for children because, unlike its predecessor,[100] 'it covers all decisions on parental responsibility independently of any link with a matrimonial proceeding'.[101] The Regulation, which is directly applicable in Member States prevails over national law[102] and supersedes Conventions already concluded between two or more Member States.[103] Moreover, the Regulation takes precedence over the Abduction Convention and a number of other specified multilateral Conventions, insofar as they concern matters governed by the Regulation.[104] The Regulation's general provisions on jurisdiction and recognition and

---

[92] For a description of the procedure in general and in England and Wales in particular, see Lowe et al, *International Movement of Children* (n 3) 411–17.
[93] In relation to the UK, see ibid 427.
[94] *Re G (A Minor)(Enforcement of Access Abroad)* [1993] Fam 216, 229 (Hoffman LJ).
[95] Art 1(c).
[96] Child Abduction and Custody Act 1985, ss 9(b) and 16(4)(c).
[97] [2003] OJ L 338/1-29. This does not apply in relation to Denmark, Brussels II bis, Art 2(3).
[98] Except for a few articles which apply from the date of entry into force. ibid, Art 72.
[99] ibid, Art 1.
[100] Council Regulation (EC) No 1347/2000 of 30 June 2000 on jurisdiction and the recognition and enforcement of judgments in matrimonial matters and in matters of parental responsibility for children of both spouses OJ L 160 (usually referred to as Brussels II).
[101] Brussels II bis, para 5 of the Preamble.
[102] ibid, Art 72; See also N Lowe, M Everall and M Nicholls, *The New Brussels II Regulation: A Supplement to International Movement of Children* (UK, Jordan, 2005) 3.
[103] Brussels II bis, Art 59.
[104] ibid, Art 60.

20 *Birth of the Convention and other Instruments*

enforcement of judgments in cases relating to parental responsibility will now be summarised briefly by way of background to a more detailed consideration of the provisions applicable to intra-EU Abduction Convention cases.

ii Jurisdiction and Judgments

The new jurisdiction rule in relation to parental responsibility provides that 'The courts of a Member State shall have jurisdiction in matters of parental responsibility over a child who is habitually resident in that Member State at the time the court is seised.'[105] However, where the child's habitual residence has changed following a wrongful removal or retention, there is a special rule.[106] In this situation, the courts of the former habitual residence retain jurisdiction until either

(a) each person[107] having rights of custody has acquiesced in the removal or retention; and
(b) the child has resided in the new habitual residence for at least one year after the holder of the rights of custody has or should have had knowledge of the whereabouts of the child and the child is settled in his or her new environment provided that one of four conditions are met:

  (i) no request for return has been lodged before the competent authorities of the State of refuge;
  (ii) a request for return which was lodged has been withdrawn;
  (iii) a case before the courts of the former habitual residence has been closed pursuant to Article 11(7);[108] or
  (iv) a judgment on custody which does not require the return of the child[109] has been issued by the courts of the former habitual residence.

This rule was designed to define exactly when jurisdiction transfers to the State of refuge, as this issue is not clarified by the Abduction Convention. The chosen rule aims to provide a balance between two competing principles.[110] On the one hand, abductions should not result in a change of the court which has jurisdiction because this provides an incentive to abduct. On the other hand, issues relating to children should be determined by the courts of the State which is most closely connected to the child, which is assumed to be the State of the child's habitual residence. Accordingly, once a year has passed, the courts of the new State of habitual residence will acquire jurisdiction provided that one of a number of conditions are satisfied, each of which indicate that the child is now unlikely to be returned. However, it is important to emphasise that, other than in cases of acquiescence, the fact that return has been refused does not per se bestow jurisdiction on the courts of the State of refuge. This will only occur after 12 months has elapsed, the child has become settled in

---

[105] ibid, Art 8(1). There are also a number of additional subsidiary jurisdiction rules for cases where another court is exercising jurisdiction in relation to matrimonial proceedings (Art 12) and for special situations (Arts 13–14) and a provision allowing transfer of jurisdiction where another court is better placed to hear the case (Art 15).
[106] ibid, Art 10.
[107] Or institution or other body, ibid.
[108] On the basis that no submissions were received.
[109] For consideration of the meaning of this phrase, see *Re A, HA v MB (Brussels II Revised: Article (11)7 Application)* [2007] EWHC 2016 (Fam).
[110] The provision is similar to Art 7 of the Protection Convention, discussed at E ii below.

his new environment and the court of the State of origin has closed the case[111] or given a judgment which does not require return.

Judgments given in a Member State are to be recognised in other Member States without the need for any special procedure,[112] subject to a number of grounds for non-recognition. For judgments relating to parental responsibility, these include: (a) if such recognition is manifestly contrary to public policy of the Member State in which recognition is sought taking into account the best interests of the child; (b) if the judgment was given, except for urgent cases, without the child having been given an opportunity to be heard, in violation of fundamental principles of procedure of the Member State in which recognition is sought.[113] The Regulation expressly provides that neither the jurisdiction of the court which gave the judgment nor the substance of the judgment may be reviewed by the Member State in which recognition is sought.[114]

iii Return Proceedings under the Abduction Convention: General Provisions

Article 11 of the Regulation makes a number of modifications to the way in which the Abduction Convention operates in cases where both the requesting and the requested States are parties to the Regulation. These modifications fall into two categories: provisions which relate generally to the operation of the Abduction Convention and provisions which restrict the scope for refusing to return the child.

Article 11(3) reiterates the Abduction Convention's exhortation to courts to act expeditiously, using the most expeditious procedures available in national law. However, the Article goes a step further by imposing upon courts an obligation[115] to issues its judgment no later than six weeks after the application is lodged, unless exceptional circumstances make this impossible. Whilst the provision appears only to relate to the decision of the first instance court, Thorpe LJ has said that it includes appeals[116] and the Practice Guide states that it should be interpreted so as to include enforcement of the return order. In other words, appeals should be heard within this time frame or return orders should be enforced, even where appeals are pending.[117] In the UK, Thorpe LJ has set down guidelines to ensure compliance with the six-week deadline in intra-EU Abduction Convention cases.[118]

A novel and most significant aspect of the Regulation is its express reference to the importance of hearing the child.[119] Article 11(2) provides

---

[111] Under Regulation 11(7), this court, upon being notified of the refusal to return, must invite the parties to make submissions.
[112] Brussels II bis, Art 21.
[113] ibid, Art 23. This article includes a further five grounds, most of which relate to lack of natural justice for another parent and inconsistency with a prior judgment.
[114] ibid, Arts 24 and 26.
[115] Lowe et al, *The New Brussels II Regulation* (n 102) 30.
[116] *Klentzeris v Klentzeris* [2007] EWCA Civ 533.
[117] Practice Guide for the Application of the New Brussels II Regulations, reproduced in Appendix 4 to Lowe et al, *The New Brussels II Regulation* (n 102) para 2.4.
[118] *Vigreux v Michel* [2006] EWCA Civ 630.
[119] Brussels II bis, para 19 of the Preamble; P McEleavy, 'Integrating the Brussels II bis Regulation in the United Kingdom' in K Boele-Woelki and C Gonzalez Beilfuss (eds), *Brussels II bis: Its Impact and Application in the Member States* (Antwerp, Intersentia, 2007) 319, suggests that this reform is likely to have the greatest impact of all the reforms in Brussels II bis. See also Baroness Hale's comment in *Re D (A Child) (Abduction: Rights of Custody)* [2006] UKHL 51 [52] that this reform would lead to many more children being heard.

> When applying Article 12 and 13 of the 1980 Hague Convention, it shall be ensured that the child is given the opportunity to be heard during the proceedings unless this appears inappropriate having regard to his or her age or degree of maturity.

It should be noted that the obligation to hear the child is not limited to cases where the child objection exception is pleaded. Rather, this provision appears to be giving recognition to the right of the child to participate in proceedings concerning him, entrenched in Article 12 of the United Nations Convention on the Rights of the Child 1989,[120] whether or not the child's views are necessary for the making of the decision.

Nonetheless, it must be appreciated that the Regulation does not regulate the method by which the child should be heard and the Preamble expressly states that the Regulation is not intended to modify national procedures.[121] One commentator has suggested that this approach is regrettable and that 'the vulnerable position of the migrant child arising out of divergent child-consultation procedures between the Member States needs to be addressed'.[122] The different methods of hearing children will be analysed in detail in chapter 14 of the book.

iv Refusing Return

The provisions of the Regulation which modify the operation of the Abduction Convention scheme in relation to refusals to return abducted children are controversial[123] and their rationale unclear. McEleavy suggests inter alia that they are based to a large extent on a misconception, on the part of the advocates of reform, that abducting parents were often able to exploit the exceptions to the Abduction Convention in order to change the court which had jurisdiction to determine the merits of the case.[124] The Regulation restricts the scope for non-return under the exceptions in the Abduction Convention in three ways.

Firstly, return cannot be refused unless the person who requested the return of the child has been given an opportunity to be heard.[125] Ironically, this provision, which is purely procedural, appears to be inconsistent with the requirement of expedition. However, use of modern technology to facilitate hearing the applicant in his home State,[126] may avoid delays.

Secondly, a court may not refuse to return a child on the basis of the grave risk of harm exception in Article 13(1)(b) of the Abduction Convention, 'if it is established that adequate arrangements have been made to secure the protection of the child after his or her return'.[127] The provision does not make it clear where the burden of proof lies. However, the better view would seem to be that the burden is on the left-behind parent to establish

---

[120] And to Art 24 of the Charter of Fundamental Rights of the European Union, referred to in para 33 of the Preamble to the Regulation.

[121] Although the fact that the child was not heard can be a ground for refusing to recognise a decision relating to parental responsibility, ibid, Art 23(b).

[122] G Shannon, 'The Impact and Application of the Brussels II bis Regulation in Ireland' in K Boele-Woelki and C Gonzalez Beilfuss (eds), *Brussels II bis: Its Impact and Application in the Member States* (n 119) 157.

[123] For a detailed discussion of the opposition to these provisions and the political forces at play, together with the diplomatic compromise that was reached, see P McEleavy, 'The New Child Abduction Regime in the European Union: Symbiotic Relationship or Forced Partnership?' (2005) 1 *Journal of Private International Law* 5.

[124] P McEleavy, 'Brussels II bis: Matrimonial Matters, Parental Responsibility, Child Abduction and Mutual Recognition' (2004) 53 *International and Comparative Law Quarterly* 503, 509.

[125] Brussels II bis, Art 11(5).

[126] See Practice Guide (n 117), para 2.3.

[127] Brussels II bis, Art 11(4). For detailed discussion of the extent to which protective measures can protect children from harm, see ch 11 at III.

that adequate protection is available.[128] The Practice Guide helpfully points out that it is not sufficient that procedures exist in the requesting State to protect the child, but it must be shown that the authorities have in fact taken concrete measures to protect the child in question.[129] This provision is of particular significance in those civil law States which did not have jurisdiction to make return orders conditional on the giving of undertakings designed to protect the child, a practice which has become quite widespread in common law States. [130]

Thirdly, where return is refused on the basis of one of the exceptions in Article 13 of the Abduction Convention, the courts of the State of habitual residence prior to the abduction retain jurisdiction and a subsequent decision by these courts ordering return will 'trump' the refusal to return[131] and be entitled to 'fast-track' enforcement[132] in the requested State without the need for a declaration of enforceability, provided that certain safeguards are satisfied.[133] This provision gives expression to the underlying principle that the requested State does not acquire jurisdiction immediately after a refusal to return and that the State of habitual residence prior to the wrongful removal or retention retains jurisdiction to make determinations relating to parental responsibility. In order to give effect to this principle, the requested State is obliged to send, within one month, a copy of the non-return order and of the relevant documents to the authorities of the State in which the child was habitually resident immediately before the wrongful removal or retention.[134] Those authorities must then notify the parties of their right to make submissions to the court of the State of habitual residence within three months.[135]

The new scheme in relation to the re-evaluation of decisions in which return has been refused is the most far-reaching of the provisions of the Regulation relating to intra-EU Abduction Convention cases. Reaction to it has been mixed. On the one hand, Lowe et al suggest that it is a reasonable compromise and that it might actually lead to more refusals to return.[136] Indeed, the fact that the courts in the requested State will determine the merits of the case removes some of the reasons for ordering return. In particular, the merits of the case will be decided by the *forum conveniens* and the abductor will not have succeeded in changing the forum which will determine issues relating to parental responsibility.[137]

---

[128] McEleavy, 'Integrating the Brussels II bis Regulation' (n 119) 321.

[129] Practice Guide (n 117), para 2.2; In the case of CA Paris 15 février 2007 [INCADAT cite: HC/E/FR 979], the French Court held that the child should be returned because the Italian authorities had taken measures to protect the child by entrusting the child to the local authority and assurances had been received from the Italian Ministry of Justice in relation to the implementation of protective procedures; cf CA Aix-en-Provence, 30 November 2006, N° RG 06/03661Référence [INCADAT cite: HC/E/FR 717], in which the French Court was not satisfied that adequate measures had been put in place to protect the child in the light of the allegations of sexual abuse, the veracity of which could not be ruled out.

[130] See ch 11 at III A.

[131] Brussels II bis, Art 11(8).

[132] McEleavy, 'Matrimonial Matters' (n 124) 510.

[133] Brussels II bis, Art 42. Where the judgment has been certified in accordance with the requirements of Art 42(2), then its recognition may not be opposed.

[134] ibid, Art 11(6).

[135] ibid, Art 11(7).

[136] Lowe et al, *The New Brussels II Regulation* (n 102) 32–33; R Lamont, 'Mainstreaming Gender into European Family Law? The Case of International Child Abduction and Brussels II Revised' (2011) 17 *European Law Journal* 366, 382.

[137] Indeed, the current author suggested more than 15 years ago that return and venue for adjudication did not necessarily have to go hand in hand and that in some cases it may be desirable not to order return but to provide for adjudication in the State of origin, R Schuz, 'The Hague Child Abduction Convention: Family Law and Private International Law' (1995) 44 *International and Comparative Law Quarterly* 771, 782.

On the other hand, there may be procedural difficulties in determining the merits of the case in the absence of the child and the abducting parent[138] and in obtaining the relevant documentation upon which the non-return order was based.[139] Also, there does not seem to be any obligation to expedite these proceedings[140] and enforcement a long time after the abduction may violate the human rights of the abductor and the child under the European Convention for the Protection of Human Rights and Fundamental Freedoms (ECHR).[141] In addition, it has been suggested that in some cases the State of refuge will be more 'in touch' with concrete situations and better placed to evaluate the child's interests[142] and that there is a risk that the court in the State of origin will not give sufficient weight to the reasons underlying the non-return order.[143] Moreover, in practice there seem to be difficulties in enforcing the subsequent return order made by the State of origin.[144]

McEleavy goes further and claims that the scheme is 'an unsatisfactory settlement which is likely to cause years of confusion'.[145] In his view, the scheme is not consistent with the mutual trust which forms the basis of the Abduction Convention.[146] If the requested State applies the exceptions responsibly, there should not be any room to allow another Member State to 're-hear' the case.[147] Thus, the regular making of trumping orders is likely to lead to ill-feeling between the courts of the Member States.[148] Accordingly, it is to be hoped that the courts of the State of origin will use their power to trump non-return orders sparingly and only in exceptional cases, such as where it is clear that the refusal to return was based on lack of evidence or a misconception by the courts of the requested State.[149]

Finally, some suggestion can be found in the case law that Brussels II bis has raised the bar for refusing return in reliance on the exceptions.[150] However, there is nothing in the Regulation which requires such an interpretation, other than the need to ensure that no protective measures are available which can alleviate the harm. Moreover, McEleavy has

---

[138] Lowe et al, *The New Brussels II Regulation* (n 102) 32–33. Although again, technology may help to overcome this problem as in the case of *Re A (Custody Decision after Maltese Non-Return Order)* [2006] EWHC 3397.

[139] McEleavy, 'The New Child Abduction Regime' (n 123) 31.

[140] The only time deadline is the three-month period in which the parties can make submissions to the courts of the State of origin, Brussels II bis, Art 11(7). In the case of *AF v T* [2011] EWHC 1315 (Fam), the Art 11(7) proceedings in England took place two years after the no-return order. The English Court did not order return, but did make a contact order since the father was not in a position to obtain such an order in Germany.

[141] A Schulz, 'The Enforcement of Child Return Orders in Europe: Where Do We Go From Here?' (2012) *International Family Law* 43, 46–47.

[142] J Long, 'The Impact and Application of the Brussels II bis Regulation in the Member States: Italy' in K Boele-Woelki and C Gonzalez Beilfuss (eds), *Brussels II bis: Its Impact and Application in the Member States* (n 119) 183.

[143] McEleavy, 'The New Child Abduction Regime' (n 123) 33. Indeed, in the case of *Šneersone and Kampanella v Italy*, no 14737/09, s 1107, 12 July 2011, the European Court of Human Rights held that an Italian order, made under Art 11(8), granting custody to the left-behind parent and requiring return of the child from Latvia, violated the abductor's human rights under Art 8 of the ECHR because the Italian Court had not given sufficient consideration to the grounds upon which the Latvian Court had previously refused to order return under the Abduction Convention.

[144] Kruger (n 66) 135.

[145] McEleavy 'Matrimonial Matters' (n 124) 509; See also Shannon, 'The Impact and Application' (n 122) 155.

[146] And indeed the basis of the Brussels II bis Regulation itself.

[147] ibid.

[148] ibid; although elsewhere, the same author (n 123) 32 does point out that mutual trust can be fostered by judicial liason between the judges in the two States.

[149] *Re A* (n 138) would seem to be such a case.

[150] See eg *Vigreux v Michel* [2006] EWCA Civ 630 (Wall LJ); *Re F (Abduction: Joinder of Child as Party)* [2007] EWCA Civ 393 (Thorpe LJ).

suggested that even where it is likely that the requesting State will trump the non-return order, a subsequent return once that State is already seised of proceedings may provide better protection for the child.[151]

D European Convention on Human Rights

i General

The ECHR of 4th November 1950 was designed to create a level of co-operation and harmonisation at political, legal and social levels which would make further military hostility within Europe as unlikely as possible and to ensure collective enforcement of basic human rights.[152] Today, 47 European countries are parties to the Convention.[153] The roles of the organs set up by the ECHR have been changed a number of times following protocols to the Convention.[154] Today, there is a permanent court of Human Rights (the 'ECtHR') situated in Strasbourg in France, to which complaints of violation may be brought against Member States by other Member States or by individuals.[155] Where they raise serious questions affecting the interpretation of the Convention, the decisions of this Court may be appealed to the Grand Chamber of the ECtHR.[156]

A Member State, which is found to be in violation of the ECHR, is bound to abide by the decision of the ECtHR. This involves not only paying compensation and/or costs as ordered by the Court, but also ensuring that in the future its national law complies with the Court ruling.[157] In addition, decisions are likely to influence other Member States who will want to avoid being taken to the Strasbourg Court.

Two provisions of the ECHR are most relevant to international child abduction cases. Article 6(1) provides that 'In the determination of his civil rights and obligations . . . everyone is entitled to a fair and public hearing within a reasonable time by an independent and impartial tribunal established by law'. Article 8(1) provides that 'Everyone has the right to respect for his private and family life, his home and his correspondence'. Article 8(1) is qualified by Article 8(2), which enacts the principle of proportionality, providing:

> There shall be no interference by a public authority with the exercise of this right except such as is in accordance with the law and is necessary in a democratic society in the interests of national security, public safety or the economic well-being of the country for the prevention of disorder or crime, for the protection of health or morals, or for the protection of the rights and freedoms of others.

---

[151] P McEleavy, 'Evaluating the Views of Abducted Children: Trends in Appellate Case–Law' (2008) 20 *Child and Family Law Quarterly* 230.
[152] A Schulz, 'The 1980 Hague Convention and the ECHR' (2002) 12 *Transnational Law & Contemporary Problems* 356, 357.
[153] See Status Chart: http://conventions.coe.int/Treaty/Commun/ChercheSig.asp?NT=005&CM=&DF=&CL=EN.
[154] For details, see Schulz, 'The 1980 Hague Convention' (n 152) 357–59.
[155] There is no requirement that an individual petitioner be a resident or citizen of a State which is a party to the ECHR.
[156] Art 30 ECHR (as revised).
[157] Art 53 ECHR; See N Lowe, 'A Supra-National Approach to Interpreting the 1980 Hague Child Abduction Convention – a Tale of Two European Courts: Part 1: Setting the Scene' (2011) *International Family Law* 48, 50.

ii The Inter-Relationship between the ECHR and the Abduction Convention

Apart from Liechtenstein, all the Member States of the ECHR are also party to the Abduction Convention.[158] Thus, there is considerable scope for parents who feel aggrieved by the handling or outcome of Abduction Convention proceedings in an ECHR Member State to petition to the ECtHR. It will be convenient to divide the discussion into two categories: petitions brought by left-behind parents and those brought by abducting parents.

a Petitions Brought by Left-Behind Parents

Left-behind parents have claimed a violation of the ECHR in cases where a return order has not been enforced; where return applications have not been processed promptly and in cases where return has been refused. The leading case is *Ignaccolo-Zenide v Romania*,[159] in which the ECtHR held that Romania's failure to take the necessary measures to ensure the return of the children to their mother in accordance with the return order was a violation of the mother's rights under Article 8 of the Convention. However, the decision made it clear that in enforcing return orders, national authorities had to strike a fair balance between the interests of the various parties and that recourse to coercive measures against children would usually not be desirable.[160] The ECtHR's emphasis in this case on the obligation to act speedily in Abduction Convention cases has been applied in subsequent petitions by left-behind parents in cases where national authorities failed to take necessary measures to process return applications expeditiously.[161] It should be noted that these cases did not involve the ECtHR in reviewing the way in which the national courts had interpreted the Abduction Convention.[162] In contrast, in recent cases, in which the left-behind parent has attacked a refusal to return, the ECtHR has reviewed the decision of the national court.[163]

b Petitions Brought by Abductors

Since petitions brought by abductors *ex hypothesi* challenge the decision of the court ordering the return of the child and not merely omission or delay on the part of national authorities, it is hardly surprising that in these cases the ECtHR has reviewed the interpretation and application of the Abduction Convention by the national courts. In the first case of this type, *Maumousseau and Washington v France*,[164] the ECtHR rejected the mother's petition,

[158] See Status Chart (n 153).
[159] *Ignaccolo-Zenide v Romania* App no 31679/96 (ECHR, 2000-I). For a detailed discussion of this case, see Schulz, 'The 1980 Hague Convention' (n 152) 380–90.
[160] *Ignaccolo-Zenide v Romania* ibid [94].
[161] See eg, *Maire v Portugal* App no 48206/99 (ECHR, 2003-VII); *Iglesias Gil and AUI v Spain* App no 56673/00 (ECHR, 2003-V) (the authorities did not take steps to locate the abductor); *Iosub Caras v Romania* App no 7198/04 (27 July 2006) (the authorities did not inform the divorce court of return application which then made a custody order inconsistent with the return order and which resulted in the overturn of the return order on appeal).
[162] Schulz, 'Enforcement of Child Return Orders' (n 141) 44.
[163] See *Monory v Romania and Hungary* App no 71099/01 (5 April 2005), where the ECtHR upheld the father's petition not only on the basis that the proceedings took more than a year, but also on the basis that the national court had misinterpreted the Abduction Convention by holding that there was no breach of custody rights where the abductor had joint custody; See discussion in N Lowe, 'A Supra-National Approach' (n 157); See also *Raban v Romania* App no 25437/08 (26 October 2010) where the ECtHR upheld the Romanian Court's refusal to return on the basis that it was consistent with the principle of the paramountcy of the best interests of the child. For a discussion of this approach, see section b.
[164] *Maumousseau and Washington v France* App no 39388/05 (6 December 2007).

which was based on a claim that the French courts had ignored the harm which would be caused to the child by being returned to the US. The Court stated that it entirely supported the policy of the Hague Convention to protect children from the harmful effects of abduction and to return them speedily to their habitual residence. Nonetheless, the emphasis of the Court on the best interests of the child and the fact that the decision was based on the finding that the best interests of the child had been duly considered, laid the foundation for future controversial statements and decisions.

Two paragraphs in the majority decision of the Grand Chamber in the leading case of *Neulinger and Shuruk v Switzerland*[165] have given rise to particular concern and so it is appropriate to quote the relevant parts in full (references omitted):

> [138] It follows from Article 8 that a child's return cannot be ordered automatically or mechanically when the Hague Convention is applicable. The child's best interests, from a personal development perspective, will depend on a variety of individual circumstances, in particular his age and level of maturity, the presence or absence of his parents and his environment and experiences ... For that reason, those best interests must be assessed in each individual case.
>
> [139] In addition, the Court must ensure that the decision-making process leading to the adoption of the impugned measures by the domestic court was fair and allowed those concerned to present their case fully. To that end the Court must ascertain whether the domestic courts conducted an in-depth examination of the entire family situation and of a whole series of factors, in particular of a factual, emotional, psychological, material and medical nature, and made a balanced and reasonable assessment of the respective interests of each person, with a constant concern for determining what the best solution would be for the abducted child in the context of an application for his return to his country of origin.

The approach described in these paragraphs appears irreconcilable with the Abduction Convention's summary return mechanism without a full investigation into the merits of the case. Technically these paragraphs are obiter because the decision that enforcement of the return order would violate the petitioners' right to family life, was based on the long period of time which had passed since the making of that order.[166] Nonetheless, such significant comments made by the Grand Chamber could not be ignored. This no doubt explains why the President of the ECtHR, Judge Costa, felt the need to defuse the concern caused by these dicta by stating in an extra-judicial speech[167] that the above passage should not be read as abandoning the swift summary approach that the Abduction Convention envisages. The UK Supreme Court seems to have treated this statement as resolving the problem.[168]

However, in the subsequent case of *X v Latvia*,[169] another petition against a return order brought by an abducting mother, the ECtHR seems to have ignored Judge Costa's remarks. The Court repeated that the child's interests are paramount[170] and expressly relied on the

---

[165] *Neulinger and Shuruk v Switzerland* App no 41615/07 (6 July 2010).
[166] Schulz, 'Enforcement of Child Return Orders' (n 141) 46–47 points out that in cases where there has been delay in enforcing the return order, the requested State is in a no-win situation. If it does not enforce the order, then it will be violating the left-behind parent's rights, but if it does enforce the order despite the delay, it will be violating the rights of the abductor and the child.
[167] Speech given on 14 May 2011 by MR Jean-Paul Costa, President of the ECtHR: www.hcch.net/upload/wop/abduct2011info05_en.pdf.
[168] *Re E (children)* [2011] UKSC 27 [25].
[169] *X v Latvia* App no 27853/09 (13 December 2011).
[170] ibid. See also *B v Belgium* App no 4320/11 (10 July 2012) [61], although in this case the interference with the decision of the Belgium Supreme Court seems to be justifiable on the basis of the grave risk of harm, without reference to best interests.

controversial paragraphs in *Neulinger*. Furthermore, it held that the Latvian courts' failure to consider fully the best interests of the child by carrying out an in-depth examination of the entire family situation and in particular its failure to consider a psychological report submitted by the mother constituted a breach of her Article 8 rights.

If the ECtHR continues with this approach, a head-on collision between that Court and those of the Member States seems inevitable. Indeed, the UK Supreme Court has recently made it clear that it fundamentally disagrees with the Strasbourg approach and that it would be entirely inappropriate to conduct an in-depth examination, of the sort described by the ECtHR, in Abduction Convention cases.[171] Nigel Lowe has helpfully suggested that one way to try to resolve the impasse is for the Hague network of judges[172] to hold a conference with the Strasbourg judiciary.[173]

In addition to the problem caused by the ECtHR's unorthodox interpretation of the Abduction Convention, the length of time which ECtHR proceedings take is a serious threat to the summary return mechanism in the Convention. The most extreme example is the *Neulinger* case,[174] in which the delay[175] in processing the mother's petition to the ECtHR was itself the cause for the ultimate non-return of the child. Even though the majority of the Grand Chamber took the view that the original Swiss decision ordering the return of the child had been within the margin of appreciation allowed to national courts, it held that enforcing the return order now would violate his rights because he had become so settled in Switzerland and the contact with his father had been further eroded. It is surely totally absurd and intolerable that the right of the child to contact with his father and the rights of the father were violated as a direct result of the proceedings in a Court which is designed to protect human rights.

However, even in cases where the time factor does not determine the final result, the fact that ECtHR proceedings take so long frustrates the Abduction Convention's central objective of immediate return. The abductor has nothing to lose from submitting such a petition, since he will be entitled to legal aid from the ECtHR and, even if ultimately unsuccessful, he has gained more time with the child in the state of refuge. In contrast, the left-behind parent does not have full party status in the proceedings before the ECtHR and is not entitled to legal aid.[176] Although the petition is technically brought against the requested State which made the return order, the decision is determinative from the point of view of the left-behind parent, in the same way as an appeal. Accordingly, he should be given procedural rights before the Court. Thus, if the ECtHR is to consider such petitions, it must adopt an effective fast track procedure in the spirit of the Hague Convention and should grant equal status and legal aid to the left-behind parent.

Furthermore, the ECtHR's willingness to review return orders at the request of abductors creates a disparity between those who abduct to European countries, which are signatory to the ECHR, and those who abduct to other countries. The right of the former to

---

[171] *Re S (a child)* [2012] UKSC 10 [38].
[172] See ch 2 at II B.
[173] N Lowe 'A Supra-National Approach' (n157).
[174] *Neulinger and Shuruk v Switzerland* (n 165).
[175] ibid. The decision of the Swiss Appeal Court ordering return was handed down on 16 August 2007; the decision of the ECtHR was given on 8 January 2009; the mother's appeal to the Grand Chamber was heard in October 2009 and the decision given on 6 July 2010. It seems that the Court did not heed its own warning that 'the passage of time can have irremediable consequences for the relations between the child and the parent with whom it does not' [140].
[176] See R Schuz, 'The Relevance of Religious Law and Cultural Considerations in International Child Abduction Disputes' (2010) 12 *Journal of Law & Family Studies* 453, 495–96.

petition the ECtHR gives them an additional 'bite of the cherry', another chance to avoid return of the child, not available to the latter.[177] Therefore, the ECtHR should be very slow to accept petitions brought by abductors against return orders and apply costs sanctions against unmeritorious claims.[178]

E The 1996 Hague Child Protection Convention

i General

The Hague Convention on Jurisdiction, Applicable Law, Recognition, Enforcement and Co-operation in Respect of Parental Responsibility and Measures for the Protection of Children ('the Protection Convention') is primarily designed to prevent conflicting decisions between different countries in matters relating to parental responsibility and protection of children. To date, 39 States are parties to this Convention, which entered into force in 2002.[179] The scope of this Convention, which is designed to replace the little used 1961 Hague Convention on the Protection of Infants,[180] is much wider than that of the Abduction Convention and will affect many more children. Nonetheless, it does have implications for Abduction Convention cases, which will be considered below after first setting out the basic scheme of the 1996 Convention.

The Protection Convention creates uniform rules in all three areas of private international law. The State of habitual residence of the child has exclusive jurisdiction to take measures directed to the child's person or property,[181] subject to a number of exceptions. In particular, in cases of urgency, the authorities of the State where the child is present may take necessary measures of protection. These measures will lapse as soon as the State of habitual residence takes measures.[182] There is also a specific exception for abduction cases, where habitual residence is changed as a result of a wrongful removal or retention.[183] In such cases, the State of origin retains its jurisdiction even where there is a change in habitual residence, until each person having custody has acquiesced in the removal or retention or the child has resided in the State of refuge for at least one year since all persons having custody rights know the whereabouts of the child,[184] there are no return proceedings pending and the child has become settled in his new environment.[185] Moreover, the jurisdiction of the State of refuge is limited to the taking of urgent measures necessary to protect the child.[186]

---

[177] This disparity, of course, is exacerbated if the standards applied by the ECtHR are different to those applied by most Contracting States. For example, it seems to the author that if the mother in the Israeli case of FamA 1855/08 *RB v VG*, http://elyon1.court.gov.il/verdictssearch/HebrewVerdictsSearch.aspx, 8 April 2009 [INCADAT cite: HC/E/IL 923] (discussed in detail in ch 11 at II Aii) had been able to petition the ECtHR, she would have had a very good chance of success, taking into account the length of time which had passed since the child had had contact with his father and the evidence of psychological harm.

[178] For attempts to speed up Strasbourg proceedings, see N Lowe, 'A Supra-National Approach' (n157) 51.

[179] Status Table: www.hcch.net/index_en.php?act=conventions.status&cid=70 (last visited 6 January 2013).

[180] No common law countries were parties to this Convention.

[181] Art 5(1).

[182] Art 11.

[183] Art 7. For implications of this provision for meaning of habitual residence, see R Schuz, 'Policy Considerations in Determining the Habitual Residence of a Child and the Relevance of Context' (2001) 1 *Journal of Transnational Law and Policy* 101, 153; for similar provision, see Art 10 of Brussels II bis, discussed above at B ii.

[184] Compare the exception in Art 12(2), under which the 12-month period starts to return from the date of the wrongful removal or retention, irrespective of whether the left-behind parent knows of the whereabouts of the child (other than in the US). See ch 9 at II Ai.

[185] Art 7.

[186] ibid.

The applicable law is the *lex fori*,[187] other than in relation to attribution of parental responsibility, which is governed by the law of the habitual residence.[188] However, a change of habitual residence cannot divest a person of parental responsibility which was attributed to him under the law of the former habitual residence.[189]

Measures taken by the authorities of a Contracting State shall be recognised by the operation of law in all other Contracting States,[190] subject to a number of grounds of refusal.[191] These include measures taken in breach of the jurisdiction provisions of the Convention; failure to provide an opportunity to hear the child or a person who claims that the measure infringes his parental responsibility and manifest incompatibility with the public policy of the requested State, taking into account the best interests of the child.

ii Interaction with the Abduction Convention

The Protection Convention specifically provides that it does not affect the operation of the Abduction Convention, but that nothing precludes provisions of the Protection Convention from being used to obtain the return of a child who has been wrongfully removed or retained or of organising access rights.[192]

Indeed, the automatic enforcement provisions should facilitate enforcement of contact orders made in another Contracting State and thus provide a partial answer to the unsatisfactory rights of access provision in Article 21 of the Abduction Convention.[193] Indeed, where the Protection Convention is in force between the two countries in question, Article 21 of the Abduction Convention would seem to be redundant.

In contrast, it is difficult to conceive of any reason why a left-behind parent would choose to invoke the Protection Convention instead of the Abduction Convention as a means of recovering a child who has been abducted. Firstly, this possibility will only exist where there has been a breach of a pre-existing custody order, which he then seeks to enforce. Secondly, the Protection Convention does not provide for the expedited treatment of cases and so this is likely to be a slower procedure. Thirdly, there is no provision for legal aid under the Protection Convention as there is under the Abduction Convention.[194]

However, there are a number of ways in which the Protection Convention may assist in the operation of the Abduction Convention. Firstly, and most importantly, where the court of the requested State orders return subject to undertakings/conditions or other protective measures,[195] these will be treated as urgent measures within Article 11. Accordingly, these measures will be entitled to enforcement in the requesting State after the return of the child, until such time as that State itself takes necessary measures.[196] This will resolve to a

---

[187] Art 15.
[188] Art 16(1).
[189] Art 16(3).
[190] Art 23(1).
[191] Art 23(2).
[192] Art 50.
[193] Discussed in ch 18.
[194] N Lowe, 'The 1996 Hague Convention on the Protection of Children – a Fresh Appraisal' (2002) 14 *Child and Family Law Quarterly* 191, 205.
[195] See detailed discussion in ch 11 at III.
[196] Revised Draft Practical Handbook on the Operation of the Hague Convention of 19 October 1996 on Jurisdiction, Applicable Law, Recognition, Enforcement and Co-operation in Respect of Parental Responsibility and Measures for the Protection of Children, *Permanent Bureau*, Preliminary Document No 4 of May 2011, www.hcch.net/upload/wop/abduct2011pd04e.pdf (Revised Draft Handbook), para 13.7.

considerable extent the problem of unenforceability of undertakings/conditions and other protective measures and will obviate the need to obtain mirror or safe harbour orders.[197]

Secondly, the co-operation provisions of the Protection Convention, which require Central Authorities to provide 'information as to the laws of, and services available in, their States relating to the protection of children'[198] are wider than the Abduction Convention obligation to provide 'information of a general character as to the law of their State'.[199] Similarly, use may be made of Article 34 of the Protection Convention, under which the authorities of a Contracting State may request information relevant to the protection of a child from the authorities of another Contracting State.[200]

Nonetheless, there are a number of respects in which the Protection Convention fails to prevent conflicting decisions in case of abduction. Firstly, there is no provision on how to treat cases where proceedings for return are brought both in the country of refuge (under the Abduction Convention) and in the country of origin (under domestic law). Whilst the expeditious nature of Abduction Convention proceedings often makes this issue irrelevant, this is not always the case and so it would be helpful to provide for a uniform procedure.[201]

However, even if such a procedure were introduced, it would not prevent the possibility of conflicting decisions where the State of refuge refused return either on the basis that, in its view, the child was not habitually resident in the requesting State immediately prior to the wrongful removal or retention or because one of the exceptions applies. Where the requesting State does not recognise this decision and insists on enforcing its own custody order, the conflict between the two jurisdictions cannot be resolved.[202] In practice, the decision of the requesting State appears to be a *brutum fulmen* because it cannot be enforced so long as the child and abductor remain in the State of refuge.[203]

The Protection Convention does not appear to prevent the conflict between the decisions of the different States in this scenario. The decision to refuse return under the Abduction Convention is not entitled to recognition under Article 23 of the Protection Convention because the jurisdiction is not founded upon the bases of jurisdiction provided by that Convention. Even if the child's habitual residence has changed, jurisdiction to make decisions in relation to the child (other than urgent measures) is vested solely in the courts of the State of origin. In theory, the custody decision of the country of origin may be entitled to enforcement in the State of refuge,[204] but it seems unlikely, as will be

---

[197] However, there will still be cases where such conditions or undertakings will be insufficient to protect domestic violence victims, M Weiner, 'International Child Abduction and the Escape from Domestic Violence' (2000) 69 *Fordham Law Review* 593, 685–86 and discussion in ch 11 at III.

[198] Revised Draft Handbook (n 196), para 13.9.

[199] Abduction Convention Art 7(2)(e).

[200] Revised Draft Handbook (n 196), para 13.11.

[201] ibid, para 13.12 (suggesting that the two Contracting States should communicate and co-operate via Central Authorities or direct judicial communications).

[202] See eg, US decision in *Ben-Haim v Ben-Haim* appeal Docketed No FD 02-906-11 (NJ Super Ct 25 August 2011) (refusing comity to an Israeli no-return decision and ordering the arrest of the abducting mother for failure to obey the US Court's decision to return the child). See ch 6 at IV Ei.

[203] In the case of FamA 5253/00 *R v L* (Unreported, 21 January 2001) (Isr) [INCADAT cite: HC/E/IL 834], the fact that the California Court would not recognise the Israeli Court's refusal to return the child (on the basis of the real risk that he would commit suicide) meant that the mother and child had to stay in Israel until the child reached 18, which effectively prevented her from finding employment (personal communication to author). The Californian criminal proceedings against the mother were only dropped after the precedent in the case of *People v Neidinger* (n 75).

[204] The refusal to return under the Abduction Convention is not per se a ground for refusing recognition, Revised Draft Handbook (n 196), example 13(a).

explained below, that that State will enforce the custody order in circumstances where it has refused return under the Abduction Convention.[205]

If the court in the requested State refused return because in its view the State of origin is not the child's habitual residence, then a custody decision of the latter State may well not be entitled to recognition under the Protection Convention.[206] If it refused return because the left-behind parent acquiesced, then provided that the State of refuge has now become the child's habitual residence,[207] it is now entitled to take measures which override those made by the former state of habitual residence. If one of the other exceptions was held to apply, then surely recognition of the custody order of the State of origin will be manifestly contrary to public policy, taking into account the interests of the child.[208] In particular, it should be borne in mind that where one of the exceptions is established, the court exercises discretion and will only refuse return where it is convinced that the best interests of the child mandate such a refusal and that these outweigh the policy of the Convention.

The only rare situation in which it is envisaged that the State of refuge would enforce the custody order of the State of origin, despite an earlier finding that one of the exceptions is established, is where there has been a significant change in circumstances, such as fresh evidence not previously available, which removes the foundation of the refusal to return. An example would be where allegations of abuse treated seriously by the court in the State of refuge have been clearly refuted in the course of subsequent proceedings in the country of origin.[209] It should be added that whilst the Protection Convention forbids review on the merits of the decision, it is difficult to see how the public policy defence can be invoked without examining the merits of the decision.

Thus, the Protection Convention will not usually provide any immediate solution to the stalemate between the State of origin and the State of refuge. Nonetheless, it does seem to provide a longer term solution to these problems. Once 12 months have passed since the date that the left-behind parent knew the whereabouts of the child and the child has become settled in his or her new environment, then unless proceedings under the Abduction Convention are still pending, the State of refuge which should now be the child's habitual residence will have jurisdiction to take all measures in relation to the child[210] and these will override measures taken by the former State of habitual residence, including a custody order in favour of the left-behind parent. Furthermore, the latter State will be obliged to recognise such an order, unless one of the grounds for non-recognition applies. Whilst the State of origin may be displeased with the situation, it is difficult to see how the public policy exception could be invoked since *ex hypothesi* the child has now been living in the State of refuge for more than a year and has become settled there. Thus, it seems that the stalemate will be resolved after a year in favour of the State of refuge.

---

[205] *cf* G DeHart, 'The Relationship between the 1980 Child Abduction Convention and the 1996 Protection Convention' (2000) 33 *New York University Journal International Law & Policy* 83, 94.
[206] Unless one of the other bases of jurisdiction exist, such as where the decision is made ancillary to divorce proceedings within Art 10.
[207] Art 7.
[208] Lowe, 'The 1996 Protection Convention' (n 194) 204.
[209] Revised Draft Handbook (n 196), example 13(a); Beaumont and McEleavy (n 11) 18 and 220 suggest the situation where refusal was based on the child's objection and he has now removed that objection.
[210] Although it will have to wait until the completion of any proceedings currently pending in the State of origin (Art 13).

However, it is not clear why it is necessary to wait a year. According to the Lagarde Report,[211] the underlying idea behind Article 7 of the Protection Convention was to prevent the abductor from taking advantage of his wrongful act 'in order to modify for his benefit the jurisdiction of the authorities called upon to take measures of protection'. However, once the court in the country of refuge has refused return because return is not mandated under the Abduction Convention, it is difficult to see what benefit is achieved[212] by a situation which perpetuates the conflict between the decisions of different countries until the one-year period has passed.[213]

Since the ultimate result is inevitable, it is not clear why the courts of the State of refuge should not acquire jurisdiction when they refuse return under the Abduction Convention,[214] where the child has now become habitually resident in that State.[215] The reason behind the Article 7 scheme seems to be the concern of some States, especially the US, that such automatic acquisition of jurisdiction would provide an incentive for courts to refuse return.[216] With respect, this reasoning is difficult to accept[217] given the extreme reluctance with which courts refuse return; the fact that the child will physically remain in the country of refuge and the fact that such courts will in any event acquire jurisdiction in the not too distant future. Thus, the scheme simply provides for diplomatic embarrassment and uncertainty and distress for the parents[218] and the child.

F United Nations Convention on the Rights of the Child 1989

All the States which are party to the Abduction Convention have ratified the United Nations Convention on the Rights of the Child 1989 ('CRC'), with the exception of the US. Whilst in many States, the CRC has not been implemented into national law, as has the Abduction Convention, courts will generally try to interpret the Abduction Convention in a way which is compatible with their Government's international obligations under the CRC. The current author drew attention to the potential inconsistencies between the CRC and the way in which the Abduction Convention was being implemented in a paper

---

[211] P Lagarde, 'Explanatory Report on the 1996 Convention, in Proceedings of the Eighteenth Sessoin' (1998) *Premanent Bureau*, www.hcch.net/upload/expl34.pdf, para 46.

[212] ibid, para 48, comments that the Special Commission wanted to avoid the situation where the jurisdiction of the State of refuge was dependent on a decision of the authorities of that State.

[213] *cf* the Brussels II bis scheme (B iv above), which expressly allows the courts of the State of origin to re-evaluate and to trump the non-return order. Thus, there is a reason to allow that State to retain jurisdiction until such time as it closes the case, where no submissions were made within three months, or makes an order, see Art 10(b), discussed at C above.

[214] See by M Weiner, 'International Child Abduction' (n 197) 523.

[215] Which will usually indicate that he has become settled in his new environment. For a discussion of the different approaches to determining the habitual residence of a child, see ch 8.

[216] P Nygh, 'The New Hague Child Protection Convention' (1997) 11 *International Journal of Law and Policy and the Family* 344, 348; G DeHart, 'The 1980 Child Abduction Convention and the 1996 Protection Convention' (n 205).

[217] *cf* A-M Hutchinson and M Bennett, 'The Hague Child Protection Convention 1996' (1998) 28 *Family Law* 35, 37 who state that courts will be reluctant to refuse return on the basis of grave risk of harm where the State of origin retains jurisdiction to make an enforceable custody order. This argument ignores the fact that where there is a grave risk, this will also be a ground for refusing to enforce the custody decision, as explained above. Furthermore, in cases where Brussels II bis applies, courts do sometimes refuse return, even though they know that the country of origin can make an order for return which will override that refusal. See above at B iv.

[218] In cases where return has been refused because of domestic violence, the lack of jurisdiction of the State of refuge may be seen as 'adding insult to injury', Nygh, 'The New Hague Child Protection Convention' (n 216) 348.

delivered at an International Conference in 2001.[219] Since then, there has been a much greater awareness among judges of the potential impact of the CRC on the operation of the Abduction Convention. Nonetheless, there are still many tensions between the two Conventions.

One of the most important parameters for analysis in the central chapters in Part III and IV of this book is the extent to which the way in which the Abduction Convention is being interpreted and applied is consistent with the rights and interests of children, as defined in the CRC. In chapter six, these rights and interests will be explained in detail.

---

[219] Subsequently published as R Schuz, 'The Hague Child Abduction Convention and Children's Rights' (2002) 12 *Transnational Law & Contemporary Problems* 394.

2

The Operation of the Abduction Convention

I Sources of Information and Statistics

A Introduction

Before analysing in detail the way in which particular provisions in the Hague Convention on the Civil Aspects of International Child Abduction ('Abduction Convention') have been interpreted and applied, it is important to explain how the Abduction Convention actually works in practice. Whilst there are considerable variations in practice between different Contracting States, a general overall picture of how the Abduction Convention operates on the ground can be obtained from a number of sources of information, most of which are available on the Hague Conference of Private International Law's website.[1] These include:

1. The conclusions of the various Special Commission meetings[2] which reflect problems that have arisen and recommended ways to address these problems.
2. The preliminary documents prepared for these Special Commission meetings including questionnaires completed by each of the Contracting States.
3. The Good Practice Guides,[3] which provide detailed guidance in relation to different aspects of the operation of the Convention, written on the basis of experience in operating the Convention in different countries.
4. The country profiles of the Contracting States.
5. The Country Reports published by the National Centre for Missing and Exploited Children.[4]

In addition, a number of empirical studies of different kinds have been undertaken into the operation of the Convention and the aftermath of Convention proceedings.

B The Empirical Studies

The Centre of International Family Law Studies at Cardiff University Law School, directed by Professor Nigel Lowe, has conducted three statistical surveys, respectively relating to

---

[1] www.hcch.net.
[2] For details about Special Commission meetings, see Dii below.
[3] To date, six such Guides have been produced: CA Practice, Implementing Measures, Preventive Measures, Enforcement, Transfrontier Contact Concerning Children and Mediation. They are all available at www.hcch.net/index_en.php?act=text.display&tid=21
[4] http://1800victims.org/doc.asp?id=159&parentID=166.

applications for return filed via Central Authorities (CAs) in the years 1999, 2003 and 2008. These surveys compile and analyse data provided by the CAs of the Contracting States. Each survey contains comparisons with the previous surveys and so most of the relevant information can be found in the latest survey.[5] However, whilst in the earlier two surveys there were individual national reports for every Contracting State, the latest survey only includes individual reports for 11 countries, which received a substantial number of incoming applications.

The surveys contain a wide range of information about the persons involved, including the gender, relationship to the child and nationality of the taking parent and the age of the children. In addition, the surveys provide statistics in relation to the outcome of the proceedings and their duration. In relation to cases where there was a judicial refusal to return, data is available in relation to the ground for that refusal.

A Belgian survey, directed by Thalia Kruger,[6] provides quantitative and qualitative analysis of 667 abduction files at the Belgian CA, Child Focus and the Belgian Ministry of Foreign Affairs, open in 2007 and 2008. The survey is not restricted to cases decided under the Abduction Convention and some useful comparisons are made between Abduction Convention cases and others. Furthermore, the interviews with parents, lawyers and others involved in dealing with abducted children provide interesting insights into the reasons for abduction and into the practical obstacles faced by left-behind parents trying to get their children back. An earlier smaller survey conducted by Marilyn Freeman for the Reunite Research Unit[7] and a follow-up which included interviews with the children[8] also provides insight into the impact of the abduction and return proceedings on the lives of the parents and the children.

Reference will be made to the data and insight from these three surveys in this chapter and throughout the book, where relevant. At this stage, an overview of the latest statistical data will be presented and the significance of return rates and duration of proceedings will be briefly discussed.

C Statistics

The scale of the operation of the Abduction Convention can be ascertained from the 2008 Statistical Survey, which reports 1,961 return applications made to 54 Contracting States.[9] Unsurprisingly, there are vast differences between the number of applications received by different States,[10] based on the popularity of such States as places of refuge. The US received

---

[5] N Lowe, 'A Statistical Analysis of Applications Made in 2008 under the Hague Convention of 25 October 1980 on the Civil Aspects of International Child Abduction, Part I Global Report', Preliminary Document No 8 (November 2011), www.hcch.net/upload/wop/abduct2011pd08ae.pdf ('2008 Statistical Survey').

[6] T Kruger, *International Child Abduction: The Inadequacies of the Law* (Oxford, Hart Publishing, 2011).

[7] Reunite Research Unit, 'The Outcome for Children Returned Following an Abduction' (September 2003): www.reunite.org/edit/files/Library%20-%20reunite%20Publications/Outcomes%20Report.pdf ('Reunite Outcomes Study').

[8] M Freeman for the Reunite Research Unit, 'International Child Abduction the Effects': www.reunite.org/edit/files/Library%20-%20reunite%20Publications/Effects%20Of%20Abduction%20Report.pdf ('Reunite Effects Study').

[9] 2008 Statistical Survey (n5), 6.

[10] The word 'State' refers to a territorial unit where there is more than one such unit within the Contracting State.

the most applications (283) and England and Wales the second highest number (200).[11] Eleven States received more than 50 applications[12] and 19 received less than five.[13]

It is perhaps tempting to assess the success of the Abduction Convention on the basis of the number of children who are returned and how quickly. This book argues that this approach is misconceived for a variety of reasons. Firstly, these figures do not provide an accurate assessment of the response to the international child abduction inter alia because in some cases there was no wrongful removal or retention. More substantially, as stated in the Introduction to this book, the success of the Convention is measured by the proper application of its provisions and not by the total number of children returned. Thus, since exceptions are part of the policy of the Convention, in cases where they do indeed apply, refusal to return does not indicate a failure of the Convention. Accordingly, the Convention has to be evaluated in the light of a number of parameters, which reflect all its objectives and consistency with general legal principles. These parameters will be discussed in detail in chapters five and six.

Nonetheless, return rates and the speed with which return is ordered do give some indication as to the way in which the Convention is operating. Accordingly, there is some value in a brief discussion of the available statistics. The return rate in the 2008 statistical survey was 46 per cent,[14] of which 19 per cent were voluntary returns. Whilst this figure might seem relatively low, it is important to take into account that 18 per cent of the applications were withdrawn and eight per cent were still pending. Furthermore, five per cent of applications were rejected by CAs because the conditions of the Abduction Convention were not met. Accordingly, only in 15 per cent of cases was return actually refused by the court. However, it may be a matter of concern that the 2008 return rate was five per cent lower than that in 2003.[15] Moreover, the wide disparity between the return rates in different States, ranging from 100 per cent in Scotland to 20 per cent in Estonia, suggests that there are real differences between the way in which the Convention is implemented in the various Member States.[16]

In the 2008 Statistical Survey, the mean duration of proceedings, from the filing of the application with the CA to the final decision was 188 days.[17] However, this figure varied depending on outcome, ranging from 121 days, in the case of a voluntary return, to 286 days, where there was a judicial refusal. It is a matter of concern that all these figures were higher than in the previous two statistical surveys.[18] Again, there were considerable disparities between different Contracting States,[19] ranging from Denmark (overall average of 44 days) to Bulgaria (overall average of 347 days).[20] Furthermore, the breakdown of the

---

[11] 2008 Statistical Survey (n5), para 34.
[12] Even though the judicial refusal rate was only 2% lower, ibid, para 35.
[13] Some of these were very small States or territorial units such as the Falkland Islands.
[14] In Kruger's study (n6) at 190, in the nine cases in which the Hague Convention applied to abductions from Belgium, the child was returned in 55.6% of the cases.
[15] Even though the judicial refusal rate was only 2% lower, ibid para 69.
[16] Although it should be borne in mind that in States which receive only a few applications, a single return or non-return can make a radical difference to the return rate.
[17] 2008 Statistical Survey (n5) at para 149. Kruger (n5) 161–72, also found that proceedings could take a long time. However, in the Reunite Outcomes Study (n7) the average length of the abduction was only 132 days.
[18] 2008 Statistical Survey ibid, para 153. The real figure will be higher than this because cases which were still pending at the cut-off date for the survey were not included in the figure ibid, para 158.
[19] Again, it should be borne in mind that in States which receive a few applications, a single case which takes an unusually short or long length of time can significantly affect the average duration.
[20] 2008 Statistical Survey (n5), para 157.

duration into the period before submission to the court and that thereafter show considerable differences between the different Contracting States[21] and in some States a marked difference between the two stages.[22] There is clearly much work to be done in many Contracting States to speed up their treatment of Abduction Convention cases.

II Institutions and other Actors Involved in the Operation of the Convention

A Central Authorities

Article 6 of the Abduction Convention obliges Contracting States to set up CAs to discharge the duties which are imposed upon these authorities by the Convention. Article 7 of the Convention provides that CAs 'shall co-operate with each other and promote co-operation amongst the competent authorities in their respective States to secure the prompt return of the child and to achieve the other objects of this Convention.' The Article then proceeds to give a non-exhaustive list of the functions of the CAs. These functions will be considered in the context of the discussion of the various stages involved in Abduction Convention cases in Part III of this chapter. Reference will also be made there to the differences in the ways in which CAs in different States carry out these functions.

Contracting States may choose where to locate the CA.[23] For the most part, the CA is situated within a Government Department, such as that of Justice, Foreign Affairs, Community Services or Police. In the US, the CA is the Office of Children's Issues in the Department of State.[24]

In light of the wide variations between the effectiveness of different CAs,[25] recommendations were made by the various Special Commission meetings designed to ensure improvement in standards and uniformity of practice.[26] The most important step towards this goal

---

[21] ibid, para 171. The figures for the period before submission of the application to court vary from Uruguay (2 days) to South Africa (270 days) and for the period after submission from Dominican Republic (7 days) to Ukraine (414). In some countries, there was a marked difference between the speed at the two stages.

[22] For example, in South Africa, despite the delays before the submission to Court, the cases were dealt with relative quickly by the courts (45 days). In contrast, in Panama, the average time before submission to court was 7 days, but the average period thereafter was 285 days. At first sight, these figures indicate that in some countries the CAs are more efficient and in others the courts work faster. However, the statistics may reflect little more than the allocation of the work between the different authorities. Thus, where the CA has collected all the relevant information, the court may be able to process the case quicker; whereas where proceedings are commenced very quickly, sometimes before the child has been located, the information will have to be obtained during the course of the proceedings. The author is grateful to Andrea Schulz for this insight.

[23] 'Guide to Good Practice under the Hague Convention of 25 October 1980 on the Civil Aspects of International Child Abduction, Part I, CA Practice' ('Guide to CA Practice'), www.hcch.net/upload/abdguide_e.pdf, para 2.3.3 states that the CA should have strong links to the internal justice and welfare system.

[24] Prior to 2008, the independent National Centre for Missing and Exploited Children handled incoming applications.

[25] Many examples of complaints against the inadequate functioning of CAs can be found in the responses of Contracting States to the Permanent Bureau's 2010 Questionnaire, www.hcch.net/index_en.php?act=publications.details&pid=5291&dtid=33.

[26] eg Conclusion 3 of the Second Special Commission Meeting in 1993, www.hcch.net/upload/abdrpt93e.pdf; Conclusions 1.1–1.8 of the Fourth Special Commission Meeting in 2001, www.hcch.net/upload/concl28sc4_e.pdf.

was the publication of the 'Guide to Good Practice'[27] in 2003. This Guide emphasises the need for CAs to be adequately resourced with suitably trained staff and modern communication equipment.[28] In recent years, efforts have been made to help newly acceding states in setting up their CAs inter alia by organising training visits from experienced CA staff from other Contracting States.[29] Beaumont and McEleavy suggest that the existing Contracting States could do more to ensure that newly acceding States do indeed set up adequately resourced CAs by making their agreement to apply the Convention to that State conditional on this.[30]

B Judicial and Law Enforcement Authorities

The Abduction Convention envisages that proceedings for the return of the child may take place before judicial or administrative authorities in the requested State.[31] In practice, in nearly all (if not all) Contracting States, only judicial authorities are empowered to decide return applications. In some States, Abduction Convention cases are heard by specialist family court judges, but in others judges without any particular expertise in family law decide these cases. Moreover, in some countries efforts have been made to ensure that Abduction Convention cases are heard by a small number of judges who then develop expertise in these cases.[32] This practice is clearly desirable, but it is not always practicable for geographical reasons, particularly in large countries in which there are few Abduction Convention cases.

The network of Hague judges is designed inter alia to address the problem of judges who have no previous experience of Abduction Convention cases. Contracting States appoint a liaison judge, or sometimes more than one, and judges in that State can contact the liaison judge if they have any questions about the application of the Abduction Convention.[33]

The police may be involved in locating children and in enforcing return orders. Their role will be discussed in relation to these issues.

C Lawyers

There are significant differences between the arrangements in different countries for providing legal representation for applicants in Abduction Convention cases. At one extreme, England provides non-means tested legal aid to all applicants and they are referred by the CA to high quality lawyers who specialise in Abduction Convention cases. Similarly, in

---

[27] (n 23).
[28] The German Response to the 2010 Questionnaire (n 25), para 3.1 reveals that some CAs are only allowed to respond to correspondence sent in the original and not to emails.
[29] See eg list of new Contracting States to which the German CA has provided assistance in the German Response to the 2010 Questionnaire ibid, 3.11.
[30] P Beaumont and P McEleavy, *The Hague Convention on International Child Abduction* (Oxford, Oxford University Press, 1999) 244.
[31] eg Arts 11 and 12.
[32] eg in England and Wales, where all cases are heard by the judges of the Family Division of the High Court; See also German amending Act of 13 April 1999 which concentrated jurisdiction to hear cases under the Hague Convention in just 24 family courts (compared to the original 600 local courts before the amendment), German Response to the 2010 questionnaire (n 25) 4.1. Similarly, Austria has concentrated jurisdiction both at first instance and Supreme Court level, Austrian Response to the 2010 Questionnaire (n 25), para 4.1.
[33] See ch 11 at III D.

Australia, applications under the Convention are made by the CA itself on its own behalf and at its own cost[34] and in some countries a State lawyer is appointed to represent the left-behind parent.[35] However, in countries where the case is filed by the public prosecutor, he is acting in the public interest and does not necessarily represent the view of the applicant.[36]

On the other hand, many Contracting States entered a reservation to Article 26,[37] which forbids Contracting States from imposing charges on applicants, except insofar as the costs are covered by its own legal aid system. This means that in Contracting States, which do not have a comprehensive legal aid system, applicants may not be able to afford to pay for legal representation and certainly not expert representation.[38] Special Commissions have repeatedly urged States to find a solution to this problem.[39] It is noteworthy that Article 7(g) of the Abduction Convention requires CAs to take measures to provide or facilitate the provision of legal aid and advice, including the participation of legal counsel and advisors.[40]

An additional problem which has been identified by researchers is the lack of knowledge about the Abduction Convention among lawyers.[41] Since the problem of child abduction is dispersed, few lawyers have made this a specialist area.[42] However, it seems that the extent of this problem could be considerably reduced if CAs and other agencies with whom left-behind parents are likely to come into contact, such as the police and welfare services, were to make readily available a list of lawyers who have expertise in child abduction matters. Similarly, concentration of jurisdiction encourages specialisation.

D The Permanent Bureau

The Abduction Convention does not impose any duties on the Permanent Bureau of the Hague Conference of Private International Law ('the Permanent Bureau') in relation to the operation of the Convention. Indeed, the Bureau is not even mentioned. Thus, for example, accession instruments are deposited with the Ministry of Foreign Affairs of the Kingdom of the Netherlands[43] and not with the Permanent Bureau. However, in practice the Permanent Bureau, despite its limited resources, has contributed greatly to the wide-

---

[34] Country Report for Australia (n 4), paras 2.4–3.5.

[35] eg Spanish Response to the 2010 Questionnaire (n 25), para 3.5. In Manitoba, the CA represents applicants in its capacity as Crown Counsel for the Minister of Justice, Country Report for Canada (n 4), para 3.3.

[36] In relation to Belgium, see Kruger (n 6) 118, who discusses the conflict of interests faced by public prosecutors. In relation to Hungary, see the Hungarian Response to the 2010 Questionnaire (n 25), para 3.5 which noted that if the applicant does not agree with the way in which the public prosecutor presents the case, he may have to hire an independent lawyer in the middle of the proceedings.

[37] See Status table, http://www.hcch.net/index_en.php?act=conventions.status&cid=24.

[38] M Freeman, The Hague Child Abduction Convention – An Uneven Playing Field, Part 11 – Legal Aid and the Role of Administrative Proceedings, Occasional Papers on the 1980 Hague Child Abduction Convention, International Child Abduction and Related Issues, Part 11, Reunite, 2002.

[39] Conclusion 8 of the Second Special Commission Meeting (n 26); Conclusions of the Fourth Special Commission Meeting) (n 26) para 3.6. In response to the question about legal aid and legal representation in para 3.4 of the 2010 Questionnaire (n 25), a number of Contracting States (eg New Zealand and South Africa) refer to delays and difficulties in finding pro bono lawyers for applicants in the US, but *cf* the Hungarian Response, which indicates that there has been an improvement in the speed with which lawyers for applicants are found there.

[40] See also Guide to CA Practice (n 23), para 4.13.

[41] Kruger (n 6) 141–44; Reunite Outcomes Study (n 7) 28.

[42] Kruger ibid.

[43] Art 38.

spread ratification of the Convention[44] and to improvements in the operation of the Convention. In view of the importance of the Permanent Bureau's role, it is worthwhile to outline briefly the most significant ways in which it promotes effective operation of the Convention.

i Provision of Information

The Permanent Bureau provides information about the operation of the Convention both to the CA personnel and to the general public. This includes publishing contact details of CAs, new ratifications and accessions and the various preliminary and information documents prepared by the Bureau and others. Much of this information is disseminated via the Child Abduction section of the Hague Conference website.[45] Perhaps the most important publications prepared and disseminated by the Permanent Bureau, in accordance with the instructions of Special Commissions,[46] are the series of Good Practice Guides, which are designed to allow Contracting States to learn from each other's experience and to promote uniformity of practice.

In addition, the Permanent Bureau established and runs a database containing summaries of Convention cases from different Contracting States, called Incadat,[47] under the professional direction of Professor Peter McEleavy. This database provides invaluable insights into the way in which the Convention is applied in different countries and is widely used by researchers and practitioners. Whilst some questions have been raised about the degree of accuracy and objectivity of the database,[48] measures have been taken to correct these problems.[49]

ii Special Commission Meetings

The Permanent Bureau has hosted the Special Commission meetings to review the practical operation of the Abduction Convention[50] which take place approximately once every four years. Contracting States are invited to send a delegation, which typically includes governmental representatives, CA personnel and judges. In addition, various non-governmental organisations have observer status.[51] These meetings 'provide a forum for discussion which facilitates the promotion of good Convention practices and is designed to help overcome operational challenges regarding the Conventions'.[52] The discussions, which are usually informed by preliminary and information documents prepared by Permanent Bureau staff,

---

[44] The role of the Permanent Bureau in this respect was recognised in the conclusions of the Sixth Special Commission Meeting in 2011, www.hcch.net/upload/wop/abduct2012concl_e.pdf, para 1.

[45] (n 1).

[46] See eg Recommendation 1.16 of the Fourth Special Commission Meeting (n 26); An additional Special Commission Meeting was convened in 2002 in order to approve the first of these Guides, Conclusions available at www.hcch.net/upload/abd2002_rpt_e.pdf.

[47] www.incadat.com.

[48] C Bruch and M Durkin, 'The Hague's Online Child Abduction Materials: A Trap for the Unwary' (2010) 44 *Family Law Quarterly* 65.

[49] Conclusions of the Sixth Special Commission Meeting (n 44), para 89.

[50] And in later years also the Child Protection Convention.

[51] The current author represented the International Society of Family Law at both parts of the Sixth Special Commission Meeting in May 2011 and January 2012.

[52] 'Report on Services and Strategies Provided by the Hague Conference on Private International Law in Relation to the 1980 Hague Child Abduction Convention', Preliminary Document No 12 of 2011, www.hcch.net/upload/wop/abduct2012pd12e.pdf, para B(i).

relate primarily to problems and issues which have arisen in the operation of the Convention. At the end of each meeting, a list of conclusions and recommendations is adopted.

There is little doubt that these meetings have played an important role in the search for solutions to problems encountered in applying the Convention and promoting uniformity in the implementation and application of the Convention. Furthermore, CA staff report that the opportunity to meet with their counterparts from other Contracting States often enhances the degree of co-operation between them.

iii Supporting the Judicial Network

The Permanent Bureau has played a central role in setting up and supporting the International Hague Network of Judges and in exploring ways in which judicial co-operation and judicial liaison can enhance the operation of the Abduction Convention.[53] In addition, since 1999, the Permanent Bureau has published the Judges' Newsletter, which contains articles and information of relevance to judges who apply the Abduction Convention and other Hague Conventions involving the protection of children.[54]

iv Regional Programmes

The Permanent Bureau runs a Latin American office, which provides support to activities in the region inter alia in relation to the Abduction and Child Protection Conventions. The Sixth Special Commission[55] expressed strong support for this work and for developing an office in the Asia Pacific Region in order to strengthen the activities of the Bureau in that region.[56]

v Expanding the Role of the Permanent Bureau

Some have suggested that the role of the Permanent Bureau should be extended to include monitoring compliance with the Convention.[57] However, at the Sixth Special Commission the majority of the delegates who addressed the issue took the view that the Bureau should not take on such a role and should remain neutral.[58]

---

[53] ibid at paras 27–33; see also 'Emerging Guidance Regarding the Development of the International Hague Network of Judges and General Principles for Judicial Communications, Including Commonly Accepted Safeguards for Direct Judicial Communications in Specific Cases, Within the Context of the International Hague Network of Judges' Preliminary Document No 3, revised July 2012, www.hcch.net/upload/wop/abduct2011 pd03ae.pdf.

[54] ibid, paras 34–38.

[55] Conclusions of Sixth Special Commission Meeting (n 44), para 88.

[56] The Permanent Bureau has also been highly involved in the Malta Process, designed to lead to co-operation with Islamic law states, see Report on Services and Strategies (n 52), paras 88–104.

[57] Report on Services and Strategies ibid, para 112.

[58] Some delegates were concerned about resource implications, but others had substantive concerns such as difficulties in identifying non-compliance and damage to mutual trust between Contracting States, Protocol of Meeting No 23 of the Sixth Special Commission Meeting (on file with author) and author's notes of that meeting.

III The Abduction Convention Process

A The Application

A left-behind parent will usually apply to the CA of the child's habitual residence (the requesting State), although he may apply directly to the CA of the requested State or even straight to the courts of the requested State.[59] Where he applies to the CA of the requesting State, that CA has to ensure that the application meets the requirements of the Convention and that all necessary supporting documentation, translated where necessary, are attached to the application before forwarding it to the CA of the requested State.[60] Thereafter, the CA of the requesting State will need to monitor the progress of the application.[61]

Upon receipt of the application, the CA of the requested State will also check whether the application meets the requirements of the Convention and where necessary ask the requesting State to supply further information. The CA of the requested State may reject the application where 'it is manifest that the requirements of the Convention are not fulfilled' or the application is not 'well-founded'.[62] The Good Practice Guide urges CAs to exercise extreme caution before rejecting applications, especially in relation to issues about which there may be differences of opinion, such as habitual residence and rights of custody, which should be determined judicially.[63]

B Locating the Child

Proceedings cannot usually be commenced under the Abduction Convention until the child has been located[64] and so the first task of the CA of the requested State is to take measures 'to discover the whereabouts of a child who had been wrongfully removed or retained'.[65]

The Guide to CA Practice[66] lists a number of measures which can be taken by those authorities to help locate children. These include searching the population register,[67] in those countries where such a register exists, and enlisting the help of local police. In some countries, the police have appointed a coordinator who is responsible for looking for missing children, with whom the CA can liaise. In addition, Interpol can play a useful role in locating abducted children and there is no need to institute criminal proceedings in order

---

[59] Art 29
[60] Guide to CA Practice (n 23), paras 5.1–5.8.
[61] ibid, para 5.13.
[62] ibid, para 4.9.
[63] ibid. For a statistical breakdown of the grounds on which applications were rejected in 2008, see 2008 Statistical Survey (n 5), para 4.6.
[64] But *cf* in England and Wales where one court has jurisdiction and that court can make a location order.
[65] Art 7(a).
[66] (n 23), Appendix 5.1
[67] In addition, information about the child may be available through other governmental agencies, such as Border Control, the Ministry of Education and Health (personal communication to author by Adv Leslie Kaufman of the Israeli CA); Conclusions of the Fourth Special Commission Meeting (n 26), para 1.9 recommends that such enquiries should be exempted from legislation or regulations concerning confidentiality of such information; In Holland, the CA itself has access to the relevant databases, see Netherlands Response to the 2010 Questionnaire (n 25), para 3.6.

to seek such help.[68] One CA has stressed the importance of sending a photograph of the child and, wherever possible, providing information as to the cities or areas of the country in which the child might be staying.[69]

Where these measures are to no avail, it may be appropriate to instruct private investigators. Some CAs reimburse these expenses[70] and sometimes it may be possible to recover the costs later from the abductor.[71]

C Protecting the Child

CAs are charged with taking measures 'to prevent further harm to the child or prejudice to interested parties by taking or causing to be taken provisional measures'.[72] Where the CA of the requested State becomes aware that the child's safety is at risk, it should immediately inform the appropriate welfare or child protection agencies.[73] Some CAs are empowered to apply directly to the court for protection orders.[74] The Good Practice Guide lists a number of examples of potential additional harm which might be caused to abducted children.[75] These include abuse by the abductor, deprivation of contact with other family members, being alienated from the left-behind parent and the risk of re-abduction.[76]

It seems that in some Contracting States, children are sometimes removed from the abducting parent pending the outcome of return proceedings. Where the applicant parent is not available to care for them, this means that the children are placed in foster or institutional care.[77] It is difficult to believe that such a step promotes the welfare of the child[78] unless there is real concrete evidence that remaining with the abductor will cause harm to the child.[79]

D Voluntary Return

CAs are instructed to take measures 'to secure the voluntary return of the child or to bring about an amicable resolution of the issues'.[80] The Good Practice Guide on CAs sets out the benefits of voluntary return, which include minimising disruption to the child, avoiding

---

[68] See conclusion 6 of the Second Special Commission Meeting (n 26). In relation to the role of Interpol, see S Kreston, Prosecuting International Parental Kidnapping, (2001)15 *Notre Dame Journal of Law & Public Policy* 533, 539-40.

[69] See Response of Brazil to the 2010 Questionnaire (n 25), para 3.6.

[70] Guide to CA Practice (n 23), Appendix 5.1.

[71] See ch 17.

[72] Art 7(b).

[73] Guide to CA Practice (n 23), para. 4.15. This obligation would also come within the Art 7(d) requirement to exchange, where desirable, information relating to the social background of the child.

[74] eg Quebec, ibid.

[75] ibid.

[76] See also the Fourth Special Commission's Meeting (n 26), para 1.12, warning that Contracting States should ensure the availability of effective methods to prevent either party from removing the child prior to the decision on return.

[77] See eg the case of *Wood v Hosig-Wood*, 24 Aug 2006, referred to in M Weiner, 'Intolerable Situations and Counsel for Children: Following Switzerland's Example in Hague Abduction Cases' (2008) 58 *American University Law Review* 335, 336

[78] See discussion on impact of separation from the primary carer in ch 3 at II D.

[79] In the Scottish case of *P v SA and West Lothian Council* (discussed in Report for Scotland in 'Special Focus: Enforcement and Return of Access Orders', Judges' Newsletter, Spring 2004 Issue 10, available at www.hcch.net/upload/spring2004.pdf at 64), the child was placed in foster care because of the real risk that the mother would abscond with the child. However, surely it would have been preferable to find other ways of preventing flight such as the use of an electronic tagging device (see *Re C (Abduction: Interim Directions: Accommodation by Local Authority)* [2004] 1 FLR 653), which would have been less harmful to the child.

[80] Art 10 and Art 7(c).

increased hostility to the parties and saving time and expense. In the 2008 Statistical Surveys, 19 per cent of cases ended in voluntary return. However, the figure varies considerably from country to country,[81] which suggests that some CAs make more effort to achieve voluntary return than others.

The Fourth Special Commission envisaged that it may be appropriate to instruct lawyers in order to negotiate a voluntary return or to refer the parties to mediation services and that the courts themselves have a role in encouraging voluntary return.[82] However, many CAs themselves take action to encourage voluntary return. This often includes sending a letter to the abductor, requesting voluntary return and explaining to him the implications of not returning the child voluntarily.[83] Before sending such a letter, it is necessary to consider whether this will cause a risk of flight. In addition, some CAs themselves provide mediation facilities.[84]

It is important that measures employed in ensuring voluntary return do not lead to undue delay in commencing or pursuing return proceedings[85] as this can lead to a frustration of the objective of prompt return and can provide an incentive to use negotiations or mediation in order to buy time.

E Commencing Proceedings

Article 7(f) of the Abduction Convention requires CAs to 'initiate or facilitate the institution of judicial or administrative proceedings with a view to obtaining the return of the child'. This wording reflects the considerable differences between the role of the CA in different Contracting States. The CA itself brings the application in Australia[86] and in some parts of South Africa.[87] In contrast, in most Contracting States the applicant himself brings the proceedings and the role of the CA is confined to giving advice and to monitoring the progress of the proceedings. In such countries, the onus is on the applicant to find a lawyer and to submit the return application himself.[88] There are a number of other models, including the public prosecutor model;[89] representation of the applicant by the CA[90] and models in which the proceedings are commenced by the CA, but are then conducted by a lawyer appointed by the court or hired by the applicant.[91]

---

[81] Countries with a high voluntary return rate include the Dominican Republic (71%, 5 out of 7 applications) and the UK – Scotland (60%, 3 out of 5). Countries with relatively low voluntary rates include Canada (0%, none out of 49) and Argentina (4.5%, 1 out of 22), 2008 Statistical Survey (n 5), para 4.3.

[82] Conclusions of Fourth Special Commission Meeting (n 26), para 1.10.

[83] eg Country Report for Germany (n 4), para 3.2.

[84] In relation to mediation generally, see ch 16.

[85] Conclusions of Fourth Special Commission Meeting (n 26), para 1.11.

[86] Regulation 14 of the Family Law (Child Abduction Convention) Regulations 1986. Following amendment of this Regulation in December 2004, a person whose rights of custody have been violated may also submit an application, *MQ and A (By Her Next Friend) & Department of Community Services* [2005] FamCA 843 [51].

[87] In South Africa, the CA is the Chief Family Advocate. Depending on the practice followed in the relevant provincial office of the Family Advocate, the CA is sometimes the applicant in the return application. In this situation, the left-behind parent is sometimes joined as a second applicant (personal communication from Justice van Heerden of the South African Supreme Court).

[88] eg the US and Israel.

[89] See section II C above.

[90] This model is used in Romania. It was also formerly used in The Netherlands and the Czech and Slovak Republic but has now been abolished there (personal communication from Andrea Schulz, Director of the German CA for International Custody Conflicts).

[91] eg in Germany (personal communication from Andrea Schulz, ibid).

F Conduct of the Proceedings

Proceedings are conducted in accordance with the procedural law of each Contracting State. Many Contracting States have enacted special laws[92] or regulations to govern procedure in Abduction Convention cases,[93] in order to facilitate expedition. In addition, in some States, the Courts themselves have developed procedural protocols for Convention cases.[94]

The role of the CA in the conduct of the proceedings varies from State to State. Sometimes, in cases involving novel legal points, the CA may be asked to submit an opinion to the court.[95] Similarly, where there are delays, the CA is expressly authorised to request a statement from the court of the reasons for the delay.[96] More often, however, the CA will provide advice through the applicant's lawyer.[97]

G Ensuring Safe Return

Article 7(h) of the Abduction Convention requires CAs to take measures 'to provide such administrative arrangements as may be necessary and appropriate to secure the safe return of the child'. This obligation may cover both measures relating to the physical return to the requesting State, as well as measures in relation to the safety of the child after he arrives there. The former may include social work accompaniment at the airport[98] or even on the journey[99] and arranging supervision during any stop-overs,[100] in order to prevent the risk of abscondment.

The role of the CAs in relation to ensuring the safety of the child after return has been discussed regularly at Special Commission meetings. In particular, reference has been made to the importance of planning arrangements for safe return in advance;[101] alerting child protection authorities in the requesting State[102] and taking steps to ensure that the abducting parent will be able to participate and be heard in custody proceedings there.[103] Significantly, the Fourth Special Commission commented that protection of the child may also sometimes require steps to be taken to protect an accompanying parent.[104]

---

[92] eg in the Netherlands, the Implementation Law 1980 on Child Abduction and in Germany, the International Family Law Procedure Act of 2005, available at www.bundesjustizamt.de/cln_349/nn_2052372/EN/Topics/citizen__services/HKUE/Legal__provisions/IntFamRVG,templateId=raw,property=publicationFile.pdf/IntFamRVG.pdf.

[93] eg in Israel, Chapter 22(1) of the Civil Procedure Regulations 1984 (added in 1995); in Hungary, Decree No 7 of 1988 of the Minister of Justice, Hungarian Response to the 2010 Questionnaire (n 25), para 4.2.

[94] See eg Response of Canada to the 2010 Questionnaire (n 25), para 1.1.

[95] eg Israeli case of ACH (SC) 4117/11 *ShB-H v OB-H*, http://elyon1.court.gov.il/verdictssearch/HebrewVerdictsSearch.aspx 12/07/11 [INCADAT cite: HC/E/IL1183], discussed in ch 10 at III B.

[96] Art 11.

[97] Guide to CA Practice (n 23), para 4.17.

[98] Country Report for Israel (n 4), para 3.7.

[99] See eg, the Scottish case of *P v S A and West Lothian Council* (n 79), in which the judge ordered the child to be accompanied back to Texas by his grandmother and two social workers who would stay for a few days to ensure that he was settled in with his father .

[100] Communication to the author by Adv Leslie Kaufman of the Israeli CA.

[101] Conclusion 4 of the Second Special Commission Meeting (n 26).

[102] Conclusions of Fourth Special Commission Meeting, ibid, para 1.13.

[103] ibid, para 5.3.

[104] ibid, para 1.13.

The Good Practice Guide on CAs provides a list of measures which may be taken by CAs to assist in ensuring the safe return of the child.[105] These include provision of information in relation to protection and other resources available to the returning parent and the child in the requesting State; making arrangements for the care of the child pending the determination in the custody proceedings and encouraging the making of mirror orders or safe harbor orders or otherwise ensuring that undertakings given to the Court in the requested State are enforceable.[106]

H Enforcement of Return Orders

No reference is made in the Abduction Convention to enforcement of return orders and thus methods of enforcement are determined by the national law of each Contracting State. Two research studies were conducted in relation to law and practice in regards to enforcement in different Contracting States on behalf of the Permanent Bureau.[107] The purpose of these studies was to ascertain the extent to which enforcement problems existed and to identify practices which were effective in preventing or overcoming enforcement problems. The research studies indicated that most return orders are complied with voluntarily without the need for coercive measures.[108]

Nonetheless, in some countries, problems of enforcement are encountered in a significant percentage of cases.[109] The causes of enforcement problems are varied[110] and include the disappearance of the child with the abducting parent[111] or without him;[112] physical resistance by the parent[113] or child;[114] the failure of an applicant to comply with undertakings;[115] lack of co-operation by the abductor in relation to travel and/or visa

---

[105] Guide to CA Practice (n 23), Appendix 5.2.
[106] See detailed discussion in ch 11 at III.
[107] 'Enforcement of Orders Made under the 1980 Convention a Comparative Legal Study', *drawn up by Andrea Schulz, First Secretary* (Preliminary Document No 6 of 2006) at Part IV, www.hcch.net/upload/wop/abd_pd06e2006.pdf ('Comparative Legal Study') and N Lowe, S Patterson and K Horosova, 'Enforcement of Orders Made under the 1980 Convention – an Empirical Study (info document no 1 of 2006)', www.hcch.net/upload/wop/abduct2006infodoc.pdf.
[108] Comparative Legal Study, ibid at Part IV; Lowe et al, ibid, 45.
[109] ibid.
[110] See generally Lowe et al 'Enforcement of Orders' (n 107), para 2; 'Enforcement of Orders Made under the 1980 Convention, Towards Principles of Good Practice', *drawn up by Andrea Schulz, First Secretary* (Preliminary Document No 7 of 2006), www.hcch.net/upload/wop/abd_pd07e2006.pdf ('Towards Principles of Good Practice').
[111] eg *Bianchi v Switzerland*, no 7548/04 (ECtHR), 22 June 2006; *Middleton v MacPherson* (October 2000, Unreported) discussed in Report for Scotland in 'Special Focus" (n 79), 62.
[112] eg RFamA (SC) 1855/08 *RB v VG* http://elyon1.court.gov.il/verdictssearch/HebrewVerdictsSearch.aspx, 8 April 2008 (Isr) [INCADAT cite: HC/E/IL 923] (child disappeared in July 2008 on the day he was supposed to meet his father at the airport and has not been found since).
[113] eg *Maumousseau and Washington v France* App no 39388/05 (ECtHR, 6 December 2007) (unsuccessful attempt by police to take children from kindergarten because of resistance by staff and other parents).
[114] eg *Re HB* [1998] 1 FLR 392 (child created scene on airplane and return order was subsequently revoked; *TB v JB (Abduction: Grave Risk of Harm)* [2001] 2 FLR 515 as reported in Report for England and Wales in 'Special Focus' (n 79), 54 (teenage children physically resisted enforcement); *Re F (Hague Convention: Child's Objections)* [2006] Fam CA 685 (child refused to board plane despite some force by the police).
[115] eg case referred to in Australian Report in 'Special Focus' (n 79), 12 (return order was not enforced because the applicant father was unable to rescind the criminal proceedings in Canada upon which return of the child was made conditional).

arrangements;[116] inability to fund travel costs;[117] lack of timeframe for return;[118] lack of response by national authorities to requests for enforcement[119] and lack of availability of appropriate coercive measures.[120] The case law highlights the fact that significant delay in enforcing a return order may make it inappropriate to return that order.[121]

The wide variations between the law and practice in different States revealed by the research studies[122] highlighted the need for a Good Practice Guide, which was prepared in accordance with the instructions of the Fifth Special Commission.[123] This Guide[124] contains advice on measures which might reduce the need to enforce return orders. These include explicitly setting out the arrangements for return in the court order;[125] taking all measures possible to facilitate voluntary compliance with the return order[126] and minimising the legal challenges to return orders and legal obstacles to enforcement.[127] In addition, the Guide provides guidance in relation to methods of making enforcement more effective. These include the availability of effective and rapid mechanisms for locating children;[128] providing bailiffs and other enforcement officers with appropriate training and information in relation to the specific case;[129] carefully choosing the place and time of the enforcement;[130] involving professionals where necessary[131] and, where the abductor and/or the child does not speak the local language, bringing an interpreter to the scene of enforcement.[132]

Whilst no doubt the detailed measures recommended in this Good Practice Guide can help to avoid enforcement problems or overcome them, the Guide does not provide a satisfactory answer to the highly sensitive question of whether and to what extent physical force should be used in enforcing return orders, where there is no other way to enforce the order. The Permanent Bureau's research reveals that quite a number of Contracting States do provide for physical removal of the child from the abductor[133] and the Practice Guide

---

[116] Lowe et al 'Enforcement of Orders' (n 107), para 2.
[117] ibid; example given in Australian Report in 'Special Focus' (n 79) at 12.
[118] Lowe et al (n 107), para 2.
[119] 'Towards Principles of Good Practice' (n 110), 5.
[120] ibid.
[121] See eg ECtHR cases of *Neulinger and Shuruk v Switzerland* App no 41615/07 (ECHR, 6 July 2010); *Ignaccolo-Zenide v Romania* App no 31679/96 (ECHR, 25 January 2000); See also Art 13 of the Swiss Federal Act on International Child Abduction and the Hague Conventions on the Protection of Children and Adults (Translation Appended to A Bucher, 'The New Swiss Federal Act on International Child Abduction' (2008) 4 *Journal of Private International Law* 139), which provides that a court may amend a return order where circumstances change significantly.
[122] See n 106. See also comment in Concluding Report of 'Special Focus' (n 79), 80–81 that whilst in common law countries courts have powers to supervise enforcement of return orders, in many civil law countries, enforcement is the exclusive responsibility of bailiffs.
[123] Which recommended that the Guide be based on the principles set out in 'Towards Principles of Good Practice' (n 110).
[124] The Guide to Good Practice, Part IV, Enforcement of Return Orders, www.hcch.net/upload/guide28enf-e.pdf ('Guide to Enforcement').
[125] ibid, para 77. See also Art 11 of the Swiss Federal Act (n 121).
[126] Guide to Enforcement (n 124), para 91–92. See also Art 11 of the Swiss Federal Act, ibid.
[127] Guide to Enforcement ibid, Chapters 2 and 3.
[128] ibid, paras 13–16.
[129] ibid, paras 105, 107 and ch 9.
[130] ibid, para 106.
[131] ibid, para 108–11.
[132] ibid, para 108.
[133] eg Austria, Canada, Germany, New Zealand and USA, ibid, fn 54; For an example of a case where force was used against children, see the Swiss case of *Arrêts du Tribunal Fédéral Suisse (ATF)* 130 III 530 ss, described and strongly criticised by Bucher (n 121) 139.

recommends that this coercive measure should be available.[134] On the other hand, the Good Practice Guide also recognises that coercive measures are not often used, out of concern for the child's best interests.[135] Thus, it is appropriate to consider in what circumstances, if at all, force should be used against a child or an abducting parent.

The European Court of Human Rights (ECtHR) has indicated the undesirability of using coercion against a child[136] and there is much to be said for the view that where a child physically resists return, then there is little that can be done to ensure compliance.[137] Indeed, the use of force is likely to cause more harm to the child than the original abduction[138] and so should be avoided. Therefore, all steps should be taken to prevent such situations arising. Ensuring that the child's voice is heard properly[139] and that he receives separate representation[140] should mean that the court is well aware of the fact that the child is likely to resist return. Accordingly, where the court still orders return despite the child's strong views, it will have to order measures, such as the provision of psychological counselling, designed to change the child's attitude.[141] However, at the end of the day, if these measures are not successful, it will have to be recognised that the order cannot be enforced.

A more difficult question arises where it is the parent, rather than the child, who is physically resisting the return. However, again, the use of force to separate the child from the parent is liable to cause considerable damage to the child. Even where it is possible to use force against the parent only,[142] this may be very traumatic if the child is present and cause him considerable psychological damage, including resentment against the left-behind parent who appears to him to be responsible for the situation. Thus again, it is necessary to take all possible measures to avoid a confrontational enforcement scene and, where this is unavoidable, to take steps to minimise the harm to the child, by ensuring that counselling and support is available. The need for great caution in the use of coercive measures, even against adults, is underlined by the ECtHR's warning that account must be taken of the rights and freedoms of all involved and in particular the rights under Article 8 of the European Convention on Human Rights (ECHR) and the best interests of the child.[143]

At the end of the day, it has to be remembered that the Abduction Convention is designed to protect children from harm. Whilst in principle abductors should not be allowed to defy court orders, enforcement should not take place at any price. Thus, as the ECtHR has said, there is a need to 'strike a fair balance between the interests of all persons concerned and the general interest in ensuring respect for the rule of law'.[144] Similarly,

---

[134] In addition to the power to impose fines on the abductor and to imprison him (eg for contempt of court), Guide to Enforcement (n 124), para 24. The ECtHR also indicates that indirect sanctions such as the imposition of fines are not sufficient, *Ignaccolo-Zenide v Romania* (n 121) [111].

[135] Guide to Enforcement ibid, para 24.

[136] See *Ignaccolo-Zenide v Romania* (n 121) [106].

[137] Comparative Legal Study (n 107), para 64; case discussed in Hungarian Report in 'Special Focus' (n 79) 32.

[138] Bucher (n 121) 153 suggests that the Art 13(1)(b) exception also applies to the enforcement of the return order and thus measures which will cause the child physical or psychological harm or place him in an intolerable situation should not be taken.

[139] Guide to Enforcement (n 124), para 6; see generally ch 14 below.

[140] See detailed discussion in ch 15.

[141] The ECtHR has criticised Member States for failing to take measures to prepare children prior to attempts to enforce return orders, eg *Ignaccolo-Zenide v Romania* (n 121); *Sylvester v Austria* (nos 36812/97 and 40104/98) (2003) 37 EHRR 17.

[142] Some jurisdictions, for eg Czech Republic, Denmark and Finland, which do not allow the use of force against the child do allow the use of force against the abductor, Guide to Enforcement (n 124), fn 54.

[143] See eg *Sylvester v Austria* (n 141) [58]. Art 12 of the Swiss Federal Act (n 121) specifically provides that the authority responsible for executing the return order shall take into account the best interests of the child.

[144] *Sylvester v Austria* ibid, [59].

Baroness Hale's warning that the Abduction Convention should not become an instrument for causing children harm[145] is pertinent in this context.

IV After Return

A Obtaining Information

In order to evaluate fully the operation of the Abduction Convention, it is necessary to consider what happens after the return of the child. In particular, it is essential to ascertain to what extent undertakings or conditions required by the court of the requested State are honoured, in order to assess whether these measures can really protect children. It is also important to know whether the merits of the case are indeed determined promptly and fairly by the court in the State of the habitual residence, so as to assess to what extent Abduction Convention proceedings are really only first aid and to what extent they are outcome determinative. In addition, information relating to the return of the abductor with the child; the child's adjustment after return; the outcome of any subsequent proceedings and the degree of ongoing contact with the non-custodial parents can help us to understand the impact of the abduction and return on the child and thereby to seek ways to minimise the harm caused.

Some of the surveys do provide some interesting data and insights in relation to the aftermath of the return of the child and these will be summarised in section B below. Whilst some tentative conclusions will be drawn from these surveys, caution has to be exercised in placing too much weight on them due to the small size of some of the samples and factors which limit their representativeness.[146] The same is true of the occasional publication of the, usually unfortunate, aftermath of particular cases.[147]

It is not surprising that little research has been undertaken into the aftermath of return because return is generally seen as the end of the process and so the relevant authorities close their files at this point.[148] Even the lawyers who represented the parties in the Abduction Convention proceedings may well not know what happens after the child has returned to the requesting States. In addition, confidentiality issues may prevent them divulging any information which they have.

Nonetheless, in view of the importance of information concerning the aftermath of return, efforts should be made to overcome these difficulties. It would seem that the body best placed to undertake follow-up research is the CA of the requesting State.[149] This

---

[145] Re D (A Child) [2006] UKHL 51 [52].

[146] eg the limited number of requesting States covered and the fact that there was an inevitable degree of self-selection. In particular, much of the information about the aftermath of return was obtained by interviewing one of the parents, which of course required the consent of the interviewee, Reunite Outcomes Study (n 7), 9; Kruger (n 6) 6.

[147] eg in Scottish Report in 'Special Focus' (n 79), 71 and in the comments section of Incadat reports.

[148] Kruger (n 6) 184, 205; see also case detailed in Hungarian Response to the 2010 Questionnaire (n 25), para 6.6, in which the Hungarian CA tried to follow up a case in which Hungary had been the requested State, but was told by the CA in the requesting State that it could not help because the file was closed. For a general discussion of the difficulties in conducting empirical research in relation to the effects of child abduction, see Preface to GL Grief and RL Hager, *When Parents Kidnap: The Families behind the Headlines* (New York, Free Press, 1993).

[149] It should be noted that some Contracting States take the view that CAs should not be obliged to provide each other with follow-up information and that it is not the function of the CA of the requested State to monitor

authority is situated in the same country as the returned child and is familiar with the local legal system. A number of parallel methods could be used to obtain follow-up information. The left-behind parent could be asked to keep the CA updated, including providing details of any lawyers representing him, and be sent periodical reminders. In addition, CAs could be given access to local court files in order to obtain information about subsequent court proceedings concerning the child. It should be easier for CAs, which are usually situated in Government departments, to obtain access to such information than outside researchers.[150] This proposal is not problem-free and it will clearly not be possible to obtain information about all cases. In addition, sources will have to be found to fund the research, since many CAs are in any event understaffed.

B The Surveys

i Information Relating to Subsequent Legal Proceedings

In the Reunite Outcomes Study, further legal proceedings took place after the child's return in 19 out of 22 cases.[151] Nine of these were considered within a month of return and the remaining 10 within one to six months after return. In most of the cases, both of the parties were represented in these proceedings,[152] although less than a quarter of the parties were legally aided.[153] In the 17 cases in which custody was considered, custody was awarded to the abductor in 10 of the cases and to the left-behind parent in five cases, with joint custody being awarded in two cases.

In 11 out of these 17 cases, the custodial parent requested leave to remove the child from the jurisdiction and in six of the cases this was granted.[154] In a study of 11 South Australian cases, conducted by the author of the Reunite study, leave to remove was granted in only three out of the nine cases in which it was requested.

Kruger's Belgian survey provides information about changes in residence arrangement following return. She does not specifically state whether this is a result of contested legal proceedings between the parties following return.[155] In a clear majority of the cases, there was a change. In 21 per cent of cases, the child's principal residence changed to be with the other parent and in 62.8 per cent of cases, the child had previously had his principal residence with both parents and now it was with only one of them.[156]

---

the effectiveness of protective measures ordered prior to return. However, others are in favour of the provision of follow-up information, see Responses to 2010 Questionnaire (n 25), Question 6.8.

[150] Although Marilyn Freeman did obtain access to files in the Family Court of South Australia, see Reunite Outcomes Study (n 7), 7.

[151] ibid, 36. In a small survey conducted in 2006 by the current author where questionnaires to lawyers in Israel were sent out in relation to cases where return had been ordered, in seven out of ten cases the lawyers knew of proceedings which had taken place in the requesting State following return.

[152] Reunite Outcomes Study (n 7). In two cases the abductor was not represented and in one case the left-behind parent was not represented.

[153] ibid.

[154] ibid, 137. In two further cases, the abducting mother unilaterally removed the child after being granted custody and in one of these cases further Abduction Convention proceedings were then commenced.

[155] Kruger (n 6) 206. The new arrangement could reflect legal proceedings instigated by the left-behind parent after the abduction prior to return or could simply reflect the fact that the abductor did not return with the child.

[156] ibid.

ii Information Relating to the Situation of the Abductor and the Child Following Return

In the Reunite Outcomes Study, 13 out of the 14 mother abductors returned to the State of habitual residence.[157] In contrast, none of the eight father abductors returned.[158] Whilst there are no figures in relation to which parent was the primary caretaker, it can perhaps be assumed that most, if not all, of the mothers were primary caretakers. This very high mother abductor return rate is particularly significant in light of the fact that in nearly half of the cases, the abducting mother expressed domestic violence as a concern relating to return.[159]

Indeed, in six of the cases, non-molestation undertakings were given and these undertakings were violated in all of them.[160] Other types of undertakings were more likely to be adhered to, but there were still frequent violations. For example, five out of seven undertakings relating to accommodation and maintenance and four out of seven undertakings not to remove the child from the care of the returning abductor were not kept.[161]

Those who attempted to enforce the undertakings often discovered that the undertakings were not effective in the requesting State.[162] Others did not have the funds available to finance proceedings to enforce the undertakings or any other proceedings.[163] Generally, abductors complained about the lack of support and assistance available to them upon return.[164]

iii Information Relating to Contact between Child and Non-Custodial Parent Following Return

Since one of the objectives of the Abduction Convention is to ensure regular contact between a child and both of his parents, it might be expected that following a return order, such contact would take place in most cases. The Reunite Study shows that this is not the case and that in less than half of the cases did regular satisfactory contact take place with the non-custodial parent.[165] However, the author of the Study suggests that the fact that regular contact was taking place in nearly half the cases, and telephone contact in another quarter of the cases is an encouraging finding, given the extremely difficult circumstances surrounding abduction cases.[166] This may be so, but as there is no correlation between this statistic and which parent abducted, it is difficult to draw any conclusions as to the extent to which the return did result in regular contact with the left-behind parent. If the emotions aroused by the forced return of abductor and child mean that it is not possible to renew satisfactory contact between the left-behind parent and the child in a significant number of cases, the value of return in these cases might be questioned. In some such cases, the abductor may have been willing to make great efforts to maintain the contact between the left-behind parent and the child if she had been allowed to stay in the country of refuge.[167]

---

[157] (n 7), 35. In contrast, in the author's Israeli survey (n 151), mother abductors returned in 4 out of 7 cases.
[158] Similarly, in the author's Israeli survey, ibid, none of the three father abductors returned.
[159] Reunite Outcomes Study (n 7), 35; there is no information as to the basis for this concern and the extent to which domestic violence was raised as a defence in the return proceedings.
[160] ibid, 31.
[161] ibid.
[162] ibid, 33–34.
[163] Reunite Effects Study (n 8), 27.
[164] ibid, 42–44.
[165] Reunite Outcomes Study (n 7), 43.
[166] ibid.
[167] Kruger (n 6) 208–09 reveals wide variations in relation to contact with left-behind parents in cases of non-return.

iv Information Relating to the Experiences of the Child Following Return

Both the Reunite and the Belgian studies report difficulties experienced by children after return. These include problems in re-adapting to life in the home country, inter alia, as a result of educational disruption[168] and psychological difficulties resulting from the awareness of the returning abductor's unhappiness; from witnessing violence against her and from separation from siblings.[169] It has to be borne in mind that some of this information was provided by returning abductors who were likely to blame the problems on the return, in contrast with left-behind parents who would be more likely to see the abduction itself as the source of any problems.[170] However, the need for the availability of counselling for returning children was mentioned by both categories of parents.[171]

v Conclusions

The data provided by the studies considered do suggest that in most cases the Abduction Convention proceedings are generally first aid proceedings and that the arrangements for the child are reconsidered following return. Thus, the return does in fact force the issue of with whom and in which country the children will live to be determined lawfully in proceedings for custody and/or leave to remove, rather than unilaterally.

Nonetheless, the information provided by the abductors in relation to the aftermath of the abduction is less encouraging. In particular, the fact that undertakings were violated in 66 per cent of the cases, including all the cases in which anti-molestation undertakings were given, is a cause for great concern. This issue will be addressed in more detail later in the book in the context of the grave risk of harm exception.[172] In addition, it seems that professional counselling needs to be made available to help returning children re-adjust socially and psychologically and in order to promote regular contact with non-custodial parents.[173] In some cases, the emotional fallout of the return may be one of the reasons for the contact difficulties and so therapy might help in relation to both of these issues.

---

[168] ibid 200; Reunite Outcomes Study (n 7), 40; GL Greif, 'The Long-Term Aftermath of Child Abduction: Two Case Studies and Implications for Family Therapy' (2009) 37 *The American Journal of Family Therapy* 273, 284.
[169] Reunite Outcomes Study, ibid.
[170] ibid, 39.
[171] ibid, 40; Kruger (n 6) 203.
[172] Ch 11 at III.
[173] Although a child's experience of such counselling is not always positive, Reunite Effects Study (n 8), 61.

3

Inter-Disciplinary Aspects of International Child Abduction

I Sociological Aspects

A Introduction

There are many questions for sociologists to research in relation to the phenomenon of parental child abduction. How many children are abducted? What are the characteristics of the families in which abduction takes place and of the abductors themselves? What are the motives of the abductors? In what ways do changes in social norms in relation to family life impact on the phenomenon of parental child abduction? What is the significance of social attitudes to and perceptions of parental child abduction?[1] How are abduction and its aftermath perceived by the children themselves?[2] Studies shed some light in relation to these issues,[3] but the picture is far from complete and there is a need for more empirical research. Moreover, it is not known to what extent the findings in the older studies are still relevant following the widespread ratification of the Hague Convention on the Civil Aspects of International Child Abduction 1980 (the 'Abduction Convention') and the resultant changes in legal response and social attitudes.

Two central issues which are directly relevant to the Abduction Convention have been chosen for discussion in this sub-chapter. The first concerns the profile and motivations of abductors. In order to assess the validity of the sociological assumptions which informed the drafting of the Convention, the available contemporary empirical evidence in relation to the profiles and motivation of abductors will be compared with the literature available in 1980. In addition, insights into the motivation of abductors are relevant in trying to assess the likely deterrent effect of the Convention,[4] in seeking more effective methods of prevention[5]

---

[1] For a historical consideration of the implications of the way in which parental abduction is portrayed, see P Fass, 'A Sign of Family Disorder? Changing Representations of Parental Kidnapping' in MA Mason, A Skolnick and SD Sugarman (eds), *All Our Families: New Policies for a New Century* (Oxford, Oxford University Press, 1998) 145.

[2] Especially in light of the recognition of the sociology of childhood as an independent field of study, N Taylor, P Tapp and M Henaghan, 'Respecting Children's Participation in Family Law Proceedings' (2007) 15 *International Journal of Children's Rights* 61, 67.

[3] eg GL Grief and RL Hegar, *When Parents Kidnap: The Families Behind the Headlines* (New York, Free Press, 1993); GL Grief and RL Hegar, 'Parents Who Abduct: A Qualitative Study with Implications for Practice' (1994) 43 *Family Relations* 283; RF Janvier, K McCormick and R Donaldson, 'Parental Kidnapping: A Survey of Left-Behind Parents' (1990) 41 *Juvenile & Family Court Journal* 1.

[4] See discussion on deterrence in ch 5 at II Cii.

[5] eg evidence that many abductions by mothers are in response to domestic violence should lead States to seek methods of providing more effective local protection and support for these women. Similarly, the provision of more community support for foreign women might have prevented these women from feeling so isolated, vulnerable and desperate that they were driven to abduct the child back to their home country, see T Kruger, *International Child Abduction the Inadequacies of the Law* (Oxford, Hart Publishing, 2011) 67.

and in determining the nature of the protection and support which abductors and their children might need on return.

The second issue to be discussed is the significance of gender in child abduction cases. This issue has become topical in recent years, largely as part of the wider 'gender wars' which have been waged in many Western countries in relation to parenting arrangements following relationship breakdown.[6] Claims of gender discrimination in Abduction Convention cases have been made both by advocates for mothers and by fathers' rights activists. Given the high emotions which these claims can rouse, it is important to consider to what extent the case law and data support them and to dispel misconceptions. Finally, it should be noted that the important issue of the child's perspective will be considered in Part IV of the book.

B Which Parents Abduct and Why

i The Assumptions of the Drafters of the Convention

The Dyer Report,[7] prepared as a preliminary document for the Special Commission Meeting in March 1979,[8] contains a chapter on the sociological background to the problem of international child abduction. This surveys the fairly obvious factors which underlie the substantial increase in the scale of the phenomenon, such as ease of international transport, increases in international relationships and the breakdown thereof.[9] In addition, a model is constructed of the typical situation which produces abduction, from which it is abundantly clear that abduction was seen as a measure of last resort by a frustrated non-custodial parent or by a parent who feared that he would lose custody.[10] There is no mention in the Report of factors which might cause a custodial parent to abduct a child.

Even though the Dyer Report does not refer specifically to fathers as abductors, the belief that only non-custodial parents abducted, combined with the fact that mothers were usually granted custody, must have led the drafters to assume that most fathers were abductors. This assumption is supported by sociological studies from that time[11] and by some later studies. For example, a study conducted in 1988–89 found that most of the international abductions in the sample were carried out by fathers who did not have custody or feared losing custody.[12]

ii The 2008 Statistical Survey

The most up-to-date data on the identity and status of the abductor in relation to the child can be found in the 2008 Statistical Survey, undertaken in preparation for the Sixth Special

---

[6] eg the campaign of fathers' groups in Australia described in R Graycar, 'Family Law Reform in Australia, or Frozen Chooks Revisited Again' (2012) 13 *Theoretical Inquiries in Law* 241.
[7] A Dyer, 'Report on International Abduction by One Parent ("Legal Kidnapping")', Preliminary Document 1 (1978), Actes et Documents of the XIVth Session, 17 ('Dyer Report').
[8] See ch 1 at I Aiii.
[9] Dyer Report (n 7), 19.
[10] ibid, 19–20.
[11] P Beaumont and P McEleavy, *The Hague Convention on Child Abduction* (Oxford, Oxford University Press, 1999) 8–9.
[12] Janvier et al, 'Parental Kidnapping' (n 3) 4.

Commission Meeting on the basis of data provided by the Contracting States.[13] This shows that globally 69 per cent of abductors were mothers and 28 per cent were fathers.[14] Interestingly, this pattern was not uniform throughout the Contracting States. Thus, in some States all, or nearly all, of the incoming applications involved abducting mothers;[15] whereas in others, a relatively small percentage of the abductors were mothers.[16] The two Contracting States with the most incoming return applications also deviated significantly from the global mean: in the USA, only 59 per cent of abductors were mothers;[17] whereas in England and Wales, the figure was 81 per cent.[18]

Information as to the status of the abductor was only available in relation to 17 per cent of the return applications made globally.[19] In these cases, 40 per cent of the abductors were the child's primary carer; 33 per cent their joint primary carer and 28 per cent a non-primary carer.[20] When this data was combined with the relationship with the taking parent, it was found that 51 per cent of taking mothers were primary carers and 37 per cent were joint primary carers; whereas the corresponding figures for taking fathers were 13 per cent and 22 per cent respectively.[21]

Since the Statistical Survey is *ex hypothesi* a quantitative survey, it does not provide any information directly relating to the motivation of the abductors. However, it is clear that the traditional assumption that parents abduct because they have lost custody cannot apply where the abductor is a sole primary carer.[22] Another possible insight into motivation might be gained from the data in relation to a correlation between the State of refuge and the nationality of the abductor. The survey revealed that 60 per cent of the taking parents abducted the child to a State of which they were a national. This suggests that in these cases, one motivation for the abduction was that the abductor wanted to return to his home State,[23] at least where the abductor was a primary carer of the child.[24]

The above figures make it clear that most of the assumptions which informed the drafting of the Abduction Convention are no longer accurate. In particular, 73 per cent of abductors are primary or joint primary carers and not non-custodial parents, as envisaged

---

[13] N Lowe, 'A Statistical Analysis of Applications Made in 2008 under The Hague Convention of 25 October 1980 on the Civil Aspects of International Child Abduction, Part I Global Report, Preliminary Document 8 (November 2011), www.hcch.net/upload/wop/abduct2011pd08ae.pdf

[14] ibid 14. In the remaining 3%, both parents abducted or the abductor was a family member or institution.

[15] eg Scotland (all 5 applications), Ukraine (29 out of 30) and Norway (9 out of 10).

[16] eg Montenegro (1 out of 5), Uruguay (2 out of 7) and Mexico (79 out of 167).

[17] N Lowe, 'A Statistical Analysis of Applications Made in 2008 under The Hague Convention of 25 October 1980 on the Civil Aspects Of International Child Abduction Part III – National Reports', Preliminary Document No 8 (May 2011), www.hcch.net/upload/wop/abduct2011pd08c.pdf, 199 ('2008 National Reports').

[18] ibid, 183.

[19] 2008 Statistical Survey (n 13), para 46.

[20] ibid, para 47; The term primary carer is used rather than custodial parent because, as will be seen in ch 7, the wide definition given to the term's rights of custody in the Abduction Convention means that parents who were traditionally treated as non-custodial parents may now have rights of custody even though the child does not live with them. Thus, the literature now refers to the de facto status of the parent as a primary carer or non-primary carer. The 2008 Statistical Survey (n 13), fn 19 states that the 'primary carer' refers to the parent with whom the child usually lived at the time of removal and the 'joint-primary carer' where the child either lived with both parents at the time of removal or, if the parents were separated, spent a substantial amount of time with each parent.

[21] 2008 Statistical Survey ibid, fn 23.

[22] Although joint primary carers might want to become sole primary carers or might fear that following legal proceedings the other parent will be given sole primary care.

[23] 2008 Statistical Survey (n 13), para 49.

[24] Non-custodial parents may also choose take the child to their home State in the hope that this State will favour a local national, Dyer Report (n 7), 20.

by the drafters. Moreover, there is a significant difference between the profiles of abducting mothers and fathers. Only 13 per cent of mothers were non-primary carers; whereas 65 per cent of fathers fell into this category.

iii Qualitative Studies

From the findings of the various small-scale qualitative studies, it is possible to compile a list of reasons which motivate parents to abduct a child. Some caution has to be exercised since in most of the studies the left-behind parent was interviewed and his perception of the reason may be different to that of the abductor.[25] The list of reasons includes the following:

(a) The desire of one parent to return to her home country,[26] often because she feels isolated and unhappy in the State of habitual residence.[27] This may occur where there has been an international marriage[28] or where the parties have moved to another country for career or other reasons.[29]
(b) Escape from violence, abuse or continuing conflict with the other parent.[30]
(c) Desire for more time with the child.[31]
(d) New partner who lives in or wishes to move to another country.[32]
(e) To promote the welfare of the child, where the abductor believes that the other parent or the environment in the State of habitual residence is harmful to the child.[33] Sometimes, the background to the abduction is disagreement about the way the child should be brought up[34] or specific issues relating to the child.[35]
(f) Revenge.[36]

---

[25] Grief and Hegar, 'Parents Who Abduct' (n 3) 283. In Reunite Research Unit, 'The Outcome for Children Returned Following an Abduction' (September 2003), /www.reunite.org/edit/files/Library%20- 20reunite%20 Publications/Outcomes%20Report.pdf, 23 ('Reunite Outcomes Study'), in 7 out of the 8 cases in which both parents were abducted, they disagreed about the reason for the abduction.

[26] Reunite Outcomes Study, ibid, 23–24.

[27] Kruger (n 5) 66.

[28] ibid.

[29] ibid 67.

[30] Grief and Hegar, 'Parents Who Abduct' (n 3) 285; Kruger (n 5) 63–64; A 2007 ISS Report, *Learning from the Links between Domestic Violence and International Parental Child Abduction*, cited in J Edelson and T Lindhurst, 'Multiple Perspective on Battered Mothers and their Children Fleeing to the United States for Safety, A Study of Hague Convention Cases Final Report', www.haguedv.org/reports/fmalreport.pdf, 5, concluded that in cases where domestic violence was present, it was the primary motivation for the abduction. The Reunite Outcomes Study (n 25), 23 reports that one parent abducted because of domestic violence, but later in the study (at 29), four abducting mothers expressed concerns about domestic violence upon return. For a detailed discussion of the relevance of domestic violence against the abductor in Convention Proceedings, see ch 11 at II Biv.

[31] Grief and Hegar, 'Parents Who Abduct' (n 3) 287; N Long, R Forehand and C Zogg, 'Preventing Parental Child Abduction: Analysis of a National Project' (1992) 31 *Clinical Pediatrics* 704. In such situations, the custodial parent's refusal to comply with visitation orders can be a trigger for the abduction, ibid.

[32] Kruger (n 5) 69; Reunite Outcomes Study (n 25), 24.

[33] eg Grief and Hegar, 'Parents Who Abduct' (n 3) 285. In extreme cases, that parent believes that the child is being abused by the other parent. See eg D Fisher, 'Why Parents Run' (1990) 5 *J Interpersonal Violence* 123; Long, Forehand and Zogg, 'Preventing Parental Child Abduction' (n 31); M Freeman, 'Effects and Consequences of International Child Abduction' (1998) 32 *Family Law Quarterly* 603, 617–19. See also reference to this situation in US Department of State, Hague International Child Abduction Convention; Text and Legal Analysis, Public notice 957, 51 Federal Regulation 10,494 at 10,510 (1986).

[34] Grief and Hegar, 'Parents Who Abduct' (n 3) 284.

[35] Kruger (n 5) 67–68.

[36] Grief and Hegar, *When Parents Kidnap* (n 3) 34; IJ Sagatun and L Barrett, 'Parental Child Abduction: The Law, Family Dynamics, and Legal System Responses' (1990) 18 *Journal of Criminal Justice* 433; Sometimes, the desire for revenge was triggered by the left-behind parent's new relationship, Kruger (n 5) 70.

58 *Inter-Disciplinary Aspects of Abduction*

(g) Mental or emotional disorder of the abductor.[37]
(h) Pressure from grandparents and/or other family members.[38]

It is not possible to rank these reasons according to frequency and in some cases there is more than one reason for the abduction. However, there is evidence to suggest that domestic violence and the abuse of children are among the most common reasons for abduction.[39] Thus, whilst clearly some abductors are still non-custodial parents, responding to loss of custody or fear of such loss, as envisaged by the drafters of the Convention, the empirical evidence shows that the picture today is much more complex.

C Gender Issues

i The Background

When the Abduction Convention was drafted, gender was not an issue. Since abductors were assumed to be non-primary carers who were taking the law into their own hands after having lost a custody battle, it made little difference whether they were mothers or fathers. Return would restore the child to the primary carer. However, now that most abductors are mothers who are primary carers, the debate surrounding the application of the Convention to primary carer abductions has inevitably taken on a gendered dimension.[40] Furthermore, the very reason for many of these abductions – the need of mothers bringing up children alone to move back home or to another country where they will receive economic and/or practical support from family and other social networks – is itself gendered.[41]

In addition, two further developments have highlighted the gendered aspects of the Abduction Convention. Firstly, many legal systems started giving legal rights to non-primary carers and in particular the right to veto removal of the child from the jurisdiction. This meant that many more mothers were unable to relocate with their children, even where they were sole primary carers.[42] Secondly, it became clear that, not infrequently, abducting mothers had been subject to domestic violence, itself a gendered issue. The response to the challenges thrown up by these developments has not been uniform and it is therefore not surprising that claims of discrimination have been voiced both by advocates of women's rights and by fathers' groups.

Furthermore, the entry of gender politics into the field of international child abduction has to be understood in light of the wider context of the 'gender wars' discourse in post-separation parenting law reform.[43] In particular, the debate concerning gendered aspects of

---

[37] Kruger ibid 64; Janvier et al, 'Parental Kidnapping' (n 3) 6.
[38] Kruger ibid 69–70; Reunite Outcomes Study (n 25), 24.
[39] 'Domestic and Family Violence and the Article 13 "Grave Risk" Exception in the Operation of the Hague Convention of 25 October 1980 on the Civil Aspects of International Child Abduction: A Reflection Paper', Preliminary Document No 9 (May 2011), www.hcch.net/index_en.php?act=progress.listing&cat=7, 4.
[40] R Lamont, 'Mainstreaming Gender into European Family Law? The Case of International Child Abduction and Brussels II Revised' (2011) 17 *European Law Journal* 366, 369–70.
[41] See IR Lamont, 'An Analysis of the EU's Commitment to Gender Equality in the Context of Private International Family Law: A Case Study of International Child Abduction under Regulation' (Doctoral Thesis, University of Liverpool, 2003) Chapter 4.
[42] C Bruch, 'The Promise and Perils of a Protocol to the 1980 Convention on the Civil Aspects of International Child Abduction' in A Büchler and M Müller-Chen (eds), *Festschrift fur Ingeborg Schwenzer aum 60. Geburtstag* (Bern, Stämpfli Verlag AG, 2011) 239.
[43] See sources quoted in H Rhoades, 'Children's Needs and Gender Wars: The Paradox of Parenting Law Reform' (2010) 24 *Australian Journal of Family Law* 160, fnn 12 and 13.

relocation law is of relevance to the abduction situation.[44] Since most primary carers are mothers, restrictive relocation regimes will prejudice women.[45] Thus, for example, it has been pointed out judicially that allowing an investigation into the reasons for the move opens the door to unjustifiably restricting the mobility rights of custodial parents, who are most often women, and so has the potential for turning a mobility issue concerning the best interests of the children into a gender issue.[46] This prejudice is compounded where mothers who wish to relocate for economic reasons are not allowed to do so. In such cases, the refusal of permission exacerbates the economic disadvantage invariably suffered by mothers as a result of structural socio-economic inequalities.[47] In addition, it is argued that the fact that courts usually only consider the mobility of the primary carer mother and not that of the father is discriminatory.[48] On the other hand, liberal relocation regimes seem to prejudice fathers by giving apparently little weight to their relationship with the child.

ii The Claims of Gender Bias

The main claims voiced by mothers are that the father's right to veto removal of the child from the jurisdiction has been interpreted as a custody right, contrary to the intention of the drafters[49] and that return is ordered even where the father was violent.[50] Ordering return in such situations, it is argued, inevitably harms the child. If the mother does not return with the child, he is separated from his primary carer and if she does return to a violent, impoverished or otherwise difficult situation, the child will also be adversely affected.

On the other hand, fathers, who are the applicants in most Convention cases, complain about financial and other impediments to bringing applications.[51] Similarly, it has been suggested that courts apply the defences less stringently in cases where the mother is the abductor. Moreover, where return is ordered, the financial undertakings required of them[52] are often so great that they cannot afford to enforce the return order.

At face value, the statistics would seem to support the fathers' claim. The 2008 Statistical Survey showed that globally in 17 per cent of cases where the mother was the taking parent, return was refused; whereas in only 11 per cent of cases where the father was the taking

---

[44] Despite the differences between the two areas of law. For a detailed discussion of relocation law and its inter-relationship with abduction, see ch 4.

[45] 'Preliminary Note on International Family Relocation', Preliminary Document No 11 (January 2012), www.hcch.net/upload/wop/abduct2012pd11e.pdf, para 29.

[46] *Stav v Stav* 2012 BCCA 154 (Court of Appeal for British Columbia) [87].

[47] As a result of labour market *discrimination* against women and/or child rearing responsibilities which have impaired career development.

[48] Preliminary Note on International Family Relocation (n 45), para 30 and ch 4 at text accompanying nn 90–93.

[49] See detailed discussion in ch 7 at III C and IV Bi.

[50] For a discussion of claims of gender bias against women in determining habitual residence, see ch 8 at V F. In addition, Lamont, 'Mainstreaming Gender' (n 40) discusses the fact that the returning mother may not have a right to residence in the requesting State if she was dependent on her former husband's residency status and that her ability to acquire residency status may be impaired by her childcare responsibilities which prevent her from working.

[51] NL Browne, Note, 'Relevance and Fairness: Protecting the Rights of Domestic–Violence Victims and Left-Behind Fathers under the Hague Convention on International Child Abduction' (2011) 60 *Duke Law Journal* 1193, 1216–20.

[52] Undertakings may be required where the abducting mother is the primary carer of the child, in order to ensure appropriate conditions for her and the child on return. See generally ch 11 at III.

parent, return was refused.[53] In the UK, the difference was even more pronounced. Return was not refused in any case where the father was the taking parent; whereas return was refused in nearly nine per cent of cases where the mother was the taking parent.[54] Moreover, globally in 52 out of the 56 cases (93 per cent) in which the sole reason for refusing return was grave risk of harm within Article 13(1)(b), the mother was the abductor.[55] However, this apparent bias can perhaps be largely explained by the fact that, as seen above, the percentage of taking mothers who are primary or joint primary carers is significantly higher than the percentage of fathers who are primary or joint primary carers.[56] Thus, the statistics may simply reflect, quite logically, that return is refused more often where the abductor is a primary carer rather than any gender bias.

The current author decided to investigate claims by Israeli fathers' groups that Israeli courts are biased against men in Abduction Convention cases,[57] by examining success rates in the reported cases from 2001 to 2011, of which there were 49. As will be seen from the table below, the statistics do not support the claim of bias. Indeed, men were successful in 63 per cent of the cases overall and enjoyed a higher success rate than women in the cases where they were applicants (68 per cent as opposed to 55 per cent). Since it was clear that the fathers groups' claims were based on the experience of Israeli fathers, it was decided to analyse the statistics according to whether the applicant was considered Israeli or foreign.[58] This analysis revealed the root of the fathers' impression of bias, viz that only 22 per cent of the Israeli male applicants were successful.[59] However the fact that this figure does not indicate gender bias against men[60] is shown clearly both by the fact that 83 per cent of foreign fathers were successful[61] and that Israeli female applicants were not successful in any case.[62]

Table 1: Relationship between Gender of Applicant and Success in Israeli Abduction Cases

Applicant Mothers	Applicant Fathers	
55% (n= 6 out of 11)	68% (n= 26 out of 38)	Success rate for whole sample
0% (n=0 out of 4)	22% (n = 2 out of 9)	Success rate for 'Israeli' applicants
86% (n=6 out of 7)	83% (n=24 out of 29)	Success rate for 'foreign' applicants

In conclusion, the author has not found any evidence of discrimination against men or women per se under the Abduction Convention. Rather, any apparent differences in treatment stem from underlying sociological factors connected to parenting and family life that

---

[53] 2008Statistical Survey (n 13), para 113.
[54] 2008 National Reports (n 17), 187.
[55] 2008 Statistical Survey (n 13), para 116.
[56] Of course, it may be countered that the very fact that more mothers are primary caretakers is itself a result of gender bias, but this is not the concern of the Abduction Convention.
[57] A letter of complaint was written to the Permanent Bureau in January 2012, bringofirhome.org/wp-content/uploads/2011/10/Hague-convention-ccfisrael-report1.pdf.
[58] Applicants who were born and brought up in Israel or immigrated to Israel before the age of 18 were considered Israeli.
[59] Most of these cases concerned Israeli couples who had gone to live abroad.
[60] A lawyer associated with the fathers' groups suggested to the author that the discrimination against men in Hague cases had only been apparent in the previous few years. However, an analysis of the cases decided between 2008 and 2011 did not reveal any significant difference.
[61] One possible explanation for this disparity is the Israeli courts' concern about their international image in cases where the applicant is perceived as foreign. See ch 6 at IV E.
[62] In three out of the four cases, it was found that there was consent on the part of the mother.

are reflected inter alia in the fact that most primary carer abductors are mothers. Whilst this and other gendered dimensions of child abduction cannot be ignored in policy making,[63] it has to be remembered that the main objective of the Child Abduction Convention is to protect children[64] and that experience shows that introducing 'gender wars' discourse into child law is liable to distract the focus from the needs of children.[65]

Accordingly, emphasis should be placed firmly on protecting the child,[66] who is the real victim of the abduction, and the claims made both by mothers and fathers should be considered in this context. Thus, the issue of whether a right to veto should be considered a right of custody should be discussed from the child's perspective, without reference to the gender of the parent who has the right to veto. Similarly, obstacles to bringing applications under the Convention should be remedied so as to provide protection for children abducted by both mothers and fathers.[67] In relation to domestic violence, giving proper weight to the harm caused to the child by being exposed to violence and by the impact of the violence or risk of violence against his primary carer on the child, necessarily involves taking into account the perspective of the victim of the domestic violence. Thus, in order to understand the implications of domestic violence for children, it is necessary to understand the gendered aspects of the dynamics of domestic violence.[68]

II Psychological Aspects of Abduction

A Introduction

This sub-chapter will consider contemporary psychological research which is relevant to policy making in the field of international child abduction in general and decision making under the Abduction Convention in particular. Reference will be made not only to the various relatively small scale studies conducted into the psychological effects of abduction and the aftermath thereof, but also to other relevant research findings relating to the effect on children of residential mobility and the impact of parental separation on children. These studies address inter alia the significance of a number of variables which will be relevant in attempting to assess the likely impact of abduction and return on children in particular circumstances. These include frequency of contact and quality of the relationship with the non-primary carer; continuing conflict between the parents and separation from a primary carer.[69]

---

[63] See detailed discussion of EU's failure to do this in enacting the Brussels II bis Regulations in Lamont, 'Mainstreaming Gender' (n 40).

[64] For the potential tension between protecting children's rights and promoting gender equality, see Lamont ibid 381.

[65] See eg Rhoades, 'Children's Needs' (n 43).

[66] For a similar child-centred approach in relation to relocation, see R Zafran, 'Children's Rights as Relational Rights: The Case of Relocation' (2010) 18 *American University Journal of Gender, Social Policy & the Law* 163, 212–16.

[67] Thus, for example, if the basis for the father's claim is that they do not qualify for legal aid (whereas mothers are more likely to do so), but still cannot afford to bring proceedings, then it is necessary to ensure that means testing is realistic.

[68] Lamont, Thesis (n 41), Chapter 5; for a discussion of the impact of violence on court decisions in Abduction Convention cases, see ch 11 at II B iv.

[69] These factors will also be relevant to relocation disputes, which will be discussed in ch 4.

It is important to consider the research evidence available in relation to the psychological aspects of abduction and its aftermath for a number of reasons. Firstly, the Abduction Convention was based on the assumptions that abduction is usually harmful to children and that prompt return is the best way to mitigate the harm. The substantial amount of relevant research published since 1980 sheds some light on the extent of the validity of these assumptions. Whilst it is most unlikely that the Convention will be amended in the near future, research findings can inform the way in which the Convention is interpreted and applied. In particular, this research can help identify factors which are liable to make the harm to which the child is at risk of being exposed upon return greater than the usual harm associated with a move, for the purposes of ascertaining whether the grave risk of harm exception is established.[70] For example, evidence as to the effect of separation of a young child from his primary carer could be relevant in cases where the child will be returning alone without the primary carer abductor. Similarly, evidence about the impact on a child of conflict and violence between his parents could be relevant in assessing whether to return the child to such a situation. Moreover, even where return is ordered, knowledge about the effect of return on children in such situations and in general can help courts and other authorities devise effective protective measures which will minimise, so far as possible, the harm to the child.

In addition, as will be seen below, not all of the research studies are consistent with each other and there is disagreement between social science scholars in relation to the conclusions which can be drawn from some of the studies. This means that experts who write opinions for courts may rely on one school of thought, without explaining that there are researchers who take a different view. In some cases, reliance on such a report may be determinative of the case.[71] Accordingly, it is important for judges, practitioners and others to be aware of the differences of opinion and the criticisms levelled against some of the research.

However, it should be emphasised that the purpose of this sub-chapter is to bring to the attention of the reader the social science research which sheds light on the psychological aspects of international child abduction and its aftermath and to explain its relevance to the operation of the Abduction Convention. There is no attempt to assess the validity of the methodology used in the various studies or the extent to which the research data support the conclusions drawn by the researchers, but reference is made in the footnotes to literature which provides such critical analysis. Moreover, at the outset it is appropriate to express a number of general caveats in relation to the populations that were studied. The findings of most of the child abduction studies may have been distorted by the fact that the subjects were selected from criminal justice or clinical samples or were self-selected. Accordingly, less serious cases where the parents and children involved got on with their lives without suffering any obvious harm are unlikely to be represented in the studies.[72]

---

[70] See ch 11 at II Aii.

[71] eg in the Israeli case of RFamA (SC) 1855/08 *RB v VG* http://elyon1.court.gov.il/files/08/550/018/r03/08018550.r03.pdf, 8/4/08 (Isr) [INCADAT cite: HC/E/IL 923], the expert psychologist's opinion that leaving the child in Israel, which in his view would result in the child losing all contact with the father, would cause him long term damage was clearly based on Gardner's Parental Alienation Syndrome (see below F). The judge, apparently unaware of the controversy surrounding this syndrome (ibid) relied on this opinion and held that whilst the grave risk exception had been established, refusing return would also cause the child damage and accordingly he should be returned (see discussion in ch 11 at II Aii).

[72] This may be one of the reasons why a survey based on telephoning randomly selected households found that most abducted children did not suffer significant harm, D Finkelhor, G Hotaling and A Sedlak, 'Children Abducted by Family Members; A National Household Survey of Incidence and Episode Characteristics' (1991) 53 *Journal of Marriage and Family* 805.

Moreover, many of the abduction studies are based on parental reports of their children's adjustment without any interviews with the children or objective assessment. Finally, some of the findings of the general divorce studies may be related to the socio-economic conditions in the US, where the vast majority of the studies were conducted.[73]

B The Impact of Moving

Both international abduction and return involve the relocation of a child from one country to another. Thus, it is appropriate firstly to consider the likely impact of these moves on the child. The research evidence in relation to the effect of residential mobility on children has been described as equivocal.[74] Whilst some studies did find significant negative outcomes, including adjustment and behavioural problems, associated with frequent residential mobility,[75] others found a positive or non-significant negative effect of residential mobility on children's well-being.[76]

Some psychologists suggest that a move following marital breakdown[77] involves special risks for children because the child does not have the support of an intact family in coping with the challenges of adjustment[78] and because the move can 'represent a second, or sometimes a third edition of the original disruption that occurred at the time of the marital breakdown'.[79] Nonetheless, even in relation to children of separated parents, the research studies are not consistent. Whilst some studies do find significant negative outcomes of relocation on these children,[80] it is difficult to isolate the relocation factor from other destabilising factors which frequently accompany moves following relationship breakdown, such as a change in the custodial parent's partner,[81] and not all studies take sufficient account of socio-demographic factors.[82] It should also be pointed out that much of the research involved children who had relocated many times and so may indicate little about the effect of a single move or a single move followed by return. Similarly, since most of the research studies deal with planned moves, they cannot tell us about the effect of the sudden and sometimes surreptitious nature of the move in abduction cases.

---

[73] B Horsfall and R Kaspiew, 'Relocation in Separated and Non-Separated Families: Equivocal Evidence from the Social Science Literature' (2010) 24 *Australian Journal of Family Law* 34, 35, point out that the level of child poverty in the USA is particularly high and its level of support for single parent families particularly low.

[74] ibid.

[75] WG Austin, 'Relocation, Research, and Forensic Evaluation, Part I: Effects of Residential Mobility on Children of Divorce' (2008) 46 *Family Court Review* 137, 140–42; Horsfall and Kaspiew, 'Relocation in Separated' (n 73) 44, suggest that socio-demographic factors might account for some of the negative outcomes,

[76] Horsfall and Kaspiew (n 73) 36–41.

[77] Divorced parents relocate at a much higher rate than intact families, Austin, 'Relocation, Research' (n 75) 140.

[78] ibid 144.

[79] S Wallerstein and TJ Tanke, 'To Move or Not to Move: Psychological and Legal Considerations in the Relocation of Children Following Divorce' (1996) 30 *Family Law Quarterly* 305, 309–11. These authors also suggest that the high risk of conflict between the parents which is likely to accompany the relocation issue can severely threaten the child's sense of security. This seems to apply a fortiori where there has been an abduction.

[80] Horsfall and Kaspiew (n 73) 55.

[81] Austin (n 75) 142; One study suggested that the mother's attitude to relocation was an important factor (see Horsfall and Kaspiew ibid 45).

[82] Horsfall and Kaspiew ibid 55.

C The Impact of Abduction

The research studies involving abducted children do indeed suggest that abduction may cause them harm,[83] sometimes long-term,[84] and there is some evidence that abduction increases the harm caused by high-conflict parental separations.[85] However, these studies do not distinguish between cases where children were concealed or otherwise lost contact with the left-behind parent during the period of the abduction and those where contact continued.[86] Thus, it is difficult to assess to what extent the harm was caused by the abduction per se, rather than by the effect of concealment[87] and/or loss of contact with the other parent. In particular, it should be noted that many of the cases referred to in the literature relate to children who were on the run, sometimes for considerable lengths of time, whereas perusal of the Abduction Convention cases reveals that in many cases the abducted child is living in a relatively stable environment.[88] Similarly, it is not possible to know to what extent the harm reported in these studies was caused or at least exacerbated by the further disruption caused by return.[89]

Nonetheless, some comments made to researchers by children who had been abducted do provide some specific insight into the possible effects of abduction on the child.[90] One adult who was abducted as a child reports that the 'thought that you can just be picked up and moved on at any moment' still causes her to feel insecure.[91] On the other hand, in other cases, the children did not report negative feelings about the abduction itself, especially where it was presented as an extension of a holiday or an outing.[92] However, some of the children interviewed reported missing siblings, extended family and friends during the period of time during which they were abducted.[93] A few children reported difficulties at

---

[83] See eg MW Agopian, 'The Impact on Children of Abduction by Parents' (1984) 63 *Child Welfare* 511; RL Hegar and GL Grief, 'Parental Assessment of the Adjustment of Children Following Abduction by the Other Parent' (1993) 2 *Journal of Child and Family Studies* 143; But note that in M Freeman, 'International Child Abduction the Effects' (the Reunite Research Center, 2006) www.reunite.org/edit/files/Library%20-%20reunite%20Publications/Effects%20Of%20Abduction%20Report.pdf, 23 ('Reunite Effects Study'), a quarter of the parents (half abductors and half left-behind parents) did not think that there had been adverse effects on the children.

[84] GL Greif, 'A Parental Report on the Long-Term Consequences for Children of Abduction by the Other Parent' (2000) 31 *Child Psychiatry and Human Development* 59, 66; GL Greif, 'The Long-Term Aftermath of Child Abduction: Two Case Studies and Implications for Family Therapy' (2009) 37 *The American Journal of Family Therapy* 273, 274–75; Reunite Effects Study ibid, 50.

[85] Greif, 'A Parental Report' ibid 70, after comparing his sample with a similar longitudinal study of the effects of divorce on children who had not been abducted, claimed that the abducted children were faring worse and suggested that the abduction experience may add to the effects of divorce. This view was echoed by some of the parents interviewed in the Reunite Effects Study ibid, 48. However, many of the comments made by the parents and children reflected the effects of the conflict between the parents (often still continuing) rather than the actual abduction, ibid, 21, 48, 58–60.

[86] In the Reunite Effects Study ibid, 58, contact was lost, at least initially, in most of the cases.

[87] Children may be severely affected by the lies they were told and were forced to tell and by the manipulation of their identities during the process of concealment, J Sagatum and L Barrett, 'Parental Child Abduction: The Law, Family Dynamics and the Legal System Responses' (1990) 18 *Journal of Criminal Justice* 433, 440.

[88] Beaumont and McEleavy (n 11) 11 note that concealment does not often arise in reported cases.

[89] Reunite Effects Study (n 83), 61, 63; Greif, 'The Long Term Aftermath' (n 84) 284–85; Freeman, 'Effects and Consequences' (n 33) 605.

[90] Although, of course, they do not have any statistical significance.

[91] Reunite Effects Study (n 83), 50; another child reported experiencing a continued fear of being kidnapped ibid, 57.

[92] ibid, 56; but some felt betrayed on discovering the truth and had difficulty thereafter in trusting one or both parents ibid, 60.

[93] ibid, 58.

school and socially in the country of refuge, often as a result of language barriers, but other children reported the experience of a new school and new friends as a positive one.[94] Importantly, some children reported suffering difficulties in re-adjusting educationally and socially in their home country after being returned.[95]

So, whilst the research does provide some, albeit equivocal, support for the assumption that a move to another country as a result of abduction or a return may cause harm to a child, it also suggests that whether or not such harm occurs, and the extent thereof, is dependent on many other factors, including the length of the abduction,[96] the conditions during the abduction,[97] the degree of contact (if any) with the left-behind parent during the abduction,[98] the information given to the child about the left-behind parent,[99] the support available on return,[100] the age of the child[101] and whether there was a separation from a sibling(s).[102]

One of the most significant factors is likely to be the impact of the move on the child's relationship with each of his parents. Most of the empirical research in relation to the effects of abduction and its aftermath does not distinguish between cases where the child was abducted by a primary carer and those where the abductor was a non-primary carer and some of the studies seem to have included only or mainly abductions by non-primary carers.[103] The differences between the short-term effects of abduction in these two situations seem obvious,[104] but the way the de facto status of the abductor affects the long-term impact of abduction and return on the child is perhaps less clear. Some insight into the differences between the two situations can be gleaned from the general research studies relating to separation of children from primary and non-primary carers. Thus, the following sections will consider the relevant research findings and the implications thereof for abduction cases.

D The Impact of a Move Away from a Primary Carer

Firstly, it is important to realise that there are cases where one parent cannot be defined as the primary carer and the other as the non-primary carer.[105] It is increasingly common for both parents to be joint primary carers. This is usually the case where the parents live together at the time of the abduction and are both active in looking after the child and

---

[94] ibid, 57.

[95] ibid, 57, 59.

[96] Greif, 'The Long Term Aftermath' (n 84), 275; Agopian, 'The Impact on Children' (n 83).

[97] See eg atrocious conditions endured by the children in the first case study in Grief ibid 279 compared with cases where the child lives in a stable environment and feels at home in the country of refuge, eg Reunite Effects Study (n 83), 56. For a discussion of the impact of having to change appearance or take on a new identity, see Grief ibid 283, 285.

[98] Reunite Effects Study ibid, 46–47, 58; Grief and Hegar (n 3) 151.

[99] Some children were told or allowed to believe that the left-behind parent was dead or did not want them anymore, Reunite Effects Study ibid, 56, 58. In some cases, the child was told that the left behind parent was dangerous, Grief, 'The Long Term Aftermath' (n 84), 279; Reunite Effects Study ibid, 14.

[100] Including support from parents and family (Grief ibid 280; Reunite Effects Study ibid, 59) and professional support (Grief ibid 285; ch 2 at IV Biv).

[101] Grief and Hegar (n 3) 143.

[102] Grief 'The Long Term Aftermath' (n 84) 284.

[103] eg ibid.

[104] In some cases where the abductor was the primary carer, the children did not perceive the move as an abduction at all, but rather as a return home, Reunite Effects Study (n 83), 56.

[105] In relation to the difficulties in defining primary care, see Reunite Outcomes Study (n 25), 17–18.

where parents share the care of the child on a more or less equal basis following separation. Similarly, the identity of the primary carer may have changed at some point before the abduction. Thus, whilst the abductor may not technically be the child's primary carer, the child may still relate to that parent as such.[106] It is not easy to apply the research findings to these situations.

The impact of the move away from a primary carer will be relevant in two Abduction Convention situations. The first is where the left-behind parent is the primary carer. This was the scenario which the drafters of the Convention had in mind when expressing their desire 'to protect children from the harmful effects of their wrongful removal or retention'.[107] The second situation is where the primary carer abducted the child and she is not able or willing to return with the child. The court will therefore have to assess the impact of returning the child unaccompanied by the primary carer, in order to determine whether the Article 13(1)(b) exception is established viz, whether return will expose the child to grave risk of harm or place him in an intolerable situation.[108] The research literature on the impact of the separation from the primary carer is highly relevant to such a determination.[109]

Whilst it is perhaps axiomatic that separation from the primary carer will cause the child short-term harm, it is less clear that it will cause him long-term harm, at least in the situation where he is being well cared for in a stable environment by a loving, capable parent, who effectively now becomes his primary carer.[110] However, there is evidence that, even in such circumstances, the separation from the primary carer may well cause long-term harm, especially where the child is very young at the date of separation.

The critical importance of continuity of primary care, which has long influenced decision making in custody disputes,[111] is largely based on the widely accepted theory of attachment.[112] According to this theory, a person's ability to form and maintain healthy intimate relationships depends on his having had a close and consistent relationship, often referred to as a primary attachment relationship, with his primary carer during infancy.[113] Disruption or straining of this primary attachment relationship during the early formative years of a child's life is likely to cause him not only temporary insecurity but also impair his ability to form secure attachment relationships throughout his life. Interestingly, research on the development of the brain provides a neurological explanation for this phenomenon. Neuroscientists have discovered that early socio-emotional experiences influence the maturation of the brain circuits in the right hemisphere of the brain.[114] Separation from the

---

[106] This seems to have been the case in the two case studies in Grief, 'The Long Term Aftermath' (n 84), in which the mothers abducted after having lost custody.

[107] Preamble to the Abduction Convention.

[108] For a discussion of the courts' attitude to this situation, see ch 11 at II Biii.

[109] In the abduction context, Hegar and Grief, 'Parental Assessment' (n 83) 155 reported on readjustment difficulties in children who had been returned to a non-custodial parent after having been abducted by a custodial parent.

[110] Two of the research studies report that some children formed strong emotional bonds with the non-primary carer abductor and wanted to remain with him, see Freeman, 'Effects and Consequences' (n 33) 615; See also Greif and Hegar (n 3) 145.

[111] eg *Burchard v Garay* 724 P.2d 486, 488–89 (Cal 1986); *re Marriage of Burgess* 913 P.2d 473, 478–79 (Cal 1996); *J v C* [1970] AC 688.

[112] Bruch, 'The Promise and Perils' (n 42) 285.

[113] Researchers also claim that children who had secure attachment relationships will be better able to cope with stressful events, often termed resilience. See A Stroufe and J McKintosh, 'Divorce and Attachment Relationships: The Longitudinal Journey' (2011) 49 *Family Court Review* 464, 465.

[114] eg A Shore and J Mckintosh, 'Family Law and the Neuroscience of Attachment, Part I' (2011) 49 *Family Court Review* 501, 506–07.

primary caregiver during the first two years of life is likely to delay this maturation and irreversibly alter the trajectory of the development of the brain.[115]

Whilst the original research which led to the development of attachment theory concerned children who were separated from both parents, many leading researchers take the view that this theory also has considerable relevance in the divorce setting in which young children are separated from their primary carer during visitation with their other parent.[116] Thus, they recommend that contact schedules should be organised in such a way as to avoid straining the primary attachment relationship with the primary carer, for example by avoiding frequent transfers of care.[117] A fortiori, complete separation at a young age from the primary carer as a result of an abduction or unaccompanied return is likely to disrupt the primary attachment relationship with that parent, which may well impair the child's ability to form an attachment relationship with the other parent, even though he is now the primary caregiver, and cause long-term psychological damage.[118]

E The Impact of a Move Away from a Non-Primary Carer

The effect on the child of a move away from a parent who was not a primary carer is primarily relevant in cases where the abductor is the primary carer. Whilst loss of contact with the left-behind parent during the period of abduction may well be damaging to the child, even where that parent was not the primary carer, once the case comes before a court, any such damage is not directly relevant to the question of whether return should now be ordered.[119] Rather, the long-term impact of reduced contact with the non-primary carer on the child is the relevant issue in determining whether the Abduction Convention should apply to this type of case[120] and, where it does, whether return should be ordered. The former question will arise in determining whether the non-primary carer's rights should be treated as rights of custody.[121] The second question will be primarily relevant in cases where the court has discretion as to whether to return the child because one of the defences has been established.[122] However, a judge's approach to this issue may also influence the way in which he applies some of the defences.[123]

The social science research literature in relation to the importance of regular contact with a non-primary carer is polarised, largely as a result of inconsistent research findings and disagreements as to the appropriate way in which to interpret those findings. The opposing positions will be briefly explained below. The first school of thought interprets the research as indicating that the most important parameter for positive outcomes for

---

[115] ibid.

[116] See the articles devoted to this subject in the special issue of (2003) 49 *Family Court Review* 3.

[117] J McKintosh 'Guest Editor's Introduction to Special Issue on Attachment Theory, Separation, and Divorce: Forging Coherent Understandings for Family Law' 49 (2011) *Family Court Review* 418, 423.

[118] For refusal to return on the basis of the damage likely to be caused by separation from a parent with whom a young child was attached, see *Steffen F v Severina P*, 966 FSupp2d 922 (E Ariz 1997).

[119] Even if return is not ordered, contact with the left-behind parent will usually be renewed.

[120] See C Bruch, 'The Promise and Perils' (n 42).

[121] See ch 7 at III.

[122] And in relocation disputes, see ch 4.

[123] Thus, if he thinks that lack of contact with the left-behind parent will cause damage to the child, he is less likely to find that the grave risk of harm defence is established, even where there is evidence that return will cause harm, as in *RB v VG* (n 71).

children after family breakup is continuing regular contact with both parents.[124] According to this view, a long distance move which will inevitably prevent regular contact with the non-custodial parent will be harmful for the child.[125]

In contrast, other researchers argue that the cumulative body of social science research does not support the proposition that there is any correlation between the amount of visitation with the non-custodial parent and the outcome for the child.[126] Rather, the quality of the relationship with the non-custodial parent is more significant than the quantity thereof.[127] Indeed, in cases of high conflict, frequent visitation ordered despite the objection of the custodial parent can in itself cause harm,[128] particularly if there is violence during transfers.[129] Furthermore, according to this second school of thought, the research shows clearly that the child's adjustment is consistently related to the psychological adjustment of the custodial parent.[130] Indeed, some scholars claim that good parenting by the custodial parent is the most effective protection for a child's well-being post-divorce.[131] Accordingly, where a long-distance move is likely to lead to a real improvement in the custodial parent's functioning, it is likely to promote the child's welfare.

The above research findings are very relevant to cases where there has been violence or a high level of conflict before the abduction. In such cases, return of the child will invariably mean that the mother will return to an environment which will cause her considerable anxiety and distress and impair, often substantially, her ability to function.[132] According to the second school of thought, this situation will cause the child more harm than the reduced contact with the non-custodial parent, which would result from non-return.[133] Moreover, the empirical studies show that even after return there are frequently contact difficulties.[134] Thus, it is far from clear that return will indeed result in substantially increased contact with the non-primary carer in the many cases where the abductor continues to be the primary carer. Alternatively, where there is regular contact following return, this may actually be damaging

---

[124] eg RA Warshak, 'Blanket Restrictions: Overnight Contact between Parents and Young Children' (2000) 38 *Family and Conciliation Courts Review* 422, 435–36; JB Kelly and ME Lamb, 'Using Child Development to Make Appropriate Custody and Access Decisions for Young Children' (2000) 38 *Family and Conciliation Courts Review* 297, 306–07. For criticism of this and similar research, see C Bruch, 'Sound Research or Wishful Thinking in Child Custody Cases? Lessons from Relocation Law' (2006) 40 *Family Law Quarterly* 281, 297–304.

[125] eg RA Warshak, 'Social Science and Children's Best Interests in Relocation Cases: Burgess Revisited' (2000) 34 *Family Law Quarterly* 83; SL Braver, IM Ellman and WV Fabricius, 'Relocation of Children after Divorce and Children's Best Interests: New Evidence and Legal Considerations' (2003) 17 *Journal of Family Psychology* 206, 216–17. For criticism, see Bruch ibid 308–09.

[126] Wallerstein and Tanke 'To Move or Not to Move' (n 79), 312; Bruch ibid 288. For a criticism of Wallerstein's opinion, see R Pasahow, 'A Critical Analysis of the First Empirical Research Study on Child Relocation' (2005) 19 *Journal of the American Academy of Matrimonial Lawyers* 321.

[127] Wallerstein and Tanke, ibid 312–313; M Hetherinton and J Kelly, *For Better or For Worse: Divorce Reconsidered* (WW Norton & Company, New York, 2002) 134.

[128] Wallerstein and Tanke (n 79) 314.

[129] Bruch, 'Sound Research' (n 124) 288.

[130] Wallerstein and Tanke (n 79) 311; Bruch ibid 291–92; This conclusion is supported, in relation to very young children, by neuroscience researchers who claim that 'the emotional relational environment provided by the primary caregiver shapes, for better or worse, the experience-dependent maturation of the brain systems involved in attachment functions that are accessed throughout the life span', Shore and Mckintosh, 'Family Law and the Neuroscience' (n 114) 502.

[131] Hetherinton and Kelly (n 127) 126; Wallerstein and Tanke (ibid).

[132] See Reunite Effects Study (n 83), 31.

[133] For a discussion of the impact of primary caregiver stress on the development of young children, see Shore and Mckintosh, 'Family Law and the Neuroscience' (n 114) 510.

[134] See eg Reunite Effects Study (n 83), 40; Kruger (n 5) 207–08

if the conflict between the parents continues. Accordingly, the child may lose out as a result of the return from every perspective.

F Parental Alienation

Whichever parent abducts, there is a risk that the abducting parent may alienate the child against the left-behind parent either consciously or sub-consciously. Moreover, the lack of contact or very limited contact with the left-behind parent is likely to increase the influence which the abductor has over the child. The effect of this situation on the child may be relevant in Abduction Convention proceedings in two contexts. The first is the extent to which in these circumstances any objections to return voiced by the child can be considered to reflect his own independent views rather than those of the abductor, for the purpose of establishing the child objection exception.[135] The second context is where the court is comparing the consequences of returning the child with those of leaving him in the country of refuge, either in determining whether the grave risk of harm exception applies[136] or in the exercise of its discretion where one of the defences has been established.

In both these contexts, left-behind parents and courts have relied on the Parental Alienation Syndrome (PAS) theory, developed by Richard Gardner.[137] This theory holds that any refusal of a child to visit one parent is evidence of incitement by the other parent. The method of treatment is to prevent continued influence by the alienating parent, which in serious cases will involve removing the child from his custody, even where this means putting the child into foster or institutional care. According to this theory, where an abducted child demonstrates signs of alienation, such as refusing to talk to the left-behind parent or shouting abuse at him, his views should not be treated as independent and thus however strongly he objects to return, the court should not refuse return under Article 13(2).[138] Some advocates of PAS have gone a stage further and claimed that the very fact of abduction is likely to put the child in the same situation as a child who has been alienated by brainwashing because he is completely dependent on his abductor.[139] An Israeli court cited this view as a reason not to even hear the views of the children since they could not possibly be independent.[140] Similarly, blind acceptance of PAS theory may lead courts to return children to harmful situations because the long-term damage caused by the alienation, which they assume will continue, is perceived to be greater than that which will be caused by return, even where there is clear evidence of the likelihood of such damage.[141]

However, none of the courts which relied on PAS theory in the abduction context seem to have been aware of the serious flaws which have been exposed in the theory by respected

---

[135] For a detailed discussion of this exception, see ch 12.

[136] For a discussion of whether such a comparison is appropriate in determining whether there is a grave risk of harm, see ch 11 at II Aii.

[137] RA Gardner, *The Parental Alienation Syndrome: A Guide for Mental Health and Legal Professionals*, 2nd edn (Creative Therapeutics, New Jersey, 1998).

[138] eg FamA (Dist TA) 1167/99 *R v L* (Unreported, 3 July 2000) [INCADAT cite: HC/E/IL 834] which expressly refers to PAS theory in holding that the child's views were not independent, but in this case return was refused under Art 13(1)(b) because the child's suicide threats were taken seriously. See also BB Soval and WM Hilton, 'Article 13(b) of the Hague Convention Treaty: Does it Create a Loophole for Parental Alienation Syndrome – an Insidious Abduction?' (2001) 35 *International Lawyer* 997.

[139] Z Bergman and A Witzum, 'Parental Abduction and Parental Alienation Syndrome' (1995) 9 *Sihot* 115, 115, 119 and 129 (Hebrew).

[140] FamA (Dist TA) 28/97 *Plonit v Almonit* 19 April 1999 Nevo.

[141] This was the case in *RB v VG* (n 71), discussed in ch 11 at II Aii.

social science and legal scholars,[142] including the lack of empirical data to support the theory. Three deficiencies in the theory are particularly relevant in the child abduction context.

Firstly, the theory does not take into account that there may be objective reasons for the child's negative attitude to the left-behind parent and his refusal to return. These may include the left-behind parent's abusive[143] or other problematic behaviour towards the child and/or other family members or the child's emotional reaction to the breakdown of his parents' relationship. Similarly, where the child is happily settled in the country of refuge and wishes to remain there, the left-behind parent's insistence that he return against his will may well be perceived by the child as showing that that parent does not care about him and trigger or exacerbate alienation.[144] In addition, the assumption that children always side with the abductor is too simplistic. Whilst children may be reluctant to express views contrary to those of the abductor as long as they are still under his control, there will not usually be any need for them to express strong views against return. Furthermore, it should be taken into account that by the time the child's views are ascertained, the left-behind parent is once again in the picture, together with the authorities and thus the child is no longer completely dependent on the abductor, although he may not always realise this. Accordingly, it should never automatically be assumed that the child's objections to return are not independent. Indeed, such an assumption renders the child objection exception redundant. Rather, it is necessary to examine carefully the reasons given for these views, together with the child's current circumstances, before concluding that the child has been influenced.

Secondly, even where there is evidence of influence by the abducting parent, this does not necessarily mean that the views expressed by the child do not to some extent represent his own independent wishes. Indeed, it should be borne in mind that even adults' views are not formed in a vacuum and are usually influenced by the attitudes of those around them. Thus, careful examination is again required rather than blanket assumptions in determining what weight should be given to the child's views.

Finally, Gardner's belief that alienation causes irreparable damage to children and so requires immediate treatment is not supported by research findings. Indeed, other research studies have shown that in all but unusual cases, a child's relationship with the alienated parent resolves itself over time.[145] Thus, the alleged long-term consequences of alienation should not be used as a basis for not refusing to order return, where there is evidence that return will expose the child to immediate and concrete harm.

---

[142] C Bruch, 'Parental Alienation Syndrome and Parental Alienation: Getting it Wrong in Child Custody Cases' (2002) 14 *Child and Family Law Quarterly* 381, 386–92.

[143] Gardner's claim that allegations of abuse against the alienated parent are fabricated is completely unsupported, Bruch ibid 384.

[144] Thus, eg in the case of *RB v VG* (n 71), the child's hostility to the father intensified as the legal proceedings progressed and he told the expert that if the father would agree to him staying in Israel, he would renew contact with him (expert opinion on file with author).

[145] Bruch, 'Parental Alienation Syndrome' (n 142) 385 and research cited there at fn 20.

4

International Relocation and its Inter-Relationship with International Child Abduction

I Introduction

It is perhaps axiomatic that child abduction and relocation are 'two sides of the same coin'.[1] Abduction is the unlawful removal of a child from his habitual residence, whereas relocation is the lawful removal of the child from that place after having obtained the consent of the other parent or the court.[2] However, this truism tells us little about relocation law or the ways in which abduction law should inform relocation law and vice versa. In this chapter, these issues will be considered. First, the current state of relocation law will be briefly summarised (Part II). This will include surveying the approaches taken by different legal systems to contested requests by custodial parents to relocate with their child(ren); scholarly analysis of the current law; the attempts which have taken place in recent years towards achieving some degree of international harmonisation in this area and the various empirical research studies that have been conducted. The chapter will then go on to consider the relevance of each of the two areas of law on the formulation of the other at the macro level and on the making of relocation and return decisions respectively at the micro level (Part III).

It should be pointed out from the outset that the common concerns of relocation law and abduction law provide scope for cross-fertilisation. In particular, both areas of law have to contend with the dilemma of which option is the lesser of two evils for a child where the custodial or joint custodial parent wishes to move to another country and the other parent does not. On the one hand, if this move is allowed (either by permitting relocation or refusing return in the case of abduction), the child is separated from the non-custodial parent. On the one hand, if the move is not allowed (by refusing relocation or returning the child), this will result either in the child being separated from the custodial parent (where that parent relocates alone or does not return with the child) or 'forcing' the custodial parent to remain in a country where she is not happy which may well have repercussions on her parenting ability. In relocation law, this issue is at the very heart of the decision whether to allow relocation. In abduction law, this issue is primarily relevant in determining whether the Article 13(b) grave risk exception applies where the custodial abductor refuses or is not able to return with the child or where it is clear that return will have a negative effect on her parenting abilities.

---

[1] *G (Children)* [2010] EWCA Civ 1232 [12] (Thorpe LJ).
[2] ibid.

To date, considerably more social science research has been published in relation to the implications of relocation decisions than in relation to decisions in abduction cases. Thus, there is clearly room for those formulating policy and making decisions in relation to abduction to learn from the research conducted in relation to relocation.

However, it is important to emphasise that despite the considerable common ground between relocation law and abduction law, there are fundamental differences, which should not be forgotten. Relocation law is domestic law which is applied in order to determine, on the merits of a particular case, whether a parent should be allowed to relocate with a child. On the other hand, the Hague Convention on the Civil Aspects of International Child Abduction 1980 ('the Abduction Convention') is an international instrument which provides a summary remedy ordering return of the child to his habitual residence, without considering the merits of the case. Thus, the decision is not meant to be a final decision on the merits of the case, but rather creates a situation where the court of the habitual residence will make such a decision. However, the fact that in reality decisions under the Abduction Convention may be outcome-determinative[3] blurs this distinction to some extent. In any event, the differences between the two areas of law does not mean that one cannot learn from the experience of the other, but rather that care has to be taken in importing the findings from one area into the other and that the differences have to be borne in mind when assessing the implications of conclusions drawn in relation to one area for the other.

II Relocation Law

A The Different Approaches

Firstly, it is important to point out that relocation law is only relevant where the relocating parent needs the consent of the other parent to change the child's country of residence. Thus, where the remaining parent does not have joint legal custody and does not have a right to veto removal from the jurisdiction, the custodial parent is free to move abroad at will. However, such a situation is becoming less common as a result of the worldwide trend over the last few decades towards granting joint legal custody, and even joint physical custody,[4] or at least bestowing on non-custodial parents a right to veto removal of the child from the jurisdiction. This fact together with the increasing number of international marriages and non-marital partnerships, higher rates of relationship breakdown, greater international mobility and the increased involvement of fathers in child-rearing has resulted in a substantial increase in the number of relocation disputes,[5] in which one par-

---

[3] Where there is no subsequent decision on the merits in the requesting State (where return is ordered) or in the requested State (where return is refused), either because the losing parent gives up or does not have the financial or emotional resources to litigate.

[4] 'Preliminary Note on International Family Relocation', Preliminary Document No 11 (January 2012), www.hcch.net/upload/wop/abduct2012pd11e.pdf, para 24–26.

[5] Conclusions and Recommendations of the Fourth Meeting of the Special Commission to Review the Operation of the Hague Convention of 25 October 1980 on the Civil Aspects of International Child Abduction, www.hcch.net/upload/concl28sc4_e.pdf, para 7.3; P Parkinson, J Cashmore and JP Single, 'The Need for Reality Testing in Relocation Cases' (2010) 44 *Family Law Quarterly* 1, 2–3.

ent ('the relocating parent' wishes to relocate and the other parent ('the remaining parent') opposes the move. Since in practice it is usually the mother who wishes to relocate,[6] relocation law has sometimes been seen as a gender issue.[7]

Research studies show that the main motive[8] for relocation is the applicant's desire to return home to be near family and friends.[9] Other common reasons for wishing to relocate are the applicant's re-partnering with a foreign resident and better employment prospects or a higher standard of living in the new country.

It has been suggested that the common denominator in relocation cases is that the relocating parent is seeking a 'better life'.[10] However, it should be borne in mind that in some cases the wish to reduce the remaining parent's involvement in the child's life is the real reason for the desire to relocate, or at least an additional motive.[11] It will be noted that there is a distinct similarity between these research findings and those in relation to the motivation of abductors, discussed above.[12]

Only a few States have enacted legislative provisions governing relocation disputes.[13] In many States, relocation is treated as an aspect of child custody determination or modification and thus will be decided in accordance with the law governing custody disputes.[14] Whilst internal relocation within the same State[15] raises many of the same issues as foreign relocation, the discussion here will be restricted to extra-State relocations as these more accurately parallel the abduction situation.

On the one hand, broadly speaking, there seems to be a consensus as to the main factors which are relevant to a relocation determination: the best interests of the child;[16] the autonomous interest of the relocating parent to choose where to live and the interests of the non-relocating parent to maintain a meaningful relationship with his children and play an active role in their life. On the other hand, however, there is no consensus as to the precise content of these parameters, especially the best interests of the child, and there seem to be almost as many different ways of balancing these various interests as there are States. The literature on US relocation law[17] divides the different approaches in the US into four

---

[6] eg in one review of 602 relocation cases, 91% of the applicants were mothers. See T Glennon 'Still Partners? Examining the Consequences of Post Dissolution Parenting' (2007) 41 *Family Law Quarterly* 105, 123. Accordingly, for simplicity, the relocating parent will be referred to as the mother.

[7] See eg R Zafran, 'Children's Rights as Relational Rights: The Case of Relocation' (2010) 18 *American University Journal of Gender, Social Policy and the Law* 163, 212–16. For a discussion of gender aspects of child abduction, see ch 3 at II B

[8] Most applicants had more than one reason for wanting to relocate, NJ Taylor and M Freeman, 'International Research Evidence on Relocation: Past, Present and Future' (2010) 44 *Family Law Quarterly* 317, 330.

[9] ibid.

[10] M Heneghan, 'Relocation Cases – the Rhetoric and Reality of a Child›s Best Interests – a View from the Bottom of the World' (2011) 23 *Child and Family Law Quarterly* 226, 227.

[11] M Freeman, 'Relocation: The Reunite Research' (Research Unit of the Reunite International Child Abduction Centre, July 2009), www.reunite.org/edit/files/Library%20-%20reunite%20Publications/Relocation%20Report.pdf, 1 ('Reunite Relocation Report').

[12] Chapter 3 at II A.

[13] 'Preliminary Note on International Family Relocation' (n 4), para 7. This legislation often adopts the best interests standard, eg In Louisiana, La Rev Stat Ann § 9:355.13

[14] ibid, para 46.

[15] In many States, the considerations are similar and, perhaps surprisingly, some courts are more restrictive about allowing inter-State relocations (Heneghan, 'Relocation Cases' (n 10) 239). Some US States have statutorily defined relocation to include relocations within the same State where the new home is more than a fixed distance from the old home.

[16] See the detailed discussion of the best interests standard below.

[17] eg L Mcough, 'Starting Over: The Heuristics of Family Relocation Decision Making' (2003) 77 *St John's Law Review* 291.

74 *International Relocation*

categories. It will be convenient to adopt these categories and to include examples from non-US jurisdictions into the appropriate categories.

i *Presumption in Favour of Relocation*

Under this approach, relocation will be allowed unless the non-relocating parent can rebut the presumption by showing that relocation will be harmful to the child.[18] Some courts have explicitly based this presumption on the right of the custodial parent to change the child's residence.[19]

Whilst such a formal presumption in favour of relocation has not been found in any non-US jurisdiction, in practice the approach of some courts amounts to such a presumption. For example, in England and Wales, the seminal case of *Payne v Payne*[20] states that the custodial parent's application to relocate will be granted unless the court concludes that it is incompatible with the welfare of the children[21] because refusing the primary carer's reasonable proposals for the relocation of her family life is likely to impact detrimentally on the welfare of her dependent children.[22] Thorpe LJ explained that 'in most relocation cases the most crucial assessment and finding for the judge is likely to be the effect of the refusal of the application on the mother's future psychological and emotional stability.'[23]

This guidance has been very influential[24] and has resulted in most relocation applications in England and Wales being allowed. It remains to be seen whether the recent Court of Appeal clarification[25] that these statements constitute guidance, not binding principles of law, and that the welfare checklist is to be applied in relocation cases will have any impact on the way in which relocation cases will be decided.[26] In particular, it is not clear whether the *Payne* guidance applies in cases where there is shared care.[27]

Similarly, in Israel, in practice relocation has eventually been allowed in every reported case,[28] since a 2000 Supreme Court decision, holding that the relocating parent did not have to justify the decision to relocate and that the only consideration is the welfare of the child.[29] As in the UK, considerable weight is given to the impact on the custodial parent of not being allowed to relocate.[30]

---

[18] eg in the US State of Wyoming, *Testerman v Testerman* 193 P3d 1141 (2008).

[19] eg *Kaiser v Kaiser* 23 P.3d 278 (Ordinary Court of Appeal, 2001); *In re Marriage of Burgess* 913 P2d at 473–86.

[20] *Payne v Payne* [2001] EWCA Civ 166 [26] (Thorpe LJ).

[21] This was also the position in Australia prior to 2003, eg *Craven v Craven* (1976) FLC 90-049 and *D and SV* (2003) FLC 93-137.

[22] A similar approach has been adopted in South Africa in *Jackson v Jackson* 2002 (2) SA 303 (SCA).

[23] *Payne v Payne* (n 20).

[24] eg *BD v AID and D (children)* [2010] EWCA Civ 50; *Re W (Children)* [2011] EWCA CIV 345; *Re H (Leave to Remove)* [2010] 2 FLR 1875; *Re G (Leave to Remove)* [2007] EWCA Civ 1497.

[25] *MK v CK* [2011] EWCA CIV 793.

[26] For an analysis of the recent decisions, see M Welstead, 'I Want to Go Home – Parent and Child Relocation outside the Jurisdiction' in B Atkin (ed), *The International Survey of Family Law*, 2012 Edition, (Bristol, Jordans, 2012), 69.

[27] In *MK v CK* (n 25), Thorpe LJ held that the *Payne* guidance did not apply in cases of shared care, but the other judges who took a more general view of the *Payne* guidance did not agree.

[28] Although sometimes relocation is refused by family courts, whose decisions are overturned on appeal, eg RFamA (SC) 5072/10 *Ploni v Ploni*, http://elyon1.court.gov.il/verdictssearch/HebrewVerdictsSearch.aspx (26 October 2010).

[29] RFamA 4575/00 *Plonit v Plonit* 56(2) PD 321.

[30] See eg ACH (SC) 9201/08 *Ploni v Ploni*, 05 April 2009 http://elyon1.court.gov.il/files/08/010/092/s10/08092010.s10.pdf; RFamA 5072/10 (n 28).

ii Presumption against Relocation

This approach, which is diametrically opposed to the first, requires the relocating parent to prove to the court that the reason for the relocation is legitimate and that the relocation is in the child's best interests.[31] This will involve the parent providing an assessment as to the likely influence on the child of the proposed move and of the ways in which the child will maintain contact with the other parent.[32] In some States, the burden is even higher and the relocating parent has to show a positive benefit which will accrue to the child as a result of the move.[33]

iii Intermediate Approaches

Most legal systems seem to fall within this category,[34] which includes two types of approach. The first type is where the burden of proof shifts from one party to the other. Typically, the relocating parent has to show that the motive for the move is bona fide and not in order to cut the child off from the other parent. Once this burden has been satisfied, relocation will be allowed unless the non-relocating parent can show that it will be harmful to the child.

The second and more common type is where there is no burden of proof. Rather, the basis for determination is the best interests of the child[35] and each party will try to persuade the court why his position coincides with the child's best interests. Factors which will be taken into account[36] include the suitability of the child's living conditions in the foreign country and the ease with which he is likely to integrate into the new country; the adequacy of the arrangements made for preserving contact with the remaining parent and the views of a sufficiently mature child. The reason for the move will usually be taken into account to the extent that this is relevant to the best interests of the child.[37] Furthermore, there is likely to be a tendency to identify the child's interests with those of the custodial parent.[38]

This approach creates a good deal of uncertainty since the determination depends ultimately on the judge's perceptions concerning the relative importance for children of the custodial parent's level of functioning and mental health on the one hand compared with that of regular contact with the non-custodial parent on the other hand.[39] These perceptions will of

---

[31] eg the recent Scottish case of *SM v CM* [2011] CSIH 65.7.

[32] M Sattler, 'The Problem of Parental Relocation: Closing the Loophole in the Law of International Child Abduction' (2010) 67 *Washington and Lee Law Review* 1709 recommends that in cases of international relocation to a State which is not a signatory to the Hague Abduction Convention, the burden should be on the relocating parent to show that the other parent will be able to enforce contact rights in the foreign country, and where appropriate to take steps to ensure such enforcement, such as obtaining a mirror order.

[33] eg US State of Louisiana, La Rev Stat Ann § 9:355.13.

[34] LD Elrod, 'A Move in the Right Direction? Best Interests of the Child Emerging as the Standard of Relocation Cases' in PM Stahl and LM Drozd (eds), *Relocation Issues in Child Custody Cases* (London, Routledge, 2007) 29 (describing 'a clear trend' away from presumptions).

[35] Heneghan 'Relocation Cases' (n 10) 227. Examples of countries adopting this approach include Canada (*Gordon v Goertz* [1996] 2 SCR 27); France ('Preliminary Note on International Family Relocation') (n 4).

[36] For a list of some of the factors and the cases which use them, see 'Preliminary Note on International Family Relocation' (n 4), paras 59–60.

[37] *Stav v Stav* 2012 BCCA 154 (Court of Appeal for British Columbia, 5 April 2012) [89].

[38] ibid [91], holding that the first instance judge erred in treating the mother as the custodial parent when in practice the parents shared the care of the children equally.

[39] In the words of one judge, the question is whether 'the enhancement to the mother's new life trickle down to the children and does the trickle-down enhancement offset the detriment to the children and the father caused by the move?' and 'there is no evidence that can be presented to a court that can prove this issue one way or another with any better predictability than rock-paper-scissors'; WD Duggan, 'International Judicial Perspectives on

course be influenced, often considerably, by the evidence of an expert psychologist or custody evaluator,[40] where this is commissioned by the court or brought by the parties. The uncertainty created by the subjective nature of the underlying perceptions is exacerbated by the fact that the best interests analysis is, as courts and scholars remind us,[41] highly fact sensitive. Thus, it is very difficult to extrapolate from previous case law as to how a given case is likely to be decided and apparently similar cases may be decided differently. This encourages litigation and appeals. This uncertainty is even more pronounced in cases where there is shared care and in jurisdictions in which legislation expresses a preference for shared care.

Indeed in Australia, the uncertainty of relocation law[42] appears to have increased as a result of the reforms to child custody law in 2003 and 2006,[43] which inter alia require judges to take into account the child's right to a meaningful relationship with both of his parents as a primary consideration and to consider whether shared parenting is practicable. Some judges have taken the view that this limits the possibilities of allowing relocation.[44] However, others have taken the view that whilst a child has a right to a meaningful relationship with both parents, there is no requirement that this is the optimal relationship and thus relocation may be permitted even where it will impact negatively on the quality of the relationship with the remaining parent.[45] The 2010 High Court decision in *MRR v GR*[46] does little to clarify the issue, other than emphasising the need to consider the practicality of both parents' situation.[47]

In New Zealand, relocation rates initially dropped after the enactment of the 2004 Care of Children Act, which emphasised joint parental responsibility and continuity of arrangements.[48] However, the rates later returned to their previous level.[49] Nonetheless, a recent Supreme Court decision stating that the fact that the current arrangements are working well is a weighty factor[50] in determining the best interests of the child seems likely to lead to a more restrictive approach to allowing relocation.[51]

Relocation: Rock Paper-Scissors: Playing the Odds with the Law of Child Relocation' (2007) 45 *Family Court Review* 193; see, for example, New Zealand cases referred to by Heneghan 'Relocation Cases' (n 10) 244–245, in which relocation was refused despite evidence of the mother's depression.

[40] WG Austin, 'Relocation, Research, and Forensic Evaluation, Part I: Effects of Residential Mobility on Children of Divorce (2008) 46 *Family Court Review* 1, 137.

[41] eg Elrod, 'A Move in the Right Direction' (n 34).

[42] P Parkinson reports significant differences between the approach of judges in different cities, P Parkinson, 'The Realities of Relocation: Messages from Judicial Decisions' (2008) 22 *Australian Journal of Family Law* 35.

[43] See generally, P Parkinson, 'Freedom of Movement in an Era of Shared Parenting: The Differences in Judicial Approaches to Relocation' (University of Sydney Legal Studies Research Paper 08/87), http://papers.ssrn.com/sol3/papers.cfm?abstract_id=1181442.

[44] Thus, there has been a reduction in the rate of relocations allowed, Parkinson, 'The Realities of Relocation' (n 42).

[45] eg *Godfrey v Saunders* [2007] FamCA 102 [33]–[36] (Kay J).

[46] *MRR v GR* [2010] HCA 4.

[47] The mother's relocation request was allowed, even though it would prevent shared parenting, because relocation would provide the mother with full employment opportunities and reasonable accommodation, which were not available in the current place of residence, and prevent her from being depressed and isolated.

[48] Heneghan, 'Relocation Cases' (n 10) 238.

[49] ibid.

[50] *Kacem v Bashir* [2010] NZSC 112 [24]; A cynic might comment that this approach provides an incentive for the relocating parent to subtly ensure that the arrangements are not working well before applying for relocation.

[51] Heneghan 'Relocation Cases' (n 10) 239–41; P Boshier, 'Judicial Approach to Relocation in New Zealand', The Judges Newsletter, Special Edition No 1, 2010, www.hcch.net/upload/jn_special2010.pdf, 47.

iv The American Law Institute Model

This hybrid model distinguishes between single custody and joint custody cases, defined according to the time spent with the child rather than the legal status of the parents.[52] Thus, a parent who looks after the child for more than 60 per cent of the time is treated as a sole custodial parent. There is a presumption in favour of a request for relocation by such a parent, provided that he is acting in good faith and can show that there is a legitimate motive for the move. However, where there is joint custody, there is no presumption and the determination is based purely on the best interests of the child.

B Empirical Evidence

The relevant research studies can be divided into two categories. Firstly, studies conducted by social scientists on the impact of residential mobility on children in general and after parental separation in particular. These studies, which do not distinguish between cases where there has been a legal dispute about relocation and those where there was consent or no need for consent, attempt inter alia to analyse the factors which determine the impact of relocation on children. Whilst some factors seem uncontroversial, such as the positive effect of support from the wider family in the new location and the extent to which the child finds new friends, there is a fundamental disagreement among researchers as to the impact of the reduced contact with the non-custodial parent. As seen in an earlier chapter,[53] some researchers take the view that the quality of the parenting by the primary caretaker is the most important parameter in determining child adjustment after divorce[54] and that therefore it is essential to protect the stability and integrity of the post-divorce family unit in which the child is living.[55] The contrary research argues that a secure father-attachment is a prerequisite for a child's long-term welfare and therefore relocations which reduce the frequency of contact with the father are generally not beneficial to children.[56]

In light of the discrepancies between the findings of different research studies and the criticism levelled at some of the research,[57] some commentators have concluded that we really know very little about the impact of relocation after parental separation on outcomes for children and there has been a call for further and rigorous research.[58] It has even been optimistically suggested that if more clear-cut evidence as to the link between relocation and child outcomes was available, relocation disputes could be prevented because parents would be able to understand the benefits or risks involved.[59]

The second type of study is that carried out by law academics, often in mixed teams with social scientists. Most of these studies specifically address cases where there has been a dispute concerning relocation. Some of these studies involve an analysis of decided cases and

---

[52] Heneghan ibid 250 also suggests guidelines which distinguish between cases of primary care and shared care.
[53] Chapter 3 II.
[54] eg S Wallerstein and TJ Tanke, 'To Move or Not to Move: Psychological and Legal Considerations in the Relocation of Children Following Divorce' (1996) 30 *Family Law Quarterly* 305.
[55] ibid 311.
[56] eg RA Warshak, 'Social Science and Children's Best Interests in Relocation Cases: Burgess Revisited' (2000) *Family Law Quarterly* 34 83–114.
[57] See in particular, C Bruch, 'Sound Research or Wishful Thinking in Child Custody Cases? Lessons from Relocation Law' (2006) 40 *Family Law Quarterly* 281.
[58] eg Taylor and Freeman, 'International Research Evidence' (n 8) 338; Parkinson et al, 'The Need for Reality Testing' (n 5) 4–6.
[59] Taylor and Freeman ibid.

others involve interviewing one or both of the parents and sometimes also the children after the conclusion of the relocation dispute. These studies do not attempt to analyse the impact of the relocation decision on the overall long-term outcomes for children, but rather to obtain information about various aspects of these disputes. These include data as to the percentage of cases in which relocation is allowed; characteristics of cases in which relocation is allowed or refused; motivation of the relocating parent; differences between the outcome in practice and the decision of the court; the legal costs involved and the direct impact of the relocation decision on the lives of the parents and children.

When considering the data obtained in this second category of studies, it should be borne in mind that most of these research studies are relatively small samples. Nevertheless, these studies do shed light on various aspects of relocation disputes which can inform policy both in relation to relocation law and abduction law.

i Violence

A significant number of the applicant mothers claimed that they had suffered violence or abuse at the hands of the fathers and this was often one of their motivations for seeking relocation.[60] Case law from a number of jurisdictions indicates that violence is a weighty factor in favour of allowing relocation.[61]

ii Resolution and Costs of Relocation Disputes

In Australia, relocation disputes have a lower settlement rate compared to other family law disputes and those that did settle tended to settle at a late stage.[62] The reasons for the difficulty of settling relocation cases include the fact that there is no middle ground, as there is in other disputes concerning children, such as those in relation to custody and contact arrangements,[63] and the considerable uncertainty as to the outcome which is a result of the large element of discretion in the decision.[64] In addition, it has been suggested that the general level of conflict between the parents may be higher in relocation cases than in other types of case, as indicated by the relatively high frequency of domestic violence allegations, and the fact that the difficulties involved in making routine arrangements concerning the child is sometimes one of the reasons behind the request to relocate.[65]

An inevitable consequence of the difficulty of settling relocation cases is that the costs involved in fighting a relocation dispute are high.[66] Research shows that these costs are liable to cause major financial distress to parents,[67] which will clearly have an impact on their children's standard of living.[68]

---

[60] In the study of Parkinson et al, 'The Need for Reality Testing' (n 5), 11 out of the 39 women mentioned violence or abuse. In the study of Berhens et al (cited by Taylor and Freeman ibid 332), the mother alleged violence in a significant majority of the cases.
[61] eg Parkinson et al, 'The Need for Reality Testing' ibid 3.
[62] ibid.
[63] ibid 18; Heneghan 'Relocation Cases' (n 10) 236.
[64] Parkinson, et al (n 5).
[65] ibid.
[66] In the Australian longitudinal study, the median cost reported by the participants was 42,000 Australian dollars, ibid 21. In the New Zealand study (Heneghan 'Relocation Cases' (n 10) 236, the average cost was 30,000 New Zealand dollars.
[67] Parkinson, et al (n 5) 23; Taylor and Freeman (n 8) 331.
[68] In some cases, this involved selling the family home, ibid.

iii Post-Relocation Contact Arrangements

The studies show that children who have relocated often travel long distances on a regular basis by various methods of transport, including by air, in order to remain in contact with the non-custodial parent. In some of these cases, the financial and physical burden of the frequent long distance travel makes it impossible to maintain the contact schedule which has been approved by the court or agreed by the parties.[69] In some cases, the relocating parent does not comply with the contact arrangements[70] and non-residential parents may face considerable difficulty and expense in enforcing a contact order in a foreign jurisdiction.[71]

iv Changes Occurring after the Relocation Decision

In some of the cases which were included in the studies, the events which occurred after the relocation decision did not reflect that decision. In one study, five per cent of the mothers that were allowed to relocate did not do so and another five per cent returned within a short time because the relocation did not bring the expected benefits.[72] In some cases, mothers whose relocation request was refused still relocated without the children and the custody of the children was transferred to the father. In the New Zealand study, there were 12 such cases and in five of them, the change in custody failed and within two years the children had moved back to live with their mothers in her new place of residence.[73] In all these cases, the father had not played a significant part in the children's lives before the transfer of custody.

C Scholarly Analysis

There is a considerable body of literature analysing relocation law and proposing different models designed to provide better mechanisms for decision making in relocation cases. A comprehensive review of this literature is outside the scope of this book. However, the spectrum of views expressed by scholars will be briefly mapped. To a large extent, this spectrum reflects the different approaches adopted by courts, discussed above.

One group of scholars is concerned that a move away from the presumption in favour of relocation results in insufficient weight being given to the detrimental consequences for children of effectively forcing the custodial parent to remain in the current country of residence.[74] Similarly, some commentators are concerned that current trends making relocation law more restrictive do not give sufficient weight to the constitutional right of the custodial parent to travel.[75] Conversely, there are commentators who believe that too much

---

[69] Parkinson et al, 'The Need for Reality Testing' (n 5) 31–32;
[70] Parkinson et al ibid 26–27.
[71] Reunite Relocation Report (n 11), 14–16, 21.
[72] Parkinson et al, 'The Need for Reality Testing' (n 5) 24; Heneghan also reports instances of return by relocating parents, Heneghan 'Relocation Cases' (n 10) 237.
[73] Heneghan ibid.
[74] eg Bruch, 'Wishful Thinking' (n 57); MH Weiner, 'Inertia and Inequality: Reconceptualizing Disputes Over Parental Relocation' (2007) 40 *University of California Davis Law Review* 1747.
[75] eg D Chipman and M Rush, 'The Necessity of "Right To Travel" Analysis in Custodial Parent Relocation Cases' (2010) 10 *Wyoming Law Review* 267, 287. In relation to the violation of free movement rights within the EU, see R Lamont, 'Free Movement of Persons, Child Abduction and Relocation within the European Union (2012) *Journal of Social Welfare and Family Law* 11.

weight is given to the distress of the mother who wishes to relocate[76] and that relocation is often allowed without adequately safeguarding the right of the remaining parent to regular direct contact with his child.[77] Similarly, some authors have expressed concern that too much weight is given to the availability of technology which facilitates virtual visitation whilst ignoring the limitations of this form of contact.[78]

A number of scholars support a hybrid approach, similar to that advocated by the American Law Institute, under which the burden of proof depends on the current de facto custody situation.[79] Thus, for example, where there is a dual residential situation, the burden is on the relocating parent to prove the benefits of relocation; whereas where the child is almost exclusively cared for by one parent, relocation by that parent should usually be allowed. Many scholars support models which do not contain presumptions,[80] but some of these have suggested that there is a need to identify a factor which carries special weight, such as the right of the relocating parent to travel, in order to avoid the uncertainty caused by the indeterminate nature of the best interests principle.[81] One author recommends limiting the right to appeal since the energy spent on the attempt to find a judge who sees the facts according to the appellant's point of view would be better spent in coming to terms with the decision and the money wasted should be used for the children.[82]

A number of scholars have suggested giving more weight to particular factors which are not usually currently emphasised in relocation case law. For example, Zafran[83] suggests that the focus should be on preserving relationships between family members in a way which best protects the child's interests and needs. She also argues that the interests of the child can be more accurately identified by considering his relational rights and that the child's right to meaningful participation and his right to identity[84] are particularly pertinent in the relocation context. The critical importance of listening to the child has also been highlighted by Wallerstein and Tanke,[85] who point out that even children as young as seven who have been living in shared custody arrangements have perceptions and feelings about their relationship with each parent based on their experiences of living in each home. Moreover, they suggest that reasonably mature adolescents should be allowed to choose whether to move with a relocating parent or to live with the remaining parent.[86]

---

[76] eg M Hayes, 'Relocation Cases: Is the Court of Appeal Applying the Correct Principles? (2006) *Child and Family Law Quarterly* 351. Two of the cases discussed in the Reunite Relocation Report (n 11) 17 appear to support such a view. In one, the main reason for allowing relocation was the impact of the disappointment on the mother, although there was no evidence that there would be serious distress. After relocation, the mother successfully thwarted contact by the father. In the second case, a relocating mother herself regretted the fact that she had been allowed to relocate so far from the father, expressing the view that a happy child makes a happy mother and not vice versa.

[77] eg Sattler, 'The Problem of Parental Relocation' (n 32); Zafran (n 7) 211.

[78] This concern is borne out by the empirical studies in which both parents and children referred to the limitations of Webcam and other forms of virtual contact. See eg Parkinson et al, 'The Need for Reality Testing' (n 5) 19; Reunite Relocation Report (n 11) 14.

[79] eg Wallerstein and Tanke 'To Move or Not to Move'(n 54) 316; Zafran (n 7) 205 (who suggests a three-pronged approach).

[80] eg Elrod, 'A Move in the Right Direction' (n 34).

[81] Chipman and Rush (n 75).

[82] Heneghan 'Relocation Cases' (n 10) 249.

[83] (n 7).

[84] Within the right to identity, Zafran includes both the right to preserve an existing identity and the right to develop a new identity.

[85] Wallerstein and Tanke 'To Move or Not to Move' (n 54).

[86] ibid 322.

A number of authors have suggested solutions which do not see relocation disputes as binary but rather try to balance the competing interests of the different parties in a better way. Thus, some scholars[87] suggest that courts should consider the possibility of the non-custodial parent relocating as well, which will enable the children to enjoy the advantages of relocation without the reduction in contact with the non-custodial parent.[88] Where there is no good objective reason for this parent not to relocate, then he can effectively prevent the relocation causing any detriment to the children. Similarly, it has been suggested that where the reason for the relocation is a new relationship, the possibility of the mother's new partner relocating to join the mother should also be considered.[89]

Another way of finding the middle ground between the two parents would be by requiring the non-custodial parent to compensate the custodial parent[90] for the costs she incurs as a result of not relocating.[91] These costs include direct financial disadvantage, such as loss of increased income and career opportunities which would have been available to the custodial parent in the country to which she wished to relocate.[92] Similarly, payment could compensate the parent who wished to relocate for higher costs of living accommodation in the current place of residence.[93] In addition, there are personal disadvantages which have economic value. For example, where the custodial parent wishes to relocate back to her home country, her family members would often be able to help her with child care and domestic tasks, such as making meals. The loss of this advantage could be recognised by payments which allow the mother to pay for child care and domestic help. Even the personal disadvantage of lack of contact with family and friends could be recognised by the non-custodial parent contributing towards the costs of visits by the custodial parent to visit her family abroad. Whilst money cannot compensate for social and family ties, it may be able to make it easier for the disappointed custodial parent to swallow the bitter pill of not being allowed to relocate and this is likely to be of benefit to the children. It might be added that the availability of this type of compensation may enable some relocation disputes to be resolved by agreement between the parties, thus saving the large sums usually spent on legal costs, together with the large sums later expended on travel for contact visits. The sums saved could be used to make the compensation payments and for the benefit of the children in general.[94]

---

[87] eg Weiner, 'Inertia and Inequality' (n 74) 1797; Zafran (n 7).

[88] Some courts do consider this factor. See eg Australian case of *U v U* (2002) 211 CLR 238, where the failure to consider this possibility was described as sexist. See also the States listed by Weiner ibid at 1783 and Duggan 'International Judicial Perspectives' (n 39) 209; in the Israeli case of RFamA 5072/10 (n 28), the Supreme Court mentioned, almost as an after-thought, the recommendation of the expert that the best solution is for the father to return to New Zealand together with the mother and children who were given permission to relocate. However, the British Columbia Court of Appeal, in the case of *Stav v Stav* (n 37) held that the trial judge's assumption that the father, who had shared care of the children, would move with the mother to Israel meant that she had not given sufficiently serious consideration to the option of the children remaining in his care in Canada.

[89] Parkinson et al, 'The Need for Reality Testing' (n 5) 18.

[90] As mentioned above, a parent's desire to relocate is quite often motivated by financial concerns. See Taylor and Freeman (n 8) 330.

[91] A Blecher-Prigat, 'The Costs of Raising Children' (2000) 13 *Theoretical Inquiries in Law* 179, 201–02; see also Duggan 'International Judicial Perspectives' (n 39) 211.

[92] Blecher-Prigat, ibid.

[93] Compared to those in the country to which that parent wished to relocate, see Parkinson et al, 'The Need for Reality Testing' (n 5) 10.

[94] For a discussion of the research findings concerning the relationship between outcomes for children and the mother's financial circumstances post-divorce, see C Bruch, 'Wishful Thinking' (n 57) 289.

Some authors[95] have emphasised the importance of reality testing before allowing relocation. In particular, it is necessary to assess whether the contact proposals are practicable from both a financial and physical perspective and the likely impact on the child of spending long periods of time travelling, instead of participating in recreational and social pursuits.[96] In addition, in cases where one of the motivations for the relocation is financial, it is important to check that any financial benefit in moving is not offset by travel costs and the reduction in child support payments as a result of the costs incurred by the father in contact visits.[97]

Furthermore, it has been pointed out that before allowing relocation, courts should check whether contact orders are enforceable in the new country, for example under the 1996 Child Protection Convention. Where they are not enforceable, steps should be taken before the relocation to ensure enforceability, such as by obtaining a mirror order.[98]

D International Harmonisation Initiatives

In 2001, the Fourth Special Commission on the Child Abduction Convention noted that 'Courts take significantly different approaches to relocation cases, which are occurring with a frequency not contemplated in 1980 when the Convention was drafted'[99] and expressed concern that a highly restrictive approach to relocation applications may have an adverse effect on the operation of the 1980 Convention. In 2006, the Fifth Special Commission went a step further and expressly 'encouraged all attempts to seek to resolve differences among the legal systems so as to arrive as far as possible at a common approach and common standards as regards relocation'.[100]

In March 2010, the Hague Conference on Private International Law took part in such an initiative, together with the International Centre for Missing and Exploited Children (ICMEC). At a conference which took place in Washington DC, USA, more than 50 judges and other experts from 14 countries were brought together to discuss cross-border family relocation and the delegates issued and adopted a document called the 'Washington Declaration on International Family Relocation'.[101] This Declaration gives 13 recommendations, including a list of 13 Principles which are to guide a judge confronted with a relocation dispute.

The central recommendation in the Declaration is that the best interests of the child should always be the paramount consideration, without any presumptions for or against relocation. Moreover, reasonable notice should be given of the relocating parent's intention to the parent left behind in the move. Perhaps the most significant step in the quest for uniformity is the list of 13 factors which the Declaration lists as relevant to the exercise of judicial discretion in relocation cases. These are:

---

[95] eg Parkinson et al, 'The Need for Reality Testing' (n 5) 33–34.
[96] See comment in Wallerstein and Tanke (n 54) 320, that 'children are not ping-pong balls'.
[97] Parkinson et al, 'The Need for Reality Testing' (n 5) 29–30.
[98] This was required by the Israeli Supreme Court in ACH 9201/08 (n 30).
[99] Conclusions and Recommendations of the Fourth Special Commission Meeting (n 5), para 7.3
[100] Conclusions and Recommendations of the Fifth Special Commission Meeting, www.hcch.net/index_en.php?act=publications.details&pid=3905&dtid=2, para 1.7.5.
[101] Set out in full in the Appendix to the Preliminary Note on International Family Relocation (n 4).

(i) the right of the child separated from one parent to maintain personal relations and direct contact with both parents on a regular basis in a manner consistent with the child's development, except if the contact is contrary to the child's best interest;
(ii) the views of the child having regard to the child's age and maturity;
(iii) the parties' proposals for the practical arrangements for relocation, including accommodation, schooling and employment;
(iv) where relevant to the determination of the outcome, the reasons for seeking or opposing the relocation;
(v) any history of family violence or abuse, whether physical or psychological;
(vi) the history of the family and particularly the continuity and quality of past and current care and contact arrangements;
(vii) pre-existing custody and access determinations;
(viii) the impact of grant or refusal on the child, in the context of his or her extended family, education and social life, and on the parties;
(ix) the nature of the inter-parental relationship and the commitment of the applicant to support and facilitate the relationship between the child and the respondent after the relocation;
(x) whether the parties' proposals for contact after relocation are realistic, having particular regard to the cost to the family and the burden to the child;
(xi) the enforceability of contact provisions ordered as a condition of relocation in the State of destination;
(xii) issues of mobility for family members; and
(xiii) any other circumstances deemed to be relevant by the judge.

It can be seen that most of these factors are in fact considered by courts under their current practice. Moreover, the fact that none of the factors is given priority and that the list is not exclusive means that this list does little to solve the problems of uncertainty and that there is still room for significant differences between the approaches of judges in different jurisdictions and even within the same jurisdiction, based on conflicting personal and social science views. However, for jurisdictions where there is not currently any list of factors, use of this list may lead to some increase in uniformity and ensure that judges do not overlook certain factors. In particular, as seen above, some of the empirical research does suggest that insufficient attention is given to whether proposed contact arrangements, which are often fundamental to the decision to allow relocation, are actually realistic.

At the 2012 Special Commission Meeting, the question of whether the Hague Conference might undertake any further work towards the harmonisation of relocation law was discussed. The majority view was that a decision whether to allow relocation is a matter of domestic law and so not directly within the purview of the Hague Conference. Thus, the reference to relocation in the Conclusions and Recommendations was limited to expressing (i) recognition of the Washington declaration[102] as a valuable basis for further work and reflection; (ii) support for 'further work being undertaken to study and gather information concerning the different approaches adopted in various legal systems to international family relocation, in relation to private international law issues and the application of the 1996 Convention'[103] and (iii) the need to encourage ratification of the 1996 Convention, which is of value to international family relocation.[104]

---

[102] Conclusions and Recommendations of Sixth Special Commission Meeting, www.hcch.net/upload/wop/concl28-34sc6_en.pdf, para 83.
[103] ibid, para 84.
[104] ibid, para 85. For a discussion of the 1996 Convention in general and in relation to recognition and enforcement of contact orders in particular, see ch 1 at II E.

Whilst these conclusions can be seen as effectively abandoning the Hague Conference's work in relation to relocation, their support for further study does reflect the recognition of the inextricable and mutual connection between international child abduction and international relocation. The next section will analyse the nature, extent, limits and implications of the inter-relationship between these two fields of law more closely.

III Inter-Relationship between Child Abduction and Relocation

In considering how each area of law can learn from the other, a distinction will be drawn between ways in which one area of law, including the literature and research in relation thereto, might inform policy making in relation to the other area of law ('the macro level') and ways in which the substantive provisions of one area of law might actually have an impact on individual decisions made within the context of the other area of law ('the micro level').

A The Implications of Abduction Law for Relocation Law

i At the Macro Level

In formulating relocation law, it should be borne in mind that the easier it is to obtain permission to relocate,[105] the less incentive there is for a custodial parent to abduct. Thus, a liberal approach to relocation ought to be a method of deterring child abduction.[106] Conversely, it seems logical that the harder it is to obtain permission to relocate, the greater the incentive to abduct.[107] However, Freeman argues on the basis of the Reunite Relocation Report that the assumption that restrictive relocation regimes will necessarily increase the incidence of abduction is overly simplistic and suggests that a restrictive relocation regime may actually change parents' expectations to the extent that they do not seriously consider the possibility of relocation while their children are still young.[108] Whilst it is true that the liberality of the relocation regime is only one of a number of factors which determine whether a parent will abduct or not, it is nevertheless a factor which should be taken into account. Thus, those formulating relocation law should consider the potential risk that making it more difficult to relocate will encourage abductions.[109]

---

[105] It should be remembered that the ease with which permission to relocate can be obtained is not only a function of the liberality of the approach adopted by the legislation and/or case law in a given State, but also the procedural hurdles and time taken. For example, in Israel, whilst a custodial mother will invariably obtain permission to relocate, this may well take her years and involve expensive litigation at three court levels.

[106] Guide to Good Practice Part III – Preventive Measures, www.hcch.net/upload/abdguideiii_e.pdf, 17–18. However, this assumes that abducting parents are aware of the fact that they need permission to take the child to another country, which is not always the case, see T Kruger, *International Child Abduction: The Inadequacies of the Law (Studies in Private International Law)* (Oxford, Hart Publishing, 2011).

[107] The Conclusions and Recommendations of the Fourth Special Commission Meeting (n 5), 14 noted that 'a highly restrictive approach to relocation applications may have an adverse effect on the operation of the 1980 Convention'.

[108] Reunite Relocation Report (n 11), 21.

[109] The converse proposition that liberal relocation regimes will encourage the non-custodial parent to abduct before a relocation decision is made is not convincing because *ex hypothesi* this parent does not have any interest in moving to another country. If he is mobile, then he may be equally able to move to the country to which the custodial parent wishes to relocate.

In particular, there will be a clear incentive to abduct if the court of the habitual residence does not allow relocation, in circumstances in which the custodial parent will be likely to be able to establish a defence to immediate return if she removes the child without permission.[110] Therefore, relocation law should take account of the defences in the Abduction Convention.

Another issue that arises, which has implications both at the micro and macro level, is the impact of a previous abduction by a parent who, after having returned with the child, now requests to relocate. On the one hand, it may be thought that a policy of not subsequently allowing abductors to relocate will discourage abduction. Whilst this may be so, it is questionable whether the deterrent effect can justify refusing relocation where this is clearly in the best interests of the child.[111]

ii At the Micro Level

It is important that a court considering a relocation request, pursuant to an abduction and return, should understand that a return decision under the Abduction Convention is not a decision on the merits of the case and should not per se be treated as a factor against allowing relocation.[112] In particular, the return decision does not indicate that the court in the requested State took the view that relocation should not be allowed or that it was in the child's best interests to grow up in the requesting State.

However, the very fact of the previous abduction would appear to be relevant in assessing the likelihood that the relocating parent will abide by contact arrangements and encourage the preservation of the relationship with the non-relocating parent, which is usually treated as an important parameter in relocation decisions.[113] Clearly, the extent to which this is true depends on the circumstances of the abduction. For example, where the abduction was retention after a holiday and contact between the child and the left-behind parent continued throughout the child's stay abroad, then little or no negative inference should be drawn. Even where a negative inference is justified, this should not always automatically lead to a refusal to allow relocation, if this is otherwise indicated, but rather to a consideration of whether mechanisms can be put in place which can guarantee continuing contact.[114]

In this respect, and this is true whether or not there has been a previous abduction, it will be relevant to consider whether there is a bilateral or multilateral treaty in force between

---

[110] eg, where a mature child has strong views about relocating with the custodial parent or where there is a grave risk that the child will suffer harm if he is not allowed to relocate, such as in cases of severe domestic violence.

[111] See discussion on deterrence in ch 5 at II Cii.

[112] Research conducted by M Freeman does suggest that the success rate for requests to relocate is relatively low were there has been a previous abduction. In the cases she examined in Southern Australia, only 30% of requests were allowed (M Freeman, Reunite Research Unit, 'Outcomes for Children Following an Abduction', www.reunite.org/edit/files/Library%20-%20reunite%20Publications/Outcomes%20Report.pdf, 44 (['Reunite Outcomes Report']), but no control data is available to make a proper comparison. The figure for the cases in the Reunite study itself is somewhat higher – 6 out of 11 applications allowed (ibid, 37).

[113] In the Australian case of *U v U* [2002] 211 CLR 238, the mother's attempts to remove the child from the father was a relevant factor in the first instance Court's refusal to allow relocation.

[114] See eg *Condon v Cooper* 73 Cal. Rptr. 2d 33, 33 (1998) where the Californian Court allowed relocation to Australia following abduction to that country and return, but took steps to ensure enforceability of the Californian visitation order. Similarly, in the Israeli case ACH 9201/08 (n 30), whilst the previous abduction was seen as a reason not to allow relocation by the District Court and by the minority in the additional hearing in the Supreme Court, the final decision of that Court (by a majority of 4 to 3) was to allow the relocation. Nonetheless, the conditions required by the Court, including obtaining a mirror order, seem to be a reflection of the earlier abduction.

the two countries which obliges the new country to recognise the decisions of the State of origin,[115] such as the 1996 Hague Child Protection Convention[116] or the Brussels II bis Regulation.[117]

Finally, the interplay between relocation and the Abduction Convention needs to be considered in the situation, albeit rare, where an appeal against a relocation order is successful after the relocation has already taken place. This situation arose in a recent Israeli case involving relocation from Canada.[118] The Canadian Court did not grant a stay of execution of the decision allowing the mother's request to relocate with the children to Israel, after the mother had given undertakings that the children would return to Canada if the father's appeal was successful. The father came to Israel with the mother and children and seven months after their arrival he won the appeal in Canada. However, when he arranged return flights for the children on the date fixed by the Canadian Appeal Court, the mother did not respond to the father's request to hand over the children's passports. Accordingly, the father applied for a return order under the Abduction Convention. The mother claimed that the children had become habitually resident in Israel and raised the defence of consent on the basis of negotiations which had taken place between the parties concerning arrangements for the children in Israel. However, her arguments were rejected and return was ordered.

The lesson to be learnt from this case is that before refusing a stay of execution of a relocation decision, the court has to bear in mind the implications of the appeal being successful. If the court is minded to refuse to stay execution, then it might be helpful to require the making of a mirror order by the courts of the country to which the children are to relocate, which could then be directly enforced in the event that the appeal is allowed.[119]

B The Implications of Relocation Law and Research for Abduction Law

i At the Macro Level

In this section, the implications of the case law, research and literature on relocation for abduction law will be examined. Since there is no real possibility of amending the Abduction Convention in the near future, this examination will concentrate on how the lessons to be learnt from relocation law might influence the general approach to interpretation and implementation of the Convention.

As stated above, we must not lose sight of the fundamental difference between the context in which abduction and relocation cases are decided. Over and above the formal distinction between the mandatory return mechanism of the Convention and the wide discretion in relocation cases, there are differences in the policies which inform the law in the two types of cases. In particular, the policies of restoring the status quo, deterrence and *forum conveniens*,[120] on which the Abduction Convention is based, are not relevant in

---

[115] The access provisions of the 1980 Abduction Convention are also relevant, but as we shall see in ch 18, these provisions do not necessarily ensure recognition of access rights awarded by the State of origin.

[116] See ch 1 at II E.

[117] See ch 1 at II C.

[118] FamA (JLM) *GS v LS* Nevo (Dist) 34551-09-12 (Unreported, 21 October 2012). An appeal is pending.

[119] cf *Sheldon & Weir (Stay Application)* [2011] FamCAFC 5 [55]–[56], where the Australian Court was satisfied with the security offered by the mother and with the belief that the child would be returned in the event of the father's appeal being successful, if necessary under the Abduction Convention.

[120] For a detailed discussion, see ch 5 at II C.

relocation cases which are decided by the *forum conveniens* before any change in the status quo. Nonetheless, there are considerable similarities in the substance of the dispute before the court. In particular, the basic competing interests of the parent are usually the same in the two types of cases and the objective of protecting the interests of children underlies both areas of law. In addition, where the Abduction Convention's policy objectives cannot be achieved in practice, such as in cases where it is no longer possible to restore the status quo because of the time which has elapsed and/or changes in circumstances, the differences between the two types of dispute largely evaporate.

It is suggested that there are a number of areas in which relocation law principles and research should be taken into account in the interpretation and application of the Abduction Convention.

a Domestic Violence

As seen above, the existence of domestic violence against the relocating parent is one of the motives for requesting relocation and is usually treated as a weighty factor in favour of relocation. Indeed, some courts have expressly stated that in cases of violence and high-conflict, the reduction in contact between the parents as a result of the relocation may be beneficial to the child.[121] On the other hand, as will be seen in detail below,[122] in Abduction Convention cases domestic violence is often not treated as a reason to refuse return of the child, either because it is not seen as presenting a risk to the child or because it is believed the risk can be obviated by undertakings or other protective measures. There has been much criticism against this policy[123] and the Sixth Special Commission recommended setting up a committee to consider how domestic violence should be treated in Abduction Convention cases.[124] This Committee, and indeed courts that are called upon to apply the Abduction Convention in cases of domestic violence, can perhaps learn from the rather different approach of relocation law to this issue.

b Mental Health of Primary Caretaker

In relocation cases, courts in many jurisdictions have recognised that the mental health of the primary caretaker (usually the mother) is crucial to the welfare of the child[125] and this factor is often treated as determinative in favour of allowing relocation, even where there is no clear-cut evidence as to the effect on the mother of refusal to allow relocation. On the other hand, a real risk to the mental health of the abducting mother is rarely treated as sufficient to establish the grave risk exception in Article 13(1)(b), even where there is clear evidence that return to the country of origin will lead to anxiety, depression and fear which will substantially impair parental functioning.[126] The argument that the Abduction Convention only acts as first aid does not provide an adequate explanation of this discrepancy because the impaired functioning of the parent can cause real and irreparable damage to the child even over a short period of time and because in practice a long period of time may elapse before the mother's request to relocate will be adjudicated. Similarly, undertakings and other protective measures

---

[121] Cases cited by Heneghan, 'Relocation Cases' (n 10) 243.
[122] In ch 11 at II Biv.
[123] ibid.
[124] Conclusions and Recommendations of Sixth Special Commission Meeting (n 102), para 82.
[125] eg often cited words of Thorpe LJ in *Payne v Payne* (n 20), quoted above at text accompanying n 23.
[126] See detailed discussion in ch 11 at II Bv.

are often inadequate to allay the concerns of the mother and so cannot prevent the detrimental impact on her mental health.

Accordingly, abduction law should take note of the importance attached by relocation law to the mental health of the primary caretaker and treat more seriously real evidence that return will have a detrimental effect on the abductor's parental functioning. The recent UK Supreme Court's decision in the case of *Re S (A Child)*[127] would seem to signal a positive change in this direction. In particular, the Court states clearly that, in assessing whether return will place the child in an intolerable situation, account has to be taken of the likely impact of the returning parent's anxieties on her mental state, whether or not those anxieties are objectively justified.[128] It is to be hoped that this approach will be widely adopted.

c Primary versus Shared Care

We saw above that relocation case law and literature increasingly distinguishes between cases where the relocating parent is the child's sole or primary caretaker and those cases where there is shared care. Furthermore, the New Zealand study shows that a change of custody to a non-custodial parent, where the primary caretaker relocates alone following refusal of her relocation application, may well not work out in practice.

The distinction between sole/primary care and shared care could also be made use of in applying the Article 13(1)(b) grave risk exception. In cases where the left-behind parent is the primary caretaker or there is shared care, it will rarely be possible to show that the exception will be established,[129] whether or not the abductor returns with the child. On the other hand, where the abductor has been the child's sole or primary caretaker, serious consideration has to be given to her reasonable refusal to return or to the impact which return will have on her.[130]

d Reality Testing

Relocation research shows that courts in relocation cases have a tendency to indulge in wishful thinking in seeking a solution which balances the interests of the parties fairly[131] and that in many cases the reality is different from that envisaged by the courts. In particular, not infrequently contact schedules agreed or imposed are simply not realistic because of the burden of frequent long distant travel. Accordingly, researchers have urged courts to reality test their decisions.[132]

A parallel can be drawn with Abduction Convention cases in which return will expose the child to harm. The courts often try to balance the parties' interests by making return subject to conditions or undertakings.[133] However, whilst these conditions appear on paper to protect the child, in practice they may not do so,[134] at least not without a mirror order[135]

---

[127] *Re S (A Child)* [2012] UKSC 10.
[128] ibid [34].
[129] Although violence should still be a basis for establishing the exception.
[130] See discussion in ch 11 at II Biii.
[131] Parkinson et al, 'The Need for Reality Testing' (n 5) 34.
[132] ibid. It is interesting to note that the necessity for reality testing is mentioned in the Guide to Good Practice on Mediation in Abduction Convention Cases, www.hcch.net/upload/guide28mediation_en.pdf, para 287.
[133] For a detailed discussion of these conditions and undertakings, see ch 11 at III.
[134] Reunite Outcomes Report (n 112), 31, which found that undertakings were violated in 66% of cases and that non-molestation undertakings were violated in all of the six cases in which they were given.
[135] Although the Reunite Outcomes Report ibid suggests that mirroring does not necessarily ensure enforcement.

or other method of ensuring the enforceability of the conditions after return.[136] Thus, the need for reality testing, one of the most important conclusions from the relocation research, should also be taken on board by courts in abduction cases, in which there is a potential risk of harm to the child.

ii At the Micro Level

a Judicial Decisions

Relocation law might be relevant in determining whether an abducted child should be returned under the Abduction Convention in a number of ways.[137] Firstly, the scope of a non-custodial parent's right to object to relocation might be relevant in determining whether this right should be regarded as a custody right for the purposes of the Abduction Convention.[138]

Secondly, relocation law could be relevant to the establishment of one of the defences. For example, where the country of habitual residence does not allow relocation or takes an unreasonably long time to decide applications for relocation, it can be argued that there is a breach of the custodial parent's basic human rights.[139] However, no case has been found where this claim has succeeded.[140] Alternatively, where evidence can be brought that the relocation dispute, which will inevitably follow return, is likely to be protracted, high-conflict and very expensive, it could be argued that the very process of resolving the relocation dispute will cause the child harm or place him in an intolerable situation.[141] Whilst, in light of the current restrictive approach to the grave risk defence,[142] this fact alone is unlikely to be sufficient to establish that defence, it could strengthen other evidence of harm to which the child would be exposed on return, especially where there has been domestic violence or return would seriously impair the mother's mental health.

Thirdly, where one of the defences has been established, the question of whether the requesting State will subsequently give permission to relocate is relevant in the exercise of the court's discretion whether to return the child despite the establishment of a defence. As will be seen below,[143] in exercising this discretion the court has to take account of the best interests of the particular child and it will usually not be in his best interests to be shunted back and forth between one State and another. Therefore, the relocation law of the requesting State is a highly relevant factor in this situation.[144]

However, it must be emphasised that where none of the defences can be established, then the mere fact that the return of the child appears pointless because permission will be

---

[136] See Good Practice Guide on Cross-Frontier Contact, www.hcch.net/upload/guidecontact_e.pdf, 38–41.

[137] In addition, Weiner, 'Inertia and Inequality' (n 74) 1823 suggests that where the abduction takes place in a situation in which the non-custodial parent should have agreed to the relocation and to relocate himself, the abductor should not be punished.

[138] See ch 7 at III C.

[139] eg *Caro v Sher* 687 A2d 354 (NJ Super Ct Ch 1996), discussed in ch 13 at II B.

[140] *cf* in relation to non-abduction cases, where the fact that there is no possibility of permission being given to relocate is relevant, *Re J (A Child) (Return to Foreign Jurisdiction: Convention Rights)* [2005] UKHL 40 discussed in ch 13 at II B.

[141] eg comments of Parkinson et al, 'The Need for Reality Testing' (n 5) 24, that 'The judge may be determining the case on the basis of what he or she considers is in the best interests of the child, but the process of so doing may of itself cause great damage to children's well-being.'

[142] See ch 11.

[143] Chapter 10 at IV Biii.

[144] eg *W v W (Child Abduction: Acquiescence)* [1993] 2 FLR 211; *Re S (Abduction: Acquiescence)* [1998] 2 FLR 115.

given to relocate is not a reason to refuse return. Thus, in one recent case, a UK judge urged the father to think carefully before enforcing the return order.[145]

b Left-Behind Parents' Decisions

Indeed, it may be suggested that those who advise left-behind parents on whether to pursue return proceedings under the Abduction Convention should take account of the aftermath of success in those proceedings and the likely result of a subsequent relocation request in particular. Where such a request is allowed, the left-behind parent may well find that his success under the Abduction Convention was a pyrrhic victory,[146] and a very expensive one at that.[147] Thus, he should first of all exhaust all avenues, including mediation,[148] to seek agreement on terms which will persuade the abducting parent to return voluntarily and to give up the idea of relocating. Alternatively, he should give serious thought to seeking an agreement on favourable visitation and contact arrangements with the children in the requested State or even of the possibility of moving to that State.[149]

Since the motivation of abducting parents and relocating parents are often similar,[150] some of the ideas developed in relocation cases might be adopted in negotiating or mediating abduction cases. For example, where one of the reasons for the abduction was the prospect of financial benefit, offers of increased child support or other payments by the left-behind parent might be sufficient, together with the prospect of a return order against her, to persuade the abductor to return. Similarly, the possibility of the left-behind parent moving to the country of refuge should be considered. Whilst this may well involve financial costs, these may be less than those which will be incurred by both parties in contested abduction proceedings followed by contested relocation proceedings. Thus, it may even be appropriate for the costs of the father's move to be shared by the two parents.

In summary, before deciding to apply for return, left-behind parents need to set their understandable anger and hurt aside and reality test the various options. They need to take into account the financial and human costs for themselves and their children of the combination of the abduction litigation followed by the relocation litigation and be sure that there is no other option which better promotes the long-term welfare of their children.

---

[145] *G (Children)* (n 1) [13].

[146] See eg comment of Singer J in *Re A, HA v MB (Brussels II Revised: Article (11)7 Application)* [2007] EWHC 2016 (Fam) [25] that his sympathy for the left-behind father who was aggrieved about the manner in which his Abduction Convention application had been dealt with in France was tempered by the fact that if a return order had been made, the mother would have applied for leave to remove the child to France and would most likely have been successful.

[147] There is no guarantee that he will be reimbursed for his costs in the Abduction Convention case, see ch 17. In the Australian relocation survey, the most expensive case was that in which abduction litigation was followed by relocation litigation, Parkinson et al, 'The Need for Reality Testing' (n 5) 22.

[148] See ch 16.

[149] In M Freeman for the Reunite Research Unit, 'International Child Abduction the Effects', www.reunite.org/edit/files/Library%20-%20reunite%20Publications/Effects%20Of%20Abduction%20Report.pdf, 41, some left-behind fathers who were interviewed questioned whether it would have been better for them to have gone to live in the requested State rather than bring return proceedings.

[150] See n 12 and accompanying text.

Part II

Parameters for Analysis

5
Parameters Relating to Text and Objectives

I Introduction

Parts III and IV of the book contain a methodical and comprehensive analysis of the core provisions of the Hague Convention on the Civil Aspects of International Child Abduction 1980 ('the Abduction Convention') and the way in which they have been implemented. As a precursor to such analysis, it is necessary to determine the nature of the analysis desired and then to construct a series of parameters which reflect the required analysis. In order to enable the structured discussion of a wide range of considerations, a two-stage approach to analysis is adopted. The first and narrower stage involves analysing the way in which the provisions of the Abduction Convention have been interpreted and applied[1] in light of parameters relating to the text and objectives of the Abduction Convention. The second and wider stage of the analysis involves considering to what extent the Abduction Convention itself and the way in which it has been implemented are consistent with general legal doctrines, principles and policies which are external to the Abduction Convention, but which are relevant to the subject matter of the Convention cases. The latter will be discussed in chapter six.

The starting point of any analysis of interpretation of the Convention must be the rules of interpretation of international treaties. Article 31 of the Vienna Convention on the Law of Treaties ('the Vienna Convention')[2] provides: '[a] Treaty shall be interpreted in good

---

[1] Whilst there is a clear analytical distinction between interpretation and application, in practice this distinction is often blurred and the two terms are often used interchangeably. In light of this reality, it is doubtful if there is any benefit to be gained from considering issues of interpretation and those of application separately. Accordingly, the analysis in this book will for the most part relate to interpretation and application together.

[2] Vienna Convention on the Law of Treaties (adopted 23 May 1969, entered into force 27 January 1980) 1155 UNTS 331. Arts 31(2) and 31(3)(a), which refer to agreements relating to the Treaty made between the parties, are not relevant because no such agreements have been made. Art 31(3)(b) which states that account should be taken of 'any subsequent practice in the application of the treaty which establishes the agreement of the parties regarding its interpretation' could in principle be relevant, although it would be extremely difficult to show that any practice, even if very widely adopted, evidences agreement of all the parties. Similarly Art 31(3)(c), which provides that account should be taken of 'any relevant rules of international law applicable in the relations between the parties' could in theory allow account to be taken of rules of customary international law and other treaties to which the States in question in a given case are also parties. The most obviously relevant treaty is the United Nations Conventions on the Rights of the Child [CRC]. However, the better view seems to be that only other treaties which have been signed by all the parties to the Convention which is being interpreted may be used (R Gardiner, *Treaty Interpretation* (Oxford, Oxford University Press, 2008) 270–74). Thus, since the US has not signed the CRC, it is not clear that this Treaty should be used as an aid to interpretation, although in practice courts are increasingly referring to provisions of the CRC in Abduction Convention cases. Accordingly, the parameter of consistency with children's rights will be discussed under the rubric of consistency with general legal doctrines in ch 6.

faith in accordance with the ordinary meaning to be given to the terms of the treaty in their context and in the light of its object and purpose.' It will be seen that whilst the emphasis is on the literal meaning of the text of the Convention, this cannot be separated from the object and purpose of the Convention. Moreover, when analysing the way in which the Abduction Convention has been applied to particular situations, the focus must be on the extent to which the actual results are consistent with the objectives of the Convention.

Accordingly, the four parameters for analysis which have been constructed are designed to reflect the rules of treaty interpretation, whilst emphasising the various objects and purpose of the Convention. The parameters are: internal coherence; consistency with the intention of the drafters; promotion of the objects and purposes of the Convention and compatibility with the summary nature of Convention proceedings. Their content and the reason why each of these parameters was chosen will be explained in detail in Part II below. It should, however, be pointed out at this stage that the question of the ordinary meaning of the words was not chosen as a separate parameter because there has only been dispute about the ordinary meaning of the words in the Abduction Convention in relation to a few specific issues.[3] In relation to these issues, the debate about the meaning of the words is closely related to the issues of internal coherence[4] and the intention of the drafters and so will be discussed within the framework of these parameters.

II Explanation of the Parameters

A Internal Coherence

Contextual interpretation requires consideration of the whole text of the treaty including the preamble[5] and includes any structure or scheme underlying a provision or treaty as a whole.[6] Accordingly, in the analysis of the main provisions of the Abduction Convention, consideration will be given to the extent to which the different possible ways of interpreting and applying these provisions are consistent with the overall scheme of the Convention. In other words, does each of the possible approaches create internal coherence or do they result in internal disharmony? This will include a consideration of whether particular interpretations result in overlap or render other provisions redundant in some other way.

B Consistency with the Intention of the Drafters

It is axiomatic that in interpreting a treaty the aim is to give effect to the intention of the drafters. Whilst the Vienna Convention does not expressly refer to this aim, the good faith

---

[3] The most notable issue is the meaning of the phrase 'custody rights' in general and whether it includes *ne exeat rights* (the right to veto removal of the child from the jurisdiction) in particular. In the case of *Abbott v Abbott* 130 S Ct 1983 (2010), the main difference between the view of the majority and the dissent was in relation to the ordinary meaning of the words used in defining custody rights in Art 5 of the Convention; for a more detailed discussion, see ch 7 at II C.

[4] Gardiner (n 2) 161–62 argues that the ordinary meaning of the words is not an element to be taken separately, but is intimately linked to context.

[5] ibid, 177.

[6] ibid, 182.

requirement in Article 31 has been invoked to justify express reference to the intention of the parties to the Convention.[7] Indeed, the intention of the drafters may shed light on what is indeed the ordinary meaning of the words in their context in light of the object and purpose of the Convention. Accordingly, courts sometimes explicitly refer to the drafters' intentions when interpreting the Abduction Convention.[8]

The best evidence available of the drafters' intentions will usually be in preparatory work. Article 32 of the Vienna Convention provides that recourse may be had to this and other supplementary sources

> in order to confirm the meaning resulting from the application of Article 31 or to determine the meaning when the interpretation according to Article 31(a) leaves the meaning ambiguous or obscure or (b) leads to a result which is manifestly absurd or unreasonable.

This effectively allows reference to such sources in all cases, but prohibits the use of such sources to support an interpretation which is inconsistent with a clear and reasonable interpretation, arrived at without reference thereto.[9]

The most frequently cited supplementary source in relation to the Abduction Convention is the Explanatory Report on the Convention prepared by the appointed Reporter, Professor Elisa Perez-Vera ('Perez-Vera Report').[10] The Perez-Vera Report states that it is designed to 'to throw light on the literal terms of the provisions' of the Convention.[11] This Report is based[12] on the *proces-verbaux* at the Fourteenth Session of the Hague Conference on Private International Law,[13] at which the text of the Abduction Convention was finalised and adopted, and the Reporter's own notes. The status of the Report is not clear. On the one hand, there is clearly room for subjectivity in the conclusions drawn by the Reporter from the materials and the Explanatory Report was not submitted to the Hague Conference for approval.[14] On the other hand, the official US analysis of the Abduction Convention[15] refers to the Perez-Vera Report as the 'official history' of the Convention and 'a source of background on the meaning of the provisions of the Convention'. The US Supreme Court declined to decide between these two approaches.[16] Little suggestion can be found that the Perez-Vera Report does not accurately reflect the proceedings at the Fourteenth Session. Thus, for the most part, it seems reasonable for the purposes of the present analysis to treat the Perez-Vera Report as accurately representing the intentions of the drafters. In a few places in relation to particularly controversial points, direct reference to the proceedings at that Session and to the preparatory documents is added.

---

[7] ibid, 148.
[8] See eg *Abbott v Abbott* (n 3).
[9] ibid 820, where Steven J holds that the meaning of the relevant provisions is clear and thus there is no need to refer to supplementary sources.
[10] Perez-Vera Report, Proceedings of the 14th Session of the Hague Conference Oct 1980, www.hcch.net/upload/expl28.pdf.
[11] ibid, para 6.
[12] ibid, para 8.
[13] Published in Actes et Documents de la Quatorzième Session, 1980, vol III ('Actes et Documents').
[14] Perez-Vera Report (n 10), para 8.
[15] Hague International Child Abduction Convention: Text and Legal Analysis, 51 Fed Reg 10503-10506 (1986).
[16] *Abbott v Abbott* (n 3) 807.

C Promotion of the Objectives of the Convention

As seen above, The Vienna Convention provides that international treaties are to be interpreted in light of their object and purpose.[17] In order to examine to what extent the construction and application of the Abduction Convention promotes the objectives of the Convention, it is necessary first to define the objectives of the Convention. At first sight, this would appear to be an easy task, since Article 1 of the Convention expressly states:

> The objects of the present Convention are-
>
> a) To secure the prompt return of children wrongfully removed to or retained in any Contracting States and
> b) To ensure that rights of custody and of access under the law of one Contracting State are effectively respected in other Contracting States.

Nonetheless, these express objectives have to be understood in light of both the Preamble and of the provisions of the Convention as a whole. The Preamble declares that:

> The States signatory to the present Convention, Firmly convinced that the interests of children are of paramount importance in matters relating to their custody, Desiring to protect children internationally from the harmful effects of their wrongful removal or retention and to establish procedures to ensure their prompt return to the State of habitual residence, as well as to secure protection for right of access.

This declaration makes it clear that the underlying objective of the Convention is to protect the interests of children[18] and to protect them from the harmful effects of abduction in particular. Accordingly, the expressed 'object' of prompt return is really the method of achieving the wider objective of protecting children and not an objective in its own right. Prompt return achieves this objective in two ways. The first is by restoring the status quo, which will negate the harm often caused to children who are suddenly removed from their environment.[19] The second is by deterring potential abductors[20] and thus preventing the harm which would be caused to the children who would have been abducted. In fact, these two methods of achieving the underlying objective of protecting children can be expressed as objectives in their own right: to protect abducted children from harm and to deter potential abductors.[21]

The remedy of prompt return is also designed to achieve a number of other subsidiary objectives. The first is that adjudication of the merits of the dispute concerning the child should take place in the State of the child's habitual residence,[22] which is assumed to be the *forum conveniens* for making decisions about the child's future.[23] Accordingly, no effect

---

[17] See also *Re B (Minors) (Abduction No 1)* [1993] 1 FLR 988, 991.

[18] See also Perez-Vera Report (n 10), para 24, stating that the struggle against the increase in international child abduction 'must be inspired by a desire to protect children and should be based upon an interpretation of their true interests'. Similarly, the Report refers throughout to the children who are protected by the Convention, para 75.

[19] Perez-Vera Report ibid.

[20] ibid, para 16.

[21] ibid, para 25.

[22] ibid, para 19.

[23] Beaumont and McEleavy, *The Hague Convention on International Child Abduction* (Oxford, Oxford University Press, 1999) 30; In *Wilson v Huntley* [2005] 138 ACWS (3d) 1107 (Can Ont Sup CT J), the judge even suggested that 'Perhaps the most important and most fundamental objective of the Convention is that the merits

is given to the artificial legal and jurisdictional links which have been created by the abduction.[24]

Secondly, whilst the Preamble leaves little doubt that the central objective of the Convention is the protection of children's interests, it can be seen from the provisions of the Convention that a further objective is achieving justice between the parents, by protecting the parental rights of the left-behind parent. In particular, recognition of rights of custody and access are referred to as objects of the Convention[25] and the obligation to order return of the child is triggered by the breach of the custody rights of one of the parents.[26] Accordingly, restoration of the *status quo ante* by returning the child is perceived as achieving justice between the parents.

Finally, the mechanism of mandatory return is also seen as a method of upholding the rule of law, in the sense of not allowing a person to benefit from taking the law into his own hands. The abductor is prevented from gaining any advantage as a result of the change of circumstances brought about by his wrongdoing.[27] Since the objectives of achieving justice between the parents and upholding the rule of law both focus largely on the actions of the parents and the implications of the abduction for the parents, it will be convenient to combine them and treat them as a single objective.

Some general observations will now be made in relation to the above objectives, each of which will effectively serve as independent parameters for the analysis of the interpretation and application of particular provisions of the Convention.

i *Protecting Abducted Children*

As stated above, the central aspect of the underlying objective of protecting the interests of children is to protect abducted children from the harmful effects of abduction. In the words of Waite LJ,

> The objective is to spare children already suffering the effects of breakdown in their parents' relationship the further disruption which is suffered when they are taken arbitrarily by one parent from their settled environment and moved to another country for the sake of finding there a supposedly more sympathetic forum or a more congenial base.[28]

The assumption underpinning the return mechanism is that the best way to protect abducted children from harm is to restore the *status quo ante*. Yet, by providing exceptions to the obligation to return, the drafters of the Convention recognised that there will be situations, where restoring the status quo will not in fact protect the child from harm and that return of the child may even cause harm to the child. Thus, the objective of protecting children from the harmful effects of abduction will be achieved by ensuring the speedy return of those children whom the Convention requires to be returned. Accordingly, prompt return is not an objective in its own right. Where one of the exceptions is established, the policy of the Convention does not require automatic return. Thus, to rely on the

---

of any custody dispute should be entrusted for determination to the courts of the child's habitual residence. The other objectives combine in this one'.

[24] Perez-Vera Report (n 10), para 15.
[25] Art 1(b), set out above.
[26] Or another person or body's custody rights (Art 3).
[27] Perez-Vera Report (n 10), para 71; FamA 1855/08 *RB v VG* http://elyon1.court.gov.il/verdictssearch/Hebrew VerdictsSearch.aspx, 8 April 2008 (Isr) [INCADAT cite: HC/E/IL 923], para 23.
[28] *Re B (A Minor) (Abduction)* [1994] 2 FLR 249, 260.

purpose of returning children in interpreting the scope of the exceptions[29] is to resort to circular reasoning.

Moreover, it is suggested that the objective of protecting children from the harmful effects of abduction should include protecting children from the harmful effects of mandatory return, which is itself a consequence of the abduction. Indeed as so powerfully expressed by Baroness Hale, 'No one intended that an instrument designed to secure the protection of children from the harmful effects of international child abduction should itself be turned into an instrument of harm'.[30]

Accordingly, it is necessary to examine whether the various ways in which the provisions of the Abduction Convention have been interpreted and applied do in fact ensure that children are returned when this will protect them from harm and are not returned where return is liable to cause them harm. In order to carry out such an assessment, certain assumptions have to be made about the type of harm caused by abduction. There is ample legal[31] and social science authority[32] for the proposition that the main harm caused to children by wrongful removal or retention is the instability caused by the unilateral, and often sudden, uprooting of the child from his familial and social environment. However, there are cases where the removal or retention do not actually cause harm to the children, such as in cases of retention after a prolonged visit to the country of refuge. Also, there are cases where any harm caused by the abduction is outweighed by the benefit of being removed from the harmful pre-abduction situation. In these cases, return does not fulfill the objective of protecting the abducted child from harm, although of course it may promote other objectives. Similarly, there will be cases where return will not in fact undo any harm which was caused by the abduction, for example because the child has already become acclimatised in the country of refuge or because the status quo cannot be restored for some other reason.[33] In particular, where return means a change in the child's primary carer, there will not in fact be a return to the status quo and the very separation from the primary carer may itself cause real harm.[34]

ii Deterrence

The intended deterrent effect of the immediate return mechanism, referred to in the Perez-Vera Report,[35] has been mentioned not infrequently by judges when applying the Convention[36] and has sometimes been used to justify a narrow interpretation of the defences.[37] However,

---

[29] As in eg *RB v VG* (n 27).

[30] *Re D (A Child) (Abduction: Foreign Custody Rights)* [2006] UKHL 51 [52].

[31] See for example the often quoted classic words of Buckley LJ in the pre-Convention case of *Re L* [1974] 1 All ER 913, 925–26 'to take a child from his native land, to remove him to another country, where, maybe, his native tongue is not spoken, to divorce him from the social customs and contacts to which he has been accustomed, to interrupt his education in his native land and subject him to a foreign system of education are all acts ... which are likely to be psychologically disturbing to a child, particularly at a time when his family life is also disrupted'; see also A Dyer, *Report On International Child Abduction By One Parent Legal Kidnapping*, Preliminary Document No 1, Aug 1978, in *Hague Conference On Private International Law*, 3 Actes et Documents De Laquatorzième Session (Child Abduction) (1980) 12, 17 ('Dyer Report'); Actes et Documents (n 13), 21.

[32] See sources cited in ch 3 at II C.

[33] eg return to country other than that of the habitual residence prior to the abduction or other changes in circumstances (*Wilson v Huntley* (n 23) [45]).

[34] See ch 3 at II D.

[35] Perez-Vera Report (n 10), para 16.

[36] In *Wilson v Huntley* (n 23) [48], deterrence is described as a 'central objective of the Convention'.

[37] See, for example, the decision of Justice Procaccia in *RB v VG* (n 27).

there has been little discussion of the critical question of whether the Convention does have any deterrent effect in practice.[38]

Doubts about the effectiveness of the deterrent do not de-legitimise the professed objective.[39] Nonetheless, if judges are going to use the deterrent effect of the Convention as a factor in determining how to interpret and apply the provisions of the Convention,[40] it is important to consider the reality of the deterrent effect.[41] This is particularly true where the need to deter abductors is used as a reason for narrow interpretation and application of the defences when other factors, such as the welfare and rights of the child would point towards a wider approach. In the absence of research into the actual deterrent effect of the Convention,[42] it is appropriate to consider in some detail the likely deterrent effect of the Convention.

Some insight into the extent to which the Abduction Convention's sanctions will in fact deter potential abductors can be gleaned from deterrence research in other areas. Whilst clearly caution needs to be exercised in drawing analogies between the effect of criminal sanctions – to which most of the literature relates – and the abduction context, the fundamental question as to the extent to which unpleasant legal consequences will deter a person from acting against the law is the same. Needless to say, the fact that in the abduction context, the sanction is return of the child and does not involve depriving the offender of his freedom[43] means that the deterrent effect of the Convention is likely to be less than in the case of criminal law. Potential abductors may consider that they have little to lose by abducting, since in the worst case scenario, they will be back in the same position as they were previously.[44] This of course means that researchers' conclusions about the limitations

---

[38] The discussion here relates to general deterrence (ie preventing potential offenders from offending) and not specific deterrence (ie preventing an offender from re-offending). See J Andenaes, *Punishment and Deterrence* (Michigan, University of Michigan, 1974) 129.

[39] Since deterrence is only one of a number of rationales for the immediate return mechanism, lack of evidence of any real deterrent effect does not per se raise questions as to the appropriateness of that mechanism.

[40] See eg *Secretary for Justice v HJ* [2007] 2 NZLR 289) [40], where it is said that when an exception is established, the court has to enquire whether the deterrent purpose prevails over the interests of the particular child; see also *Re L (Abduction: Pending Criminal Proceedings)* [1999] 1 FLR 433, 442.

[41] F Zimring and G Hawkins, *Deterrence the Legal Threat in Crime Control* (Chicago, University of Chicago Press, 1973) 18–23, comment on the strong belief of the judges and other officials in the deterrence of the criminal legal system, which is not borne out by the results of deterrence research.

[42] If there was a real deterrent effect, we might expect to see a reduced number of applications under the Abduction Convention rather than an increased number (as reported by N Lowe et al, 'A Statistical Analysis of Applications Made in 2008', Preliminary Document No 8A (2011), www.hcch.net/upload/wop/abduct2011pd08ae.pdf 0, para 28). It has been suggested that the fact that 72% of abductions are by parents who were the child's primary caretaker or joint primary caretaker (ibid, para 47) indicates that the Convention has succeeded in deterring abductions by non-custodial parents. However, this cannot be proven. On the other hand, there is anecdotal evidence from lawyers about clients who asked their advice about the consequences of a potential abduction and upon hearing about the likely application of the Convention decided not to abduct. However, some such parents may then, in light of the advice, devise the abduction in such a way that they hope to avoid the application of the Convention. For example, in FamA 9802/09 *Plonit v Ploni* http://elyon1.court.gov.il/verdictssearch/HebrewVerdictsSearch.aspx,17 December 2009 (Isr), the Court took the view that, after receiving legal advice about the Abduction Convention, the mother had planned an extended family visit to Israel for 9 months as a way of unilaterally changing the child's habitual residence. However, the plan did not succeed because the Court held that the children were still habitually resident in Sweden.

[43] As the current discussion concerns the deterrent effect of the Convention, no account will be taken of the possibility that the abductor might also be subject to criminal sanctions in some countries; see ch 1 at II Aii.

[44] This may not be entirely true. Firstly, there will be financial costs in abducting and then returning; for a discussion of the deterrent effect of requiring the abductor to pay compensation to the left-behind parent, see ch 17. Secondly, the abduction may prejudice the abductor in any future custody or relocation proceedings concerning the child; see ch 4 at III A. On the other hand, in cases of abduction by the custodial mother, her position might actually improve as a result of the undertakings required from the father as a condition to ordering return; see ch 11 at III B.

of the deterrent effect of criminal sanctions, discussed below, will apply *a fortiori* in the abduction context. Three areas of deterrence research are most relevant to the current discussion.

a Lack of Knowledge of Law

Deterrence research suggests that the ordinary citizen is largely unaware of the operation of the justice system and that this substantially weakens the deterrent effect of changes in the law or in the judicial implementation of the law.[45] Empirical research in relation to the operation of the Abduction Convention confirms that parents, particularly custodial parents, may not be aware that removing or retaining the child without the consent of the other parent was unlawful.[46] Thus, simply increasing the overall return rate, for example by interpreting the defences more narrowly, is unlikely to increase the deterrent effect of the Convention.[47]

b Influences on Deterrent Effect

The literature on deterrence explains that there are a number of variables which are likely to influence the deterrent effect of a particular legal sanction on a particular individual. The four main variables[48] will now be explained and applied to the child abduction context.

Firstly, a particular person's susceptibility to legal sanctions is likely to be affected by aspects of his personality, such as whether he is a 'present dweller' or 'future dweller';[49] whether he is naturally optimistic or pessimistic and whether he is naturally compliant or defiant in the face of authority.[50] Whilst of course potential abductors will have a variety of personality traits, the background of relationship breakdown and instability which invariably precede abduction are likely to make the potential abductor more preoccupied with his immediate needs, and what he sees as the immediate needs of his children, and less concerned about the possible long-term consequences of his actions. Thus, he will be less susceptible to being deterred by legal sanctions.

Secondly, social and ethical constraints are often a more powerful deterrent to criminal behaviour than legal sanctions,[51] although the latter might well strengthen accepted social and moral norms. In the past, parental child abduction was not considered a criminal offence at all.[52] Whilst the legal situation has changed in many countries,[53] the extent to

---

[45] See M Tonry, 'Learning from the Limitations of Deterrence Research' (2008) 37 *Crime & Justice* 279, 279 and 286 (pointing out that changes in police practices are more likely to achieve deterrent effects than changes in sentencing policies and practices and that there is no statistically significant correlation between the severity of sentencing and crime rates); similarly A Von Hirsch et al, *Criminal Deterrence and Sentence Severity: An Analysis of Recent Research* (Oxford, Hart Publishing, 1999) 45.

[46] T Kruger, *International Child Abduction: The Inadequacies of the Law* (Oxford, Hart Publishing, 2011) 61 and 103.

[47] Except perhaps in cases where the abductor seeks legal advice in advance.

[48] These are the variables identified by Zimring and Hawkins (n 41) 131. It should be pointed out that whilst many studies have been conducted since then, state of the art knowledge about the deterrent effects of the criminal justice system is little different to what it was in the 1970s, see Tonry, 'Learning from the Limitations' (n 45) 279.

[49] In the sense of whether he is mainly concerned with the present situation or whether he plans for the future.

[50] Zimring and Hawkins (n 41) 100–04, and 121–25.

[51] ibid 78; Tonry, 'Learning from the Limitations' (n 45) 282.

[52] Hence it was referred to as 'legal kidnapping'. See Dyer Report (n 31), 12.

[53] See ch 1 at II Aii.

which such behaviour is considered socially and ethically unacceptable is likely to depend inter alia on the circumstances of the abduction.[54] For example, a non-custodial father seizing his children by force would be widely denigrated. However, it is less likely that a custodial mother 'overstaying' a visit with her children to her family in her home country would be considered as morally wrong, particularly if she was treated badly by the father of her children. On the contrary, at least in the latter scenario, she is likely to receive substantial encouragement and support from her family and community. Thus, on the one hand, the legal sanction in the Convention is important because it may be the only obstacle standing in the way of the abductor.[55] On the other hand, however, this barrier is likely to be weak when there is no social or ethical norm to back it up.

Thirdly, it is clear that the higher the level of motivation, the less effective legal sanctions will be. Strength of motivation has been said to be a function of the importance of the drive which the offender seeks to satisfy by the illegal act and the availability of alternative means for satisfying that drive.[56] The reasons for abduction[57] are usually to preserve the abductor's relationship with his child and/or to promote the welfare of the children, as perceived by the abductor.[58] Such goals are likely to be very important to the abductor. Furthermore, abduction is very often a measure of last resort and thus, at least in the eyes of the abductor, there is no other way of achieving these ends. Accordingly, most abductors are likely to be highly motivated and so less susceptible to legal sanctions.

Fourthly, it is axiomatic that carefully planned acts are more easily deterred than those resulting from a sudden, emotional impulse.[59] Moreover, decisions about behaviour made when a person 'is in circumstances which provoke great emotional arousal' are less amenable to the threat of legal sanction because this mental state is likely to prevent consideration of the consequences of the proposed action.[60] Even where the decision to abduct is not made impulsively, but is the result of prior planning, the decision is invariably made at a time during which the abductor is in emotional turmoil in the aftermath of the breakdown of his relationship and/or as a result of being separated from his children or having little contact with them.

In conclusion, all of these four variables suggest that the sanction of immediate return is not likely to deter many potential abductors. Nonetheless, since deterrence is a clearly stated object of the Convention, it will be appropriate to consider in the analysis sections the extent to which the various ways of interpreting particular provisions of the Convention are likely to increase or reduce the deterrent effect.

c Exemplary Punishment

The deterrence literature refers to the philosophical debate as to the morality of exemplary punishment, when a particular offender's punishment is increased in order to deter others.

---

[54] Cultural, religious and other social factors will also be relevant.

[55] Non-return in such situations may not be criminalised and, even where it is, the criminal sanction may well not be activated in practice. See ch 1 at II Aii.

[56] Zimring and Hawkins (n 41) 135.

[57] See generally ch 3 at I Biii.

[58] Where the custodial parent wishes to relocate, she will see this as being for the benefit of the child.

[59] Zimring and Hawkins (n 41) 136; Tonry, 'Learning from the Limitations' (n 45) 282. Thus, many surveys show that it is easier to deter white collar economic crimes which are planned rationally than crimes of violence; see eg JN Galo, 'Effective Law-Enforcement Techniques for Reducing Crime' (1973) 88 *The Journal of Criminal Law and Criminology* 1475; R Keel, 'Rational Choice and Deterrence Theory',www.umsl.edu/~keelr/200/ratchoc.html.

[60] Zimring and Hawkins, ibid.

This issue is analogous to the question of the extent to which it is justifiable to mandate return of a particular abducted child, when return is not in the best interests of that child, in order to protect other children who might be abducted in the future.

The claim that exemplary punishment is unjust is based on the Kantian principle that a person should always be treated as an end in himself and not only as a means to an end.[61] According to this premise, it is unjust to punish a person solely in order to deter others. However, so long as the punishment is proportional to the offence,[62] the fact that general considerations of deterrence were taken into account in determining the severity of the sentence, seems unobjectionable, since the offender is being punished because he deserves to be punished and not only in order deter others. Nonetheless, scholars warn of violation of the principle of equality before the law and insist that alternative methods of deterrence should also be explored.[63]

A fortiori, considerations of deterrence alone cannot justify ordering return of the child, since in the child abduction context the child is completely innocent. In cases where there is no indication that return will harm the child, it is legitimate to take account of the assumption that ordering immediate summary return of this child may deter potential abductors. However, where there is clear evidence that return is not in the best interests of the child, deterrence appears to become the main justification for ordering return. Here, the welfare of the particular abducted child is sacrificed on the altar of the interests of other children,[64] in the belief that returning this child will deter abduction of other children in the future. Whilst this situation could perhaps be defended on utilitarian grounds[65] if it were indeed proven that the harm to the specific child[66] would save many other children from being abducted, there is no such proof.[67] Thus, considerations of deterrence cannot morally justify interpreting the grave risk of harm defence or any other defence narrowly.

iii Adjudication in the Forum Conveniens[68]

As seen above, the objective of ensuring that determination on the merits of the custody dispute will take place in the state of habitual residence prior to the removal or retention is based on the assumption that that state is the *forum conveniens* for making such decisions and that the abductor's attempt unilaterally to change the venue for adjudication is illegitimate forum shopping. In order to assess to what extent these assumptions are correct, it is necessary to consider briefly the basis for determining that a particular forum is the *forum conveniens*.[69]

---

[61] Andenaes (n 38) 129.
[62] ibid 134–35; Zimring and Hawkins (n 41) 39–42.
[63] See Andenaes (n 38); Zimring and Hawkins ibid 41–42 and 46–50.
[64] See A Bainham, *Children and the Modern Law*, 3rd edn (Bristol, Jordan Publishing Limited, 2005) 749–50; see comment of Waite LJ in *W v W* [1993] 2 FLR 211, 220 that 'it is implicit in the whole operation of the Convention that the objective of stability for the mass of children may have to be achieved at the price of tears in some individual cases'.
[65] Although theories basing punishment purely on utilitarian considerations have been widely rejected. See Zimring and Hawkins (n 41) 34–35, and 39–40.
[66] Whilst, under the Convention, grave risk of harm to the child is a defence to immediate return, as will be shown in detail in ch 11, the very narrow way in which this defence is interpreted means that return is ordered even when this is likely to cause harm to the child.
[67] Both Andenaes (n 38) 148 and Zimring and Hawkins (n 41) 43 take the view that society is morally obliged to evaluate the deterrent effect of the legal sanctions it imposes.
[68] As will be seen below, despite its name, this doctrine does not only relate to convenience but to appropriateness of forum in a wider sense.
[69] It should be noted that where one of the exceptions in the Abduction Convention is established and thus there is discretion to return, the issue of relative appropriateness of the competing fora (that of the requesting and

The concept of *forum conveniens* is primarily a common law concept, largely because the doctrine of *forum non conveniens*, under which a court can refuse to exercise its jurisdiction, is not recognised in most civil law systems.[70] In addition, in many common law systems, *forum conveniens* is one of the criteria for deciding whether to give leave to serve process on a foreign defendant.[71] However, this does not mean that the concept of the appropriateness of forum is not recognised by civil law systems. Rather, those systems use narrower, more focused jurisdiction rules as a method of ensuring that cases are heard in the most appropriate forum.[72] Furthermore, sometimes appropriateness of forum is used as a rule of statutory construction or even as part of a jurisdiction rule.[73] Finally, many civil law jurisdictions have *forum non conveniens* substitute rules.[74]

Nonetheless, in the search for criteria to determine appropriateness of forum, the case-law and literature[75] from common law jurisdictions will be more helpful because in order to apply the doctrine of *forum non conveniens*, these jurisdictions have had to develop a framework for determining whether a particular forum is appropriate. Whilst there are a number of differences between the formulations of the doctrine of *forum non conveniens* in the different common law systems,[76] considerable similarities exist between the criteria for determining appropriateness of forum.[77]

Traditionally, considerable weight, sometimes even conclusive weight, was given to factors relating to technical convenience in relation to the conduct of the litigation, such as the situation of the evidence, the place of residence of the witnesses and the language of any documentary evidence. However, in light of globalisation and methods of instantaneous communication in particular, which facilitate the transfer of documentation and even make it possible for parties and witnesses to participate 'virtually' in hearings without the need to travel, the weight given to these geographical factors has been reduced, but not

---

requested State) is often treated as the main consideration. See *Re A (Minors) (Abduction: Acquiescence)* [1992] 2 FLR 14, 28 and the discussion in ch 10 at IV.

[70] JJ Fawcett (ed), *Declining Jurisdiction in Private International Law* (Oxford, Clarendon Press, 1995) 10. An attempt to incorporate the doctrine of *forum conveniens* (albeit an attenuated version thereof) into an International Convention can be found in Art 22 of the Preliminary Draft Convention on Jurisdiction and Foreign Judgments in Civil and Commercial Matters, www.hcch.net/upload/wop/jdgmpd11.pdf. Work on this Convention was abandoned due to a lack of consensus.

[71] *Spiliada Maritime Corporn v Cansulex Ltd* [1987] AC 460.

[72] Fawcett (n 70) 8–9.

[73] ibid 7–8.

[74] ibid 24–27; similarly, Art 15 of the Brussels II bis Regulation, Council Regulation (EC) No 2201/2003 of 27 November 2003 concerning jurisdiction and the recognition and enforcement of judgments in matrimonial matters and matters of parental responsibility [2003] OJ L 338/1-29, provides a transfer of jurisdiction rule for cases involving custody and parental responsibility which is similar to a *forum non conveniens* jurisdiction. See discussion of this Regulation in ch 1 at II C.

[75] In addition to the country reports in Fawcett (n 70), see eg, M Karyanni, *Forum Non Conveniens in the Modern Age* (Ardsley, Transnational Publishers, 2004); M Bell, *Forum Shopping and Venue in Transnational Litigation* (Oxford, Oxford University Press, 2003); R Schuz, 'Controlling Forum-Shopping: The Impact of MacShannon v Rockware Glass Ltd' (1986) 35 *International & Comparative Law Quarterly* 374; DW Robertson, 'The Federal Doctrine of Forum Non Conveniens: An Object Lesson in Uncontrolled Discretion' (1994) 29 *Texas International Law Journal* 353.

[76] For example, in the US, public policy considerations are taken into account, but not in England, Fawcett ibid 15–16. Also, in Australia the doctrine is narrower than that in England and concentrates on the clear inappropriateness of the Australian forum rather than comparing the relative appropriateness of the competing fora, see R Garnett, 'Stay of Proceedings in Australia: A Clearly Inappropriate Test?' (1999) 23 *Melbourne University Law Review* 30.

[77] Fawcett ibid 11.

eliminated.[78] Instead, greater weight is given to factors relating to litigation efficiency[79] and substantive considerations including connections between the dispute and the competing fora;[80] the law governing the relevant transaction;[81] the legitimate expectations of the parties;[82] and fairness between the parties.[83] In proceedings relating to children, the best interests of the child are also taken into account, although there does not seem to be any consensus as to what weight should be given to such interests.[84]

In the child abduction context, where the child is taken to a country to which he had no previous connections and has only been there a short time, the country of habitual residence prior to the abduction will indeed invariably be the *forum conveniens* in terms of convenience, efficiency and substance. In particular, the information relating to the children and the parents will be most easily available in that country and the courts in that country will be most familiar with the social and cultural background in which the child had been living. Furthermore, there may have been previous litigation concerning the child in the courts of that country.

However, in what might be called non-standard cases, where the child does have significant connections with the place of refuge, either because he lived there at some stage prior to the abduction and/or because he has been living there for a significant length of time after the abduction, then it is far from obvious that the State of origin will be the *forum conveniens*. In particular, the most up-to-date information about the child may be most easily available in the State of refuge[85] and legal proceedings may also have been commenced there, in addition to the Abduction Convention proceedings themselves. Furthermore, particular facts relating to that system of justice and to the background to the dispute may be significant. For example, if there is no legal aid available in the country of habitual residence and one of the parties cannot afford legal representation, this will impede the ability of that court to ensure protection of the child's best interests.[86]

It will be apparent that the extent to which the country of habitual residence will indeed be the *forum conveniens* depends a great deal on how courts determine habitual residence. A detailed consideration of the different models for determining habitual residence of a

---

[78] Karyanni (n 75) 199–201 points out that the degree of weight to be attached to these considerations should depend on the relevance of distance and the increased cost to the particular parties.

[79] For example, the fact that all the litigation can be heard in one State rather than having to be split between States, JJ Fawcett and JM Carruthers, *Cheshire, North and Fawcett, Private International Law*, 14th edn (Oxford, Oxford University Press, 2008) 433. Karyanni ibid 98–99 and 204–11, explains that the object is 'resourceful and efficient resolution of the dispute' (ibid 204) which is not simply a function of geographical location.

[80] Such as the place of residence or the place of business of the parties, Fawcett and Carruthers ibid 431; Karyanni ibid 100.

[81] Fawcett and Carruthers ibid.

[82] Karyanni (n 75) 211–12.

[83] Fairness is the statutory criteria for determining whether to stay matrimonial proceedings under s 9 of the Domicile and Matrimonial Proceedings Act, 1973. See R Schuz, 'The further Implications of Spiliada in the Light of Recent Case Law: Stays in Matrimonial Proceedings' (1989) 38 *International & Comparative Law Quarterly* 946; *Otobo v Otobo* [2002] All ER (D) 27.

[84] See R Schuz, 'The Hague Child Abduction Convention: Family Law and Private International Law' (1995) 44 *International & Comparative Law Quarterly* 771, 785.

[85] The US Uniform Child Custody Jurisdiction Act s 3(a)(2) recognises that the fact that the child and at least one of his parents has a significant connection with the State in question may mean that it is in the child's best interests for that State to assume jurisdiction to determine or modify custody where substantial relevant evidence is available there, even though it is not the child's home State.

[86] In the case of *H v H (Forum Conveniens) (Nos 1 and 2)* [1993] 1 FLR 958, it was held that England was a more appropriate forum because in Wisconsin, the mother would not be able to put forward her case effectively without legal aid. In this case, England was in fact the habitual residence of the child, but it seems that the decision would have been the same even if the child had been habitually resident in Wisconsin.

child will be conducted in chapter eight. However, it should be remembered that whichever model is adopted, the fact that habitual residence has to be determined as at the date of the wrongful removal or retention will prevent changes taking place after that date being taken account of. This means that in some cases where there has been significant delay, the State of habitual residence is unlikely to still be the *forum conveniens*.

Similarly, the extent to which it is appropriate to see the abductor as a forum shopper will depend on the degree of connection between the child and the State of refuge prior to the abduction.[87] Furthermore, the assumption that the main motive of the abductor is to change the venue for the adjudication seems to relate mainly to non-custodial abductors who wish to acquire custody rather than to custodial abductors who wish to move to another country with the child without the need to conduct prolonged and expensive relocation proceedings. Whilst, of course, the result is the same, it is suggested that where the abductor is not really forum-shopping, it will be easier to find that in certain situations, the State of refuge has now in fact become the *forum conveniens*.

Finally, it is important to point out that the objective of adjudication in the *forum conveniens* does not per se require return of the child. In theory, it is possible to allow the adjudication of the case to proceed in the State of habitual residence whilst not returning the child, pending the outcome of the litigation in the State of habitual residence.[88] The advantage of such an approach is that it enables the court of the State of refuge to refuse return, where this is necessary to protect the child, whilst still allowing the merits of the case to be heard in the State of habitual residence, where this is the *forum conveniens*.

The Abduction Convention does not expressly provide for this possibility. However, courts can in fact achieve a similar result by staying the return order until the court in the State of habitual residence has come to a decision on the merits of the case. So far, this power has only been used in exceptional cases where the proceedings in the foreign country are already advanced and there seems to be a real chance that that court will allow the child to stay in the State of refuge.[89] In contrast, the Brussels II bis Regulation[90] does provide a procedure under which the State of habitual residence will retain jurisdiction to determine the merits of the case, even where return is refused.

iv Justice between the Parents and the Rule of Law

Care has to be taken when considering the objectives of justice between the parents and upholding the rule of law for two main reasons. Firstly, even though the act of removal or retention has been held to be wrongful, it is not necessarily morally blameworthy.[91] Abduction does not take place in a vacuum and is usually just one action in a series of actions and words on the part of both parties in a deteriorating intimate relationship. Whilst abduction is, of course, a radical step and so cannot be compared to many relatively

---

[87] In cases where the parties have been living abroad temporarily, neither an early return 'home' nor retention in the state of refuge can be seen as forum-shopping because there is a real connection with both fora.

[88] The opposite scenario is also possible where the custody proceedings were commenced in the requested State before the Abduction Convention proceedings; see eg *H v H (Child Abduction: Stay of Domestic Proceedings)* [1994] 1 FLR 530. However, such a decision will rarely be appropriate, largely because of the risk that the requesting State will not recognise the decision, unless of course it is bound to do so, eg by Brussels II bis Regulation (n 74) or the 1996 Hague Child Protection Convention (see ch 1 at II C and E).

[89] *F v M and N (Abduction: Acquiescence: Settlement)* [2008] EWHC 1525 (Fam); *JPC v SMW* [2007] EWHC 1349 (Fam).

[90] Brussels II bis Regulation (n 74), Art 11(6)–(8); see ch 1 at II Civ.

[91] per Baroness Hale in *Re D (a child)* [2006] UKHL 51, 56.

minor hurtful acts and words common in such a situation, the background to abduction is, not infrequently, serious physical, emotional and verbal abuse of the abductor by the left-behind parent.[92] In such circumstances return cannot be justified on the basis of the need to do justice between the parents. Whilst it is true that the 'correct' response to the left-behind parent's provocation would have been to seek assistance from the authorities in the country of origin rather than to take the law into her own hands, in apparent violation of the rule of law, there are often understandable reasons why this course of action was not chosen.[93] The objective of upholding the rule of law should take account of this reality.

Finally, the interests of the child must take precedence over the objective of justice between the parents and therefore a child should not be returned where it is clear that this will cause him real harm, however blameworthy the abductor might be[94] and however innocent the left-behind parent might be.

The analysis sections of the chapters in Part III and IV contain a discussion of the extent to which the interpretation and application of the Convention has been influenced by the objectives of justice between the parents and upholding the rule of law and whether the courts have indeed exercised the caution required in relation thereto.

D Compatibility with the Summary Nature of Convention Proceedings

The description of the Abduction Convention proceedings as 'summary' refers both to the fact that there is no hearing on the merits[95] and to the fact that the proceedings are expedited. The summary nature of the proceedings may be seen largely as a function of the objective of securing prompt return. Nonetheless, since the nature of the proceedings relates to the technical means of achieving the objective and is not a substantive objective in its own right, it was thought appropriate to treat it as a separate parameter. Indeed, the importance of the speed of the proceedings[96] should not be underestimated.[97] The delay caused by cumbersome proceedings may in practice make it impossible to achieve the objective of restoring the status quo.

Clearly, it is necessary to adopt special procedures in order to comply with the tight six-week time-scale set by the Abduction Convention.[98] In particular, it is necessary to limit the opportunity to examine witnesses and to seek expert reports. This means that the judge may not be in a position to make complex decisions of fact which require the consideration of a good deal of evidence and assessment of the credibility of the parties. Accordingly, interpreting the substantive provisions of the Abduction Convention in a way which is

---

[92] 'Domestic and Family Violence and the Article 13 "Grave Risk" Exception in the Operation of the Hague Convention of 25 October 1980 on the Civil Aspects of International Child Abduction: A Reflection Paper', Preliminary Document No 9 (May 2011), www.hcch.net/upload/wop/abduct2011pd09e.pdf.

[93] See ch 11 at IV Civ.

[94] See eg comment in *Steffen F v Severina P* 966 F Supp 2d 922 (E Ariz 1997) that the mother's inexcusable conduct should not obligate the court to ignore the compelling proof of the harm which would be caused to the child by return. 'Conversely the clean hands doctrine should not be used to bar an application, *Karpenko v Leendertz* 619 F 3d 259 3rd Cir, 2010).'

[95] See Arts 14 and 16 of the Abduction Convention.

[96] In relation to provisions relating to the speed of the proceedings, see ch 1 at Biv.

[97] The Perez-Vera Report (n 10), para 119, describes speedy decisions as being 'fundamental to the working of the Convention'.

[98] In Art 11.

likely to increase the need to make such findings of fact[99] or to rely on expert reports will not be compatible with the summary nature of the Convention proceedings and the need for speed. Whilst in some situations there may be other considerations which override the objective of speed, this will not invariably be the case. Thus, the extent to which the Abduction Convention has been implemented in a way which maximises the possibility of adherence to the summary nature of the proceedings, is certainly an appropriate parameter of analysis.

---

[99] eg if determination of habitual residence depends on the intention of the parties and the versions of the two parties are completely different from each other; see ch 8.

6

Consistency with General Legal Doctrines

I Introduction

As explained at the beginning of the previous chapter, the second stage of the analysis involves examining to what extent the Hague Convention on the Civil Aspects of International Child Abduction ('Abduction Convention') itself and the way in which it has been implemented are consistent with general legal doctrines, principles and policies which are pertinent to the subject matter of the Abduction Convention. Since the Abduction Convention is concerned with legal relations between parents and children involving an international element, the principles and policies of family law and private international law will be most relevant.[1]

The theory and content of family law has undergone radical change over the last few decades inter alia in response to fundamental social changes and to the widespread recognition of the human rights of family members in general and of children in particular. Accordingly, the parameters for analysis will focus largely on the rights and interests of children and their parents. Parts II and III below will discuss the nature and content of these rights and interests in light of modern jurisprudence.

Part IV will explain the private international law aspects of the Convention and then briefly discuss the main objectives of the three types of private international law rules – jurisdiction rules, choice of law rules and rules for the recognition and enforcement of foreign judgments – and the doctrine of comity. A general objective, which has been specifically identified in relation to private international law, but is arguably relevant to every area of law, is to achieve the optimal balance between legal certainty and flexibility.[2] Part V will elaborate on this objective and why it has been chosen as one of the parameters for analysis. Finally, other general legal doctrines are relevant to specific provisions of the Convention. For example, principles of contract law are relevant to the defence of consent. Similarly, tort law principles are relevant in considering how the left-behind parent should be compensated. These specific principles will be discussed throughout this book as and when they arise.

---

[1] See R Schuz, 'The Hague Child Abduction Convention: Family Law and Private International Law' (1995) 44 *International and Comparative Law Quarterly* 771. It will of course also be remembered that the Convention was drafted under the auspices of the Hague Conference on Private International Law, which still provides various services in relation to the Convention. See ch 2 at II D.

[2] P Hay, *Flexibility versus Predictability and Uniformity in Choice of Law*, Collected Courses (Dordrecht, Martinus Nijhoff, 1991) 226.

II Rights and Interests of Children

A Children's Rights and the Abduction Convention[3]

The essence of the doctrine of children's rights is that it recognises that children are independent rights-holders and not merely the objects of the rights of others. They are the subject of fundamental rights and basic liberties and not merely the object of solicitude and care.[4] The significance of this recognition is that the law determines the interests of the child and imposes on others the obligation to realise those rights – an obligation which is enforceable by the child himself or by others on his behalf.

The theoretical basis of the doctrine of children's rights is the 'interest' theory of rights[5] which holds that a person has a right where his interests are protected 'by the imposition of (legal or moral) normative constraints on the acts and activities of other people with respect to the object of one's interests'.[6] Accordingly, since children have interests which need protecting in this way, they are right-holders no less than adults, although of course their ability to enforce their rights may be limited. Indeed, one of these rights is that their parents or other suitable adults should assist them in realising their rights.[7]

Before continuing to examine the doctrine of children's rights in more detail, brief reference should be made to the criticism which has been levelled at the use of this model in the context of the parent-child relationship.[8] It has been argued that the divisive and egoistical nature of rights discourse is antithetical to family relationships and particularly those between a child and his parents.[9] It is alleged that focusing excessively on the child's interests may be to the detriment of the family as a whole, and so ultimately also to the child himself.[10] Furthermore, formulating disputes as a clash between the rights of the parties only allows for binary solutions, which is too simplistic an approach to family conflicts. Thus, a rights-based approach is liable to lead to polarisation which may destroy families rather than to encourage the search for creative solutions and compromises which can preserve family relationships, to the mutual benefit of all the family members.[11] Some writers have therefore advocated the model of relational rights which they claim preserves the interests of the child within a system which is committed to relationships.[12]

A detailed analysis of the relative merits of traditional rights discourse and the relational rights model in the context of disputes concerning children is outside the scope of this

---

[3] For a discussion of the relevance of the United Nations Convention on the Rights of the Child (the CRC) as an aid to interpreting the Abduction Convention, see ch 5 at n 2.

[4] A Loptaka, 'Introduction to the United Nations Convention on the Rights of the Child' (1996) 6 *Transnational Law & Contemporary Problems* 251.

[5] J Fortin, *Children's Rights and the Developing Law*, 3rd edn (Cambridge, Cambridge University Press, 2009) 13.

[6] N MacCormick, *Legal Right and Social Democracy: Essay in Legal and Political Philosophy* (Oxford, Clarendon Press, 1982) 154.

[7] Art 5 of the CRC.

[8] See generally M Minow, 'Rights for the Next Generation: A Feminist Approach to Children's Rights' (1986) 9 *Harvard Women's Law Journal* 1, 24.

[9] R Zafran, 'Children's Rights as Relational Rights: The Case of Relocation' (2010) 18 *American University Journal of Gender, Social Policy & the Law* 163, 185–90.

[10] ibid.

[11] ibid.

[12] ibid, 194–97; J Nedelsky, 'Reconceiving Rights as Relationship' (1993) 1 *Review of Constitutional Studies* 1.

book. However, it is appropriate to raise some doubts concerning the criticism voiced against the doctrine of children's rights and to explain why, in any event, consistency with this doctrine is an appropriate parameter for the analysis in this book.

Firstly, most of the arguments levelled against the children's rights model can be answered by appropriate formulation of the rights of the child to reflect the context of the family relationships. In particular, this doctrine recognises the child's right to meaningful relationships with other family members inter alia through the recognition of his right to contact and to identity. Secondly, a child's rights are not absolute and must themselves take into account his other rights. For example, the child's right to proper development should prevent the child's other rights being asserted in such a way which would damage his well-being within the family environment. Thirdly, where the child's rights clash with those of one or both of his parents, the balancing exercise must take into account the implications of the outcome for each of the parties and thus where upholding the child's rights will lead to the disintegration of the family, then this is unlikely to be the optimal balance. Finally, whilst adjudication is most certainly harmful to children, it is not clear that rights discourse discourages the use of alternative dispute resolution (ADR) methods more than any other approach.[13] If the parties are made to understand that their rights are not absolute and have to be balanced against the rights of others, hopefully they will understand the advantages of coming to an agreed solution.

Much of the opposition to the concept of children's rights is based on the concern that it will lead to increased external interference in the functioning of the family unit, which will harm rather than benefit children.[14] However, this concern is less relevant in the Abduction Convention context where the family unit has already broken down and the unilateral wrongful act of one of the parents makes interference by the judicial system unavoidable, unless the parties can come to an agreed solution.

Furthermore, this book is not suggesting that the doctrine of the rights of the child be used as a decision-making mechanism in abduction cases. Rather, the doctrine of children's rights is being used as a parameter for analysing the Abduction Convention and its implementation. This is particularly important in view of the fact that the Abduction Convention mechanism is expressly based on upholding the rights of the left-behind parent and no mention is made of the rights of the child. In order to undertake the proposed analysis, it is necessary to set out the rights of the child which need to be protected in the abduction scenario.

The United Nations Convention on the Rights of the Child ('the CRC'), which has been almost universally ratified,[15] provides a relatively comprehensive list of the rights which children are recognised as holding. Whilst the CRC should not be seen as the final word on children's rights,[16] the consensus that it represents makes it an appropriate tool for analysing the extent to which the Abduction Convention and the way in which it has been implemented are consistent with the doctrine of children's rights. It should be noted that Article 11 of the CRC expressly encourages States to enter into or to accede to international treaties combating the 'illicit transfer and non-return of children abroad', which clearly includes the Abduction Convention. Nonetheless, this fact does not necessarily mean that

---

[13] For use of ADR in Abduction Convention cases, see chapter 16.
[14] Fortin (n 5) 6–11.
[15] All countries apart from the US and Somalia have ratified it.
[16] MDA Freeman, 'Children's Rights Ten Years after Ratification' in B Franklin (ed), *The New Handbook on Children's Rights* (London, Routledge, 2002) 98.

the specific provisions of the Abduction Convention or the way in which it is implemented are consistent with the CRC. Indeed, as the Abduction Convention pre-dates the CRC by nine years, it is hardly surprising that in a number of respects the Abduction Convention might not appear to be 'rights compliant'.[17]

Four provisions in the CRC are widely considered to be the most important and to state general principles:[18] freedom from discrimination (Article 2); right to life (Article 6); treating the child's best interests as a primary consideration (Article 3(1)); and right to participation (Article 12). The latter two provisions together with a number of other rights recognised by the Convention, such as the right of the child to protection, his right to continued contact with both parents and his right to identity, have direct relevance to international abduction cases.

Moreover, the influence of the CRC is wider than the specific rights enacted therein. The Convention's recognition of the concept that children have rights contains a fundamental message about the centrality of children and their perspectives in matters affecting them. Thus, issues affecting the child have to be viewed through the child's eyes and not paternalistically from the viewpoint of adults. The implications of this perception go further than giving mature children the right to be heard and have weight accorded to their views. In addition, findings concerning children of all ages have to take into account the situation from the viewpoint of the child. In the context of the Abduction Convention, this conclusion is particularly pertinent in relation to the crucial finding as to the place of the child's habitual residence and also in relation to the finding as to whether the child has become settled in his[19] new environment under Article 12(2), in cases where one year has passed between the date of wrongful removal or retention and that of commencement of proceedings.

As a background to the examination of consistency with children's rights in the analysis sections in the chapters in Part III and Part IV of the book, the scope of the provisions of the CRC most relevant in Abduction Convention cases will now be briefly examined.

B The Best Interests of the Child and Article 3 of the CRC

This section will explain why the analysis in the book will distinguish between the traditional doctrine of the best interests of the child and the best interests formulation in Article 3 of the CRC.

The best interests of the child standard, synonymously referred to as the welfare principle, has been universally accepted by Western legal systems as a fundamental principle of family law. In such countries, the best interests of the child is an important consideration in all decisions relating to children and is the paramount consideration in disputes between

---

[17] But note comment of Perez-Vera Report, Proceedings of the 14th Session of the Hague Conference Oct 1980, www.hcch.net/index_en.php?act=publications.details&pid=2779, para 24 that the Convention should be interpreted in light of the 'general principle... that children must no longer be regarded as parents' property, but must be recognized as individuals with their own rights and needs'.

[18] S Dillon, *International Children's Rights* (Durham, Carolina Academic Press, 2010) 3.

[19] It will be noted that the text of the Convention refers to 'its new environment'. It seems to the current author that referring to the child as 'it' is difficult to reconcile with an approach that treats children as persons in their own right and so the human pronoun 'he', which, as explained in the Introduction, includes 'she', has been substituted.

parents.[20] In some countries, the best interests of the child standard has been elevated to a constitutional principle.[21] Thus, an analysis of the consistency of the Abduction Convention and its application with general legal principles must include consideration of the traditional best interests standard.

The best interests standard has been widely criticised largely because of the subjective and indeterminate nature of the standard;[22] because of the paternalism inherent in the assumption that adults are best placed to decide what is the best for a child and because of the child's total dependence on the discretion of the decision-maker. Accordingly, the doctrine of children's rights has been portrayed by some as a more advanced method of decision-making than the welfare principle because it determines the child's interests in advance and expresses them as rights, which the child is entitled to enforce. Thus, at first sight it might seem surprising that one of the central provisions in the CRC is Article 3 which provides that '[in] all actions concerning children, whether undertaken by public or private social welfare institutions, courts of law, administrative authorities or legislative bodies, the best interests of the child shall be a primary consideration'.

The most accepted explanation of this apparent inconsistency is that of Geraldine Van Bueren,[23] who takes the view that the best interests standard contained in Article 3 is a principle of interpretation[24] which has to be considered in relation to each of the rights in the Convention and residually in relation to all actions concerning children.[25] In contrast, the current author has suggested that consideration of the best interests standard should be treated as a right of the child.[26] Although Article 3 of the Convention is not expressed in terms of rights, such an interpretation is reasonable in light of the overall objectives of the Convention in setting out the rights to which every child is entitled and this approach enjoys a number of advantages.[27] Nonetheless, it is not necessary to determine whether Article 3 confers a right on the child in order to analyse to what extent the Abduction Convention and the way in which it has been applied are consistent with that provision. Rather, it is necessary to point out the ways in which the formulation in Article 3 differs from the traditional doctrine of the best interests of the child and to consider the implications of these differences.

Firstly, Article 3 appears to have a collective focus because it refers to all actions concerning children in the plural.[28] This would mean that decisions concerning children have to

---

[20] eg, English Children Act 1989, s 1. In England, the best interests principle is also paramount in disputes between parents and third parties. See eg *J v C* [1970] AC 688. However, this is not so in all legal systems. See eg in the USA *Re Clausen* 502 NW 2d 649 (1993) (widely known as the Baby Jessica case) and in HCJ 243/88 *Consulos v Torjeman* PD 56(2) 626 (Isr).

[21] eg South African Constitution, Art 28(2). Also the European Court of Human Rights (ECtHR) has held that the right to family life in Art 8 of the European Convention on Human Rights (ECHR) has to be interpreted in accordance with the best interests principle, *Neulinger and Shuruk v Switzerland* App no 41615/07 (ECHR, 6 July 2010) [134].

[22] The seminal article is R Mnookin, 'Child Custody Adjudication: Judicial Functions in the Fact of Indeterminacy' (1975) 39 *Law and Contemporary Problems* 226; see also S Parker, 'The Best Interests of the Child: Principles and Problems' in P Alston (ed), *The Best Interests of the Child* (Oxford, Clarendon Press, 1994) 26.

[23] G Van Bueren, *The International Law on the Rights of the Child* (Dordecht, Martinus Nijhoff, 1995) 46.

[24] This approach seems to have been adopted by the ECtHR, Fortin (n 5) 40–41.

[25] Under this approach, the child's participation rights under Art 12 are subject to the Art 3 best interests provision, Fortin ibid 268.

[26] R Schuz, 'The Hague Child Abduction Convention and Children's Rights' (2002) 12 *Transnational Law &Contemporary Problems* 393, 402.

[27] ibid.

[28] P Alston, 'The Best Interests Principle: Towards a Reconciliation of Culture and Human Rights' in P Alston (ed), *The Best Interests of the Child: Reconciling Culture And Human Rights Principle* (Oxford, Clarendon, 1994) 1; S Parker, 'The Best Interests of the Child – Principles and Problems' in P Alston (ed) ibid 208.

take into account the best interests of children generally and not only the best interests of the particular child in relation to whom the decision is being made. However, it seems that the reason for the use of the plural form is that legislatures and some of the other institutions referred to in the Article make decisions about groups of children.[29] Accordingly, where a court is making a decision about a specific child, the individual standard should be adopted, as suggested by the use of the singular form in the phrase 'best interests of the child' at the end of Article 3.[30]

Secondly, the phrase 'primary consideration' in Article 3 is preceded by the indefinite and not the definite article. In other words, there is no requirement that the best interests of the child are the sole or even the principle consideration as long as it is one of the main considerations.[31] This formulation gives considerable discretion to courts and other decision-makers to determine what weight to give to the best interests of the child viz-a-viz other considerations. Thus, the Article 3 standard allows the court to give less weight to the interests of the child than does the traditional paramountcy principle.[32] Accordingly, it is possible that the Abduction Convention and the way in which it has been applied will be compliant with Article 3, even if they are not consistent with the traditional best interests principle.

C The Child's Participation Rights and Article 12 of the CRC

One of the innovatory aspects of the CRC is its statement that children have a right to have a say in processes affecting their lives.[33] Article 12 of the CRC provides:

(1) State Parties shall assure to the child who is capable of forming his own her own views the right to express those views freely in all matters affecting the child, the views of the child being given due weight in accordance with the age and maturity of the child.

(2) For this purpose, the child shall in particular be provided the opportunity to be heard in any judicial and administrative proceedings affecting the child, either directly, or through a representative or an appropriate body, in a manner consistent with the procedural rules of national law.

From the text of this provision, it can be seen that participation consists of two components which should be treated as separate and independent rights. Firstly, the child has the right to have appropriate weight given to his views in all matters affecting him. This right is sometimes known as the right to autonomy or to have one's views respected. Secondly, the child has the right to be heard in all proceedings concerning him. Whilst both of these

---

[29] ibid.
[30] ibid; see also Justice Rotlevy in FamA (Dist- TA) 70/97 *Dagan v Dagan* tak-mech 98(3) 6307 (Isr). General Comment No 12 (July 2009) – The right of the child to be heard, drawn up by the Committee on the Rights of the Child, /www2.ohchr.org/english/bodies/crc/comments.htm, para 72, states that Art 3 is devoted to the best interests of the individual child, but that in identifying those best interests, it is also necessary to take into account the interests of children as a group.
[31] Alston (n 28) 12–13; Parker (n 28) 208.
[32] Although it should be noted that the scope of the decisions covered by Art 3 is wider than the scope of the decisions covered by the paramountcy principle in domestic law. See MDA Freeman, 'Images of Child Welfare in Abduction Appeals' in J Murphy (ed), *Ethnic Minorities, their Families and the Law* (Oxford, Hart Publishing, 2000).
[33] M Freeman, 'The Importance of a Children's Rights Perspective in Litigation' (1998) 2 *Butterworths Family Law Journal* 84 describes Art 12 as the 'linchpin of the Convention'.

rights[34] have been widely recognised in principle throughout the western world by legislatures, judges and law reform bodies, there is a considerable degree of uncertainty over the scope of these rights and how they should be translated into practice[35] and they have been implemented only partially and inconsistently throughout the world.[36] Before briefly discussing the debates concerning the implementation of the two aspects of the right to participate, it is helpful to consider the basis of this right.

i Basis of the Right to Participate[37]

The right to participate is based on the recognition of respect for the child as a separate human being, who has a personality, existence and views of his own, independent and distinct from those of his parents or other adults.[38] As an autonomous individual, he has the right to have a say in the shaping of his life. Non-inclusion of the child in decisions relating to him is effectively to treat him as the passive victim of his parents' dispute[39] rather than as a moral and social actor in his own right and can thus be seen as an insult to his self-respect.[40] In contrast, the child's participation places him in the centre of the decision-making process relating to him and gives a central position to the viewpoint of the child and to his wishes.

Furthermore, the empowerment conferred by the right to participate strengthens the status of children, both as a group and individually, and improves their ability to protect themselves.[41] Thus, the weakness and vulnerability of children is not a reason to exclude them from decision-making as was thought in the past, but rather a reason to encourage their participation.[42]

Indeed, the traditional view that children do not have the capacity to contribute to decision-making concerning their lives[43] and that adults know what is best for children, is paternalistic and inconsistent with empirical research. Various contemporary UK studies in which judges, parents and children were interviewed about the participation of children in disputes concerning residence and contact, show that children often have clear views which they are able to express articulately and cogently about their living arrangements and other matters affecting them and that sometimes they even suggest creative solutions

---

[34] Some scholars have identified lower level participation rights. See eg, R Hart, *Children's Participation, from Tokenism to Citizenship* (Florence, UNICEF, 1992); H Shier, 'Pathways to Participation: Openings, Opportunities and Obligations' (2001) 15 *Children and Society* 107.

[35] NV Lowe and MA Murch, 'Children's Participation in the Family Justice System – Translating Principles into Practice' (2001) 13 *Child and Family Law Quarterly* 137.

[36] N Taylor, RT Morag, A Bajpai and A Graham, 'International Models of Child Participation in Family Law Proceedings following Parental Separation / Divorce' (2012) 20 *International Journal of Children's Rights* 645.

[37] The child's right to participate in decisions concerning him is of course not limited to decisions made by court in legal proceedings. However, because this book *ex hypothesi* deals with the situation where there are legal proceedings, under The Hague Abduction Convention, the discussion of the right to participate will be limited to the context of legal proceedings.

[38] The Rotlevy Committee on Children's Rights, Report of the Sub-Committee on the Child and his Family, www.justice.gov.il/NR/rdonlyres/6CB85B58-07BF-496E-A073-2CC87F9C67D4/0/HayeledVeamishpaha.pdf (Hebrew) 81 (Rotlevy Child and Family Sub-Committee).

[39] Fortin (n 5) 234.

[40] P Parkinson and J Cashmore, *The Voice of a Child in Family Law Disputes* (Oxford, Oxford University Press, 2008) 199.

[41] Fortin (n 5) 234.

[42] Thus, even young children have a right to express their view, but it is necessary to adapt the method of hearing them to their abilities, Rotlevy Child and Family Sub-Committee (n 38), 93–95.

[43] Parkinson and Cashmore (n 40) 197.

to disputes which had not occurred to the adults.[44] Furthermore, most children do want to be consulted about arrangements which will have a major impact on their lives and feel dissatisfied and hurt when they are excluded from decision-making.[45]

In addition, it has been suggested that the right to participation contributes to the development of children into emotionally healthy, capable and responsible adults. Allowing the child to participate in and influence decisions relating to him is likely to strengthen his feeling of individuality, increase his self-confidence and boost his self-image. Also, participating in decision-making is a valuable learning experience in itself, provided of course that the mode of participation is suitable for the child's age and level of maturity, in accordance with the principle of the evolving capacities of the child.[46]

It should be emphasised that the child's right to express his views in relation to proceedings concerning him should be seen as 'an independent right' without any connection to the question of whether the court accepts his views or what weight the court attaches to those views. The UNICEF Implementation Handbook states that the right is not instrumental and is not simply designed to serve the needs of the legal system.[47] Thus, the purpose of hearing the child is not only to assist the court in determining what is in the child's best interests or, in the abduction context, whether the exception in Article 13(2) of the Hague Convention is established. Rather, the right exists in order to enable the child to express his views and feelings even when what he says does not add to the knowledge or information in the hands of the decision-maker.[48]

Nevertheless, it is clear that the increased participation of the child in the proceedings is likely to facilitate a more informed decision. Furthermore, children who feel that their views have been taken into account are more likely to come to terms with and co-operate in implementing the decision, even if it is not in accordance with their wishes.[49]

Finally, despite the overall benefits of participation, the potential harm which may be caused to children by becoming involved in the dispute between their parents cannot be ignored. However, risk of harm should not be used as an excuse for diluting the aims of Article 12,[50] but rather should be relevant in determining the method and extent of the child's participation. In other words, children need to be protected 'in participation' and not 'from participation'.[51]

ii Implementation of the Right to be Heard

The main debate concerns how the child should be heard. Neither the CRC itself nor subsequent international instruments which require children to be consulted and given an

---

[44] C Smart, 'Children's Narratives of Post-Divorce Family Life: From Individual Experience to an Ethical Disposition' (2006) 54 *The Sociological Review* 155; F Raitt, 'Hearing Children in Family Law Proceedings: Can Judges Make a Difference?' (2007) 19 *Child and Family Law Quarterly* 204, 214.

[45] Smart ibid; Raitt ibid; P Parkinson and J Cashmore, 'What Responsibility do Courts Have to Hear Children' (2007) 15 *International Journal of Children's Rights* 47.

[46] Art 5 of the CRC.

[47] R Hodgkin and P Newell, *UNICEF Implementation Handbook for the Convention on the Rights of the Child* (Geneva, UNICEF, 1998).

[48] Indeed, the 'Guidelines for Judges Meeting Children who are subject to Family Proceedings' published by the English Family Justice Council and approved by the President of the Family Division in a Practice Note of April 2010 (www.fnf.org.uk/downloads/Guidelines_for_Judges_Meeting_Children.pdf) expressly state (para 5) that the purpose of the meeting is to benefit the child and not for the purpose of gathering evidence.

[49] Parkinson and Cashmore (n 40) 9.

[50] Fortin (n 5) 236.

[51] Parkinson and Cashmore (n 40) 219.

opportunity to express their views proscribe a particular method by which this should be done.[52]

The prevailing practice in common law systems is for the child to be interviewed by a social welfare professional who will write a report for the court.[53] Whilst judges do have discretion to interview the child themselves, this is not routine practice,[54] although it is becoming more common in some jurisdictions.[55] In contrast, it is more common in civil law countries for the child to be heard directly by the judge who is making the decision.[56] A number of commentators have argued that this indirect method of being heard does not give adequate recognition to the child's right to participate in the proceedings.[57] In particular, it is claimed that true participation in decision-making involves access to the ultimate decision-maker and that the child's right to be treated as an individual is only fully realised if he is given the opportunity to be heard directly by the judge.[58]

The arguments for and against hearing the child directly in Abduction Convention cases will be considered in detail in chapter 14. However, it should be pointed out that the issue of meaningful participation of children in proceedings affecting them is wider and more complex than the question of whether they talk to a judge or welfare professional. In particular, children need to be provided with information appropriate to their age and to be provided with advice and support in relation to their right to be heard.[59] They should also be informed of the decision directly by the court or welfare officer and not hear about it second hand from one of their parents.[60]

Finally, it should be mentioned that there are cases where the only way to ensure that the child's voice is properly heard by the court is to order separate legal representation for the child. The scope and function of separate legal representation for children in Abduction Convention proceedings will be discussed in chapter 15.

---

[52] See Council Regulation (EC) No 2201/2003 of 27 November 2003 concerning jurisdiction and the recognition and enforcement of judgments in matrimonial matters and matters of parental responsibility ('Brussels II bis Regulation') [2003] OJ L, 338/1-29, Art 11 and the European Convention on the Exercise of Children's Rights, Art 3(a). Whilst the latter does require the court to consult the child in person in appropriate cases, this can be done through some other person or body (Art 6(b)). For a survey of different methods of child participation in a number of jurisdictions, see N Taylor et al (n 36).

[53] F Raitt, 'Judicial Discretion and Methods of Ascertaining the Views of a Child' (2004) 16 *Family Law Quarterly* 151.

[54] ibid; for a comprehensive study of ways of hearing children in Australia, see Parkinson and Cashmore (n 40).

[55] eg, Guidelines for Judges Meeting Children who are subject to Family Proceedings (n 48).

[56] See survey of practice in different countries in ch 14 at II B.

[57] eg, F Raitt, 'Hearing Children in Family Law Proceedings' (n 44) 204. R Schuz, 'The Voice of the Child in the Israeli Family Court' in B Atkin (ed), *International Survey of Family Law 2008 Edition* (Bristol, Jordan Publishing Limited, 2008) 185; Judge M Potter, 'The Voice of the Child: Children's Rights in Family Proceedings' (2008) *Family in Law Review* 2, 15, www.mishpat.ac.il/files/650/2911/3605/3606.pdf.

[58] C Piper, 'Barriers to Seeing and Hearing Children in Private Law Proceedings' (1999) 26 *Family Law* 394, comments that otherwise there is a danger of 'real children being invisible'.

[59] ibid; Lowe and Murch, 'Children's Participation' (n 35); Rotlevy Child and Family Sub Committee (n 38) recommended that an accompanying adult, usually a specially trained social worker, should be assigned to every child involved in proceedings.

[60] As provided for by Regulation 258(33)10 of the Israeli Regulations, appended to T Morag, D Rivkin and Y Sorek, 'Child Participation in the Family Courts – Lessons from the Israeli Pilot Project' (2012) 26 *International Journal on Law Policy and the Family* 1. See also comment of Thorpe LJ in *AJJ v JJ* [2011] EWCA Civ 1448 [46], that the judge is the best person to communicate the return decision to the child and General Comment No 12 (n 30), para 45.

iii Implementation of the Child's Right to Have Appropriate Weight Attached to his Wishes

While the principle enshrined in Article 12(1) of the CRC that appropriate weight should be given to the views of a child is clearly of the utmost importance, in practical terms the provision seems to be of limited value because it does not provide any guidance as to the relative weight to be ascribed to the views of the child vis-à-vis those other factors and thus considerable discretion is left to the individual judge.[61]

Van Bueren[62] and Fortin[63] point out that active participation should not be confused with self-determination. However, it may be argued that whilst it is clear that Article 12 does not provide children with complete autonomy to make decisions, it is correct and helpful to talk about the provision of a degree of autonomy, the measure of which will vary in accordance with the child's age and maturity, the nature of the decision and the implications thereof. Thus, in respect to certain types of matters, the weight to be given to the child's wishes is so great that in effect he has the right to decide for himself. Indeed, it would seem that the spirit of Article 12 and the CRC as a whole requires that where a child is old and mature enough to understand the implications of the decision, his views should be followed unless there are very good reasons to the contrary. Accordingly, throughout the book the terms 'degree of autonomy' and 'attaching appropriate weight to the child's wishes' will be used interchangeably.

One of the thorniest problems facing children's rights theorists is what happens when a child's wishes conflict with his welfare. Freeman's attempts at reconciliation, which he labels 'liberal paternalism', would appear to be one of the most acceptable and authoritative.[64] In his view, interventions in children's lives are justified where they are to protect them from irrational actions, which should be defined as actions that would undermine future life choices or impair interests in an irreversible way. However, he and others emphasise the need to limit paternalism to a minimum.[65]

Two additional dimensions are added to this dilemma in Abduction Convention cases. Firstly, the Abduction Convention is based on the premise that immediate return best promotes the welfare of the child. Thus, it may be assumed that the child's objection to return conflicts with his welfare, even where this is not necessarily true. Secondly, the child's objection to return appears to conflict with the Convention policy of immediate return of abducted children. The way in which courts have handled the inherent conflict between the right of the child to have appropriate weight given to his views and the desire to protect children from international child abduction will be examined critically in chapter 12.

---

[61] Though, as Van Bueren (n 23) 136 points out, the discretion is not unfettered because account has to be taken of both the child's age and degree of maturity. For criticism of interpreting this provision in a way which dilutes the child's participation rights, see Fortin (n 5) 43.

[62] Van Bueren ibid 138.

[63] Fortin (n 5) 236.

[64] MDA Freeman, *The Moral Status of Children: Essays on the Rights of the Child* (Dordecht, Martinus Nijhoff, 1997) 95–99.

[65] ibid; J Eekelaar, 'Interests of the Child and the Child's Wishes: The Role of Dynamic Self-Determinism' in P Alston (ed), *The Best Interests of the Child* (Oxford, Clarendon Press,1994); and also Fortin (n 5) 28.

D The Child's Right to Protection and to Survival and Development

Article 3(2) of the CRC provides:

> States Parties undertake to ensure the child such protection and care as is necessary for his or her wellbeing, taking into account the rights and duties of his or her parents, legal guardians, or other individuals legally responsible for him or her, and, to this end, shall take all appropriate legislative and administrative measures.

Article 6 provides: '1. States Parties recognize that every child has the inherent right to life. 2. States Parties shall ensure to the maximum extent possible the survival and development of the child.'

These provisions give clear recognition to the protection rights of the child. Whilst Article 3(2) was primarily designed to require States to provide care for children who were in need of care, it seems wide enough to impose an obligation on States not to make decisions which prevent a child from receiving the protection and care which is necessary for his well-being. It could be argued that returning a child in circumstances which would put him or the returning parent at risk or which would involve separation from his primary carer, are inconsistent with this obligation.

Similarly, it could be argued that return in such circumstances would violate the child's right to development, which has been interpreted to mean his right to proper development. In particular, the brain research referred to in an earlier chapter[66] shows that traumatic events in infanthood, such as separation from the primary care-taker, can have irreversible effects on the child's development.

It might be thought that these provisions do not add anything to the principle of the best interests of the child in Article 3 of the Convention. In a sense, this is true because a decision which does not protect the child's well-being will not be treating his best interests as a primary consideration. However, there may be certain advantages in invoking these child protection provisions, rather than Article 3. This is because the Abduction Convention mechanism does not allow for taking the best interests of the particular child into account. Thus, as will be seen below,[67] reliance on Article 3 has been seen as letting in the best interests standard 'through the back-door'; whereas reliance on the child's rights to protection and development does not suffer from this disadvantage. However, it must be borne in mind that these protection rights are not absolute. The State's obligation under Article 3(2) is subject to the rights and duties of the parents, which would seem to include the custody rights of the left-behind parent in abduction cases. The right to development is qualified by the words 'to the maximum extent possible', but this should not be a problem, since it is 'possible' not to return the child where this will damage his development.

E The Child's Right to Contact with his Parents

The importance for the child in maintaining regular and direct contact with both of his parents,[68] which clearly lies at the heart of the Abduction Convention, is widely recog-

---

[66] In ch 3 at II D.
[67] See ch 11.
[68] For the purposes of this book, this right will be considered to be synonymous with the right to a meaningful relationship with both parents.

nised.[69] However, the concept that contact between the child and his parents is primarily the right of the child rather than that of his parents,[70] or at least an equal right of the both of them, does not yet appear to have been widely accepted.[71] In particular, the ECtHR sees contact disputes in terms of adults' rights and not children's rights.[72] Rather, children's interests are referred to as a justification for infringing adults' rights, where contact is not in the child's best interests.[73] However, it is important to treat contact as a right of the child, and not only as an aspect of his interests, in order to place the focus firmly on the child. In particular, the frequency and logistics of the contact should be child-orientated rather than adult-orientated.[74]

The right of the child to maintain contact with both parents appears in three forms in the CRC. Article 7 provides the child with the right 'as far as possible to be cared for by his or her parents'. Article 9 demands that State parties 'respect the right of the child who is separated from one or both parents to maintain personal relations and direct contact with both parents on a regular basis, except if it is contrary to the child's best interests'.[75] Article 10(2) enjoins States to allow children and their parents to leave and enter their country for the purpose of maintaining contact with each other.

One explanation for the apparent reluctance to treat contact as a right of the child, despite the clear wording of the CRC, might be that in practice the right is not enforced against a parent who does not maintain contact[76] and such enforcement seems to be neither practicable[77] nor desirable.[78] However, lack of enforceability is not a good reason for denying the existence of the right in the first place. Indeed, the very use of rights talk might in the long run help parents to understand that they have a duty to maintain a relationship with their children.[79]

---

[69] Fortin (n 5) 493, citing inter alia the European Convention on Contact Concerning Children.

[70] For early recognition of this, see Israeli case of HC 40/63 *Lawrence v The Head of the Enforcement Agency*, 17 PD 1709, 1717.

[71] In England, whilst reference to the contact as the right of the child dates back to *M v M* [1973] 2 All ER 81 (see also *Re S (Minors: Access)* [1990] 2 FLR 166, and *Re R (A Minor) (Contact)* [1993] 2 FLR 762, 767 and *Re F* [1993] 2 FLR 830), the language of children's rights to justify decisions awarding contact with their fathers has now gradually died out, see Fortin (n 5) 493 and A Bainham, 'Contact as a Fundamental Right' (1995) 54 *Cambridge Law Journal* 255. In the US, visitation is treated as a parental right, A Blecher-Prigat, 'Rethinking Visitation: From a Parental to a Relational Right' (2009) 16 *Duke Journal of Gender Law & Policy* 1, 2; *cf* Australian Family Law Act 1975, s 60B(2) which refers specifically to the child's 'right to spend time on a regular basis with, and communicate on a regular basis with both their parents' except where that would be contrary to the children's best interests and declaration in Article 24 § 2 of the European Union's Charter of Fundamental Rights that '[e]very child shall have the right to maintain on a regular basis a personal relationship and direct contact with both his or her parents, unless that is contrary to his or her interests'.

[72] Fortin (n 5) 66, citing *Yousef v Netherlands* [2003] 1 FLR 210; Bainham ibid 257–58.

[73] Fortin (n 5) 493.

[74] For research evidence showing that shared parenting which is child-oriented is more likely to be successful, see C Smart, 'Equal Shares: Rights for Fathers or Recognition for Children?' (2004) 24 *Critical Social Policy* 484.

[75] This formulation seems to restrict the right to cases where the child has already formed a relationship with the parent in question, R Bailey-Harris, J Barron and J Pearce, 'From Utility to Rights? The Presumption of Contact in Practice' (1999) 13 *International Journal of Law, Policy and the Family* 111, 117. However, this is unlikely to be a problem in Abduction Convention cases since where there is no such relationship, the left-behind parents are unlikely to have been exercising rights of custody.

[76] Parkinson and Cashmore (n 40) 12; Bainham, 'Contact as a Fundamental Right' (n 71) 258.

[77] Over and above requiring the parent who does not turn up for visitation to reimburse child-care costs incurred by the custodial parent as a result thereof, Y Mazeh, 'Enforcement of Visitation Rights' (2001) 51 *Hapraklit* 227 (Hebrew).

[78] Because contact under duress is unlikely to benefit the child, Mazah ibid.

[79] *cf* C Smart and B Neale, 'Arguments against Virtue: Must Contact be Enforced?' (1997) 28 *Family Law* 332, 336 who suggest that lack of enforcement effectively turns the child's right into that of the father.

Nonetheless, it must be remembered that the child's right to contact with his parents is not absolute. Thus, care must be taken to ensure that the realisation of the right to contact does not violate other rights of the child, in particular his right to have his well-being protected, his right to proper development and his right to have his best interests treated as a primary consideration. In cases where contact involves a potential risk to the child's physical safety or psychological welfare, these other rights of the child will override his right to contact.[80] It might have been expected that viewing contact as the right of the child would encourage the court to take claims that contact is not in the best interests of the child more seriously,[81] than where the right is seen as a parental right.[82] Yet, the statutory recognition of the right of the child to contact in Australia[83] has not prevented the routine ordering of contact at interim hearings, without taking into consideration the child's best interests or other rights.[84] However, this may simply show that the rhetoric of children's rights has not been fully internalised by the Australian legal system[85] and so should not be seen as a reason not to recognise contact as the right of the child. Nonetheless, it might seem wise to include in statutory provisions recognising the child's right to contact, express provision that the child has a right to be protected from harm and so contact should not be ordered where this would be likely to cause harm to the child. This issue is relevant to the interpretation of the risk of harm exception in the Abduction Convention.[86]

Viewing contact as the right of the child raises the question as to whether a sufficiently mature child is entitled to waive this right where he is opposed to contact. Provided that the child's views are genuinely his own, and not the result of incitement by the other parent,[87] there is a strong argument for saying that contact should not be enforced on a child against his wishes, even where the parent has a justifiable claim to contact.[88] Indeed, it is questionable whether coerced contact will be of any real benefit to the child or even to the parent.[89] This issue is particularly pertinent to the interpretation of the child objection exception in the Abduction Convention.

---

[80] For a discussion of the growing recognition of the dangers of contact in cases where there has been a history of domestic violence, see Fortin (n 5) 502–07.

[81] In relation to the extreme difficulty in rebutting the contact presumption, see Fortin (n 5) 496–97; Blecher-Prigat (n 71) 3–4.

[82] Indeed, it may be suggested that the strength of the presumption in favour of contact is directly related to the political pressure exerted by father's groups, Fortin ibid 496.

[83] See n 71.

[84] R Graycar, 'Family Law Reform in Australia or Frozen Chooks Revisited Again?' (2012) 13 *Theoretical Inquiries in Law* 241, 252. The situation seems to have been exacerbated by later 2006 reform which requires the court to consider the possibility of the child sharing equal time with each parent. ibid 256–57 and L Young, Reflections on the Shared Parenting Experience in W Atkin (ed), *2012 International Survey of Family Law* (Family Law, 2012) 1 (discussing research into the impact of the 2006 reforms and the later 2011 reforms).

[85] This may have been because despite the language of children's rights, the reform of the law had really been motivated by the lobbying of fathers' groups, Graycar ibid 244 and 253.

[86] See ch 11.

[87] However, care has to be taken not to assume that the child's objection is necessarily the result of incitement. See discussion in ch 3 at II F and ch 12 at II Biib.

[88] Parkinson and Cashmore (n 40) 12; *cf* Mazeh (n 77).

[89] It will often be more worthwhile for the parent to continue to show his love for the child unilaterally by sending him messages and birthday presents etcetera. The author has anecdotal evidence of cases where this approach has, after a period of time, led to the rehabilitation of the relationship between the parent and the child. In some cases it may be appropriate for the child, depending on his age, to receive psychological or other therapy.

F The Child's Right to Identity

Although the child's right to identity is not expressly recognised in the CRC, it has been argued that the CRC as a whole supports the recognition of such a right in the sense of a right to protection of ties meaningful to the child.[90] The right to identity also supports the child's right to contact with his parents, at least where the child has a significant relationship with them. Ronen explains that the identity to be protected is a child-constructed identity and that culture and race are relevant to the extent that they are meaningful to the child and not to the extent dictated by 'ethnocentric identity politics',[91] although it might be added that children may be influenced by the perceptions of the society in which they live.

Identity is potentially relevant in all abduction cases since the child has been uprooted from the social and cultural milieu in which his identity was being constructed, even if he had not been living there for long. However, in order to determine to what extent his right to identity requires return, it is necessary to assess the meaningfulness of his ties with the country of origin from his perspective. As will be seen below, this issue is relevant to the determination of the child's habitual residence,[92] to the interpretation of being settled for the purposes of the defence in Article 12(2)[93] and to the weight to be given to the views of the child.[94]

III Rights of Parents

A Introduction

In the course of the analysis in this book, reference will be made to rights to which parents are entitled as human beings, such as the right to freedom of movement, and rights to which parents are entitled in relation to their children. The former do not need any specific introduction. Thus, this section will concentrate on the latter category of rights, which will be called parental rights.

As already seen, one of the objectives of the Abduction Convention is to ensure that rights of custody and access under the law of one Contracting State are respected in other Contracting States. Whilst, in theory, rights of access could refer to rights of children, it is clear that the reference here is to rights of parents. In many cases, realisation of these rights of custody or access will in fact be giving effect to the rights of the child and in particular his right to contact with both of his parents, discussed above. However, this will not invariably be so. Thus, there may be cases where the rights of the child clash with those of his parents. Furthermore, the current author's suggestion that breach of the right of the child to contact with both of his parents should be the trigger for the operation of the mandatory

---

[90] Y Ronen, 'Redefining the Child's Right to Identity' (2004) 18 *International Journal of Law, Policy and the Family* 147, 160.
[91] ibid 173–74.
[92] See ch 8.
[93] See ch 9.
[94] See ch 12.

return mechanism[95] would give preference to the rights of children. In order to gain a wider perspective about clashes between the rights of children and their parents in disputes concerning children, and in particular disputes concerning contact with children, it is appropriate to consider briefly the status and scope of parental rights in modern day jurisprudence and the various approaches for resolving conflicts between parental rights and the rights and interests of children.

B The Status of Parental Rights

At first, the increased recognition of children's rights was perceived as inevitably involving an 'eclipse of parental rights'.[96] Perhaps the clearest and most explicit example of the decline of the traditional universal approach to parental rights is the important dictum in the renowned House of Lords decision in *Gillick v West Norfolk and Wisbech Health Authority*[97] that parental rights only exist insofar as they were necessary for the protection of the children and that 'the parental right yields to the child's right to make his own decisions when he reaches sufficient understanding and intelligence to be capable of making up his own mind on the matter requiring decision'.[98] Thus, as children grow older and are capable of acting independently, the rights of their parents diminish accordingly.[99] In Israel, the Rotlevy Committee has recommended that the concept of parental rights be abolished as it is inconsistent with the recognition that children had rights.[100]

Nonetheless, at least in Europe, parental rights have been 'resurrected' in the form of human rights. In particular, the right to family life, entrenched in Article 8 of the ECHR, has been interpreted in such a way so as to give rights to parents in relation to their children.[101] Interference with those rights, whether by the State, the other parent or any other individual, will give rise to a remedy under that Convention, subject to the important qualification in Article 8(2).[102]

In the US, the rights of parents to prevent interference by the State in the way in which they bring up their children, for example by terminating their parental rights[103] or not respecting their choice of education,[104] are treated as constitutional rights and thus entitled to due process and other constitutional safeguards. Moreover, whilst it is not clear that

---

[95] See R Schuz, 'The Hague Child Abduction Convention and Children's Rights' (2002) 12 *Transnational Law and Contemporary Problems* 396, 408 and ch 7 at IV E.

[96] See J Eekelaar, 'The Eclipse of Parental Rights' (1986) 102 *Law Quarterly Review* 4; J Eekelaar, 'The Emergence of Children's Rights' (1986) 6 *Oxford Journal of Legal Studies* 161; KT Bartlee, 'Re-Expressing Parenthood' (1988) 98 *Yale Law Journal* 293.

[97] *Gillick v West Norfolk and Wisbech Health Authority* [1986] 1 AC 112. The *ratio* of the decision seems to be that a doctor could give contraceptives to a girl under the age of 16 whom (s)he believed to be competent without her parents knowledge or consent, although wherever possible this should be sought.

[98] ibid, 186.

[99] Eekelaar, 'The Eclipse of Parental Rights' (n 96); Fortin (n 5) 73; *cf* A Bainham, *Children and the Modern Law*, 3rd edn (Bristol, Jordan Publishing Limited, 2005) 102.

[100] Rotlevy Child and Family Sub-Committee (n 38).

[101] eg, decision in *Nielsen v Denmark* (1988) 1 EHRR 175, discussed by Fortin (n 5) 101–02.

[102] '... except such as is in accordance with the law and is necessary in a democratic society in the interests of national security, public safety or the economic well-being of the country, for the prevention of disorder or crime, for the protection of health or morals, or for the protection of the rights and freedoms of others'.

[103] *Santosky v Kramer* 455 US (1982).

[104] *Wisconsin v Yoder* 406 US 205, 234 (1972); Similarly, in Israel, some courts have recognised parents' constitutional rights to make certain decisions concerning their children, such as in relation to religious education, CA 2266/93 *Ploni (Child) v Ploni* PD 49(1) 121.

parental visitation rights are entitled to constitutional protection,[105] their strength is not in dispute.[106]

C The Scope of Parental Rights

Dickens, writing before the *Gillick* case, distinguishes between parental rights in relation to provision of the basic necessities of life and those where the parents have a degree of discretion.[107] In relation to the former, the parents clearly have an absolute duty and thus any rights exist only to enable them to carry out those duties and therefore are not really independent rights at all.[108] In relation to the latter, the parents do not have any duty and thus their freedom of choice may be expressed as a right; for example, the right to bring their children up in any religion or none at all; the right to choose the type of formal education the child will receive within those permitted by the State and the right to choose what extra-curricular activities, if any, the child will participate in.

However, at least under Hohfeld's analysis of legal rights, for a right to exist there must be a correlative duty. Dickens argues that in the case of parental rights, the correlative duty is that of others 'to permit or . . . to forbear from preventing' parents from discharging their duties and exercising the discretions outlined above as they choose.[109] In other words, there is a duty not to interfere in the way that parents choose to bring up their children, provided that this complies with the basic standards required by the law.

Bainham[110] suggests that, at least in the UK, the accuracy of this analysis depends on who the 'others' are. While he accepts that parents do have such rights viz-a-viz the State,[111] he doubts whether this is the case viz-a-viz courts, other third parties[112] or in relation to the child him/herself. In all these situations, the interests of the parents will only be protected insofar as they are consistent with the welfare of the child.[113] Commentators suggest that this is still the prevailing situation in the UK, despite increasing criticism of the welfare principle[114] and despite the enactment of the ECHR.[115] Nonetheless, there are countries in which rights of competent parents will automatically trump those of third parties.[116]

---

[105] For an argument in favour, see D Chipman and M Rush, 'The Necessity of "Right to Travel" Analysis in Custodial Parent Relocation Cases' (2010) 10 *Wyoming L Rev* 267, 287.
[106] Blecher-Prigat (n 71) 5.
[107] BM Dickens, 'The Modern Function and Limits of Parental Rights' (1981) 97 *Law Quarterly Review* 462.
[108] eg, the right to consent to essential medical treatment (at least in relation to a non-competent child).
[109] Dickens (n 107).
[110] A Bainham, *Children and the Modern Law* (n 99) 120.
[111] Because State interference is only permitted where the standard defined in the Children Act 1989, s 31(2) is satisfied.
[112] See *J v C* (n 20) and confirmed more recently in *Re KD (A Minor) (Ward: Termination of Access)* [1988] AC 806.
[113] S Choudhry and H Fenwick, 'Taking the Rights of Parents and Children Seriously: Confronting the Welfare Principle under the Human Rights Act' (2005) 25 *Oxford Journal of Legal Studies* 453. This is well illustrated by the quote which they bring from *Re O (Contact: Imposition of Conditions)* [1995] 2 FLR 124, 128: 'It cannot be emphasized too strongly that the court is concerned with the interests of the mother and the father only in so far as they bear on the welfare of the child.'
[114] J Eekelaar, 'Beyond the Welfare Principle' (2002) 12 *Child & Family Law Quarterly* 237; R van Krieken, 'The "Best Interests of the Child" and Parental Separation: On the "Civilizing of Parents"' (2005) 68 *MLR* 25.
[115] UK courts have argued that the difference between the ECHR approach and the welfare principle is semantic. See, in particular, *Re KD* (n 112) 812 (Lord Templeman) and 815 (Lord Oliver); *Re B (A Minor) (Respondent)* [2001] UKHL 70 [31] (Lord Nicholls). For a summary of the criticism of this approach, see Fortin (n 5) 294–97.
[116] *Re Clausen* (n 20) and in Israel, *Consulos v Torjeman* (n 20) (a two-year-old child who had been adopted bona fide by Israeli parents was returned to biological parents in Brazil from whom she had been abducted by

McCall Smith categorises parental rights differently.[117] He distinguishes between 'child-centred' and 'parent-centred' parental rights. The former are exercised predominantly for the benefit of the child[118] and the latter predominantly for the benefit of the parent.[119] Thus, this analysis recognises that the parents have independent interests which are protected by the law.[120] It is suggested that such an approach is consistent with modern thinking about human rights, as reflected in the ECHR[121] and other human rights instruments.[122] This approach is not inconsistent with recognition of the rights of children, but acknowledges that there are some rights of parents which are based on the independent interests of the parents and do not therefore automatically terminate as the child matures, as do 'child-centred' parental rights.

The 'parent-centred right' which is most relevant in the Abduction Convention context is the right of each parent to continuing direct contact with the child.[123] This right is separate and distinct from the child's own right to have contact with both of his parents. A parent's right to contact has been recognised as part of the right to family life, protected by Article 8 of the ECHR.[124]

Of course, in the abduction scenario, there will inevitably be a conflict between the rights of the two parents. If the child is not returned, then there is a violation of the left-behind's right to family life. However, if the child does return alone and the abductor stays in the country of refuge, then the return order is effectively interference with her right to contact with the child.[125] Similarly, whether or not an order of return is made, there will usually be a violation of the child's right to contact with one of his parents. However, it is quite likely that one of the two options will be more consistent with the child's other rights, such as the right to be protected from harm or his participation rights. In such a situation, the interests and rights of the child will inevitably clash to some extent with those of one of his parents.[126] There are various approaches to resolving such clashes.

D Conflicts between Children's Rights and Parental Rights

As noted above, the ECtHR has avoided directly addressing potential conflicts between the child's right to family life and that of his parents. The main reason for this is that, whilst

criminals involved in the trafficking of children. Unfortunately, as revealed in the Israeli press in 2004, the child was brought up in terrible conditions without education and at the age of 17 already had two children by different men who deserted her, www.nrg.co.il/online/archive/ART/655/873.html (Hebrew).

[117] A McCall Smith 'Is Anything Left of Parental Rights?' in E Sutherland and A McCall Smith (ed) *Family Rights, Family Law and Medical Advice* (Edinburgh, Edinburgh University Press, 1990).
[118] Examples are the right to authorise medical treatment and the right to represent the child.
[119] Examples are the right to maintain contact with the child and the right to choose what type of education the child receives (within the limits allowed by the law) and in particular what, if any, religious education.
[120] Similarly, see Israeli judges' comments that parents' rights are not merely derived from their duties (FamA (Dist TA) 1125/99 *DL v NCZ* Nevo, 28 May 2000 and that parents are not simply 'silent chattels' CA (SC) 1/81 *Nagar v Nagar* PD 38(1) 365, 412.
[121] See generally ch 1 at II C and discussion below.
[122] eg, the Israeli Basic Law: Dignity and Freedom of Man.
[123] Whereas the right to determine where the child lives would seem to be largely a 'child-centred' right.
[124] In the Matter of *Re D (Intractable Contact Dispute: Publicity)* [2004] 1 FLR 1226; *Elsholz v Germany* [2000] 2 FLR 486.
[125] eg Decision of the Grand Chamber of the ECtHR in *Neulinger and Shuruk v Switzerland* (n 21).
[126] J Herring, 'The Human Rights Act and the Welfare Principle in Family Law – Conflicting or Complementary?' (1999) 11 *Child & Family Law Quarterly* 223 argues that an analysis involving a clash of rights is inappropriate because 'this image is quite different from the ideal of co-operation hoped for in families, and is at odds with how most families see themselves'.

paying lip-service to the right of the child to contact with his parents, that Court has in practice seen contact as a right of the parents and referred to the child's interests as a justification for interference with this right under Article 8(2) of the ECHR.[127] This approach has been criticised by commentators who argue that express recognition should be given to the child's right to family life and that his rights should be balanced with those of his parents.[128]

Nonetheless, in assessing children's interests for the purposes of Article 8(2), the ECtHR has had to balance the interests of children against those of parents,[129] and has recognised that the interests of children may override those of parents.[130] If this is the case when children's rights are not treated as independent rights which clash with those of one parent, then a fortiori it will be the case if they are so recognised. In particular, since either solution will involve a violation of one party's rights, the burden of proof ought no longer to be on the party seeking to justify the interference with the parental right. Rather, there ought to be a more even-handed and express analysis of the implications for each party of violation of his rights.[131]

As mentioned above, in abduction cases, as well as other types of cases, there will invariably be a conflict between the respective rights of the two parents, as well as between the rights of the child and one of his parents. An approach which attempts to balance the rights of the three parties involved, sometimes called parallel analysis,[132] will enable consideration to be given to the independent interests of all the parties.[133] Whilst the interests of one parent will inevitably coincide with that of the child and special weight will be given to the interests of the child, it will also be necessary to examine the effect of realising the right of the other parent on the child, in comparison with the effect on that parent of interference with his rights. Where the effect on the child and the parent whose interests corresponds with his is slight and the detriment to the other parent great, that other parent's right might prevail.[134] It has been argued that the parallel analysis approach will enable a more transparent assessment of the respective interests of all the parties involved than the traditional welfare approach, without prejudicing children and that the need to consider the wider implications of the various options more carefully will lead to better quality decision-making.[135]

Accordingly, when analysing the Abduction Convention and the way in which it has been interpreted and applied, consistency with parental rights will be considered as well as consistency with the rights of the child. This analysis does not purport to prejudge the relative weight which should be given to the respective rights, but rather to assess the extent to which the scheme and implementation of the Convention reflect these rights.

---

[127] Fortin (n 5) 66. See also *Neulinger and Shuruk v Switzerland* (n 21) [151], where the Grand Chamber seems to have held that the interference in the rights of the father could be justified on the basis of the best interests of the child, but that the interference in the mother's Art 8 rights, which would be caused if she were forced to return to Israel, could not be justified. For an analysis of this decision, see ch 11 at IV E and F.
[128] eg, Choudhry and Fenwick, 'Taking the Rights' (n 113).
[129] *Johansen v Norway* [1997] 23 EHRR 134.
[130] *Sahin v Germany* [GC] App no 30943/96 (ECHR 2003-VIII) s 66.
[131] Choudhry and Fenwick, 'Taking the Rights' (n 113).
[132] ibid.
[133] This should include the legitimate interests of the primary carer, which might be affected, for example, by awarding or increasing contact with the non-residential parent. See eg R Dingwall, D Greatbatch and L Ruggerone, 'Gender and Interaction in Divorce Mediation'(1998) 15 *Mediation Quarterly* 277, 280–81; and the prison example given by Herring, 'The Human Rights Act' (n 126) 232.
[134] Choudhry and Fenwick (n 113).
[135] ibid; Eekelaar, 'Beyond the Welfare Principle' (n 114) 242.

IV Private International Law Principles

A The Abduction Convention and Private International Law

It should be pointed out from the outset that the novelty of the Abduction Convention, and perhaps also its success, lies in the fact that it eschewed traditional private international law remedies.[136] However, this does not mean that it is inappropriate to analyse the extent to which the Abduction Convention and its implementation are consistent with private international law principles. Indeed, while the main mechanism of the Convention is the restoration of the *status quo ante*, the Convention does indirectly create various private international law rules. Thus, the rule forbidding the requested State from exercising any jurisdiction it has to determine the merits of the custody dispute, where it has received notice of a wrongful removal or retention,[137] effectively confers exclusive jurisdiction on the State of habitual residence in matters concerning the custody of children.[138] Similarly, whilst the Convention does not purport to provide a choice of law rule[139] for determining the merits of a custody dispute,[140] it does provide a choice of law rule for determining whether there has been a breach of custody rights viz the law of the habitual residence.[141] Although this is only a narrow issue, it is in fact critical because if there has been no breach of custody rights, the removal is not wrongful, and so the return provisions of the Abduction Convention do not apply. Finally, the Abduction Convention expressly provides for the recognition of judicial decisions relating to rights of custody[142] made by the State of habitual residence[143] and forbids reliance on decisions relating to custody given by other States, which would otherwise be recognised, where this would lead to refusal to return.[144] Thus, it can be seen that habitual residence has been chosen as the connecting factor for all three types of private international law rules.

Furthermore, inherent in these rules are two classic methodological problems relating to the system of choice of law, in relation to which there are no universally accepted solutions. The first problem arises in relation to application of the law of habitual residence for the purpose of determining whether custody rights existed at the time of the removal or reten-

---

[136] Beaumont and McEleavy, *The Hague Convention on International Child Abduction* (Oxford, Oxford University Press, 1999) 21. The reference is to the fact that the Convention does not attempt to harmonise jurisdiction rules or to provide for the recognition and enforcement of foreign judgments as did previous Hague Conventions in this field and as does the later 1996 Child Protection Convention (see ch 1 at II E).

[137] Unless and until return is refused under the Convention, see Art 16.

[138] See Perez-Vera Report (n 17), para 16.

[139] See A Dyer, *Report On International Child Abduction By One Parent Legal Kidnapping*, Preliminary Document No 1, Aug 1978, in *Hague Conference On Private International Law*, 3 Actes Et Documents De Laquatorzième Session (Child Abduction) (1980) 39–40.

[140] Compare Arts 15–22 of the 1996 Child Protection Convention, which does provide such choice of law rules.

[141] Art 3. In relation to the breach of custody rights, see generally ch 7.

[142] This term would seem to be wide enough to cover not only decisions defining the scope of the custody or access rights of each of the parents and other relevant parties, but also decisions which effectively determine that a parent has custody rights, such as a decision determining paternity or awarding parental responsibility to an unmarried father or to the intended mother in cases of surrogacy (as in *W v H (Children) (Surrogacy: Habitual Residence)* [2002] All ER (D) 222).

[143] Art 3; The Perez-Vera Report (n 17), para 69 states that this includes decisions of a third State which are recognised by the habitual residence.

[144] Art 17. The scope of this section will be discussed in ch 7 at IV Gii.

tion, which were breached thereby. Are we to apply only the domestic family law rules of the country of the habitual residence or are we to apply the private international law rules of that law, which may lead to the application of the domestic rules of another legal system? The solution to this problem depends upon whether, and in what form, we adopt the doctrine of *renvoi*, which includes reference to the private international law rules of the applicable law. The second problem is known as the incidental question. This problem arises where the answer to the question which the court has to determine (the main question) is dependent on first answering a subsidiary question (known as the incidental or preliminary question). In the current context, in order to answer the main question of whether a particular person (usually the left-behind parent) had custody rights, it will sometimes be necessary to determine an incidental question. This may involve determining whether to recognise a judgment of a foreign court conferring custody rights on that person or terminating them. Alternatively, although less commonly, the incidental question may involve determining the marital status of the parents.[145] Should the court of the requested State determine this incidental question by using its own private international law rules (recognition or choice of law rules as appropriate) or by referring to the relevant private international law rules of the law governing the main question, the law of the habitual residence?[146]

In order to facilitate analysis later in the book[147] of the extent to which the private international rules adopted in the Abduction Convention and their application in the case law are consistent with private international law theory, the objectives which underlie each type of rule and the various approaches to the two methodological questions identified will now be briefly examined. In addition, there will be a separate discussion of the doctrine of comity of nations, which is one of the theoretical justifications for private international law rules, because courts frequently refer to this doctrine in Abduction Convention cases.

B Jurisdiction Rules

The main purpose of jurisdiction rules is to ensure that cases are heard in the appropriate forum or in one of a number of appropriate fora. It has already been shown that one of the objectives of the Convention is to ensure adjudication of the merits of the custody dispute in the *forum conveniens*,[148] and that examination of the extent to which this objective is being promoted involves questioning the assumption that the State of habitual residence is always the *forum conveniens*. Thus, there is no need to duplicate this analysis under the rubric of examining consistency with the principles of private international law.

---

[145] For example, in the case of *AAA v ASH* [2009] EWHC 636, the question of whether the father had custody rights depended on whether the Muslim ceremony of marriage between the parents was valid. In this case, the Dutch Court asked the UK Court for an Art 15 determination as to whether the removal was wrongful. This inevitably led to the application of the conflict rule of the habitual residence to the incidental question. In this case, it is highly doubtful if a different result would have been obtained even if Dutch law had been applied because the issue related to the form of the marriage, which is almost universally determined by the law of the place of celebration.
[146] For a discussion of the inter-relationship between *renvoi* and the incidental question, see R Schuz, *A Modern Approach to the Incidental Question* (Boston, Kluwer Law International, 1997) 27–30.
[147] In particular, in ch 7 at IV G.
[148] Chapter 5 at II Ciii.

C Choice of Law Rules

i The Principles behind the Choice of Law Rules

The choice of law rule in the Abduction Convention is a traditional jurisdiction-selecting rule, which points to the applicable law without considering the content of that law. Thus, the discussion here will be restricted to principles relevant to this type of choice of law rule.[149] Over the years much ink has been spilled on debating the rationales behind choice of law rules and the objectives and principles which should inform their design. Whilst it is difficult to claim that any one approach has been universally accepted, it seems that today the most widely accepted theory is that of 'justice to the parties'. Thus, leading commentators have stated that foreign rules are applied where it would be unjust to ignore the foreign elements in the case[150] and that the 'most important factor underlying choice of law rules must be the desire to achieve justice between the parties'.[151] Similarly, Brillmayer's rights-based approach to choice of law is largely based on the concept of fairness.[152]

It is important to emphasise that justice in this context refers to 'conflicts justice' and not 'substantive justice'. In other words, justice is determined by the various connections between the parties and the events with the law to be applied and not by the actual result which will be reached by application of the law. The two concepts which seem to be most widely referred to as yardsticks for assessing whether a particular choice of law rule does achieve justice between the parties are 'closest connection' and 'reasonable expectation of the parties'. The first concept is based on the objective of identifying the law which is most closely connected to the issue at hand. Closest connection has been adopted in some jurisdictions as a choice of law rule in its own right in certain contexts[153] or as an exception to a general rule based on a single connecting factor.[154] However, even in choice of law rules based on a single connecting factor, the chosen factor is intended to identify the most closely connected law in most cases. The concept of reasonable expectation of the parties has been referred to by scholars,[155] law reform bodies[156] and judges[157] as a test for the appropriateness of applying a particular law.

---

[149] In contrast to modern result-selecting and interest analysis approaches to choice of law.

[150] RH Graveson, 'Judicial Justice as a Contemporary Basis of the English Conflict of Law' in RH Graveson (ed), *Comparative Conflict of Laws* (Amsterdam, North Holland Publishing, 1977) vol I, 51; J Fawcett and JM Carruthers, *Cheshire, North and Fawcett, Private International Law*, 14th edn (Oxford, Oxford University Press, 2008) 36–37.

[151] AJ Jaffey, *Introduction to the Conflict of Laws* (Oxford, Oxford University Press, 1988) 275.

[152] L Brillmayer, *Conflict of Laws* (Boston, Little, Brown, 1991) ch 5. Under this approach, a person has a political right not to be burdened by a law which it is not fair to apply to him. It is not strictly a jurisdiction-selecting approach because its implementation requires ascertaining which party is burdened by the application of a particular law.

[153] Most notably in relation to contract both in common law jurisdictions and in Art 4(1) of the EC Convention on the Law Applicable to Contractual Obligations ('Rome I').

[154] For example, in relation to tort both at common law (*Boys v Chaplin* [1971] AC 356) and in Art 4(3) of the EC Regulation on the Law Applicable to Non-Contractual Obligations ('Rome II').

[155] eg JG McLeod, *The Conflict of Laws* (Calgary, Carswell Legal Publications, 1983) 21; Brillmayer's concept of a party's volitional affiliations with a State (n 152) 220, is similar to that of reasonable expectation as is the concept of fair notice of the applicability of a particular law, developed by A Shapira, *The Interest Approach to Choice of Law* (Hague, Martinus Nijhoff, 1970) ch 3.

[156] eg, Reports of the English Law Commission in relation to reforming choice of law rules in marriage (WP 89) and tort (WP 87).

[157] eg *Johnson v Coventry Churchill International Ltd* [1992] 3 All ER 14, 25; *Tolofson v Jensen* (1992) 89 DLR (4th) 129 (Canada).

ii Renvoi

The doctrine of *renvoi* is relevant where there is a conflict between the choice of law rules of the forum and those of the applicable law (*lex causae*). The forum has two options: it may apply the internal law of the *lex causae*, or it may apply the choice rule of the *lex causae* and thus decide the case according to the internal law directed by that choice rule. Both options have advantages and disadvantages.[158] The first option does not achieve the objective of ensuring uniformity of result between different fora because if the case had been heard by the courts of the *lex causae*, they would have applied a different law. Accordingly, the plaintiff has an incentive to forum-shop. On the other hand, the second option effectively involves surrendering the forum's choice of law rules to those of the *lex causae*. Also, use of total *renvoi*[159] may involve a series of references from one law to another and may lead to a stalemate where the choice of law rules of two countries that have adopted the doctrine of total *renvoi* refer to the law of each other.[160] Therefore, it is perhaps not surprising that the doctrine has not been widely adopted and has been expressly excluded in many of the Conventions drafted under the auspices of the Hague Conference on Private International Law.[161] Generally, the doctrine has mainly been invoked in order to produce a certain result in a given set of circumstances.[162] In particular, in relation to a few issues, *renvoi* has been used as a rule of alternative reference to enable application of the law which is perceived as producing the better result.[163]

D Rules for Recognition of Foreign Judgments

i The Principles behind Recognition Rules

Traditionally, two theories have been put forward to explain recognition of foreign judgments. The theory of comity[164] was largely discredited as an explanation for recognising foreign judgments,[165] partly because at common law there was in fact no requirement of

---

[158] For a general explanation as to the benefits of the doctrine of *renvoi*, see A Briggs, 'In Praise and Defence of Renvoi' (1998) 47 *International and Comparative Law Quarterly* 877.

[159] Here the reference is also to the *renvoi* rules of the *lex causae*.

[160] This has been referred to as a *circulus inextricabilis*, see eg, JHC Morris, *The Conflict of Laws*, 3rd edn (London, Stevens, 1984) 480.

[161] eg, The Child Protection Convention, Art 21(1), subject to exception in Art 21(2).

[162] For example, s 142 of the Israeli Succession Law 1965 provides for single *renvoi* where the choice of law rules of the law of the domicile of the deceased lead to application of Israeli domestic law, but not where those choice of law rules require the application of some other foreign law.

[163] The classic example is the rule that a marriage will be formally valid where it meets the requirements of the domestic law of the place of celebration or the requirements of the law which is applicable under the choice of law rules of the law of the place of celebration, *Tacanowska v Taczanowska* [1957] P 301. This approach increases the chance that the marriage will be valid, which is assumed to accord with the expectations of the parties.

[164] This concept has more than one meaning. See the detailed discussion at section E below. Here comity is referred to in the sense of reciprocity.

[165] Fawcett and Carruthers, *Cheshire and North, Private International Law* (n 150) 346; AT Von Mehren and DT Trautman, 'Recognition of Foreign Adjudications: A Survey and a Suggested Approach' (1968) 81 *Harvard Law Review* 1601, 1603 point out that the theory is circular. However, this problem is solved where the reciprocity is in the form of a Convention which binds both parties *ab initio*.

reciprocity.[166] However, it might be argued that this theory should be revived,[167] in light of the increasing number of multinational Conventions which provide for automatic recognition of judgments as between Member States, subject to narrow exceptions.[168] The second theory is that of obligation, according to which the forum gives effect to the legal obligation created under the law of the judgment-rendering State.[169] However, this theory is largely relevant to cases where there is a judgment debtor who is obliged to pay a sum of money. Furthermore, the theory per se does not give any indication as to which foreign judgments should be treated as creating such obligations, although it does suggest a policy in favour of recognition.[170]

The main policies which are served by rules governing recognition of foreign judgments are the desire for finality so as to protect the successful litigant from being harassed by his opponent and 'an interest in fostering stability and unity in an international order in which many aspects of life are not confined to a single jurisdiction'.[171] In the area of personal status, an additional policy is to ensure uniformity of status in different jurisdictions. The latter policy would seem to apply in relation to decisions determining whether a person has parental status or bestowing such a status on him. However, this policy is arguably much weaker in relation to decisions allocating custody and access rights between parents because such decisions are subject to change where the welfare of the child so requires.[172] Thus, at common law, foreign custody decisions were not enforceable,[173] even though the other policies would seem to be applicable.[174]

However, it is clear that none of the above policies can support the automatic recognition of all foreign judgments. In particular, it would not be fair to bar the unsuccessful opponent from continuing to pursue his claim if the decision was not given in accordance with the requirements of natural justice or by a court which did not have jurisdiction to adjudicate in the particular case. Furthermore, stability and unity will not be fostered by recognising judgments given as a result of forum-shopping in countries which do not have a real connection with the dispute.

Thus, traditionally, a universal requirement for recognition of a judgment has been that the rendering court had jurisdiction. The bases of jurisdiction for the purposes of recognising foreign judgments (sometimes called indirect or external jurisdiction rules) were not necessarily identical with the bases for determining jurisdiction of the forum court (direct or internal jurisdiction rules). For example, under the common law, in *in personam* cases

---

[166] Although in England, reciprocity is necessary in order to take advantage of the expedited registered procedure under the UK's Foreign Judgments Reciprocal Enforcement Act 1933; For the rather patchy history of the requirement of reciprocity in the US, see V Singal, 'Preserving Power Without Sacrificing Justice: Creating an Effective Reciprocity Regime for the Recognition and Enforcement of Foreign Judgments' (2008) 59 *Hastings Law Journal* 943.

[167] A Briggs, 'Which Foreign Judgments Should We Recognize Today?' (1987) 36 *International and Comparative Law Quarterly* 240, 242.

[168] In particular the Brussels Convention on Jurisdiction and Enforcement of Judgments in Civil and Commercial Matters, Sept 27, 1968, 8 ILM 229 (1969) (replaced by Council Regulation (EC) No 44/2001 of 22 December 2000) and the Lugano Convention on Jurisdiction and the Enforcement of Judgments in Civil and Commercial Matters, Sept 16, 1988, 28 ILM 620 (1989).

[169] Von Mehren and Trautman, (n 165) 1603.

[170] ibid.

[171] ibid 1603–04.

[172] For a discussion of the conflicting considerations and the balance adopted in Israeli law prior to the ratification of the Abduction Convention, see A Shapira, 'Aspects of Child Custody and Kidnapping Cases' (1989) (II) *Recueil des Cours* 129, 155–58 and 160–63.

[173] *McKee v McKee* [1951] AC 352.

[174] Fawcett and Carruthers, *Cheshire and North, Private International Law* (n 150) 731 pointing out that comity and reciprocity were outweighed by the welfare of the child.

only, residence or consent were sufficient to found jurisdiction of a foreign court.[175] Thus, a decision could not be recognised where jurisdiction had been acquired by service outside the jurisdiction, even in circumstances where the forum court would itself allow service out of the jurisdiction.[176] In cases involving personal status, only decisions of the court of the domicile of the parties or those recognised by the law of the domicile would be recognised.[177]

The inextricable link between jurisdiction and recognition of judgments can also be seen from multilateral international conventions relating to recognition of judgments. The earlier conventions tend to retain the traditional approach of making recognition of the foreign judgment conditional on the fulfillment of one of a number of prescribed jurisdiction links.[178] However, more recent conventions do not provide such indirect jurisdiction rules, but rather provide direct jurisdiction rules setting out the bases for adjudicatory jurisdiction in cases determined by the courts of the Member State.[179] Under these conventions, recognition of the judgments of the other Member States is not dependent on jurisdiction having been taken in compliance with the convention jurisdiction rules, although in some conventions non-compliance may be a basis to refuse recognition.[180] Rather, there seems to be mutual trust that the Member States will adhere to the jurisdiction rules and an assumption that the costs involved in verifying this are not justified. Thus, these conventions indicate a more liberal approach to recognition of foreign judgments, certainly as between treaty partners.

ii The Incidental Question

As explained above, in the Abduction Convention context, the incidental question may relate to recognition of a foreign judgment or of a status under foreign law. Since the former situation is likely to be more common, it is appropriate to discuss this issue under the rubric of recognition rules.

Neither the literature nor the sparse case law in relation to the incidental question provide a clear-cut answer as to whether the incidental question should be governed by the private international law rules of the forum (*lex fori* approach) or those of the law which governs the main question (*lex causae* approach).[181] The main advantage of the former approach is that it promotes conformity of decision-making within the forum; whereas the benefit of the latter approach is that it promotes the uniformity of decisions among

---

[175] *Schisby v Westenholz* (1870) LR 6 QB 155.
[176] ibid. For a suggestion that the jurisdictional bases for recognising foreign judgments should be aligned with modern direct jurisdiction rules which effectively provide for adjudication in the natural forum, see Briggs, 'Which Foreign Judgments' (n 167).
[177] Further rules were later added. See Morris (n 160) 194–96.
[178] eg Hague Convention on the Recognition of Divorces and Legal Separations 1971.
[179] See eg Council Regulation (EC) No 44/2001 of 22 December 2000 on jurisdiction and the recognition and enforcement of judgments in civil and commercial matters (Brussels I) and Council Regulation (EC) No 2201/2003 of 27 November 2003 concerning jurisdiction and the recognition and enforcement of judgments in matrimonial matters and the matters of parental responsibility [2003] OJ L 338/1-29 (Brussels II bis the 1996 Hague Child Protection Convention). However, Y Oestreicher, 'The Rise and Fall of the "Mixed" and "Double" Convention Models Regarding Recognition and Enforcement of Foreign Judgments' (2007) 6 *Washington University Global Studies Law Review* 339, argues that it was the attempt to use such a model that resulted in the failure to achieve consensus on a Hague Convention on Jurisdiction and Recognition of Judgments.
[180] eg, Art 23(2)(a) of the 1996 Child Protection Convention.
[181] For a brief review, see R Schuz, *A Modern Approach to the Incidental Question* (n 146) 5–7; for a more detailed review, see A Gottlieb, 'The Incidental Question Revisited – Theory and Practice in the Conflict of Laws' (1977) 26 *International And Comparative Law Quarterly* 734.

different fora. Some scholars have claimed that neither approach can be adopted universally and have suggested resolving the problem on a case by case basis, using a purposive approach.[182] The current author used purposive methodology to construct result-oriented preference rules, whose role it is to determine which private international law rule should take precedence in particular types of situations in which the incidental question arises.[183] The implications of these different approaches in relation to the recognition of foreign judgments of third States in Abduction Convention proceedings will be considered in chapter 7.[184]

E Comity of Nations

The idea that private international law is based on comity[185] dates back to Huber and was adopted by Story. The latter wrote:

> The true foundation on which the subject rests is that rules which are to govern are those which arise from mutual interest and utility; from the sense of the inconveniences which would arise from a contrary doctrine; and from a sort of moral necessity to do justice in order that justice may be done to us in return.[186]

It can be seen that Story's concept of comity includes a number of different elements and it is therefore perhaps not surprising that the notion of comity has been understood differently by different writers and judges. The current author has suggested that the label 'comity' has been mainly used to cover three different doctrines, which can be called reciprocity, judicial courtesy and business efficacy.[187] An analysis of the references to the concept of comity in Abduction Convention cases shows that it has been used in the first two senses, as will be explained below.

When considering the references to comity in Abduction Convention cases and in analysing the extent to which the application of the Abduction Convention is consistent with the comity in the various senses,[188] it is important to bear in mind that the exact status of the doctrine of comity is far from clear.[189] Whilst the doctrine has been rejected by leading scholars,[190] courts in common law jurisdictions do refer to comity in a variety of different private international and public international law contexts.[191] The doctrine has been most

---

[182] eg Gottlieb ibid.
[183] Schuz, *A Modern Approach to the Incidental Question* (n 146), analysing the incidental question as a conflict between different private international law rules of the forum. Where a foreign judgment is involved, the conflict is between the forum's choice of law rules and its recognition rules and in other cases the conflict is between the forum's two different choice of law rules (eg between the choice of law rule governing parental rights and that governing the validity of marriage).
[184] At IV G.
[185] The doctrine of comity is also part of public international law. See JR Paul, 'Comity in International Law' (1991) 32 *Harvard Journal of International Law* 1, 2–3.
[186] Commentaries on the Conflict of Laws (1834) s 35.
[187] Schuz, *A Modern Approach to the Incidental Question* (n 146) 38. For a longer list of the different senses in which comity is used, see Paul, 'Comity in International Law' (n 185) 2–3. It should be noted that in the US, the term comity is also used to refer to the actual 'recognition which one nation allows within its territory to the legislative, executive or judicial acts of another nation' (*Hilton v Guyot*, 159 US 113 (1895)) and not only to the rationale for such recognition.
[188] In the analysis sections of the chapters in Part III and IV of the book.
[189] Paul, 'Comity in International Law' (n 185) 44.
[190] ibid 40–41.
[191] ibid 41–44.

influential in the US, but even there it is characterised by ambiguity, in particular in relation to the extent to which it is binding.[192]

i Reciprocity

The concept of reciprocity itself has more than one meaning,[193] but that which is relevant to the current context is the idea that States are prepared to apply foreign laws and give effect to foreign judgments so that other States will apply their law and recognise their judgments.[194] Reciprocity in this sense clearly underlies the whole Convention[195] because Contracting States are only required to return children to other Contracting States. In other words, these States are prepared to take on obligations to return abducted children on the basis that other States will return children to them. Indeed, judges sometimes claim that it is necessary for them to return abducted children to other Contracting States so that those States will reciprocate by returning children abducted from their State[196] and even when this consideration is not expressed, it may well influence judicial decision-making. Furthermore, courts may be influenced by the related concern that failure to return a child may lead to their State being perceived as being non-compliant with the Abduction Convention[197] and to consequential negative international relations implications.[198] There is some evidence that this concern is

---

[192] ibid 10–11 and 78 ('comity is regarded both as legally compelled and discretionary'). Similarly, it has been said that extension of comity to a foreign judgment is 'neither a matter of absolute obligation, on the one hand, nor of mere courtesy and good will, upon the other'. (*Asvesta v Petrousas* 580 F3d 1000; 2009 US App, quoting *Hilton v Guyot* 159 S 113 (1895)).

[193] Schuz, *A Modern Approach to the Incidental Question* (n 146) 139–41.

[194] And conversely that they will not give effect to foreign judgments of States which do not recognise their judgments, as in the leading US case of *Hilton v Guyot* (n 192).

[195] Indeed, it has been said that 'comity is at the heart of the Hague Convention', *Blondin v Dubois* 189 F3d 240, 248 (2nd Cir 1999).

[196] eg the following statement of Kirby J (dissenting) in *DP v Commonwealth Central Authority* (2001) 180 ALR 402 [155]: 'To the extent that Australian courts, including this Court, do not fulfil the expectations expressed in the rigorous language of the Convention and the Regulations, but effectively reserve custody (and residence) decisions to themselves, we should not be surprised if other countries, noting what we do, decline to extend to our courts the kind of reciprocity and mutual respect which the Convention scheme puts in place. And that, most definitely, would not, in aggregate, be in the best interests of children generally and of Australian children in particular.' See also *Duran v Beaumont* 534 F3d 142 (2nd Cir 2008).

[197] The US State Department prepares an annual report on States that fail to comply with the Convention, in accordance with para 11611 of ICARA; see discussion in C Bannon, 'The Hague Convention on the Civil Aspects of International Child Abduction: The Need For Mechanisms to Address Noncompliance (2011) 31 *Boston College Third World Law Journal* 129, 150 et seq.

[198] eg, in CrimC (Dist BSH) 8150/08 *State of Israel v RB* Nevo, 16 June 2011, when sentencing the mother who had been found guilty of disobeying a court order to return her child to Belgium following the child's disappearance, the judge remarked that her conduct, which had prevented the enforcement of the decisions of the Israeli and foreign courts, had harmed the status of Israel as a State where law ruled. It seems likely that the earlier decision to return the child, despite the evidence of grave risk of harm (RFamA (SC) 1855/08 *RB v GV*, 8 April 2008 http://elyon1.court.gov.il/files/08/550/018/r03/08018550.r03.pdf [INCADAT cite: HC/E/IL 923], was motivated inter alia by similar views. The Israeli courts' concern about international image might also provide an explanation for the statistics brought above in ch 3, I C, showing that foreign applicants fared considerably better in Abduction Convention cases than Israeli applicants. In a rather different context, in devising a project for mediation in abduction cases, Reunite stated that 'it was of paramount importance that the UK's reputation as an enthusiastic and reliable upholder of the Hague Convention should not be undermined', The Reunite Mediation Pilot Scheme, www.reunite.org/edit/files/Library%20-%20reunite%20Publications/Mediation%20Report.pdf, 7. *cf* *Re M (Abduction: Leave to Appeal)* [1999] 2 FLR 550, which was the first case between England and South Africa, where Butler-Sloss LJ refused to give leave to appeal against the trial Judge's refusal to return under Art 13(1)(b) on the basis of the father's violence, since the appeal would be for the sole purpose of exploring 'the relationship between South Africa and the United Kingdom'. However, she did order that a copy of the decision be sent to the South African Central Authority with an explanation that this was an unusual decision and was not representative of the English approach to the Hague Convention.

greater where the case is one to which the Brussels II bis Regulation applies[199] and that accordingly the dictates of comity carry more weight in such cases.

Two questions arise in relation to the scope of the reciprocity between Contracting States. Firstly, what are the consequences of violation of the Convention by a particular State? No mechanism appears to exist for imposing sanctions against States who do not operate the Convention properly.[200] Nor is there any evidence that requested States, when deciding particular cases, take into account the return record of the requesting State, either generally or in relation to abductions from the requested State. Thus, there does not seem to be any concrete base for concerns that the failure of the requested State to return a child will result in the non-return of children to that particular State. Indeed, it seems that references to the need for reciprocity in operating the Convention often refer generally to the importance of mutual respect between Contracting States rather than to specific reciprocity between two particular Contracting States.[201]

The second question relates to the recognition of non-return orders. Whilst the Convention requires the requested State to give force to the judicial decisions of the State of habitual residence, there is no parallel requirement for the latter State to recognise decisions made under the Abduction Convention in the requested State. Thus, even though courts tend to give deference to the decisions of foreign courts,[202] there are cases where the requesting State later made an order which conflicts directly with the no-return order made by the requested State, on the basis that the latter was not properly made.[203] There is no mechanism for resolving this conflict and in practice, provided that the child remains in the requested State, any orders made by the requesting State will not be of any effect.[204] This situation is unsatisfactory[205] and appears to be inconsistent with the spirit of reciprocity on which the Convention is founded.[206] This approach also appears to be inconsistent with comity in the sense of judicial courtesy because it involves detailed review of the merits of the foreign court decision.[207]

[199] See eg, *Vigreux v Michel* [2006] EWCA Civ 630 (Wall LJ) and In *Re F (Abduction: Joinder of Child as Party)* [2007] EWCA Civ 393 (Thorpe LJ), [2].

[200] For rejection of the idea that the Permanent Bureau should monitor compliance, see ch 2 at II Dv. For a discussion of Bills introduced into the US Congress, which would impose economic and other political sanctions against non-compliant countries, see Bannon (n 197) 156 et seq.

[201] See eg Regulation 1A(2)(c) of the Australian Family Law (Child Abduction Convention) Regulations 1986 which provides that the Regulations are to be construed inter alia 'recognising that the effective implementation of the Convention depends on the reciprocity and mutual respect between judicial or administrative authorities (as the case may be) of convention countries'.

[202] *Diorinou v Mezitis* 237 F 3d 133(2000)142.

[203] eg, US decision in *Ben-Haim v Ben-Haim* appeal Docketed No FD 02-906-11 (NJ Super Ct Aug 25, 2011) (refusing comity to an Israeli decision which refused return on the basis of the consent exceptions, discussed in ch 10 at III A and III B); *Carrascosa v McGuire* 520 F3d 249 (3rd Cir 2008) (refusing comity to a Spanish decision which held that the mother had sole rights of custody in manifest contradiction to the applicable New Jersey law); *Asvesta v Petrousas* 580 F3d 1000; 2009 US App (refusing comity to a Greek decision which decided on the merits of the case and gave an overly wide interpretation to the grave risk exception). *cf* the approach of the Israeli courts in RFamA (SC) 672/06 *PR v TAE*, 61(3) PD 24 [INCADAT cite: HC/E/IL 885] (returning children to Italy following re-abduction by the father, despite the fact that the Italian decision refusing to return the child to Israel following the mother's abduction did not apply the Convention correctly).

[204] *cf* Brussels II bis Regulation, Art 11(8), which provides that a later decision made by the State of habitual residence trumps the Abduction Convention decision. See ch 1 at II Civ.

[205] For a discussion of the effect to which the Child Protection Convention solves this problem, see ch 1at II Eii.

[206] In *Avesta v Petrousas* (n 203), the Court recognised the importance of mutual trust but stated that the success of the Convention also relied 'upon the faithful application of its provisions by American courts and the courts of other contracting nations'.

[207] eg, *Diorinous v Mezitis* (n 202) (comity given to Greek decision that there had not been a wrongful retention despite some misgivings) and *Asvesta v Petrousas* (n 203). In the latter case, the US Court of Appeals explains that

ii Judicial Courtesy

It seems that judicial courtesy is the sense in which the word comity was originally used when justifying the application of foreign law.[208] In other words, foreign laws are applied in preference to forum law in order to show deference to other sovereign States and foreign judgments are recognised in order to show respect for other judges' decisions. Whilst it has long been recognised that comity in this sense cannot provide an adequate basis for constructing choice of law rules[209] or even recognition rules,[210] it can still provide a general justification for the need to apply foreign laws and recognise foreign judgments, in accordance with whatever choice and recognition rules have been chosen. Furthermore, comity in the sense of judicial courtesy can be used as a reason not to question the content of the foreign law or judgments,[211] unless these manifestly contradict the forum's public policy.

Perusal of the references to comity in Abduction Convention cases shows that it is most commonly used in this sense of respecting the law, legal decisions or legal system of the requesting State. For example, comity has been cited as a reason to recognise an order of the foreign court or its jurisdiction to decide the case.[212] Similarly, comity has been said to require a narrow interpretation and application of the exceptions.[213] In addition, when determining whether return will expose the child to a grave risk of harm, courts sometimes justify their assumption that the authorities in the requesting State will protect the child and returning parent from harm on the basis of comity.[214] Moreover, comity has been expressly cited as a reason not to investigate the extent to which the requesting State will protect the child upon return and to support the presumption that the requesting State will honour undertakings given to the court of the requested State.[215] Furthermore, US courts have based their opposition to the practice of requiring a mirror order to be entered in the requesting State on the basis that it offends international comity.[216] Finally, where the court has to exercise discretion because one of the exceptions to mandatory return is established, comity is sometimes mentioned as one of the Convention factors pointing to return.[217] At first sight the reference to comity as a Convention factor suggests that comity here is

the Court is in a better position to examine the merits of a decision made under the Abduction Convention because this is a framework agreed upon by all Contracting States.

[208] See eg, *Hughes v Cornelius* (1680) 2 Show 232 (US) and *Dicey's Conflict of Laws* 4th edn ((London, Stevens and Sweet and Maxwell, 1927) 9.

[209] Inter alia because it cannot determine which of a number of connected laws should apply.

[210] Mainly because recognition would be based on judicial discretion as opposed to the rights of the parties.

[211] *cf* Fawcett and Carruthers, *Cheshire and North Private International Law* (n 150) 4, who claim that courtesy is a matter for sovereigns and not judges.

[212] eg, *PR v TAE* (n 203), in which the Israeli courts specifically invoked the need to give respect to judicial decisions of fellow Contracting States. See also following comment of Purchas LJ in *Re S (A Minor) (Abduction)* [1991] 2 FLR 1, 'Is there any possible reason for this court to arrogate to itself the power of commenting upon or criticising the jurisprudential efficiency of the Minnesota court? It would fly in the face of comity which lies at the base of this very Convention' and per Thorpe LJ in the non-Convention abduction case of *Al Habtoor v Fotheringham* [2001] EWCA Civ 186.

[213] eg, *Van de Sande v Van de Sande* 431 F3d 567, 572 (7th Cir 2005).

[214] eg, CA (SC) 4391/96 *Ro v Ro*, 50(5) PD 338 (Isr) [INCADAT cite: HC/E/IL832]:; *TB v JB (Abduction: Graver Risk of Harm)* [2001] 2 FLR 515; *Murray v Director, Family Services* (1993) FLC 92-416.

[215] eg, comment of Supreme Court of Ireland in *RK v JK* [2000] 2 IR 416; *Re M (Abduction: Non-Convention Country)* [1995] 1 FLR 89, quoted in the Convention case of *Re K (Abduction: Physical Harm)* [1995] 2 FLR 550; comment of M Freeman, 'Primary Carers and The Hague Child Abduction Convention' [2001] *International Family Law* 140 that 'many courts are hypnotized by the need for comity'.

[216] *Danaipour v Mclarey* 286 F3d 1 (1st Cir 2002). The Court also mentioned that the State Department did not support the idea of mirror orders because it would smack of coercion of the foreign court.

[217] eg *Re M (Abduction: Zimbabwe)* [2007] UKHL 55 [45] (Baroness Hale). See generally the discussion on the exercise of the discretion in chapter 10 at IV.

being used in the sense of reciprocity. However, it may be that in reality the reference is to judicial courtesy towards the requesting State, the need for which is heightened by the fact that that State is a treaty partner.

In a number of the above contexts, courts seem to assume that the requesting State has a strong interest in the return of the child, which will be violated by the non-return order. However, it is not clear that this is always so. Firstly, it should be remembered that the left-behind parent and not the requesting State is the applicant in the proceedings.[218] Even the fact that the Central Authority of the requesting State is supporting the application does not mean anything other than that the basic conditions for applicability of the Convention appear to apply, since the Central Authority does not have any discretion in the matter.[219] In addition, whilst in many cases return of the child is required by substantive policies of the requesting State,[220] not only in order to restore national pride, there will be cases where some or all of these policies will not apply.[221] It should also be remembered that in some cases the connection of the parties with the requesting State may not be strong[222] and that return may place a burden on the requesting State, such as the need to provide resource-heavy protective measures against violence or the judicial time and cost involved in a relocation dispute. It would seem appropriate to take into account these considerations in determining what weight, if any, should be given to the need for comity between nations in particular cases.

In the analysis sections of the chapters in Parts III and IV of the book, the appropriateness of the reliance on the doctrine of comity in the various contexts will be examined under the rubric of consistency with private international law principles.

V Certainty versus Flexibility

The tension between certainty and flexibility is an inherent and unavoidable aspect of the application of law in all legal systems.[223] As one prominent scholar observed, 'There is and always will be in all countries a contradiction between two requirements of justice: the law must be certain and predictable on the one hand, it must be flexible and adaptable to circumstances on the other hand.'[224]

This tension is particularly pronounced in both areas of law with which the Abduction Convention is concerned: child law and private international law. In child law, as already seen, the best interests standard has been almost universally adopted as the decision-making mechanism. This standard is notoriously indeterminate and uncertain.[225] Yet, the need to retain the flexibility to ensure the best outcome for the child makes it virtually

---

[218] Chapter 2 at III E.
[219] Thus, eg, the US Central Authority has supported applications made by left-behind parents who appear to be living in the US illegally, see eg FamA (Dist TA) 1382/04, Nevo, 1 May 2006 (allowing an appeal against a return order inter alia because the applicant had had to leave the US since he didn't have a right to stay there).
[220] Such as upholding the rule of law, protecting children from abduction and assisting nationals.
[221] eg where the removal was with consent.
[222] At least under some of the approaches taken to habitual residence, see ch 8.
[223] P Hay, *Flexibility versus Predictability* (n 2) 291.
[224] D Rene, *English Law and French Law* (London, Stevens & Sons, 1980) 24, quoted in I Kanor, 'Theoretical Analysis of Private International Law in Israel – Normative Reflections through a Comparative Perspective' (2010) 32 *Tel-Aviv University Law Review* 339 (Hebrew), 374.
[225] Mnookin, 'Child Custody Adjudication' (n 22).

impossible to find an alternative test. Thus, attempts to reduce the uncertainty inherent in the best interests standard have usually involved the creation of checklists of factors which have to be taken into account in determining the best interests of the child[226] and sometimes rebuttable presumptions,[227] rather than replacing the standard itself.

The Abduction Convention is perhaps the only instrument, at least in the Western World, which provides for decisions to be made in relation to children without express consideration of their best interests. However, as seen above, these interests are reflected in the various defences to mandatory return. It was necessary to draft these defences in a way which would provide sufficient flexibility to a court to protect children and yet in a way which provided sufficient certainty so that the defences would not provide wide discretion to judges and thus reduce predictability and the deterrent value of the Convention. Moreover, judges who have to interpret these defences are faced with the same challenge of finding the optimal balance between certainty and flexibility. The analysis sections of this book will assess to what extent they have succeeded.

In private international law, tensions between different legal systems are added to the tensions existing within domestic law.[228] Furthermore, the foreign dimension increases the number of different permutations of any given situation which can arise, some of which may be difficult to foresee in advance. This problem was highlighted by the US choice of law revolution, which was characterised by result-selecting methods designed to achieve just results. A significant element in the debate between the supporters of this approach and its opponents relates to the appropriate balance between certainty and flexibility.[229] Indeed, it has been said that the tension between these two objectives was the 'hallmark of conflicts law' during that period.[230]

Nonetheless, the tension is not restricted to choice of law in tort, or even choice of law generally. The tension exists in relation to all aspects of private international law rules. For example, to what extent should personal connecting factors be rigid and thus easily applicable and to what extent should they be flexible, allowing all the circumstances of the case to be taken into account? The connecting factor of habitual residence has been widely adopted in international conventions, perhaps because it is perceived as achieving an acceptable balance between these two extremes. Nonetheless, whilst this assessment may have been largely accurate in relation to adults, the concept of habitual residence of children raises the question of the weight to be given to the intentions of the parents. The lack of any statutory definition of the concept has led to widely differing approaches to determining the habitual residence of a child in Abduction Convention cases and thus considerable uncertainty.[231] In this book, consideration will be given to ways in which this uncertainty, together with that which has arisen in relation to the definition of other concepts within the Convention,[232] can be reduced whilst preserving the necessary degree of flexibility to accommodate the many different situations which may arise.

---

[226] eg English Children Act 1989, s 1(2).
[227] eg Australian Family Law Amendment Act 2003 (introducing a rebuttable presumption of joint time with each parent); cf in Israel, draft Parents and Children Law 2012 (published for consultation by the Ministry of Justice), which abolishes the rebuttable presumption enacted in 1962 that children under the age of six should be in the custody of their mother.
[228] Hay, *Flexibility versus Predictability* (n 2) 293; Kanor, 'Theoretical Analysis' (n 224) 374.
[229] SC Symeonides, 'General Report' in SC Symeonides (ed), *Private International Law at the End of the 20th Century: Progress or Regress?* (Boston, Kluwer Law International, 2000) 21–22.
[230] Hay, *Flexibility versus Predictability* (n 2) 304.
[231] For a detailed discussion, see ch 8.
[232] In particular, the concept of custody rights, discussed in ch 7.

Part III

Conditions for Application of Mandatory Return Mechanism

7

Wrongful Removal or Retention

I Introduction

As we have already seen, the trigger for the operation of the mandatory return mechanism in the Hague Convention on the Civil Aspects of International Child Abduction ('Abduction Convention') is a wrongful removal or retention of the child.

The burden of proving that there has been a wrongful removal or retention lies with the applicant.[1] If the applicant fails to discharge this burden, his application will be dismissed. Article 3 of the Convention defines a removal or retention as wrongful where

(a) it is in breach of rights of custody attributed to a person, an institution or any other body, either jointly or alone, under the law of the State in which the child was habitually resident immediately before the removal or retention; and

(b) at the time of removal or retention those rights were actually exercised, either jointly or alone, or would have been so exercised but for the removal or retention.

The rights of custody mentioned in sub-paragraph (a) above may arise in particular by operation of law or by reason of a judicial or administrative decision, or by reason of an agreement having legal effect under the law of that State.

Accordingly, the concepts of removal and retention will be discussed first, followed by a consideration of the concepts of custody rights and the exercise of such rights. Since the issues relating to the concepts of removal and retention are rather different than those relating to the concept of custody rights and their exercise, they will be analysed separately.

A preliminary point should be made in relation to removals or retentions with the consent of the left-behind parent. Logically, such removals or retentions should not be treated as wrongful. However, the Abduction Convention clearly envisages that they should be considered wrongful, but that the abductor will be able to raise the defence of consent in Article 13(1)(a). The merits of this approach will be discussed in chapter 10, dealing with the consent defence.[2]

---

[1] Since in the vast majority of cases, the applicant is the left-behind parent, these two terms will be used synonymously. However, it should be borne in mind that occasionally the abducted child was in the custody of another person or institution, who may then apply for his return, eg *In The Interest of S.J.O.B.G.* 292 S.W.3d 764, 2009 Tex App; *Re JS (Private International Adoption)* [2000] 2 FLR 638.

[2] Chapter 10 at V A.

II Removal or Retention

A Relationship between the Concepts

Removal will be proven by showing that the child was taken out of the country of habitual residence and the date of removal will be the date when he crossed the border out of that State.[3] The concept of retention, however, is less self-evident and it has been necessary to define its scope in case law. Three particular questions have arisen. The first relates to the nature of retention and its inter-relationship with removal. The second concerns the question as to whether a lawful removal can be turned into a wrongful retention by a court order made after the removal. The final issue relates to identification of the commencement of the retention and in particular whether an anticipatory breach of custody rights constitutes a retention. The first two questions have been answered decisively by the House of Lords, whereas the third question has not received an authoritative answer.

In relation to the first question, that Court held that retention is a solitary event and not a continuing state of affairs and therefore there is no overlap between removal and retention.[4] This means inter alia that where the Convention was not in force at the time of the removal in the country to which the child was removed, the fact that the child was still in that country when the Convention did come into force there would not be treated as a wrongful retention. In relation to the second question, that Court held that retention may occur as a result of a court decision vesting custody rights given after the lawful removal of the child, provided that his habitual residence had not changed in the meantime.[5]

At first sight, there appears to be an inconsistency between these two holdings. It seems absurd that a lawful removal can become a wrongful retention, but that a wrongful removal cannot become a wrongful retention. The explanation would seem to be that it is necessary to make a clear distinction between a wrongful removal and a wrongful retention so as to enable identification of the date at which the applicability of the Convention is determined and the date from which the 12-month period starts to run. Accordingly, a wrongful removal cannot later become a wrongful retention and thus the relevant date for the above purposes is the date of the removal and not any later date. On the other hand, a removal which was lawful may later become a wrongful retention where custody rights are bestowed on another person after the removal. Here, the date of the wrongful retention is the only possible relevant date, which in this situation will be the date of the granting of the custody rights.

However, in other cases, where the original removal was with the consent of those with custody rights, it will not always be easy to identify the date of the retention, as will be explained in the following section.

B Identifying the Date of the Wrongful Retention

It may be necessary to determine the exact date of a wrongful retention in at least three different contexts:[6] firstly, in order to determine whether the conditions for making a return

---
[3] *Re H and Re S (Abduction: Custody Rights)* [1991] 2 AC 476, 499.
[4] ibid, 500.
[5] *Re S (A Minor) (Custody: Habitual Residence)* [1998] AC 750.
[6] See also ch 10, n 2.

order under Article 12 of the Convention have already been satisfied; secondly, in order to determine whether 12 months have elapsed between the date of the retention and the date of the submission of the application for the purposes of the defence in Article 12(2) and thirdly, in order to determine whether the Convention was in force on the date of the retention between the two Contracting States in question.[7]

In many cases of wrongful retention, the left-behind parent does not have any clear indication that the abducting parent is not intending to return the child until the day when the child was supposed to be coming back. In such cases, it is beyond doubt that the wrongful retention occurs on this date. However, sometimes the abductor's intention not to return is manifested[8] before the planned travel date and the question then arises as to whether this anticipatory breach of custody rights constitutes retention. Moreover, sometimes no fixed date is set for return, even though it is agreed that the stay abroad is temporary. In such cases, the retention would usually take place when the left-behind parent requests return of the child and the abductor does not comply. However, again it is possible that the abductor's intention not to return is manifested before such a request is made. So, in this situation the question also arises as to whether the anticipatory breach can be considered as retention.

Perusal of the case law shows that there are two main approaches to the issue of anticipatory breach. In the English case of *Re S (Minors) (Child Abduction: Wrongful Retention)*,[9] it was held that the mother's application to the English courts for a residence order, in breach of the parties' agreement to return to Israel at the end of the Sabbatical, constituted a wrongful retention and a return order was made, even though the Sabbatical year had not yet finished.[10] In contrast, in the US case of *Toren v Toren*[11] it was held that even if there had been clear evidence of the mother's intention not to return the children to Israel at the date agreed, the Abduction Convention did not provide a remedy where there had not yet been a breach of the custodial rights of the other parent. In other words, the Convention did not apply in the case of an anticipatory breach.

The latter approach was followed in the case of *Falk v Sinclair*[12] where it was held that the retention occurred on the date fixed for the child's return to her mother in Germany, after her holiday with her father in the US, and not on the earlier date on which the father had clearly informed the mother that he was not intending to send the child back to Germany. The consequence of this finding was that 12 months had not yet passed at the date of submission of the application; whereas if the retention had occurred on the earlier date, 12 months would have already elapsed. The Court supported their approach by referring to the analogy with anticipatory breach of contract made in the case of *Philippopoulos v Philippopoulou*.[13]

---

[7] eg *Viteri v Pflucker* 550 F Supp 2d 829 (Nd Illinois 2008).
[8] Either by direct communication to the left-behind parent (*Falk v Sinclair* 692 F Supp 2d 147 (D Maine, 2010)) or by the behaviour of the abductor, eg *Re S (Minors) (Child Abduction: Wrongful Retention)* [1994] Fam 70; *Mozes v Mozes* 239 F.3d 1067 (9th Cir 2001) (application to local court for residence order or custody); *Zuker v Andrews* 2 F Supp 2d 134 (D Mass 1998) (renting a flat); cf view of Wall J in *Re S (Minors)* ibid that the abductor's decision not to return, even if not manifested, could itself constitute an act of wrongful retention (relying on *Re AZ (A Minor)(Abduction: Acquiesence)* [1993] 1 FLR 682.
[9] *Re S (Minors)* ibid.
[10] See also *Mozes* (n 8); *P v Secretary of State for Justice* [2004] 2 NZLR 28.
[11] *Toren v Toren* 191 F.3d 23 (1st Cir 1999).
[12] *Falk v Sinclair* (n 8).
[13] *Philippopoulos v Philippopoulou* 461 F Supp 2d 1321, 1324 (ND Georgia, 2006) 500.

If one party to a contract anticipatorily repudiates the contract, the other party may bring an immediate action for a total breach or may wait to sue until after the repudiating party actually fails to perform as agreed. Although the non-breaching party can bring suit immediately upon the other party's anticipatory repudiation, the statute of limitations does not begin to run until the breach actually occurs (provided the non-breaching party does not place the repudiator in breach, but instead opts to await performance).

The Court observed that while the Petitioner probably could have filed suit immediately upon learning of the Respondent's intention to wrongfully retain the child, he had the right to wait until after the child had not been returned on the due date.

The implications of this reasoning are that there should be a split approach to determining the date of commencement of retention.[14] On the one hand, manifestation of an intention not to return a child should be sufficient to constitute retention for the purposes of allowing a return order to be made, if the left-behind parent wishes to file an application immediately. On the other hand, where the left-behind parent does not choose this course of action, the 12-month period in Article 12(2) should not start to run until the planned return date. It should be added that if the left-behind parent has the right to wait until the planned date of return, he should also be able to benefit from the fact that the Convention came into force between the two Contracting States in question during the period of time between the anticipatory breach and the planned date of return.

C Analysis in Relation to the Concept of Retention

i Internal Coherence

The House of Lords' unchallenged holdings that retention is a solitary event and is quite distinct from removal, ensure internal coherence. Any other approach could not be reconciled with the Convention's requirement to identify a fixed date for the occurrence of the removal or retention and with the fact that the two concepts are expressed in the alternative throughout the Convention. However, the split approach to the question of anticipatory breach, which is supported by some of the case law, does not create internal coherence because it treats this breach as a retention for some purposes and not for others.

ii Consistency with the Intentions of the Drafters

Professor Perez-Vera states that, in the case of a wrongful retention, the 12-month time period starts to run from the date on which the child should have been returned to his custodian or the date on which the custodian refused to agree to an extension of the child's stay in the country of refuge.[15] However, there is no discussion as to whether anticipatory breach could be considered as wrongful retention for the purpose of obtaining a return order before the planned date of return.

iii Promotion of the Objectives of the Convention

The three issues which have arisen in relation to the concept of retention will be considered separately. Firstly, it can be argued that the 'solitary event' approach taken to the concept

---

[14] Support for this can be found in the recent New Zealand case of *RCL v APBL* [2012] NZHC 1292 [86].
[15] Perez-Vera Report, Proceedings of the 14th Session of the Hague Conference Oct 1980, www.hcch.net/index_en.php?act=publications.details&pid=2779, para 108.

of retention by the House of Lords in the case of *Re H and Re S*[16] did not protect the child in question because it was held that the removal had occurred before the coming into force of the treaty between England and Canada and that there was no subsequent retention. However, it is suggested that the question of whether or not the Convention can be applied to events which occurred before its coming into force is not a relevant measure of whether its objectives are being fulfilled. Furthermore, since the decision does not relate to future abductions, it does not reduce the deterrent effect of the Convention, other than perhaps precipitating potential abductions to or from countries which are about to join the Convention.

Secondly, the decision of the House of Lords that a lawful removal may become a wrongful retention as a result of a court order[17] appears to protect the child by correcting the fact that he was not adequately protected at the time of removal.[18] However, this conclusion is based on the assumption that the court will only vest rights in the left-behind parent where it is satisfied that the unilateral removal, although technically lawful, did not serve the best interests of the child.

Thirdly, the approach of treating anticipatory breach as retention for the purposes of Article 12(1) does promote the objective of protecting the child because it enables the early commencement of proceedings and sometimes a court order for return can be made before the date planned for return. Such an order should deter the abductor from not returning the child and if he still fails to return him, speedy enforcement of the order minimises the delay and damage to the child.

On the other hand, for the purposes of Article 12(2), the objectives of the Convention are better promoted by not treating the anticipatory breach as a wrongful retention. Whilst the 12-month period is designed to encourage the left-behind parent to act speedily once a wrongful removal or retention has occurred, there is no reason to pressurise him to act on the basis of threats and he should be entitled to wait to see whether in practice the child is returned on the due date. On the contrary, the instigation of pre-emptory litigation is likely to cause further deterioration in the relations between the parents which may damage the children.

iv Certainty versus Flexibility

The House of Lords' determination that a retention is a solitary event and does not overlap with removal creates certainty.

The approach which treats anticipatory breach as retention provides flexibility, but may give rise to some degree of uncertainty, as there may be difficulty in proving the threat not to return, where it was made orally. A fortiori, Wall J's approach,[19] which treats an unmanifested intention not to return the child as a retention, creates considerable uncertainty.[20] This will be particularly problematic if the question only arises 12 months later in determining whether the Article 12(2) exception is satisfied. However, the split approach effectively removes this uncertainty by providing that the 12-month period only starts to run from the planned date of return. Thus, the advantages of the split approach to anticipatory

---

[16] *Re H and Re S (Abduction: Custody Rights)* (n 3).
[17] *Re S (A Minor) (Custody: Habitual Residence)* (n 5).
[18] *cf* P Beaumont and P McEleavy, *The Hague Convention on International Child Abduction* (Oxford, Oxford University Press, 1999) 40.
[19] *Re S(Minors)* (n 8).
[20] Beaumont and McEleavy (n 18) 41.

breach, and in particular the fact that it promotes the objectives of the Convention, justify any internal incoherence which it causes.

III Rights of Custody

A Introduction

As seen above, in order to prove that the removal or retention is wrongful, the applicant first has to show that there has been a breach of custody rights under the law of the State of habitual residence.[21] The drafters of the Abduction Convention, departing from their practice in previous Conventions, did not limit this reference to foreign law to the internal rules of foreign law and thus it includes reference to the choice of law rules of the country of habitual residence, in accordance with the doctrine of *renvoi*.[22] An example of the use of *renvoi* in this context can be found in an English case[23] which concerned a child born to unmarried British parents who were all habitually resident in Spain. The mother removed the child to England and contended that the removal was not wrongful because the father did not have custody rights in relation to the child. Relying on expert evidence as to Spanish law, the English Court found that under the Spanish choice of law rules, the issue of parental responsibility for the child would be governed by the law of the child's nationality, which was taken to be English law.[24] Accordingly the father did not have custody rights, even though he would have had such rights under the domestic Spanish law. The opposite result was achieved in a later, almost identical case,[25] because the expert evidence showed that the Spanish Court would not apply the English law on grounds of public policy. The implications of the adoption of the doctrine of *renvoi* in the Abduction Convention will be discussed in the analysis section at III F below.

While there seems to be consensus in relation to the need to create an autonomous definition of custody rights for the purposes of the Convention which is distinct from domestic concepts of custody,[26] it is not always clear what the inter-relationship is between the Convention concept of custody rights and the local law of the State of habitual residence. This problem will be considered in Part B below. Furthermore, there has not always been consensus in relation to the content of the autonomous Convention definition.[27] In particular, there has been a good deal of uncertainty as to where to draw the line between the concepts of custody rights and access rights within the Convention. This issue has arisen most frequently in two particular contexts. The first is where the left-behind parent has a right to veto removal of the child from the country of origin (often referred to as a *ne exeat*

---

[21] For a discussion of the 'Catch 22' situation, which may arise if determination of the child's habitual residence is dependent on the custody rights of his parents, see ch 8 at V Ai.
[22] Perez-Vera Report (n 15), para 66.
[23] *Re JB (Child Abduction) (Rights of Custody: Spain)* [2003] EWHC 2130.
[24] For a discussion of this assumption, see K Beevers and JP Milla, 'Child Abduction: Convention Rights of Custody – Who Decides? An Anglo-Spanish Perspective' (2007) 3 *Journal of Private International Law* 201.
[25] *K v K* [2009] EWCA Civ 986.
[26] *Re C (A Minor) (Abduction)* [1989] 1 FLR 403, 407 (Butler-Sloss LJ); *Hunter v Murrow* [2005] EWCA Civ 976 (Dyson LJ); *McCall and McCall* (1995) FLC 92-551, 81, 515-17; Beevers and Milla, 'Child Abduction' (n 24) 203.
[27] Beevers and Milla ibid 204–05.

right), in circumstances where the abductor has sole custody of the child.[28] The second context is in relation to unmarried fathers, in cases where they are not automatically granted custody rights by the law of the country of habitual residence. It will therefore be convenient to examine the definition of custody rights with reference to these two contexts in Parts C and D. Over the course of this discussion, the significance of the various sources of rights of custody referred to at the end of Article 3 of the Convention will be clarified.

To the extent that the local law of the country of habitual residence is relevant to the determination of whether the applicant has custody rights, it will be necessary to obtain evidence of the foreign law. One method of doing this is by requesting a declaration from the authorities in the requesting State under Article 15 of the Abduction Convention. The questions which have arisen in relation to this mechanism will be discussed briefly in Part E.

Finally, if the left-behind parent succeeds in proving that there has been a breach of custody rights, he then has to prove that those rights were actually exercised or would have been so exercised, but for the removal or retention. Whilst the question of actual exercise is not raised very often, an examination of the limited case law on this issue reveals divergent approaches, which will be considered in Part F.

B Local Law versus Autonomous Definition

Article 5(a) of the Convention defines 'rights of custody' as including 'rights relating to the care of the person of the child and, in particular, the right to determine the child's place of residence.' The interrelationship between this 'autonomous' Convention definition and the concept of rights of custody in the domestic laws of the various Member States, which may be different, has caused confusion. On the one hand, Article 3 of the Convention contains a clear directive to look to the 'law of the habitual residence' to determine whether there has been a breach of custody rights. On the other hand, the Convention appears to create an autonomous definition of the concept of 'rights of custody' which is to be interpreted in light of the objectives of the Convention.[29]

This apparent inconsistency has been resolved by adopting a two-stage approach. The first step is to identify the 'rights' that the respective parents or guardians have in respect of a child under the domestic law of the State of habitual residence. The second step is to characterise these 'rights' in accordance with the autonomous Convention definition, so as to determine whether they are considered to be 'rights of custody' for the purposes of the Convention or not.[30]

In theory, the autonomous Convention definition of 'rights of custody' and its application should be uniform throughout the Hague world. However, in practice different approaches have emerged in relation to the interpretation of the Convention definition[31]

---

[28] Compare eg *Croll v Croll* 229 F 3d 133 (2d Cir 2000) with *Furnes v Reeves* 362 F 3d 702 (11th Cir 2004).
[29] Conclusion No 2 of Second Special Commission Meeting in 1993, www.hcch.net/upload/abdrpt93e.pdf.
[30] *Re V-B (Minors: Child Abduction: Custody Rights)* [1999] 2 FLR 192, 196B, followed in *Hunter v Murrow* (n 26) [46]; *Fairfax v Ireton* [2009] NZFLR 433 (NZCA 100) [20]; *Re D (A Child) (Abduction: Foreign Custody Rights)* [2006] UKHL 51 [28]; *Abbott v Abbott* 130 S Ct 1983 (2010).
[31] For example, different approaches have been taken to the question whether the definition should be read conjunctively, so that there needs to be both a right relating to the care of the person of the child and a right to determine his place of residence or whether the right to determine the child's place of residence 'is just one particular qualifying instance and not a necessary qualification', *Fairfax v Ireton* ibid [62]–[66].

C Ne Exeat Rights

i The Issue

A *ne exeat* right is effectively a right of veto which allows the non-custodial parent to prevent the custodial parent from relocating to another country without the permission of a court. Such a right may be conferred on the non-custodial parent by a non-removal clause (sometimes referred to as 'travel restrictions') in a court order or agreement or *ex lege* by virtue of the status of the non-custodial parent as a legal guardian of the child.[33] Shortly after the signing of the Convention, it became clear that the leading academics, Eekelaar and Anton, held different views as to whether breach of a *ne exeat* right would be considered a breach of custody rights within the Convention.[34] In 1989, the English Court of Appeal gave a positive answer to this question in the leading case of *C v C (Minor) (Abduction: Rights of Custody Abroad)*[35] and this was followed by courts in a number of Convention countries.[36] Furthermore, Brussels II bis expressly states that

> custody shall be considered to be exercised jointly when pursuant to a judgment or by operation of law, one holder of parental responsibility cannot decide on the child's place of residence without the consent of another holder of parental responsibility.[37]

Nonetheless, academic commentators remained divided on the issue[38] and there were conflicting decisions within the US.[39] While this debate has now largely been resolved by the US Supreme Court decision in *Abbott v Abbott*,[40] in which the majority held that *ne exeat* rights are custody rights, in light of the importance of the issue and the academic controversy surrounding it, the opposing views will be briefly analysed.

---

[32] *Abbott* (n 30) 805.

[33] In the UK, a person with a residence order may not remove a child from the UK unless he has the consent of all parents who have parental responsibility (and non-custodial parents normally retain parental responsibility), Children Act 1989, s 13(1)(b); similarly, in Israel, a legal guardian has the right to determine the place of his child's residence (under s 15 of the Legal Capacity and Guardianship Law 1962) and a parent remains a legal guardian unless a court expressly dispossesses him of that status on the basis of one of the grounds set out in that Law; in relation to New York, see *C v C (Minors)(Child Abduction)* [1992] 1 FLR 163.

[34] Beaumont and McEleavy (n 18) 76–77.

[35] *C v C (Minor) (Abduction: Rights of Custody Abroad)* [1989] 2 All ER 465. This approach was later confirmed by the House of Lords in *Re D* (n 30).

[36] eg CA (SC) 5271/92 *Foxman v Foxman*, Nevo 19/11/92 (Isr).

[37] Council Regulation (EC) No 2201/2003 of 27 November 2003 concerning jurisdiction and the recognition and enforcement of judgments in matrimonial matters and the matters of parental responsibility [2003] OJ L 338/1-29, Art 2(11)(b).

[38] Compare Beaumont and McEleavy (n 18) 78–79 and L Silberman, 'Interpreting the Hague Abduction Convention: In Search of a Global Jurisprudence' (2005) 38 *UC Davis Law Review* 1049, 1068–72 (in favour) with C Bruch, 'How to Draft a Successful Family Law Convention: Lessons from the Child Abduction Conventions' in J Doek et al (eds), *Children on the Move, How to Implement their Right to Family Life* (Hague, Martinus Nijhoff, 1996); DP Nygh, 'The International Abduction of Children' in J Doek, ibid 34, and M Weiner, 'Navigating the Road between Uniformity and Progress: The Need for Purposive Analysis of the Hague Convention on the Civil Aspects of International Child Abduction' (2002) 33 *Columbia Human Rights Law Review* 303, 323–26 (against).

[39] eg, *Croll* (n 28) and *Gonzalez v Gutierrez* 311 F 3d 942 (9th Cir 2002) holding that *ne exeat* rights were not custody rights, as against *Furnes v Reeves* (n 28), holding that they were custody rights.

[40] *Abbott* (n 30).

ii The Arguments Against

Those who consider that *ne exeat* rights are not custody rights argue that such rights do not confer a right to determine affirmatively the child's place of residence because they are negative in nature, simply preventing foreign relocation.[41] Furthermore, the purpose of the right to veto is to protect the right to access and thus should be considered as ancillary to that right, rather than as creating a custody right. In particular, the *ne exeat* right is not per se indicative of the nature or strength of the relationship between the non-custodial parent and the child. Indeed, the *ne exeat* right will continue to exist even if the non-custodial parent does not exercise his rights of access and, where the right is *ex lege*, even if he does not have any rights of access.[42] Furthermore, it is argued that it is absurd to regard the non-custodial parent's right to veto foreign travel as a right relating to the care of the child when such a parent does not have any other right relating to care of the child (ie no right of 'supervision' or 'management').[43] Similarly, it is claimed that the *ne exeat* right is not a right to determine the child's place of residence because the right holder cannot determine where the child lives either inside or outside the jurisdiction.[44] All that he can do is to veto relocation outside the jurisdiction.

Moreover, it is argued that treating breach of a *ne exeat* right as a basis to trigger mandatory return effectively converts access rights into rights of custody. This blurs the clear distinction envisaged by the Convention between custody and access rights[45] and makes return a remedy for breach of access rights, even though this was not the intention of the drafters.[46]

iii The Arguments in Favour

The statutory basis for holding that *ne exeat* rights are custody rights can be found in Article 5 of the Abduction Convention which defines custody rights as including 'rights relating to the care of the person or the child and, in particular, the right to determine the child's place of residence'. It is argued that the right to veto a removal from the jurisdiction is effectively a right to determine the child's place of residence, because it gives the holder the power to determine whether the child may reside in any country suggested by the other parent and so can be distinguished from a pure access right.

Moreover, the purpose of the *ne exeat* right is inter alia to ensure that disputes concerning the child's country of residence and contact with him are determined by the courts of the country of habitual residence and not by the courts of another country, chosen unilaterally by one parent. This purpose is in keeping with the policy of the Convention that the place of habitual residence is the *forum conveniens* for making decisions concerning the child.[47] Thus, requiring return following removal in breach of a *ne exeat* right gives effect to this policy of the Convention.[48] In addition, returning the child does not per se change the

---

[41] ibid 814 (Stevens J (dissenting)).
[42] *Re D* (n 30) [32].
[43] *Abbott* (n 30) 813 (Stevens J (dissenting)).
[44] ibid 814–15 (Stevens J (dissenting)).
[45] *Croll* (n 28).
[46] C Bruch, 'The Promises and Perils of a Protocol to the 1980 Convention on the Civil Aspects of International Child Abduction' (2011) 1 *Festschrift Fur Ingeborg Schwenzer* 237, 237–38.
[47] *Re D* (n 30) [36].
[48] ibid.

nature of the rights of the non-custodial parent because often the returning child remains in the custody of the abducting parent.

iv *The Scope of the Decision in Abbott*

The case of *Abbott* concerned the mother's breach of a *ne exeat* right conferred on the father by statute in Chile, where the child was habitually resident. In interpreting the nature of this right, the majority relied inter alia on the text of the Convention; the way in which the right was viewed by the Chilean law[49]; the objective and legislative history of the Convention; foreign case law and the opinion of the US State Department. All these sources led the majority to the conclusion that the *ne exeat* right in this case was a custody right and that accordingly the mother was obliged to return the child to Chile.

While the Court was indeed concerned with the particular *ne exeat* right in question, the reasoning of the majority would seem to be wide enough to cover all cases where one parent has the right to veto removal of the child from the jurisdiction, whether that right is derived from the law of the place of habitual residence[50] or from a court order or agreement between the parties. However, the court specifically does not determine whether a *ne exeat* right held by a court will also be considered to be a custody right. Indeed, in this situation, the dissent's argument that the travel restriction is merely intended to protect the jurisdiction of the court is considerably more persuasive.[51] Furthermore, the case would not seem to provide authority in relation to rights which fall short of a right to veto foreign travel. For example, a right to be consulted or informed about taking children out of the jurisdiction would not be considered a right of custody.[52]

Nonetheless, the majority's holding that the *ne exeat* right was also a right relating to the care of the person of the child within Article 5 because it enabled the non-custodial parent to influence important aspects of the child's upbringing, such as identity, culture and language,[53] would seem to go further than the existing case law and opens up questions as to whether other rights might be considered to be custody rights. For example, it could be argued that the right to make decisions concerning the education of the child also enables the holder of that right to control an important aspect of the child's upbringing.[54]

---

[49] *Abbott* (n 30). The Court relied upon a statement in a letter from the Chilean agency that the Chilean statutory provision meant that neither parent could unilaterally establish the child's place of residence.

[50] In *Abbott* ibid, there was an express Chilean statutory provision, but the reasoning would seem wide enough to cover cases where the prohibition of removal without the consent of the left-behind parent derived from the common law of the habitual residence as in the case of *C v C* (n 35).

[51] See L Silberman, 'Taking "Ne Exeat" Rights Seriously: The US Supreme Court's *Abbott* Decision' (2010 draft) available from the London Metropolitan University website (with permission), www.londonmet.ac.uk/depts/lgir/research-centres/centre-for-family-law-and-practice/cpd-and-events/inaugural-conference-2010/conference-papers.cfm.

[52] eg *Re V-B* (n 30); Irish decision in *WPP v SRW* [2001] ILRM 371; ECJ decision in Case C-400/10 PPU J *McB v LE* [INCADAT cite: HC/E/ 1104]; cf *Gross v Boda* [1995] 1 NZLR 569 [34].

[53] *Abbott* (n 30) 803.

[54] In the case of *S v H (Abduction: Access Rights)* [1998] Fam 49, 57, it was held that access rights combined with the right 'to watch over the child's education, instruction and living arrangements' did not amount to custody rights. However, the position might be different where there is a right to determine the nature of the child's education.

D Unmarried Fathers

i Differences in Domestic Laws

In many countries today, unmarried fathers have automatic rights in relation to their children, in exactly the same way as married fathers do.[55] However, there are still countries, such as the UK,[56] some States of the US,[57] New Zealand,[58] France[59] and Holland,[60] where an unmarried father does not possess custody rights unless he acquires them by court order or by another method recognised in the State in question, such as by agreement with the mother, or registration. Accordingly, if the mother or another person succeeds in removing the child before the father has carried out the procedure necessary to acquire rights, then prima facie the removal is not wrongful.[61] This will be the case even if de facto the father has been caring for the child alone or together with the mother or another person. In a number of cases, courts have found various legal mechanisms to avoid such an outcome. However, where none of these mechanisms is applicable, the removal will not be wrongful.[62]

ii Inchoate Rights

English courts have extended the concept of custody rights to include 'the inchoate rights of those who are carrying out duties and enjoying privileges of a custodial or parental character which, though not yet formally recognized or granted by law, a court would nevertheless be likely to uphold in the interests of the child concerned'.[63] In the case of *Re B (A Minor) (Abduction)*,[64] the father, who did not have any rights in relation to the child under the local law of Western Australia, had been caring for the child with the agreement of the mother. He consented to the maternal grandmother bringing the child to the UK for an extended holiday on the condition that the legal position was formalised. A consent order was drawn up which would give the father sole custody, but due to technical difficulties this was not registered with the Court, which was necessary for the agreement to have legal effect, until after the grandmother's departure. In a majority decision, the English Court of Appeal held that there had been a wrongful removal. Waite LJ[65] held that the concept of custody rights in the Convention was not necessarily restricted to rights propounded by law or conferred by a court order but could also include inchoate rights. Subsequent case law has clarified that the test for determining the existence of inchoate rights is

---

[55] eg in Israel under s 14 of the Legal Capacity and Guardianship Law 1962.
[56] eg, *AAA v ASH* [2009] EWHC 636 (Fam).
[57] eg, *HI v MG* [2000] 1 IR 110.
[58] eg *Fairfax* (n 30).
[59] eg *Guichard v France* (App No 56838/00) ECHR 02 September 2003.
[60] eg RFam (SC) 9941/12 *AAK v ChSB*, (Isr) (17 February 2013), http://elyon1.court.gov.il/files/12/410/094/w02/12094410.w02.pdf
[61] *Re J (A Minor) (Abduction: Custody Rights)* [1990] 2 AC 562.
[62] eg, *Re W and Re B (Child Abduction: Unmarried Father)* [1998] 2 FLR 146; *Hunter v Murrow* (n 26); *AAA v ASH* (n 56); *Dellabarca v Christie* [1999] 2 NZLR 548; *Ch.S.B. v A.A.K* (n 60); *AAK v ChSB* (n 60).
[63] *Re B (A Minor) (Abduction)* [1994] 2 FLR 249.
[64] ibid.
[65] Staughton LJ, whilst concurring in the result, relied on the agreement as conferring 'something properly described as a custody right' ibid at 268. Peter Gibson LJ dissented with regret, since in his view the decision could not be distinguished from the House of Lords' decision in *Re J (A Minor) (Abduction: Custody Rights)* (n 61).

whether there is a reasonable prospect that a court would perfect those rights, if asked to do so.[66]

The concept of inchoate rights, as defined by Waite LJ, has been adopted in a number of subsequent cases in England[67] and in New Zealand,[68] but rejected by the majority of the Supreme Court of Ireland[69] and by the European Court of Justice.[70] In England, the concept has been restricted to cases where the alleged father is the primary caregiver or is sharing care-giving with someone other than the mother.[71] Accordingly, the father is not considered as having inchoate rights where he is living together with the mother and they are sharing care of the child,[72] but only where the mother had abandoned the care of the child.[73] This restriction seems to have been made in order to avoid inconsistency with the House of Lords' decision in *Re J*,[74] in which the unmarried father was held to have no custody rights, even though he had been living with the mother. The distinction has been justified on the basis that courts are prepared to do their utmost to protect children who have been abducted from their primary carers.[75] Nonetheless, it can be argued that the distinction is artificial because there are many cases where the court would most likely grant parental rights to a father who had been sharing care with the mother.

iii Court's Rights

In a number of cases, the court has overcome the lack of the unmarried father's custody rights by holding that there has been a breach of custody rights vested in the court,[76] where the court is actively seised of proceedings to determine rights of custody.[77] This has been justified on the basis that 'there is something particularly repugnant about a litigant seeking to frustrate the processes of the law in this way.'[78] It has been made clear that the proceedings must involve rights of custody and thus proceedings concerning the extent of contact alone would not be sufficient.[79] Thorpe LJ also indicated that the existence of court proceedings would not vest a right of custody in the court if the application was hopeless or

---

[66] *Re F (Abduction: Unmarried Father: Sole Carer)* [2003] 1 FLR 839.
[67] eg, ibid; *K v K* (n 25); See also *Re O (Child Abduction: Custody Rights)* [1997] 2 FLR 702; *Re G (Abduction) (Rights of Custody)* [2002] 2 FLR 703 (grandparents were held to have acquired inchoate custody rights).
[68] *Anderson v Paterson* [2002] NZFLR 641.
[69] *HI v MG* (n 57).
[70] *McB v LE* (n 52) [2011] Fam 364, sub nom *JMcB v LE* [2011] 1 FLR 518.
[71] *Re B* (n 63) was distinguished in the case of *Re W and Re B* (n 62) because the fathers in question were not 'carrying out duties and enjoying privileges of a custodial or parental character' other than their contact with the child. Thus, the fact that the father had applied for a parental responsibility order, which was later granted, was insufficient to confer on him an inchoate custody right.
[72] Per Hale J (as she then was) in *Re W and Re B* ibid, followed by Munby J in *Re C (Child Abduction) (Unmarried Father: Rights of Custody)* [2002] EWHC 2219 (Fam); *AAA v ASH* (n 56).
[73] In *Re C (Child Abduction) (Unmarried Father: Rights of Custody)* ibid.
[74] *Re J (A Minor) (Abduction: Custody Rights)* (n 61); See the Lord Chancellor's Child Abduction Unit Practice Note: 'Hague Convention: Applications by Fathers without Parental Responsibility' (1998) *Family Law* 224; [1998] 1 FLR 491.
[75] *Re W and Re B* (n 62) (Hale J).
[76] eg ibid; *Re H (A Minor) (Abduction: Rights of Custody)* [2000] 2 AC 291; *Re J (Abduction: Declaration of Wrongful Removal)* [1999] 2 FLR 653; *Secretary, Attorney-General's Department v TS* (2001) FLC 93-063; *A v B (Abduction: Declaration)* [2008] EWHC 2524 (Fam).
[77] For criticism of the concept that courts have rights of custody, see decision of Lord Prosser in *Seroka v Bellah* [1995] SLT 204.
[78] ibid.
[79] *Re V-B* (n 30).

insincere.[80] However, this caveat was not mentioned by the House of Lords in that case[81] and does not seem to have been relied on in subsequent cases.[82]

There has been some discussion as to the point in time at which the custody right is vested in the court. The House of Lords has held that the date of service, when the court is seised, will usually be the relevant date,[83] but left open the possibility of an earlier date where there was an interim order[84] or other special circumstances. This would presumably include cases where 'the matter has come before a judge who exercises a judicial discretion as to the future conduct of the proceedings' prior to service.[85]

iv Chasing Orders

While, as seen above, Article 3 refers to rights of custody existing and exercised immediately before the wrongful removal or retention, in a number of cases, involving unmarried fathers, effect has been given to custody rights bestowed on the father by a 'chasing order', issued after the removal of the child. For example, in the leading UK case of *Re S (A Minor) (Custody: Habitual Residence)*,[86] the child was removed from England to Ireland by the maternal grandmother and aunt following the death of the mother, at a time in which no-one had custody rights in relation to the child. Two days later, the father invoked the wardship jurisdiction and was granted custody of the child. In an Article 15 declaration, the House of Lords held that whilst the removal was not wrongful, there was a wrongful retention as from the date of the English court order.

Similarly in the case of *Re B-M (Wardship: Jursidiction)*,[87] the father who had been living with the mother until six weeks before the removal and had applied for a parental responsibility order, invoked the wardship jurisdiction shortly after the removal. Again, the English Court, in an Article 15 declaration, held that there had been a breach of the Court's rights.

v Access Rights

In the case of *Gross v Boda*, the New Zealand Court of Appeal held that access rights may constitute 'an intermittent right to possession and care of the child' and thus may be considered custody rights for the purpose of the Convention.[88] This decision is out of line with case law in other jurisdictions[89] and the English Court of Appeal[90] has refused to give effect to a New Zealand Article 15 declaration based on this decision.[91]

---

[80] *Re H (Child Abduction: Rights of Custody)* [2000] 1 FLR 201.
[81] *Re H (A Minor) (Abduction: Rights of Custody)* (n 76).
[82] Indeed, in the Scottish case of *O v O* 2002 SC 430, the Court of Session held that provided that the application was for custody, the Court acquired rights of custody, even though the applicant only sought access at the material time.
[83] *Re H (A Minor) (Abduction: Rights of Custody)* (n 76).
[84] As in *A v B (Abduction: Declaration)* (n 76).
[85] *Re C (Child Abduction) (Unmarried Father: Rights of Custody)* (n 72) relying on *Re J (Abduction: Declaration of Wrongful Removal)* (n 76).
[86] *Re S (A Minor) (Custody: Habitual Residence)* (n 5).
[87] *Re B-M (Wardship: Jurisdiction)* [1993] 1 FLR 979.
[88] *Gross v Boda* (n 52).
[89] *cf* obiter comment in the European Court of Human Rights (ECtHR) case of *Neulinger and Shuruk v Switzerland*, A no 41615/07 (2010) [101] of the decision of the majority, that the mother's removal was wrongful because it rendered illusory, in practice, the right of access that had been granted to the father.
[90] *Hunter v Murrow* (n 26).
[91] *M v H (Custody)* [2006] NZFLR 623.

It should be noted that in enacting the Abduction Convention, the New Zealand legislature made a slight change to the definition of custody rights in Article 5 of the Convention,[92] substituting the phrase 'the right to the possession and care of the child' for the phrase 'rights relating to the care of the person of the child'. However, it is doubtful whether the difference between the New Zealand jurisprudence and that in the rest of the Hague world can be explained on the basis of the slightly different formulation.[93]

In the later New Zealand Court of Appeal case of *Fairfax v Ireton*,[94] Baragwanath J, whilst conceding that the *Gross v Boda* jurisprudence was an incorrect interpretation of the Convention as originally drafted,[95] justified the New Zealand approach in light of the fundamental changes in attitude to the relationship between a child and his unmarried father.[96] Following the decision in *Gross v Boda*,[97] the issue arose as to whether access arrangements which had been agreed between the parties, rather than under a court order, could also be considered as rights of custody. The question hinged on whether informal agreements between the parties could be considered as agreements having legal effect. In the case of *M v H*,[98] it was held that the informal oral arrangement, under which the father saw his son at specified times twice a week, was an agreement having legal effect. The New Zealand High Court took the view that parents who were able to come to care arrangements on an informal basis should not be prejudiced, provided there was proper evidence as to the nature of the arrangements and as to the fact that they were being exercised at the time of removal.

In the later case of *Fairfax v Ireton*, the majority of the New Zealand Court of Appeal[99] confirmed that an agreement relating to day-to-day care and contact can be an agreement having legal effect and pointed out that non-recognition of such an agreement for Abduction Convention purposes would be inconsistent with the clear policy of the New Zealand legislation to encourage parents to come to agreed arrangements in relation to the care of their children.[100] The Court also pointed out that the parenting plan in the current case also had legal effect in the sense that it would be very significant if the father were to apply to the Court for a parenting order or to be appointed as a guardian.[101]

E Article 15 Declarations

Article 15 of the Abduction Convention provides that the court of the requested State may request that the applicant obtains a decision from the authorities of the child's State of habitual residence that the removal was wrongful within the meaning of Article 3 of the

---

[92] Section 4(a) of the New Zealand 1991 Amendment Act provides '(1) For the purposes of this Part of this Act, a person has rights of custody in respect of a child if, under the law of the Contracting State in which the child was, immediately before his or her removal, habitually resident, that person has, either alone or jointly with any other person or persons, – (a) The right to the possession and care of the child; and (b) To the extent permitted by the right referred to in paragraph (a) of this subsection, the right to determine where the child is to live.'

[93] *Gross v Boda* (n 52) [25] (Hardie Boys J), but compare McKay J at [32]. Ironically, the New Zealand legislation's formulation would appear to narrow the meaning of custody rights by adopting a cumulative test.

[94] *Fairfax* (n 30).

[95] *Gross v Boda* (n 52) [172].

[96] ibid [176].

[97] ibid.

[98] *M v H* (n 91).

[99] *Fairfax* (n 30).

[100] ibid [56]–[58].

[101] ibid [59].

Convention. Four main issues have arisen in relation to what have come to be known as Article 15 declarations, which will now be explored in the following sections.

i Who May Seek a Declaration?

Article 15 clearly envisages that the court of the requested State will request the declaration. However, in some countries implementing legislation or case law has provided that in fact the applicant may himself seek such a declaration.[102] Furthermore, in one English case, an Article 15 declaration was made after the foreign court had refused to order return, based on a misunderstanding of the English law in relation to attribution of custody rights.[103]

ii Who May Give an Article 15 Declaration?

Article 15 does not define which authorities can give a decision or determination in relation to wrongful removal. It seems that in most countries, courts give such declarations.[104] However, recently Dutch courts have refused to give a declaration, in two cases involving Israel,[105] on the basis that there is no internal legislation giving it authority to make such a declaration and that in Holland the practice is for the Central Authority to give such declarations.[106]

iii What is the Scope of the Declaration?

According to the narrow approach, an Article 15 declaration should only clarify the nature of the applicant's rights under local law and should not express a view as to how these rights should be classified under the autonomous Convention definition of custody rights.[107] The reason for this is that the view of the requesting State on the Convention question 'will be no more influential than the views of any other foreign court as to what is the "autonomous" law of the Convention'[108] and applicants should not be encouraged to seek an Article 15 declaration because the requesting State's interpretation of custody rights seems more favourable to them.[109] However, the House of Lords, adopting a wider approach, has held that the declaration should include the view of the requesting State as to classification of the relevant rights under the Convention because '[t]he foreign court is much better placed than the English to understand the true meaning and effect of its own laws in Convention terms'.[110]

---

[102] eg in England and Wales, s 8 of the Child Abduction and Custody Act 1985; *Re P (Abduction: Declaration)* [1995] 1 FLR 831; in Israel FamA (JLM) 1109/06 *GH v GY* Nevo (Dist) 24 December 2006 (Isr) (relying on Art 29 of the Convention) and thereafter an amendment in 2008 to Regulation 295(22) of the Civil Procedure Regulations 1984 (making it clear that the applicant can apply for an Art 15 declaration even if the authorities of the requested State did not do so); *cf* in Australia, *In the Marriage of Resina* [1991] FamCA 33.

[103] *A v B (Abduction: Declaration)* (n 76); *cf Mercredi v Chaffe* [2011] EWCA Civ 272.

[104] eg s 8 of the UK Child Abduction and Custody Act 1985, empowering the relevant courts to make such an Art 15 declaration.

[105] As reported in the decision of the Israeli District Court which had requested the declaration, Fam (TA) 1006//12 *ChSB v AAK* nevo 24 December 2012 [13].

[106] Decision of the Dutch Court (in Hertogenbosch) in 246521/FA RK 12-2169 2 of 20 December 2012 (the author relied on a translation supplied to her by the mother's lawyer in one of the cases).

[107] eg English Court of Appeal in *Deak v Deak* [2006] EWCA Civ 830; New Zealand Court of Appeal in *Fairfax* (n 30).

[108] *Fairfax* ibid.

[109] ibid.

[110] *Re D* (n 30) [44].

Sometimes the court of the requesting State also expresses its view as to whether the child was habitually resident there immediately before the removal or retention. However, there is little point in this since habitual residence has to be determined by the court of the requested State in accordance with its own approach to habitual residence.[111]

iii Is an Article 15 Declaration Binding?

Again, differing views have been expressed in relation to the binding nature of Article 15 declarations. The better view would seem to be that such a declaration is binding unless it is clearly out of line with the international understanding of the Convention's terms.[112]

F Actual Exercise of Custody Rights

Under Article 3(b) of the Convention, a removal or retention will only be considered wrongful where it is in breach of custody rights which were actually exercised immediately before the removal or retention or would have been so exercised but for the removal or retention.

Courts have interpreted the concept of exercise of custody rights widely and rarely hold that there has not been an exercise of custody rights.[113] Thus, for example, it has been held on a number of occasions that the custodial parent's delegation of care of the child to a third party is in fact a discharge of his duties to the child and thus an exercise of his right to custody.[114] Similarly, a Scottish court held that a parent who was detained in hospital for a period of time was to be treated as continuing to exercise his parental rights.[115] The nearest attempt at actually defining exercise of rights of custody can be found in the leading US case of *Friedrich v Friedrich*, where Boggs J said that courts should 'liberally find "exercise" whenever a parent with *de jure* custody rights keeps, or seeks to keep, any sort of regular contact with his or her child'.[116]

---

[111] Eg in *Tsimhoni v Eibschitz-Tsimhoni*, US District Court for Eastern District of Michigan (Unreported, 26 March 2010), the US Court, in holding that the children had not become habitually resident in Israel during their three-month stay there, did not give any weight to the finding in the Israeli Court's Article 15 declaration, that they had done so, FamC (KS) 29189-12-09 *TsL v ATsM*, Nevo 23 December 2009.

[112] ibid; Beaumont and McEleavy (n 18) 65; *cf In the Marriage of Resina* (n 102); *Hunter v Murrow* (n 26); N Lowe, M Everall and M Nicholls, *International Movement of Children: Law, Practice and Procedure* (Bristol, Jordans, 2004) 284.

[113] See eg, the statement in *the Scottish case of S v S* 2003 SLT 344 'that it can only be in the most extreme cases that a parent can be said to have failed to exercise his or her custody rights.' This approach was approved by the Inner House of the Court of Session in *AJ v FJ* [2005] CSIH 36. For an example of a refusal to return based on non-exercise of custody rights in a case where the applicant father could not be found at the time of the wrongful retention, see the 2007 decision of the Hungarian Supreme Court detailed in the response to the Permanent Bureau's 2010 Questionnaire, www.hcch.net/index_en.php?act=publications.details&pid=5291&dtid=33, para 1.2.

[114] eg, *Re W (Abduction: Procedure)* [1995] 1 FLR 878; *W v W (Child Abduction: Acquiescence)* [1993] 2 FLR 211, 217; *Police Commissioner of South Australia v Temple* (1993) FLC 92-365; 8Ob121/03g, Oberster Gerichtshof [INCADAT cite: HC/E/AT 548]; But *cf* Israeli case of CA (SC) 870/94 *Barbie v Barbie*, Nevo 22 June 1994 (Isr) [INCADAT cite: HC/E/IL 243], where the father, who had been given temporary custody over the child, allowed the mother to look after the child once her medical condition improved. Even though the father continued to have contact with the child, it was held that he was no longer exercising his rights of custody.

[115] *S v S* (n 113).

[116] *Friedrich v Friedrich* 78 F.3d 1060, 1069 (6th Cir 1996). Reference to contact as being the test for actual exercise can also be found in the German case of 11 UF 121/03, Oberlandesgericht Hamm [INCADAT cite: HC/E/DE 822].

The question arises as to whether contact is an appropriate test for determining actual exercise where the only custody rights held by the left-behind parent is a right to veto removal of the child from the jurisdiction. *Ex hypothesi*, such a right is not connected to contact with the child and can only be exercised if the right-holder is requested to consent to the relocation of the child abroad. Accordingly, the New Zealand Court of Appeal has held that a mother was actually exercising her right to veto removal from New Zealand, despite the fact that she was not involved in the day to day lives of the children,[117] because it was at all times very likely that she would exercise the right of veto.[118] This decision appears to represent a widening of the definition in *Friedrich* and it is hard to disagree with the New Zealand High Court judge, whose decision was overturned, that if this mother was actually exercising her rights of custody, it was difficult to imagine any parent who would not be doing so.[119] However, the result seems to be an inevitable consequence of treating *ne exeat* rights as rights of custody. The question to be asked, which will be discussed below, is whether in light of the wide interpretation of actual exercise of rights of custody, this requirement serves any useful purpose, especially in light of the fact that the non-exercise of rights of custody is one of the exceptions to mandatory return.

IV Analysis in Relation to Breach and Exercise of Custody Rights

A Internal Coherence

i Custody Rights

The wide interpretation given to custody rights to include inchoate rights and even pure access rights is difficult to reconcile with the scheme of the Convention. Firstly, as Beaumont and McEleavy point out,[120] the concept of inchoate rights is inconsistent with the requirement in Article 3 that custody rights have been attributed under the law of the State of habitual residence immediately before the wrongful removal or retention. In the current author's view, this technical inconsistency can be justified where this is the only way of promoting the objectives of the Convention. One way of avoiding this difficulty is by the inchoate right- holder – often an unmarried father – obtaining a chasing order which gives expression to his inchoate rights. As seen above, it has been held that the chasing order turns the lawful removal into an unlawful retention provided that it is obtained before the child's habitual residence changes.

Secondly, the Convention draws a very clear distinction between custody rights and access rights and provides different remedies for the breach of such rights. Whereas the

---

[117] *Chief Executive for Department of Courts v Phelps* [2000] 1 NZLR 168 [21]. The Court explained that 'A breach of any one of the bundle of distinct rights involved with custody may provide a basis for a finding of wrongful removal. The distinct, precisely recognised, right of custody in issue in this case is of course the mother's right to determine her children's place of residence.'
[118] See also comment in *Abbott* (n 30) 804 that the removal of the child without the consent of the *ne exeat* right-holder is a situation where the right 'would have been exercised, but for the removal or retention' within Art 3(b).
[119] *Phelps* (n 117) [19].
[120] Beaumont and McEleavy (n 18) 60.

remedy for the breach of custody rights is a return order, the remedy for the breach of access rights is to secure the exercise of such rights in the country where the children are now living via the Article 21 mechanism.[121] As seen above, one of the main arguments against recognising *ne exeat* rights as custody rights is based on the claim that the right to veto is effectively supporting a right of access and so its breach should not give rise to the remedy of return.[122] Indeed, in the case of *Abbott*, Stevens J (dissenting) [123] held that it was so clear that the literal meaning of custody rights did not include *ne exeat* rights that there was no room to look at supplementary sources of interpretation

However, it can be argued that the definitions of custody and access rights in the Convention do not necessarily require a binary approach, under which a right relating to the child has to be either a right of custody or a right of access. Indeed, the New Zealand Court of Appeal has taken the view that there is a degree of overlap between custody rights and access rights[124] and that 'the fact that a right of access includes a right to take the child for a limited period of time to a place other than the child's habitual residence, does not preclude that right being also a right of custody'.[125] Thus, that Court did not see the fact that in a given case remedies would be available both for breach of custody rights and breach of access rights as inconsistent with the scheme of the Convention. Indeed, a literal interpretation of the Convention does not require that custody and access rights be mutually exclusive, although as will be seen below, this does seem to have been the intention of the drafters.

ii *Actual Exercise of Custody Rights*

The relationship between the two references in the Convention to the actual exercise of rights of custody in the Convention has been referred to as a conundrum.[126] As seen above, Article 3(b) provides that a removal or retention is only wrongful where it violated custody rights that were actually exercised. If this condition is satisfied, how can the Article 13(1)(a) defence of the non-exercise of custody rights ever be established? At first sight, this defence is redundant.[127] Two explanations have been proffered in the case law.

The first, based on the Perez-Vera Report,[128] relies on the shift in the burden of proof.[129] The burden of proof under Article 3(b) is on the applicant, whereas the burden of proof in Article 13(1)(a) is on the abducting parent. With respect, the logic of this is difficult to follow. If the applicant has met the burden of proving that he exercised his custody rights, presumably despite the claim of the abductor that this is not the case, how can the abductor then succeed in meeting the burden of proving non-exercise of rights?[130] This would only

---

[121] See eg, the clear statement of the Canadian Supreme Court case of *Thomson v Thomson* (1994) 3 SCR 551, 'The Convention contains no mandatory provisions for the support of access rights comparable with those of its provisions which protect breaches of rights of custody. This applies even in the extreme case where a child is taken to another country by the parent with custody rights and has been so taken deliberately with the view to render the further enjoyment of access rights impossible' (La Forest J). See also *Re W and Re B* (n 62) (Hale J). In relation to Art 21, see ch 18 below.

[122] See above at II C.

[123] *Abbott* (n 30) 820.

[124] *Gross v Boda* (n 52).

[125] ibid [36] (McKay J), see also [21] (Richardson J) and [7] (Cooke J).

[126] *S v S* (n 113).

[127] A similar argument can be raised in relation to the defence of consent in Art13(1)(a). See ch 10 at VI.

[128] Perez-Vera Report (n 15) para 73

[129] *Phelps* (n 117).

[130] Indeed, in the case of *S v S* (n 113), the abductor claimed non-exercise of custody rights under Art 3(b) but did not claim the defence of non-exercise under Art 13(a). Presumably she realised that if the applicant overcame the Art 3(b) hurdle, she stood no chance of proving the Art 13(1)(a) defence.

be possible if the definition of exercise of custody rights were more stringent under Article 13(1)(a) than the very liberal test under Article 3(b). However, there is no evidence that this is the case and indeed such internal inconsistency in the meaning of the same term would be extremely difficult to justify.

The second explanation rests on the change in the wording between the two sections and on the fact that more than one person or body may have rights of custody, which have been breached. Whilst Article 3(b) simply states that the rights of custody which were breached were actually exercised at the relevant time, the Article 13(a) defence can be invoked where 'the person, institution or other body having the care of the person of the child, was not actually exercising the custody rights at the time of removal or retention'. Thus, it is possible that Article 3(b) will be satisfied because a person or body (not having care of the child), was exercising his rights, but that the Article 13(a) defence can be established because the person or body who had the care of the person of the child was not exercising his rights.[131] Whilst this explanation is consistent with the language of the Convention,[132] it is difficult to believe that the drafters specifically drafted these clauses in order to provide for the unusual case where more than one person or body, other than the abductor, has rights of custody. Interestingly, however, the reference in Article 13(1(a) to a person who had care of the person of the child does perhaps reflect the fact that exercise of rights is really only relevant to rights relating to the actual care of the child, and not to the right to determine the place of the child's residence. However, the issue of exercise of such a right arises equally under Article 3(b). Thus, no useful purpose is served by relying on this subtle change of language between Article 3(b) and Article 13(1)(a).

Rather, the duplication of the requirement of the actual exercise of rights in slightly different language causes unnecessary complication. The Convention would be more internally coherent if there was only one reference to the actual exercise of rights. Treating non-exercise as a defence is more consistent with the scheme of the Convention than making it a threshold requirement. There is no problem in treating removal or retention in breach of custody rights as wrongful, even where the rights were not exercised. Where a parent who wishes to relocate believes that the other parent is not exercising his rights, he should apply to have those rights revoked or for permission to relocate, rather than act in reliance on his own assessment of the situation. The advantage of treating non-exercise as a defence rather than a threshold requirement is that the court will have discretion to decide that, despite the non-exercise of custody rights, the child should still be returned to the country of his habitual residence, where this is in his best interests. This proposal would also avoid the conceptual difficulty, discussed above, of having to prove actual exercise of a *ne exeat* right, where that is the only custody right possessed by the left-behind parent.

B Intention of the Drafters

i Custody Rights

In general, the comments in the Explanatory Report support the prevailing judicial approach of interpreting the concepts of rights of custody and exercise of such rights widely

---

[131] *S v S* (n 113).
[132] Although the defence does not require that the applicant was the one not exercising his rights of custody, as implied in the explanation given in *S v S* ibid.

so as to allow the greatest number of cases to be brought within the scope of the Convention.[133] For example, support for treating informal arrangements as 'an agreement having legal effect'[134] can be found in the observations that this term includes a simple private transaction so long as it is not the sort of agreement prohibited by law and it can 'provide a basis for presenting a legal claim to the competent authorities'.[135]

In addition, the Explanatory Report appears to treat *renvoi* as a rule of alternative reference, allowing the court to choose whether to apply the domestic law or choice of law rules of the law of habitual residence,[136] rather than as a rule requiring that the choice of law rules of the habitual residence be applied in preference to domestic law, as in English case law.[137] On the other hand, the Rapporteur makes clear that the drafters intended to distinguish between custody and access rights. She explains that,

> Although the problems which can arise from a breach of access rights, especially where the child is taken abroad by its custodian, were raised during the Fourteenth Session, the majority view was that such situations could not be put in the same category as the wrongful removals which it is sought to prevent . . . A questionable result would have been attained had the application of the Convention, by granting the same degree of protection to custody and access rights, led ultimately to the substitution of the holders of one type of right by those who held the other.[138]

Accordingly, it seems quite clear that it was not envisaged that pure access rights would be treated as rights of custody.[139]

However, the position in relation to treating *ne exeat* rights as rights of custody is less clear, as it was not directly discussed. On the other hand, treating *ne exeat* rights as rights of custody is consistent with the expressed intention to allow the greatest number of cases to come within the scope of Article 3.[140] On the other hand, two main sources have been brought to support the view that the drafters did not envisage that *ne exeat* rights should be treated as custody rights and thus enable a non-custodial parent to obtain a return order. The first is the comment in paragraph 11 of the Perez-Verez Report that the '[F]undamental purpose' of the Convention is 'to protect children from wrongful international removals or retention by persons bent on obtaining their physical and/or legal custody' shows that the intention was that return should only be ordered where the taking parent was not the custodial parent.[141] However, it can be argued that this statement simply reflects the stereotype situation in the minds of the drafters and does not necessarily preclude the application of the mandatory return mechanism to other situations.

The second source[142] is the rejection of proposals that would have allowed visiting parents to obtain return orders[143] and given exclusive jurisdiction over visitation matters to

---

[133] Perez-Vera Report (n 15), para 67.
[134] One of the sources of rights of custody listed in Art 3.
[135] Perez-Vera Report (n 15), para 70.
[136] ibid and see discussion at section G below.
[137] See above at II A.
[138] Perez-Vera Report (n 15), para 65.
[139] A proposal by the Canadian Delegation to add 'or access' after 'breach of rights of custody' in Art 3 was rejected by 19 votes to 3. See Hague Conference on Private International Law, 3 Actes et documents de la quatorzième session (child abduction) 262 (1980) (Working Doc No 5, a Canadian proposal).
[140] Perez-Vera Report (n 15), para 67.
[141] See eg, *Abbott* (n 30) 810 (Stevens J) (dissenting).
[142] Bruch, 'The Promises and Perils' (n 46) 240.
[143] See n 139.

the country of the child's former habitual residence.[144] However, since the proposals related only to visitation rights and did not deal specifically with *ne exeat* rights, it is doubtful if they can shed much light on the approach which the drafters would have taken to this issue. Furthermore, the second proposal would have included cases in which the non-custodial parent did not even seek return, in which case there would be good reasons for enabling the courts in the new State to determine access issues.

ii Actual Exercise of Custody Rights

In relation to the actual exercise of custody rights, the Rapporteur points out that this requirement reflects the Convention's objective of protecting the child's right to stability in the emotional and social aspects of his life. Accordingly, only rights of custody which are actually exercised can found a return application.[145] In response to the concerns raised at the drafting stage that the need to prove actual exercise of rights could place a heavy burden on the applicant, Professor Perez-Vera explains that the applicant only has to provide preliminary evidence that he had physical care of the child.[146] This comment shows that she did not have in mind situations where the right of custody was the right to determine the child's place of residence, rather than a right to the physical care of the child.

In support of her interpretation that the Convention is built on the tacit assumption that a person with rights of custody will be exercising them,[147] the Rapporteur contrasts the heavy burden of proof imposed on an abductor who wishes to rely on the defence of non-exercise of custody rights by the applicant under Article 13(1)(a).[148] Whilst the Rapporteur's comments support the liberal view taken in the case law to interpreting the requirement of the actual exercise of rights in Article 3(b), they do not explain why the principle of only protecting custody rights that have been actually exercised cannot be adequately given effect to by the Article 13(1)(a) defence.

C Promotion of the Objectives of the Convention

i Protecting Abducted Children

a Custody Rights

It can be argued that, since the purpose of the Convention is to protect children from the harmful effects of a unilateral removal or retention which takes them away from their physical, social and emotional environment,[149] any removal or retention which interferes with the relationship between a child and the left-behind parent should be considered wrongful.[150] The degree of harm caused by the removal or retention is not a function of the legal status of the relationship between parents or even of the classification of the rights of the left-behind parent. Indeed, access arrangements are usually an important part of the

---

[144] Actes et documents (n 139) 281 (Working Doc No 31).
[145] Perez-Vera Report (n 15), para 72.
[146] ibid, para 73.
[147] ibid.
[148] For a discussion of the inter-relationship between these two provisions, see above at IV Aii.
[149] See ch 5 at II Ci
[150] *cf* Weiner, 'Navigating the Road' (n 38) 324–25, who argues that the Convention is only concerned to protect children from the harm caused by removing them from a custodial parent and not from the harmful effects of diminished access.

stability of the social and emotional aspects of a child's life. According to this line of reasoning, the child needs to be protected wherever the left-behind parent was in practice playing a real role in the child's day to day life,[151] regardless of whether his rights could only be described as pure access rights or even if he had no formal rights at all.[152] This is well expressed by Barron J, dissenting, in a Supreme Court of Ireland decision concerning an unmarried father, as follows:

> I am quite satisfied that the purpose of the Convention is to protect the interest of the child from harmful effects of an improper removal or retention. There can be no doubt but that to take a child of five from the only home he has ever known in which he has lived with his mother and father and to deprive him both of the security of that home and the presence of his father is a failure to protect the very interest of the child which the Convention is designed to protect. A removal in such circumstances defeats the purpose of the Convention. In my view, unless the Convention is coercive to the contrary, which it is not, it should be construed to apply to that child.[153]

Alternative remedies of enabling exercise of the access rights in the country of refuge, even where this can be done effectively,[154] may not be sufficient to protect the child from harm, especially where the removal was sudden and surreptitious. A fortiori, breach of a *ne exeat* right, which was expressly designed to protect the child from unilateral removal or retention, should give rise to the return remedy.[155]

However, some have strongly argued that return to a non-primary carer in support of an access right will not protect the child, but will actually cause him harm because he will not be returned to the environment in which he was living beforehand.[156] According to this view, the change in the identity of the caregiver is more damaging to the child, than the change of physical environment and the interference with the relationship between the child and non-primary caregiver.[157] While there is clearly much substance in the argument that a transfer of custody may well cause real harm to the child, this is not an inevitable result of ordering return in such situations. The obligation of the court is to order return to the country of habitual residence, not to the left-behind parent and normally the abducting primary carer will return with the child.[158] Furthermore, as will be seen below,[159] in such a situation, the court will commonly impose undertakings or conditions, designed to protect the welfare of the child and the returning abductor, at least until the matter can be adjudicated before the court in the country of habitual residence.

Of course there will still be cases, in particular where the abducting parent has suffered violence at the hands of the left-behind parent, in which the abducting parent cannot reasonably be expected to return with the child, even with the protection of undertakings or conditions. However, the better solution in such cases is to invoke the Article 13(1)(b)

---

[151] See *Hunter v Morrow* (n 26) (Thorpe LJ).
[152] For a similar approach, see *Fairfax* (n 30) [172].
[153] *HI v MG* (n 57).
[154] See the discussion in ch 18. In some cases, the fact that a return remedy is available may 'force' the abducting parent to agree to satisfactory access by the other parent in return for that parent's agreement that the child remains in the country of refuge.
[155] *Abbott* (n 30) 809.
[156] M Freeman, 'Rights of Custody and Access under the Hague Child Abduction Convention – "A Questionable Result?"' (2000) 1 *California Western International Law Journal* 39, 50; Bruch, 'The Promises and Perils' (n 46) 241.
[157] Bruch ibid 246 and fn 33; See also the psychological research discussed in ch 3 at II D.
[158] A report by the Reunite Research Unit, 'The Outcomes for Children Returned Following an Abduction' (2003), www.reunite.org/edit/files/Library%20-%20reunite%20Publications/Outcomes%20Report.pdf, 35.
[159] In ch 11 at III.

grave risk defence[160] and not to deny that there has been a wrongful removal or retention in the first place. In other words, the fact that there will inevitably be some cases where return of a child, who has been removed or retained by the custodial parent in breach of an access right or even a *ne exeat* right, will cause the child harm rather than protect him is not a reason not to treat the removal or return as wrongful in the first place. Rather, in determining whether one of the exceptions is established, the nature of the relationship between the child and the left-behind parent should be relevant.[161] Thus, interpreting the exceptions more flexibly in cases of breach of *ne exeat* rights, and even pure access rights, is more likely to promote the objectives of the Convention than blocking claims completely in these cases.

However, given the high standard of proof necessary to establish this defence, there will still be cases in which return does not protect the child because, despite the *ne exeat* or other rights possessed by the left-behind parent, that parent was not involved in the life of the child. Nonetheless, this fact does not justify a narrow definition of custody rights which would prevent return being ordered in the many cases where a parent with a *ne exeat* right, or even pure access rights, does have a meaningful relationship with the child. So, consideration will now be given to whether it might be possible to distinguish between these two types of cases by means of the requirement that the rights of custody were actually exercised.

b Actual Exercise of Custody Rights

The requirement of actual exercise of rights appears to be consistent with the objective of protecting the child because it is designed 'to prevent applications being made by persons who have not played any reasonably meaningful role in the life of the children'.[162] Nonetheless, a narrow interpretation of the concept of actual exercise would place an undesirable heavy burden on applicants[163] and a technical approach may well not reflect the reality of the connection between the child and that parent.[164] Accordingly, the liberal approach adopted by the courts to the concept of the actual exercise of custody rights[165] appears to provide the optimal solution. Indeed, as seen above,[166] it might even be argued that the threshold requirement of actual exercise is unnecessary because the child can be adequately protected from being returned at the request of a parent who has not been involved in his life by the defence of non-exercise in Article 13(1)(a).

On the other hand, it would seem that where the concept of rights of custody is extended[167] to include *ne exeat* rights and pure access rights, a more robust approach to actual exercise might be appropriate. The tacit assumption that rights of custody are

---

[160] eg Austrian decision OGH May 2 1992 2 OB 596.91 [INCADAT cite: HC/E/AT375], in which a travel restriction was held to be a custody right but the grave risk defence was held to apply.

[161] Usually, the relevant exception will be the grave risk exception. However, the fact that the left-behind parent did not play any real role in a mature child's life should be taken into account in determining the weight to be given to the child's objections (see ch 12). Similarly, where a year has passed since the abduction, such a fact is likely to make it easier to show acclimatisation in the new country (see ch 9).

[162] *S v S* (n 113).

[163] Perez-Vera Report (n 15), para 73.

[164] As, eg, in the Israeli case of *Barbie v Barbie* (n 114).

[165] See above at II F.

[166] At IV Aii.

[167] Where the rights of custody are in fact inchoate rights, actual exercise is in fact the very basis for the existence of the right. Barron J in *HI v MG* (n 57).

exercised, referred to in the Explanatory Report,[168] should not apply in relation to rights of access. Whilst the applicant need not necessarily show that he exercised his rights of access fully, he should be required to show that he did indeed take care of the child on a regular basis. This approach goes some way to answering the concerns about making return orders in support of pure access rights.

Similarly, we saw above that the requirement of actual exercise in the case of *ne exeat* rights appears meaningless because *ex hypothesi* the right cannot be exercised unless the custodial parent requests the consent of the other parent to relocate. Whilst in most cases the *ne exeat* right-holder also has access rights, the *ne exeat* right itself is not dependent on exercising the rights of access. Nonetheless, it can be convincingly argued that the child is not in fact in need of protection from a unilateral removal or retention if there is no contact between him and the non-custodial parent, even if that parent technically has the right to veto removal. Moreover, return in such a case is liable to cause harm. Thus, there is merit in the decision of the New Zealand High Court that the right to determine the residence of a child had not actually been exercised, where the parent was not playing any part in the child's life, even though this decision was overturned on appeal.[169] Accordingly, the requirement of actual exercise can provide a balance to the extension of the concept of rights of custody. In this context, a more stringent requirement of actual exercise can help to ensure that wide interpretation of the concept of rights of custody does not lead to return orders in cases where such an order does not protect the child because there was no real contact between the child and the left-behind parent. Thus, although in principle, treating non-exercise of rights of custody as a defence rather than a threshold requirement is preferable[170] and adequately protects children, there is a good deal of logic in treating non-exercise as a threshold requirement if it is effectively being used as part of the definition of rights of custody in cases where that concept has been extended.

ii Deterrence

The objective of deterrence seems to require interpreting the concept of custody rights widely.[171] In the words of the US Supreme Court, 'to permit an abducting parent to avoid a return remedy when the other parent holds a *ne exeat* right would run counter to the Convention's purpose of deterring child abductions by parents'.[172] It might, of course, be argued that referring to a removal or retention in such a case as an abduction begs the very question being asked. Nonetheless, it seems reasonable to aim to deter every unilateral removal or retention.

The threat of mandatory return ought to encourage the custodial parent to obtain permission from the non-custodial parent or the court in the country of habitual residence before relocating with the child. This protects the child from the harmful effects of a unilateral removal or retention in a number of ways. Firstly, the court will invariably impose in advance conditions designed to ensure the uninterrupted continuation of the relationship with the non-custodial parent,[173] which will make it harder for the relocating parent to

---

[168] Perez-Vera Report (n 15), para 73.
[169] *Phelps* (n 117).
[170] See above at IV Aii.
[171] And the concept of exercise of rights narrowly.
[172] *Abbott* (n 30) 808.
[173] Alternatively, after bargaining in the shadow of the law, the parties will come to an agreement themselves on the conditions for relocation.

frustrate the exercise of the other parent's access rights or to dictate conditions for the exercise of such rights. Furthermore, the move to the new country will be carried out in an open and planned way.

However, it would seem harder to deter abductions in situations where there is a stringent relocation policy in the country of habitual residence and the custodial parent knows that she will not obtain permission to relocate or that it will take a very long time and/or involve huge expense.[174] In such cases, it may still be worth her while to 'try her luck'. Nonetheless, this does not justify not treating the *ne exeat* right as a custodial right, but rather makes it necessary to consider whether the circumstances are such that return will place the child in an intolerable situation.

iii Adjudication in the Forum Conveniens

The principle that decisions concerning the child should be made by the courts of the child's habitual residence, which is assumed to be the *forum conveniens*, will usually be best realised by giving the widest possible interpretation to custody rights so as to include inchoate rights, chasing orders *ne exeat* rights and even mere rights of access. Where the parent who holds such a right does not consent to the removal of the child, the dispute will need to be decided by a court. Similarly, whilst the parent with pure access rights may not veto the removal, he may still ask a court to do so or even request a transfer of custody. In relation to all of these issues, the court of the child's habitual residence before the removal is usually the most appropriate forum and not the court in the country of refuge.[175] Even where the dispute only concerns future access arrangements, the country of habitual residence may still be the *forum conveniens* because evidence concerning the child's relationship with the left-behind parent will be most easily obtainable there.[176]

iv Justice between the Parents and the Rule of Law

Giving a wide interpretation to rights of custody would also seem to promote the objective of doing justice between the parties. The abductor has violated the rights of the left-behind parent and should not be allowed to benefit therefrom.

D Compatibility with the Summary Nature of Convention Proceedings

The fact that custody rights have to be determined in accordance with the law of the habitual residence makes it necessary to bring proof of that law. This requirement is likely to hinder the speedy resolution of the proceedings and, in some cases, to be inconsistent with the summary nature of Convention proceedings. Whilst Article 14 is designed to make it easier to prove foreign law, this will not help where the content of the foreign law is not clear. The need to determine the content of foreign law can be avoided by use of the Article 15 procedure, but this too may well take a long time.[177] Thorpe LJ has suggested that

---

[174] See generally ch 4.
[175] *Gross v Boda* (n 52) [27].
[176] However, this might be a case where the habitual residence should retain jurisdiction without the child being returned; see ch 5 at II Ciii.
[177] See eg *Re D* (n 30); comments of Thorpe LJ in *K v K* (n 25); responses of US and Netherlands to Question 8 of the 2010 Questionnaire (n 113).

sometimes it will be more efficient to prove foreign law by the appointment of a joint legal expert or requesting an opinion from a liaison judge in the requesting State, although such opinions will not be binding.[178]

Giving a wide interpretation to rights of custody may exacerbate the difficulty. For example, if inchoate rights are treated as rights of custody, it will be necessary to bring evidence as to how a foreign court would have been likely to decide if it had been asked to make an order conferring custody or parental responsibility on the applicant. *Ex hypothesi*, such an exercise is likely to be speculative and not suited to summary proceedings.[179] Furthermore, the adoption of the doctrine of *renvoi* seems to increase the difficulty of proving foreign law since it will also be necessary to determine the relevant private international law rules of the foreign law.[180]

In the current author's view, as will be explained below,[181] the best solution to these problems is to change the 'trigger' so that it is no longer necessary to prove breach of custody rights. However, so long as this is necessary, taking a wide and non-technical approach which places more weight on the autonomous Convention definition than on the law of the habitual residence would seem to be the best way of overcoming the problems involved in proving breach of custody rights. For example, if pure access rights which give the holder 'the intermittent right to care and possession' of the child are treated as rights of custody for the purpose of the Convention, it will often not be necessary to determine whether the left-behind parent also has inchoate rights of custody. Similarly, if *renvoi* is treated as a rule of alternative reference, it will only be necessary to determine the private international law rules of the habitual residence in cases where the applicant, or some other person, does not have custody rights under the domestic law.

In relation to the actual exercise of custody rights, one of the reasons given by the courts for their liberal approach is the recognition that 'embarking on a detailed quantitative or qualitative examination of the way in which custody rights were being exercised by the petitioning parent, at the time of the removal of the children, provided that he had established that he has *de jure* rights' would not be compatible with the nature of Convention proceedings.[182]

E Consistency with Rights and Interests of the Children

The definition of the wrongful removal or retention in terms of parental rights seems inconsistent with an approach based on children's rights because it treats children as merely the objects of the abduction. The message given is that the real victim of the abduction is the left-behind parent and that the breach of his rights in relation to his child enables him to request return of the child in much the same way as an owner who has been dispossessed of his property would request its return. In order to make the Convention consistent with the doctrine of children's rights, it is necessary to change the 'trigger' which activates the obligation to order return. Instead of focusing on breach of parental rights,

---

[178] *Re F (A Child)* [2009] EWCA Civ 416.
[179] Beaumont and McEleavy (n 18) 60.
[180] For criticism of the expert evidence in relation to Spanish rules of private international law, see Beevers and Milla, 'Child Abduction' (n 24) 221.
[181] At IV E.
[182] *S v S* (n 113) quoting *Friedrich* (n 116).

the focus should be on the violation of the child's right[183] to regular contact with both parents and his right to stability in the emotional and social aspects of his life.[184] Thus, a removal or retention should be wrongful where it violates this right of the child, unless such violation is sanctioned by a court or the right has been voluntarily waived by a mature child. There should be a presumption of violation of the child's right whenever, as a result of the removal or retention, the child is living in a different country to one parent, when previously he was living in the same country as that parent. An additional advantage of this approach is that it will avoid all the difficulties which have arisen in determining the meaning of rights of custody because there will be no need to distinguish between rights of custody and rights of access.

While, of course, in cases where the child's relationship with the left-behind parent was not significant or was damaging to him, his right to have contact with both parents may sometimes conflict with other rights of his, such as the right to proper development and the right to have his best interests treated as a primary consideration.[185] However, this balancing of rights should be carried out by the courts of the State of his habitual residence, unless the actual return will involve disproportionate violation of his rights,[186] in which case one of the exceptions should be invoked.

Nonetheless, so long as wrongful removal or retention continue to be defined in terms of parental rights, consistency with the doctrine of children's rights can best be ensured by interpreting rights of custody in the widest possible way, using the approaches and techniques illustrated in Part II above. However, it must be emphasised that it is necessary to recognise that other rights of the child may override the child's right to contact with both of his parents, in particular where return will cause the child harm, and thus the exceptions must also be interpreted in a way which gives effect to these rights.

F Consistency with Rights of the Parents

i The Right to Family Life

The issue of the parents' right to family life is particularly relevant in the case of unmarried fathers, who are not automatically accorded parental rights in some legal systems. In the case of *Re W* and *Re B*,[187] it was argued on behalf of the unmarried father that the Court should take the widest possible approach to the concept of custody rights because there are good policy reasons to remove all forms of discrimination between the children of married and unmarried parents and to give the children of unmarried parents the same protection as those of married parents. However, the learned judge rejected this argument, commenting that courts are not the appropriate forum for adequately addressing social policy debates.[188] Furthermore, no case had held that all differences between mothers and fathers

---

[183] Refreshing judicial recognition of this idea can be found in the words of Barron J in the Irish case of *HI v MG* (n 57): 'Nevertheless it seems to me that the Convention is more interested in the rights of the children than in the rights of the parents. Our courts in custody matters are well used to the proposition that the decision of the Court is dependent upon the welfare of the children and not upon the rights or wrong of the situation between the parents.'
[184] Perez-Vera Report (n 15), para 72.
[185] See generally ch 6 at II.
[186] For example, where there has been domestic violence or a mature child objects.
[187] *Re W and Re B* (n 62).
[188] ibid.

or between married and unmarried fathers are contrary to the European Convention on Human Rights (ECHR).[189] Thus, since English domestic law clearly provided that the fathers in question did not have rights of custody, there was no basis to hold otherwise in these cases.[190] While there have been changes in UK legislation since that case, which enable unmarried fathers to acquire parental rights through registration by the mother, this has not led to any change in the courts' approach to cases where there has not been registration in accordance with the provisions of the new law.[191]

With respect, it seems that this approach does not give sufficient weight to the human rights of the father and the child. Whilst it may be possible to justify discrimination against unmarried fathers in general on the basis that it is necessary to prevent unmeritorious fathers abusing their rights, this justification cannot be relied upon in specific cases where the father was playing a significant role in the life of the child prior to removal by the mother.[192] In such cases, an automatic bar on the father obtaining a return order simply because of his unmarried status, even where he was de facto caring for the child by himself or together with the mother, is a clear violation of his right to family life within Article 8 of the ECHR. The rights of the child and the father to family life should not be prejudiced by the fact that the father had not complied with the formalities of the law, where it seems clear that a court order could have been obtained.[193]

Furthermore, taking a narrow approach to the rights of unmarried fathers is likely to lead to the non-uniform application of the Convention, in light of the fact that increasingly and in different jurisdictions the relationship of the unmarried father with an abducted child is classified in domestic law as a right of custody.[194] Accordingly, consistency with the human rights of the child and the father, as well as uniform implementation throughout the Hague world, can only be ensured by finding that unmarried fathers who have been involved in the lives of their children have rights of custody. As seen above, there are a number of techniques available for achieving such a result. Of course, as already pointed out, treating breach of the rights of the child as the 'trigger' for the activation of the obligation to order return would solve the problem of unmarried fathers immediately.

ii Mobility Rights

It has been claimed that treating a *ne exeat* right as a right of custody violates the custodial parent's right to freedom of movement.[195] This argument is unsustainable for a number of reasons. Firstly, the travel restriction derives from the domestic law of the place of habitual

---

[189] This is still the approach of the ECtHR jurisrpudence. In the case of *Guichard v France* (n 59), the decision of a French court that removal from France by the mother was not wrongful because the father did not have rights of custody under French law was upheld. Similarly, see also *B v UK* [2000] 1 FLR and *McB v LE* (n 52).

[190] Similarly, Keene J in the Supreme Court of Ireland in *HI v MG* (n 57), held that the problems caused by the fact that unmarried fathers do not have rights of custody for Abduction Convention purposes in some jurisdictions had to be resolved through the Hague Conference's mechanisms and not by judicial innovation.

[191] eg *AAA v ASH* (n 56) (father registered the child instead of the mother).

[192] K Beevers, 'Child Abduction: Inchoate Rights of Custody and the Unmarried Father' (2006) 18 *Child and Family Law Quarterly* 499, 515.

[193] *cf* The decision of the EC in *McB v LE* (n 52) [58], holding that the father can exercise his rights by applying to the court for custody or access rights.

[194] *Fairfax* (n 30) (Bragnwath J) quoted by Thorpe LJ in *K v K* (n 25).

[195] This argument was accepted in the case of *Croll* (n 28); See also comment of La Forest J in *Thomson* (n 121) that treating a permanent ne exeat right as a right of custody 'has serious implications for the mobility rights of the custodian'.

residence. Thus, if there is any violation of rights, it is that law which is responsible for the violation. Secondly, the *ne exeat* right and even the return order do not technically restrict the movement of the custodial parent himself. If the custodial parent agrees to transfer custody to the other parent, the former parent can travel wherever he wishes. Alternatively, he can request the court's permission to travel or relocate with the child, where the other parent does not consent. Finally, even if there is some violation of the custodial parent's right to movement, this is a necessary corollary of that parent's duties in relation to the child and the rights of the child to continued contact with the other parent. Thus, any violation is justified and proportional.

G Consistency with Private International Law Principles

Article 1(b) of the Abduction Convention states that one of the objectives of the Convention is 'to ensure that rights of custody and of access under the law of one Contracting State are effectively respected in other Contracting States'. However, this objective is limited by Article 3 of the Convention, which provides that a removal or retention is wrongful where it is in breach of rights of custody under the law of the habitual residence of the child immediately before the removal or retention. As seen above,[196] this provision effectively creates both a choice of law rule and a rule for the recognition of foreign judgments. The law of the habitual residence governs the question of whether there has been a breach of custody rights[197] and thus judgments of the law of habitual residence have to be recognised by the requested State.[198] Consideration will now be given to the extent to which these rules are consistent with the principles of private international law, explained above.[199]

i Choice of Law and Renvoi

There are two main difficulties with the use of habitual residence as the connecting factor in the Abduction Convention's choice of law rule. One is that the uncertainty inherent in the concept of habitual residence[200] is not desirable in a choice of law rule.[201] The other is that, in some situations, the law of the habitual residence may not be the most closely connected law or the law which the parties expect to apply.[202] Obviously, this will depend to a large extent on the way in which habitual residence is determined, which will be discussed in detail in chapter 8. However, an example will be given here to illustrate the problem. Take a case where a child was born to unmarried parents in a country which automatically bestowed full custody rights on both parents. Assume that the parties move to another country, which does not recognise the father's rights and that, after the child has become habitually resident in that country, the mother removes the child without the father's

---

[196] Chapter 6 at IV A.
[197] Although, as seen above, the final determination has to be made in accordance with the autonomous Convention definition of rights of custody.
[198] This is made clear by the last paragraph of Art 3 which states that rights of custody may arise inter alia 'by reason of a judicial or administrative decision'.
[199] In ch 6 at IV.
[200] See ch 8.
[201] The English Law Commission rejected the use of habitual residence as a connecting factor in questions relating to personal status because of the inherent uncertainty in the concept (Law Com No 168, 1993, para 3.8).
[202] These are the parameters identified for testing whether choice of law rules achieve the objective of doing justice, explained in ch 6 at IV C.

consent. It seems unlikely that the parties would have expected that the migration would have effectively terminated the custody rights of the father. Yet, this would be the effect of applying the law of the country of habitual residence.[203]

Accordingly, the current author has suggested that in the relatively few cases where there is another law which is clearly more closely connected to the relationship between the child and the parties, that law should determine whether there has been a breach of custody rights.[204] It may be noted that a similar provision appears in the 1996 Child Protection Convention.[205]

It may be thought that the doctrine of *renvoi*, which the drafters seem to have included in the Convention,[206] will increase consistency with the objectives of private international law. Indeed, applying the choice of law rules of the habitual residence may lead to application of a domestic law which is more closely connected or which better accords with the expectations of the parties.[207] In addition, the use of *renvoi* should promote harmony by ensuring that the forum applies the same substantive law that the courts of the habitual residence would themselves apply.[208]

On the other hand, as Beevers and Milla point out, this harmony may well be illusory because of differences in characterisation in the laws of the respective countries[209] and because of the artificiality of only looking at the choice of law rule of the habitual residence in isolation from other rules which may be applied by that court, such as mandatory rules and public policy.[210] Moreover, the use of *renvoi* may lead to the application of a law which is less closely connected than the domestic law of the habitual residence and to a result which does not accord with the expectations of the parties and does not promote the goals of the Abduction Convention. Indeed, this is what happened in the case of *Re JB Child Abduction) (Rights of Custody: Spain)*,[211] where the Spanish law of habitual residence applied English law as the law of the nationality, even though the eight-year-old child had lived in Spain all his life and even though application of the English law resulted in a determination that the father did not have any custody rights.

However, these problems can largely be resolved by treating *renvoi* as a rule of alternative reference,[212] as envisaged by the Explanatory Report.[213] Thus, wherever there has been a breach of custody rights either under the domestic law or the choice of law rules of the State of habitual residence, the removal or retention will be wrongful. This approach effectively makes use of the advantages of the doctrine of *renvoi* whilst avoiding its disadvantages, in a way which promotes the objectives of the Convention.

---

[203] *cf* Art 16(3) of the Child Protection Convention, which provides: 'Parental responsibility which exists under the law of the State of the child's habitual residence subsists after a change of that habitual residence to another State.'

[204] R Schuz, 'The Hague Child Abduction Convention: Family Law and Private International Law' (1995) 44 *International And Comparative Law Quarterly* 771, 800.

[205] Article 15(2) provides: 'However, in so far as the protection of the person or the property of the child requires, they may exceptionally apply or take into consideration the law of another State with which the situation has a substantial connection.'

[206] See at IV Bi above.

[207] In particular, where the parties have not lived for long in the country of habitual residence.

[208] Beevers and Milla, 'Child Abduction' (n 24) 221.

[209] ibid, claiming that while English law regarded the issue as one of paternal responsibility, Spanish law would have regarded the issue as one of filiation.

[210] ibid; the issue of public policy was taken on board in the later case of *K v K* (n 25).

[211] *Re JB* (n 23).

[212] Sometimes also referred to as *renvoi in favorem*, Beevers and Milla, 'Child Abduction' (n 24) 228.

[213] See IV B above.

ii Recognition of Judgments and the Incidental Question

The Abduction Convention requires automatic recognition of judgments of the habitual residence which determine custody rights in relation to the child. Whilst there is no express provision for recognition of judgments of third States, which are recognised by the law of habitual residence, it seems clear that application of the law of habitual residence should be interpreted so as to include the recognition rules contained in that law.[214]

These recognition rules are accompanied by a partial non-recognition rule in Article 17, which expressly provides that custody orders of the forum or of a third State,[215] which are inconsistent with the custody rights under the law of the country of habitual residence, may not be used as a reason for not returning the child.[216] This would be the situation, for example, where the judgment of the third State conferred exclusive custody rights on the abductor, but under the law of the State of habitual residence the left-behind parent also possessed custody rights, despite the foreign judgment.[217] In other words, Article 17 requires giving precedence to the law of the habitual residence where that law confers custody rights rather than to the recognition rules of the forum, where these will result in denial of those rights.

This rule is an inevitable consequence of the fundamental assumption adopted by the drafters of the Abduction Convention that the habitual residence of the child is the appropriate forum for making decisions concerning custody and access in relation to children and for determining the rights of adults in relation to them. Thus, the private international law objective of giving effect to judgments of other States is overridden by the private international law objectives of ensuring adjudication in the most appropriate forum and the application of the most appropriate law. This preference is clearly correct where indeed the habitual residence is the *forum conveniens* and the most appropriate law.

However, the question arises as to whether the assumption in favour of the law of the habitual residence should also apply where recognition of the judgment of a third State will lead to return and the application of law of habitual residence would not. Take, for example, the situation where there is a judgment of a third State which confers custody rights on the unmarried father. If this judgment is not recognised by the law of the place of habitual residence, then he would not have rights of custody 'under the law of that State' and accordingly the removal is not wrongful. Thus, even though Article 17 does not expressly forbid recognition of the foreign judgment because its recognition would in fact lead to return, in practice the requested State cannot recognise that judgment for the purpose of the Abduction Convention proceedings. Nonetheless, of course, it may recognise the foreign judgment for all other purposes and can order return of the child under other laws.

In analysing whether the preference for the law of the habitual residence in this situation is in accordance with private international law principles, it will be helpful to appreciate that the incidental question arises here. In order to determine whether the removal is

---

[214] Perez-Vera Report (n 15), para 69.
[215] Entitled to recognition in the forum.
[216] Art 17. However, the Art does allow the reasons for the forum or foreign decision to be taken into consideration, presumably in determining if one of the defences is applicable. *cf* Art 10(1)(d) of the Council of Europe Convention, under which the existence of a conflicting decision may be a defence to recognition, as in *Re M (Child Abduction) (European Convention)* [1994] 1 FLR 551.
[217] Either because the foreign judgment is not recognised by the State of habitual residence or because the latter's internal law overrides the foreign judgment.

wrongful (the main question), it is necessary to decide whether the foreign judgment is recognised. The question is which recognition rules are to be used for this purpose. Application of the recognition rules of the law of the habitual residence (the *lex causae* approach) will lead to a determination that there has been no breach of custody rights and thus that the removal is not wrongful. In contrast, application of the recognition rules of the requested State (the *lex fori* approach) will lead to a determination that the father does possess custody rights and so the removal was wrongful.

Article 3 of the Convention adopts the former approach because it expressly refers to custody rights under the law of habitual residence and thus gives precedence to the recognition rules of the law of the habitual residence. The advantage of this approach is that it will lead to uniformity of result in different fora because all Contracting States will decide in accordance with the private international law rules of the State of habitual residence. However, it can be argued that the latter approach also has a number of significant advantages. In particular, it will promote internal harmony within the forum and is consistent with the general trend of increasing recognition of foreign judgments.[218] Moreover, where the forum's recognition rules are based on bilateral or multilateral treaties, refusal to recognise the judgment involves a violation of those treaties.[219]

How would a purposive approach work in this context? On the one hand, it may be argued that it is pointless to return the child to the State of habitual residence because, under the law of that country, the mother has sole custody and can leave again without obtaining permission from the father or the court. On the other hand, at least where the father has been exercising the rights which he has under the foreign judgment, the unilateral removal is uprooting the child from his environment and the relationship with his father and so prima facie comes within the purpose of the Convention's mandatory return mechanism. Furthermore, the father might be able to take steps in the country of habitual residence to obtain rights which will prevent a further unilateral removal.

Thus, it is not clear that the approach adopted in the Convention of automatically giving preference to the recognition rules of the habitual residence is indeed most consistent with private international law theory. It is tentatively suggested that those principles and the objectives of the Convention could be better reflected by the following differential rule:[220] preference should be given to the recognition rules of that State (the habitual residence or the forum) whose application will lead to recognition of the custody rights of the left-behind parent.[221]

iv Comity and Article 15 Declarations

The doctrine of comity would support the prevailing view of treating Article 15 declarations as binding.[222] However, there has been some judicial disagreement as to whether comity requires the requesting State to refuse to give an Article 15 declaration where this is inconsistent with a decision already given by the requested State under the Abduction

---

[218] See ch 6 IV D.

[219] In such a situation, either approach will lead to a violation of comity in the sense of both reciprocity and judicial courtesy.

[220] For the idea of using differential rules as a solution to the incidental question, see R Schuz, *A Modern Approach to the Incidental Question* (London, Kluwer, 1997).

[221] Or other person, institution or body, where relevant.

[222] See III E above, although it may be argued that this principle is weaker where the declaration is given by an administrative authority rather than a judicial one.

Convention.²²³ It is suggested that there is no breach of comity provided the Abduction Convention decision is still subject to appeal, since the obligation to show deference to that decision does not apply until it is final.

H Certainty versus Flexibility

Overall, the vagueness of the definition of custody rights in the Convention has provided a good deal of flexibility, which some courts have exploited in order to interpret the concept of custody rights in a broad manner, consistently with the objectives of the Convention. Indeed the Perez-Vera Report expressly stated that the fact that the list of sources of rights of custody at the end of Article 3 is not exhaustive enables flexible interpretation of the terms used.²²⁴

Moreover, the case law has to a large extent now managed to minimise the uncertainty which accompanied this flexibility. Thus, for example, following the US Supreme Court decision in *Abbott*, there is now a wide consensus that *ne exeat* rights should be considered as rights of custody.²²⁵ Similarly, it now seems clear that the New Zealand jurisprudence treating pure access rights as rights of custody is not accepted in other countries. However, uncertainty still exists as to whether inchoate rights should be recognised at all, and if so as to their scope.²²⁶

Whilst any attempt to make the activation of the mandatory return mechanism dependent on an assessment of the significance of the relationship between the child and the applicant would give rise to more uncertainty than the current position, treating the breach of the child's right to contact with his parents as the trigger²²⁷ should decrease uncertainty.

V Conclusions

The determination of whether there has been a wrongful removal or retention, which lies at the very heart of the Convention's mandatory return mechanism, has proved to be one of the most problematic aspects of the Convention's implementation. Whilst it is usually clear whether there has been a removal or retention,²²⁸ the need to decide whether there has been a breach of rights of custody has perhaps predictably given rise to considerable difficulty. Courts have been torn between the need to remain faithful to the wording of the Convention whilst at the same time promoting its objectives.

Thus, they have tried to create a *via media* under which the characterisation of the rights which have been breached is a two stage process involving consideration of both the local law of the habitual residence and the autonomous Convention definition. Similarly, courts

---

²²³ Compare the view of the Court of Appeal in *Mercredi v Chaffe* (n 103) that as a matter of comity the English Court should support the decision made by the French Court with the view of Bodey J in *A v B (Abduction: Declaration)* (n 76) that international comity required correcting the flawed advice which had been given to the French Court in relation to the attribution of custody rights under English law.
²²⁴ Perez-Vera Report (n 15), para 67.
²²⁵ Although, as seen at II C above, there is still some uncertainty as to the exact scope of the provision.
²²⁶ See Beaumont and McEleavy (n 18) 60 and comments of ECJ in *McB v LE* (n 52).
²²⁷ See Part V below.
²²⁸ Apart from in the situation of anticipatory breach, discussed in Part II above.

have seized upon the Convention definition of custody rights as including the right to determine the child's place of residence as a basis for treating *ne exeat* rights as rights of custody, although it is far from clear that this was the original intention of the drafters. Furthermore, some courts have creatively treated inchoate rights and rights vested in a court as rights of custody for the purposes of the Convention. However, nearly all jurisdictions have drawn the line at pure rights of access, even though unilateral removal of a child in breach of such rights may involve the same harmful effects as removals in breach of custody rights. Finally, the adoption of a non-technical approach to the requirement of actual exercise of custody rights has meant that only very rarely has there been held not to be actual exercise of such rights. Overall, it seems that most courts have achieved a reasonable balance between the competing considerations, although some suggestions have been made for improvement.

Nevertheless, as stated above, a trigger based on the right of the child to contact with both parents would be more consistent with all the parameters of analysis discussed above. In particular, such a trigger would convey the important message that the child is the real victim of the abduction and not the left-behind parent and that the child is not the parent's property to be reclaimed. This approach would incidentally resolve the problem of unmarried fathers since the children would have a right to contact with them in the same way as with any other parent. Furthermore, the difficulties involved in proving the foreign law and characterising the parental rights in question would disappear.

The child's right to continued contact with the other parent should be presumed to exist unless a court had decided otherwise and a removal or retention should be deemed to be in breach of the child's right unless adequate arrangements had been made by agreement with the other parent for continuing contact[229] or a mature child's waiver of the right had been sanctioned by the court. It could also be provided that the removal or retention would only be in breach of the child's right, where the left-behind parent had previously been maintaining contact with the child,[230] since, if this was not the case, the breach of the child's right was not caused by the removal or retention. However, it may well be sufficient to include the left-behind parent's failure to maintain contact with the child as a defence, akin to the current defence of non-exercise of rights in Article 13(1)(a).

Accordingly, a 'trigger' based on the breach of the child's right would be more consistent with the doctrine of children's rights; would better promote the objectives of the Convention; would be more compatible with the nature of Convention proceedings and would cause less uncertainty than the current 'trigger' based on breach of adults' rights of custody. In light of the general trend to bestow on non-custodial parents rights which are treated as custody rights for the purpose of the Convention,[231] adoption of the current suggestion would probably not result in a large increase in the number of cases in which the Convention would apply.

---

[229] It should be presumed that any such agreement does make appropriate provision for contact unless it is manifestly clear that this is not the case.
[230] This provision would fulfil a similar role to the current requirement of actual exercise of rights in Art 3(b).
[231] Many jurisdictions now routinely grant joint legal custody to both parents, Bruch, 'The Promises and Perils' (n 46) 244 and prohibit unilateral removal by the custodial parent from the jurisdiction by law, ibid 239.

8

Habitual Residence

I Introduction

A Structure of the Chapter

The drafters of the Hague Convention on the Civil Aspects of International Child Abduction ('Abduction Convention') adopted the concept of habitual residence as the sole connecting factor which determines applicability of the Convention and other issues, in the belief that the factual nature of the concept would enable the appropriate solution to be achieved in the vast majority of cases and prevent the development of legalistic and technical rules. However, this optimism was unrealistic. In particular, their view that it was not necessary to define or elaborate on the concept, since it was a 'well-established concept in the Hague Conference' ignored the fact that there had been very little case law in which courts had been required to apply the concept[1] and the need to clarify the relationship between the child's habitual residence and that of his parents. Thus, it is perhaps not surprising that habitual residence is one of the most litigated issues under the Convention and that there are significant differences between the way in which the concept has been interpreted by courts in different countries and even between judges within the same jurisdiction. This chapter will start by examining the development of the concept of habitual residence and its adoption as the sole connecting factor in the Abduction Convention. Part II will then proceed to examine the exact role played by the concept of habitual residence in the Convention. Parts III and IV will present and illustrate the different models which have been developed by the courts for determining the habitual residence of the child in the context of this Convention. Part V will analyse the different models in light of the parameters set out at chapters five and six of the book and finally Part VI will present the conclusions to be drawn from the analysis.

B Origin of the Concept of Habitual Residence

The background to and the emergence of the concept of habitual residence in Europe is examined in detail by de Winter.[2] The concept was first adopted by the Hague Conference more than 100 years ago[3] and has been used in all the Hague Conventions relating to family

---

[1] Palsson, in his book, L Palsson, *Marriage and Divorce in Comparative Conflict of Laws* (Leiden, Sijthoff, 1974) vol 1, 78, refers to it as a 'more virgin concept' than domicile.
[2] LI de Winter, 'Nationality or Domicile?' in AW Sijthoff (ed), *Recueil Des Cours* (Dordecht, Martinus Nijhoff,1970).
[3] In the Hague Convention on Guardianship (1902).

matters since then.[4] More recently, the concept has been adopted by the European Community in both family[5] and other types of Convention.[6] This widespread use of habitual residence in domestic family law legislation in common law countries, even in statutes not implementing Hague Conventions,[7] seems to reflect the influence of the Hague Conventions.[8] However, it should be noted that some domestic statutes provide a definition of habitual residence.[9]

The main reason for the adoption of the concept of habitual residence in international conventions seems to have been the need to find a connecting factor that was acceptable to both Continental and common law legal systems. In particular, there was recognition of the need to retreat from the nationality principle, which had previously dominated private international law in Europe. The concept of domicile, which had been primarily used in common law countries, was not seen as an appropriate alternative because different meanings had been given to the concept in different countries. A major attraction of the concept of habitual residence lay in its novelty. It was not associated with a particular type of legal system and there had not been any real opportunity for the development of judge-made glosses and restrictions on the apparently clear natural meaning of the term.

C Use of Habitual Residence in Relation to Children

Significantly, the connecting factor of habitual residence was first used in a substantive law Hague Convention relating to children; the Convention on Guardianship of 1902. The term was deliberately chosen so as to make clear that it was the child's actual residence and not his legal dependent domicile that was envisaged.[10] Subsequently, habitual residence was used as the main connecting factor in a number of Hague Conventions relating to children prior to the Abduction Convention.[11] The concept was considered to be particularly appropriate in relation to children, because in practice it was essential that the authorities in the place where the child was actually living should be responsible for his physical welfare and be involved in determining his financial needs.[12]

---

[4] For all the Hague Conventions, see www.hcch.net/index_en.php?act=conventions. In some of the Conventions, the term is qualified by a time period. Thus, under the Hague Convention on the Recognition of Divorces and Legal Separations (1970), some of the bases of jurisdiction to grant divorce require habitual residence by one of the parties for 12 months.

[5] eg, Council Regulation (EC) No 2201/2003 of 27 November 2003 concerning jurisdiction and the recognition and enforcement of judgments in matrimonial matters and the matters of parental responsibility ('Brussels II bis Regulation') OJ L 338/1-29.

[6] eg Convention 80/934/ECC on the law applicable to contractual obligations opened for signature in Rome on 19 June 1980 [1980] OJ L266 of 9 October 1980; Regulation (EC) No 864/2007 of 11 July 2007 on the law applicable to non-contractual obligations (Rome II) [2007] OJ L199/40.

[7] eg, in England, Part I of the Family Law Act 1986 is designed to allocate jurisdiction between different parts of the UK.

[8] Although in the UK the concept of ordinary residence, which is widely equated with habitual residence, was first used in the family law context in order to bypass the wife's domicile of dependency, Law Reform (Miscellaneous Provisions Act) 1949, it was used long before this in other contexts such as tax and bankruptcy statutes. See eg *Re Norris* [1888] 4 TLR 452.

[9] eg, Ontario Children's Law Reform Act 2 RSO ch C-12(2) (1990).

[10] See de Winter (n 2) 423–24.

[11] eg Maintenance of Children – Applicable Law (1956, Protection of Minors (1961) and Adoption (1965). The concept has also been used in a number of later Conventions, including the Convention on Jurisdiction, Applicable Law, Recognition, Enforcement and Co-Operation in Respect of Parental Responsibility and Measures for the Protection of Children ('the 1996 Child Protection Convention') and the Convention on Protection of Children and Co-Operation in Respect of Intercountry Adoption (1993)

[12] de Winter (n 2) 470–71.

Furthermore, habitual residence was clearly the most appropriate connecting factor in cases involving the abduction of children in order to avoid the determination of which country should exercise jurisdiction over a custody dispute being dependant on the idiosyncratic legal definitions of domicile and nationality of the forum to which the child happens to have been removed.[13] This would obviously undermine uniform application and encourage forum-shopping by would-be abductors.[14] Nonetheless, the factual nature of habitual residence caused problems in parental abduction cases because, under the 1961 Protection of Minors Convention, habitual residence was determined at the time of the proceedings. Thus, abducting parents who managed to avoid being detected for a sufficient enough time for the child to acclimatise were allowed to benefit from the abduction. Awareness of the lack of ability of the 1961 Child Protection Convention to deal satisfactorily with abduction cases seems to have been one of the factors behind the initiative to draw up the 1980 Abduction Convention.[15] To a large extent, this Convention solved the problems experienced under the 1961 Convention by providing that the critical date for determining habitual residence is immediately before the abduction. Thus, there could no longer be any possibility that the place of refuge had become the place of habitual residence (unless the child had previously been habitually resident there). However, this change did not resolve the difficulty of determining habitual residence in cases where immediately before the abduction, it was not clear whether the child was habitually resident in the country from which he was abducted, for example, because he had only recently moved there or was living there on a temporary basis. As a result of increasing international mobility, these situations became more common.

It should be noted that, although the concept of habitual residence has been adopted in all Hague Conventions relating to children, most of these Conventions are rarely litigated. Similarly, there is little case law applying the provisions of domestic legislation which use the habitual residence of the child as a connecting factor.[16] On the other hand, there are now around two thousand applications under the Abduction Convention per year.[17] In many of these cases, there is no real issue as to habitual residence, but there are still a significant number of cases in which it is not obvious in which country the child was habitually resident immediately before the wrongful removal or retention and thus a sizeable body of case law has developed in relation to the interpretation of the concept of habitual residence under the Abduction Convention.

In the early Abduction Convention cases, courts did sometimes refer to case law on habitual residence in other contexts,[18] in particular in relation to issues of principle relating to the nature of habitual residence and its determination.[19] Two such issues of principle will now be examined: firstly, whether the common law rule that a person has a single domicile at all times during his life applies equally to habitual residence and secondly whether the determination of habitual residence is a question of pure fact or of mixed fact and law.

---

[13] *Mozes v Mozes* 239 F3d 1067 (9th Cir 2001).
[14] ibid.
[15] See ch 1 at I A.
[16] Also, where the domestic statute provides its own definition, case law will be of limited value in relation to the determination of habitual residence in other contexts.
[17] Chapter 2 at I C.
[18] In particular, in the UK, courts adopted the judicial definition of the House of Lords in the case of *R v Barnet London Borough Council, Ex p Nilish Shah* [1983] 2 AC 309, which involved a domestic statute.
[19] For the need for caution when referring to such sources because of the different objectives of different instruments, see R Schuz, 'Policy Considerations in Determining Habitual Residence of a Child and the Relevance of Context' (2001) 1 *Journal of Transnational Law and Policy* 101.

D Does a Person have a Single Habitual Residence at all Times?

There are two aspects to this question. Firstly, is it possible for a person to be without a habitual residence and secondly, can a person have more than one habitual residence at any given time? In relation to the first question, it is widely accepted that it is theoretically possible for a person not to have a habitual residence at any given time.[20] There is no doctrine of fictitious continuity[21] and thus if a person has abandoned or otherwise lost his habitual residence and not yet acquired a new habitual residence, then he will not have any habitual residence. Whilst such a result is problematic where habitual residence is the connecting factor in a choice of law rule,[22] it does not create any difficulties of principle in the context of the Abduction Convention. A finding that the child does not have any habitual residence at the relevant time simply means that the Convention does not apply and so there can be no obligation to make a return order. In the Australian High Court decision in *LK v Director-General Department of Community Services*[23] for example, it was held that by the time of the retention the children had lost their habitual residence in Israel, whether or not they had acquired a habitual residence in Australia, which did not need to be determined. Nonetheless, it is not desirable that a child should not have a habitual residence because it means that the child is not protected, even if he is abducted to a third country. Thus, no doubt, in the case of such an abduction, the court would find that the child had acquired a habitual residence in the new country before the removal or retention from the latter.

In relation to the second question, Abduction Convention case law has rejected the idea of a dual habitual residence.[24] Courts have expressed the view that the concept of habitual residence is simply not compatible with the notion that there may be two or more such residences[25] and that the Abduction Convention and the Preamble, which refer to the State of the child's habitual residence in the singular rather than the plural, clearly envisage that a child will only have one habitual residence at any one time.

With respect, these arguments are not convincing. Some people do genuinely live in more than one country, moving on a regular basis between their two homes. Artificially finding that only one of those countries is the habitual residence is inconsistent with the factual nature of habitual residence.[26] Indeed, case law in other areas of law has recognised the possibility that a person may have more than one habitual residence.[27] Furthermore, where the child does genuinely have a home in more than one country, it is inappropriate

---

[20] eg, P Beaumont and P McEleavy, *The Hague Convention on International Child Abduction* (Oxford, Oxford University Press, 1999); *Delvoye v Lee* 329 F3d 330 (3rd Cir 2003); *M v M (Abduction: England and Scotland)* [1997] 2 FLR 263; *SK v KP* [2005] 3 NZLR 590; Lagarde Report on the 1996 Protection Convention, www.hcch.net/upload/expl34.pdf, para 41.

[21] As in relation to domicile in the US and Australia *cf*, under English law, when a person abandons a domicile of choice, his domicile of origin revives until he acquires a new domicile of choice.

[22] Beaumont and McEleavy (n 20) 113.

[23] *LK v Director-General, Department of Community Services* [2009] HCA 9.

[24] eg, *In the Marriage of Stephanie Selina Hanbury-Brown (Appellant/Wife) and Robert Hanbury-Brown (Respondent/Husband) v Director General of Community Services (Central Authority)* (1996) FLC 92-671; *Friedrich v Friedrich* 983 F2d 1396 (6th Cir 1993); *re V (Abduction: Habitual Residence)* [1995] 2 FLR 992.

[25] *SS-C v GC* [2003] RDF 845 (SC).

[26] N Lowe, M Everall and M Nicholls, *International Movement of Children: Law, Practice and Procedure* (Bristol, Jordans, 2004) 72.

[27] eg *Ikmi v Ikmi* [2001] EWCA Civ 875 relying on the dictum of Lord Scarman in *Shah* (n 18).

for the Convention to apply to removals or retentions between those two countries.[28] Where the removal or retention is to a third country, the operative habitual residence for the purposes of the Convention will be the State which is requesting return of the child and so it is irrelevant that there might also be another habitual residence.

E Nature of the Determination of Habitual Residence

It is not clear whether the determination of habitual residence is a question of fact or a question of mixed fact and law and divergent judicial views can be found in relation to this issue.[29] Ironically, the reasons given in support of both of the approaches are based on the need for uniformity in determining habitual residence.[30] On the one hand, support for the question of fact approach[31] usually relies on the official view, expressed in the Perez-Vera Report, that the determination has to be a question of fact in order to ensure uniform interpretation in all Member States and to avoid the development of restrictive technical rules.[32] On the other hand, support for the question of mixed fact and law approach is based on the view that the determination requires the application of a legal standard, which defines the concept of habitual residence, to the facts of the case[33] and that uniformity of application can only be achieved if courts can reconcile their decisions with those reached by other courts.[34] This divergence of views is more apparent than real and is based on terminological confusion.

In particular, it should be noted that a number of the cases which support the factual approach themselves provide definitions of habitual residence and list principles for its determination.[35] The internal inconsistency within these cases is evidence that the question of fact approach is too simplistic and that the underlying assumption that the '[t]he two words "habitual" and "residence" are quite capable of doing all the work required of them'[36] is unsupportable.[37] Indeed, there are many borderline cases, in which it would not be 'an abuse of language' to say that a child was habitually resident in country X or in country Y or in both of them.[38] In such cases, application of 'those ordinary principles of legal

---

[28] cf Lowe at el (n 26) 72, who suggest that the Convention should apply to removals between the two habitual residences.

[29] See the comment of Justice Sarokin (dissenting) in *Feder v Evans-Feder* 63 F3d 217, 227 (3rd Cir 1995) that 'federal and state courts have struggled over this precise issue, with some making findings of fact and others conclusions of law regarding a child's habitual residence'.

[30] Perhaps even more ironically, as will be seen below, the objective of uniformity has not been realised, but this failure cannot be attributed to the approach chosen in relation to the nature of the determination.

[31] eg, *Friedrich v Freidrich* (n 24); *In re Application of Ponath* 829 F Supp 363, 367 (D Utah, 1993); Justice Sarokin dissenting in *Feder* (n 29); *C v S (Minor: Abduction: Illegitimate Child)* [1990] 2 All ER 449, 454–55.

[32] Perez-Vera Report, Proceedings of the 14th Session of the Hague Conference Oct 1980, www.hcch.net/upload/expl28.pdf, para 66; See also Lagarde Report (n 20), para 41.

[33] eg, *Feder* (n 29) 222.

[34] *Mozes* (n 13); Justice Geifman in FamA (Dist TA) 48471/05 *Ploni v Plonit* Nevo, 11 September 2006 (Isr).

[35] eg *Re B (Minors)(Abduction) (No 1)* [1993] 1 FLR 988, 991–92; *Cooper v Casey No. EA102 of 1994*, slip op (Fam Ct Austl, 5 May 1995).

[36] As claimed by EM Clive, 'The Concept of Habitual Residence' (1997) *Juridical Review* 137. See also the reference of Lord Brandon in *Re J (A Minor) (Abduction: Custody Rights)* [1990] 2 AC 562 to 'the ordinary and natural meaning of the two words' contained in the expression habitual residence.

[37] The very fact that more than one model has developed in relation to the child's habitual residence shows that it is naive to think that the term has a natural meaning.

[38] eg, where the child relocated shortly before the date on which habitual residence has to be determined.

and common experience which are ordinarily entrusted to a finder of fact'[39] is not sufficient to determine habitual residence and thus without some legal guidance, the determination will be arbitrary and based purely on the whim of the court.[40] This reality seems to have been recognised by the judges who have given some guidance as to the meaning of habitual residence, despite their view that the issue is a question of fact.

Furthermore, the concerns of those who adopt the 'question of fact' approach can be answered in other ways. Firstly, the fear that habitual residence might become a technical term with complicated legal requirements does not mean that it has to be determined in a legal vacuum without any legal guidance at all. Rather, it simply needs to be acknowledged that the determination is fact intensive[41] and that accordingly the legal standard is intended to give guidance as to how to interpret the facts rather than to fetter the court with rigid rules. Whilst, unfortunately, some of the models of habitual residence adopted by the courts are, as will be seen below, legalistic and inconsistent with the factual emphasis approach, this does not seem to be a direct result of characterising the determination as a mixed question of fact and law. Secondly, the concern that characterisation of the determination as a mixed question of fact and law will lead to more appeals[42] can be resolved by providing that the clearly erroneous standard of review applies rather than the plenary standard.[43]

Thus, the determination of habitual residence should be treated as a mixed question of fact and law. However, in defining a legal standard, it should be remembered that the determination has a largely factual emphasis.

II Role of Habitual Residence in the Abduction Convention

A In Determining the Applicability of the Convention

The Convention is only applicable where the child has been abducted to a Member State other than that of the child's habitual residence. Thus, operation of the Convention can be maximised by finding, wherever possible, that the child had a habitual residence immediately before the abduction, and that this is in a country other than the place of refuge.[44] In removal cases, this will generally involve finding that the child has acquired a habitual resi-

---

[39] This is the test used by Justice Steven for distinguishing between questions of fact and those involving law in *Bose Corp v Consumers of Union of US Inc* 466 US 485, 501 (1984).

[40] The difficulty of determining habitual residence in borderline cases can also be seen from the divergence of opinions expressed by members of the Special Commission on the Protection Convention, see Proceedings of the 18th Session of the Hague Conference (Permanent Bureau of the Conference edn, 1998) vol 2, Minute No 4.

[41] *Karkkainen v Kovalchuk* 445 F3d 280, 291 (3d Cir 2006). See also *SK v KP* (n 20), according to which the inquiry is ultimately a question of fact but identification of principles, according to which the enquiry is to be conducted, is a question of law.

[42] Because plenary review is permissible, whereas questions of fact can only be reviewed for clear error, *Feder* (n 29).

[43] The phenomenon of characterising issues as questions of fact for some purposes and question of law for other purposes is known. See RT Cross and JW Harris, *Precedent in English Law*, 4th edn (Oxford, Clarendon Press, 1991); see also ET Lee, 'Principled Decision Making and the Proper Role of Federal Appellate Courts: The Mixed Question Conflict' (1991) 64 *South California Law Review* 235 (favouring the clearly erroneous standard in relation to questions of mixed fact and law).

[44] In *Re F (A Minor)(Child Abduction)* [1992] 1 FLR 548, the English Court of Appeal admitted that it was keen to find that the child had acquired a habitual residence in Australia so that the Convention would apply.

dence in the country where he was living before the removal;[45] whereas in retention cases it will involve finding that the child has not acquired a habitual residence in the country where he was living immediately before the retention.[46]

It is unclear from the Convention's provisions whether it is sufficient that the place of habitual residence immediately before the abduction is a Member State, or whether it is also necessary that the removal must be from the place of habitual residence.[47] While judges commonly refer to abduction from the place of habitual residence,[48] this would seem to be simply a convenient, shorthand way of describing the situation and not as indicating that a case where the child was removed from a place other than his habitual residence would not be covered by the Convention. In particular, since in these cases removal is from the place of habitual residence, no significance should be attached to the judges' use of this expression.

Support for this approach can be found in an Israeli case[49] involving the removal of the child to Israel from the Dominican Republic by the mother. The five-year-old child had been born in France, where the Israeli parents had lived for nine years before moving to the Dominican Republic, 10 months before the abduction. The Family Court, rejecting the father's argument that the Dominican Republic was the child's place of habitual residence, held that the Convention was not applicable. However, on appeal, the District Court accepted the father's alternative claim that the child's habitual residence was in France at the date of removal and so the Convention did apply.[50] Thus, it is clear that the Court took the view that it was not necessary for removal to be from the place of habitual residence, provided that at the time of the removal the habitual residence of the child was in a Contracting State, other than the requested State.[51]

This can be contrasted with the decision of the Full Family Court of Australia in *Hanbury-Brown v Hanbury-Brown*,[52] where the point was discussed in full. The Court held that taking into account the Preamble and the Convention as a whole, there was a requirement that removal be from the place of habitual residence. In particular, the Court explained that the words 'removal' and 'return' are co-relative terms and thus since return is to the place of habitual residence the only logical conclusion would be that 'removal' is from the place of habitual residence.

With respect, this reasoning is inconsistent with the objectives of the Convention since the need for the prompt return of the child arises whenever the child is wrongfully removed to a country other than that of the habitual residence, irrespective of the country from which he was removed. Furthermore, this reasoning is dependent on holding that return has to be to the place of habitual residence, which as will be seen below is questionable.

---

[45] Unless that country has not joined the Convention, In *Re A (Minors) (Abduction) (Habitual Residence)* [1996] 1 WLR 25, 33.
[46] eg *Mozes* (n 13).
[47] *cf* section 105(1)(d) of the New Zealand Care of Children Act 2004, which expressly requires that the child was habitually resident in the country from which he was removed.
[48] eg *Smith v Smith* 2001 (3) SA 845, 850 (SCA).
[49] FamA 1018/09 (Dist TA) *Ploni v Plonit* Tak-Mech 2009 (1) 12641.
[50] But the Court rejected the father's request that the child should be returned to the Dominican Republic rather than to France, see discussion at C below. Thus, since the father was not interested in returning to France, the application was dismissed.
[51] See also *In re A (Minors) (Abduction) (Habitual Residence)* (n 45), in which the Court seems to have assumed that if the children had been habitually resident in the US at the time of the removal from Iceland (which was not a Member State), then the Convention would have been applicable.
[52] *Hanbury-Brown* (n 24).

Thus, in the absence of an express provision on the point, it would be more sensible not to impose this additional restriction which is likely to lead either to a strained interpretation of the phrase 'removed from'[53] or to manipulation of the finding of habitual residence.[54] In addition, the Australian Court's reasoning does not refer to the situation where there has been a retention rather than a removal.[55]

B In Determining Whether the Removal or Retention was Wrongful

The law of the habitual residence determines wrongfulness. Thus, in cases where the removal is not considered wrongful by the law of the place of habitual residence,[56] the mandatory return provision will not be triggered even though the removal is considered wrongful by other relevant laws. Equally, where the removal or retention is considered wrongful by the place of habitual residence, the requested State will have to return the child, even though under its own internal law the removal or retention is not considered wrongful.

C As the Place to Where the Child is Returned

Whilst the Preamble states that the procedures under the Convention are to ensure the prompt return 'to the State of their habitual residence', Article 12, the main operative provision of the Convention, simply states that return should be ordered without specifying to which country. According to the Perez-Vera Report, this omission was deliberate in order to provide the courts with some flexibility.[57] Thus, if the applicant is now living in a third State, return to the applicant should be ordered.

However, the Full Family Court of Australia in *Hanbury-Brown*,[58] basing itself mainly on the Preamble, held that the correct construction of the Convention is that the child should be returned to the place of his or her habitual residence. With respect, there is no good reason to limit the powers of the court of the requested State by requiring that return be ordered to the place of habitual residence, when a wider construction of the operative provisions of the Convention is equally plausible.

The adoption of the narrower construction is likely to lead to manipulation of the determination of habitual residence where it is thought appropriate to return the child to a third State. For example, assume that the custodial parent is on a sabbatical abroad at the time of

---

[53] The Court in *Hanbury-Brown*, ibid explained that where a child is physically removed from a third country, as eg when the child is on vacation, this is considered a removal from the habitual residence since the habitual residence 'cloak' remains with the child while on vacation.

[54] eg, if the child is abducted from a third country where he was resident temporarily, a court might be tempted to find that the residence is habitual.

[55] *cf* the South African case of *Central Authority v Reynders* [2011] 2 All SA 438 (GNP), where it was held that the Convention did not apply because the father had not proven that the child was habitually resident in the USA, where she had lived for a year prior to her wrongful retention by her maternal grandmother in South Africa. However, the Court does not explain why it was not sufficient that the child's habitual residence was in Belgium and it seems that this was not argued by the father. The most obvious explanation is that the statement in *Smith v Smith* (n 48) was taken literally to mean that the removal or retention has to be from the place of habitual residence.

[56] In relation to meaning of the law in this context, see ch 7 at II A.

[57] Perez-Vera Report (n 32), para 110.

[58] *Hanbury-Brown* (n 24).

the abduction. It seems absurd to order the child to be returned to the country of origin, where there is no one to look after him.[59] Thus, the Court would have little option other than to hold that the place of the sabbatical is the place of habitual residence,[60] despite the fact that habitual residence would normally not be changed in such circumstances. Similarly, where the applicant's habitual residence has changed since the time of the abduction, it would make no sense to order return to the former habitual residence.

Support for the wider construction can be found in two Israeli cases which not only accept the principle that return can be ordered to a third country, but examine the circumstances in which it will be appropriate to do so. Analysis of these cases and the reasoning therein is helpful in trying to formulate principles which will apply to requests to order return to a third country. In *RB v VG*,[61] for two years prior to the removal to Israel, the child had been living with the mother in France after the Belgian Court had awarded custody to the mother and given permission for relocation. The father appealed against this decision and eventually the Belgian Appellate Court allowed his appeal and ordered that the child be transferred to the custody of the father in Belgium. Before the date set for the transfer the mother removed the child to Israel. The mother's argument that the Court could not order return of the child to Belgium because his habitual residence was in France was rejected. Justice Arbel stated that in most cases returning the child to a third country would not give effect to the objectives of the Convention of returning the child to a familiar everyday life. However, in cases where it is not practicable to return the child to the place of habitual residence, then it may be preferable to return the child to a third country than to leave him in the State of refuge, especially where the third country was a place with which he was familiar, for example, where he had lived there previously or had visited the left-behind parent there. Furthermore, in this particular case, if the child had not been abducted, he would have in any event moved to live in Belgium in accordance with the Belgian Court's decision, which was enforceable in France. Thus, returning the child to France, from where he would be sent to Belgium in any event, would only lead to unnecessary prolongation of the process of returning the child to his father, in contravention of the purpose of the Convention.[62]

In a later case,[63] the father, relying on the decision in the *RB v VG*, asked for the child to be returned to the Dominican Republic where the family had been living immediately before the wrongful removal, even though the Court found that the child was habitually resident in France. The District Court rejected this argument and distinguished the two cases in two ways. Firstly, return to the Dominican Republic would not give effect to the objectives of the Convention because this would not lead to return to a stable and familiar everyday life.[64] Secondly, in this case there had not been an expert opinion on the welfare

---

[59] See D Mclean, 'Return of Internationally Abducted Children' (1990) 106 *Law Quarterly Review* 376; but cf Beaumont and McEleavy (n 20) 31 (arguing that it is inappropriate to allow the left-behind parent to relocate unilaterally when such a privilege is denied to the abductor).

[60] With respect, the approach of the Court in *Hanbury-Brown* (n 24) that the child may be returned to the third country because he remains under the cloak of the country of habitual residence while there is an abuse of language.

[61] RFamA (SC) 5579/07 *RB v VG*, 7 August 2007 (Isr). http://elyon1.court.gov.il/files/07/790/055/B03/07055790.b03.pdf

[62] ibid [14].

[63] FamA 1018/09 (n 49).

[64] The evidence in the case showed that the 10 months spent in the Dominican Republic were characterised by instability and frequent moves and by the mother's allegations of violence and coercion by the father.

consequences of returning the child to a third country, as there had been in the case of *RB v VG*[65]

The reasoning in these cases can, with some clarification and refinement, form the basis of a test to determine whether return should be allowed to a third country. The following formulation would seem appropriate: return to a third country should be allowed if this best fulfils the objectives of the Convention, where return to the habitual residence is not practicable or removal was from that third county. It makes sense to allow return to a third country where return to the habitual residence is not practical. It is envisaged that return would be considered impracticable, where the abducting parent is not prepared to return with the child to the place of habitual residence and the left-behind parent does not wish to move back there.[66] On the other hand, where the abductor is prepared to move back to the place of habitual residence, but the left-behind parent is not interested in this option, then return by the abductor to the place of habitual residence should not be considered impracticable and there is no reason not to restore the *status quo ante*.[67]

However, in cases where the child was living in a country other than the place of habitual residence immediately before the abduction, return to the place of habitual residence will not in fact restore the *status quo ante*. Thus, in such a case there is room to consider whether in fact return to that third country would in fact better fulfil the objectives of the Convention than return to the country of habitual residence. This approach is consistent with that of the Court in the Israeli case which considered the possibility of return to the Dominican Republic, from where the child had been removed, despite the fact that the mother was prepared to return to France, the place of habitual residence.[68]

Even where one of the conditions is fulfilled (ie that it is impractical to return to the place of habitual residence or removal was from the third country), return to a third country should not be automatically allowed. Rather, the court should consider whether this option best fulfils the objectives of the Convention.[69] How this test might be applied can be illustrated by considering two typical scenarios.

The first situation is that which Professor Perez-Vera seems to have had in mind,[70] where the left-behind parent moves to a third country following the abduction and requests that the child is returned to him there, rather than to the place of habitual residence. If the abductor is not prepared to return to the country of habitual residence, return to such a country will be impractical and so it will not be possible to restore the status quo. Furthermore, if neither parent is living in the place of habitual residence, that country is unlikely to be the *forum conveniens*. The child's interests will depend to a large extent on whether he is familiar with the country in which the left-behind parent is now living. If this is a place where he has previously lived[71] or where he has spent time on access visits, then

---

[65] Ironically, a later expert opinion in the case of *RB v VG* (n 61) held that returning the child to Belgium would be a catastrophe for him, taking into account inter alia that he had not lived there for more than four years and had not had contact with his father for two years. See ch 11 at II Aiii.

[66] Beaumont and McEleavy (n 20) 73 doubt whether it would be appropriate for a child to be returned into foster care. See also Art 5 of the Swiss Federal Act on International Child Abduction, discussed in ch 11 at II Aiii.

[67] Unless the court in the third country has ordered the child to be transferred to the parent in that country and this order is enforceable in the place of habitual residence, as in *RB v VG* (n 61). In such a case, return to the place of habitual residence is impractical in the sense of being pointless because the child will only then be moved on to the third country.

[68] FamA 1018/09 (n 49).

[69] Set out in ch 5 at II C.

[70] Perez Vera Report (n 32).

[71] As in the case of *Central Authority v Reynders* (n 55).

return there can fulfil the deterrence objective without harming the child. However, where the child has never been to the third country and is unfamiliar with the language, culture and way of life there, then return to the left-behind parent, especially where he has had little contact with that parent over a long period of time, may well be harmful to the child. Thus, in such a case the objectives of the Convention would not be fulfilled by returning the child to the third country and the left-behind parent will have to choose between returning himself to the original place of habitual residence or litigating the custody dispute in the country of refuge.

The second situation is where the parties have travelled abroad for a fixed but temporary purpose, such as a sabbatical or diplomatic or employment assignment, and one parent then removes the child to another country (not the country of origin). Assuming that the court in the requested State holds that the child is still habitually resident in the country of origin,[72] the issue arises as at whether return should be ordered to the third country where the left-behind parent is spending the sabbatical or assignment. This is a case where the removal was from a third country (ie the one where the sabbatical or assignment is being spent) and thus, under the proposed formulation, return to that third country should be allowed where this better fulfils the objectives of the Convention. It appears that the status quo will be restored by return to the third country, rather than to the place of habitual residence. On the other hand, the place of habitual residence will often still be the *forum conveniens*. Return to either the habitual residence or the third country would seem to further the objective of deterrence since the abductor is not being allowed to gain from his unlawful behaviour. Thus, again the child's interests might well be determinative. In deciding which solution better promotes the child's interests, the court should take into account the child's age, the length of time that the child was living in the third country, the degree of his acclimatisation there, how much of the sabbatical or assignment is left, the extent to which the child retained connection with the original country and whether the abductor is prepared to return to the third country if the court orders that the child be returned there.[73] Usually, where the child has only been living for a short period of time in the third country or where his life there was not stable,[74] then his interests would require that he is returned to the place of habitual residence.[75] However, where he had a settled way of life in the third country,[76] then his interests might be best promoted by return to the third country, especially if the abductor would return there too.

---

[72] See IVii below.

[73] Whilst the abductor's refusal to return with the child is not usually considered a reason not to order return (see ch 11 at II Biii), here the issue is not whether the child will be returned but to where. If the abductor, whilst preferring to return to the country of habitual residence, will in practice accompany the child, if he is returned to the third country, this will mean that the child will be able to live in the same country as both his parents, which will usually be better for him than a situation where his parents live in different countries.

[74] As in FamA 1018/09 (n 49).

[75] As in ibid. The mother was prepared to return to France, but the father was only interested in return to the Dominican Republic where he was now living and so his application was rejected.

[76] As will be seen below, the fact that the child has a settled way of life in a particular country will not necessarily be sufficient for that country to become his habitual residence.

III The Different Models

In an article published in 2001, the current author showed how the apparently purely factual concept of habitual residence was being interpreted in quite different ways in different jurisdictions.[77] The two main models[78] used by the courts at that time were the parental intention model (referred to then as the parental rights model),[79] adopted by the UK and Commonwealth jurisdictions, and the independent or child-centred model (later referred to also as the factual model), adopted in the USA. Analysis of the case law and literature during the course of the decade which has passed since the publication of that article reveals that there is still no consensus in the Hague world as to which model represents the correct approach. Furthermore, there are some countries, where there is not even consensus on this issue among the judges at national level.[80] Two opposing trends can be identified. On the one hand, the development of a narrower version of the parental intention model in some USA circuits[81] has widened the disparity between the two models. On the other hand, attempts can be found by judges in some jurisdictions, such as New Zealand and Israel,[82] to combine the two models, in a way similar to that recommended by the current author in the 2001 article. In this section, the presentation of the different models will include an examination of their origin and theoretical basis.

A The Parental Intention Model

The modern version of this model seems to have evolved from two separate premises. The first is that the child's habitual residence should be determined by the parent who has the right to decide where the child lives.[83] In the situation where both parents have the right to determine in which country the child should live, neither may change the child's place of habitual residence without the consent of the other.[84] The second premise is that since

---

[77] R Schuz, 'Habitual Residence of Children under the Hague Child Abduction Convention – Theory and Practice' (2001) 13 *Child And Family Law Quarterly* 1.

[78] Schuz ibid, did also refer to a third model – the dependency model. It was pointed out that whilst this model is theoretically unattractive because it is too legalistic and treats the child as an appendage of the parents, the result in most of the cases is consistent with this model. Nonetheless, few cases actually use the dependency model and it has been disapproved judicially, eg, per Hedley J in *W and B v H (Child Abduction: Surrogacy)* [2002] 1 FLR 1008 (HC).

[79] This model will be referred to here as the parental intention model because most of the recent case law emphasises the parents' intentions, rather than the fact that it is based on the parents' rights to determine where the child should live.

[80] In the USA, different circuits have adopted different models, T Vivatvarapol, 'Back to Basics: Determining a Child's Habitual Residence in International Child Abduction Cases under the Hague Convention' (2009) 77 *Fordham Law Review* 3325. The US Supreme Court avoided dealing with this issue when it refused certiorari in *Stern v Stern* 132 S Ct 1540 (2012), perhaps because on the facts the result would have been the same under all the different models.

[81] CD Davis, 'The Gitter Standard: Creating a Uniform Definition of Habitual Residence under the Hague Convention on the Civil Aspects of International Child Abduction' (2006) 7 *Chicago Journal of International Law* 321.

[82] See below at C.

[83] This is why the current author, in R Schuz, 'Habitual Residence' (n 77), originally called the model the parental rights model. Under a pure version of this model a parent can intend for his child to be habitually resident in a country other than that in which he himself is habitually resident. However, this approach has been rejected, Lowe et al (n 26) 62.

[84] *Re P (GE) (An Infant)* [1965] Ch 568.

children cannot decide by themselves what the nature of their residence is in a particular place,[85] the subjective element of habitual residence has to be determined by reference to the intention of the parent who has the right to determine where the child lives.[86]

Thus, in the case of unilateral removal by one party, it will be necessary to decide whether that party has the sole right to determine where the child lives; whereas in the case where the whole family moves from one country to another, the issue that will arise is whether both parties had the requisite intention for the new country to become their own and their child's habitual residence.[87] Where only one parent had such an intention, the child will remain habitually resident in the original country.[88] Accordingly, in such cases, the focus is on the nature of the intention required in order to change one's habitual residence. In relation to this issue, a clear divergence can be found between UK and US case law.

i The UK Version: Settled Purpose[89]

Ironically, the judicial definition of habitual residence adopted in Hague cases is that laid down in the case of *R v Barnet London Borough Council, Ex p Nilish Shah* (hereinafter: the *Shah* case) [90] which did not relate to children at all, but rather concerned the meaning of the phrase 'ordinary residence' in a domestic statute relating to the entitlement of a 'foreign' university student to a local education authority maintenance grant. In this case, the House of Lords, equating habitual residence with ordinary residence,[91] provided the following definition of these concepts (hereinafter: 'the *Shah* formula'): 'a man's abode in a particular place or country which he had adopted, voluntarily and for settled purposes as part of the regular order of his life for the time being, whether of short of long duration'.[92]

It is axiomatic from the wording of this definition, from the result in the *Shah* case itself and from subsequent case law[93] that a settled purpose does not require the intention to take up long-term residence[94] and that purposes involving residence for a limited period, such as education and employment, can be considered as settled.[95]

---

[85] In *Mozes* (n 13), Konski J said that children 'normally lack the material and psychological wherewithal to decide where they will reside'.
[86] *Re N (Abduction: Habitual Residence)* [2000] 2 FLR 899; Lowe et al (n 26) 75.
[87] Where the children are sent abroad to live with relatives or for educational purposes, their habitual residence will not change where the parents intend for them to return, but may change after a period of time where there is no such intention, eg non-Convention case of *Re A and D (Children)* [2008] EWCA Civ 265.
[88] eg, *Re G (Abduction: Withdrawal of Proceedings, Acquiescence, Habitual Residence)* [2007] EWHC 2807 (Fam).
[89] In recent years, UK case law has been influenced by European Court of Justice (ECJ) case law (discussed below at III), especially following the Brussels II bis Regulation (see ch 1 at II C). This section refers to the original UK approach, which has had wide influence on the development of the case law in other common law jurisdictions.
[90] *Shah* (n 18).
[91] Compare the earlier view that they were not to bear the same meaning in, eg, J Blom, 'The Adoption Act 1968 and the Conflict of Laws' (1973) 22 *International and Comparative Law Quarterly* 109, 136, who points out that both terms are used in the Adoption Act 1968 and *Cruse v Chitum* [1974] 2 All ER 940. Also, some judges later expressed the view that there might be a difference between the two concepts, eg Lord Slynn in *Re S (A Minor) (Abduction)* [1998] AC 750; New Zealand Court of Appeal decision in *SK v KP* (n 20)[77].
[92] *Shah* (n 18) 343 (Lord Scarman).
[93] eg, *Re A (Abduction: Habitual Residence)* [1998] 1 FLR 497 (posting for three years); *Ryder v Ryder* 49 F3d 369, 373 (8th Cir 1973) (two-year employment contract); *Re R (Abduction: Habitual Residence)* [2003] EWHC 1968 (Fam) (assignment abroad for six months); *Re G* (n 88) (to stay in UK for purpose of giving birth and attempting reconciliation).
[94] cf *A v A* [1993] 2 FLR 225, 235 (Ratee J).
[95] eg *D v D* [2001] ScotCS 103.

ii The US Version: Intention to Abandon Previous Habitual Residence

Analysis of the US case law shows that the origin of the interpretation that the intention required is an intention to abandon the previous habitual residence lies in what appears to be a misunderstanding of the following words of Lord Brandon in the case of *C v S (Minor: Abduction: Illegitimate Child)*:[96]

> There is a significant difference between a person ceasing to be habitually resident in a country A, and his subsequently becoming habitually resident in country B. A person may cease to be habitually resident in country A in a single day if he or she leaves it with a settled intention not to return to it but to take up long-term residence in country B instead. Such a person cannot, however, become habitually resident in country B in a single day. An appreciable period of time and a settled intention will be necessary to enable him to become so.

In the leading case of *Mozes v Mozes*,[97] Justice Konski understands this passage as meaning that in order for a new habitual residence to be acquired, it is necessary to abandon the previous habitual residence. However, with respect, this is not what Lord Brandon says. Rather, he states that a habitual residence **may** be abandoned in a day; whereas it will take longer before a new habitual residence will be acquired. He does not consider the situation where a new habitual residence is acquired by residence for an appreciable period of time and a settled intention, even though there is no abandonment of the previous habitual residence.[98] It is axiomatic from the *Shah* case itself that such a situation is possible. The students in that case intended to return to their country of origin after the completion of their studies and so cannot have intended to abandon their habitual residence there. Rather, the fact that they were resident in the UK for a sufficient period of time for a settled purpose resulted in a holding that they were currently habitually resident in the UK and that therefore in the meantime they were no longer habitually resident in their countries of origin. Any other interpretation would mean that a person who travels abroad for a limited period of time for a fixed purpose, such as education or employment, could not become habitually resident in the new country, unless he did not have any intention to return to the country of origin.

Furthermore, it can see be seen that the *Mozes* Court's conclusion that 'a settled intention to abandon one's prior habitual residence is a crucial part of acquiring a new one'[99] subverts the use of the word 'settled' in the original *Shah* definition in two ways. Firstly, the word 'settled' in *Mozes* describes intent, whereas in Shah it was used to describe purposes. Secondly, in *Mozes*, the word 'settled' relates to the nature of the connection with the former habitual residence, whereas in *Shah* the word 'settled' relates to the nature of the residence in the new country. It seems that the source of the subversion are the words of Lord Brandon cited above, but, as already explained, this dictum simply provides an example of a person who has a settled intention not to return and does not purport to state that such an intention is a condition precedent to acquiring a new habitual residence. Furthermore, the *Mozes* Court expressly rejects the settled purposes standard on the basis that by itself it

---

[96] *C v S* (n 31).

[97] *Mozes* (n 13). A reference to lack of intention to abandon the habitual residence can also be found in the earlier case of *Harkness v Harkness* 227 Mich App 581 (Mich App 1998), but no source is given for this.

[98] Since this was not the situation in that case. In *Re R (Abduction: Habitual Residence)* (n 93), Munby J expressly rejects a proposition that a habitual residence cannot be acquired in another country unless there is a settled intention not to return to the previous habitual residence as unfounded in principle and contrary to binding authorities.

[99] *Mozes* (n 13) 1075.

is powerless to explain why temporary absences, such as during a summer camp, do not give rise to a change in habitual residence. With respect, this comment is misconceived because it is clear that a holiday or other transient purpose does not have a sufficient degree of continuity to be described as settled under the *Shah* definition. Thus, it is suggested that the *Mozes* Court's real problem with the settled purpose standard is that the judges simply do not agree with the *Shah* ratio that a move for a limited period of time for a settled purpose will lead to a change in habitual residence.

The *Mozes* requirement of intention to abandon the former habitual residence has been subsequently adopted by courts in a number of US districts. For example, in *Gitter v Gitter*,[100] the US Court of Appeals for the Second Circuit held that the child who had lived in Israel with his parents for a period of 15 months, from the age of four-months-old, retained his habitual residence in New York since the move to Israel was for a trial period and the mother had not formed an intention to abandon her habitual residence in New York. However, the US Court of Appeals for the Third Circuit attempted to reconcile the *Mozes* approach with the UK concept that a settled purpose can be for a limited period. In the case of *Whiting v Krassner*,[101] that Court held that the intent to abandon the former place of habitual residence need not be forever. Thus, in this case, where it was agreed that the child would live with the mother in Canada for two years and then return to New York, there was sufficient settled intent, from which could be inferred an intention to abandon the habitual residence in New York for two years. Accordingly, the child's habitual residence was now in Canada. It is to be hoped that the other circuits will adopt this approach.

However, in the meantime, any analysis of the parental intention model must distinguish between the UK and the US standards of parental intention. In addition, it should be noted that the US model, is not based on parental intention alone. Thus, even where the parents have the requisite intention, sufficient time must elapse to allow the child to acclimatise in the new country.[102] Furthermore, the lack of parental intention may be trumped by unequivocal evidence of settlement by the children. However, the warning that courts should be slow to find a change of habitual residence in the absence of the requisite parental intent[103] makes it clear that parental intention to abandon the previous habitual residence is the dominant element in this model.[104]

B The Independent/Child-Centred Model

Under this model, the quality of a child's residence in a particular country is determined solely by examining the quality of the connection between the child and that country.

---

[100] *Gitter v Gitter* 396 F3d 124 (2nd Cir 2005); The same result was achieved on very similar facts under the combined model in the Israeli case of FamA (BSH) 130/08 *Plonit v Ploni*, Nevo, 31 August 2008.

[101] *Whiting v Krassner* 391 F3d 540 (3rd Cir 2004).

[102] *Mozes* (n 13) 1078.

[103] ibid. In *Gitter* (n 100) 134, the Court held that this could only happen in those 'relatively rare circumstances' where it appears 'possible that the child's acclimatization to the location abroad [is] so complete that serious harm to the child can be expected to result from compelling his return to the family's intended residence'.

[104] The current author is not aware of any cases which adopt this model, where the child's habitual residence has been held to have changed despite the lack of requisite parental intention, but *cf* obiter dicta in *Koch v Koch* 450 F3d 703,717 (7th Cir 2006), in which it was held that the children would have become habitually resident in Germany, even if the parents had not intended to abandon the habitual residence in the US. On the contrary, there are cases where habitual residence has not changed despite a lengthy stay in the new country, eg *Ruiz v Tenorio* 393 F3d 1247 (11th Cir 2004).

Thus, the child's habitual residence is determined independently of the parents' intentions. The model is also called the child-centred model since it recognises that the child is an autonomous individual and that the focus is the degree of his acclimatisation in the country concerned. The model has also been referred to as the factual[105] or objective approach in contrast to the parental intention model which is highly subjective. However, this terminology will not be used here in order to leave open the possibility that the child's own subjective views can be taken into consideration.

Perhaps ironically, the earliest support which can be found for the independent model is in two English cases. In the pre-Convention case of *Re P (GE) (An Infant)*,[106] Pearson LJ and Russell LJ indicated that even if the father had formed the requisite intention to remain in Israel, the residence of the child there is still insecure and unsettled and that therefore he remained ordinarily resident in England. Later, the High Court in the unreported case of *Re Bates*,[107] which has been heavily cited in the US but not in the UK, stated that the residence whose habituality has to be established is that of the child and not of the mother.

This idea was developed further by the US Court of Appeals for the Sixth Circuit in the case of *Friedrich v Friedrich*.[108] In this case, the mother, a US servicewoman serving in Germany, was evicted by the German father from their home. She and the child went to live in the local USA army base and shortly afterwards the mother took the child to the US. The mother claimed that the child became habitually resident in the US when they were forced to move to the US army base. Boggs J, rejecting this claim, said,

> Habitual residence pertains to customary residence prior to the removal. The Court must look back in time, not forward. All of the factors listed by Mrs. Friedrich pertain to the future. Moreover, they reflect the intentions of Mrs. Friedrich; it is the habitual residence of the child that must be determined.[109]

Later on in the judgment, the honourable judge effectively rejected the parental rights theory, when he stated that '[H]abitual residence can be "altered" only by a change in geography and passage of time, not by changes in parental affection and responsibility'. Thus, the focus is shifted to the child's connection with the country in question and this shift necessitates examining past experience rather than future intentions.

The independent approach was endorsed by the US Court of Appeals for the Third Circuit in the case of *Feder v Feder*.[110] Justice Mansmann's definition of habitual residence of the child as 'the place where he or she has been physically present for an amount of time sufficient for acclimatization and which has a degree of settled purpose from the point of the child' seems to be an excellent description of the independent approach and has been quoted extensively and expressly accepted by the US Court of Appeals for the Sixth Circuit.[111] In the cases where the independent approach is applied, reference is made to a number of factors which are relevant in determining the degree of connection between the child and the country and whether he has indeed acclimatised sufficiently.[112] These fac-

---

[105] eg in Israeli case law.
[106] *Re P (GE) (An Infant)* (n 84).
[107] *Re Bates* (Unreported decision of 23 February 1989).
[108] *Friedrich v Friedrich* (n 24).
[109] ibid 1401.
[110] *Feder* (n 29).
[111] *Robert v Tesson* 507 F3d 981 (6th Cir 2008).
[112] In *Jenkins v Jenkins*, 569 F3d 549 (6th Cir 2009), the majority held that the acclimatisation test does not require comparing the living situation in the previous country with that in the new one, apart from in the situation where the children live alternately in different countries for extended periods, as in *Robert v Tesson* ibid.

tors include regular attendance at an educational establishment, participation in extra-curricular activities, social and cultural integration, formation of meaningful relationships with relatives and friends and mastering the language.[113] In addition, in some cases, the courts have given practical expression to the child-centred rhetoric by actually considering how the children would have perceived their stay in the new country on the basis of the facts and information known to them.[114]

Nonetheless, whilst many dicta can be found supporting the independent approach in subsequent US,[115] Australian[116] and Israeli[117] case law, in many of them heavy emphasis is still placed on the parents' intentions.[118] Even in the case of *Feder*[119] itself, the Court expressly held that the parents' present shared intentions could be considered in determining habitual residence and that in this case the parties had intended to settle in Australia, despite Mrs Feder's unexpressed reservations. In addition, the scope of the independent model was subsequently restricted by the same Court that decided *Feder*. In the case of *Delvoye v Lee*,[120] the US Court of Appeals for the Third Circuit clarified that in the case of very young children, the intent of the parents was of paramount importance because the children could not form independent connections with their surroundings. Thus, the degree of acclimatisation of such a child was of far less significance than of an older child, who was able to acquire a sense of environmental normalcy.[121] The confusion between the two models in judicial rhetoric is further illustrated by the *Mozes* case.[122] As seen above, in this case the appeal was allowed because the District Court had not taken into account parental intention and passages from the judgment are often quoted in support of the proposition that the child's habitual residence will not be changed, unless his parents intend to abandon their former habitual residence. Nonetheless, the judgment also states that, even where there is no settled intention on the part of the parents to abandon the child's habitual residence, there will still be a change in habitual residence where

> we can say with confidence that the child's relative attachments to the two countries have changed to the point where requiring return to the original forum would now be tantamount to taking the child out of the family and social environment in which its life has developed.[123]

---

[113] eg, *Karkkainen v Kovalchuk* (n 41).
[114] eg, ibid and *Robert v Tesson* (n 111). In the former it was significant that the girl brought with her many personal belongings, whereas in the latter relatively few clothes were brought.
[115] eg *Prevot v Prevot* 855 FSupp 915 (WD Tenn 1994); *Slagenweit v Slagenweit* 841 FSupp 264 (ND Iowa 1993).
[116] eg *Patterson, DHCS v Casse* (1995) FLC 92-629; *Cooper v Casey* (1995) FLC 92-575.
[117] In CA (SC) 7206/93 *Gabbai v Gabbai* PD 51(2), 241 Barak P said, 'Habitual residence is not a technical term. It is not domicile nor residence. It expresses a continuing reality of life. It reflects the place where the child usually lives before the abduction. The point of view is that of the child and place where he lives. The examination focuses on the day to day life of the child and not on plans for the future' (author's translation).
[118] eg in the Australian case of *De Lewinski v D-G of NSW Department of Community Services* (1997) FLC 92-737, *Cooper v Casey* (n 116) was understood as supporting the parental intention approach; cf *Tsimhoni v Eibschitz-Tsimhoni*, US District Court for Eastern District of Michigan (Unreported, 26 March 2010), where the Court expressly held that the evidence regarding the parties' intent was irrelevant to the Court's habitual residence analysis because there will be scant, if any, evidence that the children had knowledge of the relevant information.
[119] *Feder* (n 29).
[120] *Delvoye v Lee* (n 20).
[121] *Whiting v Krassner* (n 101) (confirming the distinction between very young children and older children).
[122] *Mozes* (n 13).
[123] ibid 1081, quoting from the Perez-Vera Report (n 32), para 11. See also use of this test in *In the Interest of SJOBG* 292 SW3d 764 (Tex App 2009).

Ironically, this sentence not only describes the independent approach, but provides justification for that approach and thus it is difficult to reconcile with the express adoption of the parental intention model in the *Mozes* case.[124]

In contrast to this lack of clarity, the independent approach has been adopted in its pure form in a number of continental jurisdictions including Germany, Austria and Switzerland. Courts in these countries have stated that habitual residence reflects the centre of the child's life and his social relationships and that a stay of six months is usually sufficient to acquire habitual residence, even where one parent does not agree thereto.[125]

C The Combined/Hybrid Model

The current author's 2001 article suggested that a proper application of the independent approach involves taking into account the intention of the parents insofar as they are relevant to the child's daily life.[126] This was explained as follows:

> [T]he fact that the child is living in temporary accommodation would be a factor against his having acquired habitual residence; this arrangement itself will reflect the parents' intention. Furthermore, where the child is old enough to understand, information which the parents have given him about the purpose of the residence will be very relevant, because this will affect the way in which the child behaves and the quality of the connections which he forms with the people and institutions around him.[127]

This suggestion effectively recommends a third model, which whilst continuing to emphasise the independent nature of the determination of habitual residence and the focus on the child, also recognises that the quality of the child's connections with a particular place cannot be properly assessed in a vacuum. Thus, some reference needs to be made to the intentions of the parents, at least to the extent that those intentions are manifest from their behaviour or communicated to the child.[128]

This model reflects the spirit of those US cases, in which the court purports to apply the independent model, but also takes into account parental intention[129] and those that apply a test of settled purpose, but examines this from the perspective of the children.[130] A good example of the latter approach can be found in the decision of the US Court of Appeals for the Eighth Circuit in the case of *Silverman v Silverman*,[131] where the majority, in overruling

---

[124] For this reason the model adopted in *Mozes* (n 13) has sometimes been referred to as a hybrid model, *Punter v Secretary for Justice* [2007] 1 NZLR 40 [99].

[125] eg *2 UF 115/02*, Oberlandesgericht Karlsruhe [INCADAT cite: HC/E/DE 944] (Germany); *2 BvR 1206/98*, Bundesverfassungsgericht (Federal Constitutional Court of Germany), 29 October 1998 [INCADAT cite: HC/E/DE 233] (Germany); *8Ob121/03g*, Oberster Gerichtshof, 30 October 2003 [INCADAT cite: HC/E/AT 548] (Austria); *5P.367/2005/ast*, Bundesgericht, II. Zivilabteilung (Tribunal Fédéral, 2ème Chambre Civile) [INCADAT cite: HC/E/CH 841] (Switzerland).

[126] Schuz, 'Habitual Residence' (n 77) 16.

[127] ibid.

[128] The same point was made later by the *Mozes* Court (n 13) 1079–80, when it explained that parental intent is part of the inquiry 'because the child's knowledge of these intentions is likely to color its attitude to the contacts it is making'.

[129] eg *Feder* (n 29); In the case of *Karkkainen v Kovalchuk* (n 41), the Court referred to parental intent because it affected the child's perspective and prevented one parent from unilaterally altering an agreement made by the parties.

[130] See eg *Stern* (n 80); *Barzilay v Barzilay* 600 F3d 912, 916 (8th Cir 2010).

[131] *Silverman v Silverman* 338 F3d 886 (8th Cir 2003).

the District Court's decision, which had given weight to the mother's unexpressed reservation, stated:

> The court should have determined the degree of settled purpose from the children's perspective, including the family's change in geography along with their personal possession and pets, the passage of time, the family abandoning its prior residence and selling the house, the application for and securing of benefits only available to Israeli immigrants, the children's enrolment in school and, to some degree, both parent's intentions at the time of the move to Israel.

Subsequently, a number of courts in other countries have attempted to formulate a cohesive model combining the parental intention and independent models. In *SK v KP*,[132] the New Zealand Court of Appeal, referring to the current author's article, adopted a model similar to the one advocated there, under which the Court has to undertake 'a broad factual enquiry of all factors relevant of which the settled intention of the parents is an important but not necessarily decisive factor'. In the later case of *Punter v Secretary for Justice*,[133] the Court elaborated on the factors to be taken into account which should include:

> settled purpose, the actual and intended length of stay in a state, the purpose of the stay, strength of ties to the state and to any other state (both in the past and currently), the degree of assimilation into the state, including living and schooling arrangements, and cultural, social and economic integration.

This approach has now also been approved by the High Court of Australia in *LK v Director-General, Department of Community Services*.[134]

The New Zealand Court of Appeal specifically rejected the parental intention model and explained that their model puts less emphasis on parental intent than the *Mozes* formulation. Thus, in the case of *Punter*,[135] it was held that the children had acquired a habitual residence during the two-year stay in New Zealand, the objective facts outweighing the parental intention.[136] Similarly, in the earlier case of *SK v KP*,[137] it was held that the child had lost his habitual residence in the USA as a result of the length of his stay and strength of the connections he had now acquired with New Zealand, even though the father had only ever agreed to a short-term stay in New Zealand. Nonetheless, whilst these cases put more weight on the independent factual considerations than other commonwealth jurisdictions, parental intent is still considered as an independent factor.

Similarly, two Israeli judges have attempted to combine the two models into a single cohesive model.[138] In the first,[139] Justice Hendel, after surveying the case law in Israel and a number of English speaking jurisdictions, comes to the conclusion that the Israeli Supreme Court's definition of habitual residence in the case of *Gabbai v Gabbai*,[140] which clearly adopted the independent approach, has to be understood more widely. He helpfully reminds us that the test is of habitual residence and not permanent residence. He also

---

[132] *SK v KP* (n 20).
[133] *Punter v Secretary for Justice* (n 124).
[134] *LK v Director-General, Department of Community Services* (n 23).
[135] *Punter* (n 124).
[136] McGrath J, ibid, expressly stated that settled purpose should not override the 'underlying reality of the connection between the child and the particular state', [61]–[62].
[137] *SK v KP* (n 20).
[138] Although the Israeli Supreme Court has expressly refused to decide between the parental intention and independent model, ACH10136/09 Plonit v Ploni, 21 December 2009 http://elyon1.court.gov.il/files/09/360/101/n01/09101360.n01.pdf
[139] FamA (BSH) 130/08 (n 100).
[140] *Gabai v Gabai* (n 117).

emphasises that the perspective is that of the child and not of the parents and that the inquiry is essentially factual. Nonetheless, whilst the life of the child has to be examined as it is, the intention of the parents will usually be a relevant fact because young children do not usually leave their parents. The weight to be given to the different facts, including the intention of the parents, will vary from case to case depending on the circumstances. Thus, for example, Justice Hendel suggests that where the relocation is clearly permanent, less weight will be placed on the degree to which the child has acclimatised, than where the relocation is for a fixed period. Accordingly, in his view, the outcome should be determined not by which model is adopted, but by the unique factual matrix of each case.[141]

The second reference to a combined model can be found in the concurring judgment of Justice Shtemer in *LM v MM*.[142] Relying on the current author's article,[143] she stated:

> [I]n my view, the test is factual and one of the relevant facts to be examined is the intention of the parents and the physical manifestations thereof (such as repeatedly making clear to the child that the place of residence is temporary). Sometimes this intention will influence the child's and his parents' perception of the place of residence and sometimes not. Between the child's viewpoint as to where he perceives his place of residence and the centre of his life and the intentions of his parents about the future, in my view the child's perception should take precedence. (Author's translation.)

Finally, the approach taken by the ECJ in case law concerning the meaning of habitual residence of a child for the purpose of the Brussels II bis Regulation[144] would also seem to be a hybrid approach, which takes into account parental intentions as a factor within the independent approach.[145] In its first ruling relating to the meaning of the concept of habitual residence of children in this Regulation, the ECJ adopted a factual test in which the enquiry is whether 'the residence of the child reflects some degree of integration in a social and family environment.'[146] However, whilst most of the factors used in this enquiry are objective[147] the ECJ also mentioned the relevance of the parents' intentions to settle permanently, where this is manifested by tangible steps such as the purchase or lease of a residence.[148] Moreover, in a later ruling,[149] the ECJ held that a young child shares the social

---

[141] He overturned the Family Court ruling that the child's habitual residence was in England because his parents had had the intention of spending at least two years there, on the basis that only 10 months had elapsed since the move to England and during this time the child had spent 6 weeks on holiday in Israel.

[142] FamA (Dist HAI) 4646-11-08, *LM v MM* Nevo, 13 January 2009 (Isr). The other two judges took the view that the main test was the factual test, but that there would be cases where the parents' intentions would be determinative.

[143] Schuz, 'Habitual Residence' (n 77).

[144] P McEleavy, 'Habitual Residence and Children' (2012) *International Family Law* 22 explains that the integrated manner in which child abduction and jurisdiction in matters relating to parental responsibility are dealt with in this instrument means that it is not possible for EU countries to adopt a distinct interpretation of habitual residence for child abduction cases. For consideration of the meaning of habitual residence in the Brussels II bis Regulation in the context of ECJ case law in other contexts, see R Lamont, 'Habitual Residence and Brussels II bis: Developing Concepts of European Private International Family Law' (2007) 3 *Journal of Private International Law* 261, 267.

[145] However, it is clear from Art 10 of the Regulation that habitual residence can change without the consent of both parents, see ch 1 at II Cii.

[146] *In Proceedings brought by A*, Case C-523/07 [2009] ECR 1- 2805 [38].

[147] Such as 'duration, regularity, conditions and reasons for the stay on the territory of a Member State and the family's move to that State, the child's nationality, the place and conditions of attendance at school, linguistic knowledge and the family and social relationships of the child in that State must be taken into consideration'. ibid [39].

[148] ibid [40].

[149] *Mercredi v Chaffe* Case C-497/10 PU [2011] 1 FLR 1293.

and family environment of the circle of people on whom he is dependent and thus where he is cared for by his mother, it is also necessary to assess the mother's integration in her social and family environment in the Member State in question.[150] Accordingly, the ECJ did not rule out the possibility that the young child in this case had acquired a habitual residence in the new country within a few days of his arrival there with his mother.[151]

IV Illustrating the Different Models

In this section, the practical significance of the differences between the models presented above will be highlighted by focusing on how each model will be applied in a number of problematic situations which recur in the case law.

A Permanent Relocations

Two issues may arise in relation to habitual residence in cases involving a permanent relocation. The first is how soon the habitual residence changes. This will be relevant where one parent removes the child within a short period of time after the relocation. The second issue concerns the relevance of one parent's unvoiced reservations about the relocation.

i Period of Residence Required

Under the US version of the parental intention approach, it would seem that a new habitual residence can be acquired relatively quickly upon arriving in the new country, where the parties intend to abandon the previous habitual residence.[152] In relation to the UK version of the parental intention approach, the weight of authority supports the proposition that habitual residence will only change after residence for 'an appreciable period of time',[153] although some judges have taken the view that this period can be very short.[154] In contrast, under the independent model, habitual residence will only be changed after a period sufficient for acclimatisation. Whilst time should be considered through the eyes of a child, who has a different perspective to an adult, it is unlikely that he will become

---

[150] ibid [50].

[151] ibid [51]. This seems inconsistent with Lamont's view, 'Habitual Residence' (n 144) 281, that actual residence should be required.

[152] *Mozes* (n 13) 1078 suggests that it will not be immediate.

[153] *Re J* (n 36) (Lord Brandon). Support for this view can be found inter alia in *Nessa v Chief Adjudication Officer* [1999] 4 All ER (Lord Slynn); *Re F* (n 44). In *Re A (Abduction: Habitual Residence)* [2007] 2 FLR 129, it was held that eight days was not an appreciable period. In contrast, support for the opposing view, that provided the requisite attention exists, there is no minimum period of residence, can be found in *Cameron v Cameron* [1996] SLT 306, 313; *Re M (Minors) (Residence Order: Jurisdiction)* [1993] 1 FLR 495, 503. Similarly, in the Australian case of *Patterson* (n 116), Kay J seems to have gone even further, expressing the view that once an intention to adopt an habitual residence has been reached and acted upon in a decisive way so as to provide a degree of certainty and continuity, then it may be open to a court to find that habitual residence has been changed from that point.

[154] eg, in *Re F* ibid, it was suggested that a month could be sufficient; in *V v B (A Minor)(Abduction)* [1991] 1 FLR 266, habitual residence was held to have changed after two months residence; cf P Smart, 'Ordinarily Resident: Temporary Presence and Prolonged Absence' (1989) 38 *International and Comparative Law Quarterly* 175 (suggesting that the time taken to acquire habitual residence depends on how settled the intention is and previous visits to the country concerned, but that three months is the minimum period).

acclimatised, on the basis of objective factors alone, in less than six months,[155] unless the child has previously lived in that country.[156] Nonetheless, under the combined approach which allows weight also to be given to parental intention, it would seem that a shorter period of time would be sufficient where it was clear to the children that the relocation was permanent.[157]

It should be made clear that whilst the time period is an important factor in determining acclimatisation, it is by no means the only factor. Thus, for example, the court will also look to see to what extent the child has integrated socially and culturally in the new environment. Where he is not fluent in the language of the new country and/or there are significant cultural differences in the school system and social norms, acclimatisation will take longer.[158]

It should be noted that there seems to be a difference of opinion about the significance of the young age of the child in applying the independent and combined models. On the one hand, some courts have held that since a young child cannot form connections with his environment independently of his carers, little weight should be put on the child's acclimatisation.[159] On the other hand, some courts seem to have taken the view that for a young child a short period is of greater significance and that therefore his habitual residence will change more quickly.[160]

ii Parental Reservation

Under the US version of the parental intention approach, if one parent can show that he did not have an intention to abandon the previous habitual residence, the habitual residence of the children will not change.[161] The position under the UK version of the parental intention approach is less clear. On the one hand, there is authority that there must be a settled purpose shared by both parties.[162] On the other hand, courts are reluctant to give credence to parental reservations which are not manifested in the facts.[163]

---

[155] eg, *Tsimhoni v Eibschitz-Tsimhoni* (n 118) where three months was held to be insufficient for acclimatisation; cf *Jenkins v Jenkins* (n 112) (five-month stay in the US was sufficient); Canadian case of *Droit de la famille 3713*, No 500-09-010031-003 [INCADAT cite: HC/E/CA 651] (stay of less than four months was sufficient). See also *Karkkainen v Kovalchuk* (n 41) (11-year-old girl was held to have acclimatised sufficiently to change her habitual residence after two months in the US where her father lived) where, in addition to the objective factors, the Court took into account the girl's expectations and in particular the fact that she had been led to believe by her mother and step-father that she could live permanently with her father in the US if she so wished.

[156] In *Robert v Tesson* (n 111), the Court did not completely rule out the possibility of habitual residence being re-acquired in France after a stay of three weeks, but rather relied on specific facts, including the preparations for the trip and the events of those three weeks, to show that the children retained their habitual residence in the US.

[157] per Justice Hendel in FamA 130/08 (n 100).

[158] eg, *Tsimhoni v Eibschitz-Tsimhoni* (n 118) where it was held that the fact that the children were not fluent in Hebrew and the significant differences between the Israeli school and their former school in the US 'hindered the acclimatization process'.

[159] eg, *Whiting v Krassner* (n 101). Under the combined approach, this will mean that more weight is given to the parents' intention and their integration, ECJ case of *Mercredi v Chaffe* (n 149).

[160] eg, *Falls v Downie* 871 F Supp 100 (D Mass 1994) (21-month-old child, who had spent 8 months with his father and paternal grandparent in the US, whilst his mother remained in Germany in order to resolve the parent's financial difficulties, was held to have acquired a habitual residence in the US because 'he had become completely accustomed to life in this country with his father and grandparents and he barely knew his mother').

[161] eg *Papakosnias v Papakosinas* 483 F3d 617 (9th Cir 2007); *Mikovic v Mikovic* 541 F Supp 2d 1264 (MD Fl 2007); but cf statement in *Mozes* (n 13) that the qualms of one parent will not stand in the way of finding a shared and settled purpose.

[162] *D v S (Abduction: Acquiescence)* [2008] EWHC 363 (Fam).

[163] eg *In The Matter of Z (Children)* [2008] EWHC 3473 (Fam).

In contrast, under the independent and combined models, unexpressed parental reservations will not be relevant. Thus, for example, in *Feder*, the fact that the mother regarded the move to Australia as conditional on the marriage improving did not prevent the child acquiring a habitual residence there. Similarly, in the US case of *Silverman*,[164] the Appeal Court, overruling the District Court, held that the mother's reservations about emigrating to Israel were not relevant because the emphasis should be on the facts and the children's perspective.

B Fixed Term Relocations

The situation where a removal or retention takes place during or at the end of a fixed term relocation, such as sabbaticals and employment and military assignments, perhaps illustrates most clearly both the difference between the various models and the lack of clarity within some of the models. Under the US version of the parental intention model, habitual residence will not change during a fixed term relocation so long as both parents do not intend for the child to abandon his habitual residence in the country where he lived prior to the relocation.[165] In contrast, case law shows that under the other models there will be a change in habitual residence, at least where the relocation is for more than two years.[166]

The difference between these two approaches is well illustrated by the Israeli case of *YM v AM*.[167] In this case, an Israeli couple travelled to Oxford so that the husband could undertake post-graduate study there. It was a condition of the husband's funding that he would return to work in Israel for a period of time. After more than two years in Oxford, the marriage broke down and the mother unilaterally retained the children in Israel after a holiday there. The majority in the District Court held that the children's habitual residence was in England on the basis of the children's objective connections with that country. However, Justice Drori dissenting held that the children were habitually resident in Israel, on the basis that the parents had clearly intended to return to Israel after the husband had completed his studies.

Whilst the US version of the parental intention model offers a definitive solution to all cases involving fixed term relocations, the other models are not easy to apply in relation to shorter term relocations. The UK version of the parental intention model has produced results that are difficult to reconcile with each other. On the one hand, cases can be found in which a relocation lasting for one year or less resulted in a change in habitual residence on the basis that a settled purpose existed.[168] On the other hand, there are cases where a

---

[164] *Silverman* (n 131).
[165] eg *Holder v Holder* 392 F3d 1009, 1014 (9th Cir 2004); *Tsarbopoulos v Tsarbopoulos* 176 F Supp2d 1045 (ED Wash 2001); *Paz v Paz* 169 FSupp2d 254 (SD New York, 2001). This also seems also to have been the approach adopted in RFamA (SC) 9802/09 *Plonit v Ploni*, 17 December 2009 (Isr) http://elyon1.court.gov.il/files/09/020/098/e03/09098020.e03.pdf in which, according to the father's version accepted by the Court, the parties had come to Israel for an extended holiday of eight months during the father's parental leave. Justice Amit expressly stated that habitual residence could never change during a fixed term relocation.
[166] See eg, *Re A (Minors) (Abduction) (Habitual Residence)* (n 45) (military posting to Iceland for three years); *Shalit v Coppe* 182 F 3d 1124 (9th Cir 1999) (3-year stay with father while mother attended law school); *In The Matter of Z (Children)* (n 163) (employment assignment in Israel for two years which was subsequently extended, despite mother's desire to return to England).
[167] FamA (Dist JLM) 575/04 *YM v AM* Nevo, 9 November 2004 [INCADAT cite: HC/E/IL 836].
[168] eg, *Re R (Abduction: Habitual Residence)* (n 93) (six months posting in Germany); *Moran v Moran* 1997 SLT 541 (father agreed that children would live in Scotland for a year with mother with a view to discussion about

relocation lasting between one and two years did not lead to a change in habitual residence, even though there appears to be a settled purpose,[169] in the sense stated in *Shah*.[170]

Similarly, it will not be easy to anticipate when a fixed term relocation will lead to a change in habitual residence under the independent model. In the US case of *In re Morris*,[171] the Court expressed the view that 'stays for a limited distinct period of time, especially less than one year' would not lead to a change in habitual residence. However, it is difficult to lay down any blanket rules in relation to relocations lasting more than one year because of the fact-intensive nature of the inquiry. In particular, much depends on the degree of cultural and social acclimatisation of the particular child.

An instructive example is an Israeli case[172] in which the US father and English mother, who had been living together with the children in England, came to Israel for a two-year period in order to work for international organisations. During the stay in Israel, the parties, who were not Jewish, lived in a neighbourhood of Jerusalem inhabited mainly by foreign diplomats and other foreign temporary residents and the children studied at an international school, in which the language of instruction was English. Also, the parents managed their financial affairs via their English banks and no attempt was made to learn Hebrew. In holding that the parents and the children retained their habitual residence in England, the Court emphasised the fact that they had not established any connections with Israeli life and they were living in a 'bubble'.[173]

Similarly, under the combined model, much will depend on the length of the stay, the degree to which the child has acclimatised and the connections retained with the country of origin, but more emphasis will be placed on the fact that the stay is temporary, at least where this is known to the children[174] or reflected in the living conditions of the family.

C Relocations for an Indefinite Period

Many habitual residence disputes concern cases where the child relocates with one or both parents for an indefinite period. Sometimes, the relocation is for a trial period or subject to a condition. In other cases, the parties have not clarified in advance the duration of

---

their future after the year had elapsed); *Re S (A Minor)(Abduction)* [1991] 2 FLR 1 (intention to spend one year in US sufficient); *H-K (Children)* [2011] EWCA Civ 1100 (intention to spend one year in England sufficient).

[169] eg, in *Re S (Minors) (Abduction: Wrongful Retention)* [1994] Fam 70, the children were held to remain habitually resident in Israel during a sabbatical in England which was to last at least a year with a possibility of an extension for a further year. This decision has been criticised by commentators (eg, Beaumont and McEleavy (n 20) 100, fn 74) and the New Zealand Court of Appeal in *Punter* (n 124) [150] has suggested that the decision would be different today. See also *Re H (Abduction: Habitual Residence: Consent)* [2000] 2 FLR 294 (the mother retained her habitual residence in Sweden because 'she was merely a student abroad for a finite one-year course'); *Re P-J (children)* [2009] EWCA Civ 588 (stay of a year in Wales was not part of regular order of children's lives)'; ØLK, 5 April 2002, 16. afdeling, B-409-02 (Denmark) [INCADAT cite: HC/E/DK 520] (agreed stay with father for one year while the mother was hospitalised) and *S v M* [1999] NZFLR 337 (13-month stay with father in order to give the mother a break).

[170] *Shah* (n 18) and accompanying text.

[171] *In re Morris* 55 FSupp 1156 (D Colo 1999) (10-month sabbatical).

[172] FamA (Dist JLM) 132/08 *AS v MB* Nevo, 5 May 2008.

[173] See also FamA (Dist Bsh) 3465-10-11 *DC v YAC* Nevo, 2 November 2011 (Isr) (children had not acquired habitual residence in Spain despite the three-year period of residence there because they did not have any status there, did not go to school and did not learn Spanish).

[174] eg FamC (RLZ) 41179-08-11 *EA v SA* Nevo, 11 December 2011 (Isr) (habitual residence did not change after a two-year stay in the US for a work assignment because the children had not integrated and could not wait to go back to Israel).

the relocation or the circumstances in which it will either end or alternatively become permanent.

Under the US version of the parental intention model, there will not be any change in habitual residence so long as the parents or one of them treats the relocation as temporary.[175] This can be clearly seen from two leading US cases, *Gitter v Gitter*[176] and *Ruiz v Tenorio*.[177] In the latter case, it was held that the children had not lost their US habitual residence, even though they had been living in Mexico for nearly three years and had become acclimatised there, because their mother had never intended to abandon the US as the children's habitual residence, and the move to Mexico was conditional.

Conversely, under the UK parental intention approach, the child's habitual residence will change provided that the parents have a settled purpose.[178] If there is an agreement between the parties, this may be evidence of settled purpose. Thus, in the Scottish case of *Cameron v Cameron*,[179] an agreement which provided that the father could take the children to live with him in France was evidence of settled intention, even though there was provision to review the agreement every six months and for the return of the girls to Scotland if they were unhappy.[180] Furthermore, even if it is not possible to define a purpose in advance, where the relocation lasts more than one year, it will usually be considered to be for a settled purpose.[181]

Under the independent model, the position would not seem to be any different than in relation to permanent relocations and it will be necessary to determine whether the child has acclimatised sufficiently.[182] Similarly, under the combined model, where the child is unaware that the relocation is conditional or for a trial period, the non-permanent nature of the stay will not influence the quality of the connections he forms with the new country. There would appear to be a difference between the independent and combined models in the case where it is clear that one parent considers the stay temporary whilst the other considers it to be permanent. Under the independent model, this fact has no relevance in assessing the acclimatisation of the child, whereas under the combined model it will be taken into account as a factor in its own right. Nonetheless, where the disparity of views between the parents does not affect the child's perception of the situation, then the reality of his daily life will outweigh the fact that one parent viewed the stay as purely temporary.

---

[175] However, a mere hope to return to the country of origin one day will not prevent a new habitual residence being acquired where the parties' actions and present intentions point clearly to the fact that the move is of a settled nature and not temporary, *Koch* (n 104) 716–17.
[176] *Gitter* (n 100) and accompanying text.
[177] *Ruiz v Tenorio* (n 104).
[178] eg, *Re B (Minors)(Abduction) (No 1)* (n 35) (children's habitual residence had changed after six months in Germany because the parents had a settled purpose of using the stay in Germany as a platform from which to resolve their differences and work out the future course for the marriage); *Sasson v Sasson* 327 F Supp 2d 489 (D New Jersey, 2004) (the child's habitual residence changed when the parents arrived in the US with the shared intent to settle there, even for a limited period of time, in the hope of resolving their marital difficulties).
[179] *Cameron v Cameron* (n 153).
[180] Thus, it was held that the girls had already become habitually resident in France after only three months there.
[181] eg *LJG v RTP (Child Abduction)* [2006] NZFLR 589; Clive, 'The Concept of Habitual Residence' (n 36).
[182] eg Israeli case of FamC 42721/06 (TA) *GK v YK* Nevo, 18 March 2007 (Isr) (girl had not acquired habitual residence after 20 months in the USA because she had found it hard to learn English, had studied in three different schools and had not made friends); cf comment in case of *Slagenweit v Slagenweit* 63 F3d 719 (8th Cir 1995) (suggesting that child's habitual residence had changed after eight months as a result of 'geography and passage of time').

An interesting example of a conditional relocation can be found in the Israeli case of *GS v LS*,[183] which concerned an Israeli couple who had been living in Canada for nine years. When the marriage broke down, the mother obtained permission from the Canadian Court to relocate with the children to Israel, despite the father's opposition. The father appealed, but the Canadian Court refused a stay of execution, after the mother undertook to return to Canada if the appeal was successful. The father also came to Israel and nine months later, the Canadian Court allowed his appeal. When the mother refused to hand over the children's passports to enable the father to return with them to Canada, the father applied to the Israeli Court for a return order under the Abduction Convention. The Israeli Court rejected the mother's argument that the children's habitual residence had changed when the whole family came to Israel, on the basis that the move was conditional upon the Canadian appeal being dismissed and that the Canadian Court had continuing jurisdiction to determine where the children should live. The District Court took the view that the decision would be the same under all the models for determining habitual residence. Whilst this may be correct on the facts of this case, if it had taken longer before the appeal had been decided, a different result might have been reached under the independent approach.[184]

D Shuttle Custody Arrangements

Cases where there is rotating custody arrangement, under which the child lives for a period of time with one parent in country X and then a similar period of time in country Y, do not fit easily into the Convention framework. If the child's habitual residence changes each time he moves to the other parent, the Abduction Convention will not apply to protect the child from being retained by one parent in breach of the agreement. However, to hold that the child remains habitually resident in the country he was living before the breakdown of the marriage leads to the arbitrary result that he will not be protected from retention in that country, but will be protected from retention in the other country. Not infrequently, the parents or the court try to pre-empt the problem by providing in an agreement or court order which court should have jurisdiction or even which country will be considered to be the place of the child's habitual residence. However, the prevailing view is that such provisions are not binding on a court hearing a Convention application for return inter alia because of the factual nature of habitual residence.[185] Thus, the way in which courts determine habitual residence in such cases will depend on which model is adopted.

Under the US version of the parental intention model, it would seem that, provided that one of the parents continues to live in the place where the child was habitually resident before the arrangement was made, he will remain habitually resident in that place because there was never any shared intention for him to abandon that country.[186] However, in the

---

[183] FamA (Dist JLM) 34551-09-12 *GS v LS* Dinim District 120 (114) 2012.
[184] However, in the case of FamA (BSh) 121/07 *RB v VG* Nevo, 18 June 2007, the District Court held that the child was still habitually resident in Belgium, despite the fact that he had been living in France for two years, because an appeal against the Belgian Court's decision to allow him to relocate had been pending. The Supreme Court (n 61) found it unnecessary to determine this issue because in its view even if the child had become habitually resident in France, he could still be returned to Belgium. See discussion above at II C.
[185] Report of Third Special Commission Meeting (17–21 March 1997) www.hcch.net, para 16 and see discussion below at V F.
[186] This was the outcome in the case of *Bickerton v Bickerton* No 91-06694 (Cal Super Ct 17 July 1991), but the Court does not give reasons for its decision that the habitual residence of the children had not changed during their one-year stay with the mother in the US under a rotating custody arrangement.

case of *Whiting v Krassner*,[187] the US Court of Appeals for the Third Circuit held that the intention to abandon the child's habitual residence in New York (where she had lived prior to the separation of the parents) during her agreed two-year stay in Canada with the mother was sufficient to result in a change of habitual residence because it was not necessary to show an intention to abandon forever. Nonetheless, it has to be remembered that this Court had adopted the independent model in *Feder*[188] and so, even though in this case it clarified that acclimatisation was much less important than the parents' settled purpose where the children were very young, it is not clear to what extent this court's modification of the nature of the intention to abandon will be accepted in circuits that have adopted an unadulterated parental intention model.

Under the UK version of the parental intention model, the residence with each parent would seem to be for a settled purpose and so the child's habitual residence would change with each move.[189] This would also be the outcome under the independent model, provided that the child became acclimatised in each place, which is likely as he would be living with a parent who was permanently resident there and he would know that he would be going back there again. Thus, for example, in the case of *AFJ v TJ*,[190] in which there was a two-year alternating custody arrangement, the Swedish Court held that the child had become habitually resident in Sweden, on the basis of the length of the period of residence there and her objective ties with that country, and so denied the father's application for return to the US.[191]

Similarly, under the combined model, the combination of the settled purpose and the day to day routine of the child while in each parent's care will result in serial habitual residences as the child moves to and fro between the different countries in which the parents live.[192] This would appear to be the approach adopted by the Ontario Superior Court of Justice in the case of *Wilson v Huntley*, which referred both to the settled purpose of the child's six-month period of residence in Canada in accordance with the parenting agreement and to the fact that at the moment of retention 'Canada was the child's reality, not the United Kingdom'.[193]

E Newborn Child

One of the most difficult situations in which to determine the habitual residence of the child is where the child is born during the mother's temporary absence from the place where she and the father had been residing together. The situation is complicated even further where the parents have different intentions about the future.

A pure version of the parental intention model would seem to result in such children being habitually resident in the country where the parents had last been habitually resident together,[194]

---

[187] *Whiting v Krassner* (n 101).
[188] *Feder* (n 29).
[189] See eg, *Watson v Jamieson* [1998] SLT 180; *Re S (A Minor) (Abduction)* (n 168).
[190] RÅ 1996 ref 52, *AFJ v TJ*, 9 May 1996, Supreme Administrative Court of Sweden [INCADAT cite: HC/E/SE 80].
[191] But the US Court, in *Johnson v Johnson* 26 Va App 135, 493 SE2d 668, 672 (1997) later found that it had retained jurisdiction and that it was the *forum conveniens* because the agreement between the parties had expressly stated that the child's habitual residence should remain in the US.
[192] *Punter* (n 124) [169].
[193] *Wilson v Huntley* (2005) ACWSJ 7084 [58].
[194] This assumes that the rule that one parent cannot unilaterally change the habitual residence of the child applies to a child who was not yet born at the time the unilateral decision was made, a point which does not yet seem to have been decided. In two English cases, in which the child was born in England after the mother had

even though he has never set foot in that country.[195] However, most courts have avoided such a conclusion by simply finding that the child was not habitually resident in the country where he was born and from where he was removed, without stating whether he was habitually resident in any other country.[196] Since the removal has invariably been to the country of intended habitual residence, the result is identical with that which would be reached if it were found that the child was habitually resident in that country. For example, in the leading US case of *Delvoye v Lee*,[197] the US mother and Belgian father who had been living together in the US travelled to Belgium for the birth, in order to avoid US medical expenses. The mother returned to the US two months after the birth and the father claimed wrongful removal. The US Court of Appeals upheld the decision of the District Court that the child was not habitually resident in Belgium because the parties did not have any shared intention for the child to become habitually resident in Belgium.[198] This finding was sufficient to prevent application of the Convention. Of course, if the removal were to a third country, it would be necessary to determine whether the child had a habitual residence in the US, despite the fact that he had never entered that country, or did not have any habitual residence.

Some courts have specifically stated that there must have been some actual residence in the country concerned[199] and thus children born in a country other than that intended by the parents to be their habitual residence will not have any habitual residence,[200] at least until their first visit to the country where their parents are habitually resident.[201] Thus, in the unusual case of *W and B v H (Child Abduction: Surrogacy)*,[202] the English Court held that the twins who were born to an English surrogate mother were not habitually resident in California where the intending parents lived, because they had never been there. Hedley J expressed the view that such a conclusion would involve 'a degree of artificiality, inconsistent with a proposition of fact'.[203]

---

changed her habitual residence during the pregnancy, it was held that the child had a habitual residence in England (*Re A (Abduction: Habitual Residence)* (n 93) and *Re G* (n 88). However, in both cases, the father had consented to the mother being in England and in the latter case Sir Mark Potter said that it was an open question what the situation would be if the father had not agreed to his child being born in a different country.

[195] eg, *B v H (Habitual Residence: Wardship)* [2002] 1 FLR 388 (a child, who was born in Bangladesh at a time when the mother was unable to leave that country, took the mother's UK habitual residence, even though he had never left Bangladesh, for the purposes of English domestic legislation, but Hedley J later cast doubt on this reasoning (*in W and B v H* (n 78)) on the basis that habitual residence is a question of fact. Justice Rotlevy in the Israeli case of FamA (Dist TA) 70/97 *Dagan v Dagan* Nevo, 13 December 1998 clearly envisaged that if there had been consensus between the parties about the limited nature of the stay in the US, the child would have been habitually resident in Israel, even though he was born in the US and had lived there all his life.

[196] eg, *Delvoye v Lee* 329 F3d 330 (3rd Cir 2003); Israeli case of FamA (DistTA) 1026/05 *Ploni v Almoni*, Nevo, 17 March 2005 (later upheld by the Supreme Court without discussion) (the fact that children had been born in Paraguay and lived there all their lives was not conclusive because the parents had not intended to abandon their habitual residence in Israel).

[197] *Delvoye v Lee* ibid.

[198] cf *Re G* (n 88), where at the time of birth, the mother had acquired a habitual residence in England during the pregnancy and the father had agreed that following the birth the baby should be in the mother's care in England pending any agreement on return to Canada. It should be noted, however, that the older child who had been born and lived in Canada was still habitually resident there and return was ordered. The Court assumed that the mother would return with both of the children.

[199] eg, *Re M (Abduction: Habitual Residence)* [1996] 1 FLR 887; *Re A (Abduction: Habitual Residence)* (n 93); *Al Habtoor v Fotheringham* [2001] EWCA Civ 186; *REA (Wardship: Habitual Residence)* [2006] EWHC 3338 (Fam).

[200] Clive, 'The Concept of Habitual Residence' (n 36) 146.

[201] *Cooper v Casey* (n 116) (Nicholson CJ).

[202] *W and B v H* (n 78).

[203] Hedley J also held that they were not habitually resident in the UK because neither of their biological parents had any connection with the UK. With respect, this reasoning is inconsistent with the English law approach which treats the birth mother as the legal mother of the child.

No case law has been found which attempts to apply the independent model to the newborn child situation. It would seem that since the child has only ever lived in the country where he is born, he must be habitually resident there. While it might be argued that he needs time to acclimatise, it seems that this requirement relates to a situation where a person has lived in one place and needs time to get used to another. Furthermore, acceptance of this argument would logically lead to the absurd result that no child has a habitual residence at birth.

Similarly, no attempt has been found to apply the combined model to the newborn child situation. Whilst the factual element of this model would seem to prevent a child being habitually resident in a country in which he has never lived, the relevance of other factors including settled purpose might lead to a situation where the child does not have, at least initially, any habitual residence. Thus, where the stay in the foreign country was short-term, the child would not have any habitual residence during the course of that stay. However, where the stay, although temporary, was for a longer period, or where the original period was extended, there would come a stage where the objective facts would outweigh the intentions of the parents to return to the country of origin.

F Re-Abduction

Where the child is re-abducted, sometimes after a considerable period of time, back to the country of origin, the question arises as to whether the child had become habitually resident in the country of refuge. Under the parental intention model, the answer would seem to be in the negative, provided that the left-behind parent had the right to determine the child's residence and has at no time agreed to the child remaining in the country of refuge. A particularly extreme example of this situation can be found in the case of *Isaacs v Rice*,[204] where it was held that the child was still habitually resident in the US at the time of the re-abduction, even though he had been living in Israel for 11 years since the original abduction, because the abducting father could not unilaterally change the child's habitual residence. However, in the case of *Re B (Abduction: Children's Objections)*,[205] Stuart-White J did leave open the possibility of finding that a child's habitual residence had changed in an extreme case, such as where he had been living in the country of refuge for 10 years, because any other result would be 'an affront to common sense'. Furthermore, it seems that the child's habitual residence will change where the court in the country of refuge has refused to return the child and awarded custody to the abductor.[206]

Under the independent model, the child's habitual residence will change after he has become acclimatised in the country of refuge. However, his acclimatisation may be slowed down if he is aware of the chance that he may be returned to the country of origin. Furthermore, where the child is in hiding, he will be isolated from his environment and so will not become acclimatised.[207] Similarly, under the combined approach, there will come

[204] *Isaacs v Rice* 1998 US Dist Lexis 12602; See also *Re R (Wardship: Child Abduction)(No2)* [1993] 1 FLR 249, 256.
[205] *Re B (Abduction: Children's Objections)* [1998] 1 FLR 667.
[206] This was the situation in the Israeli case of RFamA (SC) 672/06 *PR v TAE*, 61(3) PD 24 [INCADAT cite: HC/E/IL 885], but *cf* provisions of the 1996 Child Protection Convention, discussed in ch 1 at II E.
[207] See the discussion of a similar issue in relation to the establishment of settlement for the purposes of the Art 12(2) defence, in ch 9 at II Bii.

a stage at which the reality of the child's life in the country of refuge overrides the lack of shared parental intent.

V Analysis

A Internal Coherence

i The Various Models

At first sight, a model which is predicated on the right of the parents to choose where their children live, as is the parental intention model, seems to fit well with the terminology of the Abduction Convention, under which the mandatory return mechanism is triggered by a breach of custody rights, which are usually parental rights.[208] However, this apparently conceptual consonance is not in fact a good reason for adopting the parental intention model. There is a fundamental difference between the question of determining habitual residence, which defines the connection between the child and a particular jurisdiction, on the one hand, and that of determining whether a removal or retention is wrongful, which characterises the parent's action, on the other hand. Thus, whilst there is a degree of logic in answering the latter question by reference solely to the rights of the parents, such an approach is inappropriate in relation to the former issue.

In addition, there is an element of circular reasoning in the parental intention model. In order to determine which parent has the right to decide where the child should live, it is necessary to know which law determines the respective rights of the parents. Under the Abduction Convention, the rights of the parents are governed by the law of habitual residence of the child,[209] and yet the very purpose of the enquiry is to determine which country is the habitual residence. A pragmatic solution to this conundrum is to apply the law of the last common habitual residence of the two parents, on the assumption that this was also the child's habitual residence. Unless the parents had different habitual residences at the date of the child's birth,[210] there will be some baseline common habitual residence. However, this country may no longer have any connection with the child or the parties and thus may seem as inappropriate a connecting factor as the domicile of origin. Furthermore, where the parties separated before the child's birth, there may well not be any mutual intention in relation to where the child should live, in which case it will not be possible to determine the child's habitual residence on the basis of parental intention. This is more likely to be problematic where the parents are not married to each other, since some legal systems do not grant automatic parental rights to unmarried fathers. However, even with married parents, if the mother obtains a sole custody order, it is necessary to know whether this was given by a court in the country of habitual residence or recognised by the law of habitual residence in order to know whether it does indeed determine the parental rights[211]

---

[208] For criticism of the choice of breach of parental rights as the trigger, see ch 7 at IV E.

[209] This law determines whether there has been a breach of custody rights and thus whether there is a wrongful removal or retention (Art 3).

[210] cf *Re A (Abduction: Habitual Residence)* (n 93) and *Re G* (n 88), in which the fathers had consented to the mothers coming to England.

[211] eg decision in *Tahan v Duquette* 600 A 2d 472 (NJ Sup Ct, 1991) 476 in which the Court held that the child was habitually resident in Canada because of the Canadian custody order in favour of the mother.

In addition, the theoretical foundation of the parental intention model is undermined by the fact that, as mentioned above, a number of courts have acknowledged the need to deviate from the model in certain extreme situations. For example, Stuart-White J acknowledged that holding that a child's habitual residence had not changed after living in a country for 10 years was an affront to common sense.[212] Similarly, some courts have not been prepared to find that a child is habitually resident in a country in which he has never set foot, even though this is clearly what his parents intended.[213]

Finally, the parental intention model does not fit in well with the philosophy behind the Article 13(2) child objection exception,[214] because it does not take into account the views of the child at all. This might lead to rejection of a Convention application in a case where the child would have very much wanted to return to the country which he saw as his habitual residence simply because one parent had not intended for there to be a change of habitual residence.

ii Other Issues

Whichever model is chosen, a number of issues arise in relation to the finding of habitual residence for the purpose of the Convention and the relevance thereof. Firstly, it is necessary to decide whether a child should be able to have more than one habitual residence concurrently. Whilst the finding that a child has concurrent habitual residence does not appear to fit comfortably within the framework of the Convention,[215] such a finding is not in fact inconsistent with the Convention. As explained above,[216] there is no reason why in such a case the Convention cannot apply to removals or retentions to third countries and so it is appropriate to find dual habitual residence, where this reflects the situation on the ground.[217]

Secondly, as seen above, it is unclear whether the removal has to be from the place of habitual residence and whether the return has to be thereto.[218] For the reasons explained above,[219] neither the text of the Convention nor the need for internal coherence requires a positive answer to these questions. On the contrary, the scheme of the Convention requires that it should apply to removals from third countries and that return to a third country should be allowed where removal was from that place or where return to the place of habitual residence is not practicable, provided that this will further the objectives of the Convention.[220]

Finally, some courts have suggested that in cases of doubt, the child's habitual residence should be determined in such a way that the Convention will apply[221] and thus any doubt should work in favour of the left-behind parent.[222] Such a presumption does not promote

---

[212] *Re B (Abduction: Children's Objections)* (n 205).
[213] eg, *Re M (Abduction: Habitual Residence)* (n 199); *Re A (Abduction: Habitual Residence)* (n 93); *Al Habtoor v Fotheringham* (n 199).
[214] See ch 12.
[215] Similarly, the Protection Convention seems to envisage that a child can only have one habitual residence at any one time. See Lagarde Report (n 20), para 41.
[216] At I C.
[217] Such as in cases of shuttle custody agreements. See IV D above and Lamont, 'Habitual Residence' (n 144) 267.
[218] At II A and C.
[219] ibid.
[220] ibid.
[221] eg, *Re F* (n 44); see further discussion below at Ci.
[222] RFamA 9802/09 (n 165) (Justice Amit).

internal coherence because it means that the result may depend on which parent acts. [223] Take for example the case of *Re F*,[224] in which the English Court held that the child had acquired a habitual residence in Australia after three months there and that therefore the father, who had taken the child back to the UK, had to return him to Australia. Assume that the father had not removed the child, but had instead applied under the Convention to the Australian Court, claiming unlawful retention by the mother. The policy of ensuring that the child is protected by the Convention would now favour the father and thus the child would be held to be habitually resident in the UK and return would be ordered to the UK. Surely, it is absurd that the determination of the child's habitual residence should depend on whether he is removed or retained.

Moreover, a presumption in favour of application of the Convention is inconsistent with the Convention scheme, under which the applicant is required to prove that the child's habitual residence was in a Contracting State, other than the requested State at the time of the wrongful removal or retention.[225] Thus, in cases of doubt, he will not succeed in raising the burden of proving the threshold conditions which trigger the duty to order return.

B Consistency with the Intention of the Drafters

According to the Perez-Vera Report, the main reason that habitual residence was chosen as the connecting factor in the Abduction Convention was because the drafters were seeking a concept that was a pure issue of fact and not one that was technical and legalistic like domicile.[226] Accordingly, a number of commentators and judges warned against developing detailed and restrictive rules as to habitual residence, which might make it a technical term of art, like common law domicile.[227]

The parental intention model of habitual residence does not give effect to the intentions of the drafters. In particular, the principle that one parent cannot change the habitual residence of a child unilaterally, unless he has sole parental rights, will lead to an absurd result, from the factual perspective, if the child continues to live with that parent and the other parent does not agree or acquiesce. An extreme example is the US case of *Isaacs v Rice*,[228] in which it was held that the child had not become habitually resident in Israel, where he had lived for 11 years after being abducted by his father, because his mother did not intend him to be living there.

Furthermore, the need for the views and intentions of the parents to coincide introduces a highly technical element. Thus, for example, in the case of *D v S (Abduction: Acquiescence)*[229] it was held that, even though both parents had agreed that the child should spend three

---

[223] Similarly, a presumption in favour of the application of the Convention means that the determination of habitual residence will depend on the legislative context in which it is made and that a child who is found to be habitually resident in a certain country for the purposes of the Abduction Convention would have been found to be habitually resident in a different country if the finding were made in a different context, such as internal jurisdiction, Schuz, 'Policy Considerations' (n 19) 145.

[224] *Re F* (n 44).

[225] eg *Smith v Smith* (n 48) 850.

[226] Perez Vera Report (n 32), para 66.

[227] eg L Collins (ed), *Dicey and Morris and Collins on the Conflict of Laws*, 15th edn (London, Sweet & Maxwell, 2012); C Bruch, 'International Child Abduction Cases: Experience Under the 1980 Hague Convention (revised)' in J Eekelaar and P Šarčević (eds), *Parenthood in Modern Society* (Kluwer, Martinus Nijhoff, 1993).

[228] *Isaacs v Rice* (n 204).

[229] *D v S (Abduction: Acquiescence)* (n 162).

years in England, which was sufficient to found a change in habitual residence, there was no common settled purpose because the mother secretly intended to keep the child in England after the end of that period and thus the child remained habitually resident in Mexico. With respect, this result is absurd and not even consistent with the theory behind the parental rights model since from each parent's perspective, the child was resident in England with a settled purpose. The fact that they had in mind different settled purposes and that one had misled the other does not in any way derogate from the fact that each one had agreed that the child should live in England for three years or from the quality of his residence in England. Indeed, it would make far more sense to adopt a lowest common denominator approach to situations where there is a disparity between the views of the parents. Furthermore, any distinction between cases where one parent formed the intention not to honour the agreement before the relocation and cases where he changed his mind afterwards is legalistic and not consistent with the intention of the drafters.

Moreover, under the US version of the model, it is possible that a child may retain his habitual residence in a country even though he has not lived there for many years, provided that one of his parents retains an intention to return there. Indeed, such a scenario is reminiscent of the much criticised English case law in relation to the domicile of origin.[230] The *Mozes* Court's insistence that their approach does not equate habitual residence to domicile[231] is not entirely convincing. The assertion that the parental intention model does not require an intention of permanent or indefinite residence in the new country, as does domicile, ignores the fact that such an intention is often simply the corollary of intention to abandon the previous domicile. Thus, frequently the reason that a person does not acquire a new domicile despite many years residence in the new country is because he harbours an intention to return to his country of domicile someday. Accordingly, a model which makes intention to abandon the former habitual residence as a pre-requisite for changing the habitual residence retains significant features of the law of domicile, which the drafters sought to avoid.[232]

C Promotion of the Objectives of the Convention

i Protecting Abducted Children

As already mentioned, some courts have expressed the view that, insofar as possible, a child's habitual residence should be determined in such a way that he is protected by the Convention.[233] However, Beaumont and McEleavy[234] rightly point out that this view is too simplistic because it does not consider whether the child has any real connection with either the country to which he is to be returned if the Convention applies or with the parent to whom he is being returned. Thus, the objective of protecting children does not require a presumption in favour of application of the Convention per se.[235] Rather, it is necessary to ensure that the Convention applies to protect a child in circumstances where

---

[230] An extreme example is the much criticised case of *Bullock v IRC* [1976] 3 All ER 353 (tax payer retained his domicile in Canada even though he had lived in the UK for more than 40 years because he intended to return to Canada if his wife predeceased him or if he could persuade her to return there).
[231] *Mozes* (n 13) 1076.
[232] See *Punter* (n 124) [111].
[233] *Re F* (n 44) 555 and *Nessa v Chief Adjudication Officer* [1998] 2 All ER 728 (Thorpe LJ).
[234] Beaumont and McEleavy (n 20) 90.
[235] See also Aii above.

the abduction is likely to cause him harm because he was removed or retained 'from the social and family environment in which his life has developed'.[236] Thus, it is appropriate to examine to what extent the different models will accurately identify such situations.

Under the US version of the parental intention model, the focus on the parents' intention to abandon the former habitual residence means that it is possible that the country where the child is living is not his habitual residence even though it is indeed the family and social environment in which his life has developed. In such a case, there will be no remedy under the Convention where a child is removed from the place where he has been living for a substantial period of time and taken back to the country where he was living beforehand, simply because one or both of his parents never intended to abandon that country.[237] Yet, this would seem to be a situation where the child is in need of protection.

Conversely, the UK version of the parental intention approach may lead to a finding of change of habitual residence during a short and fixed stay abroad[238] or shortly after arriving for an indefinite but conditional stay.[239] It is doubtful whether in such circumstances the 'new' country can be described as the family and social environment in which the child's life has developed and consequently being suddenly uprooted therefrom may well not be harmful, at least when the child is being returned to the country where he lived previously and to where it was intended that he would return at the end of the posting or if the condition upon which relocation was based did not materialise. On the contrary, the child has been removed to the environment with which he is most familiar and return back to the new country may cause him harm. So, it also seems that this model may not always be able to distinguish between situations where protection is necessary and those where it is not.

By contrast, the independent and combined models are expressly seeking to determine whether the child has acclimatised sufficiently so that the new country can be considered to be the social and family environment in which the child's life has developed. As one US court notes, 'the child's perspective should be paramount in construing this convention whose very purpose is to "protect children"'.[240]

ii Deterrence

In the case of *Punter v Secretary of Justice*,[241] the New Zealand Court of Appeal expressed the view that the policy of the Convention is deterrence of removal or retention **from the place of the habitual residence** (author's emphasis) and not abduction or retention per se. While this view seems correct, it does not provide any assistance in determining between the different models of habitual residence. Rather, it simply reinforces the other objectives, which explain why it is necessary to deter removal or retention from the place of habitual residence: viz to protect children from being suddenly uprooted from their social and family environment and to deter forum-shopping.[242] Indeed, to consider the objective of deterrence in determining habitual residence would seem to involve circular reasoning.

---

[236] Perez-Vera Report (n 32), para 11.
[237] *Robert v Tesson* (n 111) 991. Similarly, under the UK approach, if there is no mutual intention or common settled purpose, the child might remain habitually resident in a country in which he has not lived for a number of years, eg, *D v R (Abduction: Acquiescence)* (n 162).
[238] eg, *Re R (Abduction: Habitual Residence)* (n 93).
[239] eg *Cameron v Cameron* (n 153) (three months); *Re S (A Minor)(Abduction)* (n 168).
[240] *Stern* (n 80) 452.
[241] *Punter* (n 124) [181].
[242] The potential tension between the objective of deterrence and that of decision-making in the *forum conveniens* was noted in *SK v KP* (n 20) [84].

iii Adjudication in the Forum Conveniens

The connecting factor of habitual residence was designed inter alia to identify the *forum conveniens* for the determination of the custody dispute.[243] Thus, it is necessary to consider to what extent the various models for determining the habitual residence of the child will accurately identify the *forum conveniens*. At the outset, it should be remembered that, at least in borderline cases, the identification of the *forum conveniens* is a complex exercise, highly dependent upon the specific factual matrix of the particular case and that a number of different approaches exist to determining the *forum conveniens* in general and in relation to children in particular.[244]

Furthermore, there may be some situations in which the place of habitual residence is not the *forum conveniens*.[245] Indeed, Waite J in the case of *H v H (Minors) (Forum Conveniens) (Nos 1 and 2)* expressly held that in determining the *forum conveniens* in cases concerning children, 'the child's habitual residence is a factor in all cases persuasive, in many determinative, but in none conclusive'.[246] Thus, it is not possible to state definitively that a particular model of habitual residence will always identify the *forum conveniens* most accurately.[247] Nonetheless, it is feasible to assess which models are more likely to achieve this objective.

Under the US parental intention model, the requirement of parental intention to abandon the former habitual residence may lead to a situation where the child's habitual residence is in a country where he has not lived for many years, or perhaps never lived. It is highly unlikely that such a country will be the *forum conveniens* for the determination of the custody dispute both because of the substantive connections with the new country and because most of the evidence concerning the child will be in the new country.[248]

Conversely, under the UK parental intention approach, the possibility that a temporary purpose will be considered to be a settled one means that a child's habitual residence may change fairly quickly even when the relocation is not permanent.[249] In cases of short, fixed-term relocations, it is unlikely that the new country will have become the *forum conveniens* for determining the custody dispute only a few months after arrival.

---

[243] Schuz, 'Policy Considerations' (n 19) 140.

[244] See ch 5 at II Ciii.

[245] See examples brought in R Schuz, 'The Hague Child Abduction Convention: Family Law and Private International Law' (1995) 44 *International and Comparative Law Quarterly* 771, 784–92.

[246] *H v H (Minors) (Forum Conveniens) (Nos 1 and 2)* [1993] 1 FLR 958.

[247] Indeed the US Uniform Child Custody Jurisdiction Act which adopted the child's 'home state' as the main basis for jurisdiction, which is analogous to habitual residence, found it appropriate to add alternative bases of jurisdiction to reflect the fact that there may be cases where a State other than the home State would be the *forum conveniens*. In particular, another State may assume jurisdiction where this is in the child's best interests because the child and at least one of his parents has a significant connection with that State and substantial relevant evidence is available in that State (s 3(a)(2)).

[248] See the comments of the *Punter* Court (n 124) [182] that 'the less familiar the circumstances of a prior habitual residence are, and the better able the new jurisdiction is to adjudicate on custody arrangements, the less the rationale for returning a child applies'.

[249] eg, in *Re R (Abduction: Habitual Residence)* (n 93), it is difficult to accept that Germany was the *forum conveniens*. Similarly, in *DG v Davis* (1990) FLC 92-182, the Australian Court ordered return of the children to the UK (aged eight and four) who had been taken back to Australia by the mother only three months after the family moved to the UK for an indefinite period, holding without discussion that the children were habitually resident in the UK. It is certainly arguable that Australia, where the children had lived for many years, was still the *forum conveniens* and that under the independent and combined approaches the children would still have been habitually resident there.

In contrast, the independent and combined models' focus on the factual connections between the child and the country more accurately mirror the closest connection test often used in determining the *forum conveniens*.[250] Nonetheless, the nature of the relocation, as determined by the parents' intentions, is also likely to be relevant in identifying the *forum conveniens*. Thus, the fact that the parties had intended to return to the country of origin at the end of the fixed-term relocation is significant in determining whether that country is an appropriate forum for making long-term decisions about the children. Similarly, if the relocation is not permanent, the family is likely to retain close ties with the country of origin, which will make pursuance of litigation there less inconvenient than in a case where the relocation is intended to be permanent.[251] Such factors will be taken into account under the combined model, but not necessarily under the independent model. Accordingly, the combined model is most likely to result in promoting the objective of ensuring that custody disputes are determined in the *forum conveniens*.

In a few borderline cases, courts have expressly justified their finding of habitual residence on the basis that it is consistent with the *forum conveniens* for determining the merits of the custody dispute. For example, in the case of *Wilson v Huntley*,[252] the Canadian Court explained that Canada was the *forum conveniens* both because the ties of the child with Canada were more permanent than those with the UK and because the agreement between the parents showed that they envisaged that custody disputes would be determined in Canada. Similarly, in the case of *Punter*, the Court commented that New Zealand was likely to be the more convenient forum because 'witnesses as to the children's situation over the last two years at this very critical stage of their lives will all be in New Zealand'.[253]

iv Justice between the Parties

It would seem that justice between the parties would require that the child's habitual residence be determined in such a way that the Convention should apply so that the abductor is not rewarded for his illegal act. This is because the unilateral act of the abductor unfairly prejudices the left-behind parent, even where the place of refuge is the habitual residence of the child. Indeed, some courts have based their rejection of an independent approach on the fact that this allows a parent to manipulate a consensual stay abroad in a way that ensures that the child becomes acclimatised there.[254] This problem is less acute under the combined model because the intention of both parents is taken into account, at least where the child is aware of the intentions or they impact on his daily life. In any event, the objective of justice between the parents is only subsidiary and so this consideration should only be relevant in borderline cases where the facts are consistent with a finding of habitual residence in more than one country.

However, the situation in re-abduction cases is rather different. In such cases, justice would seem to require finding that the child has not acquired a habitual residence in the

---

[250] See ch 5 at II Ciii.
[251] eg, usually, the family will have left many of its belongings behind and may even have accommodation available or which can be made available.
[252] *Wilson v Huntley* (n 193).
[253] *Punter* (n 124) [187].
[254] *Mota v Rivera Castillo* 692 F3d 108, 116 (2d Cir 2012). See also ACH 10136/09 (n 138) in which the Court took the view that the mother had planned the one-year stay of the family in Israel with the hope that this would result in a change of the children's habitual residence, even though she knew that the father expected that the family would return to Sweden.

country of refuge following the first abduction and thus the Convention does not apply to the re-abduction back to the original place of habitual residence.[255] Indeed, the need to prevent the first abductor from benefitting from his illegal act has been mentioned by the courts in such cases to support a finding that the child is still habitually resident in the original country of origin.[256] There is some merit in this approach, provided of course that the finding that the original habitual residence has been retained is indeed consistent with the facts.[257]

D Compatibility with the Summary Nature of Convention Proceedings

Under both versions of the parental intention model, it is necessary to ascertain what the parents intended at the time of the relocation and/or at the time of the removal or retention, at least in the usual situation where they both have parental rights. Case law shows that the mother and father usually present different accounts of the nature, purpose and intended duration of the move to the new country. The task of determining which party's version is accurate is extremely difficult, since invariably the main evidence is conversations between the parties, to which there were no witnesses. Moreover, very often there is evidence to support both parties' contentions and the court is simply left to determine, usually impressionistically,[258] which party is a more reliable witness or which evidence seems weightier.

The summary nature of Convention proceedings is unsuited to making such determinations,[259] which require detailed consideration of large quantities of evidence[260] and in which oral testimony is essential. Thus, in an effort not to cause delay, the court may well not consider all the evidence fully.[261] For example, amidst the sea of conflicting evidence, the court may seize on a particular fact or statement as being determinative, even though there are other plausible explanations for this fact or statement, which have not been put forward convincingly enough or have not been internalised by the court.[262] Alternatively,

---

[255] *cf* German case of 2 BvR 1206/98, Bundesverfassungsgericht, 29 October 1998 [INCADAT cite: HC/E/DE 233], in which it was held that the children had acquired a habitual residence in France during the nine months they had been there following the abduction before being re-abducted.

[256] eg, *Meredith v Meredith* 759 F Supp 1432, 1435 (D Ariz 1991), where it was said, in relation to the original abduction, that 'it would be inequitable and unjust to allow such conduct to create habitual residence'; similarly *Re R (Wardship: Child Abduction (No 2)*(n 204), where it was said that it would be wrong to allow the mother to rely on the provisions of the Hague Convention 'to overcome her disobedience to the order of this Court'.

[257] *cf Isaacs v Rice* (n 204), discussed at IV B.

[258] eg, in ACH 10136/09 (n 138), the Court preferred the father's witnesses to the mother's without saying why. Of course, where there is only affidavit evidence, it is not even possible to obtain such an impression, *Zotkiewicz & Commissioner of Police (No 2)* [2011] FamCAFC 147 [100].

[259] Vivatvarapol, 'Back to Basics' (n 80) 3363, even claims that 'an inquiry into difficult to divine and amorphous concepts is directly contrary to the summary-return mechanism contemplated by the drafters of the Child Abduction Convention. This author also argues that even in cases where the parental intention is found to be consistent with the objective evidence of acclimatisation, the need to examine parental intent is time-consuming and unnecessarily complicates litigation.

[260] In *Dagan v Dagan* (n 195), Judge Haim Porat was critical of the mother's lawyers for bringing 12 witnesses, 40 documents and 8 cassettes, most of which related to the question of the parties' intentions in relation to the issue of habitual residence.

[261] In *Re B (Minors)(Abduction) (No 1)* (n 35), it was said that in order to ensure that Convention proceedings were completed speedily, habitual residence had to be determined by taking a general view rather than by an intricate examination of every word and action.

[262] eg in RFamA (SC) 2338/09 *LM v MM*, 3 June 2009 (Isr), http://elyon1.court.gov.il/files/09/380/023/h12/09023380.h12.pdf the Court relied heavily on the fact that the mother had taken departure money from the

212 *Habitual Residence*

the trial will drag out for a long time, making the objective of immediate return unattainable.

Either way, the uncertainty involved in the forensic process of deciding which parent is telling the truth can only encourage parents to try their luck and thus to litigate abduction cases rather than come to a settlement. The hurt and bitterness caused by this litigation and by the fact that each party will see the other as distorting the truth and rewriting the facts can only harm the children.[263] This seems particularly unfortunate when the subject matter of this dispute does not even relate directly to the welfare of the children.

In contrast, under the independent model, there is no need to determine the parents' intentions and the objective connections between the child and the country in question can usually be proven relatively easily. Under the combined model, parental intentions are taken into account, but since this is only one factor, the court may not necessarily have to come to a definitive conclusion as to which parent's version is more accurate. Moreover, at least in relation to older children, the focus is on the child's perspective and so what is important is how he would have understood the parents' intentions, based on their actions and conversations with him. Thus, the scope of the relevant evidence is likely to be more limited.[264] Thus, the independent and combined models are significantly more compatible with the nature of Convention proceedings than the parental intention models.

E Consistency with Rights and Interests of Children

A weighty argument against the parental intention model is that it is inconsistent with the contemporary approach to the parent-child relationship. Under this approach, the emphasis on parental rights has given way to recognition that the child is an independent actor with his own interests and rights;[265] whereas the parental intention model bases the habitual residence on the intention of the parents, without any inquiry as to whether this is either necessary for, or even consistent with, the child's interests. The US approach is even less consistent with a child-centric perspective than the UK approach because it focuses on the parents' subjective long-term intentions, which may have little relevance to the child's day-to-day experience; whereas the UK model focuses on the purpose of the parent's residence in a particular country, which will usually be reflected in the child's daily life.

In any event, it is clear that the independent and combined models most accurately reflect the philosophy of children's rights, according to which the child is to be treated as

---

Kibbutz as showing that the parties' move to France was not temporary. However, the mother's lawyer has informed the author that the reason for taking the money was the need to finance the trip to France, to look for work. Furthermore, the Court did not take into account that the conditions in which the parties lived in France, most of the time sleeping in friends' apartments on mattresses which was evidence of the temporary/conditional nature of the stay there. See also the Full Court's criticism of the first instance decision in *Zotkiewicz* (n 258) [120].

[263] Furthermore, emphasis on parental intention may encourage one party to manipulate the facts so as to support his version of parental intention eg, in *Tsimhoni v Eibschitz-Tsimhoni* (n 118), the father, whilst persuading the mother to come to Israel with the children for a trial period, took steps to makes this look like a permanent move inter alia by applying in her name (she alleged that this was without her consent) to receive benefits due to a returning resident. These facts convinced the Israeli Court, FamC (KS) 29189-12-09 *TsL v ATsM* Nevo, 23 December 2009 to make an Art 15 declaration that the children's habitual residence was in Israel when they were removed three months after arrival. However, the US Court, applying the independent model, later found that the children had not become acclimatised in Israel.

[264] eg in *Zotkiewicz* (n 258), what was relevant was the extent to which the mother's intentions affected the integration into life in Poland and not the precise intention of the parties when they left Australia.

[265] See generally ch 6 at II.

an autonomous individual. Under these models, the child's habitual residence is determined on the basis of his own objective connections with the country concerned and not through the eyes of his parents. Whilst the combined model does takes into account the parental intentions, those intentions are viewed from the perspective of the child. The advantage of the combined model is that it does give recognition to the legal reality under which, whilst minors have independent legal rights of their own, their parents have the right and duty to care for them and provide a home for them and to the practical reality that most children are not in a position to decide where they want to live because they are physically and/or financially dependent on their parents. This fact means that the parents' choices will usually have an influence over the way in which a child perceives the place where he is living and the quality of the connections he forms with that place.

Furthermore, an older child's intentions concerning where he would like to live should be taken into account, in accordance with the child's right to participate, as enacted in Article 12 of the United Nations Convention on the Rights of the Child.[266] Clearly, the weight to be given to these views in determining the child's habitual residence will depend to a large extent on how realistic it is for him to be able to live in the place where he wants to live.[267]

Finally, the child's right to identity[268] can only be protected if the question of habitual residence is considered from his perspective. Even young children develop meaningful ties with the family and community in which they are living which deserve to be protected.[269] In order to provide this protection, it is necessary to consider what meaning the child gives to the relationships and events in his life, which may be different from that which adults might expect.[270]

F Consistency with Rights of the Parents

It is axiomatic that the parental intention approach best gives effect to the rights of the parents. Moreover, there are two particular ways in which parental rights may be prejudiced where a finding of habitual residence does not take into account their real intentions.

The first is the situation where one parent, invariably the mother, is coerced into agreeing to the family living in a particular place. There is indeed evidence that in violent relationships, women may agree to move to another country or to stay in the country where they are currently living against their will.[271] The independent and combined models

---

[266] Schuz, 'Habitual Residence' (n 77) 17–18.
[267] ibid. In the case of *Karkkainen v Kovalchuk* (n 41) 295, the Court said that 'we are presented with a unique fact pattern, in that Maria's parents agreed ... that she possessed "the material and psychological wherewithal" to decide where she would reside'.
[268] See generally Y Ronen, 'Redefining the Child's Right to Identity' (2004) 18 *International Journal of Law, Policy and the Family* 147.
[269] ibid 158.
[270] ibid 162–63.
[271] MH Weiner, 'International Child Abduction and the Escape from Domestic Violence' (2000) 2 *Fordham Law Review* 593, 641–50; K Brown Williams, 'Fleeing Domestic Violence: A Proposal to Change the Inadequacies of the Hague Convention on the Civil Aspects of International Child Abduction in Domestic Violence Cases' (2011) 4 *John Marshall Law Journal* 54–58; J Edelson and T Lindhurst, 'Multiple Perspective on Battered Mothers and their Children Fleeing to the United States for Safety' A Study of Hague Convention Cases (Final Report, November 2010) 110–20, www.haguedv.org/reports/finalreport.pdf.

cannot take this fact into account,[272] apart from in the unlikely event that the child is aware of the mother's real wishes or in borderline cases.[273] Furthermore, even the parental intention approach will only help the mother if the court is prepared to look at her real wishes[274] as opposed to those which were manifested by her behaviour.[275] However, as seen above, the concept of habitual residence is designed to test whether the child has been removed or retained 'from the social and family environment in which his life has developed'.[276] Thus, there is little justification for looking for the real reasons why the child is living in a particular place, unless they impact on his daily life. Accordingly, it is necessary to find other methods of taking into account the impact of the dynamics of domestic violence on child abduction.[277]

The second issue is the potential impact of the way in which habitual residence is determined on the parents' freedom to travel. As seen above, under some models, children's habitual residence may change during fixed-term relocations, such as sabbaticals and military postings. This fact is likely to deter some parents from travelling rather than taking the risk that they will not be able to return to the country of origin if the other parent does not consent. This danger was expressly recognised by the US District Court in the case of *In re Morris*, which stated that where the travel is for less than a year, the child's habitual residence should not change because 'to find otherwise would have significant negative policy implications by discouraging extended international travel and temporary international employment for scholastic and professional enrichment'.[278] Similarly, Israeli Supreme Court Justice Amit[279] obiter expressed concern that if children's habitual residence could change during the course of a temporary fixed-term relocation abroad, such as a diplomatic assignment for two years, then couples might hesitate to travel.[280]

This concern is legitimate and courts should be slow to find that there has been a change of habitual residence where there has been a short, fixed-term relocation.[281] However, where the relocation is for longer than two years, the policy of not discouraging foreign travel has to be weighed against the reality of the situation, where the child has become fully integrated into life in the foreign country.

---

[272] eg *Nunez-Escudero v Tice-Menley* 58 F3d 374 (8th Cir 1995).
[273] eg in *Zotkiewicz* (n 258), where the objectively evidenced lack of voluntariness of the mother's stay in Poland was relevant in determining that the child had not acquired habitual residence during the five months spent there.
[274] As in eg *Ponath* (n 31); *Tsarbopoulos v Tsarbopoulos* (n 165).
[275] *In The Matter of Z (Children)* (n 163).
[276] Perez-Vera Report (n 32), para 11.
[277] See ch 11 at II Biv.
[278] *Re Morris* (n 171) 1163.
[279] RFamA 9802/09 (n 165).
[280] ibid [14]. This policy would also seem to be behind Justice Drori's dissenting opinion in the case of *YM v AM* (n 167), in which he completely rejected the possibility that the children's habitual residence could change during a fixed-term relocation for educational or employment purposes. Inter alia, he expressed the view that a lay person would simply not comprehend the concept that a mother, who was living abroad with her husband while he was studying, would be abducting her children if she unilaterally brought them back to Israel before the completion of the father's studies.
[281] Certainty could be provided by recognising agreements between the parties. See discussion at sections H and I below.

G Consistency with Matrimonial Law

Most countries, to varying degrees, support efforts to prevent the breakdown of marriage,[282] often because it is thought that such breakdown is detrimental to the children of the marriage.[283] Two types of cases can be identified where finding that a new habitual residence has been acquired may discourage parents from trying to save their marriage and thus be inconsistent with the policy of encouraging such attempts.

The first category of cases[284] involves marriages that have begun deteriorating before one spouse expresses the desire to relocate for employment or other reasons. The other spouse will have to decide whether to accompany the relocating spouse in the hope that the move will improve the marriage. If the attempt to save the marriage fails, the accompanying parent will usually want to return to the country of origin with the child. If she knows that the child's habitual residence will change and that therefore the Convention will prevent her from taking the children back home, she may well not be prepared to take the risk of being 'stuck' with the children in the new country and so may refuse to accompany the other parent in the first place. Thus, any chance of saving the marriage will be lost. In the second category of cases,[285] the parents have already separated and one has moved to another country. Later, the custodial parent moves to the country where the other parent is living in order to attempt reconciliation. If the reconciliation fails, she will want to return with the child to the country where she was previously living. If she knows that the child's habitual residence will change during the attempted reconciliation, she may be deterred from making such an attempt and thus the policy of fostering reconciliation will be frustrated.

This concern was expressly mentioned in the Australian case of *DW v Director-General, Department of Child Safety*, where the majority commented:

> [W]e are of the view that the interests of children generally could well be adversely affected if the courts too readily find that a parent of a child who attempts reconciliation in a foreign country with the other parent in order to try to create for the child a family consisting of both its parents, has together with the child become habitually resident in that foreign country.[286]

Similarly, in the case of *Feder*,[287] the District Court was concerned that Mrs Feder should not lose out as a result of her last attempt to save her troubled marriage. However, this decision was reversed on appeal[288] and other cases can be found where children were held to have acquired a habitual residence soon after arriving in a country for the purpose of an

---

[282] eg, by funding marriage guidance services, imposing a duty on lawyers and/or courts to promote reconciliation (eg, Canadian Divorce Act, RSC, ss 9 and 10) and by providing that attempted reconciliations do not prejudice the right to petition for divorce (eg English Matrimonial Causes Act 1973, s 2.).

[283] eg some jurisdictions make divorce harder to obtain where there are minor children (eg under Swedish law there is a 'waiting' period of six months to one year), A Logdberg, 'The Reform of Family Law in the Scandinavian Countries' in AG Chlores (ed), *The Reform of Family Law in Europe: The Equality of the Spouses, Divorce, Illegitimate Children* (Deventer, Kluwer, 1978) 201–03.

[284] eg, *Feder* (n 29); *Re F* (n 44) 558; *In Re B (Minors) (Abduction) (No 1)* (n 35).

[285] eg, *In Re B (Child Abduction: Habitual Residence)* [1994] 2 FLR 915; *DW & Director-General, Department of Child Safety* [2006] FamCA 93.

[286] *DW v DG* ibid [52]. It should be noted that in this case the parents were not married.

[287] *Feder v Feder* 922 So2d 213 (Fla 3d DCA 2006).

[288] *Feder* (n 29).

attempt to save their parents' marriage,[289] without any reference being made to the policy implications thereof.

Indeed, it is difficult to see how account can be taken of the policy of saving marriages under the independent and combined approaches in the first category of cases, because usually the children will be unaware of the parent's reservation about the marriage. However, in the second category of cases, if the child is aware that the move is for the purpose of an attempted reconciliation, this will usually affect his attitude to his life there and prevent a change of habitual residence. Only under the US version of the parental intention approach[290] will it always be possible to ensure that no new habitual residence is acquired.[291]

Nonetheless, under all the models, it is suggested that in borderline cases where the court is unsure whether a new habitual residence has been acquired, it is appropriate to take into account the policy of encouraging attempts to save marriages in both categories of cases set out above. Of course, this policy can only be relevant to the determination of habitual residence for a limited period of time. If the parties continue to live together, at some stage it must be assumed that the attempt to save the marriage was successful and that the family is now settled in the current place of residence.

H Consistency with Contract Law

Parties frequently make agreements concerning the residence of their children. Such agreements may relate to the length of a family relocation abroad or, in the case where the parties are separated and living in different countries, to the periods of time that the child will spend with each parent. Such agreements may often be interpreted as implied agreements about the habitual residence of the child.[292] Moreover, sometimes the parties expressly provide in their agreement that a certain court will have jurisdiction over disputes concerning the child or that the habitual residence of the child will remain in the country of origin. Occasionally such a provision is incorporated in a court order allowing for the temporary relocation of the child with one of the parents.[293] The question arises as to what weight should be given to such agreements in determining habitual residence.

Honouring agreements is the most fundamental legal principle in contract law and a basic moral value. Even where the court's own jurisdiction is concerned, it is reluctant to allow one party to breach an agreement and thus in civil actions most courts will refuse to exercise their jurisdiction where an action is brought in breach of a foreign jurisdiction agreement, unless there are exceptional circumstances.[294] Furthermore, as seen above, the

---

[289] See eg, *Re B (Minors) (Abduction) (No 2)* [1993] 1 FLR 993. See also *Laing v Central Authority* (1996) 21 Fam LR 24, where it was held that the child would have reacquired her habitual residence after six weeks in the US during an attempted reconciliation, but in fact this was not relevant because she had never lost her habitual residence in the US.

[290] In the UK, the attempt to save the marriage has itself been held to be a settled purpose, sufficient for acquisition of a new habitual residence in Germany, *Re B (Minors) (Abduction) (No 2)* ibid.

[291] eg *Mikovic v Mikovic* (n 161).

[292] Shuttle custody arrangements per se should not be understood as an agreement about where the child's habitual residence is, unless there is an express provision that the child's habitual residence should be in a certain place or that a certain court has jurisdiction.

[293] See eg, Israeli case of FamA (TA) 90/97 *Moran v Moran*, Dinim District (2) 597.

[294] eg 2005 Hague Convention on Choice of Court Agreements, Art 6, but note that matters of personal status and family law matters are expressly excluded from the Convention (Art 2).

principle of reciprocity requires that a court should respect a decision given by an authorised judicial body in another country.[295]

Application of these principles to Abduction Convention cases would mean that an express or implied parental agreement that the child's habitual residence remains in a certain place would be given effect to by the court. Moreover, where the parties agreed that the courts of a particular State have jurisdiction, then in order to give effect to the parties' intentions, it would be found that that State is the place of habitual residence. *A fortiori*, court orders providing either expressly or implicitly that a child's habitual residence should be in a certain country would be honoured.

However, the claim that an agreement or court order as to habitual residence should be honoured gives rise to a number of difficulties. The most substantive difficulty[296] is that the principle of honouring agreements or court orders is fundamentally inconsistent with the factual nature of habitual residence. Thus, the Report of the Third Special Commission expressly rejected the power of agreements or court orders to determine a habitual residence that differs from the factual habitual residence of the child.[297] An additional problem is that unless there is an express agreement in writing, there is likely to be a dispute as to the content of any alleged agreement between the parties and, as already explained, the summary nature of Convention proceedings makes them ill-suited to determining contradicted issues of fact.[298]

Nonetheless, the policy that agreements and court orders should be honoured is so fundamental that it should not simply be ignored because of the above difficulties, formidable as they are. Rather, the scope of the application of this policy should be limited in order to minimise those difficulties. In particular, the policy should be limited to borderline cases in which it is not an abuse of language to hold that the child's habitual residence is in the place provided for in the agreement or court order.[299] In addition, the policy could be limited to cases where there is a written agreement or court order, in order to avoid the problem of proving the agreement and its content.

There are a few cases where the courts have expressly held that an agreement between the parties or court order determining jurisdiction or habitual residence should be upheld. For example, in the case of *Johnson v Johnson*,[300] the consent decree issued by the Virginia Court, which provided for a shuttle custody arrangement between the mother in Sweden and the father in the US, explicitly stated that the father's residence in Virginia was the child's 'place of residence for the purpose of all adjudications of custody and visitation' and that neither party would apply to any other court. However, before the end of the child's two-year stay in Sweden, the mother applied to the Swedish Court to vary the custody

---

[295] Chapter 6 at IV E.
[296] A further problem is that courts have traditionally been reluctant to treat agreements between spouses (at least while they are living together) as binding, either on the basis that they were made without intent to create legal relations or were against public policy. Whilst this approach has to a large extent been overtaken by the concept of private ordering, agreements concerning children usually need the approval of the court, which has to check that they are consistent with the child's welfare and sometimes also that they were entered into freely. Thus, where an agreement concerning habitual residence has not been judicially approved, it is not clear that it should be automatically enforced.
[297] Report of Third Special Commission Meeting (17–21 March 1997), para 16, www.hcch.net/index_en.php?act=publications.details&pid=2271&dtid=2.
[298] At section D above.
[299] This limitation is quoted with approval in *Punter* (n 124) [178] and [185].
[300] *Johnson v Johnson* (n 191).

agreement between the parties. The Virginia Court of Appeals[301] held that, in light of the residence provision in the consent order, not only did the Virginia courts have continuing jurisdiction, but that Virginia was the *forum conveniens*.[302] However, the Swedish Supreme Administrative Court held that the child was now habitually resident in Sweden for the purposes of the Abduction Convention and thus there was no unlawful retention.

Similarly, in an Israeli case,[303] also involving Sweden, litigation over the custody of the child between the Swedish father and the maternal Israeli grandparents[304] ended in an agreement, approved by the court, under which the father would have interim custody for a year, at the end of which the Israeli Court would review the situation and determine permanent custody. This agreement expressly provided that the Israeli courts would retain international jurisdiction in relation to custody of the child. The father did not return the child to Israel at the end of the year, in breach of the agreement, and the Israeli Court awarded custody to the grandparents, in reliance inter alia on the report of an Israeli social worker who had travelled to Sweden to examine the child's situation. The grandparents managed to bring the child back to Israel without the father's knowledge. When the father requested return of the child under the Abduction Convention, the Israeli Court held that the child's habitual residence was at all times in Israel, relying inter alia on the provision in the consent order.

The question of the extent to which the child's habitual residence can be preserved by parental agreement or court order has been discussed expressly, albeit obiter, by the Israeli District Court. In *Dagan v Dagan*,[305] Justice Porat claimed that the stipulation of continuing habitual residence made by the court in an earlier case[306] was invalid because habitual residence is purely a question of fact; whereas Justice Rotlevy took the view that such a condition would ensure that the Abduction Convention would apply to a subsequent retention in the foreign country in contravention of the original court order. The latter view was later supported by Justice Drori[307] on the basis that it is inappropriate to limit the autonomy of parents to regulate by agreement the legal consequences of a temporary relocation abroad.

Finally, it should be noted that McEleavy's proposal to allow parents travelling abroad to make an enforceable agreement, preserving their child's habitual residence for a period of up to 12 or 18 months,[308] clearly promotes the policy of honouring agreements. Moreover, the suggested time limitation is consistent with the view expressed here that this policy should only apply where the agreement is not clearly inconsistent with the factual situation.

I Certainty versus Flexibility

The wide variety of different situations means that there is a need for a degree of flexibility in determining habitual residence to ensure that the Convention applies in cases where its

---

[301] ibid.
[302] See also *Wilson v Huntley* (n 193), in which the Ontario Court took into account the provision in the parenting agreement for disputes to be resolved by the Alberta courts as indicating the parties' preference for litigation in Canada.
[303] FamC (TA) 107064/99 *KL v DSh* Nevo, 30 December 2003 (Isr) [INCADAT cite: HC/E/IL 835].
[304] The 10-year-old child had been living with the mother in Israel next door to the grandparents until she committed suicide.
[305] *Dagan v Dagan* (n 195).
[306] *Moran v Moran* (n 293).
[307] *YM v AM* (n 167).
[308] P McEleavy, 'A Protocol for the 1980 Hague Convention' (March 2010) *International Family Law* 59.

objectives will be promoted thereby and to allow relevant policy considerations to be taken into account. Indeed, it has been suggested that the need for flexibility is one of the reasons why habitual residence was not defined in the Convention.[309] Furthermore, one judge has suggested that the need for flexibility justifies allowing each judge to decide which model of habitual residence is most suitable to the case in front of him.[310]

On the other hand, there is also clearly a need for a good deal of certainty in relation to the interpretation of habitual residence, both in order to prevent unnecessary litigation and so that parties can plan their lives accordingly. For example, as noted above, if a parent knows that a trip abroad will change the child's habitual residence and that he may not be able to take the child back home without the consent of the other parent or of the court in the foreign country, he may think twice before agreeing to the trip.[311] The uniform adoption of a single model will substantially increase the possibility of predicting the impact of a move on the habitual residence of the child.

In choosing the model to be adopted, the aim should be to achieve a reasonable balance between flexibility and certainty and thus it is appropriate to examine the degree of flexibility and certainty inherent in the various models. Formally both versions of the parental intention model are not flexible because the outcome is determined by a single factor, viz parental intention. In practice, however, at least where there is evidence to support both parties' versions of the facts, the court will be tempted to choose the version that produces the result which it sees as desirable. Whilst this possibility introduces flexibility via invisible manipulation of the evidence, it makes predicting the outcome very difficult and so leads to uncertainty. Furthermore, the considerable degree of uncertainty inherent in the concept of settled purpose, which is central to the UK version of the parental intention model, is evidenced by the apparently contradictory decisions in cases concerning fixed-term relocations.[312] Accordingly, it seems that the parental intention models do not provide much flexibility and yet still involve considerable uncertainty.

The independent and combined models, on the other hand, possess an inherent element of flexibility because they involve weighing up a number of different factors in order to determine whether the child's connections with the country in question are sufficiently strong that he can be said to be habitually resident there. Thus, the court has considerable discretion in deciding what weight to give to the various factors. While this discretion clearly means that different weight will be given to the same factor in different cases, this is inevitable because the factual matrix in each case is unique.[313] Also, whilst the element of discretion clearly gives scope for manipulation in order to achieve the desired result, this process is much more transparent than in the case where the court simply has to determine which evidence to believe. Thus, in these models, the uncertainty would seem to be the inevitable price for the necessary flexibility.

Whilst at first sight it might seem that there is more uncertainty in the combined model than in the independent model because of the need to also take into account parental intentions, it can be argued that the opposite is true. By viewing the bald objective facts through the prism of parental intention, as understood by the child, it will often become

---

[309] eg FamC (JLM) 18874/07 *BM v SA* Nevo, 3 April 2008 (Isr) (Justice Elbaz).
[310] FamA 48471/05 (n 34) (Justice Geifman).
[311] *Silverman* (n 131) [30]; *Mozes* (n 13) 1072–73.
[312] See above at IV B. Thus, it is difficult to accept the view of Waite J in *Re B (Minors) (Abduction) (No 2)* (n 289) 998, that 'A settled purpose is not something to be searched for under a microscope. If it is there at all, it will stand out clearly as a matter of general impression'.
[313] FamA 130/08 (n 100) (Justice Hendel).

clearer what weight should be given to those facts. For example, it is suggested that the weight to be given to school attendance and participation in extra-curricular activities should be different in the case where a child is aware that he is only staying in a country for a relatively short period of time from that where he considers the stay to be indefinite. In the former case, he may simply be making the best use of the opportunities presented, for example, for cultural enrichment and activities which might not otherwise be available to him and thus these facts tell us very little about the depth of his connection with the country. However, in the latter case, these same facts may well indicate that he has integrated educationally, socially and culturally into the new environment. Finally, McEleavy's proposal,[314] under which parents travelling abroad for a period of up to 18 months would be able to enter into an agreement preserving their child's habitual residence would inject a great deal of certainty into the determination of habitual residence in cases where such an agreement was made. Moreover, this proposal seems broadly consistent with the combined approach because where the parents have made such an agreement it will be clear to the child that his stay is only temporary. Nonetheless, there may be exceptional situations in which the child acclimatises rapidly and fully despite the temporary nature of the stay and in such a case the proposal would not reflect the factual situation. A possible solution would be to provide that the parental agreement creates a presumption that the child's habitual residence has not changed, but that this can be rebutted by clear evidence to the contrary. The advantage of this modified version of McEleavy's proposal is that it creates certainty in most cases, whilst being flexible enough to accommodate exceptional cases.

VI Conclusions

The analysis in Part V shows that the combined approach to determining habitual residence best promotes the objectives of the Convention and is most consistent with general legal doctrines. In addition, this approach leads to internal coherence and is consistent with the intentions of the drafters that the Convention is designed to protect a child who has been removed 'from the social and family environment in which his life has developed'.[315]

The lack of uniformity between the approaches of different jurisdictions to determining habitual residence leads to significant variations in the way in which the Convention is implemented in different countries and causes confusion and uncertainty.[316] The lack of certainty is illustrated by the fact that 18 per cent of judicial refusals are based on a finding that the child was not habitually resident in the requesting State.[317] If there was more cer-

---

[314] McEleavy, 'A Protocol' (n 308).
[315] Perez-Vera Report (n 32), para 11.
[316] It may even lead to the absurd situation where the child's habitual residence has not changed under the law of requested State, even though it would have changed under the law of the requesting State. In the Israeli case of *AS v MB* (n 172), for example, it seems likely that in the eyes of English law, the children would have become habitually resident in Israel since the parents' work for international organisations would have constituted a settled purpose.
[317] N Lowe, 'A Statistical Analysis of Applications Made in 2008 under the Hague Convention of 25 October 1980 on the Civil Aspects of International Child Abduction, Part I Global Report, Preliminary Document 8 (November 2011) 28, www.hcch.net/upload/wop/abduct2011pd08ae.pdf (this figure is 50% more than in the 1999 survey).

tainty about the meaning of habitual residence, it would be expected that more cases where the requirement of habitual residence was not satisfied would be weeded out by being rejected by Central Authorities.[318]

In the absence of a Protocol,[319] which might have provided a definition of habitual residence, the best solution would seem to be for the Hague Conference to produce a Guide to Good Practice recommending adoption of the combined approach and explaining how it will be applied in common situations. It is to be hoped that the apparent adoption of the combined approach by the ECJ[320] will be a significant step towards the uniform adoption of this approach and that the EU States will apply this approach in cases concerning non-EU States.[321] In the US, dicta can be found in leading cases, such as *Mozes*,[322] which would support a combined approach, but many courts have chosen to follow the dicta emphasising the parental intention instead.[323] In light of the divergence of approaches between the different circuits, it is surely only a matter of time until the question of habitual residence is considered by the US Supreme Court and it can be expected that this Court will take into account the prevalent approach in the rest of the Hague world.[324]

However, it has to be appreciated that even the uniform adoption of a particular approach will not completely remove the uncertainty involved in determining habitual residence since this is inherent in the fact-intensive nature of the enquiry and the infinite number of different possible factual matrixes. Accordingly, courts will inevitably be influenced by policy considerations in borderline cases,[325] a number of which were discussed in the analysis section above. In order to ensure transparency, courts should refer expressly to these considerations.[326]

There is likely to be a temptation to attach significant weight to the policies of protecting children from abduction and deterring potential abductors because these appear to be so central to the Convention. The difficulty with such an approach, as explained above,[327] is that this policy only applies to situations in which the child has been removed or retained from the social and family environment in which his life has developed. Where it is not clear that the country from which the child has been removed or retained fits this description, then the very purpose of the connecting factor of habitual residence is to identify whether this is a situation to which the Convention should apply. Thus, giving weight to the policy of protecting children from abduction in determining habitual residence in such cases is circular reasoning. In contrast, the question of whether the requesting State is the *forum conveniens* is likely to cast light on whether the case is one to which the Abduction Convention was intended to apply.

Finally, there is considerable merit in McEleavy's proposal that, in order to avoid uncertainty, parents who travel abroad for a period of up to 18 months should be able to make an agreement preserving the habitual residence of their children. However, as suggested

---

[318] Only in 7 cases did Central Authorities reject on this basis, ibid 26.
[319] See ch 19 at II C.
[320] See text accompanying n 145 to 151 above.
[321] For an attempt to apply the traditional UK approach in a way which is consistent with the ECJ approach, see *H-K (Children)* (n 168).
[322] See text accompanying n 122.
[323] See III Aii above.
[324] As it did in *Abbott v Abbott* 176 L Ed 2d 789 (5th Cir Tex, 2008), discussed in detail in ch 7 at III C.
[325] Schuz, 'Policy Considerations' (n 19).
[326] ibid, approved in *Punter* (n 124) [177].
[327] At section V C.

above, treating such agreements as creating a presumption, which can be rebutted in exceptional cases, would be more consistent with the factual nature of habitual residence and the need to focus on the child. Indeed, this approach would enable the period of time to be spent abroad pursuant to the agreement to be extended to two years or even longer.

Part IV

Defences to Mandatory Return

9

Article 12(2)

I Introduction

Article 12(2) of the Hague Convention on the Civil Aspects of International Child Abduction ('Abduction Convention') provides:

> The judicial or administrative authority, even where the proceedings have been commenced after the expiration of the period of one year referred to in the preceding paragraph, shall also order the return of the child, unless it is demonstrated that the child is now settled in its[1] new environment.

This provision appears to perform two functions. On the one hand, it recognises that where a lengthy period of time has passed and the child has become settled in the State of refuge, summary return will not achieve the objectives of the Convention of protecting the child by restoring the status quo. On the other hand, the provision also makes it clear that the mere passage of time per se does not exclude the possibility of summary return.[2]

Whilst a few courts have mistakenly treated settlement as a defence in its own right,[3] it is clear beyond doubt that the two conditions of passage of 12 months and settlement are cumulative. A number of questions have arisen in relation to the interpretation of both the conditions and these have not been answered uniformly by the courts, as will be explained below. One of the causes of the difficulty in interpreting Article 12(2) is that, whilst the provision is clearly an exception to the mandatory return mechanism in Article 12(1), it is worded quite differently from the other exceptions. In particular, there is no reference to the burden of proof and the Article does not make it clear whether the court has discretion to order return, despite the establishment of the exception, as with the other defences. The latter question has been the subject of considerable judicial and academic debate, which will be discussed in detail below.[4]

In relation to the burden of proof, whilst there seems to be a consensus that, as with the other exceptions, the burden is on the abductor who pleads the defence,[5] differences of opinion have been expressed about the weight of that burden. On the one hand, there is some Australian authority that the burden of proving settlement is not particularly heavy

---

[1] In the author's view, referring to the child as 'it' is difficult to reconcile with an approach that treats children as persons in their own right and so the word 'his' will be used instead of 'its'.
[2] This aspect of the provision was passed by a very small majority. See generally Beaumont and McEleavy, *The Hague Convention on International Child Abduction* (Oxford, Oxford University Press, 1999) 203.
[3] eg, decision appealed against *In the Interest of AVPG and CCPG, Minor Children*, SW3d 117 (Tex Ct App 2008).
[4] At II C.
[5] eg, *Re N (Minors)(Abduction)* [1991] 1 FLR 413, 417; MBGA c RVM, Cour d'appel du Québec, 8 juin 2004, N° 500-09-014099-048 (500-04-034363-037) [INCADAT cite: HC/E/CA914]. This adopts the opinion expressed in the Perez-Vera Report, Proceedings of the 14th Session of the Hague Conference Oct 1980, para 109, www.hcch. net/upload/expl28.pdf. The US legislation states that the abductor has to prove the conditions in this defence on the preponderance of the evidence, 42 USC 11601(a)(4).

and is simply a question of fact to be determined on the balance of probabilities.[6] In contrast, the Scottish Inner House has held that it must be clearly shown that the settlement in the new environment is so well established that it overrides the clear duty of the court to order the return of the child.[7] The first approach may be criticised as treating the burden as a mere token,[8] whereas the second approach puts a gloss on the words of the Convention.[9] The solution seems to be the *via media* adopted in Hong Kong[10] and in some Australian case law,[11] under which the burden of proving settlement is to be treated as a significant burden, but the determination is based only on the relevant facts.[12]

II The Case Law

A Expiration of the 12-Month Period

i The Starting Point

It is clear from Article 12(1) that the starting point of the 12-month period is the date of wrongful removal or retention. While, as discussed above, there are inherent difficulties in identifying the date of retention,[13] locating the exact time of removal would seem to be a simple exercise. Nonetheless, a number of questions have arisen in relation to identifying the date on which the 12-month period starts to run.

Firstly, where the child does not depart from the country of origin immediately upon removal from the left-behind parent, does the time start to run when he is removed from the custody of the left-behind parent or only when he is taken out of the country? This question arose in the Israeli case of *Lukatz v Lukatz*,[14] in which the father removed the child

---

[6] In *Director-General Department of Families, Youth and Community Care v Moore* (1999) FLC 92-841(Aus), the Full Family Court of Australia commented in relation to a five-year-old child, 'We acknowledge that the onus of satisfying the court that a child is settled in a new environment ... may not be a difficult onus to discharge, at least where the child concerned is of the age and maturity of this child, and where he or she has been living in the same residence for a period of over six months and in the same geographic area for about eighteen months. It could perhaps be said that in such circumstances, and provided there is no evidence that the child is showing signs of particular distress, the conclusion will always be open that he or she is settled in his or her new environment'; see also *Secretary, Attorney-General's Department (AGD) and TS* [2000] FamCA 1692 (Aus). See also decision of the Swiss Federal Tribunal in the case of 5P.254/2005 /frs, Tribunal fédéral, IIè cour civile [INCADAT cite: HC/E/CH 842], which held that it could be assumed that children who had lived in the requested State for four years had settled into their environment.
[7] *Soucie v Soucie* 1995 SC 134.
[8] *AC v PC* [2004] HKMP 1238; *Secretary, Dept of Human Services State Central Authority v CR* (2005) 34 Fam LR 354 [53]–[54].
[9] *State Central Authority v CR* (2005) 34 Fam LR 354 [50].
[10] *AC v PC* (n 8).
[11] *Dept of Human Services v CR* (n 8).
[12] The Court of Session in the case of *Perrin v Perrin* 1994 SC 45 expressed the view that where only a short time had elapsed since the expiry of the 12-month period, the quality of the evidence of settlement would have to be good.
[13] Chapter 7 at II. The various approaches to defining the beginning of the retention will not be rehearsed again here, but clearly which approach is adopted may be critical in determining whether 12 months have passed since the date of wrongful retention. In the case of *In re Interest of Zarate*, No 96 C 50394 (ND Ill 23 December 1996), the mother failed to show that the retention occurred more than 12 months before the commencement of the proceedings.
[14] FamC (Dist TA) 2637/91 *Lukatz v Lukatz*, Tak-Mach 92(3)1056 (1992).

from the mother in Hungary and hid with the child for a few months before leaving that country and bringing him to Israel. The Israeli District Court held that the 12-month period began when the child crossed the border because the Abduction Convention has no application in relation to internal abductions.

The second question which has arisen is whether the relevant date is the date of leaving the country of origin or arriving in the country of refuge. This question may be relevant where the flight leaves on one day and arrives at its destination the next day or where the abductor does not travel directly to the State of refuge. The prevailing approach seems to be that the time starts to run when the child is removed from his place of habitual residence and is calculated in accordance with the local time in that place.[15] The issue was discussed obiter[16] in an Israeli case, in which the abducting parent took the child from France to Italy and the Ukraine before arriving in Israel four weeks after leaving France.[17] Justice Hendel held that the date of removal, for the purpose of starting to count the 12-month period, was the date of crossing the French border since that was when the wrongful removal occurred.[18] On the other hand, Justice Elon held that the removal was only complete when the child arrived in Israel. Clearly, the first view is to be preferred[19] because the essence of the wrongful removal is taking the child away from his habitual residence. In addition, certainty requires that the date of wrongful removal be identifiable immediately upon crossing the international border and not only retrospectively after the child has arrived at the final country of refuge. Also, it would not always be easy to determine whether a country was an interim stop on the journey or the intended destination originally. In any event, the date of arrival in the requested State will be taken into account in determining whether the child has become settled.

The final and most significant issue in relation to the starting point of the 12-month period relates to situations where the abductor has been in hiding. Some US courts have adopted the doctrine of equitable tolling under which, in cases of concealment, the 12- month period only starts to run after the abducted child is located,[20] on the basis that this doctrine should be read in to every federal statute of limitation, unless Congress states otherwise.[21] With respect, this approach, which has been rejected in other jurisdictions,[22] cannot be reconciled with the clear wording of Article 12(2) and with the intention of the drafters to take into account the fact that the child has become settled in the country of refuge.

---

[15] See *State Central Authority (SCA) v CR* [2005] Fam CA 1050 (Aus). The frontier was crossed on 21 July 2004 and the proceedings were commenced just on time (on 21 July 2005). If the flight had left on time, the removal would have in fact occurred a day earlier and the 12-month time period would have expired.

[16] Because the child had not become settled in Israel.

[17] FamA 111/07 (Dist BSH) *Ploni v Almonit* Nevo, 18/04/07 [INCADAT cite: HC/E/IL 938].

[18] He relied on *Re H and Re S (Abduction: Custody Rights)* [1991] 2 AC 476 (HL); *State Central Authority (SCA) v Ayob* (1997) FLC 92-746 (Aust); the Perez-Vera Report (n 5), para 107–08.

[19] This was the view taken by the Australian Court in *SCA v Ayob* ibid.

[20] See eg, *Furnes v Reeves*, 362 F3d 702 (11th Cir 2004). But the doctrine does not apply where there is no concealment, even where the applicant is not responsible for the delays, *FHU v ACU* 427 NJ Super 354 (2012).

[21] *Furnes v Reeves* ibid, citing *Young v United States*, 535 US 43 (2002). cf *Anderson v Acree* 250 F Supp 2d 872, 875 (SD Ohio) (2002) and *Lozano v Alvarez*, 697 F3d 41, US App (2nd Circ) (2012) (rejecting tolling inter alia on the basis that Article 12(2) is not a statute of limitations).

[22] eg *Canon v Canon* [2004] EWCA CIV 1330; *AC v PC* (n 8); RFamA (SC) 5690/10 *Plonit v Ploni* 18 August 2010 (Isr), http://elyon1.court.gov.il/files/10/900/056/z04/10056900.z04.pdf; However, in *Re H (Abduction: Child of 16)* [2000] 2 FLR 51, the English High Court did take into account the fact that the father had commenced the proceedings within 12 months of discovering the children's whereabouts in determining that they were not settled, largely on the basis that it was not fair for the abductor to rely on the fact that he had hidden the child. With respect, this is tantamount to application of the doctrine of equitable tolling and inconsistent with the mainstream of English case law.

ii The End Point

According to Article 12(1), the 12-month period ends on 'the date of commencement of the proceedings before the judicial or administrative authority of the Contracting State where the child is'. The question has arisen as to whether the left-behind parent's application to the Central Authority in the requested State[23] constitutes commencement of proceedings or whether only the submission of a formal application to the court in that State can be considered commencement of proceedings. In a number of cases,[24] it has been held that the submission of an application to the Central Authority does not stop the clock running for the purposes of the 12-month period in Article 12. The phrase 'commencement of proceedings' in this provision refers to proceedings before a body, whether it be judicial or administrative, which has the authority to order the return of the child. Since Central Authorities do not themselves have the power to make such an order, any application to them cannot be considered as commencement of proceedings for the purposes of Article 12. Furthermore, there is usually no clear timetable for the proceeding of applications by Central Authorities. However, the fact that an application has been made to the Central Authority may prevent the child becoming settled in his new environment, if this triggers negotiations between the parties[25] or if the children are aware of the application.[26]

Moreover, the Israeli Supreme Court has held that the clock stops running when the proceedings are commenced, even where the abductor does not know of the proceedings and there is a considerable delay before he is located and an *inter partes* hearing takes place.[27]

B The Child is Settled in his New Environment

A preliminary issue arises in relation to the date at which settlement is to be assessed. No case has been found where it was necessary to decide this point, but a few judges have mentioned the issue obiter. In England, it has been suggested that it is when the proceedings were commenced which is relevant.[28] However, the Supreme Court of New Zealand took the view that settlement should be assessed at the date of the hearing, as this best accommodates the interests of the child and avoids the artificiality of ignoring recent developments in the child's life.[29] In most cases, the issue will be hypothetical because the hearing will be conducted shortly after the commencement of the proceedings. However, if for some reason the hearing is delayed, it is possible that the child had become settled by the

---

[23] Application to the Central Authority in the requesting State would clearly not count because the child is not in that State.

[24] eg *Wojick v Wojick*, 959 F Supp 413 (ED Mich 1997); *VBM v DLJ*, 2004 NLCA 56; FamA (Dist JLM) 584/04 *Plonit v Ploni*, Pador 63-1-683 [INCADAT cite: HC/E/IL838]; *Re M (Abduction: Acquiescence)* [1996] 1 FLR 315 (UK HC); *Perrin v Perrin* (n 12) 47; but *cf* decision of the Paris Court of Appeal in *Époux H (13 July 1993) Cour d'Appel de Paris, 1re Ch Section A, JCP 1994, IV, No 224* cited by Beaumont and McEleavy (n 2) 205.

[25] Beaumont and McEleavy, ibid.

[26] Similarly, the fact that an application had been made to the Central Authority before the expiration of the 12-month period could be taken into account in the exercise of the court's discretion. See section C below.

[27] *Plonit v Ploni* (n 22) where proceedings were commenced by substituted service on the abducting mother's relatives, even where the whereabouts of the child within Israel were not known. The court made a return order in an ex parte hearing, but this was discharged when the mother was found two years later. After an *inter partes* hearing, return was ordered.

[28] *F v M and N (Abduction: Acquiesence: Settlement)* [2008] EWHC 1525 (Fam).

[29] *Secretary for Justice (New Zealand Central Authority) v HJ* [2007] 2 NZLR 289 [57]; see also *Director-General (D-G), Department of Families, Youth and Community Care v Thorpe* (1997) FLC 92-785.

date of the hearing, although he had not been so settled at the date of the commencement of proceedings. The likelihood of this will be reduced by the fact that the very commencement of proceedings, which gives the abductor and child notice that a return is possible, may well prevent the child from becoming settled where this has not already happened. Nonetheless, the approach adopted by the New Zealand Supreme Court is to be preferred since there is no reason why the child should be made to suffer for any delays and thus if he has settled by the date of the hearing, the defence should be established.

Three specific issues in relation to the definition of settlement[30] have been the subject of judicial debate:

(i) The extent to which the word 'settled' in this context involves an emotional as well as physical element.
(ii) The effect of concealment on the settlement of the child.
(iii) Whether a very young child can become settled.

In relation to all these issues, some judges have adopted a narrow approach and some a wider approach. Each issue will be considered in turn.

i The Need for an Emotional Element

The narrow approach can be traced back to the comment of Bracewell J, who said:

> There is some force, I find, in the argument that legal presumptions reflect the norm, and the presumption under the Convention is that children should be returned unless the mother can establish the degree of settlement which is more than mere adjustment to surroundings. I find that word should be given its ordinary natural meaning, and that the word 'settled' in this context has two constituents. First, it involves a physical element of relating to, being established in, a community and an environment. Secondly, I find that it has an emotional constituent denoting security and stability.[31]

In addition, Bracewell J, accepting the view expressed by Purchas LJ in *Re S (A Minor) (Abduction)*[32] that what was required under Article 12(2) was a 'long-term settled position', explained that this phrase involved demonstrating 'that the present position imports stability when looking at the future, and is permanent insofar as anything in life, can be said to be permanent'.[33]

Bracewell J's interpretation, requiring both a physical and emotional element, has been accepted by the English Court of Appeal[34] and by courts in some other Commonwealth

---

[30] There has also been a difference of opinion about the significance of the word 'new'. Moss J in *Director-General, Department of Community Services v Apostolakis* (1996) FLC 92-718 at 83, 649, suggested that where there is no real difference between the way of life in the two countries, then there is no new environment and so there cannot be any settlement. This view was disapproved of in *D-G v Thorpe* ibid where Lindemeyer J preferred the simple and ordinary meaning of the word 'new' as meaning an environment which was new to the child, whether or not there was a fundamental difference between the nature of that environment and that in which he had lived previously. With respect, the latter view is clearly to be preferred.

[31] *Re N* (n 5) 417.

[32] *Re S (A Minor) (Abduction)* [1991] 2 FLR 1.

[33] *Re N* (n 5) 418; *In re Interest of Zarate* (n 13) where the Court held that the mother had not proved that the child was settled because she had not shown that her environment was unlikely to change. Similarly in the Scottish case of *P v S* [2002] Fam LR 2, the child was held not to be settled because the mother did not intend to remain in the same place with the child. In this case, the need to look into the future was explained on the basis that the exception could not be justified if there was no expectation of continuity.

[34] *Canon v Canon* (n 22), overruling the decision of Singer J in *Re C (Abduction: Settlement)* [2004] EWHC 1245 (Fam), who had rejected the need to prove an emotional element.

jurisdictions.[35] Thorpe LJ's view is: 'to consider only the physical element is to ignore the emotional and psychological elements which in combination comprise the whole child'.[36] However, this interpretation was rejected in Australian cases, which preferred a wider approach to the meaning of settlement. In a decision of the Full Court of the Family Court of Australia, Nicholson CJ said:

> Nowhere in the Regulations are the words "long term" to be found and there is in our view no warrant for importing them. The test, and the only test to be applied, is whether the children have settled in their new environment.[37]

Similarly, in another case it was said that the suggestion that the degree of settlement was more than a mere adjustment to surroundings or that the word 'settled' had two constituent elements (physical and emotional) represented a gloss on the legislation and was not an accurate statement of the law.[38]

Academic comment has also been critical of the high burden of proof required by Bracewell J. In *Dicey and Morris*, it is argued that it is going too far to insist that settlement should be 'permanent in so far as anything in life is permanent'.[39] Beaumont and McEleavy, agreeing with this comment, claim that 'it would be manifestly unreasonable, if not illogical, to demand a demonstrably higher standard than would, for example, be required to indicate a change in habitual residence'.[40]

In the current author's view, it is necessary to distinguish between the two aspects of Bracewell J's definition of settlement. The requirement of an emotional element per se is not problematic. Indeed, as Thorpe LJ points out, children have emotions and their degree of attachment to a place is determined not merely by physical connections.[41] However, it is necessary to test the existence of the emotional element in light of the ways in which children become psychologically connected to their environment and not from an adult perspective. Thus, the question of security and stability must be considered in light of the child's sense of time, which does not usually include long-term future planning.[42] Accordingly, it is inappropriate to require proof of a long-term settled position.[43]

ii Concealment

Under the wider approach, concealment does not per se prevent settlement. Singer J in *Re C (Abduction: Settlement)* rejected the submissions of the father's counsel that the apparent settlement could not really be called settlement in this case because 'rumbling beneath the apparently calm surface has all this time been the deceptively quiescent volcano, representing the everyday risk of being found' on the basis that acceptance of this proposition would

---

[35] See eg *Perrin v Perrin* (n 12); *JEA v CLM* (2002) 220 DLR (4th) 577 (NSCA); and *Graziano v Daniels* (1991) 14 Fam LR 697 (Aus).

[36] *Canon v Canon* (n 22) [57].

[37] *Director General, Department of Community Services v M and C and the Child Representative* [1998] FLC 92-829.

[38] *Townsend v Director-General Department of Families, Youth and Community* [1999] 24 Fam LR 495.

[39] See L Collins, *Dicey and Morris on the Conflict of Laws*, 12th edn (London, Sweet & Maxwell, 1993) para 19–96.

[40] Beaumont and McEleavy (n 2) 207.

[41] *Canon v Canon* (n 22).

[42] Accordingly, doubts about immigration status do not per se prevent a finding that a child is settled. See *M and C and the Child Representative* (n 37) and *Lozano v Alvarez* (n 21).

[43] However, where the abductor already has plans to move on, this may well prevent the child from becoming settled either because he knows about the plans or because the temporary nature of the stay influences the social and other activities organised for the child.

mean that Article 12(2) could never apply in a case where the abductor had escaped detection and such a conclusion was impermissible.[44]

In contrast, in the Court of Appeal in that case, Thorpe LJ supports the proposition that 'it will be very difficult indeed for a parent who has hidden a child away to demonstrate that it is settled in its new environment'.[45] He justifies this conclusion inter alia[46] on the basis of the impact of concealment on settlement. He states that 'A very young child must take its emotional and psychological state in a large measure from that of the sole carer. An older child will be consciously or subconsciously enmeshed in the sole carer's web of deceit and subterfuge.'[47] Thus, in his view, it is unlikely that the emotional element of settlement will exist in a case of concealment.[48]

With respect, this is a generalisation that cannot be true in all cases. Whilst the parent may be a fugitive from justice, the child has not committed any wrong. Thus, in each case, it is necessary to examine the effect of the concealment on the child's physical and emotional connection to the place where he is living, from the child's point of view as evidenced by the child's way of life. Accordingly, where the child together with the abductor is living 'underground'[49] or 'on the run' or knows that he will be moving again in the near future in order to avoid detection, then the child will not become settled in his current environment. However, where the child has been living in the same place for a reasonable period of time; is living a perfectly normal everyday life and participating fully in educational and social activities,[50] the fact that his carer is an illegal immigrant or a fugitive from justice should not be relevant to the question of the child's settlement.[51] The mere knowledge that he might have to move on to prevent detection, or if he is found, does not per se prevent settlement.[52] After all, there are many children who know that their parents might

---

[44] *Re C* (n 34).

[45] *Canon v Canon* (n 22) [53]; *Lops v Lops*, 140 F3d 927 (11th Cir 1998) (the children were held not to have become settled in the US where they lived for more than two years, inter alia because the abducting father was committing four or five misdemeanours in his efforts not to be traced by the left-behind mother).

[46] Additional reasons are an analogy with the acquisition of habitual residence (*Canon v Canon* ibid [55]) and injustice to the left-behind parent (*Canon v Canon* ibid [58]) With respect, the analogy with habitual residence is misconceived because it ignores the Court of Appeal decision in the case of *Mark v Mark (Divorce: Jurisdiction)* [2004] EWCA Civ 168 (later upheld by the House of Lords in *Mark v Mark* [2005] UKHL 42), which held that the effect of illegality on the quality of the residence is a question of fact in each case. The issue of injustice will be discussed below at III C.

[47] *Canon v Canon* ibid [57].

[48] See also the Canadian case of *JEA v CLM* (n 35).

[49] See eg the Swiss decision in Justice de Paix du cercle de Lausanne, (Magistrates' Court) J 765 CIEV 112E [INCADAT cite: HC/E/434], where the now 10-year-old child had been living clandestinely for four years and had not attended school or developed any social relationships.

[50] eg decision of Kirkwood J in *Re C (Abduction: Settlement) (No 2)* [2005] 1 FLR 938 which held that a 10-year-old girl, who had been abducted to England and had escaped detection for more than four years, had become settled. The judge relied on the evidence which showed stability and complete integration into the local community rather than hypothesising about the effect of the changed names and risk of detection on the girl. Similarly, in the Hong Kong case of *AC v PC* (n 8), the judge commented that the children had not led a covert way of life.

[51] In *M v M* [2008] EWHC 2049 (Fam), Black J accepted that the fact that a parent is in a vulnerable and watchful state of mind does not necessarily mean that the children are unable to settle in their new environment (although relying on features concerning the children themselves held that they had not become settled during the 15 months they had been in the UK); cf the Scottish case of *C v C* [2008] CSOH 42 (upheld in *NJC v NPC* [2008] SC 571), where the likely extradition and imprisonment of the father could not be ignored.

[52] This was the approach adopted by Black J in *F v M and N* (n 28); cf the holding in the case of *JEA v CLM* (n 35) that, while the child had become settled, the detection by the father which exposed the carer mother's illegal status made her unsettled. With respect, it is difficult to accept the concept that a child who is settled can become unsettled for the purposes of Art 12(2), at least where the reason for the instability stems from the possibility of being returned under the Convention. In nearly every case, the initiation of proceedings is likely to destabilise the child's situation and thus the exception in Art 12(2) would be rendered virtually redundant.

have to move because of their employment and this cannot mean that these children are not settled in their environment.

iii Young Children

A few judges have expressed the narrow view that young children cannot become settled because they are completely dependent on the abducting parent and do not have independent connections with the local environment.[53] At the other extreme, it has been suggested that a young child may become settled very quickly where the abductor is the primary carer.[54]

The latter view seems unsupportable because in the context of the Convention, the environment cannot simply refer to the home. On the other hand, the position in the home should not be completely ignored as that is part of the child's environment.[55] Thus, a blanket rule that young children can rarely become settled is too simplistic.[56] All the facts need to be considered from the perspective of a young child.[57] These include the exact age of the child,[58] the length of time he has lived in the new environment,[59] the stability of the situation in the home, the language(s) the child speaks[60] and the nature and degree of contact with people outside the home,[61] including attendance at a nursery or other pre-school activities.[62] Furthermore, in cases where the abducting parent has become socially integrated in the State of refuge, this will inevitably have an impact on the child, which should also be given weight.[63]

---

[53] eg, *David S v Zamira* S 151 Misc.2d 630, 636; *Graziano v Daniels* (n 35), holding that the mother is not part of the new environment and so 'a child whose main relationship is with its mother and does not have a lasting relationship beyond the mother, cannot be said to have settled in the mother's new environment'.

[54] In *Dept of Human Services v CR* (n 8), Kay J referred to the paradox that 'the younger the child, the easier it will be to show that the child is settled and thriving in its new surrounds. The root it needs to develop to achieve a settled lifestyle are firmly entwined rounds its principle caregiver'. similarly, judicial comments that for a very young child 18 months is a significant length of time, Austrian decision *70b573/90 Obserster Gerichtshof* 17/5/90 (INCADAT cite: HC/E/AT 378); see also Irish decision in *P v B (No 2) (Child Abduction: Delay)* [1999] 2 ILRM 401, suggesting that very young children will become settled more quickly.

[55] *Secretary, Attorney-General's Department v TS* (2001) FLC 93-063.

[56] *Ploni v Almonit* (n 17)(Justice Hendel). See also UK case of *S v S & S* [2009] EWHC 1494 (Fam), where it was held that the child had become so integrated in his new life that he had become settled, independently of his dependence on and attachment to his mother.

[57] See eg, *Ploni v Almonit* ibid; *AGD and TS* (n 6); R 6136; M. Le Procureur Général contre MHK [INCADAT cite: HC/E/MC 510]; Präsidium des Bezirksgerichts St Gallen (District Court of St Gallen), decision of 8 September 1998, 4 PZ 98-0217/0532N [INCADAT cite: HC/E/CH 431]; CA Paris 27 October 2005, 05/15032 [INCADAT cite: HC/E/FR 814].

[58] Justice Hendel in *Ploni v Almonit* (n 17) points out that the situation of a one-year-old is quite different from that of a five-year-old; *In re Coffield* 96 Ohio App. 3d 52 (App Ct 1994), where it was held that the five-year-old boy had not settled because he had not 'developed the connections to the community which a normal child of his age would'.

[59] In *Perrin v Perrin* (n 12), it was critical that whilst the child had been in Scotland for 14 months, she had only been living in the current accommodation for three months.

[60] For example, in the French case of CA Paris, 19 octobre 2008, No 06/12398 [INCADAT cite: HC/E/FR1008], emphasis was placed on the fact that the children aged 3 and 5 only spoke French.

[61] In the case of *Collopy v Christodoulou*, No 90 DR 1138 (D Colo May 8, 1991) [INCADAT cite: HC/E/USf 210], the Court placed great emphasis on the 20-month- old child's connections with the abducting mother's wider family and also her contact with other children whom the mother looked after.

[62] Comments in the case of *David v Zamira* (n 53) and *In re Coffield* (n 58) suggest that the conclusion might have been different in these cases if the children had been enrolled in a nursery or other similar pre-school activities; see also Swiss case of 4 PZ 98-0217/0532N (n 57), where the fact that the child was happy in stable child care arrangements was taken into account; *cf* per Justice Hendel in *Ploni v Almonit* (n 17) (settlement in child care framework not relevant because it is likely to change each year).

[63] In addition, some courts have taken into account whether the child still maintains connections with the country of origin. See eg, *David v Zamira* (n 53) and *Collopy v Christodoulou* (n 61).

C Discretion to Order Return

Inconsistent answers have been given to the question of whether the court has discretion to order return despite the fact that the one-year period has expired and the child has become settled.[64] Whilst the House of Lords[65] has now held that such a discretion does exist and the New Zealand legislation expressly provides for discretion,[66] there is still much to commend the 'no-discretion approach' and so it is appropriate to consider briefly the relevant arguments and authorities.[67] Before examining the two approaches, it is appropriate to consider the significance of this question.

i The Significance of whether there is Discretion to Order Return where the Article 12(2) Exception is Established

It might be thought that, at least in common law jurisdictions, the issue of whether the court has discretion under the Abduction Convention is of little practical consequence since even if there is no discretion under the Convention, the left-behind parent can always apply for summary return under the court's inherent jurisdiction or under the relevant child law legislation.[68] Thus, apart from the inconvenience and cost[69] of having to initiate fresh proceedings, the issue appears to be of academic interest only. However, such a conclusion is misconceived because there is a substantive difference between the exercise of discretion under the Convention and the exercise of discretion outside the Convention. As the Court of Appeal reminds us,[70] in exercising discretion under the Convention the court has to have due regard to the overriding objectives of the Convention in addition to considering the child's welfare. In contrast, in proceedings under the inherent jurisdiction or specific legislation relating to children, the child's welfare is the paramount consideration. Clearly this difference could be critical to the outcome of any particular case. Moreover, in legal systems where there is no jurisdiction to order summary return in non-Convention cases, the issue is of even greater significance

---

[64] The Nova Scotia Court of Appeal in the case of *JEA v CLM* (n 35) seems to merge the question of settlement with the exercise of the discretion. Thus, in determining whether the child is settled or not, the Court takes into account the objectives of the Convention, as if it is exercising a discretion. Cromwell JA states 'The concept of being settled is one of degree and requires a careful examination and assessment of the child's circumstances here and a balancing of them with the objectives of the Convention' ([81]).
[65] *Re M (Abduction: Zimbabwe)* [2007] UKHL 55.
[66] Care of Children Act 2004, s 106(1)(a).
[67] For a detailed analysis of the two approaches, see R Schuz, 'In Search of a Settled Interpretation of Art 12(2) of the Hague Child Abduction Convention' (2008) 20 *Child and Family Law Quarterly* 1, 64.
[68] In England, the Children Act 1989.
[69] This is a real factor in the UK since applicants in Hague Convention proceedings are entitled to non-means tested legal aid. However, in other jurisdictions, the cost factor would seem to be marginal.
[70] *Canon v Canon* (n 22) [38]; *Re L (Abduction: Pending Criminal Proceedings)* [1999] 1 FLR 433.

ii The No-Discretion Approach

Whilst there are very few cases which hold that there is no discretion to order return,[71] the weight of academic authority supports this view.[72] The main arguments in favour of this approach may be summarised as follows:

Firstly, the wording of Article 12 does not contemplate the existence of discretion to order return, where the conditions of the settlement exception are satisfied.[73] In particular, the wording of Article 12 can be distinguished from that of Article 13, which states that the court 'is not bound to order return' where the exceptions in that section exists. Similarly, Article 13(2) states that the court 'may refuse to order return' where the child objects and Article 20 states that the return of a child 'may be refused'. It is reasonable to assume that similar language would have been used in Article 12 if the intention had indeed been to confer a residual discretion.

Secondly, the proponents of this approach reject the idea, adopted in some of the case law, that Article 18[74] confers a residual discretion 'within the four walls of the Convention'[75] and understand those provisions as clarifying that the Convention in no way precludes the requested State from ordering return pursuant to its own domestic law.[76]

Finally, allowing a residual discretion effectively defeats the purpose of Article 12(2) in drawing a line between cases where it is inappropriate to consider the merits and those cases where it is necessary to do so, as is explained by Singer J:

> Where more than (and it might well be much more than) the relevant year has elapsed and where settlement is established, the framers of the Hague Convention decided that the interests of the child can no longer be generalized to support a Convention order for return. Over that line, the Convention recognizes that it is in the child's best interests to investigate the merits. Investigation of the merits is not, however, an activity to be undertaken in the context of a Convention application.'[77]

iii The Discretion Approach

Most of the case law assumes that, although the existence of the conditions in Article 12(2) prevents return from being mandatory, the court still has a discretion to order return.[78] Whilst in the earlier cases the contrary view was not put to the court,[79] the discretion

---

[71] Australian decisions of Kay J in *SCA v Ayob* (n 18); *SCA v CR* (n 15); Singer J in *Re C* (n 34); Hong Kong case of *AC v PC* (n 8).

[72] Perez-Vera Report (n 5), para 112; Beaumont and McEleavy (n 2) 209; N Lowe, M Everall and M Nicholls, *International Movement of Children Law, Practice and Procedure* (Bristol, Family Law, 2004) para 17.32; Schuz, 'In Search of a Settled Interpretation' (n 67).

[73] *Re C* (n 34) (Singer J).

[74] This provision states, 'The provisions of this Chapter do not limit the power of a judicial or administrative authority to order the return of the child at any time.'

[75] *SCA v Ayob* (n 18) (Kay J).

[76] *Re C* (n 34) (Singer J); Perez-Vera Report (n 5), para 112.

[77] *Re C* (n 34) [36]; This point is also made in para 107 of the Perez-Vera Report ibid; Similarly, Lord Rodger, dissenting on this point, in *Re M (Abduction: Zimbabwe)* (n 65) [7], expresses the view that where the child has become settled, the Convention ceases to play a role because the purpose of speedy return can no longer be achieved.

[78] This approach is perhaps unsurprising because the courts are used to the fact that existence of the exceptions in Art 13 (which are much more frequently raised) simply opens the gate to the exercise of discretion.

[79] eg *Re S (A Minor)* (n 32). In the case of *Re L* (n 70), Wilson J admitted that at first he was unsure whether Art 18 referred to a power outside the Convention, for example arising in the inherent jurisdiction, but both counsel agreed that the power referred to is one arising within the Convention and he was satisfied that this was correct.

approach was later confirmed by the English Court of Appeal and the House of Lords after full argument.

In *Canon v Canon*, the Court of Appeal relied mainly on the existing case law, even though none of it was binding, and on paragraph 112 of the Perez-Vera Report, which is stated to support the view that Article 18 confers discretion to order return, even when the conditions in Article 12(2) are satisfied.[80] With respect, this statement is a misreading of that paragraph, which specifically says that Article 18 authorises the invoking of other provisions to enable return to be ordered.[81]

In the House of Lords decision in *Re M (Abduction: Zimbabwe)*,[82] Baroness Hale, giving the judgment of the majority, rehearses the competing authorities and arguments in relation to the discretion issue and finally concludes, not without considerable hesitation, that Article 12(2) does envisage that a settled child might nevertheless be returned with the Convention. She bases this decision on seven reasons.[83] Firstly, the language of Article 12(2) is open to both interpretations.[84] Secondly, the discretion approach is consistent with the position in relation to the other exceptions. Thirdly, the possibility of returning a settled child under the Convention, in the unusual event that summary return is appropriate, will save the need for separate, and probably unfunded, proceedings. Fourthly, the discretion approach recognises the flexibility in the concept of settlement, which may arise in a wide variety of circumstances and to very different degrees and, fifthly, acknowledges that late applications may be the result of active concealment of the child. Sixthly, the discretion approach leaves the court with all the options open and finally, the difference between the two solutions is by no means as great as is sometimes assumed.

With respect, whilst these arguments are more persuasive than those given by the Court of Appeal in *Canon v Canon*,[85] they are still not convincing. In particular, if the drafters had envisaged consistency with the other exceptions, then they would have used similar wording. In addition, the narrow approach adopted by the *Canon* Court to the concept of settlement can hardly be described as flexible. Indeed, the need for the discretion would have been more understandable if a wider approach to this concept had been adopted. Furthermore, treating concealment as a relevant factor is inconsistent with the child-centric approach favoured by Baroness Hale herself in this case.

Finally, the case of *Re M* itself illustrates the danger, predicted by this author,[86] that the 'discretion' approach would lead to robust judges ordering the return of settled children in order to give effect to the so-called policy of the Convention, without giving sufficient weight to the policy behind the Article 12(2) exception or the interests of the children. In this case, the first instance court and the Court of Appeal held that the children should be returned, even though the Article 12(2) exception had been established, ignoring the fact

---

[80] *Canon v Canon* (n 22). See also US case of *FHU v ACU* (n 20).
[81] *Re M (Abduction: Zimbabwe)* (n 65) [21] (Baroness Hale).
[82] ibid.
[83] ibid [31]. She does not rely on Art 18, rejecting the view that this Article confers any new power within the Convention, ibid [21].
[84] *cf* the view of Lord Bingham ibid [3]–[4], who argues that the wording of Art 12(2) clearly supports the 'discretion' approach because the absence of a direction not to return the child (in contrast to the direction 'shall' in Art 12(1), indicates that in the situation to which the 'coda' refer there is nevertheless a discretion to return the child.
[85] *Canon v Canon* (n 22).
[86] Schuz, 'In Search of a Settled Interpretation' (n 67) 74.

that disruption caused to the children by return would make the children victims twice over.[87]

III Analysis

A Internal Coherence

At first sight, the discretion approach might appear to lead to greater coherence because it treats all the exceptions the same.[88] Against this, it can be argued that the 'no discretion' approach leads to greater internal coherence within the Convention because it gives effect to the difference between the wording of Article 12(2) and the wording of the other exceptions.

In addition, the discretion approach and narrow interpretation of settlement are inconsistent with the structure and philosophy of the Convention. In particular, it should be remembered that the summary return mechanism is based on the premise that return is prompt. The Article 12(2) exception gives expression to the Convention's recognition that if return is substantially delayed, the major objective of securing swift return cannot be met[89] and it can no longer be presumed that return protects the interests of the child.[90] However, the careful balance achieved by this provision will be altered by too narrow an interpretation thereof. This was eloquently explained by Singer J as follows:

> Established settlement after more than one year since the wrongful removal or retention is the juncture in a child's life where the Hague judge's legitimate policy objective shifts from predominant focus on the Convention's aims (for the benefit of the subject child in particular and of potentially abducted children generally) to a more individualised and emphasised recognition that the length and degree of interaction of the particular child in his or her new situation deserve qualitative evaluation, free of Hague Convention considerations and constraints. If (by analogy with the judicial response to the exercise of the art 13(b) discretion) too high a threshold is set for establishing settlement, the consequence is not so much that the Hague Convention's aim of speedy return will be frustrated, but rather that a child who has in his or her past already suffered the disadvantages of unilateral removal across a frontier will be exposed to the disruption inherent in what for that child would be a second dys-location, potentially inflicting cumulative trauma.[91]

Indeed, according to this line of argument, if there is to be discretion, then the policy of the Convention should be treated as a factor pointing against summary return of a settled child[92] and so return should only be ordered where it can be clearly shown that return will promote the interests of the children in question.

---

[87] *Re M (Abduction: Zimbabwe)* (n 65) [52] (Baroness Hale). Similarly in the US case of *FHU v ACU* (n 20), no reason is given for ordering return of the settled children other than the need to uphold the Convention, even where it produces 'austere results' (ibid at 382).
[88] *Re M (Abduction: Zimbabwe)* ibid [31].
[89] ibid [7] and [47].
[90] ibid [44].
[91] *Re C* (n 34) [105].
[92] *Secretary for Justice v HJ* [2006] NZSC 97 [139] (McGrath J).

B Consistency with the Intention of the Drafters

The Article 12(2) exception reflects the drafters' recognition that where a child had spent a long time in the requested State and had become settled there, it would not be possible to restore the *status quo ante*.[93] Since no objective method of determining the child's level of integration could be found, it was necessary to fix an arbitrary time-limit. The original draft provided for a two tier system under which the time limit was six months from the date where the child's location was known with a maximum period of 12 months.[94] Later, a single time-limit of one year was adopted.[95] However, in response to the views of some delegates that it should be possible to return children even after this period has elapsed, an additional clause was added allowing the child to be returned unless it is shown that he has become settled in his new environment.[96]

The drafting history makes it clear that the drafters envisaged that the fact that the location of the child was not known would not delay or prevent the expiration of the one-year period and thus the US doctrine of equitable tolling is inconsistent with the intentions of the drafters.

Furthermore, the wording of the Convention and the Perez-Vera Report suggest that the drafters did not intend that there would be discretion to order return under the Convention where the conditions in Article 12(2) are established.[97] Whilst it may be possible to interpret Article 12(2) as conferring discretion on the court,[98] there is no evidence that this is what the drafters envisaged and no explanation as to why there was no express provision of such discretion.

Although the Court of Appeal in *Canon v Canon*[99] cites paragraph 112 of the Perez-Vera Report as supporting the view that there is such discretion by virtue of Article 18, with respect, this is a misreading of that paragraph. Indeed, Thorpe LJ seems to admit that the drafters did not envisage any discretion when he states that the global judicial community construes Article 18 as conferring discretion 'whatever may have been the drafting intention'.[100]

C Promotion of the Objectives of the Convention

i Protecting Abducted Children

As we saw above, Article 12(2) recognises that where a substantial period of time has elapsed since the wrongful removal or retention, it can no longer be assumed that return will protect the interests of the individual child and thus it is necessary to check whether he is settled in his new environment.[101] Accordingly, a child-centric approach to

---

[93] Beaumont and McEleavy (n 2) 203.
[94] Art 11 of the Preliminary Draft Convention.
[95] Beaumont and McEleavy (n 2) 203.
[96] ibid.
[97] See quote from Singer J in text accompanying n 77 above.
[98] As held by Hale in *Re M (Abduction: Zimbabwe)* (n 65) [31].
[99] *Canon v Canon* (n 22).
[100] ibid [48].
[101] As explained by a US judge in the case of *Robinson v Robinson* 983 F Supp 1339 (D Colo 1997), 'It would seem that, just as it is harmful to wrongfully remove the children from their habitual residence, it may also be harmful to remove them again if they have become connected to or "settled" in the new environment.'

the concept of settlement will best promote the objective of protecting the child from harm.

Similarly, the 'no discretion' approach protects the child because it recognises that a settled child may be harmed by summary return and thus it is necessary to conduct a best interests inquiry. However, granting discretion to the court in such a case would not be problematic if the court were indeed to give appropriate weight to the welfare of the child in exercising that discretion.[102] However, experience shows that this is not always the case and that judges in their zealousness to give effect to the objective of returning abducted children, are liable to forget that it is not the Convention's policy that children must be returned in all circumstances[103] and that the objective underlying the Convention is the protection of the abducted children themselves.

For example, in *Re C (Abduction: Settlement) (No 2)*,[104] even though return of the settled child was refused and the child's welfare was one of the four considerations taken into account by the judge,[105] the analysis does not appear to give sufficient weight to the interests of the child. In particular, in balancing the various considerations, whilst taking into account the voice of the child 'who is entitled also to look to the court for justice' and who loves her school and does not want to leave, the learned judge expressly states that her voice does not sound more loudly than any of the other matters.[106] Furthermore, in concluding that it would be wrong to order return, the judge states that 'this is an extremely unusual case in which the child has settled and got on with her life in a quite outstanding way'.[107] This comment, together which the careful and even-handed analysis of the countervailing considerations, gives the impression that return will be ordered in other cases where the period of time which had elapsed was shorter or the settlement was not as 'perfect'.

Indeed, this is what happened in a later decision of the English High Court, which was upheld by the Court of Appeal, in the case of *Re M (Children)*,[108] in which the children had been in the UK for two years and were held to still have cultural and social roots in Zimbabwe. Although mention was made of welfare considerations, including the strength of the children's connection with their father who had previously cared for them and their volatile immigration position in the UK, considerable weight was also placed on the mother's wrongdoing and little weight was placed on the children's objections and the reasons behind those objections.[109] Whilst the House of Lords' ruling, overturning this decision, seems to make clear that a more child-centric approach should be adopted in the exercise

---

[102] As did the Family Court of Australia in the case of *D-G v Thorpe* (n 29). The judge, in considering the objectives of the Convention, said 'However, in my view, part of the underlying purpose and intention of the Convention is to be gleaned from other aspects of it as well. And that includes the fact that the Convention ... recognise[s] that once a child has settled in a new environment it may no longer be appropriate to subject him or her to the summary procedure, provided for in the Regulations of an order to return him or her to the country from which he or she was taken or retained'; See also the minority opinion of Elias CJ in *Secretary for Justice v HJ* (n 29), holding that only the best interests of the child should be taken into account in exercising the discretion.

[103] See comment of Warnick J quoted in the decision of the Full Court of Australia in the case of *D-G v Moore* (n 6). See also *Re S (A Minor)* (n 32), where it was held that even if there had been settlement, which was in doubt, the discretion would be exercised in favour of return in accordance with the underlying comity of the Convention.

[104] *Re C (No 2)* (n 50).

[105] The others were the purposes of the Hague Convention, the mother's wrongdoing and the injustice to the father. ibid [27].

[106] *Re C (No 2)* (n 50) [48].

[107] ibid [49].

[108] *Re M (Children)* [2007] EWHC 1820 (Fam); *Re M (Children)* [2007] EWCA Civ 992.

[109] This seems to have been partly because the children were not separately represented. See below ch 15 at III Biv.

of discretion in settlement cases,[110] considerable leeway is still given to individual judges in balancing the countervailing considerations.

Perhaps the clearest example of using the discretion to return settled children in a way which clearly did not protect them can be found in the decision of the Family Court in the New Zealand case of *Secretary of State v HJ*, which was upheld by the High Court, before being overturned by the Court of Appeal, whose decision was subsequently approved by the Supreme Court.[111] In this case, the main reason for the mother's removal of the children from Australia and failure to inform the father of her whereabouts was the violence of the father, with whom the children had had an intermittent relationship. There was no real issue as to custody and New Zealand had now become the *forum conveniens* for determining access. Thus, this was a case where the children would be disrupted purely in order to uphold the deterrent effect of the Convention.[112] Whilst the Supreme Court decided that the potential harm to the children in this case was greater than the harm to the Convention, the majority took the view that there will be cases where the deterrent policy of the Convention will prevail over the welfare of the child,[113] particularly where there has been concealment.[114] With respect, this view is misconceived. Only in extremely rare cases will it be appropriate to return a child who has become settled, in the narrow sense of the concept,[115] without a full examination of the merits of the case.[116] Any analysis of the countervailing considerations which gives sufficient weight to protecting the child from harm will invariably result in a refusal to order summary return.[117] Thus, it would be preferable not to accord the court any discretion in the first place, so as not to leave an opening for 'misuse' of the discretion.

ii Deterrence

It may be convincingly argued that a wide interpretation of settlement and the 'no-discretion' approach will reduce the deterrent value of the Convention and encourage abductors to hide

---

[110] *Re M (Abduction: Zimbabwe)* (n 65) [52]–[53].
[111] *Secretary for Justice v HJ* (n 29).
[112] ibid [115].
[113] ibid [50].
[114] ibid [87].
[115] A possible example of such a situation can be found in the case of *F v M and N* (n 28), where custody proceedings were already well advanced in Poland. The Court held that whilst every solution had a disadvantage for the child, her best interests would be best served if those proceedings were completed as speedily and effectively as possible and so ordered return. Nonetheless, the Court expressed the hope that the Polish Court would allow the child to remain with the mother in the UK, pending the outcome of those proceedings, and suspended the return order so as to allow for the mother to make an application to this effect to the Polish Court. Thus, the judge recognised that what was in the best interests of the child was adjudication in Poland and not return to Poland, other than to the extent necessary for completion of the court proceedings there. Whilst the court in an Abduction Convention case cannot bring about a separation between adjudication and the physical location of the child (*cf* under Brussels II bis Regulation, see above ch 1 at II C), the judge in this case did in fact pave the way for the creation of such a situation. Another possible situation where it might be appropriate to order return would be where the settled child will in any event be moving from the present environment with the abductor, see Scottish case of *P v S* (n 33) and *Secretary for Justice v HJ* (n 29) [26] (Elias J).
[116] Hale J (as she then was) commented, 'Once the time for speedy return has passed, it must be questioned whether it is ever in the best interests of the child for there to be a summary return after the very limited inquiry into the merits which is involved in these cases' in *Re HB (Abduction: Children's Objections) (No 2)* [1998] 1 FLR 564.
[117] *cf Secretary for Justice v HJ* (n 29) (Elias J), suggesting that there may be cases where the long-term interests of the settled child justify the short-term disruption. With respect, it is difficult to see how the court will be able to come to such a conclusion without considering, at least to some extent, the merits of the case.

240   Article 12(2)

the child until the one-year period has passed and the child can be considered to be settled. Indeed, this concern seems to be the reason behind the equitable tolling approach adopted in the US.[118]

However, this concern, albeit legitimate, seems to be exaggerated in light of the relatively small number of cases in which the settlement defence appears to be pleaded.[119] Furthermore, and more importantly, the need for deterrence cannot justify prejudicing the welfare of the particular child in such cases. This view is expressed rather dramatically by Kirkwood J, stating,

> Nor am I professionally willing to sacrifice this child, if sacrifice it would be to order her return, in order to set an example to others of the comprehensive and rigorous enforcement of the purposes of the Hague Convention. Nor does the Convention require me to do so.[120]

In a similar vein, Baroness Hale concluded that 'These children should not be made to suffer for the sake of general deterrence of the evil of child abduction world-wide.'[121]

Rather, the deterrent effect of the Convention should be maintained by increasing international and national efforts to ensure that abductors are located as soon as possible. It is indeed instructive to note that in some of the cases where the children were not located for a while, they were actually living openly without any change in appearance[122] and it would seem that greater activity on the part of the authorities would have led to the earlier location of the child.

iii Adjudication in the Forum Conveniens

Where the child has been living in the country of refuge for a considerable period of time and has become settled there, it is likely that that country will now be the *forum conveniens* for determining the merits of the custody dispute, instead of the country of origin. Indeed, in the case of *Re C (Abduction: Settlement) (No 2)*, Kirkwood J expressly found that it was no longer the case that the Californian Court was in a better position to determine welfare issues relating to the child.[123] On the contrary, all the evidence about the child was in England, where she

---

[118] See n 22 above and accompanying text.
[119] An INCADAT search for cases relating to Art 12(2) revealed 75 cases (www.incadat.com); N Lowe, 'A Statistical Analysis of Applications Made in 2008 under The Hague Convention of 25 October 1980 on the Civil Aspects of International Child Abduction, Part I Global Report', Preliminary Document No 8 (November 2011), www.hcch.net/upload/wop/abduct2011pd08ae.pdf, shows that the Art 12(2) defence was the reason for 11% of refusals in cases where there was a single reason for refusal. This relatively low number might corroborate the claim that the exception is not often pleaded but might equally well be evidence of a narrow approach to the interpretation of the defence.
[120] *Re C (No 2)* (n 50) [38]. Compare the Canadian case of *JEA v CLM* (n 35), where in similar factual circumstances (mother thwarted the judicial process in Iowa by fleeing to Nova Scotia and there successfully avoided detection for seven years by deception), the Court appears to give almost decisive weight to the deterrence objective and does not consider the harm which might be caused to the child by return after seven years. Cromwell JA says, '[The mother] and any who have knowingly assisted her in this abduction must be made to understand how firmly and unequivocally the courts of this Province will deal with international child abduction. It also must be clear that Nova Scotia is not a haven for child abductors. In all these respects, the facts of this case call for a response stressing precisely the deterrence which is at the core of the Convention's objectives'.
[121] *Re M (Abduction: Zimbabwe)* (n 65) [54]; comment of Elias J in *Secretary for Justice v HJ* (n 29) [3] and [27], that the welfare and best interests of the child should not be modified by the deterrent policy of the Convention and so should not be balanced against concerns about sending 'wrong messages' to potential abductors.
[122] eg, *Re C* (n 34) in which the child was eventually found via an internet site set up by the father in which the child's picture appeared. Could the child's picture in such cases not be sent via email to all educational institutions in countries where the child was likely to be?
[123] *Re C (No 2)* (n 50) 949–50. See *Re M (Abduction: Zimbabwe)* (n 65) [47]; *Secretary for Justice v HJ* (n 29) [115].

had been living for the past five years. Thus, a narrow approach to settlement and exercising discretion to return settled children is likely to be inconsistent with the objective of ensuring determination of disputes in the *forum conveniens*.[124]

iv Justice between the Parents and the Rule of Law

The apparent injustice to the left-behind parent of a refusal to return on the basis of settlement is exacerbated in concealment cases. Both the moral turpitude of the abductor, who has compounded her initial wrongdoing by taking effective evasive steps, and the distress suffered by the left-behind parent, who has had no contact with his child for a long period of time, are greater than in other abduction cases. Furthermore, it is the morally repugnant act of concealment itself that facilitates the expiration of time and the settlement of the child, which lead to the establishment of the Article 12(2) exception. Thus, it is understandable that courts in such cases will try to avoid such a blatantly unjust result.[125] Indeed, this consideration seems to have been at the forefront of the minds of some of the judges who advocated a narrow interpretation of settlement and supported the 'discretion' approach. For example, Thorpe LJ in *Canon v Canon* expressly refers to 'the injustice to the deprived father that the longer the deprivation extends the less his prospects of achieving return'.[126] Similarly, the injustice of allowing the abductor to be rewarded for his misconduct is the main rationale behind the adoption of the equitable tolling doctrine in the US in concealment cases.[127]

Nonetheless, it must not be forgotten that justice between the parents is only a subsidiary aim of the Convention and that priority must be given to protecting the interests of the child.[128] Indeed, Kirkwood J accepted the submission of the abducting mother's counsel that 'the sins of the mother should not be visited on the child'.[129] Similarly, the Supreme Court of New Zealand rejected the view that the abductor should not be given the benefit of the discretion, arising where Article 12(2) was established, if he did not come to the court with clean hands because this approach did not take into account the interests of the child.[130]

It should also be remembered that in some cases the passivity or ambivalence of the left-behind parent is the cause for the delay in locating the child and/or in bringing proceedings. Whilst this parent may have been wronged in the first place, he has to understand that time does not stand still and that the child will not simply wait around for this parent to

---

[124] But *cf F v M and N* (n 28), in which the Court found that Poland was still the appropriate forum to resolve the custody dispute because proceedings there were well advanced.

[125] Bracewell J in *Re H* (n 22) went so far as to say, 'it is not good law for the abducting parent to be able to say well, I have managed to evade the wronged parent; I have managed to hide my address and whereabouts of the children and I am going to rely on that in [advancing] the argument that the children have been so long in the jurisdiction that they have now settled in that environment . . .'.

[126] *Canon v Canon* (n 22) [58].

[127] *Mendez Lynch v Mendez Lynch* 220 F Supp 2d 1347, 1362-63 (MD Fla 2002).

[128] See eg, following explanation of Denham J in *P v B* (n 54), 'However, the Hague Convention and the Act are instruments for the benefit of the child. The child's interest is paramount. Consequently, defences to the application of the father . . . may be considered by the Court in spite of the reprehensible behaviour of the mother' (upholding the establishment of the Art 12(2) defence in a case where the child had been concealed).

[129] *Re C* (no 2) (n 50) [38].

[130] *Secretary for Justice v HJ* (n 29). See also comment of Mostyn QC in *In Re SC (A Child)* [2005] EWHC 2205, 'No doubt F . . . would say that . . . I am rewarding the worst kind of turpitude and encouraging a kidnapper's charter which says that if someone can successfully abduct a child for a sufficiently long period of time then that person will get away from it. But these views have to be subordinated to the child's best interests and in my view it would be a breach of the judicial duty to sacrifice a child's best interests in order to prove a point of principle.'

242 *Article 12(2)*

seek his return, but will naturally adjust to his new surroundings. Thus, where the left-behind parent does not act promptly to secure the return of the child, the moral basis of his request for summary return is weakened.[131]

D Compatibility with the Summary Nature of Convention Proceedings

It can be argued that a court cannot properly consider whether to return a settled child without receiving detailed evidence concerning the welfare of the child, which is inconsistent with the summary nature of Convention proceedings.[132] Whilst this is true to some extent in all cases where an exception is established, in relation to other exceptions this process is inevitable and expressly mandated by the Convention.

However, in the case of Article 12(2), there is no express reference to such discretion. Moreover, the need for a summary procedure seems difficult to justify, when so much time has already passed since the wrongful removal or retention and the child has already become settled. Thus, in such cases, the issue of whether to return the child should not be determined under the Abduction Convention but under domestic procedures in accordance with the best interests standard.

E Consistency with Rights and Interests of Children

The Article 12(2) exception may be seen as giving effect to the child's need for stability and continuity, which is part of his welfare, and in some cases also to his right to identity. Thus, too narrow an interpretation is likely to be inconsistent with these rights and interests.

In addition, as explained above,[133] the concept that children have rights contains a fundamental message about the centrality of children in matters affecting them and requires that findings concerning children of all ages take into account the situation from the child's point of view. The need to consider the question of whether the child has become settled from the perspective of the child has been recognised in recent years by some judges.[134] However, the implications of such a child-centric approach have not been fully explored. For example, a child-centric approach requires that the existence of the emotional element of settlement be tested in light of the child's perceptions and sense of time and not those of adults. In addition, a wide approach should be taken to the implications of concealment and the age of the child, under which the child's degree of attachment to his new environment is assessed from his point of view in light of his daily way of life, in accordance with his age. Clearly, where the child is old enough, it is critical to hear his views in determining whether he is settled.[135] Thus, in most cases, his point of view cannot be properly put

---

[131] In the Irish case of *P v B* (n 54), the culpable delay on the part of the father in instituting proceedings was treated by the Court as a relevant factor in exercising its discretion not to return the settled child.
[132] See *Secretary for Justice v HJ* (n 29) [59].
[133] See ch 6 at II A.
[134] Justice Hendel in *Ploni v Almonit* (n 17) held that the Court has to examine the connection between the environment and the child from the child's point of view.
[135] *Anderson v Acree* 250 F Supp 2d 876 (US Dist 2002); eg decision of *Cour de Cassation* in Cass Civ 1ère 12 décembre 2006 (N° de pourvoi: 06-13177) [INCADAT cite: HC/E/FR 892]. In CA Paris 8 août 2008, N° 08/05791 & 08/07826 [INCADAT cite: HC/E/FR1006], the judge expressly relied on his impression from hearing the child in concluding that he was settled. See also the decision of the Quebec Court of Appeal in Droit de la Famille 2785, Cour d'appel de Montréal, 5 December 1997, No 500-09-005532-973 [INCADAT cite: HC/E/CA 653], overturn-

forward without separate representation.[136] Finally, a truly child-centric approach requires adoption of the 'no-discretion' approach because where a child has become settled, the only way to give proper weight to his interests is by a full investigation of the merits of the case.[137]

F Consistency with Private International Law Principles

The doctrine of comity would seem to support the discretion approach because this provides the opportunity for the court in the requested State to respect the foreign decision, despite the lapse of time and settlement. Indeed, comity is sometimes mentioned by courts as one of the factors when exercising its discretion under Article 12(2).[138]

However, it is suggested that in reality refusing to order return where this exception has been established should not be seen as inconsistent with comity, either in the sense of reciprocity or judicial courtesy. Rather the fundamental change in circumstances which has occurred since the wrongful removal or retention has made the foreign law or legal decision largely irrelevant. Thus, non-return does not imply disrespect for the foreign decision or lack of confidence in the legal system of the foreign State. Furthermore, it has to be remembered that the doctrine of comity is not absolute[139] and cannot justify harming the interests of the child. Accordingly, only in the very rare case where returning a settled child will not prejudice his interests, should considerations of comity be taken into account when exercising the discretion.[140]

G Certainty versus Flexibility

The 'no-discretion' approach provides more certainty, whilst the 'discretion' approach provides a degree of flexibility. Indeed, Baroness Hale seems to consider that this flexibility is necessitated by the flexibility inherent in the concept of settlement.[141] Nonetheless, she herself recognises that there will often be powerful reasons not to order the summary return of a settled child.[142] Thus, it can be questioned whether the slim possibility that a settled child should be returned justifies the uncertainty, as well as the time and expense, involved in the exercise of discretion in every case where the exception is established. The case of *Re M* itself[143] illustrates that this uncertainty is not illusory because the High Court and Court of Appeal did indeed decide to return the child and the House of Lords reversed the decision.

---

ing the decision of the first instance court that the child was not settled, on the basis of hearing the child, who had not been heard by the first instance court. For a full discussion of how a child's views should be heard, see ch 14.

[136] *Re M (Abduction: Zimbabwe)* (n 65) [57]. For a full discussion of the question of separate representation, see ch 15.
[137] See Ci above.
[138] eg *Re S (A Minor)* (n 32).
[139] See ch 6 at IV E.
[140] Some support for this view can be found in Baroness Hale's comment that the further away one gets from speedy return, the less weight should be given to Convention considerations such as comity, *Re M (Abduction: Zimbabwe)* (n 65) [42]–[44].
[141] ibid [31].
[142] ibid [47].
[143] ibid.

IV Conclusions

We have seen that a narrow interpretation of the Article 12(2) exception is not consistent with the intentions of the drafters or the objectives of the Convention. It has to be remembered that where 12 months have passed, the purpose of summary return cannot be achieved. Whilst, this fact per se should not prevent return, the combination of the expiry of a lengthy period of time since the wrongful removal or retention, together with the integration of the child in his new environment rebuts the presumption that the return of the child promotes his best interests, on which the mandatory return mechanism is based.

Accordingly, whilst the mere passage of time and superficial adjustment to the new surroundings do not indicate that a child has become settled in his new environment, an overly narrow definition of settlement is not appropriate. In particular, the question of settlement should be considered from the child's perspective and where he is old enough, his views should be heard and be taken seriously. It should be remembered that usually damage will be caused by returning a child who feels settled, irrespective of the long-term intentions of the abductor and whether there is concealment.

If there is to be discretion to return settled children, it should be exercised extremely sparingly. Courts should realise that the integrity of the Convention will not be undermined by the refusal to return settled children and that children should not be made to suffer for the sins of the abducting parent. Rather, the main purpose of protecting children from harm will nearly always require that a settled child is not returned without a full best interests hearing.

10

Consent and Acquiescence

I Introduction

Article 13(1)(a) of the Hague Convention on the Civil Aspects of International Child Abduction ('Abduction Convention') provides that the court is not bound to order return where the person opposing return establishes that

> the person, institution or other body, having the care of the person of the child was not actually exercising the custody rights at the time of removal or retention, or had consented to or subsequently acquiesced in the removal or retention.

This sub-article contains three separate defences. The first, non-exercise of custody rights, was discussed above in chapter seven on wrongful removal because it is inextricably entwined with the requirement in Article 3(b) of actual exercise of rights of custody. The other two defences are consent and acquiescence.

It is trite law that the difference between these two defences is one of timing: consent being given before the wrongful removal or retention[1] and acquiescence occurring after it.[2] Whilst clearly there are issues which are specific to the interpretation of only one of the defences, there are also many issues which are relevant to both.[3] Moreover, the defences are based on the same rationales. There is no need for the 'first aid' remedy of immediate summary return in order to restore the *status quo ante*, where the left-behind parent has previously consented to, or later acquiesced in, the change of that status quo.[4] Accordingly, any questions relating to the future of the children can be determined within the framework of the family justice system in the country of refuge. In addition, these defences are designed to prevent the Convention becoming a bargaining tool to be used cynically by the left-behind parent in order to gain an advantage over the other parent.[5] Thus, a left-behind parent who has consented or acquiesced is effectively estopped from demanding the immediate return

---

[1] *Re P-J (children)* [2009] EWCA CIV 588 [53].
[2] However, it is not entirely clear which defence is appropriate where the left-behind parent agrees that the child need not return at the end of a holiday abroad. If the 'abducting' parent's announcement that she does not intend to return itself amounts to wrongful retention (see ch 7 at I), then the left-behind parent's agreement to the child staying is acquiescence. However, if the 'abducting' parent's announcement is not considered as an anticipatory breach of custody rights, then the agreement is consent. The issue does not seem to have any practical implications. See eg *BT v JRT (Abduction: Conditional Acquiescence and Consent)* [2008] EWHC 1169 (Fam) in which Sumner J seems to use the terms 'consent' and 'acquiescence' interchangeably and does not analyse which is applicable in this case.
[3] 'The test regarding consent and acquiescence are the same tests in essence', *Re G and A (Abduction: Consent)* [2003] NIFam 16.
[4] CA (SC) 7206/93 *Gabbai v Gabbai* PD 51(2) 241 (Isr), 256.
[5] Per Justice Arbel in RFamA (SC) 741/11 *OB-H v ShB-H* 17 May 2011 (Isr) http://elyon1.court.gov.il/files/11/410/007/b06/11007410.b06.pdf, para 17 quoting from para 115 of the Perez-Vera Report, Proceedings of the 14th Session of the Hague Conference Oct 1980 www.hcch.net/index_en.php?act=publications.details&pid=2779.

of his child.[6] Finally, where a lengthy period of time passes before the left-behind parent tries to revoke his consent or acquiescence, the child will be likely to have become settled in the country of refuge. In light of the considerable common ground between the two defences, they will be considered together. Where the discussion relates to only one of them, this will be specified expressly.

The defences of consent and acquiescence are substantially different from the other defences in that they relate entirely to the conduct of the parents and do not per se reflect the position of the children. In other words, they are not child-centric.[7] Accordingly, the fact that the consent or acquiescence exception is established tells us little about the likely impact of return on the child and does little, if anything, to rebut the presumption that return promotes the best interests of the child. This means that where one of these defences is established, the court approaches the exercise of its discretion to return with a virtually clean slate.[8] Accordingly, there is a need to consider in some detail what factors the courts take into consideration when exercising their discretion to return in consent/acquiescence cases and this will be done in Part IV below.

A preliminary point should be made in relation to the defence of consent. Whilst logically it might be thought that a removal or retention with consent is not wrongful in the first place, the Convention seems to envisage that such a removal or retention should be considered wrongful, but that the court may refuse to order return under the Article 13(1)(a) defence. Most courts have accepted this scheme[9] and this chapter will be written accordingly. However, in the analysis section, the merits and implications of this approach will be discussed.[10]

Acquiescence was traditionally classified as active or passive, but, as will be seen below, there no longer seems to be any significance to this distinction. However, it is still convenient to categorise the various forms of consent or acquiescence since different issues will arise in relation to the different forms. Three categories are suggested, the first two of which apply to both consent and acquiescence. The first category is where the alleged consent or acquiescence is in the form of oral[11] or written statements. While such statements might seem to speak for themselves, their significance may depend on the context in which they were made. In particular, as will be seen below, it may be relevant that the statements were made in the course of negotiations or in the initial aftermath of the removal or retention. The second category is where the alleged consent or acquiescence is implied from the conduct of the left-behind parent, for example where he has helped the abductor to pack or sell household items[12] or has later shipped the belongings of the abductor and child to the country of refuge.[13] In such cases, there will often be more than one possible interpretation

---

[6] Per Justice Melzer in *OB-H v ShB-H* (n 5); *Re H (Abduction: Acquiescence)* [1998] 2 AC 72.

[7] See *Re M (Abduction: Zimbabwe)* [2007] UKHL 55 [52] (Baroness Hale).

[8] This is in contrast to the other defences, where the very establishment of the defence casts real doubt on whether the basic assumption that return is in the best interests of the child holds good in that case, see *Re D (Abduction: Discretionary Return)* [2000] 1 FLR 24, 36.

[9] eg *Re P-J* (n 1); *Re P (A Child) (Abduction: Acquiescence)* [2004] EWCA CIV 971; *Director-General, Department of Child Safety v Stratford* [2005] CA 1115 (fam); *BB v JB* [1998] 1 ILRM 136; sub nom *B v B (Child Abduction)* [1998] 1 IR 299; But *cf FC v PA, Droit de la famille* – 08728, Cour Supérieure de Chicoutimi, 28 mars 2008, N°150-04-004667-072 [INCADAT cite: HC/E/CA 969] and CA Rouen, 9 mars 2006, N°05/04340 [INCADAT cite: HC/E/FR 897].

[10] At section Di.

[11] Early English case law which held that consent had to be in writing has not been followed, *Re K (Abduction: Consent)* [1997] 2 FLR 212.

[12] eg *Re C (Abduction: Consent)* [1996] 1 FLR 414.

[13] *Dimer v Dimer*, No 99-2-03610-7 SEA (Wa Sup Ct July 29, 1999).

of the actions in question. The third and final category is where the alleged acquiescence is in the form of inaction. Here, the main questions which arise relate to the period of time which has to elapse and the circumstances in which inactivity will not be seen as indicating acquiescence. Of course, in some cases the alleged consent or acquiescence may consist of a combination of two or more of these categories. For example, in one Israeli case,[14] acquiescence was founded on the fact that the father had participated in custody proceedings in an Israeli court, together with the lack of any action on his part to secure the return of the child to the US, over a period of 10 months. Similarly, in some cases the claim of consent or acquiescence will be based on a combination of statements and actions.[15]

The consent or acquiescence must be clear and unequivocal and must be proven by clear and cogent evidence.[16] Thus, wherever the words or actions in question are ambivalent, the abductor will not succeed in establishing the defence.[17] Accordingly, whether the defence is established in a particular case depends largely on the ability of the abductor to convince the court that his version of the relevant statements and/or actions[18] is correct and that these should be interpreted as consent or acquiescence.[19] Nonetheless, guidance can be gleaned from the case law as to the circumstances in which certain types of statements and actions or inaction might be considered to constitute consent or acquiescence. So, in Part III below, the courts' approach to the different types of consent and acquiescence in a number of typical situations will be examined. Firstly, however, it is necessary to set out a normative framework, by considering what conditions need to be fulfilled for a statement, action or inaction to constitute consent or acquiescence and what the significance of such consent or acquiescence is.

II Normative Framework

A Content of Acquiescence or Consent

The first question which arises relates to the nature of the rights that the left-behind parent is waiving by his consent or acquiescence. In the case of *Re AZ (A Minor) (Abduction: Acquiescence)*,[20] the Court of Appeal stated that it was sufficient if the conduct

---

[14] CA (SC) 473/93 *Leibovitz v Leibvotiz* PD 47(3), 63 [INCADAT cite: HC/E/IL242].

[15] eg in the Israeli District Court case of FamA (JLM) 575/04 *YM v AM*, DM 34(7), 291 (Isr) [INCADAT cite: HC/E/IL 836], the finding of acquiescence was based inter alia on statements made by the father, together with his renting of a flat near the flat which the mother had rented for herself and the children in Jerusalem.

[16] *R v R* [2006] IESC 7; *Re K* (Abduction: Consent) (n 11).

[17] eg *Department of Child Safety v Stratford* (n 9), in which the father's retort to the mother's announcement that she was going to take the child to England that 'this could not happen soon enough', was not an unequivocal communication of consent on which the mother could rely.

[18] In some cases there will be no evidence other than the conflicting testimony of the parties themselves. In these cases, the court will have to decide which party is more credible. Sometimes external facts will support one party's version, eg in the South African case of *Central Authority v H* 2008(1) SA 49 (SCA), the fact that the mother had travelled with only two suitcases was more consistent with the father's version that she had travelled for an extended stay than her claim that this was the first stage of emigration. Where the court cannot decide the conflict of evidence, the abductor will fail to establish the defence. See eg *Re P (A Child)* (n 9) and *Re S (Abduction: Acquiescence)* [1998] 2 FLR 115.

[19] The strong factual basis of determinations of acquiescence was emphasised by the Supreme Court of Ireland in *RK v JK (Child Abduction: Acquiescence)* [2000] 2 IR 416.

[20] *Re AZ (A Minor) (Abduction: Acquiescence)* [1993] 1 FLR 682.

was 'inconsistent with the summary return of the child to the place of habitual residence'. Thus, in that case, the father's agreement that the child could stay with the maternal aunt in England, as indicated inter alia by his execution of a power of attorney giving her responsibility for the child's health and education for a year, constituted acquiescence, even though he had requested care and control of the child in foreign divorce proceedings.

Similarly, in the Israeli Supreme Court, Justice Elon explained that there will be cases where it is more convenient for the left-behind parent to litigate the dispute concerning the children in the country of refuge. In such cases, he waives his right of summary return, even though he continues to fight for custody of the children.[21]

In principle, the same approach should apply to consent. Thus, consent to a change of residence for the time being should be seen as a waiver of the left-behind parent's right to insist on the preservation of the status quo. However, in the case of *Re HB (Abduction: Children's Objections)*,[22] Hale J (as she then was) held that the consent to a potentially open-ended arrangement under which the children would live in the UK for the time being was insufficient. The correctness of this decision is doubted by Beaumont and McEleavy[23] and later case law in other jurisdictions supports the view that it is not necessary to show consent to a permanent change of residence and that consent to a durable stay will establish the defence.[24] Of course, it may not always be easy to distinguish between an extended visit abroad, which will not suffice, and a durable stay. So, the court will have to consider carefully the nature and scope of the consent.[25]

Finally, consent or acquiescence may be made conditional on the fulfillment of terms, provided that these terms are clear and intended to be binding on both parties.[26]

B Subjective or Objective Test

An issue which has figured prominently in the case law is whether acquiescence and consent are to be determined subjectively or objectively. In other words, is the court to consider the subjective intentions of the particular left-behind parent or can it find that the statements or actions in question constitute acquiescence because they appear inconsistent with an intention to insist on the summary return of the child? In the early English case law, a distinction was drawn between active acquiescence and passive acquiescence.[27] In relation to the former, the test was held to be objective[28] whilst in relation to the latter the subjective intentions of the left-behind parent were to be considered.[29]

---

[21] *Leibovitz* (n 14), para 6.
[22] *Re HB (Abduction: Children's Objections)* [1997] 1 FLR 392.
[23] Beaumont and McEleavy, *The Hague Convention on International Child Abduction* (Oxford, Oxford University Press, 1999) 129.
[24] eg *De Directie Preventie, optredend voor haarzelf en namens F. (vader/father) en H (de moeder/mother)* (14 juli 2000, ELRO-nummer: AA6532, Zaaknr.R99/167HR) [INCADAT cite: HC/E/NL 318]; 5P1999/2006 /blb, Bundesgericht, II Zivilabteilung (Federal Court, Second Chamber) Decision of 13 July 2006, 5P1999/2006 /blb, [INCADAT cite: HC/E/CH 896]; see also *Re K (Abduction: Consent)* (n 11) (consent to a temporary shift of base for the child was sufficient to constitute consent to a change of habitual residence).
[25] *Baxter v Baxter* 423 F3d 363 (3rd Cir 2005).
[26] *BT v JRT* (n 2).
[27] *Re A (Minors) (Abduction: Custody Rights)* [1992] 106 (Fam), 119.
[28] ibid.
[29] *Re S (Minors) (Abduction: Acquiescence)* [1994] 1 FLR 819 (Neill and Hoffmann LJJ).

However, the House of Lords decision in *Re H (Minors) (Abduction: Acquiescence)*[30] abolished that distinction and made it clear that in all cases the court has to examine whether the left-behind parent 'acquiesced in fact'. If the abductor cannot prove the required subjective intention, then he will fail to establish the exception unless the words or actions of the wronged parent clearly and unequivocally show and have led the other parent to believe that the wronged parent is not asserting or going to assert his right to the summary return of the child and are inconsistent with such return.[31] It has been suggested that this statement creates two types of acquiescence: actual and constructive.[32] The subjective test adopted in *Re H* has been followed[33] in case law in a number of jurisdictions,[34] and in some countries the subjective approach was adopted prior to that decision.[35] It has also been held that the subjective approach applies equally to consent.[36]

Whilst the outward acts of the left-behind parent will still usually provide the main evidence of his intention,[37] there seems little doubt that the adoption of a subjective test narrows the scope of the defence, as will be seen from the discussion of specific situations in Part III below. A good example of the impact of the subjective approach can be seen in the recent US Court of Appeals for the First Circuit decision in *Nicolson v Pappalardo*.[38] In this case, the US mother, who had retained the child in the US, sought a Protection from Abuse Order in a Maine State court against the Australian father, in response to harassment by him. The father, through his Maine attorney, agreed to the entering of an Order which included awarding temporary custody to the mother for a two-year period, subject to amendment by a competent court. The father did not inform that court that he was in the process of initiating return proceedings under the Abduction Convention through the Australian Central Authority. The mother's claim that the consent court order evidenced acquiescence was rejected because the father did not subjectively intend to waive his rights, as evidenced by the initiation of the Convention proceedings, and the order could not be read as an unequivocal agreement by the father that permanent custody should be determined in a Maine court and nowhere else.[39]

C Ignorance of Rights

The question arises as to the extent to which the left-behind parent can consent or acquiesce when he is unaware that he has the right to refuse permission (in the case of consent) or the right to the immediate return of the child (in the case of acquiescence). On the one

---

[30] *Re H (Abduction: Acquiescence)* (n 6).
[31] ibid at 90.
[32] *Barry Eldon Matthews (Commissioner, Western Australia Police Service v Ziba Sabaghian* (2001) PT 1767 of 2001 (Australia) [18].
[33] Although it could have been argued that this was obiter because even on an objective test there was no acquiescence in this case, Beaumont and McEleavy (n 23) 117.
[34] eg *Re G (Abduction: Withdrawal of Proceedings, Acquiescence and Habitual Residence)* [2007] EWHC 2807 [55]–[56] (England); *AQ v JQ*, 12 December 2001, Outer House of the Court of Session [INCADAT cite: HC/E/UKs 415] (Scotland); *Smith v Smith* 2001 (3) SA 845 (SCA); *Matthews v Sabaghian* (n 32); *cf* US Court in *Dimer v Dimer* (n 13), adopting an objective test.
[35] eg *Commissioner, Western Australia Police v Dormann* (1997) FLC 92-766 (Australia); *Gabbai v Gabbai* (n 4).
[36] *Re K (Abduction: Consent* (n 11); *P v P* [1998] 2 FLR 835; *Re G and A* (n 3).
[37] More weight will usually be attached to these actions than to the left-behind parent's later evidence about his state of mind, *Re H (Abduction: Acquiescence)* (n 6) 88.
[38] *Nicolson v Pappalardo* 605 F.3d 100 (1st Cir 2010).
[39] ibid 108.

hand, if the test is subjective it is difficult to see how a person can intend to waive his rights if he is unaware of their existence.[40] Accordingly, it would seem necessary to show that the left-behind parent knew about the remedy available to him under the Abduction Convention. On the other hand, it seems unduly burdensome to require the abductor to check whether the left-behind parent was aware of his rights before acting in reliance on that parent's consent or acquiescence.[41]

The case law is not consistent. Some judges have favoured a narrow approach under which it is necessary for the left-behind parent to have specific knowledge of remedies under the Convention.[42] However, more support can be found for a wider approach under which it is sufficient that the left-behind parent is aware in general terms of his rights against the abductor.[43] Thus, it is not necessary to show that he knows the 'the full or precise nature of his legal rights under the Convention'.[44] The Israeli Supreme Court has gone further, holding that there is a presumption that a parent, who knows that his child has been abducted, is aware of his legal rights or at least knows that he should obtain legal advice.[45]

Whilst it is clear that a parent who is given incorrect legal advice will not be treated as acquiescing under the narrow approach, it is not clear how such a situation will be treated under the wider approach. On the one hand, obiter dicta suggest that actions based on completely misleading legal advice cannot be treated as acquiescence.[46] On the other hand, in the case of *Leibovitz*,[47] the Israeli Supreme Court held that there had been acquiescence, even though the father had not been told by his lawyer of the possibility of obtaining an order for the return of the child.

In practice, the author has not found a case where the courts have held that there has not been consent or acquiescence because the left-behind parent was unaware of his rights, whether or not he specifically knew about the Convention.[48]

D Need for Reliance

The question arises as to whether the abductor has to show that he relied on the left-behind parent's consent or acquiescence. While it seems clear that consent or acquiescence only crystallises where the abductor is aware of it[49] and genuinely believes that there has been

---

[40] Or in the words of Lord Donaldson in *Re A (Minors) (Abduction: Custody Rights)* (n 27), 'a person cannot acquiesce in a wrongful act if he does not know of the act or does not know that it is wrongful'.
[41] See comment of Scott JA in *Smith v Smith* (n 34), 'it strikes me as quite unfair to require the respondent, who bears the onus, to establish what was said or not said in the course of privileged conversations between the appellant and his legal advisers'.
[42] eg per Balcolme LJ (dissenting) in *Re A (Minors) (Abduction: Custody Rights)* (n 27).
[43] eg *Re AZ* (n 20); *Re A* (n 27); *W v W (Child Abduction: Acquiescence)* [1993] 2 FLR 211; *Re S (Abduction: Acquiescence)* (n 18). However, it should be borne in mind that some of these cases were decided before the adoption of the subjective approach by the House of Lords in *Re H (Abduction: Acquiescence)* (n 6), which may be seen as casting doubt on the wider approach; Beaumont and McEleavy (n 23) 119.
[44] *Re A (Minors) (Abduction: Custody Rights)* (n 27) (Stuart-Smith LJ).
[45] *Leibovitz* (n 14).
[46] *Re S (Abduction: Acquiescence)* (n 18). The Court of Appeal agreed that it would be difficult to treat the actions based on the incorrect legal advice given by the first solicitor as acquiescence, but held that the actions after the advice of the second solicitor did amount to acquiescence.
[47] *Leibovitz* (n 14).
[48] cf dissenting opinion of Balcolme LJ in *RE A (Minors) (Abduction: Custody Rights)* (n 27).
[49] *Gabbai* (n 4) [21]; Similarly, the majority of the Jerusalem District Court in *YM v AM* (n 15) held that the need for 'absorption' of a unilateral legal action is a fundamental principle in Israeli law.

consent[50] or acquiescence,[51] it is unclear whether the abductor has to show that he actually changed his position in reliance thereof. Since, in the case of consent, the removal or retention itself is invariably evidence of reliance,[52] the discussion will be confined to acquiescence.

One UK High Court judge cast doubt on the need to show actual reliance. In his words:

> This is not estoppel. Even if the mother had done nothing further, where there were clear and unequivocal actions or words that led the mother to believe he was not asserting or going to assert his right to summary return of the children that might well be sufficient.[53]

On the other hand, in holding that the defence of acquiescence has been established, courts do usually expressly refer to the fact that the abductor has relied on the acquiescence.[54] Indeed, Beaumont and McEleavy state categorically that acquiescence will not be inferred where no reliance was placed on the words of the dispossessed parent.[55] Nonetheless, the current author has not found a case where the claim of acquiescence failed solely because the abductor failed to show reliance.

E Irrevocability

It seems undisputed that consent and acquiescence are irrevocable.[56] Any other conclusion would make the defence redundant because by definition it will only be raised where the left-behind parent has changed his mind and petitioned for the return of the child, despite the fact that he previously consented to or acquiesced in the change of the status quo.

However, if reliance is required in order for consent or acquiescence to crystallise, then logically consent or acquiescence could be revoked at any time before the abductor has relied on them.[57] Moreover, even if there is no general requirement of reliance, there does not seem to be any reason why consent cannot be revoked before the wrongful removal or retention.[58] If this revocation involves violating an agreement between the parties, the wronged party has to seek remedies for that violation. However, he cannot justify removing or retaining the child in reliance on the consent which he already knows has been revoked. In any event, even where the defence is established, the length of time which has passed between the consent or acquiescence and the attempted revocation, together with the degree of reliance will be of relevance in the exercise of the court's discretion to return the child.[59]

---

[50] *T v T (Abduction: Consent)* [1999] 1 FLR 916. In *Currier v Currier* 845 F Supp 916 (DNH 1994), the mother's signature on a document according the father sole legal custody of the child was not considered consent inter alia because the father knew full well that the mother wished to continue to exercise custody; See also *Re P-J* (n 1), discussed below at III C.

[51] *Re A (Minors: Abduction)* [1991] 2 FLR 241. In *Re H (Abduction: Child of 16)* [2000] 2 FLR 51, it was held that the fact that the abducting mother had tried to prevent communication with the father suggests that she knew that he did not acquiesce.

[52] *cf Zenel v Hadow* 1993 SC 612, where the majority held that consent given 15 months earlier as the basis for an attempted reconciliation sufficed to establish the Article 13(1)(a) defence, even though the removal had not been based on this consent.

[53] Per Sumner J in *A v A (Children) (Abduction: Acquiescence)* [2003] EWHC 3102 (FAM).

[54] eg, *YM v AM* (n 15) [73] of Justice Drori's opinion.

[55] Beaumont and McEleavy (n 23) 121.

[56] See eg *Re A (Minors) (Abduction: Custody Rights)* (n 27); *Leibovitz* (n 14) [10].

[57] See *Re P-J* (n 1), and discussion at Ciii below.

[58] *Re P-J* ibid [48].

[59] *Re A (Minors) (Abduction: Custody Rights)* (n 27); *Kilah v Director-General, Department of Community Services* (2008) FAm CAFC 81 (Aus). See generally Part IV below.

III Specific Situations

A Vitiating Factors

It is clear that any consent or acquiescence must be real, in the sense that there must not be any defect in the left-behind parent's agreement to waive rights, which would vitiate the consent.[60] Thus, the defence will not be established where the left-behind parent's agreement was based on a mistake or was secured by deceit, misrepresentation, duress or undue pressure.[61] The question of whether any of these vitiating factors exist is a question of fact to be decided in each case.[62] The difficulty in determining when there is a defect in expressly given consent,[63] is illustrated well by the recent Israeli case of *ShB-H v OB-H*. The father claimed inter alia that his consent to the child staying in Israel was vitiated by the pressure he was under to get the stop order which had been issued against him lifted, so that he could return to his commitments in the US on the return flight he had booked. This claim was accepted by the Family Court judge,[64] but was rejected in the Supreme Court[65] on the basis that in negotiations each party is subject to pressures and that there was no evidence in this case that the pressure overcame the father's free will or prevented him from exercising judgment.[66]

B Statements Made During Negotiations

Courts will generally not treat statements made during negotiations as evidence of consent or acquiescence.[67] This principle applies both where the negotiations are for the voluntary return of the child[68] and where the negotiations relate to the conditions upon which the left-behind parent is prepared to agree to the child staying in the state of refuge.[69] In

---

[60] *T v T* (n 50); *Gabbai* (n 4) [21].

[61] ibid; *Re B (A Minor) (Abduction)* [1994] 2 FLR 249; *Currier* (n 50).

[62] See, eg *BT v JRT* (n 2), where the judge found that there had not been any deceit. In *Director-General, Dept of Community Services & Bindle* [2009] FamCA 122 (Australia), the fact that the mother had not told the father of the exact day of departure, for fear that he may withdraw his consent, was held not to vitiate the consent that the father had clearly given.

[63] See eg FamA (Dist-JLM) 2059/07 *Ploni v Almonit*, Nevo, 1 July 2007 (Isr), in which the Court rejected the father's claim that his consent to the children staying in Israel was based on deceit, and accepted the mother's evidence that she had only decided to end the marriage after the consent was given. With respect, since the evidence showed that the father had consented in order to save the marriage, it is difficult to accept that his consent was not conditional upon the continuation of the marriage, at least until he joined the family in Israel.

[64] FamC (NAZ) 54043-08-10 *ShB-H v OB-H*, Nevo, 21 December 2010 (Isr).

[65] *OB-H v ShB-H* (n 5) [32].

[66] It might also be added that the father could have attempted to get the stop order lifted by offering appropriate financial guarantees and/or other undertakings. However, The Superior Court of New Jersey in *Ben-Haim v Ben-Haim*, appeal Docketed No FD 02-906-11 (NJ Super Ct Aug 25, 2011) preferred the approach of the Israeli Family Court judge and refused to award comity to the Israeli Supreme Court's no-return order inter alia on the basis that the defence of consent could not be established where negotiations had taken place between the parties in a situation 'laden with duress'.

[67] *P v P* (n 36); CA (SC) 7994/98 *Dagan v Dagan* 53(3) PD 254 [INCADAT cite: HC/E/IL807].

[68] *Re H (Abduction: Acquiescence)* (n 6); *H v H* [1995] 13 FRNZ 498; *Wanninger v Wanninger*, 850 F Supp 78 (D Mass, 1994).

[69] *Walker v Walker* 2012 US App LEXIS 23505 (16 November 2012); *Dagan* (n 67); FamC 4810/05 (JLM) *CA v CSh* Nevo, 8 April 2005 (Isr).

the former situation, the fact that the left-behind parent chooses to use persuasion or mediation to get the child back should not be interpreted as waiving his right to demand return under the Abduction Convention, although there will come a point where failure to institute proceedings may be seen as acquiescence.[70]

In the latter situation, the fact that the left-behind parent is prepared to consider the possibility of a change in the status quo which existed before the abduction should not be treated as consent or acquiescence for two reasons. Firstly, until the negotiations crystallise into a binding agreement, the left-behind parent's agreement to a change in the status quo is not unequivocal; it is conditional upon the abductor agreeing to his terms.[71] Secondly, treating statements made during negotiations as evidence of consent or acquiescence is liable to discourage parties from entering into such negotiations.[72] Such a situation is inconsistent with the general policy of encouraging the private ordering of family disputes and with the specific policy of encouraging voluntary return and mediations which has been adopted by successive Special Commissions.[73]

Nonetheless, in the recent case of *OB-H v ShB-H*, the majority of the Israeli Supreme Court was prepared to find consent or acquiescence[74] on the basis of a final draft agreement between the parties in which it was agreed that the child would stay in Israel. Justice Arbel justified her finding of consent on the basis that even though the agreement had not been signed, because the mother was having second thoughts about the financial provisions, the mother had started to execute the agreement by agreeing to the lifting of the stop order, which she had obtained against the father. Thus, the majority of the Court took the view that the father's acceptance of the draft agreement could be treated as consent or acquiescence for the purposes of Article 13(1)(a).[75] The claim that this decision would have the negative effect of discouraging parents from negotiating[76] was rejected on the basis that the case turned on its specific and unique facts.[77] Nonetheless, the case has caused considerable difficulties for practitioners who are not sure to what extent they should negotiate and cannot give clear-cut advice as to the implications of negotiations that have already taken place.

C Advance Consent

In a number of cases, the question has arisen whether consent has to be given immediately prior to the removal or whether consent can be given to removal at some unspecified time in the future, or upon the happening of some future event. The better view seems to be that

---

[70] *Re H (Abduction: Acquiescence)* (n 6).
[71] Per Justice Fogelman (dissenting) in *OB-H v ShB-H* (n 5) [3] approved in *Ben-Haim* (n 66). See also *BT v JRT* (n 2), where it was made clear that the conditions for the consent or acquiescence must be intended to be binding on both parties.
[72] *OB-H v ShB-H* (n 5) [5].
[73] Good Practice Guide on Mediation, www.hcch.net/upload/guide28mediation_en.pdf, 15-16.
[74] *OB-H v ShB-H* (n 5).
[75] But see criticism of this decision by the New Jersey Court in *Ben-Haim* (n 66) on the basis that an unexecuted agreement cannot constitute consent.
[76] As claimed in the dissent of Fogelman J and by the Israeli Central Authority, which supported the father's request for an additional review of this case.
[77] Per Rivlin J refusing the request for an additional review, ACH (SC) 4117/11 *ShB-H v OB-H* 12 July 2011 (Isr) http://elyon1.court.gov.il/files/11/170/041/p05/11041170.p05.pdf.

consent may be given in advance,[78] but that it is necessary to check that the consent is still in force at the time of the removal.[79] This means inter alia that the consent can be revoked before the removal.[80] Furthermore, if the consent is conditional upon the occurrence of a particular event, that event has to be reasonably capable of objective ascertainment.[81]

In the case of *Re P-J (Children)*,[82] the father persuaded the mother to return with the children to Spain after an extended stay in the UK, by agreeing that if things did not work out she could leave with the children. The Court of Appeal upheld the finding of the President of the Family Division that this consent was no longer subsisting, when she removed the children two months after their return.[83] The Court put considerable emphasis on the fact that the removal had been carried out clandestinely, which was evidence that the mother had real doubts as to whether the father did still consent to the removal.

Similarly, in an Israeli case,[84] the majority of the District Court held that an agreement signed by the father, in which he undertook not to apply to any court in relation to the child and not to prevent the mother from returning with the child to Israel at any time, was no longer subsisting at the time of the wrongful removal a year and a half later. However, in a dissenting opinion, Justice Amit took the view that the consent was still valid since the mother had agreed to come to the US for the purposes of reconciliation, and later to stay in the US with the child, despite the failure of the reconciliation, in reliance on this agreement.

D Statements Made in Immediate Aftermath of the Removal or Retention

Since the adoption of the subjective approach, courts are likely to view with suspicion statements made, or actions taken, by the left-behind parent immediately after the removal or retention on the basis that these statements were made impulsively at a time of emotional turmoil and do not accurately reflect that parent's will.[85] Accordingly, where the court takes the view that such statements or actions do amount to acquiescence, it will often expressly comment that the parent was not in a state of emotional turmoil at the relevant time.[86]

In the case of *A v A (Children) (Abduction: Acquiescence)*,[87] Sumner J seems to have widened this category of cases to include situations in which the left-behind parent did have some time to digest the fact of the removal or retention, but there are circumstances which explain his apparent acquiescence. In this case, the Court accepted the father's claim that

---

[78] But cf G Maher, 'Consent to Wrongful Child Abduction Under the Hague Convention' (1993) *Scots Law Times* 1993, 281 (claiming that consistency with the other defences in Article 13(1)(a) requires that the consent defence must relate to a specific removal).
[79] *Re P-J* (n 1) [48].
[80] ibid.
[81] ibid.
[82] ibid.
[83] The Court cast doubt on the correctness of the earlier decision of the Scottish Inner House in *Zenel v Hadow* (n 52); See also Israeli Family Court case of FamC (RLZ) 41179-08-11 *EA v SA* Nevo 11 December 2011, in which it was held that an agreement between the parties, before travelling to the US for a two-year work assignment, that if either of them wanted to return to Israel then the family would return, had not been revoked and so constituted consent to a removal nearly two years later.
[84] FamA (HA) 218/02 *Ploni v Plonit* Nevo, 15 January 2003 (Isr).
[85] *Re H (Abduction: Acquiescence)* (n 6), 89–90.
[86] eg *BT v JRT* (n 2) and *Re A (Minors) (Abduction: Custody Rights)* [1992] 2 FLR 14, 27.
[87] (n 53).

he had appeared to acquiesce because he feared that the children would disappear otherwise. However, this sort of explanation is only likely to be accepted where the parent has acted relatively quickly to recover the children, in this case within five weeks.

E Pursuance of Other Remedies

Pursuance of remedies other than return under the Abduction Convention might be seen as a waiver of the right to immediate return. In the case of In re H (Abduction: Acquiescence),[88] which involved children who were abducted from Israel to England, the father, who was an ultra-Orthodox Jew, first turned to the Rabbinical Court in Israel. Only six months later, when this Court's orders had failed to result in the return of the children, did he apply to the English court under the Abduction Convention. The Court of Appeal held that the resort to the Rabbinical Court indicated that the father had waived his rights to immediate return and thus the acquiescence defence was established, but the decision was overturned on appeal on the basis that this interpretation of the facts did not reflect the father's subjective intention. However, as Beaumont and McEleavy point out,[89] even on an objective analysis, the fact that the father chose a different route to secure the return of the children, in accordance with his religious beliefs, did not indicate any waiver of his right to demand their return under the Convention. Of course, if the father had continued to pursue this alternative route for a longer period of time, it might have been possible to infer waiver of those rights. Accordingly, pursuance of other remedies will only be treated as acquiescence where it is accompanied by statements or actions which demonstrate waiver of the right to the summary return of the child or where such waiver can be inferred from the lapse of time.[90]

F Actions for the Benefit of the Children

Sometimes after the abduction, the left-behind parent performs acts which could be read as acquiescing in the child remaining in the country of refuge. For example, he may agree to the registration of the child in kindergarten or school;[91] he may agree to the provision of health care services to the child[92] or he may send clothes and toys for the children.[93] However, the fact that a parent wants to promote the welfare of the child in the interim period, while the child remains in the country of refuge, does not necessarily mean that he has waived his rights to summary return. Thus, such actions should be interpreted as reflecting concern of the left-behind parent for the child, wherever this is a plausible explanation.[94] A parent should not be penalised for caring about his child. However, where there are other indications that the left-behind parent does not intend to seek the return of the child, such as express statements or passivity over a long period of time, these beneficial actions might help support a finding of acquiescence.

---

[88] Re H (Abduction: Acquiescence) (n 6).
[89] Beaumont and McEleavy (n 23) 118.
[90] Therefore, submitting an application for custody in the requested State, expressed to be without prejudice to the applicant's rights under the Abduction Convention is not acquiescence, RK v JK (n 19).
[91] eg, Gabbai (n 4).
[92] ibid.
[93] eg Dimer (n 13).
[94] Gabbai (n 4) [20].

G Inaction

Acquiescence will be inferred from silence and inactivity over a prolonged period of time. There are no firm rules on the necessary period of time which needs to elapse before acquiescence will be found and this will depend on all the circumstances of each case.[95] Thus, a shorter period may suffice where there is other evidence indicating acquiescence. For example, in a recent Israeli case, the nine-month delay on the part of the father in commencing proceedings for the return of his children was compared with the speed with which he initiated proceedings in the Israeli court objecting to the circumcision of his sons. Even though the latter proceedings took place after the wrongful removal, he made no protest about this to any of the authorities involved.[96]

The test is subjective and so the court has to assess what the left-behind parent was thinking during the period before he took action.[97] However, the intention of the parent will inevitably be interpreted from the facts[98] and the longer the period that has elapsed,[99] the easier it will be to infer acquiescence unless the left-behind parent can provide a convincing explanation for the delay in taking action to secure the return of the child.

Explanations for delay which have been accepted include poor legal advice,[100] employment and medical problems[101] and being misled by the abductor as to the nature of the visit abroad.[102]

H Acquiescence Following Initiation of Proceedings

The question has arisen as to whether the withdrawal of proceedings or non-enforcement of a return order can amount to acquiescence.

In the case of *Re G (Abduction: Withdrawal of Proceedings, Acquiescence and Habitual Residence)*,[103] the father had withdrawn his application for the return of his child when the parties had agreed to attempt a reconciliation. When this failed, the father issued a second return petition under the Abduction Convention. The mother's claim that the father's withdrawal of the first proceedings amounted to acquiescence was rejected because the father had not subjectively intended to acquiesce and the mother had not been led to believe otherwise.

---

[95] *Re H (Abduction: Acquiescence)* (n 6), 87–88; *AQ v JQ*, 12 December 2001, transcript, Outer House of the Court of Session [INCADAT cite: HC/E/UKs 415].

[96] RFamA (SC) 8540/11 *DC v YAC* 1 December 2011 (Isr) http://elyon1.court.gov.il/files/11/400/085/z02/11085400.z02.pdf.

[97] In *Re H (Abduction: Acquiescence)* (n 6); *Re K (Abduction: Child's Objections)* [1995] 1 FLR 977, where it was held that a delay of six months in starting proceedings did not constitute acquiescence where it was clear that the father sought the return of the children.

[98] In the Israeli case of FamA (JLM) 621/04 *DY v DR* Nevo, 18 November 2004 (Isr) [INCADAT cite: HC/E/IL 833, the fact that the father had not seen the girls for the past year and a half, even though he had been given the opportunity to do so, was held to constitute acquiescence with the current situation, despite the fact that he was pursuing proceedings under the Abduction Convention.

[99] eg *W v W* (n 43); *Leibovitz* (n 14) (10 months).

[100] eg *Soucie v Soucie* 1995 SC 134; *Re S (Minors)(Abduction: Acquiescence)* [1994] 1 FLR 819.

[101] *MM v AMR or M* 2003 SCLR 71.

[102] *Re H (Abduction: Child of 16)* (n 51).

[103] *Re G* (n 34).

In the Israeli case of *RK v ChK*,[104] the father obtained a return order in respect of his three children who had been wrongfully removed by the mother. Several days after the ruling, he took his son back to the United States, but did not make any attempt to enforce the order in relation to his two daughters and did not contact them for four months. The mother's appeal from the return order was allowed in relation to the girls on the basis that the father had waived his right to the summary return of the girls. Justice Drori held that if a parent who has not taken any action to bring about the return of his child can be considered to acquiesce in a removal, a fortiori a parent who has obtained a court ruling providing for return and does not seek to rely on it, should be treated as acquiescing.

IV Exercise of Discretion

A The Nature of the Discretion

The fact that the establishment of a defence does not automatically lead to the refusal of return was quite often overlooked in the earlier consent and acquiescence cases.[105] However, over the last decade, more attention has been paid to the discretion and to the way in which it ought to be exercised.

There are two possible approaches to the exercise of discretion in consent and acquiescence cases. Under a narrow approach, the court would exercise its discretion only on the basis of considerations directly connected to the consent or acquiescence, such as the impact of the delay in instituting proceedings on the child, where there has been such a delay, or the disruption to the new status quo, created in reliance on the consent/acquiescence.[106] In contrast, under a wide approach, the gate is opened completely and the court can take into account all considerations relating to the welfare of the child, even though these are not in any way related to the consent or acquiescence.[107] The latter approach seems to have been almost universally adopted and Baroness Hale has said that the discretion is 'at large'.[108] Some of the cases provide a list of relevant factors,[109] but these are not to be treated as exhaustive and courts do not always refer to all the factors. The weight to be given to the respective criteria seems to be flexible. Sometimes, one factor seems to be dominant. At other times, the court gains an overall impression from the evidence in relation to all the criteria. In some cases, the court has indicated that it has not found it easy to decide how to exercise its discretion.[110]

---

[104] FamA (JLM) 592/04 *RK v ChK*, Tak-Mech 04(4), 2608 [INCADAT cite: HC/E/IL 837].

[105] See eg *Zenel v Hadow* (n 52); similarly, no mention is made of discretion in *Re D (Abduction: Acquiescence)* [1998] 2 FLR 335 or the Israeli case of *YM v AM* (n 15).

[106] *Leibovitz* (n 14), where emphasis was placed on the fact that as a result of the father's acquiescence, which had been in the form of participating in court proceedings in Israel over a period of 18 months, it was not in the child's best interests to order return.

[107] In *Re A (Minors) (Abduction) (No 2)* [1993] 1 All ER 272, 278, the Court of Appeal rejected the narrow approach, praying in support the final paragraph of Art 13 which states that 'in considering the circumstances referred to in this Article, the judicial authorities shall take into account the information relating to the social background of the child ...'.

[108] *Re M (Abduction: Zimbabwe)* (n 7) [42]. In Australia, the discretion has been referred to as 'unconfined except in so far as a particular consideration is extraneous', *Kilah v Department of Community Services* (n 59) [28].

[109] eg *W v W* (n 43).

[110] eg *Kilah* (n 59) [33].

Perhaps surprisingly, few cases expressly mention burden of proof. Those that do make it clear that the abducted parent has to satisfy the court that the child should not be returned.[111] In addition, comments made in some cases about the need to uphold the underlying policy of the Convention suggest that the burden will be on the abducting parent to show why return will be contrary to the welfare of the child[112] or why, for some other reason, the policy of the Convention does not require that the child should be returned in this particular case or that there are considerations which override the policy of the Convention.

Nonetheless, the reported case law suggests that courts do not often order return where one of the defences is made out. However, it should be borne in mind that decisions on discretion are not always published. In particular, where an appeal court has, allowing the abductor's appeal, held that the consent or acquiescence defence is established, it may remit the case to the first instance court to exercise the discretion to return.[113]

B The Relevant Factors

i Welfare of the Child

The welfare of the child is always treated as an important factor, but not necessarily the paramount consideration.[114] Accordingly, courts will not get involved in a detailed best interests analysis, as if making a decision on the merits of the custody dispute. The extent to which it will be appropriate to investigate welfare considerations will vary from case to case.[115]

In practice, in many cases the abductor has already offered evidence about the welfare issues in pursuance of her alternative claim that the grave risk exception exists. Where the acquiescence or consent defence is established, the court will rely on this evidence when exercising its discretion, even though no decision has been made in relation to the grave risk exception[116] or it has been rejected. For example, in the Israeli case of *OB-H v ShB-H*,[117] the mother had invoked the grave risk exception on the basis that her position in the US would be vulnerable, since she would only have a tourist visa, and that she had always been the primary carer of her very young daughter. The Court held that the grave risk exception was not established, but that there had been consent or acquiescence. It then proceeded to rely on the mother's claims in relation to the welfare of the child when exercising its discretion and refused to order return.

In determining the effect which the return is likely to have on the child's welfare,[118] the court will consider both the degree to which he has become settled in the state of refuge[119]

---

[111] In *Re A (Minors) (Abduction: Custody Rights) (No 2)* [1993] Fam 1.
[112] eg *Townsend & Director-General, Department of Families, Youth and Community* [1999] 24 Fam LR 495.
[113] eg *Re AZ* (n 20).
[114] *Re A (No 2)* (n 111), 282 (Scott LJ).
[115] *Re M (Abduction: Zimbabwe)* (n 7) [44].
[116] eg *Re R (Abduction: Consent)* [1999] 1 FLR 828.
[117] (n 5).
[118] This was listed as a separate factor by Waite J in *W v W* (n 43).
[119] eg *B-G v B-G (Abduction: Acquiescence)* [2008] EWHC 688 (Fam); *BT v JRT* (n 2); *Re D (Abduction: Acquiescence)* [1999] 1 FLR 36; *Townsend v Department of Families, Youth and Community* (n 112). See also comment of Wall J in *Re L (A Minor) (Abduction: Jurisdiction)* [2002] 1 WLR 3208 [65] that delay in the resolution of the proceedings is relevant.

and the situation awaiting the child and abductor on return to the country of origin.[120] Accordingly, violent behaviour on the part of the applicant, even if not sufficient to establish the grave risk exception, will be relevant to the exercise of the discretion.[121] Similarly, significant weight has been placed on the lack of a home and financial support for the children in the country of origin.[122] In assessing the likely effect of return, account will be taken of any undertakings offered by the applicant[123] or conditions which can be imposed by the court.[124]

Courts have also been prepared to consider factors not directly related to the child in question, but which are liable to have an influence on his welfare. For example, in the Australian case of *Department of Community Services & Bindle*,[125] the Court took into account the fact that the return of the child to New Zealand would involve the mother having to leave behind her older son with his father in Australia and that this would have an impact on the mother's emotional state and her ability to care for the child.[126]

ii The Forum Conveniens

Lord Donaldson seems to have treated the issue of appropriateness of forum as the sole factor in the exercise of the discretion.[127] However, he did include the child's welfare within this factor by holding that return should only be refused where the interests of the child renders it appropriate that the courts of the requested State rather than the courts of the requesting State should determine the child's future.[128]

While this approach has not been widely adopted, in a number of cases the fact that the country of origin is the *forum conveniens* has been the decisive factor in favour of a return order.[129] Furthermore, appropriateness of forum is invariably mentioned as an important factor either directly[130] or indirectly. For example, in the Israeli case of *OB-H v ShB-H*,[131] the Court took into account the relative weakness of the parties' connection to the USA in comparison with their connection to Israel and the fact that their stay there was temporary. These facts are clearly relevant to the relative appropriateness of the competing fora.

In some cases, the fact that substantive proceedings have already been commenced in one of the courts may be relevant because that court will be able to resolve the dispute

---

[120] *W v W* (n 43).
[121] eg *BT v JRT* (n 2); *Re R* (116).
[122] In *Re A (No 2)* (n 111); *Re S (Abduction: Acquiescence)* (n 18).
[123] See eg *Re C (Abduction: Consent)* (n 12); In *Re D (Abduction: Discretionary Return)* (n 8), the Court took into account the mother's agreement that the children could live with the father in France until he could apply to the Court for an interim court order. Conversely, in *B-G v B-G* (n 119), the Court took into account the fact that the father had not offered sufficient undertakings to ensure the wellbeing of the mother and the children in France. Similarly, in *BT v JRT* (n 2), the Court noted that the undertakings of the father could give the mother little comfort in light of his previously violent behaviour.
[124] In *Kilah* (n 59) [95], the Court clearly stated that return should be ordered provided that the financial arrangements which it ordered could be arranged within a reasonable time.
[125] *D-G v Bindle* (n 62).
[126] It is perhaps significant that the mother only agreed to the older child moving from New Zealand to Australia with his father because the younger son's father had consented to her taking him to Australia.
[127] *Re A (Minors) (Abduction: Custody Rights)* (n 86), 29.
[128] ibid.
[129] See *U v D* [2002] NZFLR 529; *Re D (Abduction: Discretionary Return)* (n 8); *Kilah* (n 59) [34].
[130] eg *Re K (Abduction: Consent)* (n 11); *W v W* (n 43); *U v D* (n 129).
[131] *OB-H v ShB-H* (n 5).

more speedily.[132] In some cases, the issue of choice of forum is evenly balanced and then the discretion will have to be exercised on the basis of the other factors.[133]

iii Likely Outcome of Substantive Proceedings in the State of Habitual Residence

The fact that the foreign court is likely to give custody to the abducting parent and to allow her to relocate back to the country of refuge has been treated as a weighty consideration against ordering return in a number of cases.[134] The double dislocation involved in such a scenario is seen as creating unnecessary disruption to the child.

However, this factor does not always seem to be taken into account. For example, in the Australian case of *Kilah v Director-General, Department of Community Services*,[135] a simple enquiry into Israeli law would have revealed that the mother had a very high chance of being awarded custody and that Israeli courts invariably allow custodial mothers to relocate.[136]

iv Consequences of the Acquiescence

As seen above, on a narrow approach to the discretion, this would be the sole factor. Whilst the wide approach takes into account a variety of other factors, considerable weight may still be attached to the consequences of the acquiescence.[137] Thus, any delay caused in initiating proceedings is taken into account.[138] Conversely, where the left-behind parent reneged on his consent or acquiescence quickly and it is still possible to effect a speedy return, then return may well serve both the interests of the child and the policy of the Convention.[139]

v Underlying Policy of the Convention

The purpose and philosophy of the Convention are invariably mentioned in one form or another.[140] Some judges take the view that the policy of the Convention requires that the court should only exercise its discretion to refuse return in exceptional cases.[141] However, this view has now been authoritatively crushed by Baroness Hale, stating 'The circumstances in which return may be refused are themselves exceptions to the general rule. That in itself is sufficient exceptionality. It is neither necessary nor desirable to import an additional gloss into the Convention'.[142]

Whilst the policy of the Convention is usually taken as ensuring the swift return of abducted children to the country of origin, the extent to which this policy applies in cases

---

[132] eg *B-G* (n 119) (proceedings well advanced in UK) and *Re D (Abduction: Discretionary Return)* (n 8), 37 (extant order in France).

[133] eg *Re S (Abduction: Acquiescence)* (n 18), 124.

[134] eg *W v W* (n 43); *Re S (Abduction: Acquiescence)*(ibid); *BT v JRT* (n 2), See also *B-G* (n 119) where it was said that a French court was unlikely to order return to the UK.

[135] *Kilah* (n 59).

[136] See generally in ch 4. Rather, the judge seems to have regarded the issue as equivocal, no doubt reflecting the Australian position on relocation (ibid).

[137] This factor is included in the list of considerations in *W v W* (n 43).

[138] See eg *Re S (Abduction: Acquiescence)* (n 18) (child in UK 11 months); *Smith v Smith* (n 34). In *Re D (Abduction: Acquiescence)* (n 119), 53, delay was also stated to be relevant because it runs contrary to the philosophy of the Convention.

[139] See eg *Kilah* (n 59). See also the obiter comment of Justice Marcus in the Israeli case of *CA v CSh* (n 69), that even if acquiescence had been established, the Court would have ordered return in light of the short period of time which had elapsed since the children arrived in Israel (less than four months).

[140] In *W v W* (n 43), Waite J referred to 'the overall effect on the Convention of not making a return order'.

[141] See cases cited by Baroness Hale in *Re M (Abduction: Zimbabwe)* (n 7) [34].

[142] ibid [40].

of consent and acquiescence may be questioned. Hale J (as she then was) said, in *Re R (Abduction: Consent)*,[143] that 'in a case where there has been agreement to the children coming to this country, the policy that they should be returned to their home State for their future to be decided there carries much less weight than it would in other cases'.[144]

Lord Donaldson has stated that it is the policy of Convention that 'wrongful removal or retention shall not confer any benefit or advantage on the person who has committed the wrongful act'.[145] This policy is clearly inappropriate in the context of consent because the act is not really wrongful and only treated as such in order to preserve the coherence of the Convention.[146] Even in relation to acquiescence, in which context the comment was made, it can be argued that the acquiescence turns a wrongful removal into a lawful one and that it is equally unjust to allow the left-behind parent to change his mind after the abductor has relied on his waiver of his rights. Indeed, Justice Amit in the Israeli District Court held that return should be refused on the basis of justice in a case where the father violated his written agreement, on which the mother had relied, that she could come back to Israel with the child whenever she wanted.[147] Accordingly, the policy should be defined neutrally as doing justice between the parties rather than as not giving a reward to the abducting parent.

In summary, when exercising the discretion to return in cases of consent and acquiescence, courts should take care to define the policy of the Convention in a way which is suited to such cases and not assume that the generally accepted purpose and philosophy, which are premised on non-consensual removals and retentions, apply without modification.

V Analysis

A Internal Coherence

The consent defence in Article 13(1)(a) gives rise to a logical difficulty, expressed by a judge recently in the following rhetorical question: 'If a left-behind parent with rights of custody gave consent ... to the child's removal, how can he successfully complain that it was in breach of his rights within the meaning of art 3 of the Convention?'[148] Similarly, it could be argued, although rather less convincingly, that where there has been acquiescence, the removal or retention has ceased to be wrongful. Accordingly, in such cases, the conditions for triggering the mandatory return mechanism would not exist. However, such an approach would render the consent, and perhaps also the acquiescence, defence in Article 13(1)(a) redundant.[149] This problem has been described as a conundrum, caused by poor draftsmanship, to which there is no good answer.[150]

---

[143] (n 116), 826. See also her comment in the earlier case of *Re K (Abduction: Consent)* (n 11), that where there had been consent, the possibility of frustrating the Convention scarcely arose.
[144] But *cf* her Ladyship's later comment in *Re M (Abduction: Zimbabwe)* (n 7), discussed below at V F.
[145] *Re A (Minors) (Abduction: Custody Rights)* (n 86), 29.
[146] See *Re D (Abduction: Discretionary Return)* (Wilson J) (n 8), 36.
[147] *Ploni v Plonit* (n 84).
[148] *Re P-J* (n 1) [53] (Wilson LJ).
[149] An additional problem is that the applicant would have to prove absence of consent – 'a negative' as a prerequisite to obtaining relief. *Re P (A Child)* (n 9) [22].
[150] *Re P-J* (n 1) [53]. A similar conundrum arises in relation to the defence of non-exercise of custody rights. See discussion above in chapter 7 at IVA2

One solution, suggested by the English Court of Appeal, is that the specificity of the reference to consent in Article 13(1)(a) draws all issues of consent into it and out of Article 3.[151] Whether or not they accept this rationale, most judges[152] have felt it necessary to take a pragmatic view[153] and to treat consensual removals and retentions as wrongful for the purposes of Article 3.[154] The Article 13(1)(a) defence is then invoked and the Court considers whether to exercise the discretion to return. This scheme preserves the internal coherence of the Convention.

Another reconciliation which has been suggested[155] is to distinguish between cases where the issue is whether the consent was true consent, which would be dealt with under Article 3, and those where the issue is whether there had been any consent at all, which would come within Article 13(1)(a). This distinction would ensure that the burden of proving that consent given was not real consent would fall on the left-behind parent. However, this approach has been rejected in subsequent case law[156] and by commentators,[157] who point out that even under Article 13(1)(a), where the abductor proves consent, the burden of proving a vitiating factor will pass to the left-behind parent.

A further issue of internal coherence arises with regard to the inter-relationship between Article 13(1)(a) and Article 12(2); mainly in cases where there is alleged to be passive acquiescence. Under Article 13(1)(a), acquiescence may be established even though less than 12 months have passed and even though settlement of the child is not proven. Nonetheless, internal coherence requires that courts take into account the rationale behind the Article 12(2) defence when determining whether there has been passive acquiescence and in the exercise of discretion in acquiescence cases. Accordingly, since the left-behind parent has 12 months in which to invoke the mandatory return mechanism of the Convention, the fact that he does nothing for the first few months after the removal or retention should not be treated as acquiescence.[158] Similarly, even where a much longer period of time has elapsed and acquiescence has been established, if the child has not settled, then the court should carefully consider whether it might still be in the best interests of the child to return to the country of habitual residence.

B Consistency with the Intention of the Drafters

With respect, the Perez-Vera Report[159] does nothing to shed light on the intention of the drafters in relation to the interaction between the Article 13(1)(a) defence and Article 3,

---

[151] *Re P (A Child)* (n 9).
[152] See cases cited above at n 9.
[153] In *Re P-J* (n 1) [43], Ward LJ expressly states that he is leaving the debate as to whether the issue of consent should be considered under Article 3 or Article 13(1)(a) to another day, but that he does not encourage that debate because it is much better to deal with consent 'as a discrete issue' under Article 13(1)(a).
[154] Nonetheless, consent or acquiescence may enable the child's habitual residence to be changed which means that a re-abduction to the original place of habitual residence by the left-behind parent may fall foul of the Convention. See eg *Re S (A Child)* [2002] EWCA Civ 1941. Similarly, in *Re K (Abduction: Consent: Forum Conveniens)* [1995] 2 FLR 211 and in the Australian High Court decision in *LK v Department of Community Services* [2009] HCA 9, (2009) 253 ALR 202), the consensual removal was held to have enabled the children's habitual residence to have changed and thus the Convention did not apply.
[155] *Re O (Abduction: Consent and Acquiescence)* [1997] 1 FLR 924 (Bennett J).
[156] *T v T* (n 50), 918
[157] Beaumont and McEleavy (n 23), 133
[158] *Gabbai* (n 4), 259.
[159] (n 5).

but rather creates further confusion. Firstly, in paragraph 28 of that Report, the defence is described as applying where the person requesting the child's return was not actually exercising his custody rights, 'or if he had subsequently consented to the act which he now seeks to attack'. The omission of any reference there to consent given prior to the removal, together with the comment in paragraph 71 that 'from the Convention's standpoint, the removal of a child by one of the joint holders without the consent of the other is equally wrongful', suggest that consensual removals are not wrongful and thus there is no need to invoke the Article 13(1)(a) defence in such cases. Furthermore, the assertion in paragraph 115 that 'the guardian's conduct can also alter the characterisation of the abductor's action, in cases where he has agreed to, or thereafter acquiesced in, the removal which he now seeks to challenge' could be interpreted to mean that acquiescence turns a wrongful removal into a lawful one. Yet, there is no discussion of how the defence in Article 13(1)(a) can be invoked if the removal is no longer wrongful.

Accordingly, the comments of Professor Perez-Vera should be read as explaining the rationale behind the Article 13(1)(a) defence, rather than as holding that consensual removals are not wrongful. In other words, the fact that consent or acquiescence might appear to change the characterisation of the removal, simply means that there is no duty to return in such cases.

C Promotion of the Objectives of the Convention

i Protecting Abducted Children

The fact that the left-behind parent has consented or acquiesced does not per se mean that the child does not need to be protected from the harmful effects of removal or retention. Thus, it might be thought that a narrow construction of the defence will best protect the child. However, the considerations relevant to the child's need for protection may not necessarily be reflected in the test for acquiescence or consent. For example, where the child has settled in the country of refuge, the fact that the left-behind parent did not intend to acquiesce, but was given incorrect legal advice, does not affect the fact that the child no longer needs to be protected from the removal or retention and that, on the contrary, summary return might cause him harm.

Accordingly, the best way to ensure that the child is returned when he is in need of protection against the harm caused by the removal or retention, and is not returned where this will harm him, is by interpreting consent and acquiescence widely and then exercising the discretion in accordance with the objective of protecting children and promoting their welfare. However, as the discretion is at large, then a wide interpretation of the defence, together with a wide discretion might be seen as creating too much of an inroad into the policy of mandatory return. On the other hand, at the end of the day, provided that the discretion is exercised in accordance with the objectives of the Convention, then return will be ordered, wherever this will indeed protect the child.

ii Deterrence

There might seem to be a need to deter parents from abducting in the belief that the left-behind 'weak' parent will be persuaded to acquiesce in the *fait accompli* afterwards. Such deterrence will best be achieved by setting a stringent standard for acquiescence which checks that there is a genuine and informed waiver of rights. Such an approach also gives a clear message that a wrongful removal or retention cannot be easily legitimised. Similarly, the fact that even where acquiescence is established, the court still has discretion to return should discourage parents from taking the risk.

In contrast, there might not seem to be any need to deter removals and retentions where genuine consent has been given in advance. Nonetheless, requiring the abductor to provide clear evidence of real consent should discourage attempts to 'trick' the left-behind parent into agreeing and encourage relocating parents to obtain written and unequivocal statements of consent.[160] Furthermore, the fact that even where consent is established, the court still has discretion to return might encourage relocating parents to make arrangements which ensure regular contact between the left-behind parent and the child, which will reduce the likelihood that the left-behind parent will later renege on his consent. [161]

iii Adjudication in the Forum Conveniens

On the one hand, the left-behind parent is waiving his right to litigate in the *forum conveniens*. On the other hand, however, the objective of adjudication in the *forum conveniens* is not only designed to protect the left-behind parent, but is also assumed to serve the best interests of the child[162] and even the public interest by ensuring efficiency.[163] Thus, the fact of acquiescence or consent does not make this objective redundant. Accordingly, as most courts seem to have realised, the relative convenience and appropriateness of adjudication in the two fora should be a weighty consideration in exercising discretion where consent or acquiescence has been established. [164]

iv Justice between the Parents and the Rule of Law

It can be argued that where there is consent or acquiescence, then there is no need to order the return of the child in order to achieve justice between the parents or uphold the rule of law because the left-behind parent has agreed a priori or ex post facto to the removal or retention. Moreover, as mentioned above, mandatory return in such cases might actually cause injustice to the abductor by allowing the left-behind parent to manipulate the Convention for his own purposes.

On the other hand, giving a wide interpretation to the defence might well prejudice the left-behind parent. In particular, if statements made during negotiations or actions taken for the benefit of the child are treated as consent or acquiescence, it seems unjust then that his bona fide attempts to promote the welfare of the child will be used against him. Similarly, interpreting the left-behind's action or inaction, without taking into account the emotional turmoil and the quandary in which he finds himself as a result of the abduction, is likely to be unfair to him. Accordingly, the prevalent subjective approach does seem to do justice between the parents. On the other hand, preventing the left-behind parent from withdrawing his consent or acquiescence, in cases where the abductor has not acted to her

---

[160] Per Hale J (as she then was) in *Re K (Abduction: Consent)* (n 11).

[161] See comment of Thorpe LJ in *Re S (A Child)* (n 154) that often the real issue between the parties in Convention cases is not the return of the child but the extent of the contact with the left-behind parent.

[162] R Schuz, 'The Hague Child Abduction Convention: Family Law and Private International Law' (1995) 44 *International And Comparative Law Quarterly* 771,785.

[163] See ch 5 at II Ciii

[164] See IV Bii above .

detriment in reliance on that consent or acquiescence, might be seen as unnecessarily harsh on the left-behind parent.[165]

D Compatibility with the Summary Nature of Convention Proceedings

Almost inevitably, a court will have to decide between the conflicting versions of the parties in order to determine whether the left-behind parent did indeed consent or acquiesce. Often, there will be no other witnesses to the statements alleged to have been made by the left-behind parent and the court will have to base its decision on an assessment of which party's version appears more consistent with the objective facts.[166] Furthermore, since the test is a subjective one, the court will not only have to ascertain what statements were made and/or actions taken, but will also have to determine what the intentions of the left-behind parent were. Some courts, recognising the difficulties of making such findings purely on the basis of affidavit evidence,[167] have allowed oral evidence in consent and acquiescence cases,[168] despite the general approach of not hearing oral testimony in Convention cases in order to prevent delays.

Accordingly in some cases, in which deciding whether there has been consent or acquiescence involves determining disputed issues of fact, which is likely to be time-consuming, it might be more efficient for the court to consider first of all how it would exercise its discretion if the defence were established. If, in any event, the court would return the child, then there is no need to determine definitively whether the defence is established.[169] This might be the situation, for example, where the left-behind parent has revoked the alleged acquiescence or consent very soon after the removal and there are no clear welfare grounds for refusing return. However, in some cases, this approach would not have much real benefit because the facts relevant to determining whether there has been consent or acquiescence are also relevant to the exercise of the discretion.[170]

E Consistency with Rights and Interests of the Child

The fact that the left-behind parent has agreed in advance or ex post facto to the change of habitual residence does not necessarily prevent the removal or retention causing a violation of the child's right to regular contact with both parents and with his right that his best interests should be treated as a primary consideration in decisions concerning him. Whether these rights have been breached will depend inter alia on whether adequate arrangements have been put in place to ensure continuing regular contact with the left-behind parent. The very fact that the left-behind parent seeks to withdraw his consent

---

[165] See II E above.

[166] cf Re P (A Child) (n 9), where the Court allowed the parties to submit reports from handwriting experts as to whether the consent letter had indeed been signed by the father.

[167] In some cases, lawyers' attendance notes have been produced in order to cast light on the left-behind parent's state of mind. See eg Re D (Abduction: Acquiescence) (n 105), 335.

[168] eg, ibid and Dept of Community Services & Bindle (n 62); Re H (Abduction: Acquiescence) (n 6) (Lord Brown Wilkinson); but cf Re R (n 116).

[169] A similar approach can be found in U v D (n 129), in which the judge was not sure whether the mother's letter constituted acquiescence because of the emotional turmoil that she was in at the time. He resolved the dilemma by holding that there was acquiescence, but that the children should be returned.

[170] For example, where the abductor claims that he has changed his position and that of the child in reliance on the alleged consent or acquiescence.

to the removal or retention may well indicate that no such adequate arrangements have been made[171] and/or the left-behind parent's subsequent reservations as to whether the move is indeed in the best interests of the child.

Treating consensual removals and retentions as prima facie wrongful is consistent with the concept that the trigger for the operation of the Convention should be the breach of the child's right to regular contact with both parents[172] and also with the child's right that his best interests should be treated as a primary consideration in decisions concerning him because the other parent's consent may not necessarily promote the interests of the child. However, the defences of consent and acquiescence in Article 13(1)(a) appear to be based on the premise that the function of the Convention is to protect the custody rights of the parents. Thus, the parent may waive this protection. There is no suggestion that the child's right to maintain contact with his parents also needs protecting. The claim that 'first aid' is not required in cases of consent or acquiescence fails to recognise that the child has rights independent of his parents which need to be protected.

Nonetheless, since the court retains a discretion to return, there is room for the child's interests to be given effect to in the exercise of the discretion and for return to be ordered where his interests so require. Of course, it has to be remembered that there will also be acquiescence and consent cases where the child's interests and rights will be infringed by a return because he has become settled in the country of refuge; because of the difficult family situation in the country of origin[173] or for some other reason. Accordingly, the best way to ensure that the Article 13(1)(a) defence is interpreted in accordance with the best interests and rights of the child is to interpret the defence widely and then to exercise the discretion in light of the child's rights and interests. Indeed, in some cases a wide interpretation of this defence may compensate for the violation of the child's rights and interests, caused by an overly narrow interpretation of the grave risk and child objection defences.[174]

We saw above[175] that most courts do place great weight on the child's welfare when exercising the discretion to return in consent and acquiescence cases. It would be even more helpful if courts were to refer expressly to the child's rights[176] and in particular to his right of contact with both parents and to his views, where he is sufficiently mature, even where the child objection defence has not been raised.[177]

F Consistency with Principles of Private International Law

Comity is sometimes cited as one of the factors to be taken into account in exercising discretion where consent or acquiescence has been established. Indeed, Baroness Hale, when

---

[171] eg *Re S (A Child)* (n 154).
[172] See R Schuz, 'The Hague Child Abduction Convention and Children's Rights' (2002) 12 *Transnational Law & Contemporary Problems* 393, 408–09 and ch 7 at IV E.
[173] eg *Re R* (n 116) where the father was alleged to be violent and there were financial difficulties.
[174] In a number of cases where the abductor claimed that the left-behind parent had been violent, the finding that there had been consent or acquiescence enabled return to be refused without having to determine the extent of the violence and without having to rely on the controversial grave risk defence (discussed in ch 11), See eg *Re R* (n 116); *BT v JRT* (n 2).
[175] At IV Bi.
[176] See *Re M (Abduction: Zimbabwe)* (n 7) [43] (Baroness Hale).
[177] The children's views were taken into account in *Re D (Abduction: Acquiescence)* (n 119) and in *Re D (Abduction: Discretionary Return)* (n 8); but cf *U v D* (n 129), where little weight was given to one of the children's objections to return.

comparing these defences with the more child-centric defences in Articles 13(1)(b) and 13(2), voiced the following opinion: 'In consent or acquiescence cases, on the other hand, general considerations of comity and confidence ... might point to a speedy return so that her future can be decided in her home country.'[178]

With respect, where there has been consent or acquiescence, non-return should not be seen as lack of reciprocity or lack of deference to the requesting State. Rather, the non-return is a direct result of the applicant's waiver of his rights. Indeed, the waiver of rights is likely to be reflected in any future decision of the courts of the requesting State. Nonetheless, there is no reason why the child should suffer so that those courts can make such a decision, when the applicant has himself waived his right to immediate return. Thus, considerations of comity should not prevail over the welfare of the child in the exercise of discretion.

G Consistency with Contract Law

Since the issue of consent and acquiescence are essentially contractual, at least where the left-behind parent's waiver of his rights is relied upon by the abductor, the question arises as to the extent to which general doctrines of contract law should be incorporated into the application of these exceptions. The Israeli Supreme Court has held that the rules of contract do apply to consent and acquiescence[179] and thus, for example, factors which vitiate contracts, such as mistake, duress and deceit, will also vitiate any consent or acquiescence. However, recently, Justice Arbel suggested that it may be necessary to modify the general principles of contract law when applying them to family law because of the special nature of the relationship between the parties.[180] This comment effectively justified her decision that consent had been established in this case, even though the parties had not finalised the terms of the agreement between them. Justice Fogelman (dissenting) did not agree with this approach and held that there was no consent because there was no final meeting of minds.[181] He also went on to explain that, on the basis of general contractual principles, representations made by one party and reasonably relied on by the other could form the basis of consent, even where no contract was finalised between them.[182] However, in his view, on the facts of this case there was no factual basis for such a conclusion.

A more extreme version of the view expressed by Justice Arbel can be found in the English Court of Appeal decision in *Re P-J (Children)*, where Thorpe LJ commented,

> Consent, or the lack of it, must be viewed in the context of the realities of family life, or more precisely, in the context of the realities of the disintegration of family life. It is not to be viewed in the context of nor governed by the law of contract.[183]

The difficulty with the latter view is that it leaves wide discretion to the judge to determine whether the actions or statements of the left-behind parent constitute consent without any

---

[178] *Re M (Abduction: Zimbabwe)* (n 7) [45].
[179] *Gabbai* (n 4), 258.
[180] *OB-H v ShB-H* (n 5) [37], relying on S Lifshitz, 'Regulation of Family Contracts' (2004) 4 *Kiryat Hamishpat* 271 (Hebrew) (analysing in detail the various ways in which normal contract rules are inappropriate in a family context).
[181] *OB-H v ShB-H* ibid [4] (Fogelman J). The US judge who later reviewed the decision also seems to have adopted a contractual approach, stating that an unexecuted agreement does not amount to consent, *Ben-Haim* (n 66), 9.
[182] *OB-H v ShB-H* ibid.
[183] *Re P-J* (n 1) [48].

normative framework. Accordingly, there is much to be said for an approach which adopts general contractual rules as a starting point, but modifies them where necessary in order to reflect the realities of family life.

H Certainty versus Flexibility

The maximum amount of flexibility can be obtained by interpreting the defence of consent and acquiescence widely and then exercising the discretion at large. As seen above, this combination maximises the possibility of protecting the child. Nevertheless, such an approach creates considerable uncertainty since it may be difficult to predict the way in which the court will exercise its discretion. Indeed, one of the rationales behind the mandatory return mechanism was to create certainty by reducing discretion. Nonetheless, it might well be that because the implications of acquiescence or consent for the interests of the child are so variable there is no way of achieving the objectives of the Convention in all cases without resorting to discretion. Furthermore, because refusals based on acquiescence and consent are relatively rare,[184] flexible interpretation will not have the same widespread implications as would be the case with a more popular defence.[185]

VI Conclusions

Despite the logical difficulties involved in treating consent as a defence rather than as negating the unlawful character of a removal or retention, this approach gives recognition to the child's right of contact with his parents. It also maximises the protection of children since it enables the court to order return, even though the left-behind parent consented, where this is in the child's best interests. Similarly, it seems appropriate that the onus of proving consent is on the abductor rather than requiring the left-behind parent to prove lack of consent, which would be unduly burdensome.

Nonetheless, the fact that consent might more properly be seen as preventing the requirement to return the child from arising in the first place rather than simply as a defence does justify wider interpretation[186] of this concept.[187] Moreover, as explained above,[188] the objective of protecting children would seem to be best promoted by a wide interpretation of the Article 13(1)(a) defence, combined with a child-oriented approach to the exercise of discretion. On the other hand, justice to the left-behind parent and the need for certainty point in favour of a narrower approach to interpretation.

It is suggested that the optimal approach is purposive interpretation in light of the rationales behind the defence, outlined at the beginning of this chapter. Thus, for example,

---

[184] In the 2008 Survey, globally only 5% of refusals were based on consent and 5% on acquiescence. The figures in the previous surveys were almost identical. See N Lowe, 'A Statistical Analysis of Applications Made in 2008 under the Hague Convention of October 1980 on the Civil Aspects of International Child Abduction' (Cardiff University Law School, November 2011), www.hcch.net/upload/wop/abduct2011pd08ae.pdf, 29.

[185] Such as the grave risk defence, which constituted 27% of all refusals, ibid.

[186] The very question which is being asked is whether the removal or retention was unlawful and thus it is circular to argue that consent should be interpreted narrowly in accordance with the policy of the Convention.

[187] For example, to include consent given in advance, so long as it is not revoked before the removal or retention.

[188] At V Ci.

since some of these rationales assume that there has been reliance on the consent or acquiescence, the question of whether there has been such reliance should be reflected in the approach taken to interpretation. This does not mean that reliance is always necessary, but rather that where there has been reasonable reliance, the test for determining whether there has been consent or acquiescence should be less stringent than where no such reliance can be shown. For example, where there is reasonable reliance, an objective test might be adopted rather than the narrower subjective test.[189] Similarly, whilst normally the statements/actions of the left-behind parent in the immediate aftermath of the abduction and representations made by him during negotiations will not constitute consent or acquiescence, they could do so in the exceptional case where there has been reasonable reliance on them.[190] Of course, in such cases, the lack of subjective intention on the part of the left-behind parent and/or the context in which the consent or acquiescence occurred will be relevant factors in exercising the discretion to return. It may be added that reasonable reliance by the abductor is an important element in any attempt to consider what is just as between the parents and will often have a bearing on the need to protect the child.[191] Thus, this approach is also likely to promote the general objectives of the Convention.

---

[189] This is similar to the approach in *Re H* (n 6), which allows for constructive acquiescence where the abductor has been led to believe that the left-behind parent waives his rights.
[190] See dictum of Fogelman J referred to in text accompanying n 181.
[191] eg reliance may lead to the child becoming settled in the country of refuge.

11

Grave Risk of Harm

I Introduction

A The Dilemma

The drafters of the Hague Convention on the Civil Aspects of International Child Abduction ('Abduction Convention') were plagued by a difficult dilemma. On the one hand, they were determined to ensure that children were protected from abduction by being returned promptly without a full investigation into the merits of the situation. On the other hand, they could not ignore the fact that in some cases, return of the child would in fact cause harm to the child. It was clear to them that a general 'welfare' or 'public policy' defence[1] would to a large extent defeat the whole purpose of the Convention because return would invariably be delayed until all the necessary information was brought to the court and because there would be little deterrent to abduction, since the abductor would achieve his aim of reconsideration of the merits of the case.

Thus, the 'fragile compromise'[2] that was finally achieved involved restricting cases in which the welfare aspects of the case would be examined to those situations in which it was alleged that there existed 'a grave risk that return would expose the child to physical or psychological harm or otherwise place him in an intolerable situation'.[3] Whilst this defence clearly includes three separate and alternative grounds, it will be convenient to use the expression 'grave risk defence' to refer to the whole exception, unless otherwise stated.[4]

This carefully crafted scheme may have been the optimal solution in relation to the stereotypical situation in the minds of the drafters, of a dissatisfied non-custodial parent abducting the child from the custodial parent,[5] but it does not appear to be well-suited to cases where the abductor is the primary carer,[6] which has in practice become the more common scenario.[7] In such situations, return may not result in the restoration of the *status quo ante*, but in a change of custodial parent[8] or at least in a radical change in living

---

[1] See Beaumont and McEleavy, *The Hague Convention on International Child Abduction* (Oxford, Oxford University Press, 1999) 8 and 135 (describing the rejection of these defences).
[2] Perez-Vera Report, Proceedings of the 14th session of the Hague Conference Oct 1980, www.hcch.net/index_en.php?act=publications.details&pid=2779, para 116.
[3] For a discussion of the drafting history of this defence, see Beaumont and McEleavy (n 1) 135–38.
[4] For a discussion of blurring of the grounds in some jurisdictions, see below at II Aiii; *cf* The New Zealand, Guardianship Amendment Act 1991, in which the intolerable situation and grave risk of harm defences appear in separate sub-paragraphs (s 13(1)(c)(i) and (ii)).
[5] See ch 3 at I Bi.
[6] Beaumont and McEleavy (n 1) 138–39; M Freeman, 'Primary Carers and The Hague Child Abduction Convention' (2001) *International Family Law* 140; *Re E* [2011] UKSC 27 [6]–[7].
[7] See ch 3 at I Bi.
[8] Where the custodial abductor is unable or unwilling to return with the child.

conditions.⁹ Accordingly, in many such cases, return will almost certainly expose the child to psychological harm or place him in an intolerable situation. Yet, allowing the exception to block return in all such cases would substantially undermine the Convention. In light of this background, we can understand the United States Court of Appeals' comment that,

> Among the federal courts' most difficult and heart-rending tasks is the decision under the Hague Convention on the Civil Aspects of International Child Abduction whether to return an abducted child to the child's home country when a parent claims the child will face a grave risk of physical or psychological harm if returned.¹⁰

This chapter will examine in detail how the courts have responded to the challenge of protecting children from harm without violating the integrity of the Convention. Part II considers how Article 13(1)(b) has been interpreted and how it has been applied in particular typical fact scenarios. Part III explains how the courts have tried to minimise the use of the grave risk exception by putting in place protective measures which eliminate or substantially reduce the grave risk of harm or avoid the intolerable situation and considers the effectiveness of this approach. Finally, Part IV of the chapter provides analysis in light of the parameters set out in chapters five and six of the book and Part V sets out the conclusions arising therefrom.

However, firstly, it is important to discuss the scope of the investigation under Article 13(1)(b) since this difficult issue lies at the heart of the divergent opinions in relation to the application of the exception.

B Scope of the Investigation

As stated above, one of the rationales for not routinely examining the welfare implications of returning a child is that the delay involved would frustrate the primary objective of speedy return. Drafting a restrictive exception requiring proof of a grave risk of harm does not per se solve this problem. In order to determine whether the exception is established, it appears necessary to undertake a detailed investigation into the implications of return in every case where the abducting parent alleges that the exception applies. However, such an approach will simply encourage abductors to claim the grave risk exception in order to gain time, which may in itself increase the chance of avoiding return.¹¹ Thus, the challenge is to find a *via media* which is consistent with the summary nature of Abduction Convention proceedings and yet provides the courts with sufficient information on which to base a determination that the allegation of grave risk of harm is unfounded or that the defence is established.¹²

The only guidance to be found in the Convention is Article 13(3) which provides that in considering the defences in Article 13, 'judicial and administrative authorities shall take into account the information relating to the social background of the child provided by the Central Authority or other competent authority of the child's habitual residence'.¹³ However,

---

⁹ Where the custodial abductor is prepared to return with the child, but not to live with the other parent.
¹⁰ *Danaipour v Mclarey* 286 F3d 1 (1st Cir 2002).
¹¹ Per Thomas Bingham MR in *Re G (A Minor)*, 3 October 1995, transcript (UK Court of Appeal).
¹² Or at least that the claim is sufficiently founded to justify further investigation.
¹³ In RFamA (SC) 6039/12 *Ploni v Plonit*, 13 August 2012, http://elyon1.court.gov.il/files/12/390/060/w01/12060390.w01.pdf, the Israeli Supreme Court rejected an argument that this provision requires courts to delay making a decision until such information is available (based on the use of the word 'shall'), inter alia because

this provision, which is rarely used,[14] gives no indication as to what evidence courts should take into account in determining whether the Article 13(1)(b) exception is established. In particular, it is not clear what oral evidence, if any, should be heard in order to determine disputed issues of fact and what expert reports, if any, should be commissioned or admitted by the court.

Thus, it is not surprising that there are wide variations between jurisdictions, and even between courts within the same jurisdiction, in their approach to the evidence to be considered in Article 13(1)(b) cases.[15] For example, in some countries a welfare report on the child is routinely ordered,[16] whereas in other countries such reports are only ordered where a prima facie case of harm has been made out.[17] Similarly, in some cases, evidence presented is tested by cross-examination whereas in others it is not.[18] Indeed, a number of courts have commented that oral evidence should rarely be heard in Abduction Convention cases.[19]

To a large extent, these variations reflect differences in courts' perception as to their role in these cases.[20] This can be illustrated by the different approaches of courts to allegations of domestic violence,[21] which can be divided into four categories.[22] Firstly, at one end of the spectrum, some courts take the view that the court of habitual residence is best placed to investigate the allegations and thus any investigation should be deferred to that court.[23] Secondly, some courts place the emphasis on assessing the risk in returning the child, rather than on resolving issues of fact.[24] To this category should be added courts which place the emphasis on implementing protective measures which will reduce the risk to the child, if the allegations are indeed true.[25] Thirdly, some courts take the view that they have a duty to investigate the veracity of the allegations,[26] usually by appointing an independent

such an interpretation was inconsistent with the need for speed. Also, in this particular case, the first instance Court had found as a matter of fact that the allegations concerning risk to the child were unfounded and thus there was no need to wait for any further information.

[14] Apparently, in order to avoid delay, M Weiner, 'International Child Abduction and the Escape from Domestic Violence' (2000) 69 *Fordham Law Review* 593, 658 (citing Report of Second Special Commission).

[15] For a more detailed consideration of the types of evidence considered, see Permanent Bureau, 'Domestic and Family Violence and the Article 13 "grave risk" exception in the operation of the *Hague Convention of 25 October 1980 on the Civil Aspects of International Child Abduction*: A Reflection Paper', Preliminary Document No 9 of 2011, www.hcch.net/index_en.php?act=progress.listing&cat=7 ('Reflection Paper').

[16] eg, in Israel, wherever the abductor raises the grave risk or child objection defences.

[17] eg, *N v N (Abduction: Article 13 Defence)* [1995] 1 FLR 107; *Re G (Abduction: Psychological Harm)* [1995] 1 FLR 64; *Re M (Abduction: Psychological Harm)* [1997] 2 FLR 573; comments of Thorpe LJ in *Re W (A Child)* [2004] EWCA Civ 1366, that the trial Judge's suggestion that psychological assessment should be ordered before returning children in such cases would 'subvert the essentially summary nature of these special proceedings'.

[18] Reflection Paper (n 15), para 91.

[19] eg, *Re E* (n 6) [32]; *Re S (Child Abduction)(Grave Risk of Harm)* [2002] EWCA 908; *Family Advocate Cape Town v Chirume* (6090/05) [2005] ZAWCHC 94 (9 December 2005); *Cooper v Casey* (1995) FLC 92-575; cf *DT v LBT* [2010] EWHC 3177 (Fam), where full oral evidence was heard from both parties and *Re M (Abduction: Leave to Appeal)* [1999] 2 FLR 550, where the oral evidence tipped the balance in favour of refusing return.

[20] See also the difference of opinion between the majority and the dissenting opinion in the US Court of Appeals decision in *Khan v Fatima* 680 F3d 781 (7th Cir 2012).

[21] For a detailed discussion of domestic violence cases, see below at II Biv.

[22] Reflection Paper (n 15).

[23] ibid, para 76, citing *Murray v Director, Family Services* (1993) FLC 92-416; Supreme Court of Finland 1996:151, S96/2489 [INCADAT cite: HC/E/FI 360]; T.G.I. d'Abbeville, 10 June 1993, *W v G (France)* [INCADAT cite: HC/E/FR 298].

[24] eg, *Re K* [1995] 2 FLR 211 (CA); *Secretary to the Department of Human Services v Mander* [2003] FamCA 1128.

[25] *Re E* (n 6) [52]; A similar approach was adopted in the South African case of *Family Advocate v Chirume* (n 19).

[26] The US Court of Appeals in *Danaipour* (n 10) 18 that 'Generally speaking, where a party makes a substantial allegation that, if true, would justify application of the art 13(b) exception, the court should make the necessary predicate findings'. In the Court's view, it was not possible to decide whether return would expose the children to

expert.[27] Finally, some courts seem to invoke a vigorous adversarial process, requiring the parties to present clear evidence to support or refute the allegations.[28]

After examining the way in which the courts interpret the Article 13(1)(b) defence in general and in particular types of circumstances, we will be in a better position to discuss further the question of the appropriate scope of the investigation.[29]

II Interpretation and Application of the Grave Risk Defence

A General

Most courts, taking seriously Professor Perez-Vera's warning[30] that the Convention will become 'a dead letter' if the defences are interpreted liberally, have religiously interpreted[31] Article 13(1)(b) in a highly restrictive fashion.[32]

Firstly, it should be noted that the US implementing legislation imposes a higher standard of proof for proving the Article 13(1)(b) and Article 20 defences. These defences have to be proven 'by clear and convincing evidence'; instead of the usual standard of 'preponderance of evidence'.[33] Whilst other countries have not formally adopted a higher standard of proof, in practice courts frequently comment on the high burden imposed on an abductor who is claiming the Article 13(1)(b) defence.[34]

Secondly, it should be noted that the adjective 'grave'[35] qualifies the word risk and not harm. Nonetheless, courts have often required that the potential harm must be grave.[36]

---

a grave risk of harm without determining whether there had been sexual abuse, as alleged ([64]); In *Khan v Fatima* (n 20), the decision of the District Court ordering return was overturned on appeal because that Court had not made any findings of fact in relation to the allegations of violence made by the wife which, if true, could give rise to a grave risk of harm.

[27] Reflection Paper (n 15), para 77 citing inter alia *D v G* [2001] 1179 HKCU 1.
[28] Reflection Paper, ibid, para 78, citing inter alia *H v C* (Unreported), FC Lower Hutt, FP No 368/00, 9 March 2001 [INCADAT cite: HC/E/NZ 537].
[29] See below at IV D.
[30] Perez-Vera Report (n 2), para 34.
[31] The UK Supreme Court in *Re E* (n 6) [31], observes that the issue is not one of restrictive interpretation, but rather of restrictive application. However, the Perez-Vera Report, ibid, did refer to interpretation of the defences and most of the case law on the subject refers to restrictive interpretation or construction, see eg, *Re S* (n 19) [45], but *cf Director-General, Department of Families & RSP* [2003] FamCA 623. In the current author's view, the distinction between interpretation and application is not helpful in this context. The courts have consistently found that 'the defence represents a high hurdle for an abducting parent to clear', *TB v JB (Abduction: Graver Risk of Harm)* [2001] 2 FLR 515. It matters little whether this is because the words in the defence are restrictively interpreted or the defence is restrictively applied because of the difficulty in proving its establishment to the required standard.
[32] *cf DP v Commonwealth Central Authority* (2001) 180 ALR 402; *JLM v Director-General NSW Department of Community Services* [2001] HCA 39 [43]–[44] and the New Zealand High Court decision in *El Sayed v Secretary for Justice* [2003] 1 NZLR 349 (denying that a restrictive interpretation was required), but the latter decision was subsequently disapproved in *KS v LS* [2003] NZLR 387 [149].
[33] International Child Abduction Remedies Act, s 4 (e)(2)(A), 42 USC Sec 11603 (e)(2)(A).
[34] See eg, comment of Justice Procaccia in RFamA 1855/08 *RB v VG*, 8 April 2008 (Isr) http://elyon1.court.gov.il/files/08/550/018/r03/08018550.r03.pdf [INCADAT cite: HC/E/IL 923] [43], that the defence will only apply where there is proven to exist 'an extreme, exceptional and clear-cut situation' and her reference to 'grave risk of psychological harm at this special level'.
[35] This requires more than a real risk, *Re E* (n 6) [33].
[36] eg, *El Sayed* (n 32).

Two justifications for this interpretation can be found in the wording of the defence itself. Firstly, it has been observed that there is an 'ordinary language link' between the risk and the harm.[37] Accordingly, a relatively low risk of death will be considered to be a grave risk whereas a higher degree might be required for less serious forms of harm. Secondly, the word 'otherwise', which introduces the alternative 'intolerable position' ground in the defence, is seen as importing the concept of intolerability into the first two grounds of 'physical harm' or 'psychological harm'.[38] Thus, the defence will only be established where the potential harm is such that the child cannot reasonably be expected to tolerate it[39] or for some other reason return will place the child in an intolerable situation.

Perhaps the high-water mark of the restrictive approach is Boggs J's much cited attempt to define the circumstances in which the defence would apply as those where the return puts the child 'in imminent danger prior to the resolution of the custody dispute, eg by returning the child to a zone of war, famine or disease' or in cases of 'serious abuse or neglect or extraordinary emotional dependence, when the court in the country of habitual residence, for whatever reason, may be incapable or unwilling to give the child adequate protection'.[40] More than a decade ago, Beaumont and McEleavy[41] observed that, whilst this definition may seem extreme, the UK case law was to a large extent consistent with it. The following overview of the way in which each of the three grounds in Article 13(1)(b) has been interpreted and an examination of the particular situations in which the defence is pleaded will facilitate assessment of the extent to which this very restrictive approach is still followed today in the Hague world generally.

i Physical Harm

Only in relatively unusual circumstances have courts refused return on the basis that it will involve a grave risk of physical harm.[42] Firstly, restrictions on the evidence admissible can make it difficult to prove harm which was caused in the past. Secondly, even where it is proven that the applicant has previously caused harm, the court may well rely on the authorities of the requesting State to protect the child.[43]

ii Psychological Harm

Whilst psychological harm is much more frequently claimed than physical harm, courts are reluctant to find that such harm is 'of a severity which is much more than inherent in the inevitable disruption, uncertainty and anxiety which follows an unwelcome return'[44]

---

[37] *Re E* (n 6) [33].
[38] ibid [34]; *Thomson v Thomson* [1994] 3 SCR 551; *Re S* (n 19) [38]–[41]; *DP* (n 32) [9] and [132].
[39] The UK Supreme Court in *Re E* ibid [34] explains that 'Every child has to put up with a certain amount of rough and tumble, discomfort and distress. It is part of growing up.'
[40] *Friedrich v Friedrich* 78 F3d 1060, 1069 (6th Cir 1996).
[41] Beaumont and McEleavy (n 1) 142.
[42] eg, Israeli case of R FamA 5253/00 *R v L* (unreported, 21 January 2001) [INCADAT cite: HC/E/IL 834] (psychiatric evidence of grave risk that the child would attempt suicide if he were returned); Australian case of *Central Authority v Maynard* (Unreported, Family Court of Australia, Melbourne, 3 September 2003) [INCADAT cite: HC/E/AU 541] (a serious medical condition made it dangerous for the child to fly in the foreseeable future); *Re D (Article 13B: Non-Return)* [2006] EWCA Civ 146 (parents had been the target of shootings in Venezuala).
[43] eg *Re M (Abduction: Acquiesence)* [1996] 1 FLR 315, 322; *Re K (Abduction: Child's Objections)* [1995] 1 FLR 977. See generally discussion on protective measures in Part III below.
[44] *Re C (Abduction) (Grave Risk of Psychological Harm)* [1999] 2 FCR 507, 517 (Ward LJ).

and is 'more than transitory'.⁴⁵ In particular, it will be difficult to prove this harm unless there is an expert diagnosis or prognosis that the child suffers from or will suffer from a psychiatric or psychological disorder, such as post-traumatic stress syndrome.⁴⁶ However, as will be seen below,⁴⁷ some courts are now prepared to accept that exposure to violence between his parents will cause the child psychological harm and a few courts are prepared to take into account harm which will be caused by the separation of the child from his primary carer.

Even where the risk of psychological harm has been established, it is sometimes held that the harm which will be caused by remaining in the State of refuge is greater.⁴⁸ This 'comparative approach' is misconceived,⁴⁹ and the dangers of it are illustrated by the Israeli case of *VG v RB*⁵⁰ This case concerned a boy who had been brought to Israel by his Jewish mother from France, where they had been living for two years with the permission of the Belgian Court.⁵¹ After arriving in Israel, the mother and son adopted an ultra-orthodox religious way of life and the child acclimatised well. Ten months after the removal, the non-Jewish Belgian father issued Hague Convention proceedings and the mother pleaded inter alia the grave risk of harm and child objection defences. The psychological report, commissioned by the court, stated clearly that the return of the child, by then aged nine, to Belgium by himself would be a catastrophe for him both because of the separation from the mother, who had always been his primary carer, and because of the great disparity between the religious and cultural environment to which he was accustomed in Israel and the environment in which his father, with whom he had had no contact for the past two and half years,⁵² lived in Belgium. The report even suggested that the child, who was vehemently opposed to return,⁵³ would become depressed and perhaps even suicidal. On the other hand, the report expressed the view that if the child stayed in Israel, he would lose all contact with his father and that this would cause long-term harm to his psychological and emotional development.⁵⁴ Thus, the report concluded that the least detrimental alternative was for the child to return to Belgium with the mother.

The Family Court, adopting this conclusion, held that although the grave risk defence was established, the child should still be returned.⁵⁵ With respect, this approach is problematic

---

⁴⁵ *KS v LS* (n 32) [92].
⁴⁶ As eg in *Blondin v Dubois* 238 F3d 153 (2d Cir 2001); cf *Klentzeris v Klentzeris* [2007] EWCA Civ 533 where the exception was established on the basis of the welfare officer's report after interviewing the children
⁴⁷ At Biii and iv.
⁴⁸ *Re A (A Minor)(Abduction)* [1988] 1 FLR 365, 370; *N v N* (n 17).
⁴⁹ Beaumont and McEleavy (n 1) 145.
⁵⁰ FamC (BSH) 3450/07 *VG v RB* Nevo, 9 January 2008 (Isr) upheld by the Supreme Court in *RB v VG* (n 34).
⁵¹ The trigger for the removal was a decision of the Belgian Court ordering that custody be transferred to the father.
⁵² The delay was caused by appeals, remittance back to hear the child and the commissioning of a second psychological report because the first one was inadequate.
⁵³ The child objection defence was rejected because the child was not considered mature enough and his views were not considered to be independent. See generally ch 12 .
⁵⁴ cf A New Zealand case, where the first instance judge held that while there was a real risk that non-return would lead to alienation from the father, the risks attendant on return were greater (as reported in the appeal from that decision, *KS v LS* (n 32) [70]). On appeal, the finding of grave risk of harm was overturned (ibid [124]).
⁵⁵ Subject to a number of conditions. However, in the end even though some of these conditions had not been fulfilled, the Supreme Court ordered immediate return and the mother was given 24 hours' notice of the return flight booked by the father. The child did not turn up at the airport and has not been seen since. More than three years later, the mother was sentenced to a month's imprisonment for contempt of court, RFamA (SC) 1855/08 *RB v VG* (Isr) 29 February 2012. http://elyon1.court.gov.il/files/08/550/018/t26/08018550.t26.pdf. In relation to criminal proceedings brought against her, see ch 1 at n 74 and accompanying text.

inter alia[56] because the speculative long-term potential harm cannot justify creating the concrete immediate risk.[57] In such a case, the issue of future harm should be debated in a full-blown best interests enquiry in domestic proceedings in the State of refuge. Then, the court will have at its disposal more effective tools for assessing the likelihood of future harm[58] and the ways in which such harm might be prevented or minimised.[59]

The difficulty with the reasoning of the Family Court seems to have been recognised on appeal, when the District Court by a majority,[60] and then the Supreme Court unanimously,[61] held that the grave risk defence was not established, although they purported to uphold the decision of the Family Court. With respect, the reasoning of Justice Procaccia in the Supreme Court that the real cause of the psychological harm was the original abduction and not the return is unsustainable. Firstly, this approach is inconsistent with the wording of the Article 13(1)(b) defence which relates to the consequences of return and not the cause of the harm. As La Forest J of the Supreme Court of Canada said, '. . . from a child-centred perspective, harm is harm. If the harm were severe enough to meet the stringent test of the Convention, it would be irrelevant from whence it came'.[62] Secondly, it is axiomatic that if the child had not been abducted, there would have been no need to uproot him from his new environment and therefore there would be no risk of harm. Thus, Justice Procaccia's approach would make Article 13(1)(b) virtually redundant in relation to psychological harm.

iii Placing the Child in an Intolerable Situation

The intolerable situation ground has very rarely been established. A major reason for this seems to be some courts' 'conflation' of the intolerable situation and grave risk of harm defences.[63] This means that where there is no risk of physical or psychological harm, no consideration is given to the possibility that return will place the child in an intolerable situation for other reasons. Even where this issue is considered, it will be difficult to satisfy a court that there is an intolerable situation without being able to point to some physical or psychological harm. Courts have made it clear that the hurdle is high[64] and that the test is objective.[65] A further reason is the development of the practice of requiring undertakings

---

[56] For a discussion of misconceived reliance on Parental Alienation Syndrome in this case, see ch 3 at II F.

[57] See Baroness Hale's comment that it is inconceivable that a court would exercise its discretion to order return of a child where the grave risk of harm defence was established in *Re D (A Child) (Abduction: Foreign Custody Rights)* [2006] UKHL 51 [55].

[58] Including commissioning additional opinions.

[59] eg, providing for counselling for the child and the left-behind parent to support the rehabilitation of their relationship and imposing sanctions for failure to comply with the contact arrangements ordered by the court.

[60] FamA 104/08 (BSH) *RB v VG* Nevo, 20 February 2008, with a strong dissent by Justice Biton warning of the risk to the child of return.

[61] *RB v VG* (n 34).

[62] *Thomson* (n 38).

[63] MH Weiner, 'Intolerable Situations and Counsel for Children: Following Switzerland's Example In Hague Abduction Cases' (2008) 58 *American University Law Review* 335, 345–52, showing how this approach seems to originate from the State Department Commentary which gives sexual abuse as an example of an intolerable situation, even though this would also be covered by the grave risk of harm exception, thus making the two concepts 'look coterminous'; See also discussion in M Freeman, 'The Comparative Interpretation of Article 13b of the 1980 Hague Child Abduction Convention' in *Occasional Papers on the 1980 Hague Child Abduction Convention* (Reunite International Child Abduction Centre, Reunite, 2002) 67–68.

[64] eg *B v B (Abduction: Custody Rights)* [1993] 1 FLR 238 (Sir Stephen Brown P).

[65] *Re S* (n 19); *H v H* (1995) 13 FRNZ 498, 504.

or making conditions[66] which in the court's view turn what might otherwise be an intolerable situation into a tolerable one.[67]

Merle Weiner criticises the highly restrictive approach taken to the intolerable situation defence. In particular, she argues that the defence should include situations which are 'morally intolerable' for the child,[68] such as being exposed to domestic violence and being placed into foster care. The Swiss Parliament's definition of a specific situation where the intolerable situation defence will apply goes some way to meeting these criticisms. Article 5 of the Swiss Federal Act on International Child Abduction and The Hague Conventions on the Protection of Child and Adults ('the Swiss Act') of 2007 provides that return will place a child in an intolerable situation where:

a   placement with the parent who filed the application is manifestly not in the child's best interests;
b   the abducting parent is not, given all of the circumstances, in a position to take care of the child in the State where the child was habitually resident immediately before the abduction or if this cannot reasonably be required from this parent; and
c   placement in foster care is manifestly not in the child's best interests.[69]

The situation envisaged by the provision is one where it would not be possible to prove that being placed in foster care would cause the child harm. Nonetheless, there is little doubt that when return will necessarily involve removing a child from a parental carer, whose parenting ability has not been questioned, and placing him in a foster home thousands of miles away from that carer, the situation will be intolerable for the child.[70]

We will now turn to consider the courts' approach to Article 13(1)(b) in a number of typical scenarios in which this defence is often invoked.

B   Specific Situations

i   Risk of Abuse of Child

It would appear axiomatic that the grave risk exception will be established where risk of physical, sexual and/or emotional abuse at the hands of the left-behind parent is proven.[71]

---

[66] See detailed discussion in Part III below.
[67] eg, *Re O (Child Abduction: Undertakings)* [1994] 2 FLR 349 in which Singer J, whilst interpreting the concept of intolerable situation broadly, held that the undertakings offered by the father alleviated the risk that the children would find themselves in an intolerable situation.
[68] Weiner, 'Intolerable Situations' (n 63) 342.
[69] An English translation of the Swiss Act is appended to A Bucher, 'The New Swiss Federal Act on International Child Abduction' (2008) 4 *Journal of Private International Law* 139, 161. However, there do not seem to be any cases in which return has been refused on the basis of Art 5 of the Swiss Act, AC Alfieri, 'Enlèvement international d'enfants: premières expériences avec la LF-EEA', *La pratique du droit de la famille* ch–2012– 550, 555–56. In one case discussed there, the mother could not return to the US with the children because she did not have a visa, but the return was held not to be intolerable because the children had been spending half of their time with the father during the three years prior to the abduction, arrêt du TC VD du 17.11.2010, 214, consid. 3c, 15.
[70] Weiner, 'Intolerable Situations' (n 63) 367–69; See also *The Central Authority For The Republic Of South Africa v MA* Case No 11/39798 South Gauteng High Court, Johannesburg (Unreported, 20 March 2012).
[71] The US State Department gives as an example of an intolerable situation one in which a parent removes the child in order to prevent further sexual abuse by the left-behind parent, in US Department of State, Hague International Child Abduction Convention; Text and Legal Analysis, Public notice 957, 51 Federal Regulation 10,494 at 10,510 (1986).

However, there may be differences of approach as to what degree of corporal punishment is unacceptable[72] and what constitutes emotional abuse.[73]

Moreover, in many cases it will not be possible to prove the risk of physical harm without a full-scale enquiry. Thus, the critical question is whether the court in the requested State should carry out that enquiry or rely on the authorities in the requesting State to do so. As mentioned above, many courts take the view that the State of habitual residence is better equipped to undertake the necessary examination and so return the child on the express assumption that the requesting State will adequately protect the child in the meantime.[74]

In contrast, the US Appeals Court for the First Circuit held, in *Danaipour v McLarey*,[75] that where there is a serious suspicion of abuse, it is necessary for the court in the requested State to investigate fully the allegations of abuse in order to determine whether the grave risk exception is established.[76] In addition, the *Danaipour* Court probed more deeply into the realities of the protection which would be offered by the requesting State. The District Court, despite accepting that there was reason to be concerned that there had been sexual abuse, had ordered return on condition that a mirror order be made by the Swedish Court, containing inter alia the father's undertakings not to have any contact with the children pending a further evaluation in Sweden of the abuse allegations.[77] This decision was reversed on appeal on the basis that the evidence showed that the evaluation in Sweden would not satisfy US standards.[78] Furthermore, the *Danaipour* Court held that in cases of sexual abuse[79] a court is not required to seek protective measures and can simply deny return.[80] In its view, getting embroiled in extensive undertakings in such cases is not appropriate and tends to dilute the force of the Article 13(1)(b) exception.[81]

---

[72] Compare *Di Giuseppe v Di Giuseppe* 2008 US Dist LEXIS 29785, 2008 WL 1743079, at 6 (ED Mich April 11 2008) (finding a grave risk where the petitioner used corporal punishment three times a month, including slapping the child hard enough to leave marks, slamming the child's head into a cupboard, which drew blood, and biting the child in front of school officials), with *Altamiranda Vale v Avila* 538 F3d 581, 587 (7th Cir 2008) (holding that grave risk was not shown where the father 'struck his son with a video-game cord') and *Lopez v Alcala* 547 F Supp 2d 1255, 1261–62 (MD Fla 2008) (holding that grave risk was not shown where the father had hit the children a few times); In *Simcox v Simcox* 511 F3d 594 (6th Cir, 2007), the US Court of Appeals divided abuse into three categories: minor (return should be ordered); grave abuse (return should be refused) and intermediate cases (depends on the degree of risk and to what extent protective measures would sufficiently ameliorate the risk. In this case, the abuse which included physical abuse (repeated beatings, hair pulling, ear pulling and belt-whipping) and psychological abuse (profane outbursts and abuse of the children's mother in their presence) was held to come within the intermediate category.

[73] Verbal abuse per se will not be sufficient, eg In *Re DD* 440 F Supp 2d 1283, 1299 (MD Fla 2006).

[74] eg, *N v N* (n 17); *AS v PS (Child Abduction)* [1998] 2 IR 244; *Obergericht des Kantons Zürich (Appellate Court of the Canton Zurich)*, 28 January 1997, U/NL960145/II.ZK [INCADAT Ref: 426]; Finland case (n 23); *Anderson v Central Authority for New Zealand* [1996] 2 NZFLR 517; Freeman's research (n 63) fn 87, shows that in the latter case, this assumption was misguided.

[75] *Danaipour* (n 10) 15; *D v G* (n 27).

[76] Some courts commission an expert report in order to determine whether there is a serious suspicion of abuse. For eg, Scottish case of *Q Petitioner* [2001] SLT 243 (an expert report, in addition to evidence submitted in the proceedings which had taken place in France, showed that there was a real risk that the father had sexually abused the daughter); *Kufner v Kufner*, 519 F3d 33 (1st Cir 2008) (expert report showed there had not been abuse).

[77] *Danaipour v McLarey*, 183 F Supp 2d 311 (D Mass 2002).

[78] *Danaipour* (n 10) 24; see also *Q Petitioner* (n 76) (holding that on the basis of the French legal system's previous reaction, there was reason to believe that the children would not be adequately protected if they were returned to France).

[79] The Court clarifies that sexual abuse is not restricted to rape and that it is not necessary to show that the child is currently suffering from post-traumatic stress disorder as a result of the abuse (*Danaipour* (n 10) 16 as suggested by the District Court.

[80] *Danaipour* (n 10) 25.

[81] ibid.

ii *Return to a War Zone*

In a number of cases, mainly involving abductions from Israel, the abductor has claimed that the grave risk exception applies because of the security situation in the requesting State. The origin of this claim is the frequently cited dictum in the case of *Friederich v Friedrich* mentioning return to a zone of war as one of the situations in which a grave risk of harm will exist.[82]

Whilst the war zone claim has usually been rejected,[83] there are a few cases, which were heard at the height of the intifada in Israel in 2002, in which the claim was upheld (hereinafter: 'the war zone cases').[84] Whilst these decisions relate to a specific place and time, it is clear that the issue may arise again in different contexts and so it is important to highlight the defects in the reasoning in the war zone cases.[85]

Firstly, it is difficult to see how the evidence brought by the abductors in the war zone cases could have been sufficient to discharge the burden of proving the existence of a grave risk. Many of the courts relied heavily on newspaper reports and the rhetoric of politicians,[86] which are clearly designed to sensationalise events and cannot be relied upon as portraying an accurate picture of the situation. Similarly, reliance on travel warnings addressed to casual visitors[87] is misconceived because these warnings do not by themselves establish that the risk faced by a returning Israeli amounts to a grave risk of harm.[88] Indeed the objective facts showed inter alia that there was free entry to and exit from Israel at all times and businesses and schools continued to operate as usual.[89] Furthermore, it should be remembered that the phrase 'war zone' is a gloss on the Convention and what matters is not the label but whether a grave risk of harm is proven.[90]

Secondly, some of the courts took a comparative approach, holding that the children would be at greater risk in Israel than in the country of refuge.[91] This approach is inconsistent with the clear wording of the Abduction Convention, which requires that there be a grave risk of harm and not simply that the risk of harm in one country be greater than another. Furthermore, it is not possible to make any comparison of the risks other than in the most speculative way. In particular, it would be necessary to take into account all the

---

[82] *Friedrich* (n 40) and accompanying text.
[83] eg, CA Aix en Provence 8/10/2002, L. c. Ministère Public, Mme B et Mesdemoiselles L (N° de rôle 02/14917) [INCADAT cite: HC/E/FR 509]; VLK, 11 January 2002, 13. afdeling, B-2939-01 [INCADAT cite: EHC/E/DK 519].
[84] eg, *Janine Claire Genish-Grant and Director-General Department of Community Services* [2002] FamCA 346; *Silverman v Silverman* 338 F3d 886 (8th Cir, 2003) (affirmed on a different basis by a majority of the US Court of Appeals for the 8th Circuit (312 F3d 914 (2002)) on 11 December 2002. The majority did not discuss the war zone claim, but the dissenting judge rejected it); Civil case No 3875 (Bucharest Area Court VI, 15 April 2002) (English translation given to the author by the Israeli Central Authority) and the earlier Spanish decision *Menachem v Menachem, Ramirez-Ordina* (Trial Court No 2 of L'Hospitalet de Llabregat, No 369/01, 27 January 2002); *Raban v Raban* (referred to in *Raban v Romania* No 25437/08 (Sect 3) (Eng) – (26 October 2010)) There are also some cases where the return was only ordered after the court was satisfied that the place where the child was living was not close to where there had been terrorist attacks (eg *Zenou v Lebouef* (Court of Appeal, Aix-en-Provence, 8th October 2002) (translation given to author by the Israeli Central Authority).
[85] For more detailed analysis, see R Schuz, 'Returning Abducted Children to Israel and the Intifada' (2003) 17 *Australian Journal of Family Law* 297.
[86] *Silverman* (n 84).
[87] *Genish-Grant* (n 84).
[88] ibid (Holden J) (dissenting).
[89] *Freier v Freier* 969 F Supp 436 (ED Mich 1996).
[90] *Re S* (n 19).
[91] eg *Menachem* (n 84).

risks of living in the different places[92] and not only those of being harmed in a terrorist attack.

Finally, these cases show that the timing of the decision was critical. Most of the war zone cases were heard during a six-week period between 15 April and 27 May 2002, during which the frequency of terrorist bombings on civilian targets in large cities in Israel increased significantly. It seems likely that if the cases had been heard a few weeks later after a lull in the number of attacks, the decisions might have been different. Thus, even if the courts had been concerned about the risk of return at the time of the decision, it was fairly clear that the deterioration in the security situation was temporary. Accordingly, the courts could have adjourned the proceedings for a few weeks to see if the situation improved.[93] Whilst clearly speed is of the essence in the Hague proceedings, surely a relatively short delay in return would be preferable to no return at all.

iii *Harm Caused by Separation from a Primary Carer Abductor*

An obvious strategy[94] for a primary carer abductor is to state that she is not prepared to return with the child and that the consequent separation from her will cause the child psychological harm. Such claims are almost invariably rejected by most courts for reasons explained in the often cited words of Butler-Sloss LJ:

> Is a parent to create the psychological situation, and then rely on it? If the grave risk of psychological harm to a child is to be inflicted by the conduct of the parent who abducted him, then it would be relied upon by every mother of a young child who removed him out of the jurisdiction and refused to return. It would drive a coach and four through the Convention . . .[95]

Whilst this strict approach has been widely adopted,[96] not all courts have always taken such a robust stance. For example, a New Zealand judge held that if he had been satisfied that the mother would not return under any circumstances, then the grave risk defence would be made out because return into the primary care of the father could be psychologically abusive for the child[97] and a US judge refused to return a child on the basis of expert evidence that separation from the parent to whom he was attached would cause him dam-

---

[92] E Freedman, 'International Terrorism and the Grave Physical Risk Defence of the Hague Convention on International Child Abduction' [2002] *International Family Law* 60, points out that comparisons would only have validity if they related to particular neighbourhoods and if there was some way of ensuring that the child stayed within the neighbourhood.

[93] This was the approach adopted by the Buenos Aires Court in the case of *Altheim v Altheim* (decision of 5 October 2011).

[94] Sometimes the court states that it does not believe this threat (eg CA (SC) 4391/96 *Ro v Ro*, 50(5) PD 338 (Isr) [INCADAT cite: HC/E/IL 832], or even manages to get the abductor to concede that at the end of the day she will return with the child (see eg *Re A* (n 48)).

[95] *C v C (Minor: Abduction: Rights of Custody Abroad)* [1989] 2 All ER 465, 471. See also comment in New Zealand case of *B v B* [1994] NZFLR 497 that 'it is an inevitable consequence in respect of Hague Convention cases that there is likely to be harm to a child as a result of separation from a parent having primary care'; cf *Re M (Abduction: Leave to Appeal)* (n 19) in which Butler-Sloss J herself held that the trial judge's decision to refuse return was unappealable, even though the judge's decision was based on the fact that the two- year-old child could not be parted from the mother, against whom there had been 'a considerable degree of violence by father'.

[96] eg, *Ro* (n 94); *Panazatou v Pantazatos* 1997 WL 614519 (Conn Super Ct 1997); *Maurizio R v LC* 201 Cal App 4th 616 (2011); 10 UF 753/01, Oberlandesgericht Dresden [INCADAT cite: HC/E/DE 486]; *MG v RF* [2002] RJQ 2132 (Quebec); Bundesgericht, II. Zivilabteilung (Tribunal Fédéral, 2ème Chambre Civile), 5P.367/2005 [INCADAT cite: HC/E/CH 841].

[97] *Hollins v Crozier* [2000] NZLR 775; See also later case of *El Sayed* (n 32).

age.[98] Similarly, in some French[99] and Scottish[100] cases, courts refused to return children where it was clear that separation from the abducting mother would cause them real harm, despite the fact that this situation arose as a result of the mother's refusal to return with the child.[101] However, this approach seems to have been abandoned in recent cases.[102]

Some courts have adopted a *via media*, under which the reasonableness of the primary caregiving abductor's refusal to return is taken into account.[103] Where indeed her concerns are justified and separation from her will cause the child harm, return will be refused[104] unless measures can be put in place which will adequately allay her fears or protect the children.[105] As mentioned above, this approach has been adopted in the Swiss legislation, which expressly takes into account whether the abducting parent can reasonably be required to return, in cases where being placed in the care of the left-behind parent or in foster care is manifestly not in the best interests of the child.[106]

It might be thought that the fact that in practice most abducting mothers do return with their children,[107] even where there has been domestic violence[108] shows that usually the mother's threat not to return is bluff and need not be taken seriously. However, on the contrary this fact may be 'be considered to be a mark of the devotion of the mothers concerned that they are willing to sublimate their personal anxieties in order to be with their children'.[109] Thus, the relevant question should be whether it is reasonable to expect the abducting mother to return in the circumstances of the particular case, and not whether at the end of day she will accompany the child if return is ordered.

---

[98] *Steffen F v Severina* P 966 FSupp2d 922 (E Ariz 1997). See also recent the South African case of *Family Advocate v Remy* Case No 2004/2012 (unreported 15 February 2013) in which it was held that a three-year old was too young to return without her mother.

[99] eg Cour de Cassation, Première Chambre civile (France) Arrêt n° 1206, pourvoi n° 98-17902 [INCADAT cite: 498]; Cour de Cassation, première chambre civile (France) Cass Civ 1ère 12 July 1994, S. c. S. [INCADAT cite: HC/E/FR 103].

[100] eg *McCarthy v McCarthy* [1994] SLT 743 (dicta that if separation from their mother would cause them harm, the children would not be returned).

[101] See also German cases described in K Wolfe, 'A Tale of Two States: Successes and Failures of the 1980 Hague Convention on the Civil Aspects of International Child Abduction in the United States and Germany' (2000) 33 New York University Journal of International Law & Politics 285, 331–32.

[102] Cass Civ 1ère 25 janvier 2005 (N° de pourvoi: 02-17411) [INCADAT cite: 708]; *D v D* [2001] ScotCS 103; *Starr v Starr* 1999 SLT 335.

[103] Freeman (n 63) 70. For a discussion of the human rights implications of this approach, see below at IV Gii.

[104] eg Quebec Court of Appeal case of *NP v ABP* [1999] RDF 38 (mother's fears of returning to Israel, where she had been sold by the Russian mafia to the father as a prostitute and been abused by him, were reasonable); UF 260/98 Oberlandesgericht Stuttgart (Higher Regional Court), 25 November 1998 [INCADAT cite: HC/E/DE 323]; *Neulinger v Switzerland* App no 41615/07 (ECHR, 6 July 2010).

[105] As in *Re E* (n 6), in which the UK Supreme Court held that the protective measures were sufficient to prevent the deterioration of the mother's mental health. Similarly, in the case of *KS v LS* (n 32), the High Court of New Zealand held that the child would be sufficiently protected if the return were delayed until after the mother's surgery for breast cancer, so as to allow the mother to accompany her. Similarly, undertakings can remove the risk that the abductor will be prosecuted. For a detailed discussion of such undertakings and protective measures generally, see below at III.

[106] Section 5 on Swiss Federal Act on International Child Abduction (n 69), discussed at Aiii above.

[107] In M Freeman for Reunite Research Unit, 'Outcomes for Children Following an Abduction', www.reunite.org/edit/files/Library%20-%20reunite%20Publications/Outcomes%20Report.pdf, 35 ('Reunite Outcomes Study'), 13 out of 14 mothers returned. In contrast, none of the 8 abductor fathers returned.

[108] In the Reunite Outcomes Study ibid, domestic violence was raised as a concern in 44% of the cases in which the abducting mother raised a concern relating to return.

[109] ibid, 35.

iv Harm Caused as a Result of Violence against the Abductor

Much of the academic criticism against the Abduction Convention and its implementation has been directed to the impact of the Convention on domestic violence victims who abduct their children in order to escape the violence.[110] Ever since the second half of the 1990s, there has been a steady flow of literature highlighting the injustice perpetrated against such victims, invariably women, and their children when they are forced to return to the country from which they fled.[111]

Whilst this problem was mentioned indirectly in the documents of previous Special Commission Meetings,[112] and was discussed at the Fifth Special Commission Meeting,[113] it wasn't until the Sixth Special Commission Meeting in June 2011 that a detailed preliminary document, containing research into cases involving domestic violence, was published by the Permanent Bureau.[114] Interestingly, William Duncan, in presenting the subject, commented that the issue of how the Convention treats domestic violence was a matter of concern among some of the States which were considering acceding to the Convention.

Most of the discussion of the treatment of spousal domestic violence under the Convention has focused on the way in which the Article 13(1)(b) defence is interpreted and applied in cases where domestic violence is alleged.[115] This is hardly surprising since this defence would seem to be the most natural way of protecting domestic violence victims and their children. Yet, the available evidence suggests that the defence is successful in only around a quarter of cases in which there are allegations of domestic violence[116] and that there is a lack of consistency in the way in which the defence is applied by different

---

[110] The term 'domestic violence' is used here, in accordance with the definition in Art 3(b) of the Europe Convention on Preventing and Combating Violence against Women and Domestic Violence (adopted 7 April 2011), to refer to 'all acts of physical, sexual, psychological or economic violence that occur within the family or domestic unit or between former or current spouses or partners, whether or not the perpetrator shared or has shared the same residence with the victim'.

[111] eg C Bruch, 'The Unmet Needs of Domestic Violence Victims and their Children in Hague Child Abduction Convention Cases' (2004) 38 *Family Law Quarterly* 529; M Kaye, 'The Hague Convention and the Flight from Domestic Violence: How Women and Children are Being Returned by Coach and Four' (1999) 13 *International Journal of Law, Policy and the Family* 191; Weiner, 'Escape from Domestic Violence' (n 14) 634; R Hoegger, 'What If She Leaves? Domestic Violence Cases under the Hague Convention and the Insufficiency of the Undertakings Remedy' (2003) 18 *Berkeley Women's Law Journal* 181, 187–88; K Brown Williams, 'Fleeing Domestic Violence: A Proposal to Change the Inadequacies of the Hague Convention on the Civil Aspects of International Child Abduction in Domestic Violence Cases' (2011) 4 John *Marshall Law Journal* 39, 42–45.

[112] eg Preliminary Document No 5 of March 2001 (Checklist of Issues Raised and Recommendations Made in Response to Questionnaire Concerning the Practical Operation of the Hague Convention of 25th October 1980 on the Civil Aspects of International Child Abduction) (provided to the author by the Permanent Bureau) recommends 'close co-operation between judges and Central Authorities to ensure that the court's order includes appropriate safeguards and protections for the child's return, especially when abuse and violence allegations are raised' and the Appendix to the Fifth Commission's Conclusions, www.hcch.net/upload/concl28sc5_e.pdf refers to protecting an accompanying parent.

[113] MH Weiner, 'Half-Truths, Mistakes and Embarrassment: The United States Goes to the Fifth Meeting of the Special Commission to Review the Operation of the Hague Convention on the Civil Aspects of International Child Abduction' (2008) 1 *Utah Law Review* 222, 282 et seq.

[114] Reflection Paper (n 15).

[115] *cf* MH Weiner, 'Strengthening Article 20' (2004) 38 *United States Family Law Review* 701, 703 (suggesting using Art 20 in such cases). It should also be noted that where there are older children who object to returning, the existence of domestic violence can be relevant in a decision to uphold their objections under the Art 13(2) defence. In the research reported in the Reflection Paper (n 15), out of the 44% of cases in which return was refused, in 27% the refusal was based on grave risk and in 17% on child objections.

[116] In samples examined in Reflection Paper ibid, in 27% of the cases and in that examined by JL Edelson et al, 'Multiple Perspectives on Battered Mothers and their Children Fleeing to the United States for Safety, A Study of Hague Convention Cases Final Report', www.haguedv.org/reports/fmalreport.pdf, in 26% of the cases.

courts.[117] Perusal of the case law suggests that there are four main reasons why the defence is not successful in most cases.

Firstly, courts require proof of an established pattern of domestic violence.[118] Often, even where there was indeed regular violence, abductors are not able to prove this to the satisfaction of the court.[119] Their invariably weak financial situation means that they often do not have access to skilled lawyers to represent them.[120] Similarly, the psycho-social effects of, often prolonged, abuse and violence, impede their ability to collect reliable evidence both contemporaneously and retrospectively.[121]

Secondly, even where serious violence or abuse is established, many courts take the view that violence against the mother does not per se present a grave risk to the child or place him in an intolerable situation,[122] in the absence of evidence of violence or threats of violence against the child and/or clear expert evidence that the child has suffered from post-traumatic stress syndrome[123] or is likely to suffer therefrom if returned.[124] Accordingly, commentators[125] have argued that most courts take insufficient account of modern research literature, which shows that there is a correlation between child abuse and spousal violence and provides evidence that long-term damage is caused to children who are exposed to violence between their parents.[126]

Thirdly, even where the risk of violence is proven, some courts assume or feel obliged to assume that the authorities in the requesting State are willing and able to protect the abductor and children,[127] if requested to do so by the returning abductor.[128]

Fourthly, even where the judge is not prepared to simply rely on the foreign authorities, he will often believe that the risk of harm can be eliminated or reduced substantially through undertakings given to or imposed by him and/or other protective measures which

---

[117] Reflection Report ibid, para 148; Weiner, 'Half-Truths, Mistakes and Embarrassment' (n 113) 284–86. One of the reasons for the inconsistency might be the different standards of proof required in different States, see n 33 above and accompanying text.

[118] eg *Chirume* (n 19); *Charalambous v Charalambous* 627 F3d 462 (1st Cir 2010).

[119] eg *Kovacs v Kovacs* (2002) 59 OR (3d) 671 (Ohio CA), although return was refused on the basis that the father was a fugitive from justice.

[120] Edelson, et al (n 116) 233–34.

[121] Reflection Report (n 15), para 18.

[122] eg, *B v B* (n 95); *Ro* (n 94); *Antonio v Bello* 2004 US Dist LEXIS 17254 (ND Ga, 7 June 2004); *Dallemagne v Dallemagne* 440 F Supp 2d 1283, 1299 (MD Fla 2006); cf *Sonderup v Tondelli* 2001 (1) SA 1171 (CC) (S Afr) [34] (that violence not directed at the child can activate the grave risk defence); per Wall LJ in *Re W (A Child)* (n 17), 'If the effect on the mother of the father's conduct is severe it is, in my judgment, no hindrance to the success of an Article 13 (b) defence that no specific abuse has been perpetrated by the father on the child'; *Van de Sande v Van de Sande* 431 F3d 567 (7th Cir 2005) (that violence in front of children meant that children would face grave risk of harm).

[123] Edelson et al (n 116), identified five factors which appeared relevant to the success of an Art 13(1)(b) claim: (1) whether children were maltreated by the petitioning parent; (2) whether the children witnessed domestic violence; (3) whether the children suffered from post-traumatic stress disorder; (4) whether the abuser made threats to kill the children or others, and (5) whether there was expert testimony available. They found that grave risk was found in all of the seven cases in which four or five of these factors were present, but infrequently in the other cases. These factors were used as a basis to uphold the defence in *Acosta v Acosta* 2012 US Dist LEXIS 83063.

[124] As in *Blondin* (n 46).

[125] eg, Edelson et al (n 116) xi; Weiner, 'Half-Truths, Mistakes and Embarrassment' (n 113).

[126] For details of the relevant social science literature, see Reflection Report (n 15), para 19–22 and sources cited there and Edelson, et al ibid 26–29.

[127] eg, *Ro* (n 94); *Murray* (n 23); *TB v JB* (n 31); cf *El Sayed* (n 32), where the High Court overturned the return order because the trial judge had erred in holding that there was no grave risk because the Australian system could be relied upon to protect the children.

[128] Thus, in *TB v JB* ibid [97]. Arden LJ was not prepared to take account of the fact that the mother was too frightened of her husband to seek the protection of the New Zealand courts.

he puts in place.[129] Accordingly, he will still order return, albeit conditional on these measures. Increased judicial use of such measures[130] and the reference to the importance of protective measures in Permanent Bureau publications[131] does suggest that the academic exposure of the problem of domestic violence has led to much greater awareness of the dangers of returning children to situations of domestic violence.[132] Indeed, as mentioned above,[133] some courts prefer to concentrate on devising appropriate protective measures on the basis that the allegations are true, instead of getting involved in determining their veracity. These measures will be discussed in greater detail below, but it is appropriate to comment here that the benefit of the greater concern shown by courts for domestic violence victims and their children will be largely illusory[134] if the protective measures are not enforceable or effective in the requesting State.

v Harm Resulting from Abductor's Psychological Condition

In a number of cases, the claim of harm is based on the impact which the return of the child will have on the mother's psychological condition. Even though the mother will not be considered as responsible for a refusal to return where this would lead to a deterioration in her mental health,[135] the defence will only be made out if it can be shown that the return of the child without the mother or with the mother (where she is likely to return too), will create an intolerable situation for the child. Thus, for example, in the English case of *Re S (Child Abduction) (Grave Risk of Harm)*,[136] the mother's panic disorder caused by the security situation in Israel would not, in the Court's view, make the situation upon return with the mother intolerable for the children. In contrast, in the Australian case of *D-G v RSP*,[137] the risk that the mother might commit suicide if the child were returned to the father in the USA did meet this requirement.[138] Finally, in a recent English case, the Supreme Court refused return on the basis of the unusually powerful medical evidence which proved the devastating effect of the father's behaviour on her mental health.[139] The importance of the decision lies in its express recognition that the mother's subjective perceptions are relevant in determining the consequences of return on her and the child.

---

[129] eg, *Re H (Children)(Abduction)* [2003] EWCA Civ 355 (a case involving serious and repeated violence against the mother and the children, in which the Court of Appeal ordered return with protective measures, overturning the first instance judge's refusal to return decision on the basis that the father was an 'uncontrollable risk'.

[130] In the sample in the Reflection Paper (n 15), para 38, such measures were ordered in 25 out of the 49 cases in which return was ordered. See generally below at III.

[131] eg, Conclusions and Recommendation of Fifth Special Commission Meeting (n 112), para 1.8.

[132] Some courts have expressly referred to this literature, eg *Tsarbopoulos v Tsarbopoulos*, 176 F Supp 2d 1045, 1056 (ED Wash 2001); *Ostevoll v Ostevoll* 2000 WL 1611123 (SD Ohio); *Mander* (n 24); *Khan v Fatima* (n 20).

[133] At I B.

[134] Indeed, the very possibility of ordering protective measures may mean that courts order return when otherwise they would not do so. Furthermore, under the Art 11(4) of Council Regulation (EC) No 2201/2003 of 27 November 2003 concerning jurisdiction and the recognition and enforcement of judgments in matrimonial matters and the matters of parental responsibility, (Brussels II bis Regulation)[2003] OJ L 338/1-29, the court is not allowed to refuse return where 'adequate arrangements have been made to secure the protection of the child'.

[135] See eg *JLM v D-G* (n 32) [80].

[136] *Re S* (n 19).

[137] *D-G v RSP* (n 31).

[138] The Court specifically held that there were no conditions which could be imposed which would alleviate the risk. ibid [48]–[49]; See also *Armstrong v Evans* [2000] NZFLR 984, discussed in Freeman (n 63) 75; *Harries v Harries* [2011] FamCAFC 113.

[139] *Re S (A Child)* [2012] UKSC 10; see also *Re G (Abduction: Psychological Harm)* (n 17).

vi Harm Caused by Separation from Siblings

There are a number of situations in which a return order may result in the separation of siblings.[140] The first is where the child objection defence is established in relation to the mature sibling, but not in relation to a younger sibling.[141] The second less common situation is where the grave risk of harm defence is established in relation to only one of the siblings, as for example, where there are allegations of abuse in relation to one of the children only.[142] The third scenario is where there is a half or step-sibling being cared for by the abductor together with the abducted children. If this sibling remains in the country of refuge, the sibling who is returned will be separated from him. [143] Finally, in rare cases the Convention might apply to one sibling and not to the other, for example if they had different habitual residences at the time of removal or retention [144] or if the father had custody rights in relation to one and not the other.[145]

A number of approaches can be found in the case law to the question of whether and in what circumstances separation from siblings will activate the Article 13(1)(b) defence. Under the liberal approach, the court will readily find that returning one child alone will give rise to a grave risk of psychological harm or place that child in an intolerable situation.[146] This approach seems to be based on the recognition that 'the sibling relationship is generally the most enduring of all human relationships and of great importance and value to children' [147] and the assumption that keeping the family unit together is of 'paramount importance'.[148]

In contrast, the Israeli Supreme Court has adopted a strict approach, requiring that specific proof be brought of the harm to be suffered as a result of the separation of the siblings.[149] Furthermore, this approach relies on the fact that the return order does not create a permanent separation between the siblings and that it is for the court in the country of

---

[140] For convenience, reference will be made to the situation where there are only two siblings. However, this should be read as including a situation where there are more than two siblings of whom only some will be returned.

[141] In this situation, the issue of separation may also be relevant to the exercise of discretion to return in relation to the mature sibling. See ch 12 at II Ciii.

[142] As in the Scottish case of *Q Petitioner* (n 76).

[143] As in *Re C (Abduction: Grave Risk of physical or Psychological Harm)* (n 44).

[144] eg Israeli case of RFamA 2338/09 *LM v MM* http://elyon1.court.gov.il/verdictssearch/HebrewVerdictsSearch.aspx 3 June 2009 [INCADAT cite HC/E/IL 1037], in which the Abduction Convention proceedings only related to the five--year-old boy who had lived with the parties in France before the retention and not to the baby who had been born in Israel and remained there since his birth.

[145] RFam 2270/13 *DZ v AMVD*, 30th May 2013, http://elyon1.court.gov.il/files/13/700/022/t04/13022700.t04.pdf, in which the unmarried Dutch father had registered his rights in relation to the older son, but not the younger one.

[146] See eg *B v K (Child Abduction)* [1993] 1 FCR 382; *Urness v Minto* [1994] SC 249; *The Ontario Court v M and M (Abduction: Children's Objections)* [1997] 1 FLR 475. In *Re T (Abduction: Child's Objections to Return)* [2000] 2 FLR 192, Ward LJ said that the test was stringent but was willing to find that separation would lead to an intolerable situation on the basis of limited evidence. See also the Scottish decision in *PW v ALI* [2003] SCLR 478 [16], where the judge held that his decision not to order the return of the objecting child 'has the inevitable consequence' that the younger three siblings would not be returned. However, this case was overturned on appeal inter alia because there was no evidence to support this finding (*W v W* [2004] SC 63). See also *Ramirez v Buyauskas* 2012 US Dist LEXIS 24899 (separating siblings would not further the objective of the Abduction Convention of protecting the interests of children, as stated in the Preamble).

[147] *WF V RJ* [2010] EWHC 2909, [68]. In the case of *Miltiadous v Tetervak*, 686 F Supp 2d 544 (2010), 557, the court quoted the dictum that 'children's relationships with their siblings are the sort of intimate human relationships that are afforded a substantial measure of sanctuary from unjustified interference by the State.'

[148] *PW v ALI* ibid.

[149] *LM v MM* (n 144). See also *O v O* [2002] SC 430.

habitual residence to decide the implications of such a separation, when determining the merits of the dispute as to the place of the child's residence.[150] Similarly, it has been stated that a decision to give effect to the wishes of one child 'ought not to be regarded as necessarily sealing the fate of all the children.'[151]

In those cases in which courts have not been prepared to invoke the grave risk defence in relation to the younger sibling, they have invariably exercised their discretion to order return of the older sibling(s) despite his/their objections.[152] However, the Israeli Supreme Court recently distinguished the foreign cases and ordered return of a child on the basis that there was no objective reason why the mother should not return as well with the younger brother, to whom the Convention did not apply.[153] Likewise, in cases involving a half-sibling where the reason for the separation is seen as being the abductor's decision not to return with the half-sibling to the country of origin, the situation is treated as akin to that of separation from the primary carer caused by the abductor's refusal to return. Thus, in a number of cases, courts have ordered the return of a child, despite the fact that an older half-sibling, who was not the subject of the Convention application, was refusing to return and this caused an intractable dilemma for the mother.[154] In all these cases, the court emphasised the fact that the mother had herself caused this situation by removing or retaining the child. However, insufficient weight seems to have been given to the potential separation from the mature halfsibling who refuses to return.[155] The reason for this seems to be that since the Convention does not apply to the half/sibling, there is no need to consider his objections to return independently.[156] However, surely from the point of view of the returning child, the degree of intolerability of separation from a sibling is caused by the strength of the de facto connection between the siblings and not by the blood relationship.[157]

vii Harm Resulting from the Child's Integration into his New Environment

As seen in an earlier chapter,[158] the fact that the child has integrated fully in the environment in which he lives in the requested State is not a defence to return, unless 12 months passed between the date of the removal or retention and the commencement of proceedings under the Convention, in accordance with Article 12(2). Nonetheless, the abductor sometimes claims that the fact of integration means that return will expose the child to a grave risk of harm or otherwise place him in an intolerable situation. This claim is often raised in cases where, even though the application was submitted within 12 months, a long

---

[150] *LM v MM* (n 144) (Jubran J). However, in this case, the ultimate result was that the children were separated because the mother refused to return with the older child; Israel response to Permanent Bureau's 2010 Questionnaire, www.hcch.net/index_en.php?act=publications.details&pid=5291&dtid=33), para 6.6.

[151] *W v W* (n 146), para 17.

[152] eg *Zaffino v Zaffino (Abduction: Children's Views)*[2005] EWCA Civ 1012.

[153] *DZ v DMVD* (n 145), following *LM v MM* (n 144).

[154] *Re C (Abduction: Grave Risk of Psychological Harm)* (n 44); *Re C(B)(Child Abduction: Risk of Harm)* [1999] 3 FCR 510 (CA); *S v B & Y* (Abduction: Human Rights) [2005] EWHC 733 (Fam).

[155] eg, comments of Ward LJ in *Re T* (n 146), that the separation would be from the abductor if he decided to stay.

[156] Although the Court did take into account the half-sibling's difficult situation in the case of *S v B & Y* (n 154), but it was held that the half-sibling's rights could not prevail over the rights of the father and the abducted child. Similarly in *Re E* (n 6), [50] it was held that the interference with the right to family life of the the step-sibling could readily be justified on the basis of the interests of the abducted child and the left-behind father.

[157] Ward LJ in *Re T* (n 146), also distinguishes the cases on the basis of the fact that in *Re T*, the children are full-blood siblings, without explaining the significance of this distinction.

[158] In ch 9.

period of time has subsequently elapsed before the making of a final judicial determination.[159] However, the claim has invariably been rejected on the basis that since neither lapse of time nor integration are defences in their own right, they could not form the basis of the Article 13(1)(b) defence.[160] In the case of *RB v VG*, the Israeli Supreme Court recognised that the lapse of time, during which the child had become well integrated into the ultra-orthodox community in the Israeli town where he lived, would substantially increase the difficulty of returning him.[161] However, the Court held that the lapse of time could not form the basis of the grave risk defence, inter alia because to allow the mother to benefit from this lapse of time would be rewarding a wrongdoer.[162]

Nonetheless, in the US case of *Blondin*, the post-abduction stability of the children was treated as a relevant factor in determining that the grave risk defence was established because a return to France would, in the words of the expert, 'undo the benefit of the psychological and emotional roots' which the children had established with the mother and her family in the USA which had helped them in their recovery from the 'severe trauma' which they had suffered as a result of being exposed to the serious abuse of the mother by the father.[163]

Furthermore, in two European Court of Human Rights (ECtHR) cases, lapse of time together with integration in the receiving State do seem to have formed the basis for the refusal to return the child, even though proceedings were started within the 12-month period. In the case of *Neulinger and Shuruk v Switzerland*,[164] the reason given by the majority of the Grand Chamber for allowing the appeal was that the additional period of a year and a half which had elapsed since the decision of the lower court had tipped the balance against return.[165] It was pointed out that return after a certain period of time would undermine the pertinence of the Convention. It was also held that in determining whether return was a proportional measure in cases where a child had settled, account had to be taken of the difficulties which would face the child as a result of being uprooted from his familiar environment and the nature of his ties with the country to which he was being returned.[166] While the principles set out by the Court cannot be faulted, it is difficult to accept that their application should have led to non-return in this case. There was no evidence that the now seven-year-old child would suffer any harm over and above the usual harm associated with moving from one environment to another. Similarly, in the case of *Raban v Romania*,[167] where the children had been living in Romania for five years, the decision that the children should not be returned because they had integrated into the environment in Romania is

---

[159] eg *Neulinger* (n 104) (5 years); *Raban v Romania* (n 84) (5 years); *RB v VG* (n 34) (2 and a half years).
[160] eg, decision of the Dutch Supreme Court in the case of *Van den Berg*, as reported in *Van den Berg and Sarri v The Netherlands*, no 7239/08, 2 November 2010; *Walsh v Walsh* 221 F3d 204, 220 (1st Cir 2000); *KG v CB* 2012 (4) SA 136 (SCA).
[161] *RB v VG* (n 34). See also the comment of Kirby J in *De L v Director-General, NSW Department of Community Services* (1996) FLC 92-706: 'The assumption is that the return of a child to a foreign jurisdiction, if concluded within a very short time, will not ordinarily cause irreparable harm to the child. The longer the delay, the greater the potential for harm to the child.'
[162] *RB v VG* ibid [9]. However, Justice Arbel did place considerable weight on the lapse of time and integration of the child in coming to the conclusion that the return should be delayed in order to attempt to reduce the harm to the child by preparing him for the enormous change in his life (ibid [17]).
[163] For criticism of this aspect of the decision, see MH Weiner, 'Navigating the Road between Uniformity and Progress: The Need for Purposive Analysis of the Hague convention on the Civil Aspects of International Child Abduction' (2002) 33 *Columbia Human Rights Law Review* 275, 345–49.
[164] *Neulinger* (n 104).
[165] ibid [146]–[7].
[166] ibid.
[167] *Raban v Romania* (n 84).

difficult to justify. No evidence was presented of any difficulties which would be involved in returning them to Israel.

In contrast, in the later case of *Van den Berg v The Netherlands*,[168] the ECtHR upheld the decision of the Dutch Supreme Court ordering return of the seven-year-old girl to Italy, despite the fact that she had fully integrated into Holland during the three years during which she had lived there.[169] However, it should be pointed out that in this case, the child had already been returned to Italy in accordance with the decision of the Dutch Supreme Court. The decision may have been different if the execution of that judgment has been stayed and the child had remained in Holland for an additional three years pending the decision of the ECtHR, as happened in the *Neulinger* case. Thus, it is not entirely clear that this case really represents a change in the approach of the ECtHR to the integration of the child over a long period of time. Of course, this issue will be less likely to arise if the ECtHR adopts a fast-track procedure in petitions involving Abduction Convention cases.[170]

Finally, an additional factor which might be relevant is the likelihood that the court in the requesting State will in fact give permission for the relocation of the child back to the requested State. It has been suggested that where there is a high degree of probability that such permission will be given, returning the child is an 'empty gesture' because it causes additional and unnecessary upheaval for the child.[171] Adopting this approach in all cases is problematic as it would seem to undermine the very basis of the Convention. However, in cases where there has been substantial delay and the child has become well integrated in the State of refuge, the fact that it is extremely likely that he will later be allowed to return to that State means that return will place him in the intolerable situation of being disrupted just for the sake of upholding the Convention.

viii Financial Hardship

The claim that the reduction in the child's standard of living which will be caused by the return will place the child in an intolerable situation is hardly ever accepted.[172] The main reason for this would seem to be the practice of accepting or requiring undertakings from the left-behind parent that he will provide financial support for the child and the returning parent.[173] In addition, courts have commented that the mere reduction in the living standard of the child would not constitute a grave risk of harm or create an intolerable situation because otherwise there would be an unchecked power to abduct children from poorer countries to more developed countries.[174]

---

[168] *Van den Berg* (n 160).
[169] This overturned the lower courts' decision that leaving the stable environment in Holland would expose the girl to grave risk.
[170] See ch 1 at II Diib.
[171] Freeman (n 63) 70; For the suggestion that this is a situation in which the intolerable situation defence might apply, see JM Eekelaar, 'International Child Abduction by Parents' (1982) 32 *University of Toronto Law Journal* 281, 313.
[172] eg Australian case of *De Lewinski* [1997] 21 Fam LR 41; *De L v D-G, NSW Department of Community Service* [1996] 20 Fam LR 390; 2007 decision of the Hungarian Supreme Court detailed in the response to the 2010 Questionnaire (n 150), para 1.2, holding that the Art 13(1)(b) defence was not established simply because the mother had a job in Hungary and so could provide for her children better than in Israel, where she had had to rely on State benefits.
[173] See III below.
[174] *Cuellar v Joyce* 596 F3d 505 (9th Cir 2010) (holding that the mother's living conditions in Panama, where her home had no indoor plumbing and 'no climate control, no refrigeration, and very little furniture', did not create a grave risk of harm).

Thus, provided that the returning parent will be entitled to State benefits, or have some other source of income, and would not be left homeless and destitute, the defence will not be established.[175] Similarly, it has been held that the fact that the abductor will not be able to afford legal representation in the custody proceedings is irrelevant.[176]

ix Immigration Restrictions

In a number of cases, the abductor has claimed that return will place the child in an intolerable situation because she is not able to accompany him due to immigration restrictions in the country of origin. In some of these cases, courts have indicated that they would be willing to accept this claim if all efforts to obtain permission to enter the following country fail.[177] Indeed, in the Australian case of *Victoria v Ardito*,[178] return was refused when the mother was unable to obtain a visa to re-enter the US because the Court was satisfied that there was a grave risk that the child would be placed in an intolerable situation if returned alone. The Court also noted that the reason that the mother's request for a visa was refused was because the father had commenced divorce proceedings against her in the US. However, at the end of the day, it seems that it is usually possible, often after considerable efforts by the Central Authority, to obtain the necessary visa or permission for the accompanying parent[179] and so it will be very rare for return to be refused under Article 13(1)(b) because of immigration restrictions.

The grave risk defence has also been raised in cases where the left-behind parent's immigration status in the requesting State is uncertain. However, courts have invariably taken the view that where the requesting State supports the application under the Convention and will allow the child to return, then the courts of that country are best placed to consider the implications of immigration status on the custody issue.[180]

III Protective Measures

A Introduction

The use of measures to protect returning children has now become quite widespread. As will be seen below, there are a number of different types of protective measures which may be put in place by courts and administrative bodies. These include undertakings, which may be offered voluntarily or imposed by the court (in the latter case, they are effectively conditions to return), mirror orders, liaison between Central Authorities and judicial

---

[175] eg, *Re M (Abduction: Undertakings)* [1995] 1 FLR 1021,1026–127 (Butler-Sloss LJ); cf *Re O* (n 67) 362 (Singer J).
[176] eg, *Emmett v Perry* [1996] FLC 92-645, 85 and 525; *Re O* ibid.
[177] eg, South African case of *Chirume* (n 19) (the Court said that the mother could apply for variation of an order if all her attempts to get a visa failed); cf Swiss case of *arrêt du TC VD du 17.11.10*, consid. 3c, 15 (n 69).
[178] *State Cent Auth of Victoria v Ardito*, 29 October 1997, Family Court of Australia (Unreported).
[179] Personal communication from Adv Leslie Kaufman of the Israeli Central Authority; Conclusions and Recommendations of the Fourth Meeting of the Special Commission to Review the Operation of the Hague Child Abduction Convention (2001), www.hcch.net/upload/concl28sc4_e.pd, rec 5.3 (urging Contracting States to take measures to ensure that abducting parents can enter the country for the purpose of participating in custody proceedings).
[180] eg *Jabbaz v Mouammar* (2003) 226 DLR (4th) 494 (Ont CA).

co-operation. As Beaumont and McEleavy point out,[181] in cases where the obstacles to return are relatively minor, undertakings given by the left-behind parent to remedy these obstacles should be viewed as a bonus. However, the more difficult situation, which will be addressed below, is that where there are serious obstacles to the return of the child and protective measures are designed to overcome those obstacles.

The better view seems to be that the availability of ameliorative measures which protect the child effectively prevents the grave risk defence from being established and thus the court does not have any discretion not to return the child.[182] However, a few judges have taken the view that where the defence is established (without taking into account the possibility of protective measures), such measures are simply a relevant factor in exercising the court's discretion.[183] The former approach is expressly adopted in Article 11(4) of the Brussels II bis Regulation,[184] which provides that a court cannot refuse to return a child on the basis of the grave risk exception 'if it is established that adequate arrangements have been made to secure the protection of the child after his or her return'.

On the one hand, it may seem that the difference between the two approaches is more apparent than real because if a court thinks that it is not appropriate to return the child, despite the suggested protective measures, it will simply hold that those measures are not sufficient to prevent the defence being established. On the other hand, if the burden of proving that the proposed protective measures are not adequate is placed on the abductor, then the difference between the two approaches will be significant.[185] The wording of the Brussels II bis Regulation suggests that the burden is on the left-behind parent, but there are some non-European cases where the court appears to place the burden of proving inadequacy on the abductor.[186] A third possible approach is that the court simply has to be satisfied as to the adequacy of the proposed measures, without either party being required to discharge the burden of proof.

The issue of determining the adequacy of the proposed measures also gives rise to an important question of policy. On the one hand, careful scrutiny of the efficacy of these measures does not seem consistent with the spirit of reciprocity on which the Convention is based.[187] On the other hand, however, where the grave risk defence would be established but for the proposed ameliorative measures, surely the court has a duty to check carefully that these measures do indeed eliminate the risk to the child or sufficiently reduce it so that it can no longer be described as grave.[188] The different types of protective measures and their respective advantages and disadvantages will now be discussed.

---

[181] Beaumont and McEleavy (n 1) 158.
[182] This is the position in Israel eg *Ro* (n 94); *RB v VG* (n 34).
[183] eg *DP* (n 32) (Glesson CJ); *JLM v D-G* (n 32) [40].
[184] Council Regulation (EC) No 2201/2003 of 27 November 2003; see generally ch I at II C.
[185] Weiner, 'Escape from Domestic Violence' (n 14) 660.
[186] eg, *S v S* [1999] 3 NZLR 513, 523 (Fisher J).
[187] Wolfe, 'A Tale of Two States' (n 101) 331 argues that the adequacy of the safeguards should not be checked because this will lead to differential treatment of different countries.
[188] eg *Danaipour* (n 10); *Blondin* (n 46). It should also be remembered that because of the 'power dynamics' between batterer and victim, the abductor may be 'subtly coerced' into agreeing to undertakings even though they are not adequate, Weiner, 'Escape from Domestic Violence' (n 14) 680–81.

B Undertakings

Neither the Abduction Convention nor the implementing legislation of the various countries make any mention of the possibility of undertakings being given in respect of arrangements in the requesting State upon return of the child. Rather, the use of undertakings is 'a judicial construct, developed in the context of British family law'.[189] Beaumont and McEleavy[190] point out that undertakings had long been used by English courts in family cases involving an international element, including in pre-Convention abduction cases. Thus, it is hardly surprising that such undertakings soon became a common feature of Abduction Convention cases in the UK and other common law jurisdictions.[191] Some civil jurisdictions have adopted a similar practice under which protection orders can be made as a condition for return.[192]

Undertakings are often offered voluntarily by the left-behind parent in support of his application for return. However, where there is no such offer or it is not viewed as adequate, courts have been prepared to impose undertakings as a condition to ordering return. Whilst imposed undertakings, sometimes called conditions, may be more difficult to justify legally than voluntary ones,[193] in practice there does not seem to be any difference of substance between the two types of undertakings and so the following discussion will not differentiate between them.

A perusal of the case law reveals that there are five main categories of undertakings. The first and most common type of undertaking deals with financial and material matters, most commonly the cost of return[194] and the provision of accommodation and support for the child and returning parent.[195] The second type of undertaking is designed to prevent criminal proceedings being commenced or continued against the abducting parent on return. This may involve a commitment by the left-behind parent not to bring criminal charges or to withdraw charges which have already been brought[196] and/or to obtain assurances from the prosecuting authorities in the requesting State[197] that criminal charges will not be instigated or will be dropped.[198] The third category concerns the custody of the child

---

[189] *Danaipour* ibid 21.

[190] Beaumont and McEleavy (n 1) 157.

[191] *Re A* (n 48) 371; *C v C* (n 95); *MacMillan v MacMillan* 1989 SLT 350 (Scot Ex Div 1989); *Damiano v Damiano* [1993] NZFLR 548; *Police Commissioner of South Australia v Temple* (No 2) (1993) FLRC 92-424.

[192] See eg Austrian Response to Questionnaire of 2010 (n 150), para 1.2(2); cf Swiss decision in Urteil AppGer BS vom 17 November 2011, consid. 7.1 (discussed in Alfieri (n 69) 564), in which it was held that there was no legal basis to make the return conditional on the left-behind parent making payments to support the child.

[193] Beaumont and McEleavy (n 1) 161.

[194] Which the Court might otherwise require the abductor to cover under Art 26 of the Convention, see ch 17.

[195] eg *Sonderup* (n 122); *Ro* (n 94). Occasionally, this also includes financing the abductor's legal costs in the foreign custody dispute, eg *Re W (A Child)* (n 17)).

[196] eg, *Tabacchi v Harrison*, 2000 WL 190576 (N D III. 2000); *Re C* (n 44).

[197] Conclusions and Recommendations of the Fourth Meeting of the Special Commission to Review the Operation of the Hague Child Abduction Convention (n 179), rec 5.2., urging prosecuting authorities to give such assurances. cf comment of California Court of Appeal in *Maurizio* (n 96) 644 that the 'trial court overstepped its bounds by making an order for Leo's return contingent on Father's provision of an assurance from the Italian government that it will not arrest or prosecute Mother' because this requires an action which is not within the father's control.

[198] eg, *Sonderup* (n 122) [52], requiring an order from the Court of British Columbia confirming that criminal proceedings were no longer pending against the mother. In the Israeli case of *RB v VG* (n 34), the Supreme Court required inter alia that such assurances be obtained from the prosecution authorities in France, where proceedings had already been commenced against the abducting mother. However, when there was a delay in obtaining these assurances, the Israeli Supreme Court held that the child should be returned immediately; for the aftermath, see

pending legal proceedings in the requesting State. Where the left-behind parent has obtained a custody order prior to or in the wake of the abduction, then the undertaking/condition may provide that he will not enforce that order until there has been a full hearing on the merits.[199] In such a case, an undertaking may be essential to restore the *status quo ante*[200] and reflects the fact that 'chasing orders' made in response to the abduction are not usually based on a full best interests analysis. The fourth type of undertaking is designed to protect the returning child and parent from violence or other forms of abusive behaviour by the left-behind parent. Typically, such an undertaking will include a commitment not to approach the returning parent, and sometimes also the child, without permission from the courts in the requesting State.[201] Finally, the left-behind parent may undertake to commence custody proceedings in the requesting State promptly following return of the child.[202]

Undertakings only remain in force for a limited time, often only until the court in the requesting State becomes seized of the case. However, it has been suggested that in order to ensure adequate protection, it is necessary for the undertakings to remain in operation at least until a reasoned interim judgment is given.[203]

The wide use of undertakings has been subject to criticism both from the viewpoint of the abductor and from that of the left-behind parent. On the one hand, it is claimed that undertakings may not be of any real value, because they may well not be enforceable and so 'may simply be sophisticated forms of judicial conscience appeasement'.[204] On the other hand, it has been argued that 'undertakings are used too broadly and allow abducting parents to gain significant advantages from the abduction'.[205] The latter view seems extreme since it is unlikely that abductions are motivated by the hope of obtaining such advantages when return is ordered. However, courts should clearly ensure that undertakings do no more than provide for a basic standard of living immediately on return.[206] The abductor will of course be free to apply to the courts of the requesting State for a higher level of financial support when she has returned.

In support of the former view, there is a good deal of evidence to support the claim that undertakings may not achieve their purpose in adequately safeguarding the child from harm. The main problem is that the undertakings are not usually enforceable in the requesting

---

n 55 above. Compare *Neulinger* (n 104) [149], in which one of the reasons given by Grand Chamber of the ECtHR for allowing the appeal was the risk of prosecution of the mother in Israel, even though there was a letter from the Israeli Central Authority stating that the mother would not be prosecuted if the child was returned, provided she complied with future court orders. Surely if this assurance was not sufficient, clearer guarantees could have been requested from the Israeli authorities (see concurring judgment of Cabral Barreto [2]).

[199] eg *Sonderup* ibid [49]; Israeli case of *RB v VG* ibid (custody order obtained prior to abduction).
[200] *Thomson v Thomson* [1994] 3 SCR 551, 559.
[201] eg, *Ro* (n 94); *Damiano* (n 191).
[202] eg, *Re S (A Minor)(Abduction)* [1991] 2 FLR 1; 21, *Re K (Abduction: Child's Objections)* (n 43); *Suarez v Carranza* (2008) 2008 CarswellBC 1829, 2008 BCSC 1187.
[203] See Beaumont and McEleavy (n 1) 170, citing *Medhurst v Markle* (1995) 26 OR (3d) 178 (Gen Div) 190.
[204] Freeman, 'Primary Carers' (n 6) 146.
[205] Report of the Third Special Commission,www.hcch.net/upload/abduc97e.pdf, para 64. See also letter from US State Department to the Lord Chancellor's Office, written in response to British concerns that US courts were not enforcing undertakings, quoted in *Danaipour* (n 10) 22 stating that the scope of undertakings should be limited and should not include detailed provisions in relation to custody, visitation and maintenance.
[206] At the first part of the Sixth Special Commission meeting, one delegate commented that exaggerated conditions for return, such as to provide the returning abductor with a car and other non-essential items, etc often created an impossible burden for the left-behind parent (author's notes).

State.[207] In particular, in non-common law jurisdictions,[208] the concept of undertakings is unfamiliar.[209] Thus, the abductor is effectively dependent on the left-behind parent's willingness to keep his word or on the possibility of obtaining appropriate protection quickly from the courts of the requesting State. This will often not be the case[210] and frequently the fact that such immediate protection is not available was the reason for the abduction or for the imposition of undertakings. The problem is particularly acute in domestic violence cases, both because of the likelihood that the sort of people that abuse their spouses will not balk at violating their undertakings[211] and because of the real risks involved in renewed violence.[212] Indeed, one research study showed that in all of the six cases in which undertakings were given relating to violence or non-molestation, these undertakings were violated.[213]

However, the problem of non-enforceability has often not been taken seriously. Some judges have assumed that it is more apparent than real[214] and some have taken the view that comity requires them to assume that courts and other authorities in the requesting State will take 'the same serious view of a failure to honour undertakings given to a court (of any jurisdiction)'.[215] Other judges, whilst appreciating that the undertakings might not be enforceable, are prepared to rely on their own assessment that the left-behind parent genuinely intends to comply with the undertakings.[216]

Nonetheless some courts have realised the naivety of the above approaches[217] and there has been express judicial reference to the unenforceability of undertakings[218] and to the fact that there are cases where unenforceable undertakings will not protect the child[219] and that

---

[207] Interviews with left-behind parents reveal that some of them had been advised by their lawyers in advance to agree to the undertakings because they were not enforceable, Reunite Outcomes Study (n 107) 33.

[208] Even common law jurisdictions will not always enforce undertakings, eg *Roberts v Roberts* 1998 US Dist LEXIS 4089 (D Mass 27 February 1998).

[209] per Baroness Hale and Lord Wilson in *Re E* (n 6) [7]; 'Swedish Report in Special Focus: Enforcement and Return of Access Orders' (Judges' Newsletter, Spring 2004 Issue) 46, www.hcch.net/upload/spring2004.pdf.

[210] eg the Scottish case of *PW v ALI* (n 147), in which after return to Australia, the Court there reduced the sums of maintenance which the father had undertaken to the Scottish Court that he would pay. When the father didn't pay even the reduced amount, the mother took the children back to Scotland, Report for Scotland in Special Focus ibid, 65.

[211] eg comment in *Simcox* (n 72) that the traits which the applicant had exhibited ('an arrogance, a need to be in control and a tendency to act out violently') raised questions as to his willingness to abide by the Court's undertakings; *Walsh* (n 160) (the Court took into account the fact that the father had previously breached court orders when refusing return).

[212] eg case studies in Edelson et al (n 116) 180–83.

[213] Reunite Outcomes Study (n 107) 31.

[214] eg the view expressed in *JLM v D-G* (n 32) [146], 'Too much should not, in my view, be made of the difficulty of enforcing such undertakings.... Undertakings are now a common feature of such cases. There is no mention in the casebooks that I could find of practical difficulties that have arisen in conforming to such undertakings. This Court need not be concerned about such problems where they are not shown to exist.'

[215] *Re M (Abduction: Non-Convention Country)* [1995] 1 FLR 89, quoted in the Convention case of *Re K (Abduction: Physical Harm)* [1995] 2 FLR 550. Alternatively, it is assumed that considerations of comity will motivate the courts in the requesting State to give effect to the undertakings, *RK v JK (Child Abduction: Acquiescence)* [2000] 2 IR 416.

[216] eg *Re O* (n 67).

[217] The US Court of Appeals in *Danaipour* (n 10) 16 commented that the District Court had 'made incorrect assumptions that its own order could and would be enforced by a foreign court'.

[218] eg *McOwan and McOwan* [1994] FLC 92-451, 80691.

[219] *Danaipour* (n 10) 26 (stating that, where one of the exceptions was established, the Court should not return the child on the basis of undertakings, unless enforcement could be guaranteed); *Simcox* (n 72) (reversing and remanding a decision to return two children due to concerns that the undertakings would not be enforceable). See also the South African case of *Family Advocate v Remy*, Case No 2004/2012 (unreported, 15 February 2013), [36] in which the judge recognises that an order requiring the father to provide accommodation for the mother might not be effective because of the father's inability to finance two households and the mother's ineligibility for public assistance.

the burden is on the applicant to prove the efficacy of the undertakings.[220] Accordingly, there have been various attempts to find ways to overcome the problem of lack of enforceability of undertakings in the requesting State, which will be discussed in the next section.

C Ensuring Enforceability of Undertakings/Conditions

i Compliance before Return

Some types of undertakings can be drafted in such a way as to require compliance before return of the child. For example, in relation to financial commitments, the left-behind parent can be required to deposit the money up-front[221] and to bring evidence that there is separate accommodation available for the returning parent's use.[222] Similarly, undertakings designed to prevent commencement or continuation of criminal proceedings can be fulfilled before the return by withdrawing complaints and obtaining confirmation from the relevant prosecution authorities.[223]

ii Mirror Orders/Safe Harbour Orders

Where the undertakings relate to the behaviour of the left-behind parent after the return, the only way to ensure enforceability is to provide for the making of a court order in the requesting State prior to return. In some cases applicants requesting return of children to the US obtain a safe harbour order from a US court, in addition to the undertakings given to the court of the requested State.[224] Similarly, sometimes the court of the requested State requires the applicant to obtain an order from the court of the requesting State (known as a mirror order), containing parallel undertakings.[225] The advantage of safe harbour orders is that they avoid the unseemliness of the court in the requested State requiring the foreign court to make an order and the foreign court's possible non-compliance.[226] The advantage of mirror orders is that the undertakings will be enforceable both in the requesting and requested States.[227] Both types of order solve the problem of the limited duration of undertakings given to the court of the requested State. Since the undertakings are included in a court order of the requesting State, they can remain in force until that court cancels them. However, the evidence suggests that neither safe harbour orders nor mirror orders are commonly made.[228]

---

[220] *Simcox* ibid.
[221] See eg, *Ro* (n 94); *Sonderup* (n 122); *Re W (Abduction: Domestic Violence)* [2004] EWHC 1247.
[222] eg *KG v CB* 2012 (n 155); FamA (Dist TA)1382/04, Nevo, 1 May 2006 (Isr), where appeal against return was allowed inter alia because after a considerable amount of time the father had not yet shown that there was accommodation available for the child and mother. Compare Misc Application 2282/09 *DCM v PM*, Nevo, 7 October 2009 (Isr), in which the Israeli Court held that it could not help the mother, who upon returning to the US discovered that the father had not vacated the apartment, which was a condition of the Israeli Court's return order, and that she should not have returned until she had checked that the apartment had been vacated.
[223] eg *Sonderup* (n 122) [52]; *KG v CB*, ibid.
[224] Working Paper No 1 of 2001, Proposal by the Delegation of Australia, Facilitating the Safe and Prompt Return of Children (provided to the author by the Permanent Bureau).
[225] eg, *C v C* (n 95) 471; *Re G (A Minor) (Abduction)* [1989] 2 FLR 475; *Re W (Abduction: Domestic Violence)* (n 223).
[226] *Danaipour* (n 10) 22.
[227] Working Paper No 1 of 2001 (n 224).
[228] eg, in the Reflection Paper (n 15), mirror orders were mentioned in only three of the cases surveyed; *Sonderup* (n 122), *Re W (A Child)* (n 17) and *Re M (Abduction: Intolerable Situation)* [2000] 1 FLR 930.

It is not entirely clear whether the sparse use of this apparently effective method of making protective measures enforceable can be explained by the lack of awareness of this possibility among judges and lawyers or whether there are more substantive reasons. Two problems with mirror orders are mentioned by the US Court of Appeals in the case of *Danaipour v McLarey*.[229] Firstly, it is claimed that the practice of conditioning return upon the making of an order by the court in the requesting State 'would smack of coercion of the foreign court'.[230] Secondly, the court takes the view that expecting the foreign court simply to copy and enforce the order of the court of the requested State 'offends notions of international comity'.[231] Neither of these reasons is convincing. The court in the requested State has a duty to protect the child and in some circumstances the only way in which it can be sure that the child's safety can be protected on return is by dictating the conditions of return. If the foreign court does not like the conditions, then the child will not be returned. Of course, as stated above, the court of the requested State should limit the conditions to those necessary to protect the child upon return.

Other reasons which spring to mind for the limited use made of safe harbour and mirror orders are that some legal systems do not have the necessary procedures for giving such orders, or for the making of particular undertakings,[232] and the delay involved in obtaining them.[233] All these problems could be solved by relatively simple procedural reform in the Member States. The Conclusions of the Fourth Special Commission expressly recommend that Contracting States 'should consider the provisions of procedures for obtaining, in the jurisdiction to which the child is to be returned, any necessary provisional protective measures prior to the return of the child'.[234] However, this recommendation does not seem to have had any real impact[235] and the Fifth Special Commission Conclusions raised the possibility of providing a clear legal framework for the taking of protective measures to secure the safe return of the child (and where necessary the accompanying parent) in a Protocol to the Convention.[236] More recently, the UK Supreme Court urged the Hague Conference to consider whether procedures might be put in place which will enable protective measures to be enforceable in the requesting State.[237]

iii International Conventions

Where both of the States involved have ratified the 1996 Child Protection Convention, protective measures ordered by the court in the requested State will be automatically enforceable in the requesting State.[238] Similarly, the European Union's proposed Protective Civil Order Regulation[239] will make protective orders issued in one EU State effective in all others.

---

[229] *Danaipour* (n 10).
[230] ibid 23.
[231] ibid.
[232] eg, in the case of *Danaipour* ibid 12, the Swedish Court did not enter an identical order to that given by the US Court, holding that 'the majority of the conditions imposed by Federal Court for a return of the children under the Hague Convention cannot for formal reason be confirmed'.
[233] See eg, Israeli case of FamC (Jer) 87403/07 *YDG v TG*, Nevo, 1 November 2007 (Isr).
[234] The Fourth Special Commission Conclusions (n 181), rec 5(1).
[235] See L Silberman, 'Patching Up the Abduction Convention: A Call for a New International Protocol and a Suggestion for Amendments to ICARA' (2003) 38 *Texas International Law Journal* 41, fn 97.
[236] The Fifth Special Commission Conclusions (n 112), rec 1.8.3. In relation to a Protocol, see ch 19 at II C.
[237] *Re E* (n 6) [37].
[238] See ch 1 at II E.
[239] European Union's proposed Protective Civil Order Regulation, COM(2011) 276.

D Judicial Liaison

The International Hague Network of Judges,[240] which includes more than 70 judges from 48 States,[241] facilitates both general communication between judges in relation to the Hague Conventions[242] and direct communication between judges from different countries in specific cases. The idea that liaison between the judge hearing an application for the return of a child under the Abduction Convention and a judge in the requesting State can assist in overcoming obstacles to return, has become increasingly accepted over the last decade.[243] However, there are quite a number of Contracting States where such liaison is not possible because there is no legal basis for such judicial communications.[244]

In order to promote uniformity in the practice of direct judicial communications in those States where it is possible, the Permanent Bureau has published a document containing guidance and general principles in relation to judicial communications,[245] the use of which was approved at the Sixth Special Commission.[246] This document lists seven examples of matters which may be subject to communication.[247] Five of these are relevant to the need to protect the returning child from harm.

> b) [A]re protective measures available for the child or other parent in the State where the child would be returned?
> c) [C]an the foreign court accept and enforce undertakings offered by the parties in the initiating jurisdiction?
> d) [I]s the foreign court willing to entertain a mirror order (same order in both jurisdictions) if the parties are in agreement?
> e) [W]ere orders made by the foreign court?
> f) [W]ere findings about domestic violence made by the foreign court?

Whilst it is clear that judicial liaison may provide the judge in the requested State with information which enables him to make a more informed decision as to whether the child can be safely returned to the requesting State, some reservations have been expressed.

Firstly, where the relevant information simply relates to the law and practice in the foreign country, it is not clear why it could not be obtained by communication between

---

[240] For recommendations in relation to the appointment of liaison judges, see 'Emerging rules regarding the development of the International Hague Network of Judges and draft general principles for Judicial communications, including commonly accepted safeguards for direct judicial communications in specific cases, within the context of the International Hague Network of Judges', Preliminary Document No 3A revised July 2012, www.hcch.net/upload/wop/abduct2011pd03ae.pdf, Rule 1.1–1.8 ('Emerging Rules').

[241] ibid, 7.

[242] This includes both dissemination of information by the liaison judges to other judges in his country and general discussion between liaison judges from different countries within the framework of conferences, ibid.

[243] The first reported case of judicial liaison in a specific case is *YD v JB* [1996] RDF 753 (Que CA); See also Preliminary Document No 3B of April 2011 – 'Report on Judicial Communications in Relation to International Child Protection', www.hcch.net/upload/wop/abduct2011pd03be.pdf, para 4.

[244] 'Note on the Desirability and Feasibility of a Potential Legal Instrument Providing a Basis for Direct Judicial Communications', Preliminary Document No 3D of 2012, www.hcch.net/upload/wop/abduct2012pd3d_e.pdf, para 25. The Sixth Special Commission recommended that consideration should be given to the inclusion of a legal basis in any relevant future Hague Convention, 'Conclusions and Recommendations of the Sixth Special Commission', www.hcch.net/upload/wop/abduct2012concl_e.pdf, para 78.

[245] 'Emerging Rules' (n 240).

[246] Conclusions and Recommendations of the Sixth Special Commission (n 244), para 79(a).

[247] 'Emerging Rules' (n 240), 12.

lawyers in the respective Central Authorities, instead of involving valuable judicial time.[248] One answer might be that judicial communication will increase mutual respect and trust between judges which enhances the operation of the Convention. Also, where there is a need to obtain information about the exercise of judicial discretion or where the judge in the requested State wishes to convey his views about the case to the judge in the requesting State, then this can only be done by direct judicial communication.

Secondly, some concerns have been raised about the ethical issues involved and the possibility that judges' impartiality might be compromised.[249] This is of course a reason to restrict the use of judicial communications to cases where communication between Central Authorities will not be adequate. However, it seems that appropriate safeguards ensuring the transparency of the communications should satisfy ethical concerns.

Finally, there is a danger that judges will be too easily satisfied by information about provisions in the foreign legal system that are available to protect the child and returning parent, without receiving adequate information as to the likelihood and ease with which these provisions could be invoked in the particular circumstances of the case. Is a foreign judge likely to volunteer information showing that in practice provisions to protect domestic violence victims are not enforced in his country? Furthermore, there is a risk that informal judicial assurances will be accepted instead of requiring mirror orders. On the other hand, it can be argued that since few courts in any event require mirror orders, judicial communication in practice provides the best form of protection and the author is not aware of any cases where children returned on the basis of judicial communications have not been adequately protected. Nonetheless, consideration should always be given as to whether there is a need to obtain a mirror order, even where the information provided by the foreign judge suggests that adequate protection is available.

Support for some of the reservations expressed above can be found in the UK Supreme Court case of *Re E*.[250] In this case, the abducting mother alleged serious psychological abuse at the hands of the father. A psychiatrist diagnosed the mother as suffering from an adjustment disorder and predicted that there was a high risk that an enforced return to Norway would exacerbate the disorder which may evolve into a depressive order. The psychiatrist advised that the risk of deterioration could be substantially reduced by the provision of appropriate psychological treatment and by obtaining a court order preventing the father from knowing the mother's address or physically approaching her. The English judge hearing the case, Pauffley J, in addition to requesting an assurance from the mother's doctor in Norway that she could obtain the necessary treatment immediately upon return, sought information from the Norwegian liaison judge in relation to the legal position in Norway. The Supreme Court summarised that judge's replies as follows:

> if both parents have parental responsibility, relocating the child to another country without agreement is not possible; but it is possible to apply for sole parental responsibility in order to do this; normally a mediation certificate is required but an interim order can be made without this; the court can prohibit a parent from visiting the property to protect the children; there is also a power to do this under the Marriage Act (presumably in order to protect the wife); and it is possible to ask the local police for a restraining order. Means tested legal aid is available.

---

[248] Response of New Zealand in Preliminary Document No 3C of June 2011 – 'Collection of Responses on the Draft General Principles for Judicial Communications', www.hcch.net/upload/wop/abduct2011pd03c.pdf.
[249] Eg Response of New Zealand ibid.
[250] *Re E* (n 6).

Pauffley J, had also asked what view the Norwegian courts would take of undertakings given to the English Court, but the Norwegian judge does not seem to have understood the question and Thorpe LJ, who was in charge of international judicial communications in the UK, was not prepared to send a follow-up question to a busy Norwegian judge. Nonetheless, Pauffley J took the view that on the basis of the information provided by the Norwegian judge and doctor, a return to Norway subject to the undertakings offered by the father would not expose the children to a grave risk of harm.

With respect, the failure to seek further clarification from the Norwegian judge in relation to the issue of the undertakings demonstrates a real limitation of the usefulness of judicial liaison. Since questions may be misunderstood and the answers may give rise to further questions, there needs to be the possibility of follow-up communication. Partial information may be misleading and sometimes worse than no information at all. In addition, it is difficult to avoid the conclusion that the information provided by the Norwegian judge could have equally well been provided by a lawyer in the Norwegian Central Authority. Presumably, there would have been no hesitation to write back to such a lawyer with a follow-up request. Moreover, arguably Pauffley J was too easily satisfied by the information provided. There is no assurance at all that the undertakings would be enforced if the father decided to renege on them. No enquiry is made as to the possibility of a mirror order. Whilst Norwegian law might provide for restraining orders, no information is provided of how readily such orders are given and how long it takes to obtain one. Furthermore, there is no reference to the psychiatrist's recommendation that the father should not know the mother's address.

In summary, judicial communication can be helpful in providing the information necessary to ensure that protective measures are effective. However, care needs to be taken that judicial liaison does not serve as a replacement for effective and enforceable provisional measures.

IV Analysis

A Internal Coherence

Neither a very narrow nor a very wide interpretation of the grave risk exception can be reconciled with the overall conception of the Abduction Convention.[251] An overly narrow interpretation, under which the defence is hardly ever made out,[252] seems to ignore the statement in the Preamble that the signatory States are convinced that the interests of children are of paramount importance in matters relating to their custody.[253] Also, it has to be

---

[251] See comment of Gleeson CJ in the High Court of Australia in *DP* (n 32) [43]–[44] that 'there is no need to choose between a "narrow" and a "broad" construction. Rather, the "exception" is to be given the meaning its words require'; *JLM v D-G* (n 32).

[252] eg comment in *Simcox* (n 72), that 'although the "grave risk" threshold is necessarily a high one, there is a danger of making the threshold so insurmountable that district courts will be unable to exercise any discretion in all but the most egregious cases of abuse'.

[253] Whilst a decision under the Convention does not change rights of custody, it can have a drastic impact on the exercise of such rights in practice and on future determinations of custody.

remembered that the exceptions are part of the scheme of the Convention[254] and their invocation, from time to time, represents fulfilment of that scheme and not a departure therefrom.[255] Furthermore, to require the abductor to show that the requesting State cannot provide protection from a proven risk is to add a requirement that does not exist in the text of the Convention.[256]

On the other hand, a very wide interpretation, which effectively introduces a best interests assessment of the merits of each case via this exception, as appears to be suggested by the European Court of Human Rights in the *Neulinger* case,[257] is inconsistent with the fundamental premise of immediate mandatory return and with the Article 16 provision forbidding the court in the requested State from determining the merits of the custody dispute.

The question of whether settlement of the child can form the basis of the grave risk exception raises the issue of the inter-relationship between that defence and the defence in Article 12(2), which applies where 12 months have passed between the date of the unlawful removal or retention and the date of the commencement of proceedings and the child is now settled in his new environment.[258] On the one hand, if settlement per se can establish the grave risk defence, then the one-year requirement in Article 12(2) seems redundant. On the other hand, it should be remembered that the rationale behind the Article 12(2) defence is that the basic presumption that return promotes the child's best interests no longer applies where there has been a considerable lapse of time together with settlement of the child. Since there are cases where the lapse of time occurs after the commencement of the proceedings, denying the possibility of attaching any weight to settlement over a long period of time in such cases, is inconsistent with this philosophy.

It is suggested that internal coherence can be preserved by taking the approach that whilst settlement per se cannot lead to the establishment of the grave risk defence, it should be possible to establish this defence where evidence is brought showing that in the particular circumstances of the case, the fact that the child is settled creates a grave risk that return will expose this child to harm.[259] The difference between this approach to settlement and that in Article 12(2) is that under Article 12(2) there is no need to prove specific harm that will be caused by returning the child. Thus, the proposed *via media* preserves the distinction between the two defences, whilst remaining consistent with the rationale behind them.

A further question which arises in relation to the internal coherence of the Convention relates to the practice of ordering return subject to undertakings or other protective measures. Is this practice, which is not mentioned in the Convention, consistent with the provisions and overall scheme of the Convention? Although there has been little discussion of the issue, a number of justifications for the use of undertakings have been offered. For example, the Supreme Court of Canada has suggested that undertakings are within the spirit of the Convention because they enable the child to be returned in accordance with

---

[254] eg comment of Family Court of Australia in *State Central Authority v Papastravrou* [2008] FamCA 1120 [147] that 'the exceptions are as much a part of the philosophy of the Convention as prompt return and respect for rights of custody and access between contracting states'.

[255] *JLM v D-G* (n 32) [139], referring specifically to the grave risk exception.

[256] See eg comment in *Khan v Fatima* (n 20) that '[t]he Convention says nothing about the adequacy of the laws of the country to which the return of the child is sought – and for good reason, for even perfectly adequate laws do not ensure a child's safety.'

[257] *Neulinger* (n 104) [137]–[139].

[258] For a detailed discussion of this defence, see ch 9.

[259] Over and above the mere fact of being uprooted from his environment, see II Aii above.

the requirement of Article 12, by ameliorating any short-term harm to him.[260] Other courts have justified the use of undertakings as a means of protecting children or preventing establishment of one of the defences.[261] Beaumont and McEleavy[262] take the view that the practice can best be justified on the basis of the principle of non-exclusivity, according to which other legal rules may be invoked together with the provisions of the Convention.[263] Since all of these rationales show that the practice of making return subject to protective measures is consistent with the scheme of the Convention, nothing is to be gained by analysing which rationale is to be preferred.

B Consistency with the Intention of the Drafters

The drafters were clearly concerned that the grave risk exception should be interpreted restrictively and the Perez-Vera Report warned that otherwise the Convention would become a dead letter.[264] However, this widely cited warning has to be understood in light of the drafters' awareness that they faced an uphill task in altering the conditioning of judges, who were used to applying the best interests standard in all cases concerning children, including abducted children. Thus, it should not be thought that the drafters believed that the interests of specific children should be completely ignored in order to benefit children in general.

Indeed, Professor Perez-Vera herself states that the exception in Article 13(1)(b) is designed to cover cases 'where the return of the child would be contrary to his or her interests, as that phrase is understood in this sub-paragraph'[265] and that the exceptions are 'concrete illustrations of the overly vague principle whereby the interests of the child are stated to be the guiding criterion in this area'.[266] Thus, it is suggested that it would not have occurred to the drafters that courts would be prepared to return children in cases where this would jeopardise their safety.[267] Indeed, the proceedings of the 14th Session show that it was intended that the phrase 'intolerable situation' would cover the situation where the mother was fleeing from domestic violence.[268] Similarly, a learned observer at the Conference considered that it would cover the case where the child would inevitably end up in the requested State because there was very strong evidence that the Court in the requesting State would award custody to the abductor and allow him or her to return to the place of refuge.[269]

Moreover, a hint that there may be situations in which the abductor cannot reasonably be expected to return to the country of origin can be found in the Rapporteur's Comment that 'it has to be admitted that the removal of the child can sometimes be justified by objective reasons which have to do either with its person, or with the environment with which it

---

[260] Thomson (n 38).
[261] eg Re G (A Minor)(Abduction) (n 225); P v B (Child Abduction: Undertakings) [1994] 3 IR 507; C v C (n 95).
[262] Beaumont and McEleavy (n 1) 160.
[263] eg Arts 18, 34 and 36 of the Convention.
[264] Perez-Vera Report (n 2), para 34.
[265] ibid, para 116.
[266] ibid, para 25.
[267] The fact that their concerns were rather different is illustrated by the comment in the Special Commission Report, Proceedings of the 14th Session of the Hague Conference (Oct 1980 Vol III), 203 that the exception would not apply simply because the return would place the child at an educational or financial disadvantage.
[268] Proces-verbal No 8 ibid, 302. See also comments of Professor David McClean at the Fifth Special Commission Meeting as reported by M Weiner, 'Half-Truths, Mistakes and Embarrassment' (n 113) 293.
[269] Eekelaar, 'International Child Abduction' (n 171).

is most closely connected'.[270] Furthermore, her comment that the 'interest of the child in not being removed from its habitual residence ... gives way before the primary interest of any person in not being exposed to physical or psychological danger or being placed in an intolerable situation'[271] clearly supports non-return in cases of domestic violence and abuse. Moreover, it has been noted that the Explanatory Report 'says nothing about a reviewing court's duty to assess the home country's ability to protect a child from harm – it says only that return need not be ordered when the risk of grave harm exists'.[272]

It is not clear how the drafters would have viewed the possibility of return orders being made subject to undertakings or other protective measures as there is no express discussion of this option in the Perez-Vera Report or other *travaux préparatoires*. On the one hand, it has been suggested that the Rapporteur's reference to undertakings in the context of orders in relation to access rights under Article 21 of the Convention[273] indicates that no reason would have been seen not to use them also in relation to return orders.[274] On the other hand, the comment of the Rapporteur that '[T]he return of the child cannot be made conditional upon [a] decision or other determination being provided [by the court of the country of habitual residence]'[275] could be understood as precluding the possibility of making return conditional on the obtaining of a mirror order or safe harbour order by a court in the requesting State. Nonetheless, it is clear from the context of this comment that the reference is to decisions or determinations requested from the State of habitual residence for the purpose of determining whether the Convention applies. Thus, this comment is not relevant to the situation, in which the court in the requested State takes the view that it is necessary to obtain an order from the court of habitual residence in order to ensure that return will not expose the child to a grave risk of harm or place him in an intolerable situation.

In summary, the policy advocated in this book of taking a more flexible approach to the interpretation and application of the grave risk exception, together with wider cautious use of protective measures is perfectly consistent with the intentions of the drafters.

C Promotion of the Objectives of the Convention

i Protecting Abducted Children

As already explained, the Abduction Convention is based on the rebuttable assumption that prompt return of the abducted child will protect him from the harm caused by unilateral removal or retention. Yet, as the drafters of the Convention recognised, in some cases such return will not protect the child from harm and may even cause him harm. In the latter situation, the objective of protecting children from harm can be realised by not returning the child in accordance with the Article 13(1)(b) grave risk exception[276] or, where applicable, one of the other exceptions.

---

[270] Perez-Vera Report (n 2), para 25.
[271] ibid, para 29.
[272] *Baran v Beatty* 526 F3d 1340 (US App 11th Cir, 2008).
[273] Perez-Vera Report (n 2), para 128. See also para 110 of the Special Commission Report (n 267).
[274] Beaumont and McEleavy (n 1) 160.
[275] Perez-Vera Report (n 2), para 120.
[276] Described as 'a "longstop" defence ... in any case where it appears that the risk of harm which the Convention assumes as a result of the wrongful removal would be intolerably compounded by an order for return', *S v B & Y* (n 156) (Potter P)

However, the prevalent view that the grave risk exception has to be interpreted very narrowly has meant that children have not been adequately protected from harm. In particular, the reluctance of many courts to rely on the grave risk defence in cases of domestic violence ignores the considerable social science evidence about the damage caused to children by being exposed to domestic violence[277] and the real risk that those that abuse their partners will also abuse their children.[278]

Similarly, ignoring harm caused to the child by separation from the abducting primary carer is inconsistent with the objective of protecting the child. Expressing trust that the requesting State can protect the child who returns alone in such a situation[279] is wishful thinking.[280] Even though taking into account the abductor's refusal to return is problematic, as it gives her control and rewards her for her bad behaviour,[281] these considerations cannot take precedence over the need to protect the child, [282] especially where the abductor's refusal to return is reasonable.

Likewise, ignoring harm caused by separation of half-siblings (or siblings, where the Convention only applies to one of them) on the basis that the abductor is responsible for the situation seems to be punishing the child for the sins of the abductor. It should also be borne in mind that whilst the abductor may have created the problem by removing or retaining the children, she may well now be powerless to avoid the separation, if the sibling or half-sibling refuses to return or will be harmed by return. Furthermore, it can be argued that because of the relative rarity of cases involving potential separation of siblings, a more lenient view can be taken than in relation to harm caused by separation from the primary carer, which can be claimed in very many cases.

In addition, courts are sometimes so zealous about giving effect to the principle that difficulties caused by being uprooted from a familiar environment are insufficient to activate the grave risk defence, that they ignore the existence of exacerbating factors which will make the situation on return intolerable for the child or result in real harm to him. For example, they appear to forget that the purpose of return is to restore the *status quo ante* and that, where this will not be the case, it is much more likely that the return will cause harm or give rise to an intolerable situation even in the short term.[283] Furthermore, particular psychological characteristics of the child and his objections to return[284] may tip the balance and make the situation on return intolerable.

Finally, the policy of relying on the authorities of the requesting State or on undertakings or other protective measures to protect the child against a risk of harm, without checking that such protection will be effective, is clearly inconsistent with the objective of protecting children from harm. Experience has shown that undertakings/conditions are

---

[277] See sources cited at n 126.
[278] See evidence of this phenomenon in case studies in Edelson et al (n 116) 179–80.
[279] eg *Maurizio* (n 96) 641–42.
[280] See discussion of psychological literature in ch 3 at II D.
[281] *Maurizio* (n 96) 641–42.
[282] Potter P in *S v B & Y* (n 156) points out that the principle that an abductor should not be able to rely on a situation which she has created by her own conduct 'is not a principle articulated in the Convention . . . and should not be applied to the effective exclusion of the very defence itself, which is in terms directed to the question of risk of harm to the child and not the wrongful conduct of the abducting parent'.
[283] eg, Israeli case of FamA *RB v VG* (n 34) where the return to Belgium would not restore the status quo because for two years before the wrongful removal, the child had been living in France with the permission of the Belgian Court.
[284] Even if the child objection defence is not established due to lack of maturity or independence of views.

rarely enforceable and are often violated.[285] Moreover, even where mechanisms are theoretically available to protect the child in the requesting State, they may not be activated and are not always adequate.[286] In particular, there are limits on the ability of any legal system, however child focused and advanced, to protect children and their parents in all circumstances.[287] Thus, it is incumbent on courts to be sure that the protective measures do not simply pay lip-service to the need to protect the child, but can be enforced and will be effective.[288]

In summary, when considering whether the Article 13(1)(b) defence is established, courts should remember Baroness Hale's clear warning: 'No one intended that an instrument designed to secure the protection of children from the harmful effects of international child abduction should itself be turned into an instrument of harm.'[289]

ii Deterrence

The need to deter potential abductors is sometimes given as a justification for interpreting Article 13(1)(b) restrictively.[290] However, as pointed out above, the deterrent effect of the Convention is unproven.[291] In particular, the Convention is unlikely to act as a deterrent to abductions in the sort of cases in which the restrictive application of Article 13(1)(b) is significant, such as in cases of domestic violence.[292] Furthermore, it is not clear why applying the exception in these sorts of cases should reduce the deterrent effect in other types of cases. A possible explanation for the consistently high percentage of abductions by primary carer mothers is that these are the types of abductions which the Convention has not succeeded in deterring, despite the prevailing restrictive application of Article 13(1)(b).[293] Reasons for this might include lack of awareness about the Convention among custodial parents,[294] as well as the fact that mothers desperate to escape from violence, or what they perceive as intolerable situations, are less likely to be deterred by the possibility of a Convention application.

Whilst allowing a full-blown best interests examination in every case may well reduce the deterrent effect because it gives the abductor a 'second bite at the cherry', taking into account the short-term welfare interests of the child should not have a significant impact on the deterrent effect of the Convention. In any event, mere speculation that a restrictive application of the defences will deter potential abductors cannot justify returning a particular child when there is a real risk that this will cause him harm or place him in an intolerable situation.

---

[285] See above at III B.
[286] Weiner, 'Escape from Domestic Violence' (n 14) 680.
[287] In the words of Judge Shireen Fisher, 'no court can protect against domestic violence. Court orders are not bullet-proof', in 'How Far Did the Conclusions and Recommendations of the Fifth Meeting of the Special Commission Advance the Interpretation of Article 13(1)(b)?' (2007) 12 *The Judges' Newsletter* 55, 58.
[288] eg decision of the Australian Full Court in *Harris & Harris* [2010] FamCAFC 22 [150]-[159].
[289] *Re D* (n 57) [52]; See also comment in New Zealand case of *Ryding v Turvey* [1998] NZFLR 313 that in cases of abuse returning the child 'however protected, may be to provide a cure that is worse than the original disease'.
[290] eg, E Sthoeger, 'International Abduction and Children's Rights: Two Means to the Same End' (2011) 32 *Michigan Journal of International Law* 511, 537; *RB v VG* (n 34); dissenting opinion in *Khan v Fatima* (n 20).
[291] Chapter 5 at II Cii.
[292] Weiner, 'Escape from Domestic Violence' (n 14) 631.
[293] N Lowe and A Perry, 'International Child Abduction – The English Experience' (1999) 48 *International Child Law Quarterly* 127, 133.
[294] See T Kruger, *International Child Abduction the Inadequacies of the Law* (Oxford, Hart Publishing, 2011) 53.

iii Adjudication in the Forum Conveniens

Prima facie the objective of adjudication in the *forum conveniens* requires a very restrictive approach to all the exceptions. However, there will be cases where the presumption that the place of the habitual residence is the *forum conveniens* is rebutted because of the dangers involved in the return of the child and abductor to that place.[295] In particular, the effect of previous violence and the fear of future violence may prevent the abductor from being able to present his position fully in the state of origin.

A possible method of promoting the objective of adjudication in the *forum conveniens* without exposing the child and abductor to risk is to allow the country of habitual residence to determine the merits of the custody dispute while the child remains in the country of refuge.[296] This approach has indeed been adopted in the Brussels II bis Regulations,[297] but there is not yet sufficient case law on which to base any real assessment of the operation of this split scheme.[298]

iv Justice between the Parents and the Rule of Law

The policy adopted by some courts of not allowing abductors to rely on a situation which they have created themselves[299] appears to promote justice between the parents and the rule of law. However, it is not possible to evaluate justice between the parents without considering the background to the abduction and the reasonableness of the abductor's refusal to return.

In particular, in cases where the main reason for the abduction was the left-behind parent's violence or other morally blameworthy behaviour, justice between the parties may well not be attained between the parties by restoring the *status quo ante*. On the contrary, unless adequate safeguards can be provided, the most just solution will be to allow the child to remain with the abductor pending a decision on the merits of the case.

Similarly, since the left-behind parent was in breach of the law, it is not self-evident that the rule of law requires the immediate return of the child. On the other hand, it can be argued that the rule of law requires that even victims of violence should not take the law into their own hands, but should turn to welfare and law enforcement authorities in the country of origin in order to protect themselves. However, this argument can only be valid if the relevant authorities would have indeed been able and willing to provide sufficient protection. Where there is a real immediate danger of serious harm, victims may justifiably feel that the only real guarantee of safety is to flee abroad.[300] Furthermore, it has to be

---

[295] For a general discussion of the extent to which the habitual residence is the *forum conveniens*, see ch 8 at V Ciii.

[296] See R Schuz, 'The Hague Child Abduction Convention: Family Law and Private International Law' (1995) 44 *International and Comparative Law Quarterly* 771, 782; Weiner, 'Escape from Domestic Violence' (n 14) 698 et seq, suggesting that the return proceedings are stayed until the country of habitual residence determines the custody dispute. This also seems to be the concept behind Fisher's suggestion of 'virtual returns' to 'virtual courtrooms', Fisher, 'How Far Did the Conclusions' (n 287) 59.

[297] See ch 1 at II C.

[298] In *Re A (Custody Decision after Maltese Non-Return Order)* [2006] EWHC 3397 (Fam), the UK Court ordered return following the Maltese non-return order. Video links were used to enable the boy and the father to participate in the trial from Malta. In *Re A, HA v MB (Brussels II Revised: Article 11(7) Application)* [2007] EWHC 2016 (Fam), the English Court confirmed the French Court's non-return order.

[299] eg claims of harm caused by separation from the primary carer or siblings, discussed above at II Biii and iv.

[300] Weiner, 'Escape from Domestic Violence' (n 14).

remembered that the dynamics of domestic violence may effectively make it almost impossible for the victim to take legal action in the country of origin.[301]

D Compatibility with the Summary Nature of Convention Proceedings

As seen above,[302] one of the problems which arise in applying the grave risk defence is the difficulty of determining serious disputes of fact within the summary Convention proceedings. On the one hand, the Court needs facts in order to ascertain whether the defence is established. On the other hand, it is difficult to see how the Court can decide which side is telling the truth without a full blown examination of all the relevant evidence. The UK Supreme Court recently held that the emphasis should be on implementing protective measures which will reduce the risk to the child, if the allegations are indeed true, rather than on fact finding.[303] However, whilst this approach seems pragmatic in cases where the allegations are not serious, it is not clear how it will work where the allegations are of such severity that, if they are founded, no protective measures would be adequate. In such a case, the court cannot decide whether to order return without making a decision in relation to the facts in dispute.

One solution adopted by some courts is to appoint an expert witness instead of hearing the parties themselves. This has the advantage of saving court time and may avoid the need for the applicant to attend the hearing.[304] However, the commissioning of expert testimony will usually cause delay and prevent determination within the six-week deadline.[305] Also, reliance on expert testimony has other disadvantages. In particular, there is a risk that the expert will in fact be usurping the fact-finding function of the court without the protection provided to the parties by legal procedure. In addition, experts' conclusions may well be influenced by their own personal and professional world-view.[306]

Accordingly, it has to be recognised that in some cases the court itself will have to resolve disputes of fact, so that it is in a position to determine whether the grave risk defence is established. This will necessitate some deviation from the summary expedited nature of Convention proceedings, but this is essential in order to ensure that children are protected from harm. Clearly, courts should try to minimise the inroad into the summary nature of the proceedings, without prejudicing their ability to make reliable findings of fact. Tight, but realistic, timetables should be fixed for the hearing of evidence and the submission of expert reports. The difficulties in obtaining information about events which took place in a foreign country can be usually overcome by means of modern technology. Where it is necessary to hear evidence from the parties themselves, use of video conferencing and satellite facilities may avoid the cost and delay caused by the need to travel. Experts should be appointed to determine the implications of the facts for the child rather than to determine facts and courts should be careful to define closely the questions which the experts are asked to address.

---

[301] ibid; Edelson et al (n 116).
[302] At I B.
[303] *Re E* (n 6) [52]; *Chirume* (n 19).
[304] Although Weiner, 'Escape from Domestic Violence' (n 14) 350, claims that if the expert evidence is critical he will have to travel to meet with the expert.
[305] ibid.
[306] eg, in *RB v VG* (n 34) the expert's view that leaving the child in Israel was not a good solution, despite the risk involved in return, because of the long-term effects of losing contact with his father, were clearly influenced by Gardner's controversial Parental Alienation Syndrome theory, see ch 3 at II F.

E Consistency with Rights and Interests of Children

i The Potential Inconsistency

The phrase 'interests of the child' does not appear in the body of the Abduction Convention and, at least until the recent jurisprudence of the ECtHR,[307] it was trite law that the Abduction Convention does not take into account the welfare of the child in the full sense of the word, but only in the limited sense allowed by the exceptions.[308] Thus, courts hearing cases under the Convention have consistently refused to consider the argument that returning the child is not in accordance with his best interests and on occasion returned children with the knowledge that return did not accord with their best interests.[309] Furthermore, it has been suggested that it is inevitable that 'the best interests of individual children are occasionally sacrificed in the more general interests of the wider class of children in the international community'.[310] Whilst the question of whether the mandatory return mechanism of the Abduction Convention is consistent with the fundamental principle of the best interests of the child in fact relates to the whole scheme of the Convention, it is appropriate to discuss this question within the context of Article 13(1)(b) because this exception provides the most natural means of taking the child's interests into consideration within the framework of the Convention.[311] Accordingly, a restrictive interpretation of this exception is liable to lead to violation of the best interests principle.[312]

It has been claimed that the Abduction Convention contravenes the best interests standard, as entrenched in internal State law[313] and/or international human rights instruments.[314] In particular, it will be remembered that Article 3 of the United Nations Convention on the Rights of the Child (CRC), provides: '[in] all actions concerning children, whether undertaken by public or private social welfare institutions, courts of law, administrative authorities or legislative bodies, the best interests of the child shall be a primary consideration'. Thus, the discussion of the inter-relationship between the Abduction Convention and the best interests standard relates both to consistency with a fundamental principle of family law and to consistency with the human rights of the child. As seen above,[315] there are differences between the formulation of the best interests standard in these two contexts.

---

[307] Discussed below.

[308] eg, In the case of *In the Marriage of Gsponer* (1988) 94 FLR 164, 175 the Full Court makes reference to the decision of Latey J of the High Court of Justice in the unreported case of *Re Corrie (A Minor)* (Unreported, 14 October 1988), as follows, 'I remind myself that under the... Convention, the welfare of the child is not the primary consideration or indeed a consideration at all save to the extent that it may properly influence a decision under article 13'. Similar comments are found in the leading US case of *Friedrich* (n 40) and in many cases in other jurisdictions.

[309] eg, the Israeli Supreme Court decisions in *Ro* (n 94) and CA 5332/93(SC) *Gunzburg* PD 49(3) 282, 298 [INCADAT cite: HC/E/IL 355].

[310] A Bainham, *Children: The Modern Law*, 2nd edn (Bristol, Jordan, 1998) 582. See also comment of Waite J in *W v W* [1993] 2 FLR 211, 220 that 'it is implicit in the whole operation of the Convention that the objective of stability for the mass of children may have to be achieved at the price of tears in some individual cases'.

[311] Bucher, 'The New Swiss Federal Act' (n 69) 155. The other exceptions may also be understood as manifestations of the best interests standard, Schuz, 'Family Law and Private International Law' (n 289) 777–78; *Re E* (n 6) [16].

[312] And in some cases, of the child's right to protection, see Ch 6 IID.

[313] eg *Ciotola v Fiocca* 86 Ohio Misc 2d 24, 684 NE 2d 763, 765 (Ohio Com Pl 1997); *Sonderup* (n 122); *McCall and McCall: State Central Authority* (1995) FLC 92-551 (Austl).

[314] See eg, *Murray* (n 23); *Maumousseau and Washington v France* App no 39388/05 (ECHR, 2007-XIII) [64]–[73]; See also the dictum of Justice Rotlevy in CA 7994/98 *Dagan v Dagan*, PD NG (3) 254 (IsrSC) that in some respects the Abduction Convention is not consistent with Art 3 of the CRC.

[315] Chapter 6 at II B.

There is no doubt that the traditional paramountcy principle takes an individualistic approach, under which the court has to decide in accordance with the best interests of the particular child who is the subject of its determination. However, the position in relation to Article 3 of the CRC is less clear. To the extent that this provision relates to the need to take into account the best interests of children generally, then it seems clear that the Abduction Convention and the way in which it has been implemented comply with the provision. The whole scheme of automatic return subject to narrow exceptions, without examining the merits of the case, benefits most abducted children by ensuring that the ill effects of abduction are reversed as quickly as possible[316] and benefits all children by reducing the chance that they will be abducted[317] and by increasing the chance that one parent will agree to temporary visits abroad to the other parent.[318] However, the better view is that Article 3 of the CRC also involves an individualistic element[319] and thus it is necessary to consider to what extent the Abduction Convention can be reconciled with the obligation to treat the best interests of the particular child as a primary consideration.[320]

The use of the phrase 'a primary consideration' in the CRC is significant because, in contrast to the paramountcy formulation, it allows room to take into account other considerations, which if sufficiently weighty can override the interests of the child.[321] It has been argued therefore that the need to deter abductors and the need to ensure that abducted children are returned speedily are considerations which may override the interests of the specific child and that therefore the Convention scheme complies with the requirements of Article 3.[322] However, surely whilst these considerations are legitimate, they cannot override the interests of the specific child in cases where return will cause him real harm. Any other conclusion would be inconsistent with the requirement to treat the child's best interests as a primary consideration.

In light of the obviously potential inconsistency between the Abduction Convention and the best interests standard, it is hardly surprising that various attempts have been made to reconcile the Convention's mechanism with the best interests standard in general. These attempts have generally not distinguished between the different formulations of the best interests standard.

ii *The Attempted Reconciliations*

The first attempted reconciliation is that the best interests principle is only relevant in substantive custody disputes and is not relevant in applications for return which are 'concerned with where and in what court issues in relation to the welfare of the child are to be determined'.[323] This argument is, even on the face of it, inconsistent with the paramountcy

---

[316] Schuz, 'Family Law and Private International Law' (n 298) 774–76.
[317] *Re L* [1999] 1 FLR 433 (Wilson J).
[318] eg per Justice Hale (as she then was) in *Re HB (Abduction: Children's Objections)* [1997] 1 FLR 392, 399–400.
[319] Chapter 6 at II B.
[320] In *El Sayed* (n 32), Hammond J explains, '[T]he Hague Convention scheme addresses the general welfare of all children in the sense mentioned by Kirby P but the direct interests of a particular child are underpinned by the [grave risk] exception.'
[321] R Schuz, 'The Hague Child Abduction Convention and Children's Rights' (2002) 12 *Transnational Law & Contemporary Problems* 393, 441 and 450. These comments were ignored by Sthoeger, 'International Abduction' (n 290) 537, incorrectly asserting that the current author does not allow room for such considerations.
[322] eg Sthoeger ibid.
[323] *Murray* (n 23); Similarly, Justice Dorner in *Gunzburg* (n 302) took the view that jurisdiction to determine what is in the best interests of the child is transferred to the courts of the country from which he was abducted.

principle and with Article 3 of the CRC, which requires that the best interests of the child be a primary consideration in **all** actions concerning the child. A decision to return a child, and even a decision as to which court hears the case, must surely be included. [324] Moreover, it is palpably clear that the child's welfare may be affected by being **returned** to the requesting State, inter alia because the return may cause the child actual harm, which cannot be neutralised by the application of the welfare principle by the foreign court when it eventually hears the case.

The second attempted reconciliation is that there cannot be any inconsistency between the Abduction Convention and the CRC because the CRC itself, in the words of the *Murray* Court, 'clearly contemplates the negative impact on children of their abduction or non-return and the necessity of States concluding or acceding to bilateral and multilateral agreements to prevent such occurrences'.[325] This explanation is obviously inadequate. The fact that the CRC is concerned about preventing abduction and expressly encourages the conclusion of treaties like the Hague Abduction Convention does not mean that the specific provisions of that Convention are consistent with those of the CRC. Moreover, there is nothing in the CRC to suggest that the need to combat abduction should override the interests of the specific child. A fortiori, this explanation cannot provide a reconciliation with the paramountcy principle.

The third attempted reconciliation claims that the Abduction Convention is based on the best interests principle. This claim relies on two premises which underpin the Convention. The first premise is that the child's welfare rights 'are best protected by having issues as to custody and access determined by the Courts of the country of the child's habitual residence, subject to the exceptions contained in Article 13'[326] and the second premise is that that the best interests of the child require his immediate return to the country from which he was abducted.[327] However, these premises do not ensure consistency with the best interests principle. Even when the first premise is correct, it does not necessarily follow that it is in the child's best interests to reside in the place of habitual residence pending determination of the dispute, as required by the Convention.[328] Furthermore, it is clear that the second premise is a presumption which is not true in all cases and that the purpose of the exceptions, especially the grave risk exception, is to 'catch' those cases where this premise is not true.[329] However, if, in determining whether the grave risk exception is established, the court is not allowed to examine the interests of the particular child, there can be no guarantee that the exception will indeed 'catch' all cases where the premise is not true.

The fourth attempted reconciliation can be found in the jurisprudence of the ECtHR in a series of cases over the last few years, of which the most prominent is the Grand Chamber decision in the case of *Neulinger*.[330] The issue of the relationship between Article 3 of the CRC and the Abduction Convention arose because the right to family life, entrenched in Article 8 of the ECHR, is interpreted in light of the best interests standard, as expressed in Article 3 of the CRC.[331] The majority decision included a statement that it follows from

---

[324] *Dagan* (n 314) [16] (Rotlevy J).
[325] *Murray* (n 23), citing Arts 11 and 35 of the CRC.
[326] ibid.
[327] eg *Gunzburg* (n 311) (Dorner J).
[328] *cf* Brussels II bis Regulation, discussed in ch 1 at II C, under which the merits may be heard in the country of habitual residence even where return is refused.
[329] *Re E* (n 6) [15]–[16].
[330] *Neulinger* (n 104).
[331] ibid [134].

Article 8 that a child's return cannot be ordered automatically or mechanically without consideration of the child's best interests.[332]

This passage appears to signify a radical shift in the way in which the Abduction Convention has been applied hitherto. Whilst it answers the concerns about the inconsistency of the Abduction Convention with the best interests standard, it appears to undermine the very foundation of the Abduction Convention mechanism of summary return without a full investigation into the merits of the case. This no doubt explains why the President of the ECtHR felt the need to explain in an extra-judicial speech[333] that the above passage should not be read as abandoning the swift summary approach that the Abduction Convention envisages. Nonetheless, the President's comments, whilst making clear that the problematic passage in *Neulinger* is not to be taken at face value, do little to advance the search for a means of reconciling the best interests standard with the Hague mechanism.[334] In contrast, Thorpe LJ's subsequent explanation[335] of the apparently revolutionary statements in *Neulinger* does contain a (fifth) reconciliation which is, in the current author's view, more successful than previous attempts.

iii A Successful Reconciliation?

Thorpe LJ distinguishes between the immediate and the ultimate best interests of the child. The former are to be taken into account in determining whether the grave risk exception exists, whereas the latter are only relevant in the later custody determination.[336] This distinction between the short and long-term interests of children can also be found in the earlier case of *Sonderup v Tondelli*.[337] Furthermore, the UK Supreme Court decision in *Re E*,[338] whilst not expressly adopting the distinction between immediate and long-term interests, is consistent with it.

The distinction between short and long-term interests fits well into the Article 3 'primary consideration' formulation. Considerations such as the benefits to abducted children generally, deterrence, justice between the parents and the rule of law justify not taking into account the long-term interests of the child in applying the Abduction Convention, because those interests can be given effect to by the court in the country of habitual residence. However, these considerations cannot justify harming the short-term interests of a particular child.[339] In particular, it must be remembered that the deterrent effect of the Convention is largely speculative. Furthermore, whilst allowing a full blown best interests examination in every case would substantially impair the speedy return mechanism, considering the short-term interests of children in those cases where there is prima facie evidence that return will cause immediate harm should not have any effect on the very many cases where there is no such evidence.

In contrast, it is not clear that the distinction between the child's short and long-term interests can resolve the inconsistency between the Abduction Convention's summary return

---

[332] ibid [138]–[139], quoted in ch 1 at II Diib.
[333] In a speech given on 14 May 2011 at an Irish-British-French Symposium on Family Law, Information Document No 6 of the Sixth Special Commission, www.hcch.net/upload/wop/abduct2011info05_en.pdf.
[334] Also, subsequent ECtHR case law is inconsistent with this speech. See ch 1 at II Diib.
[335] *Re E* [2011] EWCA Civ 361.
[336] ibid [69].
[337] See *Sonderup* (n 122).
[338] *Re E* (n 6).
[339] Decision of 29 May 2000, (2001) 42 *Zeitschrift für Rechtsvergleichung (ZfRV)* 30, cited by Bucher, 'The New Swiss Federal Act' (n 69) fn 28.

mechanism and the paramountcy principle. The UK case law in non-Convention cases sheds some light on this question. Whilst in the early 1990s the UK Courts held that Hague Abduction Convention principles should also be applied in non-Convention cases,[340] they later resiled from this approach.[341] The House of Lords made it clear that the statutory requirement to decide cases concerning children in accordance with the paramountcy principle applies to non-Convention abduction cases.[342] Although UK courts have long accepted that the best interests of a child will often require summary return,[343] Baroness Hale expressly refused to accept that there is any presumption that summary return is likely to be in the child's best interests, stating:

> The most one can say, in my view, is that the judge may find it convenient to start from the proposition that it is likely to be better for a child to return to his home country for any disputes about his future to be decided there.[344]

Her Ladyship then goes on to mention a number of factors which will be relevant in determining the best interests of the child, including his real connection with the foreign country,[345] the amount of time that he has spent in both countries[346] and the legal framework for making decisions concerning children in the foreign country.[347] In particular, the fact that the norms according to which custody disputes are determined in the foreign country are different from those in the UK is a significant factor, the implications of which have to be considered carefully in light of the circumstances of the particular case.[348] It is clear that these considerations are not restricted to those relevant to the short-term interests of the child. Thus, whilst UK courts will not necessarily conduct a full investigation into the merits of the case, they may well have to hear considerable evidence about the short and long-term implications of the factual and legal position in the foreign country before deciding whether to order summary return. It is clear therefore that the Abduction Convention's return mechanism, subject only to the defences in Article 13, is inconsistent with the paramountcy principle as applied in the UK non-Convention cases.[349]

On the other hand, the South African Supreme Court took the view that there was no conflict in principle between the Hague Convention and the paramountcy of the best interests of the child, entrenched in the South African Constitution, because the objective of the Hague Convention is to promote the interests of children and the long-term interests of children would be best met in the country of habitual residence. However, that Court accepted that, in practice, the operation of the Convention might be inconsistent with the Constitution, where return does not serve the short-term interests of the

---

[340] *G v G (Minors) (Abduction)* (1991) 2 FLR 506; *Re F (A Minor) (Abduction: Custody Rights)* [1991] Fam 25.
[341] *Re P (A Minor) (Child Abduction: Non-Convention Country)* [1997] Fam 45.
[342] *Re J (A Child)* [2005] UKHL 40 [18].
[343] eg, *Re L (Minors) (Wardship: Jurisdiction)* [1974] 1 WLR 250, 264; *Re R (Minors)(Wardship: Jurisdiction)* [1981] 2 FLR 416, 425.
[344] *Re J* (n 335).
[345] Which may not be the same as his 'technical' habitual residence for the purpose of the Abduction Convention, ibid [32].
[346] ibid [34]; *cf* the later case of *Re F (Children) (Abduction: Removal Outside Jurisdiction)* [2008] EWCA Civ 854, where it was shown that the children's long-term welfare required return, even though they had been in the UK for three years, because there was no chance that the mother would be allowed to stay in the UK permanently.
[347] *Re J* (n 335) [37] et seq.
[348] ibid; see discussion in R Schuz, 'The Relevance of Religious law and Cultural Considerations *in International Child Abduction Disputes*' (2010) 12 Journal of Law and Family Studies 453, 469–70.
[349] *Re P (A Minor)* (n 334); *Re Z* [1999] 1 FLR 1270.

child.[350] Nonetheless, in the Court's view, such inconsistency could be justified under the proportionality principle in light of the objectives of the Hague Convention. The South African Supreme Court's resort to the flexible proportionality doctrine, as an ingenious way of avoiding a head-on clash between the Abduction Convention and the South African Constitution, should not detract from that Court's express recognition of the potential inconsistency between the Abduction Convention and the paramountcy principle and of the fact that the way to limit such inconsistency is to interpret the exceptions in Articles 13 and 20 in a non-restrictive way, in light of the best interests of the child.

F Consistency with Rights of the Parents

In *Neulinger*, the Grand Chamber held that returning the child would violate the mother's right to family life because her refusal to return was not totally unjustified inter alia in light of the risk of criminal prosecution.[351] Judges Lorenzen and Kalaydjieva, in their concurring opinion in that case, went a step further stating that any decision which requires the abductor to return with her child violates her human rights because only she can judge whether it is reasonable to return and that otherwise the abductor would be 'condemned' to live outside his country of origin for many years.[352] With respect, the latter approach, which would drive 'a coach and four' through the Convention, cannot be supported. The whole basis of the Convention is that the future of the child should be decided in his place of habitual residence and therefore if the abductor wishes to relocate with the child, she has to seek permission from that court. In other words, the indirect restriction on her freedom of movement[353] is justified by the need to protect the child's rights not to be removed unilaterally by one parent.

However, in cases where it is not reasonable to expect the abductor to return, such as in cases where there is a risk of further domestic violence, then an order of return would violate the basic rights of that parent, unless effective measures can be taken to protect her. Whilst the abductor is not obliged to return with the child, where she is the primary carer, returning the child alone is liable to be damaging to him. The abductor should not be placed in the invidious position of having to choose between her own safety and the well-being of her child.[354] The claim that she put herself in this position is not convincing in cases where she was abused by the left-behind parent prior to the abduction. It should also be noted that in cases of domestic violence, the short and long-term interests of the child are usually primarily dependent on the safety of the abductor.[355] Furthermore, if the return

---

[350] *Sonderup* (n 122) [29]. *cf* later case of *Central Authority v Reynders* (12856/2010) [2011] 2 All SA 438 (GNP), in which the North Gauteng High Court, relying on the Constitution, stated obiter that the best interests of the child required that return should be refused. While the Art 13 exceptions were mentioned, the Court did not explain how they applied here.

[351] *Neulinger* (n 104) [150].

[352] Judges Jocienne, Sajo and Tsotsoria agreed with this approach, stating that 'the underlying assumption that the mother has to follow the child indicates a disregard of the mother's Article 8 rights, her freedom of movement and her personal autonomy', ibid [7] of their opinion.

[353] Of course, the parent is free to relocate by herself.

[354] See proposal put forward at the Fifth Special Commission Meeting, stating that return should not be privileged over 'the primary interests of any person in not being exposed to physical or psychological danger or being placed in an intolerable situation', Working Document No 11 of 8 November 2006 (provided to the author by the Permanent Bureau), discussed by Weiner, 'Half-Truths, Mistakes and Embarrassment' (n 113) 289–90.

[355] Weiner, 'Escape from Domestic Violence' (n 14) 703.

of the child leads to a separation between the child and the abductor because the abductor is unable to return for objectively valid reasons, then there will be a violation of both the abductor's and the child's right to family life.

Similarly, where there are immigration restrictions preventing the abductor's entry to the requesting State or making him liable to deportation, an order of return will be in breach of both the parent's and child's right to family life. Accordingly, return should only be ordered after appropriate assurances have been received from the relevant authorities of the requesting State that the abductor will be able to remain there, at least until a final decision has been given there on the merits of the custody dispute.

G Consistency with Private International Law Principles

Courts, mainly in the US, have quite frequently referred to the doctrine of comity in cases concerning the grave risk defence. Perusal of the case law reveals at least three different contexts in which comity is mentioned in these cases. The following discussion considers to what extent the reference to comity in each context is appropriate.

i As a Reason to Interpret the Grave Risk Defence Restrictively

In a much cited quotation, the US Court of Appeals for the 7th Circuit stated[356] that '[c]oncern with comity among nations argues for a narrow interpretation of the "grave risk of harm" defense; but the safety of children is paramount'. With respect, there is a logical inconsistency in this statement. If the safety of children is paramount, then the only relevant consideration in determining whether the grave risk of harm exception exists is whether return of the child does threaten his safety. Thus, it is not clear how considerations of comity can influence the interpretation of the defence.

Furthermore, comity in the sense of reciprocity simply requires each Contracting State to apply the Convention. Accordingly, where the grave risk defence or any other defence can reasonably be held to exist, refusal to return does not in any way violate the obligation of reciprocity.

ii As Basis of Assumption that the Requesting State can Protect the Child

The concept of comity has also been used to justify an assumption that other Contracting States will be just as willing and able to protect children as the requested State[357] and to prevent courts from examining whether this is indeed the case.[358] Accordingly, *ex hypothesi* return can only expose the child to a grave risk of harm if circumstances outside the control of the requesting State exist, such as famine or war.[359] Similarly, in the name of comity, courts have assumed that the requesting State will enforce undertakings given by the left-behind parent and refused to check whether this is indeed the situation.[360]

---

[356] *Van de Sande* (n 122) 572 cited eg in *Norinder v Fuentes* 657 F3d 526 (2011) and *Estrada v Salas-Perez* 2012 US Dist LEXIS 139897, 28 September 2012.
[357] *cf Danaipour* (n 10) where it was held that the Swedish evaluation would not satisfy US standards.
[358] See eg *Gsponer* (n 310); *Murray* (n 23).
[359] See eg *Friedrich* (n 40) 1068.
[360] eg *Re K (Abduction: Physical Harm)* (n 217) quoting the non-Convention case of *Re M (Abduction: Non-Convention Country)* (n 217). Alternatively, courts sometimes assume that considerations of comity will motivate the courts in the requesting State to give effect to the undertakings as in *RK v JK* (n 215).

This approach involves an exaggerated view of the doctrine of comity. As clarified earlier, there is no absolute obligation to give deference to foreign States[361] and so there can be no justification for using the doctrine as an excuse not to check up on the reality of the situation in the requesting State,[362] especially in light of the clear evidence that there is a problem in enforcing undertakings.[363] Thus, this approach seems inconsistent with the clear ruling in *Van de Sande v Van de Sande*[364] that the safety of the child overrides considerations of comity.[365] Moreover, as Judge Richard Posner noted in that case, '[t]here is a difference between the law on the books and the law as it is actually applied, and nowhere is the difference as great as in domestic relations'.[366] Accordingly, acknowledging that 'even the most robust and well resourced legal systems suffer from enforcement gaps is not to denigrate mutual trust and comity; it is simply to embrace reality'.[367]

Indeed, it is perhaps ironic that the concept of comity has been invoked by courts in requested States to justify their presumption that the undertakings/conditions will be honoured, but does not seem to have been taken on board by requesting States as a basis for enforcing undertakings/conditions.

iii As a Reason not to Require Undertakings or Mirror Orders

US Courts have held that undertakings which require action or enforcement by foreign courts violate international comity.[368] Indeed, when agreeing to accept undertakings which can be fulfiled by the left-behind parent, they sometimes expressly comment that these undertakings do not offend notions of international comity because they do not require the involvement of foreign authorities.[369]

With respect, the approach of the US Courts cannot be justified. Where the court of the requested State takes the view that return of the child will expose him to a grave risk of harm unless certain actions are taken by the administrative or judicial authorities of the requesting State, then it has a choice between refusing return on the basis of the grave risk defence or making the return conditional on the taking of those actions. Thus, the latter option does not show lack of respect for the legal system of the requesting State, but rather a desire to return the child to the country of habitual residence where this can be done without risk to the child.

In conclusion, the reliance on comity to support a restrictive interpretation of the grave risk defence or to limit the court's ability to check that the child can be returned safely and to put in place protective measures to this end is inappropriate. It has to be remembered

---

[361] See ch 6 at IV E.
[362] This includes not following up unsatisfactory answers provided by foreign judges in order not to waste valuable judicial time, as in the English case of *Re E* (n 6).
[363] See above at III B.
[364] *Van de Sande* (n 122).
[365] See also comment in *Klentzeris v Klentzeris* [2007] EWCA Civ 533 [19], that preference was given to the need to protect the children from harm over 'regard for the Greek judicial authorities'.
[366] *Van de Sande* (n 122) 570–71.
[367] N Browne, 'Relevance And Fairness: Protecting The Rights Of Domestic-Violence Victims And Left-Behind Fathers Under The Hague Convention On International Child Abduction,' (2011) 60 *Duke Law Journal* 1193, 1212.
[368] *Danaipour* (n 10), 22-23; *Maurizio* (n 96), 644. The US State Department has stated that it 'does not support conditioning the issuance of a return order on the acquisition of [an] order from a court in the requesting state' see *Danaipour* ibid.
[369] eg *Kufner* (n 76); *Krefter v Wills* 623 F. Supp. 2d 125; 2009 U.S. Dist; *Wilchynski v Wilchynski* 2010 U.S. Dist. LEXIS 25903 (18 March 2010).

314 *Grave Risk of Harm*

that comity is not an absolute obligation[370] and can be overridden by other considerations. Thus, even if the review of the factual and legal situation in the requesting State and/or making return conditional on the taking of actions by the authorities of that State can be considered as breaches of comity, these can be justified on the basis of the need to ensure the child's safety. Whilst some courts have recognised that the latter consideration is paramount, others have unfortunately preferred the so-called dictates of comity.

H Consistency with Domestic Abuse Policy

Ignoring domestic violence in abduction cases is inconsistent with and liable to undermine policies adopted in many countries to combat domestic violence.[371] There is no reason why the policy of combating international abduction should take precedence over that of combating domestic violence. Thus, the approach that taking into account domestic violence will turn the exception into a rule, because of the prevalence of domestic violence,[372] is unacceptable and liable to undermine the struggle against domestic violence.

In the case of *Danaipour*, the US policy of protecting children from sexual abuse informs the grave risk analysis and that returning children in cases where there is evidence of sexual abuse is contrary to US policy.[373] Therefore, in such cases return should be refused rather than attempting to put in place extensive protective measures. Whilst the case refers specifically to the sexual abuse of children, there is no reason why the same approach should not be adopted in relation to physical and psychological abuse. Furthermore, it can be argued that this clear stance against abuse could be extended to cases where the abuse has been directed against the abducting parent. Thus, in cases of serious violence, refusing return will broadcast the message that violence does not pay. In cases where the abuse was not serious, the imposition of protective measures as a condition for ordering return may be seen as promoting policies against violence since the obligations and/or restrictions therein are effectively sanctions against the violent parent.

I Certainty versus Flexibility

There is a good deal of uncertainty surrounding the interpretation and application of Article 13(1)(b). Much of this uncertainty is caused by the different approaches of judges to the concepts of harm and intolerability, particularly in cases involving domestic violence. A specific defence of domestic violence, akin to that in the Federal International Parental Kidnapping Act,[374] would go a long way to reduce this uncertainty.[375]

In addition, uncertainty in other types of case might be reduced by identifying specific situations in which the defence will be established. A good example of this approach can be

---

[370] See Chapter 6 at IV E.
[371] For a discussion of these policies, see UN General Assembly, *Intensification of Efforts to Eliminate all Forms of Violence against Women: Report of the Secretary-General*, 2 August 2010, A/65/208, available at www.unhcr.org/refworld/docid/4cf4e25a2.html; Reflection Report (n 15), Appendix II.
[372] eg In the Matter of LL Children, NY LJ, 22 May 2000 [INCADAT cite: HC/E/USs 273].
[373] *Danaipour* (n 10) 16.
[374] International Parental Kidnapping Act 1994 18 USC s 1204(C)(2).
[375] For the advantages and disadvantages of this idea, see Weiner, 'Escape from Domestic Violence' (n 14). For a discussion of this idea in Australia, see J Caldwell, 'Child Welfare Defences in Child Abduction Cases – Some Recent Developments' (2011) 13 *Child and Family Law Quarterly* 121, 129.

found in Article 5 of the Swiss Law,[376] which defines a specific situation in which return will place the child in an intolerable situation. This provision covers the situation where the abductor who is the child's primary carer is not in a position to return to the place of habitual residence, often because of a history of domestic violence.[377] As seen above,[378] there is currently a lack of uniformity in the approach of courts to such cases. The cumulative conditions in the Swiss provision appear to inject some certainty into the determination of whether the child would be placed in an intolerable situation. Whilst the provision is not exclusive and the defence could be established even where one or more of these conditions do not exist, they provide a good guideline as to how that section should be interpreted. Thus, in the author's view, if there were to be a protocol to the Convention, it should have included an appropriate version of the Swiss provision and perhaps also similar provisions in relation to the other common scenarios outlined above, such as the implications of immigration restrictions.

In the absence of such a protocol,[379] the best method of increasing certainty is by soft law guidelines. Thus, it is to be hoped that the recommendation of the Sixth Special Commission in 2012, that a Working Group be set up to develop a Guide to Good Practice in relation to Article 13(b),[380] will indeed result in the publication of detailed guidelines as to the sort of situations in which the grave risk defence is likely to be established. Furthermore, it is to be hoped that the inclusion of cross-disciplinary experts in the Working Group will ensure that the realities of the various situations involved, in particular domestic violence, will be considered and that account will be taken of policy considerations over and above the perceived need to interpret the grave risk defence narrowly.

V Conclusions

As explained at the beginning of this chapter, in interpreting and applying the Article 13(b) exception, courts are faced with the challenge of protecting children from harm without violating the integrity of the Convention. The prevailing restrictive approach to the exception demonstrated in this chapter suggests that only too often courts have failed to provide adequate protection for children and that their zealousness not to determine the long-term interests of children has also led them to ignore their immediate interests. Whilst undertakings, judicial liaison and other provisional measures appear to provide the optimal solution to the tension between the need to protect the child and the danger of undermining the Convention, these measures are of little value unless courts ensure that they are really effective. Some courts have applied the grave risk exception more liberally and have been cautious about the effectiveness of undertakings.[381] These approaches are to be welcomed,

---

[376] The Swiss Act (n 69).
[377] Bucher, 'The New Swiss Federal Act' (n 69) 157–58.
[378] See above t II Biii.
[379] See ch 19 at II C.
[380] Conclusions and Recommendations of the Sixth Special Commission (n 246) para 82.
[381] eg Australian case of *Harris* (n 288) where the Court stated that 'Primary carers who have fled from abuse and maltreatment should not be expected to go back to it, if this will have a seriously detrimental effect upon the children. We are now more conscious of the effects of such treatment, not only on the immediate victims but also on the children who witness it' ([142]) and that it was not possible to 'construct enforceable conditions for the child's return which would moderate the gravity of the risk of harm to the child to a level which would reasonably address his safety needs or place him in anything other than an intolerable situation' ([161]).

but the resulting lack of consistency and consequential uncertainty is clearly undesirable. Accordingly, it is necessary to adopt a two-pronged approach, in order to improve the protection provided for children by the grave risk defence and to ensure consistency with the CRC and the ECHR.

Firstly, methods of ensuring effectiveness of provisional measures need to be developed and universally adopted. In parallel, whilst such improvements may increase the number of cases in which children can be safely returned, courts need to internalise the fact that there will still be cases in which there are no measures, however effective from a legal point of view, which will adequately protect the child and returning parent.

Secondly, steps need to be taken to clarify the meaning of 'grave risk of harm' and 'intolerable situation'. In view of the rejection of the idea of a protocol to the Convention, this can best be done in the form of a Good Practice Guide, which should give examples of the sort of situations in which the defence is likely to be established, together with advice about the type of evidence to be heard where the grave risk exception is raised.

At the end of the day, we have to remember that the most fundamental objective of the Abduction Convention is to protect individual children from harm.[382] Where this objective conflicts with other objectives such as adjudication in the *forum conveniens*, the right to regular contact with the other parent, and the need to deter child abduction, protection has to take precedence.

---

[382] As seen above (Ch 6, IID). Art 3(2) of the CRC recognizes the child's right to protection.

12

Child's Objection

I Introduction

A The Dilemma

The child objection exception appears in the text of the Hague Convention on the Civil Aspects of International Child Abduction ('Abduction Convention') as a separate paragraph immediately after Article 13(1)(b):

> The judicial or administrative authority may also refuse to order the return of the child if it finds that the child objects to being returned and has attained an age and degree of maturity at which it is appropriate to take account of its views.

This paragraph, which is not numbered in the official text of the Convention, is usually referred to as Article 13(2) of the Convention.[1] It is not clear why the exception appears as a completely independent paragraph rather than simply as a further reason to refuse return in addition to those already set out in Article 13(1)(a) and (b). In particular, the phrase '[t]he judicial or administrative authority may also refuse to order the return of the child' appears to simply repeat the opening words of Article 13.[2]

One possible explanation for the independent paragraph is that the burden of proof is intended to be different for Article 13(2) than for the other exceptions because there is no requirement that the person opposing return has to establish anything. Rather, the exception appears to be activated wherever the court finds that the child objects. The attraction of this interpretation is that it imposes the obligation on the court to investigate whether the child objects even if the abductor does not raise this defence. However, as will be seen below, the orthodox view is that the burden of proof is on the person opposing return as with the other exceptions.[3]

At first sight, it might appear that the child objection exception in Article 13(2) of the Abduction Convention is designed to recognise the child's right to participate in decisions concerning him,[4] albeit that this Convention predated the United Nations Convention on the Rights of the Child (CRC) by nearly 10 years. Indeed, Ward LJ expressed the view that

---

[1] This is the notation which has been adopted by the Central Bureau of the Hague Conference on their database (www.incadat.com) although some authors refer to Art 13(c).
[2] '[t]he judicial or administrative authority is not bound to order return of the child if the person . . . which opposes its return established that . . .'.
[3] The US legislation provides that the Respondent bears the burden of proving this defence by a preponderance of the evidence, 42 USC § 11603(e)(2)(B), which is a lower standard of proof than for the grave risk exception. In Australia, Regulation 16(3)(c) of the Child Abduction Regulations was amended to make it clear that the burden of proof is on the person opposing return, *Director-General, Department of Child Safety & Milson* [2008] FamCA 872[80].
[4] See ch 6 at II C.

The sentiments in both conventions are the same and they give strong support to the idea that the purpose of the exception to the general rule of immediate return is to defer to the wishes of the child for Convention purposes, even if the child's wishes may not prevail if welfare were the paramount consideration.[5]

However, with respect, this comment appears to be wishful thinking and to be attributing to the drafters of the Abduction Convention ideas which had not yet gained acceptance in 1980. Perusal of the proceedings at The Hague shows that the inclusion of the child objection exception was motivated by pragmatism rather than recognition of the child's right to participate.[6]

In any event, whatever the motivation of the drafters, it is clear that the exception in Article 13(2) provides the means to give effect to the child's right to participate[7] if courts are prepared to give weight to the views of children and to exercise their discretion to refuse to return children against their wishes. However, as will be seen below, in practice many courts have not exploited this potential inherent in Article 13(2).[8] The prevailing judicial tendency to construe the exception narrowly,[9] apparent from the case law, is confirmed by the empirical evidence. In the 2008 Statistical Survey, only 10 per cent of judicial refusals were based solely on the child's objections.[10] This figure is slightly more than that in 2003 (9 per cent), but less than that in 1999 (13%).

There appears to be two explanations for this situation. Firstly, some judges still do not seem to be aware of or have internalised the concept of children's rights and still see all issues relating to children in terms of welfare, which is seen as irrelevant in Convention proceedings. Secondly, even where there is an awareness of the children's rights, the fundamental Convention policy of mandatory return is usually preferred and thus the exception is interpreted narrowly[11] without even referring to the tension between the concept of mandatory return and the child's right to participate,[12] a tension which appears to be inherent in every case where the child does not wish to return. One of the few judges who has expressly noted this tension is New Zealand's Judge Boshier, who described it as follows,

---

[5] *Re T (Abduction: Child's Objections to Return)* [2000] 2 FLR 192.

[6] P Beaumont and P McEleavy, *The Hague Convention on International Child Abduction* (Oxford, Oxford University Press, 1999) 177–78.

[7] See comment of Wilson LJ in *Re W (Minors)* [2010] EWCA Civ 520 [17] that '[f]ortunately Article 13 was drawn in terms sufficiently flexible to accommodate this development in international thinking'.

[8] For relatively rare use by US courts, see R Nanos, 'The Views of a Child: Emerging Interpretation and Significance of the Child's Objection under the Hague Child Abduction Convention' (1996) 23 *Brooklyn Journal of International Law* 437, 448.

[9] AM Greene, 'Seen and Not Heard?: Children's Objections under the Hague Convention on International Child Abduction' (2005) 13 *University of Miami International and Comparative Law Review* 105.

[10] N Lowe, 'A Statistical Analysis of Applications Made in 2008 under the Hague Convention of 25 October 1980 on the Civil Aspects of International Child Abduction', Part I Global Report, Preliminary Document 8 (November 2011), 29 www.hcch.net/upload/wop/abduct2011pd08ae.pdf ('2008 Statistical Survey'). When judicial refusals based on multiple reasons were taken into account, the percentage of refusals in which the children's objections were one of the reasons stayed more or less constant (18% in 1999 to 13% in 2003 and 17% in 2008), ibid, 30.

[11] eg, the Israeli Supreme Court decision in RFamA 672/06 *TAE v PR*, PD 61(3) 24 [INCADAT cite: HC/E/IL 885] which paid lip service to the children's rights including reference to Art 12 of the CRC and to the Hebrew version of the current author's article R Schuz, 'The Hague Child Abduction Convention and Children's Rights' (2002) 12 *Transnational Law & Contemporary Problems* 393, but then proceeded to interpret the requirement of Art 13(2) even more narrowly than in previous case law (see eg at II Bii below). Ironically, in the first instance decision in this case, Justice Asulin had warned that reference to the child's rights should not become an empty declaration.

[12] Greene, 'Seen and Not Heard' (n 9) 109, refers to this tension as one between the 'child's individual interests and the treaty's overall interest in preventing abductions'.

the defense gives rise to a philosophical dilemma. On the one hand, rights of children, particularly those mature enough to express a view, must be heard, respected and implemented if possible. It seems to me that this is inevitable given this country's ratification of the United Nations Convention on the Rights of Children. . . . On the other hand, the scheme of the Act is clear and it requires a return of children to the country of origin in most circumstances.[13]

The tension between the child's right to participate and the perceived need to interpret the Article 13(2) exception narrowly is so germane to any discussion of Article 13(2) that it will be referred to throughout the examination of the case law in this chapter, as well as in the analysis section.

It should also be pointed out from the outset that the often expressed fear that a wider interpretation of the exception will lead to reliance on children's objections becoming the rule rather than the exception and thus thwart the Convention's return mechanism[14] is exaggerated.[15] In particular, it should be remembered that this exception cannot apply in relation to very young children and is rarely used in relation to children under eight.[16] Since 36 per cent of children in relation to whom applications are made are under four-years-old and a further 41 per cent are aged between five and nine,[17] the exception will only be potentially relevant in a minority of cases.[18] Thus, it should not be assumed that giving greater recognition to the child's right to participate will substantially undermine the Convention.

B The Scope of the Court's Discretion

The structure of Article 13 requires a two-stage decision-making process. At the first stage, sometimes referred to as the gateway stage,[19] the court must determine if one of the exceptions is made out. Then, if this stage is passed, the court must exercise its discretion as to whether to return the child or not. Whilst it is clear that at the first stage it is necessary to determine whether the child objects to return to the requesting State and whether the age and maturity of the child are such that it is appropriate for the court to take account of those objections,[20] different opinions have been expressed in relation to the stage at which the weight to be given to the child's views should be considered.

---

[13] *Secretary of Justice v Penney* [1995] NZFLR 827.
[14] See eg, Nanos, 'The Views of a Child' (n 8) 463; BB Sobal and WM Hilton, 'Article 13(b) of the Hague Convention Treaty: Does it Create a Loophole for Parental Alienation Syndrome – an Insidious Abduction' (2001) 35 *International Lawyer* 997.
[15] Whilst there is evidence that Germany overused the child objection exception in the past (see Greene, 'Seen and Not Heard' (n 9) fn 93, referring to Lowe's report according to which between 1990 and 1996 a return was refused in every case where the child's objection was raised), this no longer seems to be the case and in 2008, only 22% of German refusals were based on the child's objections, and the overall judicial refusal rate in Germany was 18% (compared with 15% globally), German National Report 102–05, www.hcch.net/upload/wop/abduct-2011pd08c.pdf.
[16] In the 2008 Statistical Survey ibid, 32, 14% of the 86 children whose objections led to refusal were under the age of 8; 28% were aged 8–10; 42% aged 11–12 and 16% were over 13.
[17] ibid, 19.
[18] It should be noted that the child's objections are a much more frequent basis for refusal where the father is the abductor (31% as opposed to 13% (figures include cases where the child objection was one of multiple reasons for refusal)), ibid 33.
[19] P McEleavy, 'Evaluating the Views of Abducted Children: Trends in Appellate Case-Law' (2008) 20 *Child and Family Law Quarterly* 230.
[20] *Re T* (n 5) 203–04.

The main dispute seems to be between the approaches advocated by Balcolme LJ and Millett LJ in the case of *Re R (Minors)*.[21] Balcolme LJ, with whom Sir Ralph Gibson agreed, took the view that where the child was of an age and maturity at which it was appropriate to take into account their views, the Court should then exercise its discretion to decide whether the weight to be given to those views when set against the fundamental policy of the Convention, justified not ordering return. In his words,

> In exercising that discretion, it is clear that the policy of the Convention and its faithful implementation by the courts of the countries which have adopted it, should always be a very weighty factor to be brought into the scales, whereas the weight to be attached to the objections of the child or children will clearly vary with their age and maturity. The older the child, the greater the weight; the younger the child, the less the weight.[22]

This approach, which has become known as the 'shades of grey' approach,[23] enables the judge to take a relatively lenient view in relation to the gateway conditions in Article 13(2)[24] because even where those conditions are satisfied, he can still decide to return the child on the basis that the weight to be given to the child's views does not override the policy of the Convention. Thus, in the case of *Re R* itself, Balcolme LJ was able to hold that the children, who were aged six and seven, were old enough and mature enough for their views to be taken into account, but not to override the policy of the Convention and thus they had to be returned.[25]

On the other hand, Millett LJ adopted what has been coined the 'in or out' approach.[26] In his view, where the child is of sufficient age and maturity for his views to be taken into account, the Convention envisages that he will not be returned against his wishes unless there are countervailing factors which require his wishes to be overridden. In his words, 'It seems to me that either the child must be old enough and mature enough for his views to prevail in the absence of countervailing considerations or he is not, and must be returned.'[27] Under this approach, the judge is likely to take a more stringent approach to the conditions in Article 13(2) because once those conditions are satisfied, he cannot return the child unless there are strong reasons for overriding the child's wishes. Thus, in the case of *Re R* itself, Millett LJ, in contrast to Balcolme LJ, held that the children were not old or mature enough for their views to be considered.[28] Accordingly, both judges decided that the children should be returned and thus it can be seen that the two approaches will not necessarily lead to different outcomes.

Whilst Millett LJ's approach was adopted by some judges both in the UK[29] and abroad,[30] later appeal court decisions in two different jurisdictions unequivocally prefer the 'Balcolme approach'.[31] In the English case of *Zaffino v Zaffino*,[32] all three judges expressly preferred the

---

[21] *Re R (Minors)* [1995] 1 FLR 716.
[22] ibid 730.
[23] *White v Northumberland* [2006] NZFLR 1105 [29].
[24] *Re W (Minors)* (n 7) [22].
[25] *Re R (Minors)* (n 21).
[26] *White v Northumberland* (n 23) [28].
[27] *Re R (Minors)* (n 21) 734.
[28] ibid.
[29] eg, Ward LJ in *Re T* (n 5).
[30] eg, Harrison J in the New Zealand case of *Collins v Lowndes* (Unreported, High Court, Auckland, 6 March 2003).
[31] *cf* Israeli case law, which seems to adopt the most stringent aspects of both approaches. Thus, age, maturity and strength of objection are treated as threshold conditions, but even where these conditions are satisfied, in exercising its discretion great weight is given to the policy of the Convention. See *TAE v PR* (n 11).
[32] *Zaffino v Zaffino* [2005] EWCA Civ 1012.

'Balcolme approach' both because it was binding on them and as a matter of principle. Neuberger LJ, although apparently minimising the difference between the two approaches to one of burden of proof, lists three problems with the 'Millett approach':

> Firstly, it fails, or at least it runs the risk of failing to give sufficient weight to the principle and purpose of the Hague Convention as embodied in the first paragraph of Article 12. Secondly, it fails to acknowledge that the weight to be given to the child's views must depend on the age and maturity of the child, the strength of the views and reasons for the views. Thirdly, it introduces a presumption into what is expressed in the second paragraph of Article 13 as an unqualified discretion.

Similarly, in the case of *White v Northumberland*,[33] the New Zealand Court of Appeal, deciding between conflicting High Court authorities, expressly preferred the approach of Balcolme LJ and ordered the return of an 11-year-old boy to England, even though he was recognised to be sufficiently old and mature enough for weight to be given to his views. Interestingly, the New Zealand Court of Appeal was influenced inter alia by a change in the wording of the local legislation enacting the Hague Convention. In its original form, the child objection exception referred to a child who had attained an age and degree of maturity at which it was appropriate to **take account of the child's views** (author's emphasis).[34] However, the amended form of legislation[35] referred to a child who had attained an age and degree of maturity at which it was appropriate to **give weight to the child's views** (author's emphasis). In the view of the Court, the change in wording represented Parliamentary endorsement of the 'Balcolme approach'.

Indeed, the 'Balcolme approach' has a number of advantages. In particular, this approach gives clear recognition to the potential relevance of even a younger child's views and should increase the chance that the court will perceive the tension between the child's right to have weight given to his views and the policy of the Convention. Nonetheless, this advantage is largely neutralised by Balcolme LJ's fundamental premise, which is also inherent in Neuberger LJ's first criticism of the Millett approach that the child objection exception should only apply in exceptional cases. In other words, he has decided in advance that in most cases the so-called policy of the Convention is to prevail over the child's right to have weight given to his views and the justification for this is to prevent the objectives of the Convention being undermined. With respect, this approach, which has now been rejected by Baroness Hale,[36] is misconceived. In particular, the policy of the Convention is to return children whom the Convention requires to be returned and thus the exceptions should be interpreted in light of the purpose behind each exception and not in light of the general policy of returning abducted children.

Thus, there is much to commend the 'Millett approach', according to which a mature child whose objections are to be taken into account will not be returned unless there are countervailing factors. Neuberger LJ's second criticism, that the 'Millett approach' fails to recognise that the weight to be given to the child's views depends on age and maturity, etc, is unconvincing. Millett LJ simply sees the question of the weight to be given to the child's views as a clear-cut issue rather than as one of degree. Under his approach, if the child is not sufficiently mature or (presumably) if his objections are not strong or valid enough,

---

[33] *White v Northumberland* (n 23).
[34] Guardianship Amendment Act 1991, s 13.
[35] Care of Children Act 2004, s 106.
[36] *Re M (Abduction: Zimbabwe)* [2007] UKHL 55 [46].

then no weight will be given to his wishes. However, if he is sufficiently mature and his objections are sufficiently strong and valid, then they should be given effect to, notwithstanding the mandatory return policy of the Convention, unless there is some countervailing reason to the contrary. On the other hand, under the 'Balcolme approach', the weight to be given to the child's views (which depends on age, maturity, strength, etc) is balanced against the objectives of the Convention.[37] This equation is problematic since it is not dealing with like factors. Provided that the child is of an appropriate age and maturity and his wishes are sufficiently clear-cut and independent, why should more weight be given to the so-called policy of the Convention because he is 11 rather than 14 or because he is unable to express his wishes as forcibly as another child?

Finally, whilst Neuberger LJ's third criticism that the creation of a presumption is inconsistent with the unqualified discretion given in the Convention appears correct on a literal interpretation of the Convention, it can be argued that the presumption introduced by Millett LJ reflects the norm introduced by the CRC, which is binding on all the countries which ratified that Convention apart from the US. Thus, although the greater flexibility in the 'Balcolme approach' is attractive, the great weight it places on the so-called policy of the Convention means that the 'Millett approach' gives greater recognition to the child's right to participate. Whilst this conclusion is affected to some extent by Baroness Hale's rejection of the 'exceptionality test',[38] courts continue to apply the 'Balcolme approach' of balancing the weight to be given to the views of the child in the particular case against the policy of the Convention, which is still referred to as 'a powerful factor militating in favour of return'.[39]

However, even under the 'Balcolme approach', the division between the two stages is not always clear. Whilst strength, validity and independence of the objections are taken into account in the exercise of its discretion as to whether to return the child or not,[40] the question of the independence of the child's views may be treated as part of the gateway issue of whether the child actually objects to return.[41] Nonetheless, whichever approach is chosen, the quality of the children's objections seem to be tested according to the same criteria, whether these are perceived as part of the threshold requirements or as relevant to the exercise of discretion. Thus, it is appropriate to categorise the examination of the case law concerning the interpretation and application of Article 13(2) on the basis of these criteria and not according to the stage at which they are considered.

---

[37] See also *Re W (Minors)* (n 7) [26].
[38] *Re M (Abduction: Zimbabwe)* (n 36).
[39] eg *Re W (Minors)* (n 7) [26]; *JPC v SMW* [2007] EWHC 1349 (Fam). McEleavy, 'Evaluating the Views' (n 19), claims that despite the conceptual importance of Baroness Hale's ruling in *Re M (Abduction: Zimbabwe)* (n 36), it is not clear that it will have much impact on the everyday application of the Convention.
[40] eg, *S v S (Child Abduction) (Child's Views)* [1992] 2 FLR 492, 501; *Singh v Singh* 1998 SLT 1084; *Re HB (Abduction: Children's Objections)* [1997] 1 FLR 392; *LJG v RTP* [2006] NZLR 589; *Ryding v Turvey* [1998] NZFLR 313; *De L v Director-General, NSW Department of Community Services* (1996) FLC 92-674 (Nicholson J) and approved by the High Court of Australia.
[41] eg *In the Matter of Z (Children)* [2008] EWCA Civ 1545.

II Interpretation and Application of Article 13(2)

A Age and Maturity

i Age

The drafters of the Convention could not agree on a minimum age at which a child's objections should be taken into account and thus no 'threshold age' was fixed.[42] Whilst the US Court in *Tahan v Duquette*[43] held that a nine-year-old was too young for the exception to apply, most judges have not been prepared to lay down such a blanket minimum age[44] and thus each judge has discretion to decide at what age a child's views may be taken into account. Thus, it is not surprising that there is inconsistency not only between courts in different countries but between different judges in the same country.[45] For example, German courts are reported to have upheld the views of a four-year-old[46] whilst in some jurisdictions children of ten have been held not to be old enough to weigh up all the circumstances.[47] Furthermore, within the US, in contrast to the approach taken in *Tahan v Duquette*, other judges have stated that the objections of children aged eight[48] can be taken into account.

The case law suggests that whilst the views of children under the age of 10 are sometimes ascertained,[49] little weight is usually given to their views[50] unless they are considered to be mature beyond their years.[51] Conversely, children over 10[52] are generally considered prima facie to be old enough for their views to be taken into account.[53] Nonetheless, even in

---

[42] The Perez-Vera Explanatory Report, Proceedings of the 14th Session of the Hague Conference Oct 1980, www.hcch.net/upload/expl28.pdf, [a30] states that 'All the ages suggested seemed artificial, even arbitrary.' The original suggestion of 12 was dropped during legislative process, Beaumont and McEleavy (n 6) 180.

[43] *Tahan v Duquette* 613 A 2d 486 (NJ Super Ct 1992); see also *Re G (A Minor)(Abduction)* [1989] 2 FLR 475 (the first instance judge, without interviewing the child or receiving any report about his maturity, found that 'his worldly understanding at the age of 9 was not sufficiently broad to comprehend all the complex factors of the case').

[44] eg, in FamA (Dist Bsh) 121/07 *RB v VG*, Nevo, 21 October 2007 (Isr) [4], Justice Hendel refused the invitation of counsel for the father to declare that 8 was too young in view of research that a child under 9 should not be allowed to cross the road by himself (which was being publicised by the Israeli Government at the time of the case).

[45] eg comment of US Court of Appeals that 'Given the fact intensive and idiosyncratic nature of the inquiry, decisions applying the age and maturity exception are understandably disparate.' *de Silva v Pitts* 481 F3d 1279, 1287 (10th Cir 2007).

[46] N Lowe and A Perry, 'The Operation of the Hague and European Convention on International Child Abduction between England and Germany, Part IV' (1998) 1 *International Family Law* 52, 55.

[47] eg, the Australian case of *Police Commissioner of South Australia v Temple* [1993] FLC 92-365.

[48] *Blondin v Dubois* 238 F3d 153 (2d Cir 2001); *Rajmakers-Eghage v Haro* 131 F Supp 2d 953 (ED Mich, 2001).

[49] For methods of ascertaining wishes, see ch 14.

[50] M Everall, N Lowe and M Nicholls, *International Movement of Children (Practice and Procedure)* (Bristol, Jordans, 2004) 165; *Re R (Minors)* (n 21); HCJ 6056/93((SC) *Eden v Eden* 51(4) PD 197 (Isr); cf *Re W (Minors)* (n 7) (objections of children aged 8 and 6 upheld even though their maturity was commensurate with their ages).

[51] eg, leading English case of *Re S (A Minor)(Abduction: Custody Rights)* [1993] Fam 242 (nine-year-old girl held to have a mental age of 12); Scottish case of *Cameron v Cameron* [1996] SLT 306 (judge found no basis for attributing to the seven and a half-year-old girl maturity greater than her years); Hong Kong case of *S v S* [1998] 2 HKC 316 (six was held to be too young because there was no evidence that the boy was precocious or mature beyond his age).

[52] The 2008 Statistical Survey (n 10), 31 shows that the average age of the children whose objections were upheld was 10 and that the lowest age was 5. For the percentage of objecting children in each age band, see n 16.

[53] In the Netherlands, the objections of children over the age of 12 will be upheld provided they are supported by reasonable grounds (answer to question 7.3 of the Permanent Bureau's 2010 Questionnaire, www.hcch.net/index_en.php?act=publications.details&pid=5291&dtid=33).

relation to older children, courts have not infrequently based their refusal to uphold their views on the basis of lack of maturity[54] and some judges may still require evidence that the child is mature beyond his years.[55] Whilst the recognition that even relatively young children are capable of making choices and expressing views[56] is welcome and in accordance with their right to participate, this is of little value unless the test of maturity is realistic.

ii Maturity

Whilst the requirement of degree of maturity appears in Article 13(2), the Convention does not provide any method of determining the degree of maturity of the child. Thus, practice varies between judges, with some relying on their own impression of the child, whilst others rely on the report of an expert who has examined the child. Furthermore, since there are no criteria for determining maturity, each judge or expert will make his assessment in accordance with his own concept of maturity.[57] The subjective nature of the assessment of maturity is illustrated well by the US case of *England v England*.[58] The majority, overruling the first instance decision, cites the facts that the 13-year-old girl, who was adopted, had had four mothers during her life and took Ritalin for attention deficit disorder as evidence of immaturity. Judge De Moss, dissenting, convincingly explains why this conclusion does not follow from the facts[59] and expresses surprise that the majority is willing to draw such conclusions without medical evidence. The learned judge then goes on to explain the unavoidable uncertainty in the concept of maturity:

> The words 'degree of maturity' as used in Article 13 are inherently relative and subjective in their concept. But it seems self-evident to me that a 'degree of maturity' contemplates something less than actual, full, final, complete maturity. For that reason, I recognize that judges reading the same record (or hearing the original testimony) could come to different conclusions on the subject of Karina's degree of maturity.[60]

Indeed, judges' explanations as to why the children in question do or do not possess sufficient maturity reveal fundamentally different perceptions as to the degree of maturity required. At one extreme is the holding of a German judge that because a child of seven was old enough to decide whether he wanted to join a judo or football club, he was sufficiently

---

[54] eg, US cases of *Bickerton v Bickerton* No 91-06694 (Cal Sup Ct 1991) (Unpublished) in which a 12-year-old's objections were not upheld because of lack of maturity; *Navarro v Bullock* No 86481 (Cal Sup Ct 1989) (12 and 10-year-old held not to have sufficient age and maturity); Swiss decision in TF, 30.3.2012, 5A_764/2011, consid 3.3., discussed in AC Alfieri, Enlèvement international d'enfants: premières expériences avec la LF-EEA, *La pratique du droit de la famille* ch–2012– 550, 560 (11-year-old child not sufficiently mature).

[55] eg, in the US case of *Escaf v Rodriguez* 200 Supp 2d 603 (ED V a 2000), the Court based its decision that the Art 13(2) exception was not established partly on the fact that the 13- year-old boy was not exceptionally mature. In the later Canadian case of *Innes v Innes* 2005 BCC LEXIS 1425, the judge felt it necessary to distinguish this case on the basis that in the case before him the 12-year-old was found to have a high degree of maturity for his age.

[56] A Smith, 'Interpreting and Supporting Participation Rights: Contributions from Sociocultural Theory' (2002) 10 *The International Journal of Children's Rights* 73, 83–84.

[57] See Nanos, 'The Views of a Child' (n 8) 447, and sources quoted there.

[58] *England v England* 234 F3d 268 (5th Cir 2000).

[59] DeMoss J (dissenting) said, 'While that is factually true [that the girl had had four mothers], I would interpret it as enhancing maturity. She has experienced adversity and rejection and has had several occasions to form an opinion as to the impact on her own life of changes in adoptive parents and changes in places of living. . . . There is nothing in the record which would compel a conclusion that Karina evidences immature behaviour as the result of taking Ritalin' ibid, 274.

[60] ibid.

mature.[61] At the other end of the spectrum, some judges impose demanding tests of maturity which many adults would fail to meet ('the stringent approach').[62] For example, at first instance, in the English case of *Re T (Abduction: Child's Objections to Return)*, Wall J concluded as follows:

> She did not have the degree of maturity to be able to appreciate that things were not entirely black and white and indeed the very force with which she had taken sides was an indication that her level of maturity was that consistent with an 11 year old rather than with a child of more mature years who would be able to understand the pros and cons in a much more balanced way.[63]

Even more stringently, Waite LJ requires that the child's views be based on 'the discernment which a mature child brings to the question's implications for his or her own best interests in the long and short term'.[64] Similarly, in *A v A (Child Abduction)*,[65] maturity was equated with the ability to provide valid reasons for not wishing to return.

These more stringent tests open the door to a paternalistic approach under which the court judges the minor's maturity according to whether his decision is consistent with his best interests, as perceived by the judge or expert. A clear example of such a paternalistic approach can be seen in the Israeli Supreme Court decision in the case of *TAE v PR*.[66] Justice Procaccia refers to the psychiatrist's opinion that whilst the children, aged 13 and 11, were mature and developed for their ages both mentally and physically, their insight was partial and their vision was only short term. In her view, the fact that they were unable to understand that separation from their mother would cause them damage in the long term demonstrated an error of judgment. Whilst such an error was common for children of their age, it was still considered an error of judgment by adults. The expert's view is particularly difficult to justify in this specific case because there is no clear basis for the conclusion that separation from the mother will cause the children any more damage than separation from their father, which was the consequence of their return to Italy and does not take into account that the children were previously abducted to Italy by the mother.[67]

A more moderate version of the paternalistic approach can be found in another Israeli Supreme Court case concerning children aged 12 and 10, in which it was held that a persuasive level of proof is required to show that the children have the ability to take into account all the family, cultural and other implications of the decision whether to return to Holland and that this requirement was not met in this case.[68] With respect, the approach in these two cases virtually turns the child objection exception into a dead letter.

---

[61] In the case of *Lady Catherine Meyer* discussed in Sobal and Hilton, 'Article 13(b)' (n 14).
[62] M Freeman, 'The Hague Child Abduction Convention – an Uneven Playing Field: The Voice of the Child in Hague Convention Proceedings' in M Freeman, *Contemporary Issues Concerning International Child Abduction and the Hague Child Abduction Convention* (Reunite, 2002) 34.
[63] Quoted in the judgment of Ward LJ in *Re T* (n 5). See also *McManus v McManus* 354 F Supp 2d (62) (2005), where ambivalence is seen as a sign of maturity, indicating an ability to weigh up both sides of the question. *cf* cases where the fact that the child shows awareness of the disadvantages of his decision, is treated as evidence that his views are not strongly enough held; eg, RCA 3052/99 (SC) *Shevach v Shevach*, 2 June 1999 (Isr) http://elyon1.court.gov.il/files/99/520/030/L03/99030520.l03.pdf
[64] *Re S (Abduction: Acquiescence)* [1994] 1 FLR 819, 827.
[65] *A v A (Child Abduction)* [1993] 2 FLR 225, 241. See also *Haimdas v Haimdas* 401 Fed Appx 567 (2nd Cir 2010).
[66] *TAE v PR* (n 11).
[67] Indeed, the return does appear to have caused damage because of the obstacles put in the way of access by the mother (personal communication from lawyers involved in the case).
[68] RFamA 902/07 *Plonit v Plonim*, 26 April 2007, http://elyon1.court.gov.il/files/07/020/009/A06/07009020.a06.pdf

Furthermore, the very axiom on which the paternalistic approach is based – that adults need to make hard decisions for children because they are not capable of making decisions themselves – is questionable. It can be convincingly argued that the more evenly balanced the considerations between the options facing a child, the more weight should be given to his views. Whilst adults in general and courts in particular, are more capable of weighing up competing considerations from an intellectual point of view, in borderline cases, the final result is often largely based on instinct and speculation. Who is to say that the instinct of a child who has personally experienced life with both parents and in both countries is not more reliable than that of the judge who is deciding on the basis of written reports and an impression of the parties gained briefly from their oral testimony (where there is such testimony)?

Thus, it can be seen that the paternalistic approach substantially undermines the child's right to participate because he is only considered old and mature enough if his wishes happen to coincide with the perception of adults (the expert and the judge) as to the correct decision. In this context, it should be remembered that the concept of allowing mature children a right to participate in decisions concerning them necessarily involves the possibility that they, like adults, may make mistakes.[69]

Refreshingly, a few judges have taken a more realistic and less paternalistic approach to the issue of maturity. Thus, Ward LJ in the Court of Appeal in *Re T* said,

> I would not wish to venture any definition of maturity. Clearly the child has to know what has happened to her and to understand that there is a range of choice. A child may be mature enough for it to be appropriate for her views to be taken into account even though she may not have gained that level of maturity that she is fully emancipated from parental dependence and can claim autonomy of decision-making.[70]

Similarly, in *Clarke v Carson*, in which the children were aged 8 and 11, the judge states,

> The position at which it is right to take into account the views of children seems to me in the normal course to be the time when they are able to reason. That is a position supported by the Convention on the Rights of the Child.[71]

The approach of these judges emphasises the child's cognitive abilities in relation to the current situation rather than discernment in relation to the future. The child is required to understand the options available and the immediate consequence of those options, but does not have to display insight in relation to the long-term implications thereof. In addition, whilst he is required to be able to reason, his reasons do not have to be valid in the eyes of the judge. It is submitted that this approach is preferable to the 'stringent approach' explained above both as a matter of principle and practicality. Firstly, as already stated, very often the long- term implications are far from clear and imposing an adult's assessment of them is paternalistic. Secondly, it is much easier to assess the child's ability to understand the current situation and to reason than to assess his ability to weigh up long-

---

[69] J Eekelaar, 'Emergence of Children's Rights' (1986) 6 *Oxford Journal of Legal Studies* 161, 182 refers to the right to make mistakes as the most precious of rights.
[70] *Re T* (n 5).
[71] *Clarke v Carson* [1995] NZFLR 926. However, this apparent liberality was neutralised when, in the exercise of his discretion whether to uphold the children's views, the judge concluded that the children lacked the maturity to be able to assess the potential prize for them in re-establishing their relationship with their father and to choose between their United States and New Zealand heritages.

term implications. Finally, there is social science evidence that there is little difference between adult reasoning and children's reasoning.[72]

B The Child's Objections

i Form of the Objections

In some cases, courts have interpreted the requirement that the child objects to return narrowly in two respects. Firstly, some courts have insisted that the child's views be expressed in the negative.[73] Thus, there must be an aversion to returning. A desire to stay is not sufficient.[74] Even if the views are expressed as an objection, little weight will be attached to them if the real reason is a desire to stay with the abducting parent in the country of refuge.[75] For example, in the Israeli case of *Shevach v Shevach*, the first instance judge interpreted the child's objection to return to the US as a mere preference to stay in Israel because he did not express any real complaints about life in the US, but rather had emphasised the advantages of life in Israel.[76] Secondly, some courts have insisted that the objection be to return to the country of habitual residence rather than to the other parent.[77] The reason for this seems to be that the objection must be 'to that which would otherwise be ordered under Article 12, viz. an immediate return to the country from which [he] was wrongfully removed'.[78]

It is submitted that both of these requirements are artificial and are unnecessary limitations on the child's right to have appropriate weight attached to his views. Whilst Article 13(2) does refer to an objection to being returned, the substance of the child's views should be examined rather than the way in which they are expressed. Thus, if the child does not really mind whether he stays or returns, an expression of a preference to stay in the country of refuge would not appear to come within Article 13(2). However, often the child's expression of a desire to stay is simply another way of saying that he does not want to return.[79] This was recognised in the Scottish case of *Urness v Minto*,[80] where it was held that the desire to stay in Scotland implied a rejection of American culture.

Moreover, the requirement that the objection is to return to the country and not to the other parent has no basis in the wording of Article 13(2). Indeed, the English Court of Appeal has quite rightly recognised that 'there may be cases where this is so inevitably and inextricably linked with an objection to living with the other parent that the two factors

---

[72] Smith, 'Interpreting and Supporting' (n 56) 83.
[73] eg, *Re R (A Minor: Abduction)* [1992] 1 FLR 105.
[74] eg *Norden-Powers v Beveridge* 125 F Supp 2d 634, 641 (EDNY, 2000); 5A.582/2007Bundesgericht, II. Zivilabteilung (Tribunal Fédéral, 2ème Chambre Civile), [INCADAT cite: HC/E/CH 986].
[75] *Re S (A Minor) (Abduction: Custody Rights)* (n 51) 252 (Balcolme LJ).
[76] As reported in the appeal from that decision in FamA 128/99 (Dist HAI) *Shevach v Shevach* Nevo, 30 April 1999 (Isr).
[77] *B v K (Child Abduction)* [1993] 1 FCR 382. In *Re J (Children) (Abduction: Child's Objections to Return)* [2004] All ER (D) 72, the first instance Court found that 'the dominant feature of his view is his wish to live with his mother. He does not have a real objection to a return to Croatia in his mother's care' (quoted at [27] (Wall LJ)).
[78] *Re S (A Minor) (Abduction: Custody Rights)* (n 51) (Balcolme LJ).
[79] Nicholson CJ commented in the case of *D-G, Department of Community Services v De Lewinski* (1996) FLC 674, 83, that '... a Court should not expect children to necessarily express their views within adult formulations'.
[80] *Urness v Minto* 1994 SC 249; comment of Sumner J in *Re H (Children) (Abduction: Children's Objections)* [2004] EWHC 211 [122], that 'a preference to stay here can be as much an objection to returning to Australia'; *D-G & Milson* (n 3) [115], where a strong wish to stay and an objection were said to amount to 'two sides of the same coin'.

cannot be separated'.[81] Furthermore, from the point of view of the right of the child to participate, there is no logical basis upon which to differentiate between objections to places and objections to parents.[82]

ii Strength of the Objections

Many courts have made it clear that expressing a mere preference not to return is not sufficient and that the objections must be strongly held.[83] These requirements seem designed to exclude situations where the child is ambivalent or his view wavers or where he does not reject either option but simply prefers not to return.[84] Yet, most courts have refused to put a gloss on the words of Article 13(2) by requiring a standard higher than the usual ascertainment of the wishes of the child in a custody dispute.[85]

However, following an amendment in 2000, Regulation 16(3) of the Australian Family Law (Child Abduction) Regulations 1989 now provides that the objection must show a strength of feeling beyond the mere expression of a preference or of ordinary wishes.[86] Similarly, the Israeli Supreme Court has held that the child's wishes must be 'dominant and of special force'.[87] This requirement will discriminate between children with different personalities; between those who by nature express themselves forcibly and those who have a more moderate temperament. Furthermore, the Israeli Supreme Court's interpretation that the views of a child who was in a situation of conflict cannot be of sufficient force is highly problematic. By definition, children in abduction cases are in a situation of conflict and even where they are absolutely sure that they do not wish to return, they are likely to display some signs that they miss the left-behind parent, the extended family and friends in the country of origin. Such signs should not be automatically interpreted as evidence of ambivalence or that the child's views are not strongly held. The child has a right to have appropriate weight attached to all his views and not only to those which are dominant and expressed forcibly. As pointed out by the first instance judge in the same case, the requirement that the child's objection to return be of special force makes the child's right to have his views considered virtually redundant.[88]

This point is also relevant where the strength of the child's objections is relevant to the exercise of discretion, rather than as a threshold condition. Courts may underestimate the

---

[81] In *Re T* (n 5); *Re M (A Minor) (Child Abduction)* [1994] 1 FLR 390; *Re M (Abduction: Psychological Harm)* [1998] 1 FCR 488.

[82] Comment of Butler-Sloss LJ in *Re M (A Minor) (Child Abduction)* ibid 395, that to refuse to listen to the child because he objected to returning to the other parent rather than to the country of origin was inconsistent with Art 12 of the CRC.

[83] eg, *Escaf v Rodriguez* (n 55); *Trudrung v Trudrung* 686 F Supp 2d 570, 577–79 (MDNC 2010) (ordering return of a 15-year-old because he had merely testified that his preference was to remain in the United States while expressing no strong objection to returning to Germany); cf *de Silva v Pitts* (n 45) (return of a 14-year-old refused on the basis of what appeared to be a preference).

[84] eg, *N v N (Abduction: Article 13 Defence)* [1995] 1 FLR 107, 112; *Western Australian Police v Dorman* (1997) FLC 92-766.

[85] *Re S (A Minor) (Abduction: Custody Rights)* (n 51), 50, rejecting approach of Bracwell J in *Re R (A Minor: Abduction)* (n 73); Australian case of *L v Director-General, NSW Department of Community Services* (1996) FLC 92-706 [22] (prior to the change in the Regulations); New Zealand case of *Ryding v Turvey* (n 40). Similarly, it has been held that there is no need to show that the child objects to return for the purpose of determining the custody dispute, *D-G & Milson* (n 3) [100]–[108].

[86] For application of this test, see *Richards & Director-General, Department of Child Safety* [2007] FamCA 65; *D-G & Milson* (n 3).

[87] *TAE v PR* (n 11); RFamA 902/07 (n 68).

[88] FamC 14830/05 (BSH) *PR v TAE* tak-mish 05(4), 266 (2005).

strength of views which are not expressed forcibly and so give little weight to them. For example, in *Re HB (Abduction: Children's Objections)*, Justice Hale (as she then was) considered that 'that the real strength of her objections, the reasons for them and the evidence of relationships at home were not enough to set against the policy of the Convention'.[89] The aftermath of this case suggests that this assessment was wrong because the girl protested violently and had to be let off the plane.[90] With respect, the learned judge seems to have been downgrading the strength of the girl's objections on the basis of the reasons given, which do not seem to her convincing.[91] This illustrates the point that just because the reasons do not seem to be convincing to the judge, it does not mean that the views are not strongly held.

iii Independence of the Objections

At the time of drafting the Convention, concerns were expressed that the inclusion of the child objection exception would open the door to influence by parents and other family members and impose great responsibility on the child.[92] Thus, it was said that it would be for judges 'to apply it with discernment'.[93] These concerns have been repeated many times by judges in cases where the child objects. For example, in *S v S (Child Abduction)*, Balcombe LJ said:

> ... if the court should come to the conclusion that the child's views have been influenced by some other person, e.g. the abducting parent ... then it is probable that little or no weight will be given to those views. Any other approach would be to drive a coach and horses through the primary scheme of the Hague Convention.[94]

A more direct reference to the effect of parental influence on the scope of the child's rights was made by Judge Clarkson in *Winters v Cowen*:

> The tension between the Hague Convention and art 12 of the United Nations Convention on the Rights of the Child is demonstrated in this case. The Convention directs the return of the children unless their expressed objection is accepted and acted upon by the Court. The real question to be answered is whether it is honoring children's rights to be heard, if one allows them to operate merely as the mouthpieces of adults. To do so would, in fact, derogate from their rights to be heard and considered independently.[95]

From these quotations it can be seen that, where there is a suggestion that a child's views are not authentic or are not independent, the Court has to decide two issues: firstly,

---

[89] *Re HB* (n 40).

[90] *Re HB* [1998] 1 FLR 422; The lesson from this case seems to have been learnt, as seen from *G (Children)* [2010] EWCA Civ 1232, where the Court of Appeal allowed the appeal against the return order because of the 13-year-old girl's threat that no-one was going to force her onto the plane. Again, the first instance Court did not seem to have appreciated the strength of her objection because they were not expressed forcibly enough.

[91] In *Shevach* (n 76), Justice Kenan's conclusion that the boy's objection was a mere preference was based on her view that his reasons for objecting were not sufficiently strong. On appeal, the District Court found that this conclusion could not be justified on the facts (ibid), but this decision was later overturned by the Supreme Court (n 63). However, afterwards the mother consented to the child staying in Israel, R Schuz, 'Protection versus Autonomy: The Child Abduction Experience' in Y Ronen and CW Greenbaum (eds), *The Case for the Child: Towards a New Agenda* (Antwerp, Intersentia, 2008) 296–97.

[92] For this reason the United States opposed the exception. See Comments of the Governments on Preliminary Document No 6 in Actes et Documents de la Quatorzième session (1980) 243.

[93] Per the Canadian Delegate in Comments of the Governments on Preliminary Document No 6 in Actes de Documents ibid, 234.

[94] *S v S (Child Abduction)* (n 40) 501; See also comment in *Escaf v Rodriguez* (n 55) that most adolescents are susceptible to suggestion and manipulation.

[95] *Winters v Cowen* [2002] NZFLR 927.

whether there has indeed been influence and secondly, if this question is answered positively, whether this influence effectively nullifies the child's objections. In relation to both of these questions, wide and narrow approaches exist.

In relation to the first issue, the wide approach treats the very act of abduction or the circumstances arising as a result thereof as influencing the child. An extreme example of this can be seen in the Israeli case of *Ploni v Plonit*[96] in which the Court stated that an abducted child is like a person who has been brainwashed because he is completely dependent on the abductor for his survival and thus his views cannot be independent. An apparently more moderate example is the approach of Judge Clarkson in the case of *Winters v Cowen*, who explains:

> It is extremely complicated to interpret the objections of these already fragile and vulnerable children, and one must take account of the influences described by the dynamics of their grandparents' response and the length of time this process and the investigations have taken.[97]

However, his conclusion that the children have been reinforced in their behaviour and beliefs by the conduct of the mother and grandparents in not returning them to their father on the due date, leads to a similar result. He is effectively saying that the very fact of the retention influences the views and prevents them from being independent. Similarly, the Israeli Supreme Court has stated that it is very difficult to separate the child's wishes from the inevitable direct or indirect influence of the abducting mother.[98]

In the US case of *Giampolo v Erneta*,[99] the inevitable influence of the abductor is related to the period of time which has elapsed since the abduction.[100] In this case, where the 11-year-old child had been in the US for more than two years at the time of the hearing, the judge found that the child had naturally become accustomed to the US and had been influenced by her mother's preference for her to remain in the US. Thus, whilst not implying that the child had expressed no independent thoughts, the Court would exercise its discretion to order return of the child. The implications of this reasoning would seem to be that wherever the child has been in the care of the abductor for a considerable period of time, his objection to returning to the country of habitual residence will not be treated seriously. With respect, this approach is absurd because the longer the child has been away from the country of habitual residence, the more reasonable it will be for him to object to return from an objective point of view since he will usually have become settled in the country of refuge. Thus, the approach in these cases is incompatible with the child's rights to have appropriate weight given to his views.

A rather different, but equally problematic, example of not treating the child's views seriously is found in the first instance decision in the Israeli case of *Shevach*,[101] where Justice Kenan decided that the child's objection to return was influenced by the fuss that was being made of him by his father's relatives and new friends at school and the apparent attractions

---

[96] FamA (Dist TA) 28/97 *Ploni v Plonit* Nevo, 19 April 1999 (Isr).
[97] *Winters v Cowen* (n 95).
[98] eg RFamA 902/07 (n 68).
[99] *Giampolo v Erneta* 390 F Supp 2d 1269 (2004).
[100] Similarly, in RFamA 9114/07 *RB v VG*, 30 October 2007, http://elyon1.court.gov.il/files/07/140/091/B01/07091140.b01.pdf, the Israeli Supreme Court held that the child's views were not independent because having spent so much time in close contact with his mother (two years in France before the abduction and a further almost two years in Israel after the abduction), it was inevitable that he would be aware of and identify with her feelings, even if she did not share her views with him.
[101] *Shevach* (n 76).

of life in Israel and that he would change his mind when the initial euphoria ended.[102] With respect, this paternalistic approach is unjustified on the facts of the case. Firstly, many of the advantages of life in Israel, such as greater freedom, are not transient. Secondly, it is artificial to look only at the influences in favour of staying in Israel without also considering the counter-influences, such as the difficulties in adjusting to a different educational and social environment and the separation from the mother. The boy had simply weighed up these factors in a different way to the judge, but this does not mean that his decision is not independent. To force upon him the judge's assessment of the situation is effectively to deprive him of any autonomy.

Similarly, the Israeli Supreme Court in *TAE v PR*, took the view, in reliance on the expert's opinion, that the children's objections to returning to Italy were not independent. In their words:

> The act of abduction, the bringing of the children to Israel without the knowledge or agreement of the mother, the pressure placed on them by the father and the extended family, mainly by enveloping them with everything good and various benefits, resulted in confusion, instability and inability to form a real opinion capable of being taken into consideration in relation to their return to their mother in Italy.'[103] (Author's translation.)

With respect, as pointed out by the first instance judge in that case, the automatic association of the child's views with the fact that he is receiving a lot of attention from the family of the abducting parent makes the child's right to have his viewpoint considered redundant.[104]

In contrast, the narrow approach assumes that whilst the child will inevitably be influenced by those around him, such influence only vitiates the independence of the child's objections where it is beyond a normal level.[105] In the words of Justice Miller in the US case of *Robinson*,

> It is likely that the abducting parent desperately desires to keep his or her child from leaving the country. It is unrealistic, indeed inhuman, to expect a caring parent not to influence the child's preference. Accepting that there will be some influence, the question really becomes when is it undue.[106]

Under this approach, the court looks for evidence of express incitement against the other parent,[107] continually 'running down' the other parent or the country of origin in the eyes of the child[108] or coaching of the child.[109]

---

[102] A similar approach can be found in the Israeli case of CA (SC) 6327/94 *Isik v Isik*, nevo, 1 December 1994, where the child's views are found to have been influenced by the fact that he had been given a mobile phone.

[103] *TAE v PR* (n 11). See also the decision of the Swiss Federal Supreme Court in 5P.1/2005 /bnm, Bundesgericht, II. Zivilabteilung (Tribunal Fédéral, 2ème Chambre Civile) [INCADAT cite: HC/E/CH 795], holding that in light of the circumstances of the flight from Spain and reception with open arms in Switzerland it was not possible for children aged 9 and 10 to say anything other than that they did not want to return to Spain. Thus, since their views could not be independent, they did not have the maturity required by Article 13(2).

[104] *PR v TAE* (n 88).

[105] eg US decision in *de Silva v Pitts* (n 45) (father's largesse not treated as preventing the child's views from being independent); *Central Authority of the Republic of South Africa v B* 2012 (2) SA 296 (GSJ) [17] (holding that whilst the active involvement and participation of the father in the life and activities of his son might have influenced his objection, they cannot be said to have manipulated or unduly influenced him).

[106] *Robinson* 983 F Supp 1339, 1343 (D Colo 1997).

[107] eg, FamA (Dist TA) 1167/99 *R v L* (Unreported, 3 July 2000) [INCADAT cite: HC/E/IL 834] (holding that there had been incitement); *cf* FamA (Dist HAI) 6591/97 *AB v YB* Nevo, 31 December 1997 (Isr) (Court did not accept the psychologist's report that there had been incitement).

[108] eg, per Wall J in the first instance Court in *Re T* (n 5).

[109] eg, *Robinson* (n 106), where the child's main reason for objecting was that he was now settled in the USA. The judge found that this is what he had been told to say by the abducting father and his counsellor; *cf McManus* (n 63), where the judge expressly stated that neither he nor the guardian *at litem* found indications that the testimony had been coached or otherwise unduly influenced by the father.

The narrow approach is clearly to be preferred. As Justice Miller indicates, the idea that a child's views can be truly independent is misconceived.[110] Even in cases where parents are careful to avoid influencing their views, it is inevitable that the child will be influenced by the words and actions of those around him. This is true in all situations and not only those of abduction. Thus, an insistence that the child's views are completely independent will mean not only that that the exception in Article 13(2) can never apply, but that the child's right to have appropriate weight attached to his views is meaningless. Thus, it is essential that only undue influence should affect the weight to be given to the child's views.

This leads us to the second issue: the implications of the finding of undue influence. Under the prevalent wide approach, if the court finds that the child's views have been shaped or even coloured by undue influence, their views will not be taken into account.[111] For example, in an Israeli case, the conclusion of the Court that the child was suffering from Parental Alienation Syndrome (PAS) as a result of the mother's incitement automatically led to the conclusion that the requirements of the Article 13(2) exception were not satisfied.[112] No effort was made to consider whether even without such alleged incitement the child would have objected, although there was factual evidence to support such a conclusion.

Similarly, in *TAE v PR*,[113] even though it was expressly found that there was no actual incitement, the Israeli Supreme Court assumed that the influence of the paternal family, together with the fact that the children had not yet started learning full time in Israel completely vitiated the relevance of the children's wishes. This approach is particularly problematic in this case, where there were clear objective reasons to support the children's objections to return to Italy, not least the fact that the mother had originally abducted them from Israel to Italy and that, according to the evidence of the father, they themselves had asked him to bring them back to Israel. Moreover, the assumption that the children's views were influenced by the holiday-like conditions they were living in is highly paternalistic, especially in view of the fact that the children had previously lived and attended school in Israel and were therefore in a position to make a comparison between life in the two countries.[114]

However, an alternative and more refreshing approach can be found in a few cases, under which the court will attempt to discount the influence and consider whether, even without influence, it is likely that the child would have held those views. This will include looking at the views of the child before the influence, other objective reasons why the child might hold those views and an assessment of the extent to which the objections are likely to be mollified on return and, where it is the case, on removal from any pernicious influence from the abducting parent.[115]

---

[110] Robinson ibid. See also words of Charles J in *Re S (Abduction: Children's Representation)* [2008] EWHC 1798 (Fam), 'As with everybody's minds the decisions they make are influenced by what others think, what others say, what others have done and their perceptions of what others have done, but to my mind it is clear that all three of these children are expressing, for understandable and sound reasons, a real and compelling wish to stay in the UK.'

[111] See eg, Hague Convention Analysis, 51 Fed Reg at 10,509; Scottish case of *AQ v JQ* (12 December 2001, unpublished) [INCADAT cite: HC/E/UKs 415].

[112] *R v L* (n 107). However, the child was not returned because his threats of suicide were taken seriously and thus the grave risk of harm exception in Art 13(1)(b) was satisfied.

[113] *TAE v PR* (n 11).

[114] Similarly, in *RB v VG* (n 100), the Israeli courts did not take into account that there were many objective reasons for the objections of the 8-year-old child, who was happily settled in school in Israel and had adopted an orthodox Jewish way of life which was completely different from the one that he would have to adopt if he returned to Belgium, where he had no connections other than his father, with whom he remembered negative experiences.

[115] *Re T* (n 5).

The difference between the two approaches is well illustrated by contrasting the relevant extracts of two judgments in the English case of *Re T*.[116] At first instance, Wall J said,

> I have to say I feel strongly that [G] herself has been placed under very substantial pressure by her father. Her father . . . filed a second affidavit . . . which is effectively a diatribe against his wife and her capacity, or lack of it as a mother. . . . Although he tried to assure me that he had never run their mother down in the children's presence or to the children, I find that submission impossible to accept. It is very plain to me that [G], although she may well have had unhappy experiences in her mother's care, has wholly absorbed her father's negative views and is repeating them and, although she may feel them genuinely, I am equally satisfied that the additional pressure which has been placed on her is her knowledge that, under no circumstances, will her father return to Spain, as he said. That makes it impossible, in my view, for her to exercise any independent judgment. In these circumstances I have to say that I do not think, sympathetic as I am to [G], that she is of an age and maturity where it is appropriate for me to take account of her wishes to the extent that I decline to order her return to Spain.[117]

In contrast, in the Court of Appeal, Sedley LJ said,

> There is no shadow of doubt that the father has played a conscious role in alienating the children from their mother, both before and after the abduction. The mother for her part has tried, but with less success, to do the opposite. But there comes a point at which, for better or for worse, an intelligent and articulate child's views, whatever their genesis, have to be taken for what they are – and the views of G, who at 11 is perceptibly both intelligent and articulate, are now made disturbingly apparent by the letter she wrote to her mother on 1 February 2000, about four weeks after the abduction to England.[118]

In other words, the Court was prepared to look beyond the clear influence for evidence of the child's own views.[119] With respect, this approach is more consistent with the child's right to have appropriate weight attached to her views[120] and with the dynamics of the process of the formation of the child's opinions. Incitement and other forms of influence do not operate in a vacuum and social science research suggests that parental alienation, even where there has been incitement, is often rooted in the child's negative experiences with the alienated parent.[121] Thus, the issue of independence of view is one of degree and not of absolutes. Accordingly, even where there is evidence of influence, the court has to decide to what extent the views expressed by the child represent input by him based on his own experiences and his own interpretation of events and to what extent he is simply repeating blindly the views fed to him directly or indirectly by those around him.

---

[116] ibid.
[117] ibid.
[118] ibid.
[119] See also *Re S (Abduction: Children's Representation)* (n 110) (Charles J); *Re M (Abduction: Child Objections)* [2007] EWCA Civ 260 [78] (holding that even though the child's views were no doubt coloured by the unseemly tug of war going on between her parents, the unsettling experiences involving the police interrogation of her mother could quite independently explain the fears expressed by the eight-year-old child).
[120] eg comments of Fisher J in *S v S* [1999] NZFLR 625 (overruling the first instance decision not to give weight to the views of the children because the various influences operating on the mind of a child of this age and maturity had inhibited their capacity to express views consonant with their own reality) that 'it would be patronising in the extreme, and contrary to the international conventions and legislation to which I have referred, to fail to give substantial weight to their wishes'.
[121] See C Bruch, 'Parental Alienation Syndrome and Parental Alienation: Getting it Wrong in Child Custody Cases' (2002) 14 *Child and Family Law Quarterly* 381, 386–92.

Thus, the view that giving significant weight to children's wishes under Article 13(2) creates a loophole for PAS[122] is a generalisation that cannot be supported. Where there is clear evidence that the incitement and undue influence of the abductor is such that the child's views cannot be said to be his own, then the exception in Article 13(2) should not be established.[123] However, this does not mean that the very fact of abduction or the consequential close relationship between the child and the abductor or other types of influence necessarily prevent the child from forming an independent view that he objects to returning to the country of origin. Furthermore, in light of the controversy surrounding PAS and the lack of scientific basis for this theory,[124] judges should not treat a diagnosis of PAS as a reason not to give weight to the child's views, without examining carefully the nature, extent and impact of the alleged incitement.

More generally, the question of the function of experts' reports also arises in the context of the issue of independence of the child's views. There is clearly room for different experts to form different opinions on this issue, as happened in the New Zealand case of *Hollins v Crozier*.[125] Thus, it is important, as indeed happened in this case, that judges should meet with the child and form their own opinion as to the independence of the child's opinions.[126]

iv Validity of Objections

Some courts have required that objections be valid. Whilst the basis of this requirement has not been explained,[127] it seems that lack of validity can be seen either as evidence that the child is not really old and mature enough for his reasons to be taken into account or, alternatively, as relevant to the discretion of the court in deciding whether to order return, despite the fact that the exception has been established.

Two approaches to the validity of objections can be identified. The first analyses the quality of the reasons given by the child. For example, the Israeli Supreme Court has held that the child's 'objection must be entrenched in reasons which are of significant weight, stable and reasonable'.[128] There seems to be a tendency to find that the reasons are valid where they are rooted in the bad behaviour of the applicant, such as alcoholism,[129] previous abduction[130] or violence,[131] or a real difference between the quality of their life in the two countries.[132] On the contrary, reasons which are simply associated with moving from one country to another – such as not wanting to change schools or to leave family and friends

---

[122] Sobal and Hilton, 'Article 13(b)' (n 14) Part V.

[123] Thus, indeed it would seem that the exception should not have been established in the Lady Catherine Meyer case, which is discussed in detail by Sobal and Hilton ibid, and it is almost certain that courts in most other Convention countries would not have upheld the children's wishes in this situation. Accordingly, it seems unfortunate to base general conclusions about the exception in Art13 (2) on this case.

[124] See ch 3 at II F.

[125] *Hollins v Crozier* [2000] NZFLR 775.

[126] See generally ch 14 below.

[127] And some judges discount objections as being invalid without explaining why the objections do not qualify. See Greene, 'Seen and Not Heard' (n 9) 137.

[128] *TAE v PR* (n 11).

[129] *Re T* (n 5).

[130] *B v C* [2002] NZFLR 433; *cf TAE v PR* (n 11) where this factor does not seem to have been taken into account by the appeal courts.

[131] *Re J* (n 77); *Ostevoll v Ostevoll* 2000 WL 1611123 (SD Ohio).

[132] eg *Castillo v Castillo* 597 F Supp 2d 432, 441 (D Del 2009) (girl's objections to returning to Colombia were based on the fact that she received little help with homework there, performed relatively poorly in school, was often unable to play outside due to safety concerns, spent much of her time at home alone, and had few friends).

in the country of refuge – will not be considered sufficiently weighty by courts which interpret the exception narrowly.[133]

In some cases, whilst the reasons are prima facie weighty and convincing, they may be neutralised, in the eyes of the court, by arrangements or mechanisms which were unknown to the child. Thus, for example, in the English case of *Re J and K (Abduction: Objections of Child)*,[134] where the reason given by the nine-year-old child for his objection to return was that he did not want to return to the care of his grandparents, an undertaking by the applicant father that there would not be any contact with the grandparents reduced the weight to be given to the child's views and the Court decided to order return in accordance with the policy of the Convention. Similarly in the case of *Zaffino v Zaffino*,[135] the English Court took the view that the girl could be protected from her father's bullying, about which she had expressed concern, by the Canadian courts and thus this was not a reason to refuse return.

However, in other cases, even where the child's reasons are genuine and cannot be neutralised, the court simply does not accept that the reasons given justify not returning the child. A striking example is the Scottish case of *Marshall v Marshall*,[136] which involved a girl of 14 who ran away from Ireland because she was unhappy living with her mother and new partner who both drank a lot. The judge found that whilst part of her evidence was exaggerated, she did object and was unhappy in Ireland and was not influenced by her father who lived in Scotland. However, he concluded that despite the girl's age and maturity, it had not been established that there was sufficient substance in the reasons given for her objection to returning.

With respect, allowing the judge to review the substance of the reasons of a mature child where there is not alleged to be any undue influence, where the reasons are not based on objectively incorrect information[137] and where there is no evidence that upholding the child's wishes will be harmful is unnecessarily paternalistic and inconsistent with the child's right to have appropriate weight attached to his views.

The second approach to validity considers to what extent the reasons for objection are rooted in reality or might reasonably appear to the child to be so grounded.[138] This approach is clearly preferable because it is not paternalistic and looks at the situation from the child's perspective.[139] It accepts the subjective effect of past experiences on the child without attempting to assess 'objectively' whether those experiences justify the objections.[140]

---

[133] eg *Zaffino v Zaffino* (n 32); FamA 902/07 (n 68); *TAE v PR* (n 11).
[134] *Re J and K (Abduction: Objections of Child)* [2004] EWHC 1985.
[135] *Zaffino v Zaffino* (n 32).
[136] *Marshall v Marshall* [1996] SLT 429.
[137] As, eg, in *Vigreux v Michel* [2006] EWCA Civ 630, where the child's objections were based largely on his perception (which has been created by his father) that he would not be able to participate in the custody trial in France, whereas in fact he would be entitled to separate representation there.
[138] *Re T* (n 5) (Ward LJ).
[139] eg comment of Lord Ordinary in Scottish case of *PW v ALI*, (Unreported, Outer House of the Court of Session, 25 February 2003) that 'it is wrong to adopt a strictly analytical approach to the child's reasons for his or her wishes' and that 'the fact of a strongly felt objection is of significance in itself.' However, this decision was overturned on appeal in *W v W* [2004] SC 63, on the basis that the reasons advanced by H for objecting to return were not 'of sufficient "validity and strength" to take them to the conclusion that it was appropriate to take account of the child's views.'
[140] eg *LJG v RTP* (n 40) (holding that the child's views have validity 'as they are based on his experiences'); *D-G & Milson* (n 3) [115] (holding that 'whether realistic or unrealistic, it is plain that J nonetheless holds the fear he expressed'.)

C Considerations Relevant to the Court's Exercise of its Discretion

Where the child objection exception is established, the Court is obliged to take into account the welfare of the child, as well as the policy of the Convention, in exercising its discretion whether to order return or not.[141] In examining how the courts apply the welfare principle in this situation, a distinction will be made between cases where the welfare considerations point in the direction of returning the child despite his objections and those where the welfare considerations are seen as supporting the child's objections. This will be followed by a separate examination of how the courts take into account welfare considerations in the situation where the objecting child has younger siblings and a brief consideration of other policy considerations which are expressly mentioned by the courts when exercising their discretion in child objection cases.

i Welfare Considerations in Favour of Returning the Child

A good example of a decision not to uphold the child's objections because to do so would be inconsistent with his welfare can be found in the English case of *Zaffino*.[142] The Court of Appeal held that the first instance judge, in upholding the objections of the 13-old-girl and her nearly 10-year-old brother whilst sending the younger siblings back to Canada, had failed to consider the practical consequences of leaving the two teenagers behind by themselves in England, since no details of the proposed arrangements had been provided.

Whilst this conclusion seems to be based on a careful weighing up of the different considerations,[143] in some cases the reasoning is very vague and seems to reflect an instinctive assessment of the judge.[144] Moreover, sometimes the reason given for the conclusion that it is not in the best interest of the child to allow him to stay is a general one and whilst expressed in relation to the particular child, could apply to most other cases. For example, some judges have held that to require a child to choose between two parents may cause him psychological harm and thus they are not prepared to give any weight to any expressed objection. For example, in the US case of *Robinson*,[145] it was said, 'Forcing a child to choose between parents may be the ultimate Hobson's choice, particularly when massive geographic or cultural differences separate the parents. I decline to impose that responsibility on this youngster.'[146] Similarly, at first instance in the Israeli case of *Shevach*,[147] Justice Kenan concluded that a return order would remove from the boy the responsibility of

---

[141] *Re M (Abduction: Zimbabwe)* (n 36) [43]. For a discussion of different views in relation to the scope of this discretion, see I B above.
[142] *Zaffino v Zaffino* (n 32).
[143] See also Northern Ireland case of *Foster v Foster* (decision of Family Division of 24 May 1993).
[144] eg, Scottish case of *AQ v JQ* (n 111) (holding that, '[h]aving regard also to the comments of Dr. Robson relative to the attachment of the children to their mother and Germany, I am of the view that the general welfare considerations also point to the interests of the children lie in their being returned to the care of the petitioner in Germany'; *TB v JB (Abduction: Grave Risk of Harm)* [2001] 2 FLR 515 (holding that it was in the best interests of the 14- year-old girl to return, together with her mother and siblings). However, Arden LJ's reasoning in that case (at 530) seems to show why it is in the interests of the mother for the girl to return with her rather than why it is in her own interests.
[145] *Robinson* (n 106).
[146] But the child was not returned because of the exception in Art 12(2) (a lapse of 12 months before submission of the application and the child was settled in his new environment).
[147] *Shevach* (n 76).

having to decide between his parents. However, as Justice Ya'akov-Shvili pointed out on appeal, this was not necessarily true since in the custody hearing in the US he would be asked with whom he wished to live.[148] In other words, so long as the court in the requesting State take into account the child's views in custody disputes, ignoring them in Hague Convention proceedings is not going to protect the child from being involved in the decision about his future.

A further example is the suggestion that the message which the child receives from having his objections upheld may be damaging educationally. For example, in the Israeli case of *Shevach*, Justice Kenan found that

> a youth of thirteen has to internalize values of discipline and respect for parents and the rule of law and if *ex post facto* it becomes clear that the abduction has succeeded, he will learn the dangerous lesson that disobedience and breaking the law pay'. (Author's translation.)[149]

With respect, such views reflect the educational philosophy of the particular judge and thus illustrate the subjective nature of the welfare principle. Such an approach would militate against upholding the child's objections in nearly every case and severely impairs the child's right to participate in decisions concerning his life.

ii *Welfare Considerations against Returning the Child*

Conversely, a finding that return will not promote the child's welfare clearly strengthens the weight to be given to the child's objections.[150] In this situation, the principle of autonomy and the principle of protection of the particular child are in harmony, both requiring that the child is not returned. In most cases, the finding that return is inconsistent with the child's welfare is based on facts which are specific to that case. For example, in the leading English case of *Re S (A Minor) (Abduction: Custody Rights)*,[151] the nine-year-old girl who objected to being returned to France, stammered when she spoke in French.[152] Similarly, the facts that the child has been in the county of refuge for a relatively long time and had acclimatised are sometimes mentioned by courts who exercise their discretion not to return children under Article 13(2).[153]

In contrast, the finding of Justice Ya'akov-Shvili in the District Court in the Israeli case of *Shevach*[154] that it was not in the child's best interests to be returned against his will is

---

[148] ibid.
[149] ibid. A hint of a similar idea that it is not necessarily in the boy's best interests to let him have what he wanted can be found in Hale J's first judgment in *Re HB* (n 40). In a similar vein, Judge Clarkson in the New Zealand case of *Winters* (n 95) commented, 'However, there is a great risk that if one allows children to believe that some niggling complaint is serious or indeed "tragic" that that is going to allow the complaint to assume much greater importance in the mind of the child, rather than assisting them to simply get on with a difficult situation of having parents in two different countries, as best they can.'
[150] Although the English Court of Appeal in the case of *Vigreux v Michel* (n 137) held that peripheral welfare considerations should not be introduced into the discretionary consideration.
[151] *Re S (A Minor) (Abduction: Custody Rights)* (n 51).
[152] See also *D-G & Milson* (n 3) [136]. Similarly, in the Scottish case of *PW v ALI* (n 139), the first instance judge came to the conclusion that the child's special educational needs were being better met in Scotland than in Australia, but this decision was overturned on appeal in *W v W* (n 139).
[153] eg, *Re B (Abduction: Children's Objections)* [1998] 1 FLR 667, where the judge concluded, 'I am wholly unable to find that the welfare of the children would in the unusual circumstances of the case, where they have indeed become well and firmly established in England during the last 2 1/2 years since April 1995, be advanced by a return to Ireland'; *Re M (Abduction: Zimbabwe)* (n 36) [52] (Baroness Hale); *Re W (Minors)* (n 7) [26].
[154] *Shevach* (n 76).

general and could apply in many, if not most cases.[155] The learned judge opined that 'breaking the will' of the 13-year-old boy was liable to 'cause anger and antagonism against the mother', which in turn could lead to his treating his mother in a 'humiliating way' (as had already happened on one occasion) and could even result in physical resistance to enforcement of the order. Thus, in the view of the judge, the order to return the child infringed the biblical injunction against 'placing an obstacle in front of the blind'.[156] In a later case, the same judge limited this reasoning to older children, explaining that a younger child was much less likely to rebel against the court order and the parent who had requested it.[157] However, the judge's approach is consistent with the view that in general the welfare of a mature child is best served by giving effect to his wishes.[158]

A further welfare reason given by Justice Ya'akov-Shvili in the case of *Shevach*[159] is also of very wide application potentially. He held that since the Court in the US was likely to decide the custody dispute in accordance with the child's wishes, he would be sent back to Israel and the disruption caused by the unnecessary return to the USA was not in the boy's best interests.[160] However, in a later case, the same judge refused to uphold the objections of a nine-year-old and sent him back to the USA despite the fact that it was fairly clear in the circumstances of the case that the USA Court would allow the mother to return with him to Israel.[161] Thus, it would seem that the disruption argument will be used as an additional reason for refusing to return the child where there are already good reasons for upholding the child's wishes, but will not by itself be sufficient to persuade the court that the child's views should be upheld where it is in doubt about this.

iii The Relevance of Siblings

a Non-Mature Siblings

In a number of cases, the question has arisen as to the significance of the presence of younger siblings on the exercise of the discretion where the child objection exception applies. There are a number of options open to the court. The first is to return the younger child(ren) alone.[162] The second is to refuse to return the older child on the basis of his objections and then to refuse to return the younger child(ren) on the basis that his/their return without the older child creates a grave risk of placing the younger child(ren) in an

---

[155] See similar approach in the non-Convention case of *Re S N and C (Non-Hague Convention Abduction: Habitual Residence: Child's Views)* [2005] NI Fam 1.

[156] Leviticus, chapter 19, v 14.

[157] FamA (Dist HAI) 218/02 *Ploni v Plonit*, Tak-Mech 2003(1) 22302.

[158] This is the reason why some systems of law tended to give effect to a child's wishes in custody disputes well before the concept of children's rights was thought of. See eg, the position under Jewish law, as explained in E Shochetman, 'Taking into Consideration the Wishes of a Minor in Child Custody Disputes' (2005) 4 *Mozney Mishpat* 545 (Hebrew).

[159] *Shevach* (n 76).

[160] In relation to the relevance of this consideration, see also discussion in ch 10 at IV Biii.

[161] FamA 218/02 (n 157). The US Court did indeed allow the child to return to Israel with his mother (personal communication from the father's lawyer).

[162] eg *In the Matter of LL Children* (Unpublished, 22 June 2000) [INCADAT cite: HC/E/USs 273], in which the Court held that if the 15-year-old child was mature enough to have her objections taken into account, she was also mature enough to decide whether or not to be separated from her sibling. However, the Court seems to have been influenced by the girl's statement that if the younger child was returned, she would go too. See also *Rajmakers-Eghage v Haro* (n 48), in which the Court adjourned the case in relation to the older child in order to ascertain his views, but felt that it had no choice but to order immediate return of the younger child. Whilst the Court advised the petitioner not to avail herself of the order made but to wait for the outcome of the hearing in relation to the older child, this does not seem to have been binding.

intolerable situation under Article 13(1)(b).[163] The third is to return all the children, including the older child, despite his objections. Such a decision may be justified either on the basis of the welfare of the older child himself[164] or on the basis that since upholding his objections would require not returning all the children, the policy of the Convention prevails over his wishes.

None of the options is ideal. On the one hand, it is clear that separating children from their siblings, in a situation where such children have inevitably already suffered separation from family members, is likely to cause them harm or to place them in an intolerable situation.[165] On the other hand, refusing to return younger siblings simply because an older one objects to return appears inconsistent with the objectives of the Convention and may well also be inconsistent with the rights of those children to contact with the left-behind parent.[166] Similarly, returning an older child against his will just because he happens to have siblings would seem to be in violation of his right of participation.[167] With respect, the Court of Session's suggestion that a view should be reached on the Article 13(1)(b) defence before considering the child objection defence[168] is not helpful because the issue of harm or intolerable situation does not arise until it is has been decided not to return the older child because of his objections.

It is suggested that while each case has to be determined on its merits, in most cases the option of relying on the grave risk/intolerability defence in relation to the younger child will be the most appropriate solution. Indeed, it has been suggested that use of the grave risk exception in this scenario is more acceptable than in the step-sibling cases because the intolerable situation on which the abductor relies is caused by the older child's refusal to return, rather than by her own actions.[169] In addition, the arguments in favour of invoking the grave risk/intolerability defence will be strengthened where the reasons for the older child's objections also apply to the younger children and so it is reasonable to assume that he would have objected if he were old enough to do so.[170]

However, there may be unusual cases where the separation will cause harm only or mainly to the older objecting child. In such a case, this fact might be a reason for exercising the discretion to override his objections.

---

[163] eg English cases of *B v K* (n 77); *The Ontario Court v M and M (Abduction: Children's Objections)* [1997] 1 FLR 475; *Re W (Minors)* (n 7); Australian case of *Bassi* (1994) FLRC 92-465; Scottish cases of *Urness v Minto* (n 80) and *PW v ALI* (n 139) (overturned on appeal in *W v W* (n 139). See discussion in ch 11 at II Bvi.

[164] As in *Zaffino v Zaffino* (n 32); *Re HB* (n 40).

[165] See the discussion in chapter 11 at IIB vi. .

[166] See comment of Court of Session in *W v W* (n 139), that a decision to give effect to the wishes of one child 'ought not to be regarded as necessarily sealing the fate of all the children'.

[167] See comment of Ward LJ in *Re T* (n 5) that 'there does appear to be something odd about refusing to return an elder child who is old enough to articulate an objection to return because of fears expressed for herself and for her young sibling because of what had happened to them without also inferring that if the younger was of an age and maturity where he had a voice and vote, he would echo the objection and vote with his elder sister'; cf Australian decision in *Wolfe & Director-General, Department of Human Services* [2011] FamCAFC 42 [74], where one of the reasons for ordering the return of an objecting 15-year-old was so that he could give support to his younger sister. It might also be noted that two cases where older siblings were returned against their wishes in order to avoid separation from their younger siblings did not have successful outcomes. In *TB v JB* (lAbduction: Grave Risk of Harm) [2001] 2 FLR 515, the children resisted return and were eventually allowed to stay in the UK (see comment at Incadat cite: HC/UKe/419) In *HB (Abduction: Child's Objections)(No 2)* [1998] 1 FLR 564, it is reported that the older child who returned was in foster care. In this case, ironically the younger child had resisted return and was allowed to stay in the UK.

[168] *W v W* (n 139).

[169] *Re T* (n 5) (Ward LJ), although of course it could be argued that the whole situation would not have arisen if it were not for the abduction.

[170] See comment of Ward LJ quoted at n 167.

b Mature Siblings

It has been held that each child should be considered separately for the purpose of deciding whether he objects and whether he has attained sufficient age and maturity, but that for the purpose of exercising the discretion, each child should not be treated in isolation but rather as a part of the family unit.[171] Thus, the Court should first decide whether each child satisfies the criteria in Article 13(2) and only then go on to exercise the discretion in relation to those children. With respect, this statement oversimplifies the situation. Firstly, the fact that there are two or more siblings whose objections are being considered together at the same time may affect the assessment of maturity or strength of objection. The younger will inevitably seem less mature than the older and his reasons will invariably seem less cogent.[172] Furthermore, the suspicion will arise that the views of the older child influenced those of the younger one, particularly where they are interviewed together.[173] Secondly, it is not clear how the court can exercise its discretion in relation to two mature objecting siblings simultaneously because the fate of each sibling is relevant to the decision. If the court decides not to return the older one, this clearly affects the younger one as in the case of a younger non-mature sibling. Similarly, if the court decides to return the younger one, then this may affect the decision in relation to the older one.

Accordingly, the preferable approach is to exercise the discretion in relation to the older child first as in the US case of *McManus v McManus*.[174] Here, the Court first held that it was in no doubt that the 14-year-old twins' objections should be upheld. It then proceeded to hold that whilst the case for respecting the objections of the younger children (aged 13 and 11) was not so strong, 'the additional factor of the psychological harm that the younger two would likely suffer if the children were separated gives support for the conclusion that they also should have their objections to return honoured'.[175] Clearly, this approach may result in a younger child's objections being upheld in circumstances where he would have been returned if he had been an only child. However, this is legitimate since the younger child's objections have to be viewed in light of the reality of the situation. In addition, as in relation to younger non-mature siblings, there can be no justification for not upholding the older child's objections simply because the court is not convinced that the younger child's objections should be upheld.

On the other hand, the situation might be different where the younger child actually wants to return. This was the situation in the New Zealand case of *LJG v RTP*,[176] where the children were aged 10 and 11. The fact that the younger child wanted to return to Australia, together with the decision of the parties to treat the children as one unit and the fact that the older child's objections were not strong resulted in a decision to return both children. Whilst this decision seems reasonable on the facts, if the older child's objections had been strong, the Court would have had to weigh up the damage which would be caused to both

---

[171] *Zaffino v Zaffino* (n 32) [34] (Wall LJ).
[172] eg first instance decision in *Singh* (n 40).
[173] As in eg *Zaffino v Zaffino* (n 32) where the CAFCASS officer commented that the younger child 'echoed his sister's feeling'. Ward LJ suggested that it was unfortunate that the two children were interviewed together.
[174] *McManus* (n 63).
[175] ibid 72. Similarly, in the case of *Singh* (n 40), an appeal was allowed from a decision ordering the return of the younger mature child, despite his objections, whilst upholding the objections of the older mature child. The Court of Session held that the first instance judge had erred in not considering the effect of the separation on the welfare of the younger child when exercising its discretion.
[176] *LJG v RTP* (n 40).

children by separating them as against the harm which would be caused to the older one by sending him back against his will.

iv The Policy of the Convention

In exercising their discretion, courts often refer to the policy of the Convention, meaning the policy of returning abducted children,[177] and pit this against the child's objections. For example, in the case of *JPC v SMW*, Sir Mark Potter held that the 14-year-old girl should be returned to Ireland 'in accordance with the plain intention of the Hague Convention' despite her age and maturity, the clarity of her objections and the fact that ordinary welfare considerations might well militate in favour of allowing her to stay with her father in England.[178] Similarly, the English Court of Appeal has held that, as a matter of principle and policy, where a child goes abroad on an agreed vacation his wishes will not be a sufficient basis to refuse return, unless there are exceptional circumstances.[179]

As explained above,[180] this approach is problematic inter alia because the policy of the Convention is to return children whom the Convention requires to be returned and where one of the defences is established, this is the very question which the court has to determine. So, with respect, there is no basis for the assumption that the Convention intends for the child to be returned just because the situation appears to fall squarely within the Convention. Sometimes courts refer specifically to particular aspects of the policy of the Convention and two of these will now be considered.

a The 'Guilt' of the Abductor

In some cases, the court specifically mentions the guilt of the abductor as a reason for ordering return despite the child's objections.[181] For example, in one Israeli case, the fact that the mother was in flagrant breach of the Dutch Court's decision of refusing to allow her to relocate was held by the Supreme Court to be relevant in exercising the discretion.[182] Furthermore, in the English case of *Re M (Abduction: Psychological Harm)*, it was said that the conduct of the abducting parent is 'crucial and in most cases determinative'.[183] Similarly, in the US it has been held that the child's objections should not be upheld where 'the passage of time during the years of wrongful retention and litigation creates the child's desire

---

[177] eg *Re R (Minors)* (n 21); *Re HB* (n 40); *Re M (Abduction: Zimbabwe)* (n 36); In the case of *G (Children)* (n 90), the Court of Appeal did not criticise the judge's exercise of his discretion in which he gave precedence to the primary objective of the Convention, but overturned the appeal on the basis of fresh evidence.

[178] *JPC v SMW* (n 39) [49]. However, the execution of the decision was delayed until a directions hearing by the Court in Ireland which would consider whether to postpone the return further.

[179] *Nyachowe v Fielder* [2007] EWCA Civ 1129. It should be noted that the Court emphasised that there was nothing exceptional about this case and so the decision might be different today following the rejection of the exceptionality requirement a month later in *Re M (Abduction: Zimbabwe)* (n 36); Similarly, the Swiss Supreme Court has said that the child's objections should not be used as a means to circumvent the provisions and goals of the Abduction Convention, ATF 131 III 334, consid. 5 notamment, discussed in Alfieri (n 54) 560.

[180] At I B.

[181] See also discussion on the relevance of guilt to the discretion in cases of 'settlement' under Art 12(2) in ch 9 at III Civ.

[182] FamA 902/07 (n 68). Similarly, the Israeli Family Court decision in the case of *Shevach* (n 76) (which was later upheld by the Supreme Court, n 63) was clearly influenced by the bad behaviour of the abducting father who had unilaterally withdrawn money from an account held jointly with his wife.

[183] *Re M (Abduction: Psychological Harm)* (n 81), but the Court did go on to explain that there were rare cases where the court has to look past the parent's conduct 'to the manifest needs of the child concerned'.

to remain in the new location, as this would reward the abducting parent for his wrongful actions'.[184]

However, other judges have expressly refused to attribute weight to the guilt of the abductor on the basis that children should not be punished for the sins of their parents.[185] For example, in *Re B (Abduction: Children's Objections)*,[186] the Court held that although it was exceptional for the mother's defiance of the previous English court order not to result in an order being made which was adverse to her, it had to be remembered that the children were not at fault.

b Forum Conveniens

Sometimes, in exercising its discretion as to whether to uphold the child's objections, the court refers to the policy of ensuring that disputes are heard in the *forum conveniens*. For example, in the case of *Klentzeris v Klentzeris*,[187] the fact that the children had lived in England all their lives apart from five months supported upholding their objections to return to Greece, which had been their habitual residence immediately before the abduction.

However, the more common and difficult situation is where the *forum conveniens* is in the country of habitual residence to which the child does not wish to return. For example, in the New Zealand case of *LJG v RTP*,[188] the likelihood that most of the relevant evidence relating to the children would derive from Australia was treated as a relevant factor in deciding to return the objecting child.[189] Similarly, in the New Zealand case of *Secretary of Justice v Abrahams ex parte Brown*,[190] the facts that South Africa was the appropriate forum for resolution of the many issues in dispute and that, if the children remained in New Zealand, the mother would not be in a position to challenge custody was a factor of significant weight in the decision to return the children against their wishes.

With respect, while there is little doubt that *forum conveniens* is a legitimate consideration, it is not clear that it should carry great weight in child objection cases, unless the consequences of the hearing taking place in the less appropriate forum are liable to impact negatively on the child. Thus, the fact that hearing in a less appropriate forum may increase costs and be inconvenient for the parties should not per se be a reason to override the views of the child. However, where not conducting the hearing in the *forum conveniens* is liable to impede proper assessment of the welfare of the child, then this factor should be weighed against the damage which will be caused by returning the child against his will.

---

[184] *Tsai Yai Yang v Fu-Chang Tsui* 499 F3d 279, 270 (3d Cir 2007) 280 cited in subsequent cases, such as *Haimdas v Haimdas* 720 F Supp 2d 183 (2010).
[185] eg Israeli District Court in *Shevach* (n 76) (Ya'akov Shvili J).
[186] *Re B (Abduction: Children's Objections)* (n 153).
[187] *Klentzeris v Klentzeris* [2007] EWCA CW 533.
[188] *LJG v RTP* (n 40).
[189] See also *Vigreux v Michel* (n 137) where the fact that France was 'clearly the right forum to decide the child's future' appears to have been a decisive factor.
[190] *Secretary of Justice v Abrahams ex parte Brown* [2001] FP 069/134/00 (Fam Ct) (Taupo NZ) [INCADAT cite: HCE/NZ 492]; See also Australian decision in *Wolfe* (n 167), in which the fact that parenting proceedings were already underway in New Zealand was an important factor in the decision to order return.

III Analysis

A Internal Coherence

There is no doubt that Article 13(2) is an independent defence separate from Article 13(1)(b) and that there is no need to show that returning the objecting child will cause him harm. Nonetheless, in some cases the circumstances which point to a grave risk will be seen as justifying the objections and sometimes the very fact of return in the face of strong objections would itself give rise to a grave risk of harm or place the child in an intolerable situation.[191] Indeed, it has even been suggested that a less strict standard can be applied in considering a child's wishes where those wishes are part of a broader analysis involving the issue of grave risk of harm.[192] Similarly, in settlement cases, it is quite common for the child to object to return and the fact that he does so is evidence of settlement. Some courts may prefer to rely on the settlement defence rather than the objection defence in such cases because the former is less likely to perceived as undermining the Convention, since the passage of time inherent therein means that hot pursuit is no longer possible.[193] Others will refuse return on the basis of more than one exception.[194] Thus, the potential overlap between the objections defence and the other defences does not create any lack of internal coherence.

Moreover, the claim that narrow interpretation of the exceptions is necessary in order to preserve the internal coherence of the Convention is even less cogent[195] in relation to the child objection exception because this exception reflects a value in its own right and is not simply a defence to return. Indeed, a few courts have referred expressly to the function of the Article 13(2) exception in upholding the child's right to participate and the impact of this on the way the defence is interpreted.[196] For example, Israeli Family Court judge Nili Maimon explained,

> The Hague Abduction Convention has to be interpreted in harmony with the Basic Law: Dignity and Freedom of Man and with the UN Convention on the Rights of the Child . . . in such a way as not to violate the right of decision-making, the autonomy of a person as to his destiny. . . . Thus, great and even determinative weight should be placed on the wishes of a child who has formed a

---

[191] per Inglis J in *Ryding v Turvey* (n 40).
[192] *de Silva v Pitts* (n 45) 1286.
[193] *Re M (Abduction: Zimbabwe)* (n 36) [47] (Baroness Hale); see generally ch 9.
[194] Thus, as noted above (n 10), whilst only 10% of judicial refusals were based solely on the child's objections, when judicial refusals based on multiple reasons were taken into account, the child's objections was one of the reasons in 17% of the refusals. It has been suggested that where more than one exception is established, their cumulative effect will weigh more heavily in favour of refusing return, J Caldwell, 'Child Welfare Defences in Child Abduction Cases – Some Recent Developments' (2001) 13 *Child and family Law Quarterly* 135.
[195] It should be remembered that the exceptions are part of the scheme of the Convention and their invocation, from time to time, represents fulfilment of that scheme and not a departure therefrom. See eg comment of Family Court of Australia in *State Central Authority v Papastravrou* [2008] FamCA 1120 [147] that 'the exceptions are as much a part of the philosophy of the Convention as prompt return and respect for rights of custody and access between contracting states'; *JLM v D-G NSW Department of Community Services* [2001] HCA 39 [INCADAT cite: HC/E/AU 347] [139].
[196] See, eg *Re T* (n 5) (Ward LJ); *Shevach* (n 76) (Justice Ya'akov Shvili); per Justice Rotlevy in the Israeli case of FamA (Dist TA) 3/98 *Biton v Biton* Nevo, 9 November 1998 (Isr) who points out that the narrow approach taken by the trial judge in that case effectively nullifies the independent status of the minor's rights to be heard and to express his opinion.

view and is able to express and stick to his view. Therefore, Article 13 which gives weight to the views of an abducted child should not be interpreted narrowly, but the opposite.' (Author's translation.)[197]

Accordingly, internal coherence will not be violated if the interpretation and application of the Article 13(2) exception is informed by the need to realise the child's right to participate and not by the alleged need to interpret the exception narrowly.

Nonetheless, it is important to clarify that recognition of the child's right to participate does not mean that the child's wishes will always be respected, because this right does not grant the child complete autonomy.[198] Furthermore, in accordance with the express wording of Article 13(2), the exception will only apply where the child objects to return. Whilst courts should look to the substance of the child's views and not the form in which they are expressed,[199] where the child is really only expressing a preference to remain in the requested State, the exception will not apply. Any other approach would threaten the internal coherence of the Convention by treating the Convention proceedings as substantive custody proceedings.

B Consistency with the Intention of the Drafters

The drafters' concern was that the forcible repatriation of teenagers against their will would give the Convention a bad name.[200] In addition, the provision satisfied those who wished to reduce the age at which the Convention applied to lower than 16.[201] Indeed, the drafting of the provision suggests that it was not based on a desire to give effect to the child's rights to participate. Firstly, there is no requirement that the court ascertain the views of the child. Thus, in the admittedly rare case where the abductor does not raise the child's objection, there need not be any consideration of the child's views.[202] Secondly, there is no provision for the method of ascertainment of the child's views.[203] Thirdly, even where the exception is proven, the court still has discretion to return the child and no guidelines are given as to how this discretion should be exercised.

On the other hand, the following comments of Professor Perez-Vera in her Explanatory Report, whilst not specifically referring to the child's rights, are consistent with the concept that the child objection exception is intended to allow the mature child a considerable degree of autonomy:

> The Convention also provides that the child's views concerning the essential question of its return or retention may be conclusive, provided it has, according to the competent authorities, attained

---

[197] FamC (Dist JEM) 430/01 *Ploni v Almonit* (Unreported), quoted in Shochetman, 'Taking into Consideration' (n 158) 580.
[198] See ch 6 at II Ciii.
[199] See above at II Ci.
[200] Beaumont and McEleavy (n 6) 177–78. Indeed, experience has shown that the Convention may not be effective even in relation to younger children, who are determined enough not to return. Thus, in two English cases the violent protests of the child on the airplane led to the child being taken off the airplane and reconsideration of his case. See *Re HB* (n 90); *TB v JB* (n 144). Similarly, in *Re M (A Minor)(Abduction: Child's Objections)* [1994] 2 FLR 126, the 13-year-old boy ran away and would not return until a stay of the return order was granted.
[201] Beaumont and McEleavy ibid.
[202] See ch 14 at I.
[203] For a detailed discussion see ch 14 at II and III.

an age and degree of maturity sufficient for its views to be taken into account. In this way, the Convention gives children the possibility of interpreting their own interests.[204]

It is perhaps hardly surprising that the drafters did not think in terms of children's rights in 1980 and did not anticipate that the views of relatively young children would be ascertained and taken into account.[205] However, this does not mean that an interpretation of the Article 13(2) exception that does give effect to those rights is necessarily inconsistent with the intention of the drafters. In particular, as already seen, the drafters were clearly concerned to protect the interests of children. Perceptions as to children's interests may change over the years as new social and legal norms become accepted and today the right of even relatively young children to participate is widely accepted as one of their interests.[206]

Finally, it should be noted that the Perez-Vera Report refers to the situation where under the law of the habitual residence a child under 16 has the right to choose his place of residence. The Report explains that a proposal that the Convention should not apply in such a case was rejected. However, in the view of the Rapporteur, in such a situation decisive weight would be given to the child's objection to return to the country of habitual residence under Article 13(2).

C Promotion of the Objectives of the Convention

i Protecting Abducted Children

As seen above, the main rationale behind the general policy of immediate return of abducted children is the desire to neutralise the harm caused to the child by the abduction. The very fact of a mature child's objection to return creates a presumption that his remaining in the country of refuge will not cause him damage. Moreover, there is a real risk that ordering the return of a mature child against his wishes will actually cause him harm.[207]

Clearly, there may be exceptional cases where the welfare of the particular child does require his return despite his objections and in such cases the court will exercise its discretion to order return, despite the fact that the exception has been established.[208] However, courts should be slow to find that upholding a child's wishes is inconsistent with his welfare.[209] The summary nature of Convention proceedings means the courts only have limited information on which to base their assessments of the child's welfare and so it is unlikely that they will be in a position to conclude that non-return is inconsistent with the welfare of the child, where the conditions of the child objection exception have been established.

Thus, the policy of protecting children from harm does not require a narrow interpretation of the Article 13(2) exception. On the contrary, a narrow interpretation is likely to mean that children are returned against their wishes which may well cause them harm.

---

[204] Perez-Vera Report (n 42), para 30.
[205] See *Re W (Minors)* (n 7) [17] (Wilson LJ).
[206] ibid.
[207] In extreme cases, it will lead to physical resistance by the child (as in eg cases cited in n 200) or to the disappearance of the child (as in Israeli Supreme Court case of *RB v VG* (n 100), in which the then 9-year-old child has not been seen since the day on which he was supposed to be returned in July 2008). See also *Ryding v Turvey* (n 40) 318 (Inglis J).
[208] See above at II Dia.
[209] See general discussion of the situation where a mature child's wishes appear to conflict with this welfare in ch 6 at II Ciii.

ii Deterrence

A number of judges have expressed concern that a liberal interpretation of the child exception objection will significantly undermine the deterrent effect of the Convention. An Israeli judge explained this concern as follows:

> If we give too much weight to the wishes of the abducted child and this leads to many abducted children remaining in the country to which they have been abducted, the Convention will become redundant.... The success of the Convention in preventing abductions will be reduced the more that courts are influenced by their impressions of the wishes of the child. There is also a fear that this will encourage parents who are considering abducting their children, who will say to themselves, "I will abduct and then I will influence the child to say to the judge that he wants to stay in the place to which he has been abducted and so the abduction will succeed." Therefore, it should be made known to the public that only in exceptional cases will a court, in reliance on the wishes of a young child; decide to leave him in the place to which he has been abducted.' (Author's translation.)[210]

With respect, the fear that wider use of the child objection exception will encourage abduction is exaggerated. Many cases involve very young children who are clearly too young to express a view.[211] Moreover, even with older children, it cannot always be guaranteed that the child will in fact want to stay in the country of refuge and where the views he expresses are not his own, the exception will not be established. Thus, a parent relying on the strategy referred to is taking a significant risk. In any event, even if there is some reduction in the deterrent effect of the Convention, violating the rights of particular children cannot be justified on the speculative basis that this may prevent other children from being abducted in the future.

It has been suggested that a wide interpretation of the child objection exception will be particularly damaging to the interests of children whose parents live in different countries,[212] because custodial parents will be reluctant to send their children to stay with the other parent, for fear that the child will be persuaded to object to return. This concern is valid, because usually non-custodial parents have little to lose if they decide to retain the child. However, there are other methods that can be used to deter retentions in such situations, such as the deposit of financial guarantees. In addition, this concern does not justify a narrow approach to the exception in all cases. Rather, it might perhaps justify checking more carefully whether the requirements of maturity and independence of objections are met in cases of children refusing to return after access visits.

iii Forum Conveniens

It may be argued that the child's right to participate is not really relevant in Convention proceedings because those proceedings simply determine jurisdiction and thus his right is sufficiently realised if his views will be given appropriate weight in the proceedings on the

---

[210] Judge Ya'akvo-Shvili in FamA 218/02 (n 157); This view seems to be diametrically opposed to the view which this judge expressed in the earlier decision in *Shevach* (n76), in which he explained that the child objection exception also reflected the independent value of the child's right to have his views taken into consideration and so should not be interpreted narrowly. The explanation for this apparent contradiction seems to be rooted in the age of the child. In the case of *Shevach*, the child was 13 and in the current case he was 9.

[211] See text accompanying n 18.

[212] See per Hale J (as she then was) in *Re HB* (n 40) 399–400; comments of Judge in the NZ case of *Winters v Cowen* (n 95), 'Parents must have confidence in New Zealand Courts to enforce the Convention, or they will not be able to properly operate access agreements or orders between the two countries.'

merits in the country of origin. This approach would justify giving great, even determinative weight, to the policy of ensuring that disputes are heard in the *forum conveniens* in the exercise of the courts' discretion, even where the child objection exception has been established.[213]

However, this argument is not convincing because the decision under the Convention does not only determine which court should hear the case, but also determines where the child will live until a decision on the merits is made, which may take a long time and in some cases will not happen at all. Moreover, the place where the child lives in the interim may have a determinative influence on that final decision. Thus, the decision directly affects the child and he has a right to have his views taken into account.

In some cases, the hearing of the custody dispute in the *forum conveniens* may be of real benefit to the child because that court is in a much better position to assess the best interests of the child efficiently. In such situations, it will be necessary to weigh up the damage caused to the child by the case not being heard in the *forum conveniens* against the breach of his right to have his views respected. Thus, as suggested above, the court should consider the *forum conveniens* from the child's point of view when treating it as a factor in the exercise of discretion to return in child objection cases.

Finally, the ideal solution from the child's perspective would often seem to be for the court in the country of origin to hear the dispute, without the need for the child to return there, other than for the purposes of being heard by the court or examined by welfare professionals. However, as already noted, the Hague Convention does not provide for such a situation[214] although it may occur under the Brussels II bis Regulation.[215]

iv Justice between the Parents

From the point of view of the left-behind parent, his child's objections to return may be adding insult to the injury caused to him by the abduction. However, this cannot be a reason not to respect that child's wishes. In particular, where the child has settled into the new country and is happy there, returning him against his wishes will turn him into a victim twice.[216] Where the choice is between the child being the victim or the left-behind parent, preference has to be given to the interests of the child. Thus, the degree of guilt of the abductor should not be a relevant factor in exercising the discretion where the objection defence is established.

Where the child's objections are a result of incitement by the abductor, the exception will not usually be established.[217] However, as explained above, care must be taken not to assume that there is incitement without clear proof and, even where incitement is proven, it is necessary to check that there aren't other objective reasons for the objections, unrelated to the incitement. Also, occasionally, the damage that will be done by trying to break

---

[213] See II Ciiib above.
[214] But a similar result may be achieved by creative means. eg in *JPC v SMW* (n 39), the English Court suspended the execution of the return order to allow for the Irish Court to consider whether it was necessary for the child to return to Ireland pending the decision on the merits by that course.
[215] Council Regulation (EC) No 2201/2003 of 27 November 2003 concerning jurisdiction and the recognition and enforcement of judgments in matrimonial matters and the matters of parental responsibility [2003] OJ L 338/1-29, see ch 1 at II C. Yet, in *Vigreux v Michel* (n 137), the Court of Appeal overruled the non-return order made by the judge, even though the latter had envisaged that the French Court would still decide about the future of the child.
[216] *Re M (Abduction: Zimbabwe)* (n 36) (Baroness Hale).
[217] See above at II Ciib.

the incited child's will by forcible return will mean that the grave risk exception is established.[218] Again, the child's interests have to take precedence over the clear injustice of this situation from the point of view of the left-behind parent.

D Compatibility with the Summary Nature of Proceedings

It has been suggested that the need for a welfare professional to examine the child to assess his maturity and the quality of his objections is inconsistent with the summary nature of Convention proceedings.[219] However, Article 13(2) clearly envisages that the child's maturity will be assessed. Furthermore, it is difficult to see how it will be possible to consider the quality of the child's objections without someone interviewing the child. At the end of the day, the issue here is one of procedural efficiency. There is no real reason why the child cannot be heard by the judge and/or a report be received from a welfare professional who has spoken to the child within a relatively short time scale if the system is set up with this need in mind.

E Consistency with Rights and Interests of Children

It is not easy to analyse to what extent the implementation of Article 13(2) is consistent with the right of the child to have appropriate weight attached to his views because of the uncertain scope of that right.[220] Whilst the right to participate does not mean giving unfettered autonomy to all children, only taking into account forceful objectively justifiable views of obviously mature teenagers makes the right to participate meaningless in most cases. However there will be situations in which other rights of the child[221] or other considerations will justify violating the right to participate. In particular, the 'weaker' the right of the particular child, whether because of doubts as to his maturity or the quality of his objections, the easier it will be for other considerations to take precedence. Accordingly, there will be borderline situations in which it will be difficult to state with certainty that the child's right to participate requires upholding his views.

Nonetheless, the case law discussed above shows that the narrow approach of many judges to children's objections does not give sufficient weight to their right to participate. This narrow approach can be seen in a number of ways: stringent tests of age and maturity;[222] a restrictive approach to the form and quality of objections[223] and in particular a tendency to disregard completely the views of the child where there is evidence of some influence by the abductor or the new environment[224] and liberal exercise of the discretion of the court to order return despite the valid objections of a mature child.[225]

---

[218] eg in Israeli case of *R v L* (n 107).
[219] L Silberman, 'The Hague Child Abduction Convention Turns Twenty: Gender Politics and Other Issues' (2000) 33 *New York Journal of International Law and Politics* 221, 244.
[220] See ch 6 at II Ciii.
[221] Such as the right to contact with both parents. However, it should be remembered that forcing contact on a child against his wishes may well not be practicable or of any real benefit to either parent or child.
[222] II A above.
[223] II Bi and ii above.
[224] II Biii above.
[225] II C above.

As explained above,[226] recognition of the concept of children's rights does not only mean giving effect to certain defined rights, but also requires that findings concerning children take into account the situation from the viewpoint of the child. Nowhere is this more necessary than in relation to conditions determining the scope of the child's right to participate. Yet, only too often courts assess maturity and the quality of objections through adult eyes, expecting children to behave in a way in which adults are perceived as behaving.[227] However, it is gratifying to note that some judges have taken a more child-centric view in implementing Article 13(2). In particular, some have understood that not every sign of influence invalidates the child's objections[228] and that the strength and validity of the objections have to be assessed from the child's perspective.[229]

Finally, it should be noted that giving insufficient weight to the objections of a mature child may constitute a violation of the child's right to freedom of movement within the EU.[230]

F Consistency with Private International Law Principles

Comity is often mentioned as one of the Convention considerations against which the court must balance the child's objections when exercising its discretion under Article 13(2).[231] In the case of *Re T (Abduction: Child's Objections to Return)*,[232] Ward LJ held that 'in the particular and exceptional circumstances of this case, the interests of the children in remaining here should not be sacrificed on the altar of comity between nation states'. Whilst the outcome is to be welcomed, the implication that in other cases the child's interests should be so sacrificed is problematic. With respect, it is difficult to see how comity can justify overriding a child's wishes. In particular, even if it were appropriate to sacrifice a particular child's interests for the benefit of children as a whole, there is no clear relationship between comity and protecting other children. As shown above, there is no evidence of 'reciprocity' in the sense that States do not return children to other Contracting States who have not returned children to them in the past.[233] Furthermore, where return is based on the child's objections to return there cannot even be the slightest suggestion of lack of confidence in the legal system of the requesting State. Similarly, since the Convention itself expressly sanctions non-return on the basis of the child's objections, such non-return should be seen as giving effect to the Convention, rather than a breach of judicial courtesy.

G Certainty versus Flexibility

The case law examined above shows that the way in which the child objection exception is interpreted depends on how the particular judge constructs age, maturity and capability.[234]

---

[226] Chapter 6 at II A.
[227] Although sometimes the tests take an idealised view of the capacities of adults. See II Aii above.
[228] eg *Robinson* (n 106) (Miller J); and *Re T* (n 5) (Sedley LJ).
[229] eg *LJG v RTP* (n 40); *PW v ALI* (n 139).
[230] R Lamont, 'Free Movement of Persons, Child Abduction and Relocation within the European Union' (2012) 34 *Journal of Social Welfare and Family Law* 231.
[231] eg *Vigreux v Michel* (n 137) [59] (Wall LJ).
[232] *Re T* (n 5).
[233] Chapter 6 at IV Ei.
[234] Smith, 'Interpreting and Supporting' (n 56) 75.

In order to reduce uncertainty and lack of uniformity, there is a need to inject some objectivity into the assessment of whether the child is sufficiently old and mature enough for his objections to be taken into account. Whilst the most effective method would be to provide a fixed age,[235] this is too inflexible.[236] Indeed, child sociologists warn against stereotyping our expectations of how children should participate according to age and claim that rigid assumptions about what children can and cannot do at different ages are inappropriate because this depends on the activities and social contexts in which they have participated.[237]

Thus, the current author has suggested a *via media*,[238] according to which there would be a presumption that children over a fixed aged are sufficiently mature,[239] without precluding the possibility of taking into account of the views of a younger child who was shown to be sufficiently mature.[240] Similarly, the fact that a child over the fixed age was shown in fact not to be mature could be taken into account at the discretion stage. Since the age is not decisive but simply creates a presumption, the arbitrariness of the age chosen[241] and the fact that the cognitive functioning of children is influenced not only by age but also by environmental influences[242] are much less problematic. In any event, social science theories are likely to provide better guidelines than criteria invented by judges, based purely on a lay perspective. Thus, the suggested approach provides a practical combination of the need for certainty with that of flexibility.

Commissioning expert reports may also appear to bring a degree of objectivity to the decision. However, this will not necessarily be so because, whilst most experts will use standard psycho-diagnostic tests in assessing maturity, there is considerable room for different interpretation by different experts. The dangers of the subjective views of the expert as to the correct outcome of the case influencing the apparently objective 'scientific' parts of her report are illustrated by the Israeli case of *TAE v PR*.[243] On the other hand, such dangers are substantially reduced where such reports are prepared by social workers who work within the court system and receive appropriate training, as in England and Wales.

---

[235] This approach has been adopted by some legislatures in relation to minors' decision-making in particular areas. See Schuz, 'Protection versus Autonomy' (n 91) 301.

[236] It also does not seem consistent with the 'evolving capacities' approach adopted in Art 5 of the CRC.

[237] Smith, 'Interpreting and supporting' (n 56) 81; General Comment No 12 (July 2009) – The right of the child to be heard, drawn up by the Committee on the Rights of the Child, www2.ohchr.org/english/bodies/crc/comments.htm, paras 20 and 29.

[238] Schuz, 'Protection versus Autonomy' (n 91) 302.

[239] The age of 10 or 11 was suggested as being broadly consistent with child development theory. For example, the influential Piagetian theory holds that children over the age of 11 can engage in pure thought independent of actions they see or perform, are able to imagine the past, present and future conditions of a problem and to create hypotheses which might logically occur under different conditions. See a summary of this theory and other child development research in WJ Mlyniec, 'A Judge's Ethical Dilemma: Assessing a Child's Capacity to Choose' (1996) 64 *Fordham Law Review* 1873, 1878–85.

[240] Thus, it would still be appropriate to hear children younger than this. *cf* decision of Swiss Appellate Court in 5P.3/2007 /bnm; Bundesgericht, II. Zivilabteilung [INCADAT cite: HC/E/CH 894] holding that children under the age of 11 or 12 need not have their views heard since they will usually not be able to understand that the issue of return is distinct from that of custody. With respect, it is difficult to see how this conclusion follows from psychological theory since understanding this distinction does not require the cognitive capacities which are thought to be acquired at the age of 11 (Mlyniec, ibid). In relation to ascertaining children's views generally, see ch 14.

[241] See n 42.

[242] eg, BJ Zimmerman, 'Social Learning Theory: A Contextualist Account of Cognitive Functioning' in CJ Brainerd (ed), *Recent Advances in Cognitive Developmental Theory* (New York, Springer, 1983); N Taylor, P Tapp and RM Henaghan, 'Respecting Children's Participation in Family Law Proceedings' (2007) 15 *International Journal of Children's Rights* 61, criticising Piagetian theory.

[243] *TAE v PR* (n 11); see discussion at text accomapnying n 66.

IV Conclusions

The above analysis of the case law indicates a not inconsiderable degree of inconsistency between the approaches of different courts to the weight to be given to the views of the child. This difference in approach is seen in relation to the interpretation and application of each of the conditions in Article 13(2) and in the exercise of the discretion. Whilst the decision not to uphold the views of a particular child is always based on non-fulfillment of one of the conditions (such as lack of age and maturity or insufficient strength) or the existence of factors which affect the weight to be given to the child's objections (such as lack of independence of the objections) or particular considerations of welfare or policy, it seems that the determination will be greatly influenced by the worldview of the judge in relation to children's rights in general and the child's right to participate in particular.

Since the US is not a signatory to the CRC, it is perhaps not surprising that US Courts have often paid little attention to children's views in Hague abduction cases. This approach has been criticised by US commentators who claim that the courts frequently do not even provide satisfactory legal reasons to support their decisions[244] and that this 'return at all costs' mentality' policy violates the rights of children who, through no fault of their own, have become involved in international custody proceedings.[245] However, some recent decisions do indicate a change in approach in the US.[246]

Outside the US, awareness of the CRC and its implications is increasing among judges. However, this awareness only leads to a wider interpretation of Article 13(2) if it is also recognised that the need to uphold the child's rights can take priority over the policy of returning abducted children on which the Abduction Convention is perceived to be based. For example, in Israel, some judges pay lip-service to the rights of the child whilst continuing to interpret Article 13(2) narrowly and to return apparently mature children against their wishes.[247] On the other hand, other judges are prepared to give precedence to the child's rights.[248]

Similarly, the experience in the UK, Australia and New Zealand is a mixed one. The need to treat the child's right to participate seriously is epitomised in the words of Justice Gillen in *Re S, N, and C*, 'if this court is to pay more than vacuous lip service to the contents of Article 12 of the UNCRC then I must take the child's views firmly into account when reaching my decision'.[249] In a similar vein, Judge Doogue in the New Zealand case of *Hollins v Crozier*[250] says 'The Court has a duty not to pay just lip service to this requirement. The Court has a

---

[244] SC Nelson, 'Turning Our Back on the Children: Implications of Recent Decisions Regarding the Hague Convention on International Child Abduction' (2001) 2 *University of Illinois Law Review* 669, 687–88.
[245] ibid.
[246] eg *McManus* (n 63); *de Silva v Pitts* (n 45).
[247] eg, Justice Proccacia in *TAE v PR* (n 11). Similarly, in *RB v VG* (n 100), Justice Arbel, despite having remitted the case back to the District Court so that the child could meet with the judges in accordance with his right to be heard, upheld the District Court's decision that the child was not sufficiently mature and his objections were not independent, which was based on a narrow approach to Art 13(2).
[248] eg, FamC (HAI)1515/06 *Ploni v Plonit* Nevo, 28 August 2006 (Isr) 'Whilst the purpose of the Convention is to frustrate abductions, ... the child should not be punished by ignoring his wishes in order to punish the abducting parents. Art 13(2) which deals with the child's wishes comes, inter alia, to respect an additional value and that is the value of respecting the child and, as far as possible and appropriate, his wishes' (author's translation); *Ploni v Almonit* (n 197); *PR v TAE* (n 88); *Biton v Biton* (n 196).
[249] *Re S N and C* (n 155).
[250] *Hollins v Crozier* (n 125) in the penultimate para.

duty to listen to Joshua, to take into account his emphatic objections to being returned. The Court has a duty to see him as a person in his own right.' The Court continues,

> To do other than respect his ardently expressed views at this time would be Draconian in the extreme. To do so would be to elevate the remedial and normative objectives of the Hague Convention unduly ahead of the defence contained in the s.13 (1)(d) [this is the section containing the child objection exception in the New Zealand implementing legislation – RS] and the obligation this Court has in administering the principles and article of the United Nations Convention on the Rights of the Child. It would result in treating Joshua as an 'object of concern' and not the person he is in his own right.

However, despite this eloquent advocacy in favour of children's rights, the Court, mindful of the floodgates argument, is also careful to point out that the facts[251] put this case in a truly exceptional category.

Indeed, as recently as March 2007, English judges continued to hold that only in exceptional cases would an objecting child not be returned.[252] However, hopefully, the following statement by Baroness Hale in the House of Lords in December 2007 will finally put an end to this erroneous approach:

> I have no doubt at all that it is wrong to import any test of exceptionality into the exercise of discretion under the Hague Convention. The circumstances in which return may be refused are themselves exceptions to the general rule. That in itself is sufficient exceptionality. It is neither necessary nor desirable to import an additional gloss into the Convention.[253]

Moreover, Baroness Hale seems to accept the argument put forward by counsel for the children in this case that the child-centric exceptions, of which Article 13(2) is one, need to be analysed primarily from the child's perspective.[254]

The suggestions made in this chapter advocating a more child-centric approach to the interpretation of Article 13(2) would allow proper weight to be given to the child's right to participate and inject some degree of certainty into the implementation of the provision. Firstly, a more objective approach should be adopted to age and maturity, based on widely accepted social science parameters. This would prevent particular judges or experts from taking an overly restrictive approach to age and maturity based on personal opinions. Secondly, the courts should look at the substance of the objections and not their form. Thirdly, there is no justification for requiring that views be expressed forcibly. Fourthly, the assessment of the strength of views should simply check for lack of ambivalence and not be based on the objective reasonableness of the views in the eyes of the court. Fifthly, in considering the independence of the views, courts should be wary of making assumptions based on instinct[255] or unproven theories, such as PAS. Sixthly, even where there is evidence that the children's views have been influenced, the court should try to assess the effect of the influence, rather than ignore the objections completely. As explained above, it is unrealistic to expect that children, or even adults, are not influenced by those around them

---

[251] In particular, the child's fear was manifested by physical symptoms and his ability to communicate his wishes in a genuine and articulate fashion.
[252] *Re M (Abduction: Child Objections)* (n 119).
[253] *Re M (Abduction: Zimbabwe)* (n 36) [40].
[254] ibid [52].
[255] eg comment of German Constitutional Court in of 2 BvR 1206/98, Bundesverfassungsgericht, 29 October 1998 [INCADAT cite: HC/E/DE 233] that if the judge was concerned that the children had been influenced by the father, he should have obtained the opinion of a psychologist before discounting their views.

in making decisions and forming their views. The question is the extent and legitimacy of the influence. Finally, to the extent that the validity of the objections is relevant in determining the appropriate weight, this has to be assessed from the perspective of the child and not only from that of adults. If courts remember that Article 13(2) creates a child's defence rather than a defence for the abducting parent,[256] they will understand that giving appropriate weight to the objections of sufficiently mature children is not contrary to the policy of the Convention and that a child-centric approach has to be taken in determining whether the defence is established.

---

[256] *B v C* (n 130).

13

Violation of Fundamental Human Rights and Freedoms

I Introduction

Article 20 of the Hague Convention on the Civil Aspects of International Child Abduction ('Abduction Convention') provides that a court may refuse to return a child if return 'would not be permitted by the fundamental principles of the requested State relating to the protection of human rights and fundamental freedoms'.[1] This Article was included in the Convention after much debate, as a compromise between those delegates who wanted a wide public policy defence and those who were opposed to such a defence.[2] However, the defence is not often pleaded[3] and is rarely successful.[4] As Beaumont and McEleavy point out, is it ironic that this provision, which caused such difficulty during the drafting of the Convention, 'has now nearly faded without trace'.[5]

Merle Weiner[6] argues that one of the main reasons[7] for the demise of Article 20 is the highly restrictive interpretation adopted by Professor Perez-Vera, the Rapporteur of the Convention, according to which,

> [t]o be able to refuse to return a child on the basis of . . . Article [20], it will be necessary to show that the fundamental principles of the requested State concerning the subject matter of the Convention do not permit it; it will not be sufficient to show merely that return would be incompatible, even manifestly incompatible, with these principles.[8]

---

[1] The UK and Finland did not include this Art in their implementing legislation.

[2] See eg M Weiner, 'Strengthening Article 20' (2004) 38 *United States Family Law Review* 701, 708–11; AE Anton, 'The Hague Convention on International Child Abduction' 30 (1981) *International and Comparative Law Quarterly* 537, 550–51.

[3] A search conducted on the Hague Abduction Convention database 'INCADAT' (www.incadat.com) in July 2012, for cases in which the 'legal basis' was Art 20, produced 35 cases. In contrast, 276 cases came up in which the Art 13(1)(b) grave risk defence was discussed.

[4] N Lowe, 'A Statistical Analysis of Applications Made in 2008 under the Hague Convention of 25 October 1980 on the Civil Aspects of International Child Abduction, Part I Global Report', Preliminary Doc 8 (November 2011), www.hcch.net/upload/wop/abduct2011pd08ae.pdf shows that in 1999 there were no cases in which a refusal to return was based even partly on Art 20; in 2003, there were eight cases where Art 20 was one of multiple reasons for refusal to return and that all of these cases were from Chile and that in 2008, there were two cases in which Art 20 was one of multiple reasons for refusal to return. It should be mentioned that the US implementing legislation requires that this exception (in common with Art 13(1)(b)) be proven by clear and convincing evidence (42 USC § 11603(e)(2)(A) (1988)).

[5] P Beaumont and P McEleavy, *The Hague Convention on International Child Abduction* (Oxford, Oxford University Press, 1999) 172–76.

[6] Weiner, 'Strengthening Article 20' (n 2) 715–18.

[7] Other reasons Weiner gives are (1) a legal memorandum written by the US State Department, stating that the defence will only apply where the claimed violation of human rights will 'utterly shock the conscience', (2) the view taken by some courts that Art 20 is redundant in light of the grave risk exception in Art 13(1)(b).

[8] Perez-Vera Report, Proceedings of the 14th Session of the Hague Conference Oct 1980, www.hcch.net/upload/expl28.pdf, para 118.

Weiner takes issue with this interpretation and advocates reading the phrase 'would not be permitted' as meaning 'return could not occur consistently with those principles'.[9] The implications of the two different interpretations will be considered in the analysis section below. Weiner also argues that Article 20 should be revived in light of the internationally recognised, expanded notions of human rights. A possible trigger for a wider interpretation of Article 20, at least in European countries, might be the intervention of the European Court of Human Rights (ECtHR) in Hague Abduction cases. Accordingly, as well as examining the case law on Article 20, the relevant jurisprudence of the ECtHR will be considered.

In addition, there are some indications that courts might become more willing to use the Article 20 defence if countries with non-Western religious and cultural norms join the Convention. So, in the analysis of the case law, specific consideration will be given to the relationship between culture and human rights in the child abduction context.

II The Case Law

Firstly, it should be pointed out that, unlike the other exceptions, Article 20 is not specifically directed at a particular person. In other words, the exception will be established where the relevant human rights of either the child or the abductor, or in theory someone else, will be violated by the return of the child. Perusal of the case law indicates that there are three main categories of claims under Article 20: claims based on inconsistency with the best interests of the child; claims based on lack of due process in the requesting State; and claims based on breach of the right to freedom of movement or similar rights. The claim, made in European countries, that return of the child violates the right of the abductor and the child to family life within Article 8 of the European Convention on Human Rights (ECHR) will be treated under the rubric of the best interests of the child since the ECtHR has held that the right to family life is to be interpreted in light of the best interests of the child.[10] Each category will be examined in turn.

A Claims Based on Inconsistency with the Best Interests of the Child

There are two variations of the claim that the return order is inconsistent with the best interests of the child, which is a fundamental principle in the local law of many States[11] and under Article 3 of the United Nations Convention on the Rights of the Child (the CRC).[12]

---

[9] Weiner, 'Strengthening Article 20' (n 2) 715–18.

[10] J Fortin, *Children's Rights and the Developing Law*, 3rd edn (Cambridge, Cambridge University Press, 2009) 69–71; cf Norweigan case, detailed in the Response to the 2010 Questionnaire, www.hcch.net/index_en.php?act=publications.details&pid=5291&dtid=33, para7.6, in which Art 20 was established because the applicant, who had obtained custody of the children in the requesting State, was not the biological father of one of the children and that accordingly there would be a breach of the mother's right to family life under Art 8 of the ECHR and also to her custody rights under Norwegian law.

[11] A few countries, such as South Africa, have entrenched the paramountcy of the best interests standard in the Constitution, and in many countries the standard is enacted in family law legislation, eg in England in the Children Act 1989 s 1 and in Australia in the Family Law Act s 64(1)(a). Moreover, the ECHR ruling that the right to respect for family life, entrenched in Art 8 of the ECHR, must be interpreted in light of the best interests of the child (n 10) effectively confers constitutional status on this standard in ECHR Member States.

[12] It should be remembered that this provision only requires that the child's best interests be a primary consideration and not the paramount consideration. See generally ch 6 at II B.

The first is where the abductor claims that the non-application of the best interests standard by the courts of the requested State when deciding to return the child violates the fundamental principles of that State and this means that there is a breach of Article 20 of the Convention.[13] Prima facie, this argument is absurd because the mechanism of immediate mandatory return at the heart of the Abduction Convention does not allow for consideration of the best interests of the child. Thus, if non-consideration of the best interests were in breach of Article 20, the Convention would be internally inconsistent and unworkable.[14] Accordingly, most courts have dismissed the claim out of hand.

Nonetheless, the claim was taken seriously in the South African case of *Sonderup v Tondelli*.[15] The Court explained that there was no conflict in principle between the Hague Convention and the principle of the paramountcy of the best interests of the child, entrenched in the South African Constitution. This is because the objective of the Hague Convention is to promote the interests of children and because the long-term interests of children would be best met by adjudication in the country of habitual residence. However, in practice, the operation of the Convention might be inconsistent with the Constitution, where return does not serve the short-term interests of the child.[16] Nonetheless, the Court concluded that such inconsistency could be justified under the proportionality principle in light of the objectives of the Hague Convention.[17] Furthermore, any inconsistency could be severely limited by interpreting the Article 13 and Article 20 exceptions in light of the paramountcy principle, rather than as narrowly as in other countries that do not have to comply with a similar constitutional provision, and by imposing conditions to safeguard the welfare of the child.[18]

Further support for the view that not giving sufficient weight to the best interests of the child might lead to violation of human rights can be found in the decision of the Grand Chamber of the ECtHR in the case of *Neulinger and Shuruk v Switzerland*.[19] The majority held that in determining whether domestic courts, in applying and interpreting the provisions of the Hague Convention, have given effect to the right to family life, secured by Article 8 of the ECHR, the decisive issue is

> whether a fair balance between the competing interests at stake – those of the child, of the two parents, and of the public order – has been struck, within the margin of appreciation afforded to States in such matter bearing in mind, however, **that the child's best interests must be a primary consideration**, as is indeed apparent from the Preamble to the Hague Convention . . .'[20] (author's emphasis added).

---

[13] See eg *Ciotola v Fiocca* 86 Ohio Misc 2d 24, 684 NE 2d 763, 765 (Ohio Com Pl 1997); *Sonderup v Tondelli* 2001 (1) SA 1171 (CC) [INCADAT cite: HC/E/ZA 309]; *State Central Authority and McCall* (1995) FLC 92-552; *Emmett and Perry and Director-General Department of Family Services and Aboriginal and Islander Affairs Central Authority and Attorney-General of the Commonwealth of Australia (Intervener)* (1996) 92-645 [INCADAT cite: HC/E/AU 280]; *CK v CK* [1994] 1 IR 260; *Kufner v Kufner* 519 F3d 33 (1st Cir 2008).

[14] In the US case of *Ciotola v Fiocca* ibid, the Ohio District Court held that an examination of the child's best interests in accordance with local law would 'violate the aim and spirit of the Convention'. Similarly, the Irish High Court pointed out that if there had to be a best interests enquiry in Convention cases, this would render meaningless the requirement in Art 16 of the Convention to stay custody proceedings pending child abduction return (*CK v CK* ibid [3]–[4]).

[15] See *Sonderup* (n 13).

[16] ibid [29].

[17] ibid, 30–32.

[18] ibid, 33–36. This analysis is very similar to the one advocated by the current author in R Schuz, 'The Hague Child Abduction Convention and Children's Rights' (2002) 12 *Transnational & Contemporary Problems* 393, 440–49.

[19] *Neulinger and Shuruk v Switzerland* App no 41615/07 (ECHR, 6 July 2010).

[20] ibid [133]–[134]. See also [4] of the concurring opinion of Justices Jociene, Sajo and Tsotsoria.

With respect, quoting the reference to the best interests of the child in the Preamble to the Convention does not solve the problem that individual assessment of the best interests of the child in each case, as advocated by the Grand Chamber,[21] is inconsistent with the mechanism of mandatory return.[22] Whilst the Grand Chamber does not mention Article 20, its approach leads to the inescapable conclusion that the failure of the courts in the requested State to attach sufficient weight to the interests of the child will lead to a breach of the child's right to family life, which would appear to be a fundamental right protected by Article 20 in ECHR Member States.

The second variation of the best interests claim is where the abductor asserts that the court in the requesting State will not determine the merits of the custody dispute in accordance with the best interests standard. Such a claim was accepted in the Spanish case of *Re S*.[23] In this case, the Spanish Court received evidence from the Israeli Consul of Honour in Spain, who was the uncle of the abducting mother, stating that an Israeli Rabbinical Court would not allow the mother to have contact with her daughter because she would be declared 'a rebellious wife'. On the basis of this evidence, which was completely false and unfounded, the Court held that the Article 20 exception applied and refused to return the child.[24] The decision is understandable on the information before the first instance court, and the Israeli High Court of Justice – which later discussed the case[25] – agreed that Article 20 would apply if the evidence were correct, but it is difficult to understand why the Spanish courts did not overturn the decision on appeal once the true facts became known.[26] Also, the reliance of the Spanish courts on the opinion of the Consul of Honour, who did not have any qualification of expertise in Jewish law, may be questioned.[27]

For the purposes of the present discussion, it is important to note that, according to the false opinion given by the Israeli Consul, the reason why the best interests standard was not applied was to punish the mother for her misconduct. Moreover, not only would she not receive custody, but she would also lose all her rights in relation to the child. Thus, the case should not be viewed as authority for the proposition that Article 20 will be established in a case where there are non-punitive reasons for the non-application of the best interests standard in the foreign country, and/or where the abductor would not lose all rights in relation to the child.

The only other known case in which the Article 20 defence was claimed on the basis of the non-application of the best interests standard in the requesting State is the *Eskinazi & Chelouche v Turkey* case.[28] In this case, a mother, who had abducted her daughter from Israel to Turkey, petitioned the ECtHR claiming that the return order of the Turkish courts violated her rights and that the Turkish courts should have invoked the Article 20 defence. She argued that the Israeli Rabbinical courts, in whom jurisdiction to hear the custody

---

[21] ibid [138].
[22] See eg comment of the Court that 'it follows from art 8 that a child's return cannot be ordered automatically or mechanically when the Hague Convention is applicable'. ibid at [138].
[23] *Re S*, Auto de 21 abril de 1997, Audiencia Provincial Barcelona, Sección 1a [INCADAT cite: HC/E/ES 244].
[24] ibid.
[25] HCJ 4365/97 *Tur Sinai v The Minister of Foreign Affairs* 53 (3) PD 673, 713. The left-behind father requested an order requiring the relevant Israeli ministries to intervene in order to change the decision of the Spanish Court. The petition was refused because, in the Court's view, the Ministries had done everything they could.
[26] It seems that the Spanish Appellate Court wrongly interpreted the Israeli Rabbinical Court's decision to award custody to the father as evidence of the correctness of the Consul's opinion. *Tur Sinai v The Minister of Foreign Affairs* ibid, 698–99.
[27] ibid, 690.
[28] *Eskinazi & Chelouche v Turkey* App no 14600/05 (ECHR, 2005-XIII) (extracts).

dispute was vested, in practice give preference to religious considerations over the advice of experts, despite the fact that they are obliged by statute to apply the best interests standard. The rejection of the mother's claims by the Turkish Court was upheld by the ECtHR, largely because of the jurisdiction of the secular Israeli High Court of Justice to review the decisions of the religious courts.

B Claims Based on Lack of Due Process in the Requesting State[29]

A good example of such a claim can be found in the New Jersey case of *Caro v Sher*.[30] In *Caro*, the Respondent claimed that the return to Spain would violate her fundamental interest in procedural due process because of the four-year delay which would take place in hearing her relocation petition.[31] The Court explained that the Spanish Court's procedures clearly did not correspond in all respects with those in the US, but that there was no reason to prefer the jurisprudential precepts of one signatory over that of another and one of the objectives of the Convention was to ensure mutual respect for rights of custody and access.[32]

However, there are indications from other cases that extreme examples of procedural unfairness could lead to the application of Article 20. For example, in the Australian case of *State Central Authority of Victoria v Ardito*,[33] the Court refused to order the return of a child to the US because the mother was unable to obtain a visa to re-enter the US on the basis of the Article 13(1)(b) intolerability defence. The Court held that it was probable that the Article 20 defence (which had not been pleaded) could also be established because it was contrary to all concepts of fairness that the question of the custody of the child should be determined in circumstances in which the mother was denied the right to appear.[34]

In addition, the New Zealand legislation implementing the Abduction Convention expressly requires the court to consider whether returning the child would result in 'discrimination against the child or any other person on any of the grounds on which discrimination is not permitted by the United Nations International Covenants on Human Rights' in determining whether the Article 20 defence is established.[35]

Furthermore, both the Spanish case of *Re S*[36] and the ECtHR case of *Estkinazi*[37] indicate that the Article 20 defence might be established on the basis that the abductor would be discriminated against in the courts of the requested State. In the former case, the claim was

---

[29] Occasionally, it is claimed that there has not been a fair trial in the Convention proceedings themselves, eg *NJC v NPC* [2008] CSIH 34, 2008 S.C. 571 [INCADAT cite: HC/E/UKs 996]. Whilst Art 20 may be mentioned, such claims are effectively made under the local human rights law of the requested State itself.

[30] *Caro v Sher* 687 A.2d 354 (NJ Super Ct Ch 1996); See also *Escaf v Rodriquez* 200 F Supp 2d 603.

[31] *Caro v Sher* ibid [17].

[32] It was also found that the Respondent did have methods of redress in the Spanish courts, ibid [361]. See also *Escaf v Rodriguez* (n 30) [40] stating, in reliance on State Department Legal Analysis, that 'Art 20 does not contemplate that courts applying the provision must copy the due process safeguards provided in the petitioner's country with those provided in the respondent's country or with some ideal notion of due process.'

[33] *State Central Authority of Victoria v Ardito*, 29 October 1997, Family Court of Australia (Melbourne) [INCADAT cite: HC/E/AU 283].

[34] A similar view was voiced by the Israeli District Court in FamA (TA) 70/97 *Dagan v Dagan* Nevo 13/12/98 but was not decided finally because in the end the mother did acquire a visa, following the intervention of the Israeli Central Authority.

[35] Care of Children Act s 106(2)(b).

[36] *Re S* (n 23).

[37] *Eskinazi* (n 28).

accepted on the basis of the false opinion of the Consul concerning the negation of the mother's rights. However, in the latter case, the mother's argument that the Turkish return order violated her right to a fair trial and her right to family life under the ECHR, because she would be discriminated against in the Rabbinical courts,[38] was rejected.[39]

The question of the availability of the Article 20 defence in cases of discrimination was addressed expressly, albeit obiter, by Baroness Hale in *Re J*,[40] a non-Convention case, involving abduction from Saudi Arabia. In considering how the case would be decided if the Hague Convention applied and Article 20 had been incorporated into the UK legislation, her Ladyship took the view that discriminatory law in the requesting State, which distinguished between the two parents on the basis of gender and in violation of Article 14 of the ECHR, would entitle, but not require, the court in the requested State to refuse return under Article 20.[41]

With respect, it is unclear why inconsistency with Article 14 of the ECHR should automatically lead to the establishment of Article 20. Baroness Hale herself stated that the Human Rights Act (which incorporates the ECHR into UK law) allows the UK Court to return a child, despite the fact that the law in the requesting State discriminates against the abductor, unless this would involve a flagrant breach of the provisions of the ECHR.[42] Since it was held that there was no such breach in this case,[43] it is difficult to see how the Article 20 requirement that return is not permitted by the fundamental principles of the requested State is satisfied.[44]

Furthermore, even where there is a breach of the abductor's human rights, it has to be remembered that most human rights regimes include a doctrine of proportionality or a

---

[38] ibid, part B and C. The mother's claim of bias in the Rabbinical courts in the context of custody is weak in light of the fact that custody is awarded to women in around two-thirds of cases. Moreover, in this particular case, Jewish law's arguably discriminatory 'tender years' presumption in relation to children under six, and gender identity presumption in relation to older children, would have worked in the mother's favour. However, it is worth noting that the arguments of a Muslim mother in a similar situation would appear somewhat stronger. While the Sharia Courts in Israel are also mandated by the Legal Capacity and Guardianship Law to apply the best interests standard, it seems that in practice they give effect to Muslim law rules on custody on the basis that these reflect the best interests of the child, See A Zahalka, *The Sharia Courts: Between Adjudication and Identity* (Tel-Aviv, Israel Bar Association, 2009) (Hebrew) 66; These rules discriminate against women in various ways, See U Khaliq and JR Young, 'Cultural Diversity, Human Rights and Inconsistency in the English Courts' (2001) 21 *Legal Studies* 192, 217–19.

[39] Similar claims were raised before an English court in the case of *Re S* [2000] 1 FLR 454, under the Art 13(1)(b) grave risk provision, because Art 20 was not incorporated into the UK legislation. However, the claims were rejected inter alia because it is not appropriate to treat Israel as a case separate and apart from the other signatories to the Hague Convention because of the dual system available in that country ibid [463].

[40] *Re J (A Child) (Return to Foreign Jurisdiction: Convention Rights)* [2005] UKHL 40 [45].

[41] ibid. However, a US court held that the mere fact that the child, if returned, would be living in a community in which there was cultural gender inequality is not sufficient to activate the Art 20 defence, *Walker v Kitt*, 2012 US Dist LEXIS 153611.

[42] *Re J* (n 40) [42].

[43] See also Khaliq and Young, 'Cultural Diversity' (n 38) 221; However, it might be suggested that outright procedural discrimination against one party in the foreign court on the basis of race, religion or gender could amount to a flagrant breach of the Art 6 right to a fair trial. A possible example could be the Sharia law provision requiring evidence from two male witnesses or one male witness and two female witnesses (s 1685 of the Majella). Similarly, in exceptional circumstances, discrimination might lead to a fragrant breach of the of the child's and/or the abductor's Art 8 right to family life, as in the immigration case of *EM (Lebanon) v Secretary of State for the Home Department* [2008] UKHL 64. Nonetheless, as Baroness Hale pointed out (at [46]–[47]), this case was different from the usual child abduction case, since the child had never had any family life with his father. It should also be noted that only Baroness Hale was prepared to accept unequivocally that it was the discriminatory law in Lebanon itself which was the reason for the likely flagrant violation of the Art 8 rights.

[44] See at I above; although if Weiner's interpretation (n 2 and accompanying text) is adopted, it might be possible to claim that return would not be consistent with the principles of the ECHR.

similar doctrine. Thus, in practice, courts will usually have discretion in determining to what extent the objectives of the Convention justify returning the child, despite the violation of the mother's rights. This analysis is different from that of Baroness Hale, since discretion is exercised in determining whether or not the Article 20 exception is established (ie whether return is permitted), rather than whether return should be ordered, despite the fact that the exception has been proven. Nonetheless, in practice, there is probably no significant difference between the two approaches.

It should be noted that the proportionality analysis is more complicated in this situation because the human rights of the abducting parents are being balanced against the purpose of the Abduction Convention and against the rights of the child who is protected by the Convention. This issue will be investigated further in the analysis section below.

C Claims Based on Right to Freedom of Movement

In a number of cases, abductors have claimed that a return order would be in breach of their fundamental right to freedom of movement.[45] This claim has invariably been rejected,[46] on the basis that the return order applies to the child and does not require the abductor to return with the child.[47] Whilst technically accurate, this reasoning has been described as unsatisfactory where there are good objective reasons behind the mother's flight from the place of habitual residence, such as violence, abuse or persecution because it forces the mother to choose between her responsibility to her child and her own basic liberty interests.[48] Some abductors have tried to overcome the ruling that the return order does not require the abductor to return by claiming that the return order is in breach of the child's right to remain in the State of his nationality or not to be extradited therefrom.[49] However, these claims have been rejected either on the basis that there is no breach under the local law[50] or on the basis that these rights are subject to the Hague Convention.[51]

A further reason for rejecting the abductor's claim based on his right to freedom of movement by the return order can be found in the US case of *Freier v Freier*.[52] In this case, the mother's claim, that the temporary injunction which had been granted against her by

---

[45] This right is widely recognised as a fundamental human right. See eg Art 2 of the Fourth Protocol of the ECHR and s 6(1) of the Canadian Charter of Rights and Freedoms (providing that no Canadian citizen can be forced to leave Canada against his free will).

[46] *cf* TGI Niort 09/01/1995, *Procureur de la République c. Y.* [INCADAT cite: HC/E/FR 63]; Similarly, the freedom of movement argument was accepted by the Swiss Court of Appeal, but this ruling was later overturned by the Swiss Supreme Court in 5P.1/1999, Bundesgericht (Tribunal Fédéral) (f 29 March 1999) [INCADAT cite: HC/E/CH 427].

[47] eg *Fabri v Pritikin-Fabri*, 221 F Supp 2d 859, 873 (2001); decision of Cour d'Appel at Aix-en-Provence of 23 March 1989, referred to in Beaumont and McEleavy (n 5) 175; *cf* Comments in separate concurring opinions in the Grand Chamber decision in *Neulinger* (n 19), suggesting that 'condemning' a parent to spend years in another country because it was in the best interests of the child to have access to the other parent would be in breach of his right to respect for private life (per Judges Lorenzen and Kalaydjieva) and referring specifically to the mother's right to freedom of movement (per Judges Jociene, Sajo and Tsortsoria at [7]).

[48] Weiner, 'Strengthening Article 20' (n 2) 732.

[49] eg *Parsons v Styger* (1989) 67 O.R. (2d) 1 (LJSC), aff'd (1989) 67 O.R. (2d) 11 (CA)]; *YD v JB* [1996] R.D.F. 753 (Que CA) [INCADAT cite: HC/E/CA 369]; *G and G v* Decision of OLG Hamm, January 18 1995, 35 ILM 529 (1996) [INCADAT cite: HC/E/DE 310].

[50] eg, because the right not to be extradited only applied to criminal extradition. See *YD v JB* ibid.

[51] *Parsons v Styger* (n 49). In *Carrascosa v McGuire* (520 F3d 249 (3rd Cir 2008)), the US Court mentioned that if courts could refuse to order the return of children on the basis that this violated the fundamental freedom of the right to travel, the Convention would be rendered meaningless.

[52] *Freier v Freier* 969 F Supp 436 (ED Mich 1996).

the Israeli courts preventing her from leaving Israel violated her human rights, was rejected on the basis that she had a due-process right to challenge such an injunction. Similarly, it can be argued that a return order does not violate the parent's right to freedom of travel because after returning he can request permission from the courts in the requesting State to relocate

This reasoning gives rise to the question as to whether Article 20 could be established where there is no relocation jurisdiction in the requesting State. Beaumont and McEleavy[53] suggest that there may be some merit in applying Article 20 in such cases. However, this suggestion is problematic for a number of reasons. Firstly, it will be difficult to distinguish between countries which do not allow relocation and those where relocation is only allowed in exceptional cases. In both situations, the abductor will not have any real chance of being allowed to relocate. Secondly, applying Article 20 in such a situation involves unwarranted interference in the internal law of the requesting State.[54]

III Analysis

A Internal Coherence

As explained above, accepting a claim that Article 20 is established because returning the child is inconsistent with the best interests of the child, which is a fundamental principle under the law of the requested State, would be totally inconsistent with the whole philosophy of the Convention, which is based on summary return without a best interests investigation. Similarly, an interpretation of Article 20 which requires the requested State to examine the internal law of the requesting State to check whether it is consistent with the best interests standard or other fundamental human rights norms, appears to be contrary to the principle of reciprocity which underlies the Convention. In particular, it should be remembered that each Member State can decide whether it wishes to engage in reciprocal treaty obligations with each acceding country.[55] Thus, a Member State's confirmation that the Convention is in force between it and an acceding State can be seen as a statement that the relevant internal law of that State is acceptable to it.[56] Accordingly, it has been held that Article 20 will usually only apply where there has been a change of regime in the requesting State since accession to the Convention.[57]

A further problem with Article 20 is that it seems to be redundant, since it is difficult to envisage situations in which it will apply which are not already covered by the grave risk exception. It has been suggested that Article 20 acts in a purely legal context, whilst

---

[53] Beaumont and McEleavy (n 5) 175.
[54] For a discussion of the different approaches to relocation, see ch 4.
[55] Except countries which were party to the Hague Conference on Private International Law in 1980. See ch 1 at I C.
[56] cf Thorpe LJ in *Re E (Abduction: Non-Convention Country)* [1999] 2 FLR 642 who took the view that '[t]he number and the diversity of the states that have joined the Hague club have made it impossible to formulate minimum standard requirements of other family justice systems before recognizing accession'.
[57] FamC (RG) 74430/99 *P v P* (Unreported, 14 December 1999) (Israel), citing Beaumont and McEleavy (n 5) 174, which quotes P Nygh, 'Children on the Move' in JE Doek, H van Loon and P Vlaardingerbroek (eds), *Children on the Move* (Dordecht, Martinus Nijhoff, 1996) 41. Similarly, courts are likely to dismiss out of hand the abductor's allegations that he has been or is liable to be mistreated by the authorities in the requesting State. See eg *Janakakis-Kostun v Janakakis*, 6 S.W.3d 843 (Ky Ct App 1999).

Article 13(1)(b) is primarily concerned with factual matters.[58] Thus, for example, return could be refused under Article 20 on the basis that the child is a refugee.[59] However, with respect, in such a situation it seems that the grave risk exception would also be established. The only advantage of relying on Article 20 appears to be that it may not be necessary to bring concrete proof of the harm to the child or the intolerable situation which will be caused by the return.

B Consistency with the Intention of the Drafters

The rather dramatic legislative history of Article 20 makes it difficult to identify the intention of the drafters with any degree of certainty. The final wording of Article 20 replaced an earlier version which would have allowed States not to return children where such return would be 'manifestly incompatible with the fundamental principles of law relating to the family and children in the requested State'.[60] Delegates and Permanent Bureau staff who opposed this wording, out of concern that such a general public policy exception would substantially undermine the value of the Convention, worked to find a narrower exception which would be acceptable to the majority of delegates. The result was the current Article 20, which changed the earlier version in two ways. Firstly, the type of fundamental principles which may be referred to was narrowed to include only those 'relating to the protection of human rights and fundamental freedoms'. Professor Perez-Vera took the view that this change diminishes the importance of the internal law of the requested State since human rights and fundamental freedoms are to a large extent governed by international agreements.[61]

The second change involved replacing the words 'manifestly incompatible' with the phrase 'would not be permitted'. Professor Perez-Vera understood this change as increasing the 'extent of incompatibility' required between the fundamental principles and the result of ordering return.[62] Thus, in her view, it is necessary to show that return is not permitted by those fundamental principles. Weiner argues that this interpretation is unduly technical since it involves consideration of the relative position of human rights legislation and the Abduction Convention in the legal hierarchy of the requested State.[63] She advocates reading the phrase 'would not be permitted' as meaning 'return could not occur consistently with those principles'.[64]

Persual of the case law suggests that this debate is academic. Whilst, as Weiner states, courts have cited the Perez-Vera Report to support a narrow interpretation of Article 20, no case has been found where Article 20 was not established purely because the relevant fundamental principles were not higher in the legal hierarchy of the requested State than

---

[58] Beaumont and McEleavy (n 5) 174, citing an interview with Dyer.

[59] ibid; *Entscheid OGer BE vom 5. Mai 2010, consid. 7 notamment*, a Swiss decision relying on Art 20 in this situation and discussed in AC Alfieri, 'Enlèvement international d'enfants: premières expériences avec la LF-EEA' (2012) *La pratique du droit de la famille* 550, 556.

[60] This version was accepted by a majority of one *Proces-verbal* No 9 at 307, Beaumont and McEleavy (n 5) 23 and 137.

[61] Perez-Vera Report (n 8), para 33, but later in the Report, at para 118, the Rapporteur makes it clear that the exception can only be invoked where there is an inconsistency with principles which have been incorporated into the internal law of the requested state.

[62] ibid, para 33.

[63] Weiner, 'Strengthening Article 20' (n 2) 712–13.

[64] ibid.

the Hague Convention. Nonetheless, it is appropriate to consider which interpretation appears to be most consistent with the intention of the drafters.

The approach of the Rapporteur is indeed understandable because some effect has to be given to the change in wording from the earlier version of Article 20 and it does seem to have been designed to avoid clashes between the Abduction Convention and States' constitutional provisions. However overall, there is much to commend Weiner's view that an interpretation which depends on the legal hierarchy in the requested State is unsatisfactory. In particular, this approach will result in disparity between the situations in which Article 20 can be invoked in different Member States.[65] Nonetheless, it seems to the current author that the words 'would not be permitted' indicate the drafters' intention that the exception be interpreted narrowly.[66] Accordingly, the exception should only be established where return of the child would be clearly inconsistent with the relevant fundamental principles, or in the words of the UK courts, where return would result in a flagrant breach of those principles.[67]

C Promotion of the Objectives of the Convention

i Protecting Abducted Children

As we have already seen, the Preamble to the Convention recites that the Member States are convinced that the interests of children are of paramount importance in matters relating to their custody. We have also seen that the Abduction Convention is based on the assumption that the best interests of the child are usually served by having issues of custody and access determined by the courts of the country of habitual residence.[68] The question arises therefore as to whether this latter assumption can be rebutted in cases where the requesting State will not determine the custody of the child in accordance with the best interests standard.[69] If so, then it could be argued that Article 20 should be invoked in such cases, where the best interests standard can be defined as a fundamental principle under the law of the requested State.[70]

However, this argument is too simplistic inter alia because the fact that the requesting State does not apply the best interests principle does not necessarily mean that the actual outcome will not be in accordance with the best interests of the child, as understood in the requested State. This is why UK Courts have, not infrequently, returned children in non-Convention cases to countries where custody is not determined in accordance with the best interests of the child.[71]

Moreover, it should be remembered that even where the paramountcy of the best interests standard is a fundamental principle, it will usually be necessary, as in the *Sonderup*

---

[65] This disparity was envisaged by UK academics who stated that Art 20 would have had less relevance in the UK than elsewhere because of the lack of a written Constitution or Bill of Rights, Beaumont and McEleavy (n 5) 173. This situation has since been changed by the enactment of Human Rights Act 1998.

[66] The Rapporteur also claims that the situation of Art 20 at the end of the chapter indicates the clearly exceptional nature of the provision's application, Perez-Vera Report (n 8), para 118.

[67] *Re J* (n 40) [42] and cases cited there.

[68] See eg, *Murray v Director, Family Services* (1993) FLC 92-416 [416].

[69] ibid [438].

[70] Or perhaps under international law, see Art 3 of the United Nations Convention on the Rights of the Child.

[71] See *Re J* (n 40) and cases discussed there.

case,[72] to consider the question of proportionality. This would involve examining the extent of the foreign law's deviation from the best interests standard and the likely consequences of such a deviation, and weighing these against the purpose of the Convention.[73] It is suggested that this sort of balancing exercise is likely to lead to the conclusion that deviation from the best interests standard will be proportional unless this will result in harm to the child and in such cases the Article 13(1)(b) defence should be invoked. Accordingly, the restrictive interpretation of Article 20 per se is not inconsistent with the objective of promoting the best interests of the child. However, if courts are not prepared to use Article 13(1)(b) in situations where deviation from the best interests standard will cause harm to the child, then Article 20 should be interpreted more widely so as to include such cases.

ii Deterrence

In theory, a wide interpretation of Article 20 might weaken the deterrence effect of the Convention. Thus, if for example it were held that the religious law of custody, as applied in a particular Member State, violates fundamental principles because it deviates from the best interests standard and/or is discriminatory, then there would effectively be no deterrent to abduction from that particular Member State. Moreover, such a wide interpretation would create an obstacle to the extension of the Convention. Clearly, the more Member States, the greater deterrent there will be to international child abduction worldwide. However, as already stated, the deterrence objective cannot justify harming the interests or violating the rights of children or adults. Thus, where a balance of the competing rights and interests[74] leads to the conclusion that the child should not be returned, Article 20 should be invoked if there is no other way of preventing return.

iii Adjudication in the Forum Conveniens

It may be argued that if the legal system in the requesting State violates basic human rights norms, it should no longer be seen as the *forum conveniens* for determination of the custody dispute. Indeed, under the doctrine of *forum non conveniens*, as developed in common law countries, the court will not stay proceedings, even where it is satisfied that there is another forum which is the natural forum for determining the dispute, where it can be shown that justice will not be done in that forum.[75]

Whilst there is some attraction in this argument, it should be remembered that 'justice' has been interpreted narrowly in this context and the claim of injustice has usually only been successful where it relates to unfairness in the dispensing of justice rather than in the content of the foreign law. Accordingly, although it has been held that justice will not be done in cases where one party will be discriminated against on the basis of nationality,[76] it is not clear that a gender preference rule would satisfy the condition of injustice. Indeed,

---

[72] *Sonderup* (n 13).
[73] See *Sonderup* ibid. eg, the harm caused to the child by not being returned immediately to his familiar environment may be greater than the harm caused to him by the fact that custody will be determined in accordance with a discriminatory gender preference rule.
[74] eg, the adult's right not to be discriminated against may have to be balanced against the child's right to be protected from the harmful effects of abduction.
[75] *Spiliada Maritime Corporation v Consulex Ltd* [1987] 1 AC 460.
[76] eg, *Mohammed v Bank of Kuwait* [1996] 1 WLR 1483 (CA); CA (SC)165/60 *Union Insurance v Ezra* 17(1) PD 646 (Isr).

such a finding would appear to be inconsistent with UK case law in non-Convention cases, in which children have been returned to Muslim law countries with such a rule.[77]

Furthermore, it has to be remembered that the Convention's primary concern is the interests of the child and thus the fact that one of the adults will not obtain justice in a particular country, as perceived through Western eyes, does not necessarily mean that that country is not the *forum conveniens* for the determination of the dispute from the child's point of view.[78]

D Compatibility with the Summary Nature of Convention Proceedings

Any interpretation of Article 20 which requires any more than a cursory examination of the legal system of the foreign country is likely to be incompatible with the summary nature of Convention proceedings. Thus, the approach adopted by the House of Lords, in non-Convention cases, under which it is necessary to carry out a detailed enquiry into the practical implications of the foreign cultural norms,[79] appears unsuitable for Convention cases. The suggestion that Article 20 should rarely be invoked in such cases and that reliance should be placed instead on Article 13(1)(b), does not solve this problem because it will still be necessary to obtain evidence about the likely scenario in the foreign country so as to determine whether indeed there is a grave risk of harm to the child.

However, it seems that this situation is unavoidable. The only way of avoiding this enquiry is to refuse return automatically where the foreign country has different cultural norms or to ignore the differences between the two legal systems. Neither of these approaches is tenable. The former will seriously undermine the Convention and the latter involves risk of harm to the child. Thus, the best solution is to find methods of obtaining reliable information[80] relatively quickly via the Central Authority of the requesting State and/or the liaison judge.[81]

In the current author's view, a more serious threat to the summary return mechanism in the Convention is the increasing intervention of the ECtHR in abduction cases in which issues of human rights arise.[82] As seen above, in cases where the requesting State has different religious or cultural norms from the European requested State, the abductor may try to avoid having to comply with a return order by petitioning the ECtHR and claiming that the return order violated his human rights under the European Convention. By giving serious consideration to these claims, the ECtHR is undermining the Hague Convention.

E Consistency with Rights and Interests of Children

To the extent that the Article 20 claim is based on inconsistency with the best interests standard, the discussion in relation to the grave risk defence[83] is equally relevant here and

---

[77] See eg, *Re J* (n 40); *Re E* (n 56).
[78] See comment of Baroness Hale in *Re J* (n 40) [39], in the context of abduction from a Muslim country, that in many cases 'the connection of the child and all the family with the other country is so strong that any differences between the legal systems here and there should carry little weight'.
[79] *Re J* ibid.
[80] The dangers of non-reliable information can be seen from the Spanish case of *Re S* (n 23) and accompanying text and from the judgment of Justice Steiner in *Neulinger* (n 85).
[81] For a discussion about obtaining information via liaison judges, see ch 11 at III D.
[82] See generally ch 1 at II Di.
[83] Chapter 11 at IV E.

will not be repeated. However, where the Article 20 claim is based on lack of due process or the parent's right to freedom of movement, the implications for the rights and interests of the child are not self-evident. In some cases, discrimination or other violation of the parent's right to due process will also violate the rights of the child or harm his interests. In such cases, the rights and interests of the child will require that return is refused under Articles 20 or 13(1)(b). However, there may be cases where, despite the threat to the abductor's human rights, refusal to return the child to his natural family environment will in fact be inconsistent with the child's rights and interests. In such cases, there is a clash between the rights of the child and the parent.

In most cases of this nature, the Article 20 defence will not be established because the violation of the parent's human rights will be for a justifiable reason and so will satisfy the proportionality principle. However, even if the defence is established, the court in exercising its discretion should give primary weight to the interests and rights of the child and consider whether the harm caused by not returning the child may be greater than the harm caused to the parent by the lack of due legal process.

F Consistency with Rights of the Parents

At first sight the restrictive approach taken to Article 20 in cases where the abductor claims a breach of her human rights seems inconsistent with contemporary Western ideology which gives increasing weight to human rights in general and the right to equality and freedom from discrimination in particular. On the other hand, in recent years there is also increasing recognition of the right to culture and the right to freedom of religion, which may well clash with equality rights. As seen from the case law discussed above, a number of the cases where abductors claimed breach of their human rights within Article 20 involved cultural differences between the requesting States and requested States. So, any discussion as to the extent to which the way in which Article 20 has been applied adequately protects parental human rights needs to be informed by a basic understanding of the different approaches to the relationship between human rights and culture.[84]

According to the universalistic approach, human rights norms will always trump and thus children should not be returned to countries whose laws violate Western human rights norms, such as gender equality.[85] Such an approach would appear to allow Article 20 to be used in any case where the cultural norms in the requesting State are different from the secular norms[86] widely accepted in modern Western democracies and effectively closes the door of the 'Hague club' to courts with non-Western legal systems. At the other extreme, a relativist approach would hold that all cultural norms have equal value and thus the requested State

---

[84] For an excellent discussion of the different approaches, see M Freeman, 'The Morality of Cultural Pluralism' (1995) 3 *International Journal of Child Rights* 1.

[85] See eg the dissenting judgment of the Austrian judge, Justice Steiner, in the ECtHR decision in *Neulinger* (n 19), who described the majority's rejection of the mother's claim that she would not be able to exercise any influence over the religious upbringing of the son as 'theoretical optimism' because, in the Israeli legal system, matters of personal status are justiciable before religious courts which apply traditional religious rules 'sometimes significantly different from those with which we are familiar with in Europe' (the case was later overturned by the Grand Chamber on other grounds).

[86] See eg Justice Steiner's reference to the 'principles of tolerance and secularism that prevail in the States Parties to the Convention', *Neulinger* ibid.

cannot criticise the norms of the requesting State.[87] Under this approach, Article 20 could never be invoked on the basis of different cultural norms.

Finally, the *via media* of cultural pluralism, whilst accepting that there are many reasonable conceptions of good and right, which are all valid from a moral perspective, holds that overriding primary values also exist, according to which it is possible to assess the reasonableness and moral validity of cultural practices.[88] Under this approach, whilst local norms should not automatically be preferred to foreign norms,[89] the differences between the norms in the different countries cannot be ignored. Rather, the Court has to consider whether a particular norm violates primary values inter alia by considering the implications of the differences between the conflicting norms in the particular case.[90] Whilst the latter approach has much to commend it and has been adopted by the House of Lords in non-Convention cases,[91] at first sight it does not seem consistent with the summary return mechanism because it requires a careful examination of the implications of the differences between the norms in the two countries in the particular case, which is likely to involve an assessment of the best interests of the child.

Nonetheless, this approach can be adapted to the constraints of the Abduction Convention by focusing the enquiry on the question of whether the foreign norms violate the overriding primary value of preventing significant harm to the child.[92] Where the breach of the parent's human right will cause significant harm to the child, the Article 13(1)(b) exception can be invoked. Situations where the abducting parent would not be allowed to have contact with the child or where he is likely to be persecuted or abused in the foreign country[93] should be seen as exposing the child to harm. However, if courts are not prepared to accept that violence against the parent harms the child,[94] Article 20 should be invoked[95] because the 'primary value' of the parent's physical integrity has to take precedence over all other considerations.

---

[87] See eg, comment of Nolan LJ in *Re S* (n 23), 305 that 'it is implicit in s1(1)(a) [of the Children Act 1989] that the paramountcy of the child's welfare is to be observed consistently with the law to which the child is subject'; see also Thorpe LJ's reference in *Re E* (n 56) to Islamic law as a system which 'is conceived by its originators and operators to promote and protect the interests of children within that society and according to its traditions and values'.

[88] P Alston, 'The Best Interests Principle: Towards a Reconciliation of Culture and Human Rights' in P Alston (ed), *The Best Interests of the Child* (Oxford, Clarendon Press, 1994) 20 explains that 'Just as culture is not a factor which should be excluded from the human rights equation, so too must it not be accorded the status of a metanorm which trumps rights.'

[89] In the words of Baroness Hale in *Re J* (n 40) [37], 'It would be wrong to say that the future of every child who is within the jurisdiction of our courts should be decided according to a conception of child welfare which exactly corresponds to that which is current here. In a world which values difference, one culture is not inevitably to be preferred to another. Indeed we do not have any fixed concept of what will be in the best interests of the individual child. . . . Once upon a time, it may have been assumed that there was only one way of bringing up children. Nowadays, we know that there are many routes to a healthy and well-adjusted adulthood. We are not so arrogant as to think that we know best.'

[90] Thus, eg, it is very relevant whether there is a genuine issue as to whether it is in the best interests of the child to live in one country. Also, the strength of the connection of the child with the two countries is a relevant factor. *Re J* ibid [39].

[91] *Re J* ibid.

[92] It is suggested that the harm would have to be imminent. Thus, eg, where there was a real threat that a forced marriage would be imposed on an adolescent girl within the coming year, the exception would be established. However, the threat that a forced marriage may be imposed on a four-year-old in 10 years' time would not be sufficient.

[93] See Weiner, 'Strengthening Article 20' (n 2).

[94] See ch 11 at II Biv.

[95] This possibility prevents Art 20 from being redundant, a consequence which is criticised by Weiner, 'Strengthening Article 20' (n 2).

On the other hand, where the foreign norm cannot be shown to cause significant harm to the child or to violate some other primary overriding value, the policies of protecting children from the harmful effects of abduction, together with that of respecting foreign cultural norms will require returning the child, despite the likely violation of the human rights of the parent in the requesting State.[96]

G Consistency with Private International Law Principles

The very restrictive approach to Article 20 adopted in the case law is consistent with comity in all senses. Indeed, in the case of *Caro v Sher*,[97] where the Spanish law did not meet the standards of due process in the USA, the Court justified its refusal to invoke the Article 20 defence on the basis that one of the objectives of the Convention was to ensure mutual respect for rights of custody and access.

In cases where foreign cultural norms will cause harm to the child, Article 13(1)(b) is to be preferred over Article 20 as a basis for refusing return since it focuses on the harm to the particular child in the particular circumstances and does not discredit the foreign norms per se. Thus, this approach is more consistent with the doctrine of comity. Furthermore, it enables non-Western countries to join the Hague Convention,[98] whilst at the same time leaving the current Member States with an opening not to return children in cases where the non-Western cultural norms will cause them real harm.

H Certainty versus Flexibility

The current situation, in which Article 20 is rarely invoked and almost never successful, provides a considerable degree of certainty. Some have argued, however, that this situation reflects an overly restrictive interpretation of the provision. This criticism is not convincing since it is clear that Article 20 was intended to be a provision of last resort. Indeed, the very fact that many of the parties to the Convention are parties to the ECHR or have equivalent human rights legislation and that all but one are parties to the CRC makes it unsurprising that the conditions in the exception will rarely be established. Starting to interpret the section more liberally is likely to cause a good deal of uncertainty, in particular if inconsistency with the best interests standard were to be accepted as a basis for establishing the exception. Nonetheless, as Weiner has pointed out,[99] the exception does potentially contain the flexibility to compensate for an overly restrictive interpretation of the grave risk defence in cases of domestic violence against the abductor. Furthermore, as stated above, the existence of the exception may be seen as a necessary safeguard if States with non-Western cultural norms are to join the Convention.

---

[96] Thus, eg, the Muslim law rule that children over a certain age will be in the custody of the father, whilst violating the mother's right to equality, should not lead to the non-return of the child, unless it can be shown on the facts of the case that application of this gender preference rule will cause the child significant harm.

[97] *Caro v Sher* (n 30).

[98] Thorpe LJ once commented that 'The further development of international collaboration to combat child abduction may well depend on the capacity of states to respect a variety of concepts of child welfare derived from differing cultures and traditions' *Osman v Elasha* [2000] Fam 62, 70.

[99] ibid.

IV Conclusion

The above analysis suggests that the restrictive interpretation of Article 20 adopted by most courts is consistent with the objectives and philosophy of the Convention and the intention of the drafters and is not clearly inconsistent with the rights and interests of the child and his parents, even in an era of increased recognition of human rights. However, this conclusion is dependent on the willingness of courts to interpret Article 13(1)(b) so as to cover situations where harm will be caused to the child as a result of the breach of the abductor's human rights.

Even though this approach renders Article 20 largely redundant, because situations which might come within it will be covered by Article 13(1)(b), it is preferable to focus on the harm to the child than to base refusals to return on breach of human rights for a number of reasons. In particular, the main objective of the Convention is to protect children from harm. Similarly, the doctrine of comity requires that findings that other Contracting States breach human rights should be avoided where possible. Finally, this approach is most consistent with the widely accepted theory of cultural pluralism.

Moreover, Article 20 is not completely redundant because it can be used as a last resort, for example if courts are not prepared to accept that abuse or persecution of the abductor will cause harm to the child. Finally, as Beaumont and McEleavy point out, the inclusion of the provision gives the Convention a certain moral authority and should pre-empt any claim that the Convention per se is inconsistent with the constitutions of Member States.[100]

---

[100] Beaumont and McEleavy (n 5) 176.

Part V

The Voice of the Child

14

Ascertaining the Child's Views

I Requirement to Ascertain the Child's Views

As seen above, courts take into account the views of a mature child in various contexts in Convention proceedings. The most common context is when the abductor raises the child objection defence in Article 13(2). However, the child's views may also be relevant in determining his habitual residence;[1] whether the grave risk defence applies;[2] and whether the child is settled for the purposes of the Article 12(2) defence.[3] In addition, the child's views may be a consideration in exercising the court's discretion, where one of the defences is established.[4]

Before addressing the question of how the court ascertains the child's views,[5] a preliminary question arises and that is whether the court is under an obligation to ascertain the child's views if the abducting parent does not raise the child objection defence. On a literal interpretation of Article 13(2), there is no such obligation.[6] Indeed, Waite J in *P v P (Minors) (Child Abduction)*[7] expressly rejected the argument that the Court had any obligation to enquire into the children's objections and refused to follow an earlier dictum by Eastham J which appeared to suggest that Article 13(2) did impose such a duty on the Court.[8]

With respect, such an approach is clearly inconsistent with the child's right to be heard,[9] which *ex hypothesi* is not restricted to cases where the parent raises the issue of the child's views. The issue might seem hypothetical because in the normal course of events the abducting parent, looking for any possible defence, will bring to the court's attention the

---

[1] See ch 8 at V E.
[2] See P Beaumont and P McEleavy, *The Hague Convention on International Child Abduction* (Oxford, Oxford University Press, 1999) 193.
[3] See generally ch 9.
[4] eg *Re D (Abduction: Acquiescence)* [1999] 1 FLR 36 and in *Re D (Abduction: Discretionary Return)* [2000] 1 FLR 24. In relation to discretion to return, see generally ch 10 at IV.
[5] The word 'views' is used as opposed to 'wishes' because it is not restricted to the question of the desired outcome of the case. Whilst indeed the establishment of the child objection defence does depend on the child's wishes, in the other contexts in which the child's views may be relevant, what is important is how the child sees his life at the present and not necessarily his desires about the future.
[6] But see the suggestion in ch 12 at I A that the reason that the child objection exception appears in a separate paragraph is that there is no need for a person opposing the return to satisfy the court that the exception exists. Rather it is sufficient if the court finds that the conditions in the exception apply. This interpretation lends support to the idea that the court might, of its own initiative, consider whether the child objects and is of sufficient age and maturity, although it is difficult to see that it imposes any requirement to do so.
[7] *P v P (Minors) (Child Abduction)* [1992] 1 FLR 155.
[8] In *Re C*, CA 281/1990 (Unreported).
[9] See decision of German Constitutional Court in 2 *B v R* 1206/98 Bundesverfassungsgericht, 29 October 1998 [INCADAT cite: HC/E/DE 233], holding that failure to hear the child in order to ascertain his wishes was a breach of his constitutional rights.

374 *Ascertaining the Child's Views*

child's views. However, this is not inevitably so[10] and there have been cases where the child's objections have not been brought to the attention of the court.[11] Accordingly, courts should, as a matter of practice, make arrangements to ensure that the children's views are made known to it wherever they are old enough that their views might possibly be relevant.[12]

In Israel, this requirement appears to be satisfied by Regulation 295(9) of the Civil Procedure Regulations ('the Israeli Regulation'),[13] which provides that

> Where a child is of sufficient age and level of maturity that it is appropriate to take into account his views, the Court shall not decide the case before it hears the child unless the Court does not see any need for this for special reasons which will be recorded' (author's translation).

Until a few years ago, no similar provision existed in most Contracting States[14] and thus courts did not enquire into the child's views if these were not raised by the abducting parent.

Since then, the position in EC countries has been changed as a result of the enactment of Council Regulation (EC) No 2201/2003 of 27 November 2003 concerning jurisdiction and the recognition and enforcement of judgments in matrimonial matters and the matters of parental responsibility ('Brussels II bis' or the 'Regulation') [2003][15] Article 11.2, which provides:

> When applying articles 12 and 13 of the 1980 Hague Convention, it shall be ensured that the child is given the opportunity to be heard during the proceedings unless this appears inappropriate having regard to his or her age or degree of maturity.

Compliance with this provision should prevent repetition of the situation where there is neither documentary evidence of the minor's wishes nor any independent assessment of them.[16] In particular, it should be noted that the obligation to ascertain the child's views applies in all cases where Articles 12 and 13 are being applied. Since Article 12 is the main operative provision of the Convention, it seems that the obligation to hear the child applies in all Convention cases. The wide scope of this provision is to be welcomed because, as mentioned above, the child's views are relevant to a number of issues under the Convention and not only to the establishment of the child objection defence. Furthermore, the child's participation is not simply instrumental, but has an independent value.[17] Thus, the fact

---

[10] This may happen, eg, where the abducting parent does not have legal representation or is not aware of the child's views.

[11] eg, the English case of *Re M (A Minor)(Child Abduction)* [1994] 1 FLR 390, in which the child's objections were not put before the Court until he had created a violent scene on the aircraft on which he was supposed to be returning to Australia and the captain refused to take off with him on board.

[12] Beaumont and McEleavy (n 2) 193, point out that it may not be possible to determine a child's maturity without ascertaining his views.

[13] For a discussion of the implementation of this Regulation, see below.

[14] *cf* s 17 of the Norwegian Child Abduction Act of 1988 which provides that 'Before reaching a decision on (...) an application for the return of a child pursuant to Section 11, the Court shall ascertain the child's views unless this is impossible having regard in particular to the child's age and degree of maturity' (brought in para 7.2 of the Norwegian Response in Replies to the Permanent Bureau's 2010 Questionnaire, www.hcch.net/index_en.php?act=publications.details&pid=5291&dtid=33) and Art 34 of the Civil Code of Québec which states that, in every application brought before it affecting the interests of a child, the court must give the child an opportunity to be heard if his or her age and power of discernment permit (brought in para 7.3 of Canadian Response in Replies to 2010 Questionnaire, ibid).

[15] OJ L 338/1-29

[16] *TB v JB (Abduction: Grave Risk of Harm)* [2001] 2 FLR 515 (Arden LJ).

[17] Chapter 6 at II Ci.

that the child's views rarely influence the outcome of the Convention proceedings is not a reason not to hear children.[18] Rather, it is important to explain to the child the limited framework of the Convention proceedings.[19]

II Methods of Ascertaining the Child's Views in Abduction Convention Cases

A Introduction

There are considerable differences between levels and mechanisms for child participation in different jurisdictions.[20] In the current context, the focus is on methods of child participation which seek to ascertain the views of the child about the legal proceedings concerning him. Four main methods of ascertaining children's views can be identified. The first is to commission a welfare officer, other social worker, psychologist or psychiatrist ('an expert') to examine the child and then report on the child's maturity and views. In some cases, the remit of the expert may be much wider and his report may include a general survey of the social background and his opinion in relation to the welfare of the child. The second is for the judge to meet with the child in person and interview him. The third is to allow the child to testify in court and the fourth is to order separate legal representation for the child. It is possible to pursue more than one of these options simultaneously. The third option is relatively rare and the fourth option, separate legal representation, will be discussed in chapter 15.[21] Thus, the present chapter will focus on the first two options.

In Continental Europe it has traditionally been common practice for judges to meet directly with children of sufficient age and understanding.[22] On the other hand, in common law jurisdictions, courts came to take the view that it was preferable to rely on the reports of experts.[23] Nonetheless, clear signs of a change in this approach can be seen in some jurisdictions in recent years. In order to illustrate the lack of uniformity in this area, Part B will survey the law and practice in relation to ascertaining children's views in Abduction Convention cases in a number of different countries.[24] Part III will then analyse critically the current law and practice in light of the principle of the child's right to participate and the findings of empirical research into child participation in legal proceedings concerning him.

---

[18] *cf* S Vigers, *Mediating International Child Abduction Cases* (Oxford, Hart Publishing, 2011) 84.
[19] See III C below.
[20] See generally, N Taylor, RT Morag, A Bajpai and A Graham, 'International Models of Child Participation in Family Law Proceedings following Parental Separation / Divorce' (2012) 20 *International Journal of Children's Rights* 645.
[21] It should be mentioned at this stage that the appointment of a separate representative does not per se make it unnecessary to use other methods to ascertain the child's views.
[22] P Parkinson and J Cashmore, *The Voice of a Child in Family Law Disputes* (Oxford, Oxford University Press, 2008) 56; this approach is reflected in Art 6 of the European Convention on the Exercise of Children's Rights, which provides for the judge to consult the child in person in appropriate cases.
[23] ibid 55.
[24] See generally responses of Contracting States to Questions 7.3–7.5 of the 2010 Questionnaire (n 14).

B Specific Jurisdictions

i England and Wales

As mentioned above, prior to the Brussels II *bis* Regulation, there was no requirement in English law for courts to ascertain the views of children and a fortiori no regulation of the method of hearing children in those cases where the court thought it appropriate to do so. Furthermore, the judges themselves refused invitations from counsel to lay down guidelines for the procedure to be adopted in ascertaining the child's views and degree of maturity.[25] In practice, it is rare for judges to meet with the child and usually a Children and Family Court Advisory and Support Service (hereinafter CAFCASS) Officer[26] will interview the child and report to the court either in writing or, if there is insufficient time, orally.[27] However, occasionally the court will give leave for the report to be written by an outside expert.[28]

Whilst following the passing of the Brussels II *bis* Regulation it is necessary to hear the child's views in far more cases,[29] this Regulation simply requires that the child is given the opportunity to be heard without specifying in what manner.[30] Furthermore, the Practice Guide specifically states that '[i]t is not necessary for the child's views to be heard at a court hearing, but they may be obtained by a competent authority according to national laws.'[31] Baroness Hale has stated that normally it should be sufficient for the child to be interviewed by a Court Welfare Officer, although there will be exceptional cases where it will be appropriate for the judge to meet with the child in person.[32]

Nonetheless, there are some indications from recent case law of a changing approach to judges directly hearing children. One reason for this seems to have been the publication of 'Guidelines for Judges Meeting Children who are subject to Family Proceedings' by the Family Justice Council with the approval of the President of the Family Division.[33] Thorpe LJ, making short shrift of counsel's arguments that these Guidelines do not apply to

---

[25] *Re S (A Minor) (Abduction: Custody Rights)* [1993] Fam 242 (Balcombe LJ); in contrast in Scotland prior to a change in the rules in 1996, it was routine practice for a child to be interviewed by both a child psychologist and a judge, see Beaumont and McEleavy (n 2) 184.

[26] It should be noted that there is no CAFCASS or similar organisation in Scotland and that where a professional assessment of the child's views is required, the parties themselves instruct experts, see Reply to the Permanent Bureau's 2006 Questionnaire, www.hcch.net/upload/wop/abd_pd02efs2006.pdf.

[27] Country Report for the United Kingdom in Country Reports, published by the National Centre for Missing and Exploited Children, http://1800victims.org/doc.asp?id=159&parentID=166, para 3.5; see also, eg *Re M* (n 11) (expressing the view that the court welfare officer can 'perform the dual roles of assessment and conveying the child's wishes to court'); *Re S* (n 25) (reporting that the first instance judge did not think it appropriate for him to see the child in person).

[28] See eg, *Re R (Child Abduction: Acquiescence)* [1995] 1 FLR 716.

[29] In the case of *Re F (A Child) (Abduction: Obligation to Hear Child)* [2007] All ER (D) 452, the Court of Appeal remitted a case back to the first instance judge because the 7-year-old girl had not been heard. The Court commented that the question of how and whether to hear the child in discharge of its obligation under Brussels II bis Regulation should be considered at the first directions appointment.

[30] Article 19 states that '[t]he hearing of the child plays an important role in the application of this Regulation, although this instrument is not intended to modify national procedures applicable.'

[31] Practice Guide for the Application of the New Brussels II Regulations (drawn up by the European Commission 2005) updated 1 June 2005, ec.europa.eu/civiljustice/divorce/parental_resp_ec_vdm_en.pdf.

[32] *Re D (A Child)* [2006] UKHL 51.

[33] 'Guidelines for Judges Meeting Children who are subject to Family Proceedings' (President of the Family Division, April 2010), www.fnf.org.uk/downloads/Guidelines_for_Judges_Meeting_Children.pdf.

Abduction Convention proceedings and have not been implemented in practice,[34] has made it clear that they reflect the recognition of the importance of engaging children directly in the legal process, where this is indicated by the facts.[35] However, it remains to be seen whether other English judges share this commitment to the right of the child to participate in proceedings concerning him.

ii Other European Countries

As stated above, some Continental legal systems have traditionally heard children directly, but there are variations between different countries. In France, where a child wishes to be heard, the judge will hear him either alone or in the presence of a lawyer or other person of the child's choice approved by the court.[36] In Germany, the child will invariably be heard personally by the judge wherever the objection defence is raised and the opinion of a child psychologist will be requested by the court in exceptional cases only.[37] In Italy, where the child objects, he may be heard by the expert sitting in the Juvenile Court or a child psychologist appointed by the Court.[38] In the Netherlands, a child over the age of 12 will always be heard by the judge and children over nine may be heard.[39] In Sweden, the child's views are usually ascertained by a social worker.[40]

iii North America

The US Reply to the 2010 Questionnaire[41] suggests that a child's views are usually conveyed to the court by mental health professionals or the guardian *ad litem*. However, the Country Report for the US also refers to judicial interviews of children and of children giving testimony and examples where these methods have been used can be found in the case law.[42] No discussion can be found in the case law as to the criteria for choosing the appropriate method in each case.

The procedure for ascertaining a child's views vary in Canada from State to State.[43] In some States, such as Manitoba and Nova Scotia, courts do not usually hear children directly and prefer the children's views to be conveyed by social services professionals,[44] but in other States such as Quebec and British Columbia, children are commonly heard by the judge.[45]

---

[34] *AJJ v JJ* [2011] EWCA Civ 1448 [38].
[35] ibid [42].
[36] Country Report for France in Country Reports (n 27), para 3.5; see also French Response to 2010 Questionnaire (n 14).
[37] Country Report for Germany in Country Reports (n 27), para 3.5; but *cf* decision of German Constitutional Court in 2 BvR 12 06/98, Bundesverfassungsgericht, 29.10.1998 [INCADAT cite HC/E/DE 233], holding that it is not necessary to hear children in Abduction Convention proceedings, unless there are special circumstances, as there were in this case.
[38] Country Report for Italy in Country Reports (n 27), para 3.5.
[39] Netherlands Response to 2010 Questionnaire (n 14).
[40] Swedish Response to 2010 Questionnaire, ibid.
[41] US Response to 2010 Questionnaire, ibid.
[42] eg *Giampaolo v Erneta* 390 F Supp 2d 1269 (ND GA 2004) (judge interviewing children in camera); *Navarro v Bullock* Calif Super Ct, Placer Cty 15 Fam L Rep 1576 (1989) (expert report and testimony of children); *Ramirez v Buyauskas*, 2012 US Dist LEXIS 24899 (child testifying in open court).
[43] For a discussion on law and practice in Ontario in relation to the judicial interview of children, see N Bala and R Birnbaum, 'Judicial Interviews with Children in Custody and Access Cases: Comparing Experiences in Ontario and Ohio' (2010) 24 *International Journal of Law Policy & the Family* 300.
[44] See Canadian Response to 2010 Questionnaire (n 14).
[45] ibid.

iv South America

In Brazil, children are usually heard by experts.[46] However, in Argentina, the court will hear the child, but his maturity will be assessed by the court's interdisciplinary team.[47]

v The Antipodes

Children are very rarely heard directly by judges in Australia.[48] Where the child's objection defence has been raised, the court will order an independent assessment of the child by a court counsellor who reports back to the court.[49]

In New Zealand, section 6 of the Care of Children Act 2004 provides:

> In proceedings involving the guardianship of, or the role of providing day-to-day care for, or contact with, a child; ... a child must be given reasonable opportunities to express views on matters affecting the child; and any views the child expresses (either directly or through a representative) must be taken into account.

A Practice Note of March 2011[50] provides that in every Abduction Convention case, the courts should consider whether section 6 applies and that it is expected that it will apply in those cases where the following defences are raised: more than a year and settled (s 106(1)(a)); grave risk of harm or intolerable situation (s 106(1)(c)); child's objections (s 106(1)(d)). Whilst neither section 6 of the 2004 Act nor the Practice Note mandate hearing the child directly, in practice judicial interviews with judges have become increasingly more common.[51]

vi Israel

As noted above, Israel has enacted a regulation providing that in Abduction Convention cases a child of sufficient age and maturity should be heard by the court unless the court does not see any need for this for special reasons which will be recorded. Nonetheless, the case law shows that whilst there are judges who do hear abducted children directly,[52] there are other judges who, preferring to rely on expert reports, invoke the exception to the

---

[46] Brazil's Response to 2010 Questionnaire (n 14).

[47] Argentina's Response to 2010 Questionnaire, ibid.

[48] R Chisholm, 'Children's Participation in Family Court Litigation' in J Dewar and S Parker (eds), *Family Law: Processes, Practices and Pressures* (Oxford, Hart Publishing, 2003); Parkinson and Cashmore, *The Voice of a Child* (n 22) 57 confirm that judicial interviews are very rare, but report on a new and vigorous debate among Australian judges as to the appropriateness of interviewing children.

[49] Country Report for Australia in Country Reports (n 27), para 3.5; Australian Response to 2010 Questionnaire (n 14).

[50] 'Practice Note: Hague Convention Cases: New Zealand Family Court Guidelines (on the appointment of lawyer for the child/counsel to assist, specialist reports and on views of the child)' (New Zealand Ministry of Justice,2011),www.justice.govt.nz/courts/family-court/practice-and-procedure/practice-notes/practice-note-hague-convention-cases-new-zealand-family-court-guidelines-on-the-appointment-of-lawyer-for-the-child-counsel-to-assist-specialist-reports-and-on-views-of-the-child.

[51] I Mill, 'Conversations with Children: A Judge's Perspective on Meeting the Patient Before Operating on the Family' (2008) 6 *New Zealand Family Law Journal* 72; Parkinson and Cashmore (n 22) 57; RM Henaghan, 'Why Judges Need to Know and Understand Childhood Studies' in M Freeman (ed), *Law and Childhood Studies, Current Legal Issues* (London, Oxford University Press, 2011) vol 14.

[52] An analysis of Abduction Convention cases heard in the years 2005, 2006 and 2007 concerning children over six years of age showed that in half the cases the children were heard directly. When cases involving children under nine were excluded, the child was heard directly in three out of four cases, R Schuz, 'The Right of the Child to Participate: Between Theory and Law in Practice in the Family Courts' (2008) 2 *Family in Law Review* 207, 251 (Hebrew).

requirement to hear the child directly. Three main reasons for not hearing a mature child[53] can be found in the case law, none of which can really be described as 'special'. Firstly, the judge may take the view that there is no need to hear the child because it is clear from the other evidence either that the exception is established[54] or, more commonly, that it is not.[55] Secondly, some judges consider that they do not have the professional tools to be able to assess the maturity of the child and the quality of his views.[56] Finally, judges sometimes state that hearing a child who is in a situation of conflict will be harmful to the child.[57]

However, the 2007 Supreme Court decision in *RB v VG*[58] refutes these reasons. Justice Arbel, citing Article 12 of the United Nations Convention on the Rights of the Child 1989 (the CRC), explained that hearing the child directly shows respect for the child as an individual and sends him the message that his views about his future are important. Where there is felt to be a need for professional tools, an expert opinion can be commissioned in addition to the direct hearing. Harm is unlikely to be caused where the child wishes to speak to the judge, but in any event advice can be sought from the expert. Thus, in this case, the majority held that the lower instance judges were wrong not to hear the child directly and ordered that the case should be remitted for the District Court to hear the child,[59] unless the psychologist who would be examining the child considered that such a meeting would be harmful to the child. An analysis of Abduction Convention cases heard after this decision shows that children are usually heard directly in cases where their views may be relevant.[60]

In 2004, the Rotlevy Committee on the Rights of the Child recommended that children be given the opportunity to be heard by the judge. In the wake of these recommendations, a scheme has been introduced which allows for children over the age of six to participate in family proceedings concerning them.[61] Under this scheme, each child is interviewed by a specialist court social worker, referred to as a 'participation social worker', who listens to the child's views about the family situation and explains to him that he has a right to meet directly with the judge deciding this case. If the child decides not to meet with the judge, then a report of the meeting with the participation social worker is made available to the judge. This report and the protocol of the meeting with the judge, where this takes place,

---

[53] In addition, a judge can decide that the child is not of an age or maturity that his views should be taken into account, eg FamAC (KS)7400/08 *Z v RNS* Nevo, 17/8/08 (girl aged seven).

[54] eg FamC (BSH) 14830/05 *PR v TAE* Nevo, 08/12/05.

[55] eg, FamA (Dist TA) 28/97 *Ploni v Plonit* Nevo, 19/04/99.

[56] eg, RFamA (SC) 672/06 *TAE v PR*, PD 61(3) 24 [INCADAT cite: HC/E/IL FamA 393/06 *Plonit v Ploni* (Unreported, 22 January 2007) [22].

[57] eg, 28/97 *Ploni* (n 55); *PR v TAE* (n 54).

[58] RFamA 5579/07 *RB v VG*, 7 August 2007, http://elyon1.court.gov.il/files/07/790/055/B03/07055790.b03.pdf

[59] A similar approach was taken by Rubenstein J in a minority opinion in the Supreme Court a few months earlier in RFamA 902/07 *Plonit v Plonim*, 26 April 2007, http://elyon1.court.gov.il/files/07/020/009/A06/07009020.a06.pdf. He thought that the case should be remitted to the District Court to hear the child directly, commenting that whilst that Court's obligation as an appeal court to hear the child was not the same as a court of first instance, in his view 'everyone who hears the child should be praised'.

[60] Out of seven reported cases involving children over nine years of age, decided between 2008 and 2011, the child was heard directly in five. In the two other cases return was refused for reasons not connected with the child (acquiescence and no breach of custody rights).

[61] The Rotlevy Committee on Children's Rights, Report of the Sub-Committee on the Child and his Family (Rotlevy Child and Family Sub-Committee), www.justice.gov.il/NR/rdonlyres/6CB85B58-07BF-496E-A073-2CC87F9C67D4/0/HayeledVeamishpaha.pdf (Hebrew); for a detailed discussion of the project, see T Morag, D Rivkin and Y Sorek, 'Child Participation in the Family Courts – Lessons from the Israeli Pilot Project' (2012) 26 *International Journal on Law Policy and the Family* 1 (a translation of the regulations governing the project is appended to the article).

are confidential and not passed to the parents or their lawyers. A pilot of the scheme ran in two family courts from 2006 to 2009 and was accompanied by research.[62]

This research indicated high levels of satisfaction by all those involved, including the children. Whilst the percentage of children who opted to meet with the judge was relatively low,[63] the conversations with the participation social worker were perceived by most of the children as very helpful. Indeed, it should be remembered that the purpose of the scheme is to give the child the right to direct hearing and not to force this upon him.[64] In light of the success of the pilot project, the participation scheme is now being implemented nationally.[65] Abduction Convention cases were excluded from the pilot stage, but they are included in the final scheme.[66] However, it is too early to ascertain what impact this scheme has on the direct hearing of children in Abduction Convention cases.

III Analysis

The brief survey above shows that children's views are usually ascertained either by commissioning an expert report or by the judge hearing the child directly in his chambers. Whilst some countries provide which method is to be used, in others it is left to the discretion of the individual judge. In this section the arguments which have been mooted in favour of and against these two methods of ascertaining the child's views will be analysed. In addition, there will be a brief discussion of the meaningfulness of the participation of children from a social science perspective, which is relevant to both methods.

It should be acknowledged at the outset that the literature relating to the methods of ascertaining children's views concerns mainly custody and access disputes and not abduction cases. However, since the issue currently under discussion is the method of ascertaining the child's views and not the scope of their relevance, the findings and views presented in this literature are prima facie equally relevant to the ascertaining of children's views within the framework of Abduction Convention cases. In the conclusion to this section, the significance of the child abduction context will be considered specifically.

A Arguments in Favour of Judges Hearing Children Directly

i The Child's Rights

As seen above, Article 12 of the CRC entrenches the child's right to participate in decision-making that affects him and provides that the child should be given the opportunity to be heard in proceedings affecting him/her 'either directly or through a representative or an

---

[62] See Morag et al, ibid.
[63] In the second stage of the pilot project, 32%, ibid.
[64] Also, even where there is no meeting with the judge, an indirect hearing by a specialist social worker whose only function is to report on the child's views is a considerable improvement on the traditional situation in custody disputes in which an expert reports on the child's views as part of a wider welfare report in which she also interviews other persons involved and is expected to give her opinion as to the best interests of the child.
[65] Morag et al, ibid.
[66] Regulation 258(33) 2 of the Civil Procedure Regulations (as amended in 2011).

appropriate body'.[67] It may be argued that this provision requires that the child be heard directly or by means of another person who will represent him in the proceedings. Since a welfare officer is an agent of the court and a professional expert is either an agent of the court or of one or both parents, they cannot be said to be a representative of the child for this purpose. Thus, indirect hearing through a welfare officer or expert would not seem to satisfy the requirements of the CRC.[68] Indeed, the Israeli Rotlevy Committee on the Rights of the Child concluded that where a child is old enough to be able to form a view about the issue in question, being heard indirectly through an expert does not fully realise the right of the child to participate.[69] Similarly, Shier regards the involvement of children in the decision-making process as a higher level of participation than simply having their views taken into account.[70]

This conclusion is consistent with the rationale behind the right to participate. True participation in decision-making involves access to the ultimate decision-maker.[71] Thus, the child is only really empowered and his right to be treated as an individual is only fully realised if he is given the opportunity to be heard directly by the judge.[72] Having his views 'translated' by an intermediary is not sufficient.[73] Indeed, it has been suggested that the use of court welfare services to ascertain children's views acts as 'a barrier towards seeing the child as an individual' and 'both actively and passively disables children'.[74] Furthermore, the tendency of some experts to place an adult construction on children's views and feelings may mean that the report does not accurately reflect the child's perception of the situation and thus effectively the child is denied a voice.[75]

In addition, hearing the child directly shows respect for the child as an individual and sends him the message that his views about his future are important and that he is not simply a chattel to be shuttled around by his parents.[76] Raitt suggests that the fact that a judge is willing to see the child conveys affirmation.[77] Similarly, the view which sees the child as a

---

[67] E Shochetman, 'Consideration of the Wishes of a Minor in Child Custody Cases' (2005) 4 *Netantya Academic College Law Review* 545, 568 (Hebrew) argues that the general constitutional right of a person to be heard in relation to issues concerning him applies also to a minor who is old enough to express his views.

[68] General Comment No 12 (July 2009) – The right of the child to be heard, drawn up by the Committee on the Rights of the Child, http://www2.ohchr.org/english/bodies/crc/comments.htm, recommends that children are given the opportunity to be heard directly (para 35) and emphasises that the representative must represent only the child (para 37); M Freeman and AM Hutchinson, 'Abduction and the Voice of the Child: Re M and After' (2008) (September issue) *International Family Law* 163, suggest that 'reporting a child's views, which is an inherently subjective exercise, may not be sufficient to allow the child to be heard, both in terms of the Brussels II bis Regulations as well as the wider human rights obligations'.

[69] Rotlevy Child and Family Sub-Committee (n 61) 93–94.

[70] H Shier, 'Pathways to Participation: Openings, Opportunities and Obligations' (2001) 15 *Children and Society* 107.

[71] F Raitt, 'Hearing Children in Family Law Proceedings: Can Judges Make a Difference?' (2007) 19 *Child and Family Law Quarterly* 204.

[72] C Piper, 'Barriers to Seeing and Hearing Children in Private Law Proceeding' (1999) 26 *Family Law* 394 comments that otherwise there is a danger of 'real children being invisible'.

[73] Per Justice M Cohen in the Israeli case FamA 3140/01 *AB v Almoni* Nevo, 13 June 2001 (Isr); See also the comment of Ryder J in *Re C (Abduction: Separate Representation of Children)* [2008] EWHC 517 (Fam) [44], 'However expert any CAFCASS officer may be in obtaining a child's views, much will depend on the way that that officer elicits those views i.e. what questions he asks and how he interprets the answers. . . . The process of reporting does not allow a child to engage in the proceedings.'

[74] AL James, A James and S McNamee, 'Turn Down the Volume? Not Hearing Children in Family Proceedings' (2004) 16 *Child and Family Law Quarterly* 189.

[75] J Fortin, *Children's Rights and the Developing Law*, 3rd edn (Cambridge, Cambridge University Press, 2009) 255.

[76] per Justice Arbel in Israeli Supreme Court decision in *RB v VG* (n 58).

[77] Raitt, 'Hearing Children' (n 71).

social actor[78] requires that his experiences are understood on his own terms. This can only be achieved if his voice can be heard, 'untrammelled by professional discretion or interpretation'.[79]

An additional argument in favour of direct hearing is that if the child's conversation with the judge is treated as confidential, he will not feel constrained in expressing his true feelings by being concerned about the reaction of his parents. Whilst under the Israeli scheme, discussed above, the parents and their lawyers are not present at the hearing and do not have access to the protocol of the conversation, this approach is not universal.[80] For example, in England and Wales, in the few cases where the child is heard directly, the parents' lawyers will be present and take notes.[81]

ii To Inform Judicial Decision-Making

The judge will be in a better position to make an informed decision about the child's views when he can form an impression of the child. He may gain insights from a face to face meeting which could not be gleaned from reading a written report.[82] In particular, hearing the child express his views and respond to questions can give the judge a better appreciation of the child as a person and the strength with which those views are held.[83]

In addition, it should be remembered that behavioural sciences are not exact sciences in which a result or a theory can be proven to be correct or not. Thus an expert's report will inevitably be coloured inter alia by whether he supports a particular psychological or other theory (such as Parental Alienation Syndrome (PAS) theory)[84] or by his subjective views as to the ability of children to make decisions and as to the importance of returning abducted children. It is well known that different experts will take different views and it is wrong that the fate of the child should depend on which expert is appointed.

Whilst it is true that different judges may come to different conclusions, this is an inevitable consequence of the legislature's decision to confer discretion on the judge. Accordingly, the judge has to exercise the discretion himself and he should not abdicate his responsibility to ascertain the views of the child and determine whether they should be taken into account by substituting the assessment of experts for his own. Thus, even if there is an expert report, he should analyse it critically and not simply rubber stamp the conclusions. The only way in which the judge can analyse the report effectively is by seeing the children himself and checking whether his impressions are consistent with those of the expert.[85]

---

[78] MA Murch and NV Lowe, 'Children's Participation in the Family Justice System – Translating Principles into Practice' (2001) 13 *Child and Family Law Quarterly* 137, 145–46.
[79] I Butler and H Williamson, *Children Speak: Children, Trauma and Social Work* (Longman, 1994), cited in Murch and Lowe ibid.
[80] Although in Continental systems, the child also seems to be heard without the presence of the parties. See II Bii above.
[81] eg *JPC v SMW* [2007] EWHC 1349 (Fam) [47].
[82] Per Justice Arbel in *RB v VG* (n 58).
[83] ibid; see also P Boshier, 'Contact and Relocation: Focusing on Children – Involving Children in Decision Making: Lessons from New Zealand' (New Zealand Ministry of Justice, 2006), www.justice.govt.nz/courts/family-court/publications/speeches-and-papers/contact-and-relocation.
[84] See chapter 3 at II F.
[85] R Nanos, 'The Views of a Child: Emerging Interpretation and Significance of the Child's Objection Defense under the Hague Child Abduction Convention' (1996) 22 *Brooklyn Journal of International Law* 437, 463 also takes the view that in addition to the expert report the court should conduct an independent inquiry through an *in camera* hearing.

Two recent English cases illustrate how a meeting with the child can be critical to the outcome of a case. In the case of *Re G*,[86] after hearing the 13-year-old girl, the Court of Appeal held that the child objection defence was established and thus set aside the return order. Thorpe LJ commented that if the first instance judge had had the advantage of meeting with the girl he might well have refused return. In the later case of *AJJ v JJ*,[87] after meeting with the children (aged 15, 13 and 10), the Court of Appeal gave permission for the children to be separately represented so that their case could be independently presented to the Court.

iii Benefits to the Child

Research suggests that the child's experience of being heard could well be as important, if not more important, than the final outcome [88] and that children find it easier to come to terms with what they see as an unfavourable outcome if they feel that their voice has been heard.[89] Where the child is heard directly by the judge, he is more likely to feel that his wishes are being taken seriously[90] than when his views are conveyed by a third party.[91]

One of the few published empirical studies in relation to child abduction also suggests that children's lack of involvement may cause them to lose faith in the adult world. One previously abducted young person reported that the 'major stress' was not moving countries, but the fact that decisions were made without taking children seriously or giving sufficient weight to their views.[92]

In addition, Thorpe LJ commented that it may well be of benefit to the child if the judge who has heard the child also communicates the return decision to the child, in cases where the child has objected. In his view, the impartiality and authority of the judge may help the child to accept the decision.[93]

---

[86] *G (Children)* [2010] EWCA Civ 1232.
[87] *AJJ v JJ* (n 34).
[88] Raitt, 'Hearing Children' (n 71) 209, and sources cited there at 214–15, where she refers to children who were hurt or felt excluded when they were not given the opportunity to be heard; see also F Raitt, 'Judicial Discretion and Methods of Ascertaining the Views of a Child' (2004) 16 *Child and Family Law Quarterly* 151.
[89] Raitt, 'Hearing Children' ibid; Y Ronen, *The Child's Participation in the Determination of his Custody* (Tel Aviv, Boursey, 1997) (Hebrew) 70–73.
[90] Justice Porat in FamA (Dist TA) 33/96 *Ploni v Plonit*, Nevo 31 December 1996 (Isr) explained, 'It is important to know that a conversation with the child is required not only in order to clarify his opinion. It is important for children, like adults, to know what is happening around them when their fate is being decided.... It is important for the child to participate in the process being conducted in relation to him and to be aware of it, even if someone else is making the decision' (author's translation).
[91] Studies show that some children lack confidence that professionals who interview them were really paying attention to them, Raitt, 'Hearing Children' (n 71) 217; in JE Timms, S Bailey and J Thoburn, 'Your Shout Too! A Survey of the Views of Children and Young People Involved in Court Proceedings when their Parents Divorce or Separate, www.nspcc.org.uk/inform/research/findings/yourshouttoo_wda49588.html, 40% of the children who were not heard directly, said that they would have liked to have had the opportunity to talk to the judge; Some surveys also reported children's frustration when their words were reinterpreted by welfare officers, Fortin (n 75) 216.
[92] M Freeman, 'International Child Abduction the Effects' (Reunite Research Centre, May 2006), www.reunite.org/edit/files/Library%20-%20reunite%20Publications/Effects%20Of%20Abduction%20Report.pdf
[93] *AJJ v JJ* (n 34) [42] and [46]; See also comment of Potter P that it was important to convey to the child the nature of his task under the Abduction Convention, which led him to the conclusion that it was necessary to order return, despite her objections. *JPC v SMW* (n 81) [47].

B Arguments against Judges Hearing Children Directly

i Professional Skill and Experience

It has been claimed by judges themselves that experts are more skilled and experienced in talking to children than judges[94] and that judges do not have the tools to ascertain the genuineness and independence of child's views. For example, Justice Procaccia in the Israeli Supreme Court commented that it was doubtful if any benefit would result from the court meeting with the children since ascertaining their genuine views was extremely difficult in light of the pressure and influence to which they were subject from the father's extended family.[95] Thus, identifying the child's real wishes, as opposed to the external verbal expression of them, should be left to experts who had reliable professional tools at their disposal.[96]

Whilst there is clearly some force in this argument,[97] the situation could be remedied to a considerable extent by providing appropriate training for family court judges.[98] Furthermore, there are also reasons why experts, despite their skill and experience, may not be able to ascertain the relevant information and present it to the court accurately. In particular, experts may have difficulty in separating the issue of the child's views from that of his welfare, since they are used to giving reports about the welfare of the child for the purposes of custody disputes. Thus, they may fail to convey accurately the child's views and the reasons advanced for them and are liable to put their own gloss on what the child wants in light of the overall view which they take of the child's needs.[99] It has also been suggested that they tend to 'stifle' and 'filter out' the child's voice.[100] In particular, since their reports will be seen by the parents, they may edit out comments which are critical of the parents in order to protect the children from parental reactions.[101]

Moreover, experts may have more difficulty in assessing the situation objectively than judges, the essence of whose work is to be objective. In particular, as stated above, behavioural sciences are not objective and thus experts are liable to be influenced by the theories which they prefer. Experience in Israel provides support for concerns about the objectivity of experts' reports. For example, in one case the psychiatrist did not limit her report to the issue of the children's maturity and their objections, but expressed her opinion that it was in the children's best interests to return to their mother in Italy.[102] Furthermore, whilst she accepted that the 12 and 10-year-old children were mature for their age, she expressed the belief that no weight should be given to the views of a child under 15 in relation to his place of residence. Thus, in her view, the children's judgment in relation to the long-term was

---

[94] Per Baroness Hale in *Re D (A Child)* (n 32).
[95] *TAE v PR* (n 56) [24].
[96] ibid.
[97] Fortin (n 75) 283; *cf* Murch and Lowe, 'Children's Participation' (n 78) 33, who suggest that judges' assumption that court welfare officers have the necessary skills and understanding to provide support for and listen properly to children is mistaken.
[98] Fortin, ibid; Rotlevy Child and Family Sub Committee (n 61).
[99] Fortin, ibid 216; Rotlevy Child and Family Sub Committee, ibid 94.
[100] Raitt, 'Hearing Children' (n 71) 204; C Smart, B Neale and A Wade, *The Changing Experience of Childhood: Families and Divorce* (Oxford, Polity Press, 2001) 163 refer to the Court Welfare Officer's selective use of what is said by the child.
[101] See James et al (n 74); in contrast where the judge hears the child directly he can take into account the child's views, although he faces the problem of how to protect the child's confidence and yet give a transparent judgment (see Raitt 'Hearing Children' (n 71) 220–23 who reports some creative solutions adopted by the judges she interviewed).
[102] *PR v TAE* (n 54).

defective and partial because they were children. The first instance judge disregarded this aspect of her report, commenting that it evidenced the expert's view of a universal truth rather than her assessment of the minors in the concrete case before the Court.[103] Thus, he upheld the children's objections. However, on appeal, the District Court and later the Supreme Court relied on the expert's views and held that the requirement of maturity in Article 13(2) was not proven in this case.[104] It seems clear that an expert with a different worldview would have found that the children were sufficiently mature and that the Court would have adopted such a conclusion.

Thus, it is difficult to agree with the conclusion of Justice Rubenstein in the Supreme Court in this case[105] that the children's position had been adequately brought to the notice of the Court. With respect, how could an expert who did not accept the authenticity of the girl's views and thought that children of their age did not have sufficient insight to make such decisions possibly convey accurately the children's views to the Court? In particular, the court record of the expert's evidence does not even refer to the reasons given by the children for their objections.

Of course, measures can be taken to reduce the deficiencies of expert reports illustrated above. Thus, experts who are trained properly, given clear instructions and have wide experience in abduction cases are less likely to fall into these traps.[106]

ii Harm to the Child

As seen above, some Israeli judges have claimed that requiring a child to choose between his parents will cause him conflict and emotional turmoil which is likely to result in psychological harm.[107] For example, in one case, the Supreme Court took the view that the damage which would be caused by the judge meeting the children was liable to be greater than any potential benefit therefrom.[108]

While clearly the risk of harm cannot be ignored, it should not be overestimated. Is a conversation with an appropriately trained judge conducted in an informal manner really likely to be more harmful than being interviewed by a Welfare Officer or other expert? In particular, it must be remembered that the question is not which parent the child prefers,[109] but what are his views about being returned to the country of habitual residence pending the resolution of the custody dispute. Thus, arguably the risks of hearing the child in such a case are less than in other cases where the views of the parents are mutually exclusive, such as in relocation cases.[110] Furthermore, the pressure placed on children can be substantially reduced if it is made clear to them that their views are not decisive.[111]

---

[103] ibid.
[104] *TAE v PR* (n 56).
[105] ibid.
[106] In *Re D (A Child)* (n 32), Baroness Hale points out that the CAFCASS officers who practice in the English High Court are not only skilled and experienced in talking with children, but also understand the scope of the relevance of the children's views in Hague cases.
[107] Raitt, 'Hearing Children' (n 71) 213, suggests that this view is common among child welfare professionals. Indeed, this concern may lead to reluctance among welfare officers to ascertain the child's wishes, Piper, 'Barriers to Seeing' (n 72).
[108] *TAE v PR* (n 56).
[109] Perez-Vera Report, Proceedings of the 14th Session of the Hague Conference Oct 1980, www.hcch.net/upload/expl28.pdf
[110] Parkinson and Cashmore (n 22) 209.
[111] Ronen (n 89) 153: See also comment of Justice Porat in 33/96 *Ploni v Plonit* (n 90) that The child should not be empowered by transferring to him the power of determination, 'The determination is in the hands of the court

In addition, the 'harm' argument ignores the possible benefits, mentioned above, which might accrue from the child meeting with the judge and the harm which might be done to him where he wishes to be heard directly, but is refused the opportunity to speak to the judge. Moreover, in a case where there is concern that meeting the judge might cause harm, then it is possible for the court to request an expert opinion on this point before the meeting.[112] The dangers with this solution are that child welfare professionals tend to take a paternalistic view about the need to safeguard children from the burden of the responsibility of being involved in decision-making[113] and they have an interest in retaining a monopoly on examining children's views.

C Making Participation Meaningful

It has been argued that in order to make children's participation meaningful, they should receive appropriate support and guidance within a social context which is capable of communicating information effectively to them.[114] In particular, often children have gleaned partial information or even disinformation from the adults around them. It has even been suggested that it is unethical to give children an opportunity to express their views without providing them with relevant information about the legal process, the role they are being offered and the consequences of the views they express.[115] Accordingly, in the Abduction Convention scenario, children need to understand the summary nature of the proceedings and that a return order is not a final determination of custody rights and other living arrangements. Thus, it is critical that accurate information is conveyed to children in a manner appropriate to their stage of development and that they are able to discuss the implications of this information with an appropriate adult before formulating and expressing their views.

The optimal mechanism for this purpose is the appointment of a separate representative,[116] who in the course of an ongoing relationship with the child can ensure that he is properly informed, listen to the child's concerns and generally provide support before the child expresses his views to the judge directly or via the separate representative. Alternatively, an appropriately trained social worker should meet with the child and provide him with relevant information before he expresses his views either to the judge or indirectly to that social worker. The main drawback with this method is that the social worker will usually not be familiar with the details of the case in the same way that the separate representative would be. Accordingly, it may be that the judge himself[117] should be trained to perform the

and it should be made clear to the child that his right is to express his views and to have his views heard, but the power and jurisdiction to decide do not belong to him. Furthermore, he is not responsible for the decision and it is not his function to determine the dispute between his parents. This clarification can be made to the child by the court and it is important that this be done.' (author's translation); See also comments of judges interviewed by Raitt, 'Hearing Children' (n 71) 214, who talked about avoiding putting the child under pressure to state a clear preference.

[112] Per Justice Arbel in *RB v VG* (n 58).
[113] Raitt, 'Hearing Children' (n 71) 213.
[114] AB Smith, 'Interpreting and Supporting Participation Rights: Contributions from Sociocultural Theory' (2002) 10 *International Journal of Children Rights* 73, 75; General Comment No 12 (July 2009) – The right of the child to be heard, drawn up by the Committee on the Rights of the Child, http://www2.ohchr.org/english/bodies/crc/comments.htm, [41].
[115] Taylor et al, 'International Models' (n 20) 74.
[116] See generally ch 15 below.
[117] Smith, 'Interpreting and Supporting' (n 114) 85.

role of providing information to the child before hearing his views. The difficulty with this is that the child needs time to digest and process the information and thus it would seem necessary for the judge to meet the child more than once. In addition, the child may not feel comfortable enough to ask the judge questions.

IV Conclusions

The arguments presented above point to the need to ascertain the views of every abducted child who is old enough to express his views and to the importance of providing such children with the opportunity to express their views directly to the judge hearing the case, where they wish to do so. However, it may be claimed that some of these arguments are not relevant in the child abduction context because the proceedings are of a summary nature and designed only to be 'first aid' in order to restore the *status quo ante*. Thus, it may be thought to be sufficient that the child's voice will be heard by the court which decides the substantive custody dispute. This argument is misconceived for three main reasons.

Firstly, the summary nature of the proceedings does not change the fact that the decision as to whether to return the child has very significant, sometimes irreversible, consequences for the child and is clearly a decision relating to him within the meaning of Article 12 of the CRC. Returning him without at least considering his wishes is to treat him like a chattel who can be moved around at will by adults. Secondly, in some cases there will not be a later substantive hearing.[118] Where the child is returned to the country of habitual residence there are many reasons, including financial ones, why the abducting parent will not contest custody in that country. Thus, the Hague Convention proceedings may be the only opportunity for the child's voice to be heard.[119] Whilst these facts cannot and should not change the nature of the proceedings, it does mean that the court in the abduction proceedings has a responsibility to ensure that the child is heard and cannot safely assume that those rights will be realised later by the court in the country of habitual residence.[120] Thirdly, it should be reiterated that involving the child directly in the legal process is an independent right, without any connection to the question of whether the court accepts his views and what weight the court attaches to the wishes expressed by the minor. Thus, even if the weight to be attached to the minor's views in abduction proceedings is limited and less than that attached to his views in other types of proceedings, this does not provide justification for not giving effect to his right to be heard.

---

[118] See M Freeman, 'The Hague Child Abduction Convention – An Uneven Playing Field Part 1: The Voice of the Child in Hague Convention Proceedings' in M Freeman, *Occasional Papers on the 1980 Hague Child Abduction Convention, International Child Abduction and Related Issues* (Reunite International Child Abduction Centre, 2002).

[119] It has also been pointed out that in EU cases where the child is not returned and a substantive hearing then takes place in the requesting State under Brussels II bis Art 11(6)-(8) (see ch 1 at II B), there may be difficulties in ensuring that the child is actually heard in those proceedings. However, it has been held that it is sufficient if the child is given a genuine opportunity to be heard, see Case C-491/10 PPU Zarraga, nyr 22 December 2010, discussed in R Lamont, 'Free Movement of Persons, Child Abduction and Relocation within the European Union' (2012) 34 *Journal of Social Welfare and Family Law* 231, 237, dx.doi.org/10.1080/09649069.2012.718537.

[120] Nanos, 'The Views of a Child' (n 85) explains that in some countries children are not given the opportunity to express their wishes in custody disputes.

On the contrary, it is submitted that the advantages of direct hearing apply equally, and perhaps more so, to Abduction Convention cases for a number of reasons. Firstly, unlike in the custody context, the child's wishes are not being ascertained as part of a welfare investigation. Thus, the tendency of child welfare professionals to examine the child's views as part of his welfare[121] is more problematic in the abduction context. Secondly, the serious and often fateful consequences of returning a child to another country against his will make it even more important that he is given a proper opportunity to express his views and feel that his voice has been heard. Thirdly, the child is likely to find it easier to accept the return order if the judge explains to him the limited nature of his discretion under the Convention and the rationale behind mandatory return. Finally, as Thorpe LJ has pointed out, in cases where an adolescent is likely to resist enforcement of the order, a direct meeting will enable the judge to assess the practicalities of the situation and so avoid dramatic scenes on the day of return.[122]

The next chapter will discuss the importance of separate representation. Whilst the provision of such representation may reduce the need for the child to be heard directly by the judge, such a hearing will usually still be desirable. In particular, there will still be an advantage to the judge from gaining a first-hand impression of the child and the child will benefit from participating directly in the legal process, where he wishes to do so. Furthermore, there may be cases where the child is not confident that his representative will indeed present his position fully and accurately. Thus, even a separately represented child should usually be given an opportunity to meet with the judge.

---

[121] See eg the report of the psychiatrist in *PR v TAE* (n 54).
[122] *AJJ v JJ* (n 34) [40].

15

Status of the Child in Abduction Convention Proceedings

I Introduction

In this chapter, two related issues concerning the child's participation in Abduction Convention (Hague Convention on the Civil Aspects of International Child Abduction) proceedings will be examined. The first question relates to the status of the child in proceedings brought for his return[1] by the left-behind parent and in particular, whether and in what circumstances he should be provided with separate legal representation, independent of that of his parents. The second question concerns the possibility of an abducted child applying for a return order under the Convention when the left-behind parent has not done so. In most cases, whilst the child is the focus of the proceedings, he is not a party to them.

In most jurisdictions, courts have the power to order separate representation of the abducted child in proceedings under the Hague Convention,[2] which has the effect of making the child a party to the case either formally or de facto.[3] To the best of the author's knowledge, the only countries which mandate the separate representation of children in Hague Abduction cases are Switzerland and South Africa.[4] Under Article 9(3) of the Swiss Federal Act on International Child Abduction of 2007,[5] it is compulsory for the court to appoint a representative for the child, with the requisite professional skills, as soon as it

---

[1] In some English cases, a sibling or half-sibling of the child whose return is being sought has applied to be joined as a party to the Abduction Convention proceedings so that he can express his views. In *S v B (Abduction: Human Rights)* [2005] 2 FLR 878, the 13 year older half-sibling was joined under Rule 6.5 of the Family Proceedings Rules (FPR) 1991 No 1247 (L 20) on the basis that his position was analogous to a child who was subject to a Convention application. In the later case of *W v W* [2009] EWHC 3288 (Fam), the 17-year-old sister was joined under Rule 6.5 of the FPR 1991 ibid on the basis that she was a person who had 'a sufficient interest in the welfare of the child'.

[2] See E Pitman, 'Making the Interests of the Child Paramount: Representation For Children in the Hague Convention on the Civil Aspects of International Child Abduction' (2009) 17 *Cardozo Public Law, Policy & Ethics Journal* 515, 527–28; for a list (albeit outdated) of statutory provisions in the US under which separate representation might be ordered, see T Eitzen, 'A Child's Right to Independent Legal Representation in a Custody Dispute' (1985) 19 *Family Law Quarterly* 53, 73–77. The Conclusions and Recommendations of the First Part of the Sixth Special Commission 2011, www.hcch.net/upload/wop/concl28sc6_e.pdf, para 51 note that an increasing number of States provide for the possibility of separate legal representation of a child in abduction cases.

[3] In some jurisdictions, such as the UK, party status is officially accorded to the child. In other jurisdictions, such as Israel, there is no formal granting of party status, but in practice the child's guardian ad litem will be able to raise issues and address the court in the same way as the parties themselves.

[4] Although in France, it seems that a children's lawyer is appointed wherever the child is old enough to have his wishes taken into account, AM Hutchinson and H Setright, *International Parental Child Abduction* (Bristol, Jordan, 1988) 148.

[5] A translation can be found in A Bucher, 'The New Swiss Federal Act on International Child Abduction' (2008) 4 *Journal of Private International Law* 139, 161–65.

receives an application for return.[6] Section 279 of the South African Children's Act 38 of 2005 provides for the legal representation of children in all Abduction Convention cases.[7]

In other jurisdictions, the extent to which courts do order separate representation in Abduction Convention cases is variable. In England and Wales, the policy under which this discretion[8] was used only in exceptional cases[9] has been relaxed somewhat in recent years. The current position would seem to be reflected in Baroness Hale's opinion in the case of *Re M (Abduction: Zimbabwe)*.[10] In this case she stated that separate representation should become routine in the small number of cases where the settlement defence in Article 12(2) is raised because the separate point of view of the child is particularly important in such cases. In all other cases, the question for the judge is 'whether separate representation of the child will add enough to the court's understanding of the issues that arise under the Hague Convention to justify the intrusion, the expense and the delay that may result'.[11] Following this decision, the lower courts do seem to have been more willing to order separate representation in abduction cases.[12]

In New Zealand,[13] separate representation seems to have been ordered relatively frequently in abduction cases.[14] However, in 2007, the New Zealand Court of Appeal held that there was a need for a more liberal approach to separate representation in abduction cases in line with the approach in other types of cases[15] and in March 2011 Principal Family Court Judge Boshier issued a Practice Note on the appointment of a lawyer for the child in abduction convention cases.[16] This provides that the appointment of a legal representative

---

[6] ibid.

[7] The section is subject to s 55, which provides that where a child, involved in a matter before the children's court is not represented by a legal representative, and the court is of the opinion that it would be in the best interests of the child to have legal representation, the court must refer the matter to the Legal Aid Board referred to in s 3 of the Legal Aid Act 22 of 1969.

[8] FPR 1991, Rule 6.5 (n 1) now updated by the Family Proceeding Rules 2010 No 2955 (L17) Rule 16.2.

[9] The exceptional circumstances test can be traced back to the decision of the Court of Appeal in *S v S (Child Abduction) (Child's Views)* [1992] 2 FLR 492; Thorpe LJ commented in *Re H (A Child: Child Abduction)* [2006] EWCA Civ 1247 that separate representation had only been ordered in cases where 'there was something close to a public law dimension', and expressed the opinion that the test should be applied even more stringently.

[10] *Re M (Abduction: Zimbabwe)* [2007] UKHL 55.

[11] ibid [57]. This seems to update the test her Ladyship set out in the earlier case of *Re D (A Child)* [2006] UKHL 51 that 'whenever it seems likely that the child's views and interests may not be properly presented to the court, and in particular where there are legal arguments which the adult parties are not putting forward, then the child should be separately represented'.

[12] See M Freeman and AM Hutchinson, 'Half Price for Children? The Voice of the Child and the Child's Fight for Party Status in Cases on International Child Abduction' (2007) 29 *International Family Law* 177; for example, *JPC v SMW* [2007] EWHC 1349 (Fam); *Re C (Abduction: Separate Representation of Children)* [2008] EWHC 517 (Fam); *F v M* [2008] EWHC 1525 (Fam); *De L v H* [2009] EWHC 3074 (Fam); *In The Matter of M (A Child)* [2010] EWCA 178; but cf *Re F (Abduction: Removal Outside Jurisdiction)* [2008] EWCA Civ 842; *AJ v JJ* [2011] EWCA Civ 1448.

[13] Statutory provision under which separate representation is ordered for the child in nearly every disputed residence or contact case, Care of Children Act 2004 s 7(2) does not apply to cases under the Abduction Convention.

[14] Hutchinson and Setright (n 4) 95 claim that separate representation is always ordered where the child objects. Examples of cases where separate representation was ordered are *Clarke v Carson* [1996] 1 NZFLR 349; *B v C* [2002] NZFLR 433.

[15] *B v Secretary for Justice* [2007] 3 NZLR 447; However, in *ST v MW* (HC 7/10/2008 CIV 2008-404-4916), the High Court rejected the claim that separate representation should have been ordered for the five-year-old child, pointing out that it was not a universal practice in Abduction Convention cases (see New Zealand Response in Replies to the Permanent Bureau's 2010 Questionnaire, www.hcch.net/index_en.php?act=publications.details&pid=5291&dtid=33, para 1.2.

[16] www.justice.govt.nz/courts/family-court/practice-and-procedure/practice-notes/practice-note-hague-convention-cases-new-zealand-family-court-guidelines-on-the-appointment-of-lawyer-for-the-child-counsel-to-assist-specialist-reports-and-on-views-of-the-child.

for the child should be considered wherever any of the defences to mandatory return is pleaded, unless the court is satisfied that this would serve no useful purpose.

In Australia, judges started ordering separate representation on a regular basis[17] but then the legislature intervened and limited its use to exceptional circumstances only.[18] In the US, federal legislation mandates separate representation where this is necessary for the child's protection,[19] but in practice courts do not order separate representation on a regular basis.[20]

In order to determine to what extent it is appropriate for separate representation to be ordered routinely, or at least more widely, in Abduction Convention cases, it is first necessary to consider the theoretical basis for and the scope of the child's right to separate representation (Part II). The arguments against and in favour of ordering separate representation in Abduction Convention proceedings will then be presented (Part III). The possibility of a child applying for a return order under the Convention will be considered in Part IV and finally Part V will set out conclusions.

II The Child's Right to Separate Representation

A The Source of the Right

Article 12(2) of the United Nations Convention on the Rights of the Child (CRC) recognises the possibility that a child may be represented but does not appear to confer on him any right to separate representation.[21] Whilst the right to be represented in legal proceedings to which one is a party or which have a direct effect on one's life is universally recognised as a basic human right. In the case of children this right was traditionally realised through the parents who would represent the child, usually by means of a lawyer instructed by them. However, the growing acceptance of the fact that children have rights independent of their parents,[22] together with the acknowledgment of the fact that parents may not be able to represent their children's interests adequately[23] have led to an increasing recognition that

---

[17] See KM Bowie, 'International Application and Interpretation of the Convention on the Civil Aspects of International Child Abduction' (March 2001) 23–24, www.Familycourt.gov.au/wps/wcm/resources/file/eba9d-849d350cf0/bowie.pdf.

[18] Section 68L(3) of The Family Law Act 1975 (as amended) provides that a separate representative for the child can only be appointed in 'exceptional circumstances'. This 2000 amendment, which was designed to minimise potential delay, was vehemently opposed by a number of family lawyers and judges, Bowie ibid. See also comment of Bennett J in *State Central Authority & Best (No 2)* [2012] FamCA 511 that there exists 'a tension between the "exceptional circumstances" threshold in s 68L(3) and our national responsibilities under UNCRC as well as to conformity with the practice of other contracting states to the 1980 Convention in relation to a requirement to hear children, directly or indirectly, or permit their interests to be represented.'

[19] The Federal Rules of Civil Procedure provide that 'The court shall appoint a guardian ad litem for an infant or incompetent person not otherwise represented in an action or shall make such other order as it deems proper for the protection of the infant or incompetent person', Federal Rules of Civil Procedure 17(c).

[20] Pitman 'Making the Interests' (n 2).

[21] The UN Children's Rights Committee takes the view that a separate representative should be appointed wherever there is a conflict of interests between him and his parents. R Hodgkin and P Newell, *UNICEF Implementation Handbook for the Convention on the Rights of the Child*, Fully Revised, 3rd edn (Geneva, UNICEF, 2007) 150–51.

[22] J Fortin, 'Children's Representation through the Looking Glass' (2007) 37 *Family Law* 500, 503.

[23] In the US, this has been phrased in constitutional terms, viz that the child is not afforded due process when he is represented by his parents or by the State. See Eitzen, 'A Child's Right' (n 2) 61–62; see also General Comment No 12 (July 2009) – The right of the child to be heard, drawn up by the Committee on the Rights of the Child, http://www2.ohchr.org/english/bodies/crc/comments.htm, para 36.

children have a right to be independently represented in certain situations.[24] Furthermore, the State has an obligation to provide such representation in the same way that it has an obligation to meet the other needs of the children that are not met by their parents, in order to prevent real damage being caused to children's needs and interests.

It is important to point out that whilst separate representation is one method of enabling the child to participate in legal proceedings,[25] the right to separate representation is wider than the right of the child to participate. Thus, separate representation is not only a method of enabling the child's voice to be heard, but is a method of ensuring that the child's case is presented to the court in a persuasive and professional manner. It should also be understood that hearing the child indirectly or directly does not per se satisfy his right to representation because it does not allow him to engage in the proceedings[26] and does not provide him with an opportunity to have his position put forward in an equal manner to the others involved in the case (invariably his parents) who are usually represented by professional lawyers.[27]

It has also been argued that not providing independent representation to children involved in private law disputes might be a violation of their rights under the European Convention on Human Rights (ECHR). Since the result of their parents' dispute will affect the children's family life, their procedural rights guaranteed by Article 8 would be infringed if they are not provided with an opportunity to influence the outcome directly.[28] Similarly, it could be contended that their right to a fair trial under Article 6, which includes the right to participate effectively in proceedings concerning them, would be breached.[29]

B The Scope of the Right

The report of an official Israeli Committee on the subject of separate representation[30] identifies six main reasons why a minor needs to be properly represented in proceedings concerning him. Firstly, proper representation helps to ensure that the child is seen as a separate individual and not simply as an attachment to his parents or the State. Secondly, proper representation facilitates a child-centred approach to decision making concerning children. Thirdly, proper representation is necessary in order to ensure due process and access to justice for the child. Fourthly, representation facilitates participation by the child. Fifthly, representation helps the court to make the best decisions for children. In particular, in adversarial systems where the judge is dependent on the information submitted to

---

[24] Eitzen ibid, 64–66.
[25] Although separate representation per se does not always give effect to the child's right to participate. See ch 14 at IV and the discussion in relation to the role of the child's representative at Bii below.
[26] See per Ryder J in *Re C* (n 12) [44]; J Fortin, *Children's Rights and the Developing Law*, 3rd edn (Cambridge, Cambridge University Press, 2009) 264.
[27] The child's representative may decide to pursue different arguments from the lawyer representing the abducting parent. For example, in the case of *De Lewinski and Legal aid Commission of New South Wales v Director General, New South Wales Department of Community Services* (1997) FLC 92-737, the child's representative appealed against the trial judge's finding that grave risk of harm had not been established, whilst the mother's lawyer did not appeal on this ground ([10]).
[28] Fortin, *Children's Rights* (n 26) 238–39.
[29] ibid.
[30] The Rotlevy Committee on Children's Rights, Report of the Sub-Committee on Separate Representation, www.justice.gov.il/NR/rdonlyres/72BC55E2-D418-483D-BAC6-C614D1A606CA/0/DOCHITZUG.pdf (Hebrew), 48–52 (Rotlevy Representation Sub-Committee).

him by the parties, lack of proper representation for the child may mean that critical facts and arguments concerning the child's interests may not be presented to the court. Sixthly, proper representation can help children to cope with the difficulties of being involved in legal proceedings. Family crises are usually a time of uncertainty and bewilderment for children. They need access to an understanding adult who can provide them with appropriate information and explanation about the legal proceedings, together with a sympathetic ear.

From this list, it can be seen that whilst there will be situations in which parents may indeed be able to represent their child in a way which promotes the child's interests in all these ways, there will be a significant number of situations in which the parents will not be able to do so. In particular, even responsible parents who are usually able to identify and take into account their child's interests separately from their own interests and to give him emotional support in times of difficulty, may well not be able to do so when they themselves are going through the trauma of marital breakdown. Furthermore, the very fact that there is a dispute between the parents makes it difficult for them to view the importance of the child's relationship with the other parent objectively. Whilst it might be argued that the subjectivity of the two parents will cancel each other out, this is not the appropriate way to promote the interests of the child. In addition, in some cases, there will be clearer conflicts of interests, where, for example, the parent can gain advantages in the financial agreement by agreeing to arrangements in relation to the child, which may not be in his best interests.

The main dilemmas faced by courts and policymakers concern the identification of those cases in which there is a need for separate representation and the role of the representative. Two of these will be addressed.

i When is Separate Representation Necessary?

Two main models can be found for identifying cases in which separate representation is required. Under the narrow view, it is necessary to show that on the facts of the particular case, the child will suffer real damage if he or she is not represented separately;[31] whereas under the wide view, it is sufficient if the case belongs to the category of cases where a conflict of interests may arise.[32] Experience in a number of countries has shown that under the first approach, courts are usually reluctant to exercise their discretion to appoint separate representatives in private law cases and do so only in exceptional circumstances where it is abundantly clear that the child's interests will not otherwise be represented.[33] On the other hand, it may be argued that the wide approach is inconsistent with the principle of family autonomy and that unnecessary intervention in the family unit may be harmful to the child.[34] Furthermore, in some jurisdictions, concerns have been expressed about the financial implications of such a wide approach.[35]

---

[31] eg FamC (t TA) 2860/96 *Ploni v Almonim*, Takdin Fam 2/97 (1987) (Isr) [12].
[32] eg the South African provisions discussed above at text accompanying n 7; *MC v SC* [2008] EWHC 517 (Fam).
[33] eg England (at least until recently), see Fortin, 'Children's Representation' (n 22) 501; in Israel, see Rotlevy Representation Sub-Committee (n 30) 39–41.
[34] Rotlevy Representation Sub-Committee ibid, 55.
[35] This seems to be the main motivation behind the English Department for Constitutional Affairs' (DCA) recommendation to restrict the appointment of separate representatives in private proceedings, *Separate Representation of Children* (CP 20/06), www.dca.gov.uk/consult/separate_representation/cp2006.htm, discussed in Fortin, 'Children's Representation' (n 22).

Thus, the Israeli Rotlevy Representation Sub-Committee suggested a *via media* in relation to private law family proceedings. In determining whether lack of representation will cause real damage to the child's rights, needs or interests, the court is required to consider whether there is a conflict of interests between the child and his parents or whether one of a list of circumstances exists.[36] Whilst the existence of a conflict of interests or one of the listed circumstances does not mandate the court to order separate representation, it alerts the court to the likelihood that the child's interests will be harmed without separate representation and thus results in serious consideration being given to this question. The list approach is also designed to increase uniformity between judges.[37]

For reasons which will become clear below, Abduction Convention cases should be included in any list of types of cases in which separate representation is required or should be seriously considered. If this is thought to be too wide, at least particular categories of Abduction Convention cases, such as those where the grave risk, child objection or settlement exceptions are raised, should be included.[38]

ii The Role of the Child's Separate Representative

The child's separate representative is called by different names in different countries, such as counsel for the child, separate representative, independent children's lawyer[39] and guardian *ad litem*.[40] However, the name does not necessarily reflect the duties expected of the representative[41] and the debate as to the role of the child's representative seems to be virtually universal. Three discrete functions may be involved in representing the child.[42] Firstly, the representative may be expected to evaluate which outcome best serves the welfare of the child[43] and to justify his conclusion to the court. Secondly, the representative may be seen as an amicus curiae, ensuring that all relevant information is presented to the court. In particular, there may be information to which the parents do not have access or are not interested in disclosing to the court. Last, but certainty not least, the child's repre-

---

[36] Rotlevy Representation Sub-Committee (n 30) 29. These circumstances are:
- Minor is under 12 and has expressed a clear opinion on the matter under discussion.
- There is a difficult dispute between the parties.
- There is lack of contact or lack of cooperation between the child and his parents.
- The minor does not have parents, or the parents cannot be identified, or one of the parents has been declared incompetent.
- It is alleged that the minor is a victim of a sexual offence, violence, abuse or neglect by a parent or other party to the proceedings.
- There is a cultural or religious dispute between the parties, which affects the minor's way of life.
- There is a dispute about the medical treatment for the minor.
- The length of the proceedings is likely to harm the minor.
- The issue that arises is particularly complex or the minor's position is under discussion in parallel in more than one court.

[37] ibid 65.

[38] This is the approach taken in the New Zealand Practice Note (n 16); see also R Schuz, 'The Hague Child Abduction Convention and Children's Rights' (2001) 12 *Transnational Law & Contemporary Problems* 393, 431–32.

[39] See P Parkinson and J Cashmore, *The Voice of the Child in Family Law Disputes* (Oxford, Oxford University Press, 2008) 49.

[40] This term seems to be used differently in different countries. For example, in the US an attorney may be appointed as a guardian '*ad litem*'. See Pitman, 'Making the Interests' (n 2) and Eitzen, 'A Child's Right' (n 2) 66; whereas under the tandem system operating in the UK, the term guardian '*ad litem*' refers to a social worker who himself instructs a lawyer on behalf of the child, Fortin, 'Children's Representation' (n 22).

[41] Eitzen, ibid 66.

[42] Parkinson and Cashmore (n 39) 51–53.

[43] This may involve consulting with experts.

sentative may be expected to act as an advocate for the child, presenting the child's views and position to the court in the most persuasive way.

It will be apparent that there may be a conflict between these different functions. In particular, if the representative does not agree with the child's view of the situation, the first and third function would appear to be incompatible.[44] Perhaps for this reason, much of the debate on the role of the child representative has become polarised into a 'welfare' approach versus a 'voice' approach.[45] Thus, some legal systems have adopted a two-tiered scheme for the representation of children. In cases where the court requires information about the welfare of the child or the child is too young to instruct a lawyer, the court will appoint a guardian *ad litem*[46] who is expected to provide an independent view on the best interests of the child. On the other hand, where the child is older, a lawyer will be appointed to act as an advocate for the child in accordance with his instructions.[47] Nonetheless, it now seems to be recognised that a single function approach rarely provides adequate representation for the child. A guardian who provides information and/or assesses the best interests of the child without ascertaining and taking into account the wishes of the child is simply an assistant to the court and does not really represent the child or enhance the realisation of the child's rights.[48] On the other hand, an advocate who simply presents the child's wishes ignores the child's need for protection. In particular, this approach will effectively force the child to become more directly involved in the litigation between his parents,[49] which may cause lasting damage to his relationship with one of them.

Accordingly, a number of commentators have put forward hybrid models. Eitzen suggests the creation of a new legal entity of separate representative, whose role will include elements of the advocate and elements of the guardian *ad litem*.[50] The representative is expected to put forward the child's position, whilst at the same time protecting him. Thus, the representative will have to treat the child differently than an adult client.[51] The child may require more intensive accompaniment and the lawyer needs to be sensitive to the child's reactions to developments in the case. Similarly, the representative has a duty to provide the child with information relevant to the dispute, but the amount of information and the way in which it is conveyed needs to be adapted to the age and emotional and intellectual maturity of the child.[52] Parkinson and Cashmore suggest that if the child's representative focuses on the child's perspectives and views rather than on his wishes, this will provide the court with a child-centric approach to the dispute without the need for the

---

[44] In the UK, where a mature child disagrees with his guardian *ad litem*'s views, he may apply to rid himself of the guardian and to instruct his own solicitor, see Fortin, 'Children's Representation' (n 22) 506. See also the discussion of how child representatives handle this conflict in Parkinson and Cashmore (n 39) 136–37. Compare the European Convention on the Exercise of Children's Rights, Art 10, which provides that the representative does not have to convey the child's views to the court where he considers that this would be 'manifestly contrary to the best interests of the child'.

[45] Parkinson and Cashmore (n 39) 52–53; Fortin, 'Children's Representation' (n 22) 505–06.

[46] In most systems, the guardian *ad litem* is a lawyer, but *cf* the tandem system in the UK, discussed above (n 40). In South Africa, it has been held that where a young child is involved, the separate representative appointed in child abduction cases is more akin to a curator *ad litem*, *B v G* 2012 (2) SA 329 (GSJ).

[47] *B v G* ibid; in the Israeli case of *Ploni v Almonim* (n 31), it was suggested that a lawyer should he appointed for children aged 15 and over. The Rotlevy Representation Sub Committee (n 30) recommended that a lawyer should be appointed for children over the age of 14 and for mature children over the age of 12.

[48] Parkinson and Cashmore (n 39) 53; N Taylor, P Tapp and M Henaghan 'Respecting Children's Participation in Family Law Proceedings' (2007) 15 *International Journal of Childrens Rights* 61, 71.

[49] Parkinson and Cashmore, ibid 205; Fortin, 'Children's Representation' (n 22) 508.

[50] Eitzen, 'A Child's Right' (n 2) 68–69.

[51] ibid.

[52] ibid.

child to take sides against one parent.[53] Whilst neither of these models completely resolves the debate about the role of the child's representative, both of them have much to commend them. In particular, as in many other aspects of children's rights law, recognising that children have rights does not mean that they are to be treated exactly the same as adults. Rather, existing institutions for realising rights, such as via legal representation, have to be adapted to take into account the vulnerability of the child. Thus, there is a need for further development and clarification of the role of the child's separate representative and for special training for such representatives.[54]

In any event, the dilemma as to the role of the child's representative would seem to be less acute in the context of Abduction Convention cases than in the context of custody and contact cases, to which the literature refers, because the court is not determining the best interests of the child. Rather, the court has to determine whether the conditions for return exist and, if so, whether the abductor can establish any of the defences. Only when a defence is established will the best interests of the child be relevant in the exercise of the court's discretion to return. Accordingly, *ex hypothesi*, the welfare aspect of the role of the separate representative will be less pronounced and the advocate model would appear to be more appropriate, at least where the child is old enough to express his views. Nonetheless, the role of the separate representative is wider than simply presenting the views of the child. Rather, he should present a child-centred perspective on the legal issues in dispute. For example, where it is not clear whether the habitual residence of the child has changed or whether the child has settled, it is his responsibility to collect information which shows how the child views his connection with the relevant environment. Furthermore, his conduct of the case will have to reflect the interests of the child and thus he may need to initiate steps to protect the child. For example, where a child is to be returned, he should raise the need for undertakings or other protective measures.[55] Moreover, there will be occasions in which his position as advocate for the child may be compromised, such as where he becomes aware of information relating to the welfare of the child, which appears to be inconsistent with the wishes of the child. Thus, lawyers who represent children in Abduction Convention cases should receive training as separate representatives, as well as being experts in Abduction Convention law.

III Separate Representation in Abduction Convention Cases

A The Arguments Against

i No Need

It is argued that there is rarely any need for separate representation in Hague Abduction proceedings, because the court is not undertaking a welfare investigation and has little discretion.[56] In addition, it is sometimes contended that the motivation which caused a parent

---

[53] Parkinson and Cashmore (n 39) 205.
[54] Rotlevy Representation Sub Committee (n 30) 93–116, 124–27.
[55] As in *Danaipour v Mclarey* 286 F.3d 1 (1st Cir 2002); Pitman, 'Making the Interests' (n 2) 525; See generally, ch 11 at III.
[56] eg *Re H (A Child: Child Abduction)* (n 9) (Wall LJ).

to remove or retain the child will be enough to ensure that such a parent will put forward the best available evidence to show that the child objects to return or that a grave risk of harm exists.[57] Finally, it may be argued that the existence of the child objection exception is sufficient to ensure that the child's objection to return will be taken into account, at least where his wishes are ascertained by direct or indirect hearing.[58]

Merle Weiner refutes the first argument, contending that the very fact that there is not a best interests adjudication means that the parents and the court will not necessarily be focused on the child's interests and thus, on the contrary, there is a greater need to appoint a representative who is responsible for putting forward those interests.[59] Furthermore, a determination of whether the grave risk defence is established directly concerns the child's interests and welfare.[60] Moreover, in relation to the second argument, experience shows that abducting parents do not always adequately present their children's interests.[61] For example, in the recent UK case of *AJJ v JJ*,[62] at the trial the mother agreed to return with the children to Poland until the litigation there was completed and thus effectively abandoned her reliance on the objections of the 15-year-old child and his siblings. The children subsequently obtained leave to be represented and to appeal the return order. However, if they had been represented from the beginning, the Court could not have accepted the mother's concession without taking into account the children's views.[63]

Finally, even where the child's views are ascertained, without separate representation his participation will be limited to the question of whether he objects to return. For example, he will not be able to present arguments about the exercise of the discretion where the child objection exception, or some other defence, is established or about the adequacy of undertakings offered by the left-behind parent or even about the timing of his return.

ii Delay

Separate representation is seen as an unnecessary complication in summary proceedings, which causes delay when speed is of the essence.[64] However, there is no good reason why separate representation should cause significant delay, provided that it is ordered promptly after initiation of the proceedings.[65] If properly trained children's lawyers are readily available, they will be able to meet with the child and other relevant persons within a short period of time.[66] Whilst it might take time to obtain relevant information, for example in

---

[57] *De L v Director-General, NSW Department of Community Services* (1996) FLC 92-706 (Kirby LJ).
[58] See generally ch 14.
[59] MH Weiner, 'Intolerable Situations and Counsel for Children: Following Switzerland's Example in Hague Abduction Cases' (2008) 58 *American University Law Review* 335, 379.
[60] Pitman 'Making the Interests' (n 2) 532.
[61] ibid 536 and see discussion below at Bii.
[62] *AJ v JJ* (n 12).
[63] However, perhaps surprisingly, Thorpe LJ does not fault the original decision not to order representation, but holds that the judge erred in not engaging the children in the process by initiating a meeting with them.
[64] *Re H* (n 9) [7] (Thorpe LJ) [7]; *Re F (A Child)* [2007] EWCA Civ 393.
[65] In England and Wales, the issue of appointing a separate representative for the child is to be discussed 'as soon as practicable after the issue of proceedings', FPR 2010, Rule 12.6 (n 8) (applied to abduction proceedings by virtue of 12.1(1)(e) of those Rules).
[66] In *Re M (Abduction: Zimbabwe)* (n 10) [57], Baroness Hale states that allowing separate representation routinely in settlement cases would not cause additional delay. She then goes on to state, as seen above, that the test for ordering separate representation in other cases is whether this 'will add enough to the court's understanding of the issues that arise under the Hague Convention to justify the intrusion, the expense and delay that may result'. cf *Re C* (n 12) [47], where Ryder J took the view that ordering separate representation for the children would not result in any delay (or only minimal delay) in the listing of the final hearing.

relation to conditions in the country of origin, this information ought to be obtained whether the child is separately represented or not. As the High Court of Australia commented, 'Prompt listing for hearing is one thing; an over-hasty and insufficient hearing is another.'[67] Thus, in the view of the majority, separate representation 'should not hinder and indeed should assist the prompt disposition of Convention applications'.[68]

iii Cost

Thorpe LJ has expressed concern about the burden on public funds of separate representation abduction cases, in particular in view of the fact that in the UK legal aid is given automatically without being means tested.[69] Whilst this is not the case in other jurisdictions, the question of who will fund the child's representative will always arise. Unless the parents can be required to pay and have the means to do so, the public purse will inevitably have to bear the cost.

Merle Weiner has expressed the view that parents are morally obliged to pay for separate representation for their children caught up in Abduction Convention proceedings and that where the parents cannot pay, the State should do so.[70] It should be borne in mind that in countries where there are not many abduction cases, the overall costs will not be great. Even in countries where the number of cases is larger, the cost of providing separate representation in these cases is only a small proportion of the sums which are expended by public funds in providing such representation in public law proceedings.

iv Harm to the Child

It has been suggested that separate representation of children in proceedings between their parents could 'drive a wedge between children and their parents and make divorce proceedings more acrimonious rather than less'.[71] Similarly, there is a risk that the child's involvement in the litigation will be exploited by one parent in order to improve his own position in the battle with the other parent.[72] Arguably, this risk is greater in the particularly fraught atmosphere following an abduction.

However, properly trained separate representatives should be able to minimise the occurrence of such phenomena. The representative can make it clear to the child that he does not have to express any preference between his parents and should focus on presenting the child's perspectives and views, rather than simply his wishes.[73] He should also be able to identify signs of exploitation of the child and to combat it. Indeed, the appointment of a separate representative may prevent the exploitation of children which would other-

---

[67] *De L v Director-General* (n 57).
[68] ibid; see also comment of Baroness Hale in *Re D (A Child)*(n 11) at para 61 that delay is caused not by the appointment of a separate representative per se, but by the request for such an appointment being made at a late stage in the proceedings; the Rotlevy Representation Sub Committee (n 30) 54, also took the view that an independent representative could help prevent delay and recommended that the definition of the function of the independent representative should include ensuring compliance with time limits.
[69] *Re H* (n 9) [19].
[70] Weiner, 'Intolerable Situations' (n 59) 400.
[71] Fortin, *Children's Rights* (n 26) 220 refers to the 'corrosive effect of being sucked into divisive litigation between their parents'.
[72] ibid 231; See eg *Re HB (Abduction: Children's Objections) (No 2)* [1998] 1 FLR 564, where Butler-Sloss LJ criticised the father for allowing his 11-year-old daughter to fight his battles with her mother for him.
[73] Parkinson and Cashmore (n 39) 205.

wise occur. For example, in the Israeli case of *Isik v Isik*,[74] the children, after a visit with their Israeli mother, applied for a change in the custody order in her favour and the father responded with an application under the Hague Convention. The Court, being concerned that the children's application really reflected the mother's interests, ordered separate representation for the children.

Furthermore, as Ryder J points out,[75] where the children have already been exposed to the issues in the proceedings, their involvement in the proceedings is unlikely to cause them further harm, particularly where they have clear views on those issues. On the contrary, in his view, 'not having the opportunity to say what they think and why they think it, is more likely ... to cause them harm than allowing them to express their views and wishes and to have their positions advocated professionally by lawyers.'[76] According to this approach, not allowing the children's views to be 'properly, independently and specifically advocated' by a separate representative may be emotionally harmful for the children.[77]

v Sending the 'Wrong Message'

Baroness Hale has suggested that routinely allowing separate representation in abduction cases would give an exaggerated impression of the relevance and importance of children's views in abduction cases.[78]

With respect, this concern is misplaced for a number of reasons. Firstly, without separate representation, it may not be possible to know in which cases the child's views are relevant. Secondly, as seen above, the role of the separate representative is not confined to putting forward the views expressed by the child, but also includes presenting the facts and arguments from the child's point of view. Thirdly, the granting of separate representation per se will not determine the relevance and importance of the child's views, but rather the weight given by the court to those views. Finally, even if there is a risk of sending a wrong message, this is not sufficient reason to deny the child the right to be separately represented.

B The Arguments in Favour

Abduction Convention cases contain a number of particular characteristics which make it highly likely that the parents will not be able to provide adequate representation for the child. Accordingly, on a wide approach, such cases should be classified as cases in which separate representation should be ordered or at least give rise to a presumption that separate representation is necessary. Alternatively, on a narrow approach, in considering whether to exercise its discretion to award separate representation, the court should examine to what extent the following reasons for ordering separate representation are present in the particular case.

---

[74] CA (SC) 6327/94 *Plonit v Ploni* Nevo 1 December 1994.
[75] *Re C* (n 12).
[76] ibid [46].
[77] ibid [44]; see also *Mabon v Mabon* [2005] 2 FLR 1011 (Thorpe LJ).
[78] *Re M (Abduction: Zimbabwe)* (n 10) [57].

i The Nature of Abduction Convention Cases

Abduction Convention cases are frequently complex and involve delicate issues.[79] In addition, such cases often involve high-conflict custody disputes, which not infrequently include allegations of domestic violence and child abuse.[80] It is widely accepted that separate representation is required in such situations.[81] Furthermore, the stakes are usually higher than in a normal custody case because the implications of the decision for each parent and the child[82] are far-reaching. If the child is returned to the country of origin, this may well lead to a dramatic change in his way of life, whether or not the abducting parent returns as well. If the abducting parent does not return, the child's contact with that parent will be significantly reduced. If the child is not returned, this will invariably result in significantly reduced contact with the left-behind parent.

ii Provision of Critical Information

Even though the court rarely has any discretion in Hague cases, its findings as to whether the criteria for the application of the Convention or for one of the exceptions are met depend on the information provided to it by the parties. Since the parents' lawyers are under a duty to represent their client's interests, they will only present information which they consider promotes their client's case. The left-behind parent and his lawyer may not have access to all the relevant and current information concerning the child.[83] Similarly, where the abducting parent is not legally represented, he may not know what information is relevant.[84] Furthermore, an older child may provide information not known to the parties or a different perspective.[85] Thus, the child's separate representative may provide the court with relevant information to which it would not otherwise have access.[86] Of course, in cases where one of the exceptions is established and the court has discretion as to whether to return the child, it is critical that all the relevant facts are presented to the court from the child's perspective.

---

[79] Bucher, 'The New Swiss Federal Act' (n 5) 150.
[80] Weiner, 'Intolerable Situations' (n 59) 381.
[81] ibid.
[82] This may make it more difficult for the parent to distinguish between his own interests and those of the child. This is also true in relocation cases and it is noteworthy that the idea of the routine appointment of a guardian for the child received wide support from parents who had been involved in relocation disputes, M Freeman, 'Relocation: The Reunite Research', Research Unit of the Reunite International Child Abduction Centre (July 2009), http://www.reunite.org/edit/files/Library%20-%20reunite%20Publications/Relocation%20Report.pdf, 25.
[83] Weiner, 'Intolerable Situations' (n 59) 381.
[84] See examples given by Weiner ibid, at 227. Even where the parent is represented, the question of whether all the relevant information is presented depends to a large extent on the competence of the lawyer. The current author has come across two unreported cases where the abducting parent failed to prevent immediate return because her lawyer did not put forward all the relevant arguments or did not produce the necessary material to support those arguments. After return, the abductor eventually obtained permission to relocate, but considerable suffering was caused to the children as a result of the unnecessary return (cases on file with author).
[85] See eg W v W (n 1) [30].
[86] See Weiner, 'Intolerable Situations' (n 59) 383–84.; State v Best (n 18), [72]. Such a lawyer may even raise arguments which the abducting parent does not raise. For example, in State Central Authority & Young [2012] FamCA 563 [77], the court ordered that the independent children's lawyer should raise the issue of the separation from siblings, even if the mother does not.

iii Particular Difficulty in Ascertaining the Child's Wishes

It will often be more difficult to ascertain the genuine wishes of an abducted child, because during the period prior to the proceedings he has little, if any, contact with the left-behind parent and so the scope for undue influence by the abducting parent is greater. Thus, judges quite often find that a child's expressed objections do not reflect his independent views.[87] The child's representative will be in a better position than the judge, court welfare officer or other expert to ascertain the child's genuine wishes because he is in continuing contact with the child throughout the proceedings. Where appropriate, he will be assisted by experts. However, the provision of separate representation does not mean that it is no longer necessary for the judge to meet directly with the child.[88] Indeed, the existence of a separate representative may alleviate some of the difficulties involved in such a meeting because the representative can prepare the child for the meeting and attempt to counter efforts by the parents to influence the child. In addition, as pointed out above,[89] the separate representative can make the child's participation more meaningful by ensuring that the child is in possession of relevant accurate information concerning the case.

iv Negative Impact of Having Child's Interests Presented by the Abductor

The child's separate representative is only concerned with the child's interests and so he is best placed to present those interests properly and objectively, putting the emphasis on issues concerning the child. Conversely, where the child's interests are presented by the parents, they will invariably be intertwined with the individual interests of that parent.[90] Thus, for example, there may be certain legal arguments which neither party is interested in putting forward.[91] Furthermore, the fact that the abducting parent clearly has a strong interest in the outcome of the case and is perceived to be the guilty party is likely to affect the way in which the court treats the abductor's arguments in relation to the child's interests.[92] For example, where the abducting parent claims that there is a grave risk that returning the child will cause him harm, the court's approach to this claim will inevitably be coloured by the fact that abductors routinely make such claims and by the perception that the abductor is the one who has caused the child harm by abducting him in the first place.[93] On the other hand, if the claim of harm is raised by the child's independent representative, it will be easier to focus on the present and future situation of the child rather than on who is responsible for the harm.

The difference between the child's interests being represented by a separate representative rather than the abducting parent can be clearly seen from the UK case of *Re M (Abduction: Zimbabwe)*. At first instance and in the Court of Appeal,[94] where the children

---

[87] See ch 12 at II Cii.

[88] For a discussion on the direct hearing of children by judges, see ch 14. For examples of cases where the judge has personally heard a child who was separately represented, see *De L v H* (n 12).

[89] Chapter 14 at II C.

[90] In *Re M (Abduction: Zimbabwe)* (n 10) [57], Baroness Hale recognises the risk that the child's point of view may be 'lost in the competing claims of the adults'.

[91] *Re D (A Child)* (n 11) [50] (Baroness Hale).

[92] P McEleavy, 'Evaluating the Views of Abducted Children: Trends in Appellate Case-Law' (2008) 20 *Child and Family Law Quarterly* 230, suggesting that 'the association of the objections with the abductor may create a negative impression in the mind of the court'.

[93] See comments to this effect by Justice Procaccia in RFamA (SC) 1855/08 *RB v GV*, 8 April 2008 (Isr) http://elyon1.court.gov.il/files/08/550/018/r03/08018550.r03.pdf [INCADAT cite: HC/E/IL 923] [44] 44http.

[94] *Re M (Children)* [2007] EWCA Civ 992.

were not separately represented, the settlement and child objection exceptions pleaded by the abducting mother were analysed more from the parents' perspective[95] than from that of the children and thus return was ordered even though the Article 12(2) settlement defence was established. In the House of Lords,[96] Baroness Hale acknowledged that the 'comparative moral blameworthiness of mother and father has had an effect upon the judgments in both of the courts below'.[97] In contrast in the House of Lords,[98] where the children were separately represented, their counsel emphasised child-centric considerations, and in particular the impact that the return order would have on the children.[99] Baroness Hale, with whom all the other Lords agreed on this point, accepted these arguments and held that the policy of the Convention could carry little weight against them. Thus, the Court allowed the appeal and refused to order return.[100]

It should be emphasised that the negative impact of the child's interest being represented by the abductor is unique to abduction cases, because in standard custody and contact cases neither party is automatically seen as a guilty party. Accordingly, this is a persuasive reason for mandatory, or at least widespread, representation of children in Abduction Convention cases, whether children are represented in other types of private law proceedings or not.

v Ensuring that Undertakings will be Effective

In cases where it is proposed to make return of the child conditional on undertakings designed to reduce the harm to the child, there is a need to check to what extent such undertakings will indeed be effective. The child's separate representative can conduct such an examination objectively.[101] Similarly, if the court makes conditions relating to the child, which have to be fulfilled before the return, the separate representative can accompany the child and ensure that the conditions are indeed fulfilled.[102]

vi Accompanying the Children and Enforcement of the Order

It is important that mature children should understand the limited nature of the weight given to the views of children in Abduction Convention proceedings and, where return is

---

[95] Much of the High Court decision was concerned with resolving the 'considerable gulf' between the facts presented by the two parents, which were 'resolved by the judge's crucial findings as to credibility'. ibid [2] (Thorpe LJ).

[96] *Re M (Abduction: Zimbabwe)* (n 10).

[97] ibid [52]. Wood J at first instance [121] expressly referred to the 'nature and seriousness of the wrongful removal, including the many layers of deception deployed by the mother in bringing about that wrongful removal, keeping the children at an address unknown to the father for many months' (quoted in *Re M (Children)*(n 94) [7] (Thorpe LJ)).

[98] *Re M (Abduction: Zimbabwe)* (n 10).

[99] Summed up by Baroness Hale, ibid [52] as follows, 'In short, having been the victims of one international relocation contrary to their wishes, they stand to be the victims of another.'

[100] For analysis of their Lordships' decision that there is discretion to order return when Art 12(2) is established, see ch 9 at II C.

[101] *State v Best* (n 18), [64]. Even where there is direct communication between the judiciary of the two countries (through the liaison judge – see ch 11 at III D), the input of the separate representative may be valuable.

[102] For example, in the Israeli case of *RB v VG* (n 93), the Court ordered that the child undergo preparation for the return, including meetings with the father, but social services did not start the preparation until a long time after the Court order. Whilst the Court subsequently delayed the return date by two weeks, this did not fully compensate for the lost time. It seems likely that this situation would not have arisen if there had been a separate representative, who would have liaised with social services.

ordered, the fact that return is a 'first aid' remedy. As the parents themselves may not fully comprehend these issues, they cannot be relied upon to explain them to the children. Where the judge meets with the child, he should clarify these matters to the child and ideally the decision should be conveyed to the child directly by the judge, or at least by a welfare officer.[103] However, as seen above,[104] children often do not meet the judge and few judges take the time to explain their decision to the child.

This lacuna can be filled by a separate representative who has an ongoing relationship with the child. He can explain to the child, more than once if necessary, the nature of the Abduction Convention proceedings and the implications of a return order. In particular, where proceedings have been initiated, or are likely to be initiated, in the country of habitual residence, he can ensure that the child understands the relationship between the two sets of proceedings.[105]

In addition, where there is a return order, the separate representative should continue to accompany the child until the order is enforced. Where he is aware that the child may not co-operate with the return order, he may be able to take steps to pre-empt the problem, including bringing the child's stance to the attention of the court.[106] Similarly, if inappropriate force is used against the child, he may be the only person who is in a position to protest about this.[107]

IV Application by the Child

A The Legal Provisions

The Abduction Convention does not specifically provide for a child to initiate a return application and the author is not aware of any attempt to bring such an application. However, since there is no requirement that the applicant be a person whose rights have been breached, the text of the Convention does not create an absolute barrier to such an application.

In Israel, section 3d of the Family Court Law provides that a minor may make an application in any 'family matter' in which there is liable to be a real violation of his rights. This condition will clearly be satisfied in a case where the child has been abducted and no application has been made for his return. In England and Wales, special provisions were introduced enabling children to apply for orders under section 8 of the Children Act, which includes residence orders and contact orders.[108] However, this would not seem to cover applying for a return order under the Abduction Convention.

---

[103] See *AJ v JJ* (n 12) [40] and [46] (Thorpe LJ).
[104] In ch 14.
[105] In *AJ v JJ* (n 12), Thorpe LJ instructed the child's lawyer to explain to the child the respective functions of the English and Polish courts and why the latter would be deciding his future.
[106] Weiner, 'Intolerable Situations' (n 59) 390. Indeed, in the case of *RB v VG* (n 93), a separate representative may have been able to alert the Court to the likely problem in enforcing the order requiring immediate return and so have prevented the child's disappearance.
[107] Weiner, ibid 390.
[108] Subject to the court's duty to consider whether the child has sufficient understanding to make the proposed application (Children Act 1989 s 10(8)). For a discussion of the judicial interpretation of this provision, see Fortin 'Children's Representation' (n 22) 224–29.

B The Need for Provision for Application by Children

Whilst abducted children may often not be in a position to initiate a return application,[109] the issue is not entirely hypothetical and yet there does not seem to be any direct discussion of this possibility in the literature. In the current author's view, it is necessary to allow applications by mature abducted children in order to comply with the obligation in Article 12(1) of the CRC of enabling the child to express his views in all matters affecting him, since the abduction is clearly a matter affecting the child. Whilst it might be argued that this right should be assured to the child through domestic proceedings, it is unlikely that these will be as appropriate as the Convention mechanism, which is specifically designed to deal with abduction.

There appear to be two main objections to such a proposal. Firstly, if the abducting parent refuses to return with the child, who will take care of the child?[110] However, the fact that the left-behind parent has not made an application for return does not necessarily mean that he does not want or is not able to take care of the child. There may be other reasons for his lack of action, such as passivity, lack of knowledge of rights, fear of legal proceedings or lack of financial resources.[111] Accordingly, prima facie, there is no reason not to order return at the request of the child. However, in cases where the abductor refuses to return and the left-behind parent does not wish to or is not able to take care of the child and there are no other suitable arrangements in the country of origin,[112] return will be refused under Article 13(1)(b).

The second objection is the potential harm of allowing children to become a party to proceedings involving their parent. Whilst this argument was rejected above as a reason not to allow separate representation of the child in proceedings which are already in existence, it has far more force in the context of an application made by the child. The child is not only expressing a clear preference for the left-behind parent, but is actively initiating proceedings against the abductor. In such a situation, even a cautious approach by the separate representative cannot avoid a head on clash between the child and the abducting parent. Thus, it seems inevitable that such action will cause serious damage to his relationship with the abducting parent. On the other hand, if the child is not allowed to make an application, the issue of return will not be brought before any court and the child's rights to contact with the left-behind parent, together with his participation rights, will be violated. Thus, whilst the harm caused to the child by requesting return should not be ignored, it must be weighed against the harm caused by not allowing the child to express his desire to return.

One possible way of ameliorating the situation would be to provide that in such cases, the return application is submitted by the Central Authority or some other governmental

---

[109] Largely because they are dependent on the abductor.

[110] In Beaumont and McEleavy, *The Hague Convention on International Child Abduction* (Oxford, Oxford University Press, 1999) 73, this problem is raised in relation to applications made by third parties.

[111] In the Israeli case of FamC (Dist HAI) 44182/99 *KGL v YL* Nevo, 11/09/00 (Isr), the Court had to reject the application because the applicant did not submit a declaration or appear, apparently due to lack of finance. It is not clear why he did not apply for legal aid in Israel.

[112] In the case of *Re S (Abduction: Children: Separate Representation)* [1997] 1 FLR 486, it was envisaged that the children would be returned to foster care. Beaumont and McEleavy (n 111) 73 doubt if this is appropriate. In this particular case, the children did not want to return, but surely if they had wanted to do so, it would have been appropriate to return them to foster care. Otherwise, since they had been removed from foster care (which was stated to have been successful), it would not have been possible to give effect to the Convention.

body, as routinely occurs in Australia.[113] Whilst the change in the formal identity of the applicant does not change the fact that the child has initiated the application and is rebelling against the abducting parent, the fact that the abducting parent is not being sued directly by his child and that the proceedings are being handled by a third party might reduce some of the tension which will inevitably be caused by such an application.

V Conclusions

The above analysis shows that in most Abduction Convention cases, there is a need for the separate representation of children, whether the abducting parent contests the proceedings or not. With proper management, there is no reason why separate representation should cause significant delay in deciding the case. Whilst appointing separate representatives in more cases would clearly create a burden on public funds, abducted children have the right to be separately represented just as much as children who are the subject of care and other public law proceedings. In fact, the relatively small number of abducted children in comparison with those involved in public law proceedings makes the cost argument less convincing. Furthermore, the potential damage which might be caused to the child-parent relationship by separate representation can be prevented by the provision of proper safeguards and training for separate representatives. Indeed, if the child is going to be involved in the proceedings in any way, such as by being heard directly or indirectly, the provision of a professional to accompany him should enable him to be protected from the dangers of such involvement. Thus, the advantages of separate representation outweigh the possible disadvantages.

Whilst, ideally, separate representation should be ordered in all Hague Convention cases, as in Switzerland and South Africa, there are certain types of cases where it is clearly essential.[114] In particular, separate representation is necessary where 12 months have elapsed since the date of the wrongful removal or retention and the commencement of proceedings and so the issue of settlement arises[115] where there is evidence that the child objects to being returned and where there is evidence that return is likely to expose the child to harm. In addition, where one of the defences in Article 13(1)(a) has been established and so the court must exercise its discretion, the child's best interests are an important factor in the exercise of such discretion[116] and so it is vital that the court is provided with objective information and, where the child is old enough, his views on the matter.[117] Finally, separate representation should be ordered wherever there is a serious question as

---

[113] See ch 2 at III E.

[114] But see comment in *State v Best* (n 18), [86] that it is not always possible to foresee what issues may arise and thus it is desirable that a separate representative be appointed at an early stage so that he will be available when necessary.

[115] In *Re M (Abduction: Zimbabwe)* (n 10) [57], Baroness Hale suggests that separate representation should become routine in such cases because these cases 'are the most child-centric' of all abduction cases and so 'the separate point of view of the children is particularly important and should not be lost in the competing claims of the adults'.

[116] See ch 10 at IV.

[117] Ryder J in *Re C* (n 12) [45], treats the fact that welfare considerations, including having regard to the children's views, are more important in the exercise of the discretion as an additional reason for ordering separate representation.

to where the child was habitually resident. As seen above,[118] courts have considerable discretion in determining habitual residence in borderline cases and are likely to be influenced by policy considerations. Thus, it is necessary that the relevant information and arguments are presented to the court from the child's perspective.

In addition, in the highly unusual situation where the abducted child wishes to return and the left-behind parent has not instituted proceedings, the child should be able to do so. In order to reduce the harm that this will cause to his relationship with the abducting parent, such applications should be submitted by the Central Authority or some other governmental body.

---

[118] In ch 8.

Part VI

Related Proceedings and Processes

16

Mediation

I Introduction

In recent years, there has been growing recognition of the advantages of mediating international child abduction disputes; although in practice the use of mediation is still limited in abduction cases. This chapter will briefly examine these advantages, together with the problems associated with mediation in these disputes and possible solutions to these problems. For the purposes of this chapter, mediation may be defined as 'a voluntary structured process whereby the mediator facilitates communication between the parties to a conflict, enabling them to take responsibility for finding a solution to their conflict'.[1] The term is used to include both court based and out of court mediation.

The Permanent Bureau of the Hague Conference on Private International Law has been working on promoting the use of mediation in cross-border family disputes for a number of years.[2] The recent publication of the Guide to Good Practice on Mediation in Abduction Convention cases[3] may be seen as the culmination of this work to date. Whilst this Guide discusses many of the issues which arise in mediation in cross-border family disputes in general, and abduction cases in particular, it does not provide definitive answers to all of these. Moreover, it is not clear that this Guide will provide the necessary motivation to States to set up mediation schemes for Convention cases, especially where this requires local legislation.[4] Thus, there may still be a need for an international instrument on cross-border mediation.[5]

---

[1] Good Practice Guide on Mediation, www.hcch.net/upload/guide28mediation_en.pdf, 7 ('Mediation Practice Guide'). For the differences between mediation and other forms of alternative dispute resolution, see ibid.

[2] For details, see ibid, 14–17. This includes the use of mediation to solve disputes involving non-Contracting States, in particular those where Shari'ah law is applicable (known as the Malta Process). For work in this field by other bodies, see ibid, 18–19.

[3] ibid.

[4] The Swiss Federal Act on International Child Abduction, Art 4 expressly provides that the Central Authorities may initiate mediation and mandates them to encourage parties to participate in mediation. Furthermore, Art 8 requires the court to initiate mediation procedures (see translation of the law in A Bucher, 'The New Swiss Federal Act on International Child Abduction' (2008) 4 *Journal of Private International Law* 139, 161). For a discussion of the implementation of these provisions, see AC Alfieri, 'Enlèvement international d'enfants: premières expériences avec la LF-EEA' (2012) *La pratique du droit de la famille* 550, 552–54.

[5] Israel put forward a proposal for such an instrument in 2009, referred to in Preliminary Document 13 of 2011 Guide To Part II Of The Sixth Meeting Of The Special Commission [38]

II Advantages of Mediation

It is now widely recognised that there are many advantages to solving family law disputes by agreement rather than by litigation and that mediation is often the best method of achieving agreement. In particular, the concept of private ordering is consistent with modern doctrines of individual autonomy and family privacy.[6] In addition, parties are more likely to comply with agreed solutions which they themselves have devised than with those imposed by a court.[7] Furthermore, the facilitation of communication between the parties will provide a basis for solving future problems which may arise in relation to the arrangements for the children.[8] Similarly, agreed solutions prevent the damage often caused by the accusations hurled by each party at the other in contested proceedings and avoid the perception that one party is a winner and the other a loser.[9] Accordingly, mediation is likely to reduce, rather than exacerbate, the conflict between the parties. The improved relationship between the parents increases the chance of ongoing contact between the child and the non-residential parent and generally benefits the child.[10] Furthermore, mediation may save costs and avoid the delay involved in the legal process.[11]

In the child abduction context, the gains may be even greater. The return of the child will usually do little to resolve the underlying problems between the parties[12] and there will usually be a need for further litigation in relation to custody and/or relocation after return. In contrast, in mediation the parents can address a broader range of issues than the return of the child[13] and they can focus on the principal question of where the child should live in the long term and how each of the parents should exercise his parental responsibility.[14] Accordingly, a mediated agreement can resolve the substantive dispute between the parties and will avoid the need for both the return proceedings and subsequent proceedings on the merits. Thus, the potential saving in financial and emotional costs may be considerable.[15] However, even where the mediated agreement only relates to the return and the conditions thereof, it may still be of benefit because it will usually reduce antagonism, prevent enforcement problems and ensure that the child's interests are protected upon return.[16]

It has even been suggested that the use of mediation may help to allay some of the concerns[17] arising from the fact that the typical abduction today is by a primary carer mother and not by a non-custodial father, as envisaged by the drafters of the Hague Convention on

---

[6] A Diduck and F Kaganas, *Family Law, Gender and the State*, 3rd edn (Oxford, Hart Publishing, 2012) 718–19.

[7] R Emery, 'Divorce Mediation: Research and Reflections' (2005) 43 *Family Court Review* 22. Empirical support for this hypothesis can be found in the research follow-up to the Reunite Pilot Medication Scheme, T Buck, 'An Evaluation of the Long Term Effectiveness of Mediation in Cases of International Child Abduction', http://www.reunite.org/edit/files/Library%20-%20reunite%20Publications/Mediation%20research%20report.pdf

[8] Mediation Practice Guide (n 1), para 34.

[9] ibid, para 33.

[10] Emery, 'Divorce Mediation' (n 7).

[11] ibid.

[12] Per Thorpe LJ in *Re G (Children)* [2010] EWCA Civ 1232 [16].

[13] J Zawid, 'Practical and Ethical Implications of Mediating International Child Abduction Cases: A New Frontier for Mediators' (2008) 40 *The University of Miami Inter-American Law Review* 1, 24–27.

[14] S Vigers, *Mediating International Child Abduction Cases: The Hague Convention* (Oxford, Hart Publishing, 2011) 39–40.

[15] Mediation Practice Guide (n 1), para 35.

[16] Vigers (n 14) 67–70. In particular, where the agreement is enforceable, it will be preferable to non-enforcable undertakings or conditions, see ch 11 at III.

[17] Ibid 64–69.

the Civil Aspects of International Child Abduction ('Abduction Convention').[18] However, this view seems unduly optimistic since mediation, like other forms of negotiation and alternative dispute resolution, is conducted 'in the shadow of the law'.[19] Thus, where the left-behind parent knows that he can obtain a return order,[20] he will usually have little incentive, other than avoiding litigation, to agree to the child remaining in the country of refuge, unless it is clear that the abductor has a very good chance of ultimately obtaining leave to relocate.[21] Similarly, there will be little motivation for him to agree to the terms demanded by the abductor for returning, unless he knows that the court in the country of refuge would in any event be likely to make return conditional on similar undertakings or protective measures. Accordingly, the wider use of mediation should not be viewed as an alternative to responding to the concerns about the operation of the Convention. On the contrary, dealing with these concerns is likely to make mediation a more attractive option. Moreover, it must be remembered that in many cases the level of conflict between the parents, which was the catalyst for the abduction in the first place, or which arose as a result thereof, is so high that there is no possibility of an agreed solution. In such cases, attempts to mediate are a waste of time[22] and resources.

Finally, some mention should be made of the reservations expressed in relation to family mediation. In particular, it is alleged that the autonomy which mediation purports to confer on the parties is illusory[23] inter alia because mediation cannot correct, and may even heighten,[24] the imbalances of power between the parties and because the parties may be pressurised into coming to an agreement.[25] This means that women, who are invariably the weaker party,[26] may be prejudiced and the welfare of the children may be jeopardised.[27] However, it seems to be widely believed that these concerns can largely be answered by introducing appropriate professional standards for mediators and that the advantages of mediation outweigh the disadvantages. Nonetheless, there are still a number of problems which are unique, or particularly relevant, to international child abduction cases, that need solving before mediation can become more widespread in these cases.

---

[18] Chapter 3 at IA.
[19] R Mnookin and L Kornhauser, 'Bargaining in the Shadow of the Law: The Case of Divorce' (1979) 88 *Yale Law Journal* 950.
[20] Of course, the situation is different in borderline cases where it is not clear whether the threshold requirements for application of the Convention are met or there is a real chance that one of the exceptions will be established, Zawid, 'Practical and Ethical Implications' (n 13) 20–23.
[21] In many jurisdictions there is considerable uncertainty in relation to relocation determinations (see ch 4 at II Aiii) and thus settlement rates are relatively low (ibid at II Bii).
[22] Mediation Practice Guide (n 1), 23.
[23] Diduck and Kaganas (n 6) 721.
[24] eg PE Bryan, 'Killing Us Softly: Divorce Mediation and the Politics of Power' (1992) 40 *Buffalo Law Review* 441.
[25] C Bruch, 'And How Are the Children? The Effects of Ideology and Mediation on Child Custody Law and Children's Well-Being in the United States' (1988) 2 *International Journal of Law and the Family* 106, 121.
[26] eg M Shaffer, 'Divorce Mediation: A Feminist Perspective' (1988) 46 *University of Toronto Faculty of Law Review* 162.
[27] Diduck and Kaganas (n 6) 721; C Bruch, 'And How Are the Children?' (n 25) 120.

III Problems and Solutions

A International Nature

The international nature of Abduction Convention proceedings creates practical and substantive difficulties for the use of mediation. Ex hypothesi two legal systems are involved and the parties, who are often of different nationalities, are living in two different countries. Modern technology has provided solutions to many of the practical problems caused in cross-border mediation. In particular, virtual mediation sessions are possible by use of various online and teleconferencing facilities.[28]

In addition, a special bi-national co-mediation model has been developed in which there are two mediators, one from of each of the States involved.[29] However, it has been argued that this scheme is onerous, restrictive and unnecessary[30] and that there is no reason why mediation should not take place in the country of refuge with a local mediator who understands the influence of culture on mediation.[31] Since the mediator does not represent the parties, it is not necessary for there to be one mediator of each nationality[32] and interpreters can be used where necessary.[33] Nonetheless, it seems to be widely recognised that mediation in cross-border cases is a specialist discipline requiring distinct training and procedures.[34]

B Delay

As seen above,[35] time is of the essence in Abduction Convention proceedings and all those involved are required to use the most expeditious procedures possible. Accordingly, the leisurely pace of domestic family mediations is inconsistent with the nature of Abduction Convention proceedings. In particular, there is a risk that the abductors will use mediation as a delaying tactic to buy time.

However, the limited experience in practice has shown that it is possible to mediate Convention cases expeditiously and without any significant delay in the making of a judicial decision, where the mediation is not successful.[36] Where a return application has been filed prior to the mediation, the court may fix a time frame for the mediation.[37]

---

[28] Vigers (n 14) 51–52.
[29] ibid 35; Zawid, 'Practical and Ethical Implications' (n 13) 12–13.
[30] Vigers ibid 36.
[31] ibid.
[32] ibid.
[33] ibid 37.
[34] ibid 57.
[35] Chapter 1 at I Biv.
[36] Vigers (n 14) 43.
[37] ibid. However, Vigers points out that the strict six-week deadline in Brussels II bis cases (Council Regulation (EC) No 2201/2003 of 27 November 2003 concerning jurisdiction and the recognition and enforcement of judgments in matrimonial matters and matters of parental responsibility, [2003] OJ L 338/1-29) may restrict the possibility of mediation and so suggests that in these cases mediation should take place, before the filing of the application, ibid 46–47.

C Enforceability

Some jurisdictions make the enforceability of agreements relating to children dependent on court approval or a procedure such as registration. In addition, there may be limits on party autonomy in relation to certain issues, such as the level of child support payments.[38] Accordingly, even if the agreement is binding in the country of refuge, where the mediation took place, this does not mean that it will be enforceable under the law of the country of origin. This issue needs to be considered before embarking upon the mediation. Where an agreement has been reached, implementation should not usually start until enforceability in all the relevant jurisdictions has been ensured,[39] either by obtaining a declaration of recognition and/or enforceability of the order made in the state of refuge or by obtaining a mirror order.[40]

However, there may be real obstacles to ensuring enforceability. In particular, where the court in the country of refuge does not have jurisdiction to deal with substantive matters relating to custody and contact, any order which it makes approving a mediated agreement[41] which includes these matters, may not be enforceable in other countries. This may well be the case where the parties agree to the custody and contact arrangements which will apply after the voluntary return of the abductor and child to the country of habitual residence.[42] This scenario may result in a Catch 22 situation.[43] The country of habitual residence may not be prepared to approve the mediated agreement unless the parties are present in that State.[44] Yet, the abducting parent will not return until she can be assured that the mediated agreement will be enforceable in the country of origin.

As yet, there are no clear solutions[45] and the Sixth Special Commission in 2012 recommended setting up a working group of experts to consider the practical and legal problems that exist in the recognition and enforcement of mediated agreements in other countries.[46] It is to be hoped that progress will be made speedily with this project since the uncertainty which currently surrounds the issue of enforceability of mediated agreements is liable to hamper the increased use of mediation in Abduction Convention cases. This issue alone may justify an international instrument on cross-border mediation.

---

[38] Mediation Practice Guide (n 1), para 41–42,
[39] ibid, para 48.
[40] ibid, para 296. Buck (n 7), 46-47 reports confusion and difficulty in obtaining mirror orders.
[41] A Swiss court approved an agreement including issues relating to custody because the principle of amicable solutions was held to take priority over the norm that the country of refuge did not have jurisdiction over custody matters, *Beschluss und Urteil* OGer ZH, 4 April 2011, NH110001-O/U, discussed in Alfieri (n 4) 555.
[42] Where the left-behind parent agrees to the child remaining in the country of refuge, then the latter will usually become the child's habitual residence and will acquire jurisdiction in relation to matters of parental responsibility as a result of the left-parent's acquiescence (eg Art 7 of the 1996 Protection Convention). However, there may be technical problems of the court seised with the Convention proceedings from approving an agreement relating to substantive matters, see Preliminary Document No 13 (2011), www.hcch.net/upload/wop/abduct2012 pd13_e.pdf, para 45(b).
[43] Although it has been suggested that the court in the State of refuge might in appropriate cases have jurisdiction under Art 11 of the 1996 Convention (protection measures in case of urgency) or Art 12(3) of Brussels II bis (on the basis of substantial connection, Vigers (n 14) 55. Also, it may be possible to use the transfer of jurisdiction provisions in Arts 8 or 9 of the 1996 Convention, Preliminary Document No 13 ibid, para 47.
[44] Mediation Practice Guide (n 1), para 310. There may also be a requirement to hear the child, ibid.
[45] It has been suggested that judicial communications may help, Mediation Practice Guide ibid, para 312. However, it is difficult to see how this liaison can overcome legal obstacles, such as lack of jurisdiction.
[46] Conclusions of the Sixth Special Commission (25–31 January 2012), www.hcch.net/upload/wop/abduct2012 concl_e.pdf, para 76–77.

D The Voice of the Child

In contrast to the trend of greater child participation in legal proceedings concerning them,[47] including in Abduction Convention proceedings,[48] child participation in mediation seems to be relatively rare.[49] There are both policy and practical reasons for the exclusion of children from mediation.[50] Any requirement to hear the child is seen as inconsistent with the principle of party autonomy, which underpins mediation.[51] Moreover, parental permission is required and this is rarely given.[52] In addition, many mediators do not feel comfortable with child participation, as they feel that it compromises their neutrality.[53] Furthermore, some have argued that involving children in mediation between their parents may lead to long term damage to their relationship with one of their parents and involves the risk of giving children too much power.[54]

Nonetheless, there are cogent reasons for including children in mediation concerning their lives.[55] In particular, their exclusion is clearly inconsistent with their right to participate in decisions concerning them.[56] Moreover, various models of child inclusive mediation have been developed which take account of the need to safeguard children's interests[57] and research has demonstrated the benefits of involving children in mediation.[58]

Whilst it may be difficult to overcome the reluctance to include children in currently existing domestic mediation schemes,[59] especially where these are private, the development of a specialist mediation procedure for Convention cases provides an opportunity to ensure that children's voices are indeed heard. Vigers gives a number of justifications for hearing

---

[47] See ch 6 at II C.
[48] See ch 14.
[49] Canadian Department of Justice, 'The Voice of the Child in Separation/Divorce Mediation and Other Alternative Dispute Resolution Processes: A Literature Review' (2009), www.justice.gc.ca/eng/pi/fcy-fea/lib-bib/rep-rap/2009/vcsdm-pvem/pdf/vcsdm-pvem.pdf, 26–48 ('Literature Review').
[50] ibid, 13–14.
[51] Vigers (n 14) 77.
[52] ibid.
[53] L Parkinson, 'Family Mediation and Children' in P Delauran (ed), *Conflict Management in the Family Field and in other Close Relationships – Mediation as a Way Forward* (Copenhagen, Dejof, 2011) 75, 87.
[54] ibid.
[55] For arguments in favour of including children in child protection mediation, see Literature Review (n 49), 9–13; K 'Jordan, Need to Be Heard: Increasing Child Participation in Protection Mediation through the Implementation of Model Standards' (2009) 47 *Family Court Review* 715; Parkinson, 'Family Mediation' (n 53) 88.
[56] General Comment No 12 (July 2009) – The right of the child to be heard, drawn up by the Committee on the Rights of the Child, www2.ohchr.org/english/bodies/crc/comments.htm, para 52 states that 'all legislation on separation and divorce has to include the right of the child to be heard by decision makers and in mediation processes'.
[57] Literature Review (n 49), 26–48; J McIntosh, 'Child Inclusion as a Principle and as Evidence-Based Practice: Applications to Family Law Services and Related Sectors', www.aifs.gov.au/afrc/pubs/resource/resource1/resource1.pdf.
[58] Literature Review ibid, 12–14; J Mcintosh et al, 'Child-Focused and Child-Inclusive Divorce Mediation: Comparative Outcomes from a Prospective Study of Post-Separation Adjustment' (2008) 46 *Family Court Review* 105.
[59] The Israeli child participation regulations include a provision that parents who apply for the approval of an agreement which they have reached should be sent an explanation about the importance of hearing their children and allow courts to order hearing of the child where they are not satisfied that the child's parents have heard him, Regulation 258(33)12 of the Civil Procedure Regulations 1984 (as amended)(translation appended to T Morag, D Rivkin and Y Sorek, 'Child Participation in the Family Courts – Lessons from the Israeli Pilot Project' (2012) 26 *International Journal on Law Policy and the Family* 1). However, this provision has not been implemented in practice.

children in Convention mediation, even though this is not the practice in domestic mediation.[60] In particular, she advocates that mediation should be seen as part of the Convention proceedings and so, since State authorities are already involved in the case, the mediation does not take place entirely within the private domain, Moreover, the Brussels II bis Regulation may require hearing the child and there may be difficulties in enforcing the mediated agreement in other countries if the child has not been heard. Accordingly, she suggests that a report should be prepared on the child's views from the outset[61] and that this should be available for use in the mediation[62] and later by the judge, if the mediation fails. The difficulty with this proposal is that it envisages that the child will not usually be heard by the judge. Whilst there are clear disadvantages to the child being interviewed on a number of occasions by different professionals, he should always have the right to be heard directly by the decision-maker.[63] Thus, where the mediation fails, the child should be offered the opportunity to talk to the judge.

E Domestic Violence

Where there has been domestic violence, the conducting of mediation may threaten the physical or psychological integrity of one of the parties. This is particularly pertinent in the Abduction Convention context because, as already seen, allegations of domestic violence are relatively common.[64] Commentators are divided between those who consider that mediation is never appropriate in cases where there is a history of domestic violence[65] and those who consider that, provided that appropriate safeguards are introduced, mediation can work in such cases[66] and even be advantageous.[67] It has been suggested that in international cases, where the mediation is being conducted between parties in different countries by distance telecommunications, violence is less of a problem.[68] Whilst there is some logic in this view, account has to be taken of the potential impact on the victim of communication with the perpetrator, albeit from afar, and care has to be taken to ensure that the dynamics of the previous violence do not continue to impair the autonomy of the victim. The better view would seem to be that ruling out mediation completely where the victim genuinely wishes to mediate is unduly paternalistic.[69] Rather, it is necessary to decide on

---

[60] Vigers (n 14) 86–87.
[61] ibid 89.
[62] Parents should only be informed of the child's views to the extent that the child agrees to this, ibid.
[63] See ch 14 at III Ai; *cf* Swiss decision in Entscheid OGer BE vom 5. Juli 2011, ZK 10655, consid. III. 5. (discussed in Alfieri (n 4) 560), in which the judge held that there was no need for him to hear the child because the child's right to be heard had been realised when he was heard by his representative and the mediator.
[64] Chapter 11 at II Biv.
[65] eg J Krieger, 'The Dangers of Mediation in Domestic Violence Cases' (2002) 8 *Cardozo Women's Law Journal* 235; LG Lerman, 'Mediation of Wife Abuse Cases: The Adverse Impact of Informal Dispute Resolution on Women' (1984) 7 *Harvard Women's Law Journal* 57.
[66] eg D Bagshaw, 'Family Violence and Family Mediation in Australia' in P Deleuran (ed), *Conflict Management in the Family Field and in other Close Relationships – Mediation as a Way Forward* (Copenhagen, Dejof, 2011) 93, 100–03; 'Mediation in International Parental Child Abduction: The Reunite Mediation Pilot Scheme' (2006), www.reunite.org/edit/files/Mediation %20Report.pdf, 48, did include cases where domestic violence had been alleged and concluded that such allegations did not preclude mediation.
[67] eg it is argued that it can empower the victim, Bagshaw ibid 101; J Alanen, 'When Human Rights Conflict: Mediating International Parental Kidnapping Disputes Involving the Domestic Violence Defense'(2008) 40 *The University of Miami Inter-American Law Review* 49, 69.
[68] Vigers (n 14) 68.
[69] Alanen, 'When Human Rights Conflict' (n 67) 54–55.

the facts of each case whether or not mediation is appropriate and what safeguards are necessary.[70] Thus, it is essential that all cases are screened for domestic violence before mediation is commenced[71] and that mediators are on the lookout for signs of violence within the relationship throughout the mediation.[72]

IV Conclusions

Mediation can be used to resolve international abduction cases in a way that benefits all the parties involved and avoids many of the drawbacks of adjudication. The distinct features of Abduction Convention cases, including their international nature and the need for speed, mean that mediation in Convention cases has to be treated as a specialist discipline involving particular procedures and requiring appropriate training.[73] Thus, the work which has been done by the Permanent Bureau and others to promote mediation in Abduction Convention cases is to be welcomed. However, the little use of mediation in practice suggests that more proactive steps are needed and thus serious consideration should be given to the drawing up of an international instrument which regulates family mediation in cross-border disputes. Any such instrument and any national or regional regulation should ensure inter alia uniform standards for the training of mediators and quality of mediations;[74] that the voice of sufficiently mature children is heard; that agreements are freely made without fear or duress and that agreements can be enforced in all relevant States.

---

[70] Alanen, ibid 106–07, suggests that, in the light of the different professional and ethical codes in relation to mediation in such cases, there is a need for a uniform standard to be adopted in Abduction Convention cases.
[71] Mediation Practice Guide (n 1), para 40.
[72] Bagshaw, 'Family Violence' (n 66) 93–94.
[73] Mediation Practice Guide (n 1) paras 98–105.
[74] For existing initiatives, ibid, paras 96–97.

17

Compensating the Left-Behind Parent

I Introduction

As seen above, one of the objectives of the mandatory return mechanism is to restore the *status quo ante*. However, the return remedy per se does not put the left-behind parent in the position he was in before the abduction. In particular, the process of recovering the child often places a considerable financial burden on the left-behind parent. For example, he may incur costs in identifying the whereabouts of the child, in travelling to and staying in the State of abduction, and in paying the legal costs of submitting an application for the child's return in the courts of the requested State. Furthermore, the discovery that his child has been abducted, together with the uncertainty as to whether and when he will recover the child and the lack of or reduced contact with the child will often cause considerable emotional distress. This chapter briefly considers[1] the extent to which it is appropriate to require the abductor to compensate the left-behind parent and various possible frameworks for the provision of such compensation. The word compensation is used broadly to refer to the reimbursement of expenses incurred and to payments for non-financial loss, such as emotional distress.

Three models for compensation will be discussed: the tort model; the criminal model and the Hague Convention on the Civil Aspects of International Child Abduction ('Abduction Convention') model.[2] Examples will be given of the use of each of the models and the advantages and disadvantage of each analysed.

II To What Extent is Compensation Appropriate?

A Arguments in Favour of Compensation

The most obvious argument in favour of compensating the left-behind parent is the basic principle of corrective justice which underpins tort law. In other words, the abductor's wrongful behaviour has caused financial loss, and sometimes also emotional distress, to the left-behind parent, for which the latter is entitled to be compensated. In addition, it is a basic principle of civil litigation in many systems that the losing party has to pay the costs

---

[1] A detailed discussion of the subject can be found in R Schuz and B Shmueli, 'Between Tort Law, Contract Law and Child Law: How to Compensate the Left-Behind Parent in International Child Abduction Cases' (2012) 23 *Columbia Journal of Gender and Law* 64.
[2] A fourth model, the contract model (ibid 99–101), is not discussed here because no cases have been found where this model alone was used and because of its similarity to the tort model.

incurred by the other party in conducting the litigation. Moreover, an award of compensation appears to promote the objectives of the Abduction Convention[3] in a number of ways. It will restore the *status quo ante*; may enhance the deterrent effect of the mandatory return mechanism[4] and will do justice between the parties.

B Arguments against Compensation

Some legal systems take the view that in matters relating to children, there are no winners and losers and thus it is not appropriate for one party to pay the other's costs.[5] Yet, it can be argued that whilst there is much to commend this approach in domestic cases in which both parties have behaved lawfully and the court simply has to decide what custody arrangements are in the best interests of the parties, the situation in abduction cases is different because the abductor has violated the custody rights of the left-behind parent.

Nonetheless, the latter argument does not take into account that abduction does not usually occur in a vacuum, but is often the 'straw which broke the camel's back' in an ongoing conflict between the parties. In particular, as already seen, there are many abduction cases in which the background to the abduction was violence, abuse or other provocative behaviour on the part of the left-behind parent.[6] In such cases, it seems unjust that the victim of the violence should have to pay compensation to the perpetrator from whom she fled. However, while in some cases it will be obvious where the moral blame lies, in other cases the facts will be less clear and any attempt to assess fault is liable to lead to a full-scale futile and damaging investigation into the marital life of the parents.

A further problem with an award of compensation against the custodial parent is that it may impair that parent's ability to provide for the child's basic needs. On the other hand, the award will be to the child's advantage in cases where the left-behind parent is now the custodial parent. It may be argued that in either situation there is little relevance to any payment of compensation by one parent to the other, because this does not actually affect the combined financial position of the parents, who are both responsible for supporting the child. On the other hand, in practice, the child's standard of living is usually dependent upon the financial position of his custodial parent.

Finally, it should be remembered that the main concern of left-behind parents, who are often in a state of emotional trauma and bewilderment, is the return of their child and so they may not give thought to the financial implications at that point in time. This suggestion is supported by the fact that many left-behind parents actually offer to pay for the costs of returning the child, even though the court could clearly require the abductor to do so.[7] Furthermore, courts sometimes make a return order conditional on the left-behind parent undertaking to waive his rights to the reimbursement of costs, on the basis that ensuring financial support for the child and custodial parent in the country of origin is necessary in order to prevent the return exposing the child to a grave risk of harm.[8]

---

[3] See ch 5 at II C.
[4] But see reservations about the deterrent effect, ibid at II Cii.
[5] *EC-L v DM (Child Abduction: Costs)* [2005] EWHC 588 (Fam).
[6] See ch 11 at II Biv.
[7] Of course, this may be because waiting for the abductor to fund the travel costs would delay the return of the child. However, it may be noted that Art 26(2) of the Abduction Convention provides that the applicant can be required to pay for the travel costs.
[8] In relation to conditions for return, see generally ch 11 at III.

Nonetheless, these facts do not justify not recognising the basic principle that the left-behind parent is entitled to compensation. Rather, they explain why there will be cases where the left-behind may be prepared or required to waive his right.

III Analysis of the Various Models

A The Tort Model

In two Israeli cases,[9] left-behind fathers succeeded in tort actions against their ex-wives who had abducted the children to other countries, following the return of the children under the Abduction Convention. The mother's action in abducting the child was held to constitute the tort of breach of statutory duty[10] because it violated a provision of the Penal Law,[11] making it an offence to remove a child from the custody of his lawful guardian without the consent of each person having legal custody. In both cases, the fathers received reimbursement of expenses, which they had not claimed from the foreign courts in the Abduction Convention proceedings. In the second case, the father was also awarded the costs of psychotherapy and compensation for emotional distress.[12]

The tort model is consistent with the objectives of the Abduction Convention, but it does have a number of drawbacks. Firstly, it is necessary to instigate separate proceedings and the continued litigation between the parties is likely to make it more difficult for the child to maintain contact and a healthy relationship with both parents. Secondly, since the court does not have any discretion to reduce or exempt the abductor from tort liability, the latter will have to pay even where he does not appear to be morally blameworthy[13] and it will not be possible to take into account the impact on the material welfare of the child.

B The Criminal Model

Under this model, a parent who was convicted of the offence of child abduction[14] would be ordered to pay compensation to the left-behind parent within the framework of the criminal proceedings where the legal system in question makes provision for this.[15] For example, in *United States v Cummings*,[16] in which the father had been convicted of abducting his children to Germany, the sums expended by the left-behind mother in trying to recover her children from Germany were held to be recoverable under the United States Victim

---

[9] FamC (TA) 42273/99 *Dr. ZM v RMP* Nevo, 09/08/05 (Justice Shochat); RFamA (SC) 3241/09 *Plonit v Ploni* (2 October 2009), http://elyon1.court.gov.il/files/09/410/032/b01/09032410.b01.pdf

[10] Section 63 of the Israeli Civil Wrongs Ordinance (New Version). The tort of negligence could also be relied upon in countries where intentional actions can constitute this tort.

[11] Section 373 of the Israeli Penal Law, 1977.

[12] *Plonit* (n 9).

[13] Unless the previous behaviour of the left-behind parent could be seen as contributory negligence or a separate tort, making set-off possible, Schuz and Shmueli 'Between Tort Law', (n 1) 98.

[14] See ch 1 at II Aii. Alternatively, in some countries disobeying a court order might be a criminal offence, eg s 287 of the Israeli Penal Law (n 11).

[15] eg United States Victim and Witness Protection Act of 1982 (VWPA) 8 USC s 3663(a)(1)(A) (2006); s 77 of the Israeli Penal Law (n 11).

[16] *United States v Cummings* 281 F3d 1046 (9th Cir 2002).

and Witness Protection Act of 1982 (VWPA). The Court also held that a parent who is convicted under the Federal International Parental Kidnapping Crime Act[17] can be ordered to pay restitution to the other parent to reimburse him for legal expenses incurred in trying to recover his child.[18] Moreover, the Supreme Court of Minnesota upheld a decision reimbursing the mother for the costs she incurred in re-abducting her children from Algeria to the country from which the father had unlawfully removed them.[19]

The criminal model has two main advantages. Firstly, there is no need for separate proceedings. Secondly, abductors are usually not prosecuted where they are not morally blameworthy.[20] However, the rarity of criminal prosecutions is also a disadvantage because it means that only in a very limited number of cases will the left-behind parent be able to obtain compensation.

C The Abduction Convention Model

Article 26(4) of the Abduction Convention provides that the court hearing the application for the return of the child may,

> where appropriate, direct the person who removed or retained the child . . . to pay necessary expenses incurred by or on behalf of the applicant including travel expenses, any costs incurred or payments made for locating the child, the costs of legal representation of the applicant and, those of returning the child.

In the United States, Article 26(4) has been enacted in section 11607(b)(3) of the International Child Abduction Remedies Act (ICARA),[21] which provides that

> [a]ny court ordering the return of a child pursuant to an action brought under section 11603 of this title shall order the respondent to pay necessary expenses incurred by or on behalf of the petitioner, including court costs, legal fees, foster home or other care during the course of proceedings in the action, and transportation costs related to the return of the child, unless the respondent establishes that such order would be clearly inappropriate.[22]

It will be noted that while this provision purports to implement Article 26(4) of the Abduction Convention, it in fact makes a substantive change by reversing the burden of proof and requiring the court to make an order unless the abductor shows that it is clearly inappropriate to do so.[23]

In general, it is difficult to obtain a complete and accurate picture of the expenses awarded by courts because this issue is often dealt with after the main case and is not reported anywhere.[24] However, the evidence suggests that, at least outside the USA, the

---

[17] Federal International Parental Kidnapping Crime Act 18 USC s 1204 (2006). It should be noted that this Act also provides remedies for the left-behind parent to reacquire the child, mostly in cases involving countries with which the US has criminal extradition treaties.
[18] *Cummings* (n 16) 1052.
[19] *State v Maidi* 537 NW2d 280 (Minn 1995).
[20] See ch 1 at II Aii.
[21] International Child Abduction Remedies Act 42 USC s 11607(b)(3) (2006).
[22] ibid.
[23] Schuz and Shmueli, 'Between Tort Law' (n 1) 108; *Acosta Saldivar v Rodela* 2012 US Dist LEXIS 141126.
[24] eg, FamC (TA) 7300/01 *B v B* (Unreported 20 June 2001) (Israel) (stating that the Court would make a decision on expenses after the applicant had submitted a declaration listing the expenses claimed); *Kufner v Kufner* 519 F3d 33 (1st Cir 2008) (stating that there are very few reported cases on fee and expenses petitions under the fee-shifting provision of 42 USC § 11607(b)(3)).

Analysis of the Various Models 421

power to award expenses is not frequently used.[25] Whilst Article 26(4) has also been enacted in Australia by regulations,[26] there is little sign of its use in the case law. In England and Wales, it is extremely unusual for any expenses, even legal costs, to be awarded to the left-behind parent.[27] This may be largely because left-behind parents receive State-funded non-means-tested legal aid[28] and thus there are no legal costs to recover.[29] Moreover, the legal aid scheme may even cover the costs of the parent's participation in the legal proceedings, including travel expenses, where he is required to give evidence.[30] In Israel, a number of cases have been found in which some expenses were awarded to the left-behind parent in addition to legal costs.[31]

The apparently limited use made of Article 26(4) seems to have been expected by the Rapporteur, who referred to it as 'an optional provision' whose 'scope is particularly symbolic, a possible deterrent to behaviour which is contrary to the objects of the Convention.'[32] Professor Perez-Vera does not give reasons for this approach, but it can perhaps be understood in the context of the pre-existing legal situation, under which parental child abduction was not usually considered to be illegal,[33] and in light of the fact that the drafters saw the mandatory return mechanism as the main method of dealing with the increasing phenomenon of international child abduction.[34] In any event, the half-hearted attitude of the Pérez-Vera Report to Article 26(4) might help explain why lawyers representing left-behind parents do not routinely make claims under the provision. It may well be that lawyers and judges in some countries are not even aware that there is a possibility of awarding expenses other than lawyers' fees.[35]

The Abduction Convention model possesses a number of advantages over the other models. In particular, no separate proceedings are required and the court has wide discretion which enables it to take into account the relative moral blameworthiness of the parties and the impact on the child of an award of compensation. However, it may be argued that the unfettered discretion is a disadvantage because it promotes uncertainty and allows

---

[25] Schuz and Shmueli (n 1) 109–10.
[26] Family Law (Child Abduction Convention) Regulations 1986 (Cth) reg 30 (Australia).
[27] *EC-L v DM* (n 5).
[28] ibid.
[29] This may also be the case in other countries where the left-behind parent is represented by the Central Authority or some other Government Agency eg, *Family Advocate, Cape Town v Chirume* 2005 (6090/05) ZAWCHC 94 [40], www.saflii.org/za/cases/ZAWCHC/2005/94.pdf; *cf* in the US, where it has been held that the legal aid fund can recover costs from the abductor, *Acosta Saldivar v Rodela* (n 23). Similarly, in New Zealand, the abductor has been ordered to pay the costs of the State in defending her unsuccessful appeal against return, *TB v JPB* HC [2011] NZHC 1135.
[30] Emails from Marcus Scott-Manderson, QC (20 April 2010 and 26 April 2010) (on file with author). Similarly, the German legal aid scheme will cover the travel and associated costs of the left-behind parent, remark of a member of the German delegation at the 6th Special Commission Meeting at the Hague (3 June 2011) (author's notes).
[31] eg, FamC (Hai) 15480/00 *D v D* (Unreported, 2 December 2000) (Isr) (awarding travel and accommodation costs for the duration of the trial); FamC (TA) 5063/97 *Pekan v Dolberg* Nevo, 16 April 1999 (Isr) (awarding travel and accommodation costs and income lost for the duration of the trial).
[32] Perez-Vera Report, Proceedings of the 14th Session of the Hague Conference Oct 1980, www.hcch.net/upload/expl28.pdf, para 136.
[33] See ch 1 at I A.
[34] Perez-Vera Report (n 32), paras 16–18.
[35] eg Justice Arbel in *Plonit* (n 9) [5] expressed the view that the Court in the Abduction Convention proceedings was not in a position to compensate the left-behind parent for his expenses and other damages, apart from legal costs. It is also significant that the provision is not mentioned in P Beaumont and P McEleavy, *The Hague Convention on International Child Abduction* (Oxford, Oxford University Press, 1999), the leading text on the Abduction Convention.

courts not to order compensation without giving any reason. Furthermore, Article 26(4) limits the award of compensation to cases where return is ordered[36] and yet, where the reason for non-return is not a result of the applicant's behaviour, it is not clear why he should not be compensated for his costs and other losses.[37] Another drawback is that Article 26(4) only allows for the reimbursement of expenses and not for compensation for non-financial loss, such as emotional distress.

IV Conclusion

It is necessary to design a model for awarding compensation to left-behind parents which is as efficient as possible and which takes into account compensatory principles, whilst being flexible enough to allow the arguments against compensation to be taken into account where relevant. The analysis in Part III shows that the optimal method of providing compensation is within the framework of Abduction Convention proceedings, although the return of the child should not be delayed whilst issues of compensation are litigated.[38] However, in order to ensure better promotion of the objectives of the Abduction Convention and tort law, it is necessary to widen the scope of the provision in Article 26(4) and increase the use of the provision in practice. Accordingly, it is suggested that the power to award compensation should also exist where return is refused and that compensation should not be limited to the reimbursement of expenses. Moreover, it is proposed that, in accordance with US practice, courts should exercise their discretion to award compensation unless the abductor shows why an award should not be made or why it should be reduced.[39] In order to reduce uncertainty, the grounds for not making or reducing an award should be limited to two:[40] that the award is inappropriate because of the behaviour of the left-behind parent[41] or that there is a grave risk that the award will expose the child to physical or psychological harm or otherwise place the child in an intolerable situation.[42]

---

[36] *Ramirez v Buyauskas* 2012 US Dist LEXIS 24899; although legal costs could be awarded on some other basis, eg the South African case of [zRPz]*Central Authority v Reynders* [2011] 2 All SA 438 (GNP), in which costs were ordered against the respondent grandmother even though the child was not returned and in *Cummings* (n 16), compensation was paid within criminal proceedings even though the children were not returned.

[37] Schuz and Shmueli (n 1) 119–20.

[38] ibid 118–19.

[39] In most of the reported US cases in which the Court found a basis for the abductor's claim that it was not appropriate to require him to make an award against him, the award was reduced rather than eliminated completely, *Silverman v Silverman* 338 F3d 886 (8th Cir, 2003).

[40] The good faith of the abductor or the legitimacy of the dispute do not make the award inappropriate, *Neves v Neves* 637 F Supp 2d 322, 345 (WD North Carolina, 2009); *Maynard v Maynard* 2007 US Dist LEXIS 46838.

[41] eg *Silverman* (n 39) (emotional abuse by the left-behind parent).

[42] This wording is chosen because it mirrors the exception to mandatory return in Art 13(1)(b) of the Convention, see ch 11. This condition may be satisfied where the abductor is the custodial parent and is impecunious, eg *Wilchinsky v Wilchinsky* 2010 US Dist LEXIS 25903, 35.

18

Enforcing Rights of Access

I Introduction

The Preamble to the Hague Convention on the Civil Aspects of International Child Abduction ('Abduction Convention') recites that the drafters of the Convention desire to secure protection for rights of access and Article 1(b) of the Abduction Convention provides that it is an objective of the Convention 'to ensure that rights of custody and access under the law of one Contracting State are effectively respected in other Contracting States'. While at first sight the objective of protecting rights of access[1] appears to be of equal standing to the objective of securing the prompt return of children provided for in Article 1(a), only two provisions of the Convention refer to rights of access. Firstly, the list of measures which Central Authorities are obligated to take includes making 'arrangements for organizing or securing the effective exercise of right of access'.[2] Secondly, Article 21 provides:

> An application to make arrangements for organizing or securing the effective exercise of rights of access may be presented to the Central Authorities of the Contracting States in the same way as an application for the return of a child.
>
> The Central Authorities are bound by the obligation of co-operation which are set forth in Article 7 to promote the peaceful enjoyment of access rights and the fulfillment of any conditions to which the exercise of such rights may be subject. The Central Authorities shall take steps to remove, as far as possible, all obstacles to the exercise of such rights.
>
> The Central Authorities, either directly or through intermediaries, may initiate or assist in the institution of proceedings with a view to organizing or protecting these rights and securing respect for the conditions to which the exercise of these rights may be subject.

Not surprisingly, the limited and ambivalent nature of these provisions has meant that they have not been widely used. In 2008, there were only 360 access applications received by 42 Contracting States.[3] Moreover, only in 21 per cent of cases did the applications result in

---

[1] The term 'access' is used in this chapter because that is the term used in the Abduction Convention, even though many legal systems use other terms such as 'visitation' and 'contact'. Thus, access should be understood broadly to refer to the various ways in which the parent with whom the child does not have his main residence (referred to as the non-custodial parent) maintains a personal relationship with the child, see W Duncan, 'Transfrontier Access/ Contact' Preliminary Document No 5 (2002), www.hcch.net/upload/abd2002_pd05e.pdf, para 8 ('Duncan Report').

[2] Art 7(f).

[3] N Lowe, 'A Statistical Analysis of Applications Made in 2008 under the Hague Convention of 25 October 1980 on the Civil Aspects of International Child Abduction, Part I Global Report', Preliminary Document 8A (November 2011), www.hcch.net/upload/wop/abduct2011pd08ae.pdf, 50 ('2008 Statistical Survey'). However, it should be noted that this represents a 40% increase from 2003. For figures in relation to return applications, see ch 2 at I C. Nonetheless, in 2008, access applications constituted only 16% of all the applications under the Convention, ibid, 70.

access being granted, either by agreement or by court order.[4] Concern at the inadequacy of the access provisions was expressed at Special Commission Meetings[5] and after thoroughly investigating the problems arising in relation to cross-frontier contact,[6] the Permanent Bureau published a Good Practice Guide relevant to both the Abduction Convention and the 1996 Child Protection Convention.[7]

Part II of this chapter will briefly examine the case law in relation to Article 21 and then analyse the way in which the provision has been interpreted and applied in light of those of the parameters set out in chapters five and six which are appropriate in this context. Part III will then consider the provisions of the 1996 Hague Child Protection Convention[8] and relevant regional instruments which relate to the enforcement of access rights. Finally, in Part IV, conclusions will be drawn as to the role which the Abduction Convention can and should play in ensuring respect for rights of access.

II Article 21 of the Abduction Convention

A Interpretation and Application of Article 21

i The Nature of the Provision

Article 21 has been interpreted differently in different countries. The narrow approach takes the view that this provision does not provide any independent source of jurisdiction[9] and does not impose any duty on courts.[10] Thus, requests to enforce access rights have to be submitted under domestic legislation.[11] In contrast, according to the wider view, the provision does confer jurisdiction. In some countries which have adopted the latter approach, it has been based on internal legislation implementing the Convention.[12] However, even among the countries who take a wider view, some treat the provision as

---

[4] ibid, 58. The figure was 33% in 2003.

[5] eg 'Conclusions and Recommendations of the Fourth Meeting of the Special Commission to Review the Operation of the *Hague Convention of 25 October 1980 on the Civil Aspects of International Child Abduction*' (22–28 March 2001) www.hcch.net/upload/concl28sc4_e.pdf, para 6.1.

[6] See Duncan Report (n 1).

[7] Good Practice Guide on Transfrontier Contact Concerning Children, www.hcch.net/upload/guidecontact_e.pdf ('Contact Guide').

[8] See generally ch 1 at II E.

[9] English Child Abduction Unit Practice Note (5 March 1993) [1993] 1 FLR 804; *Cantor v Cohen* 442 F3d 196 (4th Cir 2006) (holding that US Federal courts do not have any jurisdiction in relation to access). Thus, it is assumed that the reference to judicial orders for access made by US courts in the 2008 Statistical Survey (n 3) refers to decisions of State courts; *cf* recent US Appeals Court decision in *Otzalin v Otzalin* (2d Cir, 2013) www.gpo.gov/fdsys/pkg/USCOURTS-ca2-12-02371/pdf/USCOURTS-ca2-12-02371-0.pdf (holding, contrary to the decision in *Cantor v Cohen*, that 'ICARA 42 U.S.C. § 11603(b) creates a federal right of action to enforce "access" rights protected under the Hague Convention.')

[10] *Re G (a Minor)(Enforcement of Access Abroad)* [1993] Fam 216, where Butler-Sloss LJ said 'There are no teeth to be found in art 21 and its provisions have no part to play in the decision to be made by the judge.'; *cf* per Thorpe LJ in *Hunter v Morrow* [2005] 2 FLR 1119, suggesting adoption of the wider approach adopted in other common law countries.

[11] eg Israeli case of FamC 89790/00 *MAB v ER* Nevo, 8 February 2001, relying inter alia on *Re G*, ibid.

[12] eg in Scotland on Rules of the Court of Session which provided for applications for access under the Convention to be made by petition (*Donofrio v Burrell* 2000 SLT 1051); in Australia in Regulation 25 of the Child Abduction Regulations, which provides that the Central Authority may apply to the court for an order specifying with whom the child should spend time (*State Central Authority v Peddar* [2008] FamCA 519).

providing a basis for a court to grant access rights, whilst others understand it as a conferring jurisdiction on the Central Authority to apply for an access order under domestic legislation.[13]

However, it should be noted that it is not clear whether the approach taken to Article 21 affects the final outcome. The statistics in the 2008 Statistical Survey, suggest that access is more likely to be granted where the case is decided under the domestic law than under the convention.[14]

ii The Threshold Requirements

Article 21 does not spell out the prerequisites for its invocation. Whilst most courts have taken the view that there is no need for a wrongful removal as in return applications, it seems clear from the wording of Article 4 that it is necessary to prove breach of access rights and that the child was habitually resident in a Contracting State immediately before the breach of access rights.[15] However, there have been some differences in opinion as to the time at which the habitual residence requirement has to be satisfied. The better view is that the requirement will be satisfied where the child is habitually resident in the Contracting State to which the application is submitted at the date when enforcement is sought.[16] The position can be contrasted with return cases since in the case of access, the decision relates to the merits of the case and so usually only the court of the habitual residence has jurisdiction to make such an order. Whilst the breach of the access order may have started before the arrival of the child in the requested State, the continued breach after the change in habitual residence is sufficient to fulfill the requirement in Article 4.

iii The Decision-Making Mechanism

In those jurisdictions which treat Article 21 as conferring jurisdiction, the question arises as to the basis upon which the court should make a decision as to whether to enforce access rights. Are they to be enforced automatically, in a way similar to the mandatory return mechanism, or is the court to determine the issue of access in accordance with its own internal criteria, which will usually mean assessing the best interests of the child?

Different approaches can be found to this question. In the Australian decision of *Director General, Department of Families, Youth and Community Care v Reissner*,[17] Lindenmayer J took the view that in applications under the Convention, the object was to respect foreign access rights and therefore although the child's best interests should be taken into consideration, they were not paramount. However, in the later case of *State Central Authority v Peddar*, Barnett J rejected this view and held that access applications under the Convention

---

[13] eg in New Zealand, *G v J* [2001] NZFLR 593.
[14] 2008 Statistical Survey (n 3) 58.
[15] N Lowe, M Everall and M Nicholls, *International Movement of Children: Law, Practice and Procedure* (Bristol, Jordans, 2004) 570.
[16] *Re G (a Minor)* (n 10), overruling *B v B*, in which it was held that the Article referred to habitual residence in the Contacting State in which the access rights originally existed. The view taken in *Re G* has been followed inter alia in Australia, eg *Peddar* (n 12) and in New Zealand, eg *G v J* (n 13); cf the approach of the Israeli Supreme Court that there has to have been a change of habitual residence shortly before the breach of the access rights, RFamA 8872/09 *Ploni v Plonim*, 1 December 2009 [4] http://elyon1.court.gov.il/files/09/720/088/b02/09088720.b02.pdf.
[17] *Director General, Department of Families, Youth and Community Care v Reissner* [1999] FamCA 1238.

should be decided according to the best interests standard, as in domestic cases.[18] Nonetheless, considerable weight will be given to the access order made by the foreign court,[19] unless this is overridden by welfare considerations.[20] Yet, it should be borne in mind that an access order made at a time when all the parties were living in the foreign jurisdiction may well not be appropriate for the new situation in which the applicant is living in a different country and therefore will need longer periods of access during holiday periods rather than on a weekly basis.[21] Thus, it may quite often be necessary for the court in the State where the child is now living to modify the original access order.

iv The Obligations of the Central Authority

There is lack of clarity as to the extent of the obligations imposed on Central Authorities by Article 21. According to the narrow view, the provision is so vague that it does not create any rights even against Central Authorities, which have considerable discretion and whose powers may well be limited by local law.[22] On a wider view, the duty of the Central Authority is to make efforts to secure respect for the access rights either by promoting agreement between the parties or assisting in the submission of an access application.[23]

v Speed, Representation and Funding

It might be thought that even if Article 21 does not create an independent mechanism for enforcing access rights, it should at least entitle the applicant to the procedural benefits of the Convention, including entitlement to legal aid and a fast-track procedure.[24] However, not all courts agree that applications under Article 21 should be expedited[25] and not all jurisdictions apply the favourable legal representation and funding schemes, available for return cases, to access applications.[26] Indeed, the time taken to determine access application is significantly greater than that taken for return applications.[27]

B Analysis

i Internal Coherence

Article 21 does not fit comfortably within the framework of the Abduction Convention.

---

[18] *Peddar* (n 12) para 41. Reliance is placed inter alia on Regulation 25(A) of the Australian Child Abduction Regulations which makes clear that the court has wide discretion in the making of access orders under the Convention.

[19] This is likely to be greater the more recently the order was made, *Reissner* (n 17), para 86. Even in jurisdictions which don't treat art 21 as creating an independent source of jurisdiction, weight is likely to be given to the foreign access order, see eg *MAB v ER* (n 11).

[20] *Reissner* ibid, para 51, relying on the approach of Butler-Sloss J in Re G *(a Minor)* (n 10); comment of New Zealand Court in *G v J* (n 13) that 'Prima facie in these cases, the Court can generally assume that the order was for the welfare of the child at the time it was made. Such an approach gives practical effect to the Convention.'

[21] As in eg *Donofrio v Burrell* (n 12); *cf* the situation where the access order was made as part of an order allowing relocation, as in eg *G v J* ibid.

[22] Duncan Report (n 1), para 20.

[23] Contact Guide (n 7), 21–23.

[24] This is the situation in Israel, *MAB v ER* (n11). In Australia, the Central Authority will bring the application in the same way as in return cases, Duncan Report (n 1), para 35.

[25] eg *Donofrio v Burrell* (n 12).

[26] eg *Re T (Minors)(Hague Convention: Access)* [1993] 2 FLR 617; Duncan Report (n 1), para 35–37.

[27] 339 days as opposed to 188 days, 2008 Statistical Survey (n 3), 71.

Whilst there appears to be a common denominator between this provision and those relating to return, because both are based on the breach of the rights of the applicant and are designed to secure respect for those rights, there is a fundamental difference between the mechanism and substance of the remedies in the two types of case. Article 21 is not simply a first aid remedy designed to restore the status quo, but rather aims to provide a long term substantive solution by ensuring contact between the child and the applicant.

Thus, it is indeed understandable that many have simply seen Article 21 as an administrative provision, aimed at overcoming practical difficulties encountered by parents who live in foreign countries in organising contact with their children and in gaining access to the legal system of that country. In this respect, the plight of the non-custodial parent seeking to exercise his access rights is similar to that of the left-behind parent, and providing him with the opportunity to apply via his own Central Authority may be of considerable assistance to him. Whilst the need for speed cannot be compared to that in return applications because the place of the child's residence is not in issue, the long term implications of lack of contact between the child and the non-custodial parent still justify expedition.[28] This is even more so in international cases where access is less frequent and thus at the time of breach, significant time may have already elapsed since the applicant last saw the child.[29] Furthermore, it can be argued that the greater difficulties encountered by foreign applicants seeking access with their children[30] justifies special help with funding.

Finally, it may be commented that if the access provisions in the Convention had related only to situations in which there had been a wrongful removal or retention, there would have been greater internal coherence and perhaps greater willingness on the part of Contracting States to give them greater effect.

ii Intention of the Drafters

The drafters chose to include reference to access rights because these were seen as the corollary of custody rights[31] and because lack of access to their children was believed to be one of the motivations for abduction by non-custodial parents.[32] Conversely, the fear of abduction was seen as a common reason for breach of access rights by the custodial parents. Thus, measures taken by the Central Authority to ensure that the child would be returned at the end of a visit to the non-custodial parent might remove obstacles to the exercise of the latter's access rights.[33]

From the comments of the Rapporteur in relation to Article 21, it can be seen that the provision was indeed seen as an administrative provision, which sought to utilise the Central Authority structure in order to facilitate solving problems in relation to the exercise of access rights and, where necessary, to assist in the initiation of legal proceedings.[34] Thus, the narrow interpretation by some courts does not seem to be contrary to the intention of the drafters.

---

[28] Indeed, the Art 2 obligation to use the most expeditious procedures available also applies to ensuring respect for rights of access, cf Art 11, which only applies to return applications.
[29] Duncan Report (n 1), para 107–08.
[30] ibid, para 64.
[31] Perez-Vera Report, Proceedings of the 14th Session of the Hague Conference Oct 1980, www.hcch.net/upload/expl28.pdf, para 125.
[32] Duncan Report (n 1), para 11(d).
[33] ibid, para 128, gives the example of the making of undertakings to the Central Authority and informing the latter of the place where the child will be staying during the visit.
[34] ibid, para 126.

iii Promotion of the Objectives of the Convention

As already seen, a stated objective of the Abduction Convention is to 'ensure that rights of custody and of access under the law of one Contracting State are effectively respected in other Contracting States'.[35] Whilst Article 21 does promote this objective, its limited scope means that it can only play a relatively minor role in its achievement. In particular, there is nothing in the provision which requires States to respect rights of access existing under the law of other Contracting States. Rather, the provision provides little more than a framework for the applicant parent to apply for an order for exercise of access under the local law of the Contracting State where the child is living. Thus, the extent to which his existing rights are respected depends entirely on the internal law of the latter State. In other words, from a substantive perspective, a non-custodial parent who applies under Article 21 does not seem to be in a more favourable position than such a parent who lives in a non-Contracting State and applies directly under the local law of the State where the child is now living.

The objective of 'protecting children internationally from the harmful effects of their wrongful removal or retention'[36] could be promoted by ensuring respect for rights of access of a left-behind parent to his abducted child pending a decision in return proceedings.[37] Whilst both Articles 7(f) and 21 appear to require Central Authorities to assist in making arrangements for access in such situations, there is nothing in the Convention to empower the courts of the requested State to order access,[38] where the Central Authorities' attempts are not successful. Accordingly, whether or not there is jurisdiction to make such an order depends entirely on the local law of the requested State.[39] It would have been helpful if the Convention had expressly defined the powers of the court in the requested State to make decisions concerning access whilst the return proceedings are continuing.[40] In addition, where return is ordered and the abductor does not return with the child, then the abductor may have difficulty in maintaining contact with the child.[41] This will be particularly harmful to the child where the abductor was the child's primary carer. As seen above,[42] in such a situation agreements made about contact before return or even orders made by the court in the requested State may well not be enforceable in the requesting State.

Moreover, there are return applications in which the real motive of the left-behind parent is to maintain contact with his child. The reason that he applies for return is that there is no similar expeditious and summary method of acquiring enforceable rights of access.[43] In addition, he may well fear that any application for access in the courts of the requested State would be interpreted as acquiescence and thus would prevent him from seeking return if he were not satisfied with the access arrangements ordered or the method of

---

[35] Art 1(b).

[36] Preamble to the Convention.

[37] In relation to the harm caused to the abducted child by lack of contact with the left-behind parent, see generally ch 3 at II.

[38] Equally there is nothing to prevent making such an order because Article 16 only forbids decision on the merits of rights of custody, see per Baroness Hale in *Re D (A Child) (Abduction: Foreign Custody Rights)* [2006] UKHL 51 [67].

[39] Duncan Report (n 1), para 32.

[40] Of course, if cases were decided within six weeks, as envisaged by Art 11, this need would be considerably less. See ch 2 at I C.

[41] Contact Guide (n 7), 23.

[42] See ch 16 at II C.

[43] The Duncan Report (n 1), para 39 even suggests that the difficulty in enforcing access rights is one of the reasons why courts have been prepared to treat ne exeat orders as custody rights. See generally ch 7 at IIC.

enforcing them. In order to facilitate optimal solution of these cases, Baroness Hale has suggested that a procedure should be devised 'whereby the facilitation of rights of access in this country under Article 21 were in contemplation at the same time as the return of the child under Article 12'.[44]

iv Consistency with Children's Rights and Interests and Parental Rights

It seems clear that the reference to rights of access in the Convention refers to parental rights of access[45] and not to the right of children to maintain contact with both of their parents.[46] Accordingly, the access provisions in the Convention are consistent with the concept that parents have a right to contact with their children,[47] although, as seen above, in practice they do not per se do a great deal to give effect to those rights.

Moreover, provisions which ensure the exercise of parental rights of access will also give effect to the rights of the children, apart from situations in which mature children do not want contact with the other parent or contact is contrary to their welfare. As seen above,[48] even courts which enforce rights of access under Article 21 have held that this is subject to the overriding consideration of the best interests of the child. Nonetheless, it would clearly be preferable if the Convention specifically referred to the rights of children to contact with their parents[49] and provided a mechanism for children themselves to initiate applications for contact. Whilst it is questionable whether there is any benefit in forcing parents to maintain contact with their children when they do not wish to do so,[50] there may be cases where non-custodial parents do not take steps to exercise their rights of access out of apathy, ignorance or impecunity, but would be more than happy to respond to an initiative taken by the child.

v Certainty versus Flexibility

The uncertainty inherent in Article 21 has given rise to a considerable lack of uniformity between the practice in different Contracting States, which is clearly not desirable. However, it can be argued that Article 21 mandates a minimum standard of action by Central Authorities and that there is nothing wrong with the fact that some Contracting States want to do more to assist non-custodial parents to exercise their access rights within the framework of this provision. Nonetheless, it would obviously be preferable to attempt to create a clear and complete framework for the enforcement of access rights in international cases and indeed a number of such attempts have been made in various regional and global instruments. These will now be surveyed and will inform the discussion as to the appropriate role of the access provisions in the Abduction Convention.

---

[44] Re D (n 38) [67]. P McEleavy, 'A Protocol for the 1980 Hague Convention' [2010] *International Family Law* 59 suggests that such left-behind parents could be offered equivalent assistance in securing and enforcing access rights in the State of refuge in return for giving up their return application.
[45] See definition in Art 5.
[46] See ch 6 at II D.
[47] See ch 6 at III.
[48] At Aiii.
[49] Contact Guide (n 7), 4 starts by stating the general principle that 'all possible steps should be taken to secure the rights of children to maintain personal relationships and have regular contact with both of their parents'.
[50] See ch 6 at II D.

III Other International Instruments

A The 1980 European Custody Convention

As seen above,[51] the 1980 European Custody Convention provides for recognition and enforcement of access decisions made in another Contracting State, subject to the exceptions set out in Articles 9 and 10, and thus this instrument seems to provide a better remedy for enforcing access rights than the Abduction Convention. Although the Convention does not appear to address the fact that a change of circumstances may make it inappropriate to enforce the foreign access decision without modifying it,[52] the English courts appear to have found a solution by interpreting flexibly the power accorded by Article 11(2) to fix the conditions for the exercise of the rights of access.[53] Similarly, even where recognition of the foreign order is refused,[54] it has been suggested that the court refusing recognition can itself determine the access application on the merits under Article 11(3).[55]

B The 1996 Hague Convention on the Protection of Children

The 1996 Convention[56] may improve the remedies available to enforce access orders in the Abduction Convention in two ways. Firstly, the recognition and enforcement provisions mean that access orders made in one Contracting State will be recognised and enforced in other Contracting States, subject to defences in Article 23(2). This mechanism is enhanced by the possibility of obtaining advance recognition of an order.[57] Secondly, the level of co-operation required between Contracting States is greater than that under the Abduction Convention. Article 31(b) specifically requires Central Authorities to facilitate, by mediation or other means, agreed solutions for the protection of children; Article 35(1) provides that the authorities of one Contracting State may request those of another Contracting State to assist in implementing measures of protection 'especially in securing the effective exercise of rights of access' and Article 35(2) provides for authorities of a Contracting State to gather information or evidence relevant to the exercise of access in that country.

Nonetheless, there are limitations on the usefulness of remedies provided by the 1996 Convention. In particular there does not appear to be any method of modifying the foreign access order, even where there has been a change of circumstances and it remains to be seen how widely courts will interpret the defence that 'recognition is manifestly contrary to the public policy of the requested State, taking into account the best interests of the child'. In addition, Article 7 of the 1996 Convention makes it clear that where return has been refused,

---

[51] Chapter 1 at II B.
[52] Because Art 9(3) prohibits reviewing the substance of the decision.
[53] eg in *Re G (Children) (Foreign Contact Order: Enforcement)* [2003] EWCA Civ 1607, it was held that the French decision providing for staying access with the father in Italy could be 'enforced' by short periods of contact in London, where the children were now living with the permission of the French Court, in light of the children's refusal to travel to Italy.
[54] For example, under Art 10(1)(b), on the basis that the effects of the original decision are manifestly no longer in accordance with the welfare of the child, as a result of change of circumstances, however this defence has been interpreted narrowly, eg *Re A (Foreign Access Order: Enforcement)* [1996] 1 FLR 561.
[55] Lowe et al, *International Movement* (n 15) 590.
[56] See generally ch 1 at II E.
[57] Under Art 24. This will be useful in relocation cases.

the courts of the requested State will not have jurisdiction to make an access order[58] until a year has passed or one of the other conditions in that provision is satisfied.[59]

C The 2003 European Convention on Contact Concerning Children[60]

In light of the limitations of the existing regional and international instruments in regulating trans-frontier contact, the Council of Europe decided to draft a new instrument.[61] A major difference between the Convention on Contact Concerning Children ('Convention on Contact') and the existing instruments is that it is not confined to international aspects of contact between children and parents, but also sets out the substantive general principles which should inform decisions in relation to contact. The rationale behind this approach was that if the principle according to which contact orders were made were similar in different States, it would be easier to give effect to foreign orders.[62] These principles include the need to provide information to children with sufficient understanding and to give due weight to their ascertainable wishes and feelings.[63]

The Convention on Contact does not itself provide for the recognition and enforcement of foreign contact orders,[64] but it does provide a number of innovations designed to facilitate the exercise of trans-frontier contact. In particular, Article 10 provides that Contracting States are required to promote the use of safeguards and guarantees to ensure that contact orders are carried into effect and that the child is returned at the end of the period of contact.[65] Furthermore, this Convention contains a specific provision enabling a court which recognises a foreign contact order 'to adapt the conditions for its implementation, as well as any safeguards or guarantees attaching to it', where this is necessary for facilitating the exercise of the contact.[66]

D The Brussels II bis Regulation[67]

As already seen,[68] in intra-EU cases, orders relating to parental responsibility are to be recognised and enforced subject to narrow defences. Moreover, decisions on rights of access issue in one EU State are directly recognised and enforceable in another EU State if accompanied by a certificate, which means that their recognition cannot be opposed.[69] This effectively

---

[58] Although there would seem to be jurisdiction to make an interim access order pending the return decision on the basis of urgency under Art 11.
[59] See ch 1 at II Eii.
[60] conventions.coe.int/Treaty/en/Reports/Html/192.htm ('Convention on Contact'). As of 6 January 2013, eight States have ratified this Convention which entered into force on 1 September 2005, conventions.coe.int/Treaty/Commun/ChercheSig.asp?NT=192&CM=8&DF=06/01/2013&CL=ENG.
[61] Lowe et al, *International Movement* (n 15) 597.
[62] Preamble to the Convention on Contact.
[63] Arts 6 and 7.
[64] But it does require State parties to have a system for recognition and enforcement of such orders, Art 14.
[65] These include deposit of security, fines, surrender of passports and charges on property.
[66] Art 15.
[67] Council Regulation (EC) No 2201/2003 of 27 November 2003 concerning jurisdiction and the recognition and enforcement of judgments in matrimonial matters and matters of parental responsibility.[2003] OJ L 338/1-29.
[68] Chapter 1 at II Cii.
[69] Art 41(1). By virtue of Art 46, this also applies to agreements provided that they are enforceable in the Member State where they were drawn up, N Lowe, M Everall and M Nicholls, *The New Brussels II Regulation: A Supplement to International Movement of Children* (Bristol, Jordans, 2005) 24.

leaves no room to use the 1980 European Convention in relation to access orders in intra-EU cases.[70]

IV Conclusions

Despite the fact that the access provisions in a number of other instruments are considerably more developed than those in the Abduction Convention, the latter can still play an important role in cases involving the many Contracting States which are not party to the other Conventions. Whilst it was not expected that the very limited and vague access provisions in the Abduction Convention could provide a complete solution to the highly complex problem of cross frontier access, Article 21 does in fact provide a real basis for promoting respect for access rights, if authorities and courts are prepared to interpret it purposively.

Firstly, it is clear that in many cases the obstacles to exercise of access are mainly administrative because the foreign non-custodial parent is not in a position to make arrangements for access in the country where the children are living. The Central Authority structure, if properly used, can go a long way to resolving this problem.[71] In particular, Central Authorities can be instrumental in promoting agreements, which are very often the most effective way of securing respect for access rights.[72] Moreover, where it is necessary to initiate proceedings, Central Authorities can provide much needed assistance to the applicant. Indeed, it will be noted that all the later instruments adopted the Abduction Convention model of Central Authorities. Whilst, as seen above, some of these instruments impose more detailed duties on Central Authorities, the vague wording of Article 21 is in fact wide enough to enable Central Authorities to undertake most of these tasks, if they wish to do so, provided local law allows.[73] Moreover, an advantage of the Abduction Convention is that it provides for legal aid[74] and other procedural benefits, which can be extended to access cases. In light of the relatively small number of access cases under the Convention, extension of these benefits should not create a great burden, although of course the granting of benefits might increase the number of cases.[75]

Secondly, whilst the Abduction Convention does not mandate recognition or enforcement of foreign access decisions, this may not be a serious disadvantage provided that courts give considerable weight to such decisions and only refuse to respect them where this is necessary in the best interests of the child.[76] Indeed, as seen above, the need to modify foreign access decisions where there has been a change of circumstances can be problematic where recognition is mandatory. It seems necessary to distinguish between foreign

---

[70] Lowe et al, ibid.
[71] See generally Contact Guide (n 7).
[72] ibid, 6–11.
[73] Often, the capacity of Central Authorities to act is limited by resource implications, W Duncan, 'Transfrontier Access Contact General Principles and Good Practice', Preliminary Document No 4 (2006), www.hcch.net/upload/wop/abd_pd04e2006.pdf, 38.
[74] Although reservations might be entered under Art 26.
[75] It has also been suggested that the requiring equality of treatment between the two types of case might lead to a reduction in the benefits given by some States in abduction cases, Duncan, 'Contact General Principles' (n 73), 39.
[76] Whether or not access orders are given under Art 21 itself or under domestic law. See at II Aii above.

access orders which were made as part of a decision allowing relocation, which should generally be enforced without change, and those which were made on the basis that the parties would be living in the same country, which may well need modification.

Perhaps the most serious lacuna in the access provisions in the Abduction Convention is that they do not regulate issues concerning access which arise within the context of abduction proceedings, which arguably should have been their main focus. In particular, they do not make express provision for access orders to be made pending a return decision[77] and after no-return decisions. Similarly, they do not make provision for return to be made subject to provisions for access which will then be enforceable in the requesting State, at least until such time as a decision can be given there on the merits.[78]

---

[77] The conclusion of the First Part of the Sixth Special Commission Meeting, www.hcch.net/upload/wop/concl28sc6_e.pdf, para 20, that access may be provided pending return proceedings under Articles 7(2)(b) and 21 of the Abduction Convention seems over simplistic as it does not take into account the question of whether a Court in the requested State, which is not the habitual residence of the child, has jurisdiction to make an access order under its own internal law. It is difficult to see that Art 21 can be interpreted as conferring such jurisdiction.

[78] This lacuna has been filled to some extent by the use of undertakings, mirror orders and judicial liaision, see ch 11 at III. It should be noted that these techniques, developed in relation to return orders, can also be used in relation to access orders generally, see Contact Guide (n 7), 13, 17 and 39.

Part VII

The Way Ahead

19

Conclusions and Recommendations

I Introduction

In a concluding chapter, it is only possible to draw together the main threads of the wide-ranging and detailed analysis contained in the book and to set out the most significant of the conclusions that can be derived therefrom. A recurring theme throughout the book has been that today the approach to the Hague Convention on the Civil Aspects of International Child Abduction ('Abduction Convention') has to take into account the social and legal developments that have taken place since the drafting of the Abduction Convention more than 30 years ago and the empirical evidence relevant to the operation of the Convention. Thus, Part II of this chapter will discuss the significance of the most important relevant changes and research findings since 1980 for the interpretation and application of the Convention. Part III will then set out some general conclusions and specific recommendations for improving the application and operation of the Convention, based on the analysis in the book.

It is obvious that non-compliance with the Convention by Contracting States, who fail to take steps to locate abducted children, to process return applications speedily and to order return where this is mandated, frustrates the attainment of the objectives of the Convention. Thus, efforts need to be made to ensure that all Contracting States understand and fulfil their obligations under the Convention. However, in addition, it needs to be recognised that returning children in situations where this will cause them real harm is also inconsistent with the purpose of the Convention and is in effect also non-compliance therewith. Moreover, it is suggested that the latter type of non-compliance is more susceptible to correction than the former type because it is likely to be caused by a misconceived approach to interpretation or application of the Convention and not by lack of goodwill or incapacity on the part of the authorities in the Contracting States. Accordingly, the author expresses the hope that the insights which have been gained from the analysis in this book will enable courts and others involved in the operation of the Abduction Convention to protect better the interests of the vulnerable children to whom the Convention applies.

II Significance of the Developments Since 1980

A Children's Rights

The most important relevant legal development has been the widespread recognition that children are independent persons who hold rights, as evidenced by the almost universal ratification of the United Nations Convention on the Rights of the Child 1989 (the CRC).[1] On the one hand, the acceptance of the fact that a child has a right to contact with both parents[2] can be seen as strengthening one of the main premises on which the Abduction Convention is based, namely that the separation of a child from one of his parents, which is an almost invariable consequence of an unlawful removal or retention, violates the interests of the child. On the other hand, in situations where the return of the child will lead to separation from the abductor, the return remedy will not result in the realisation of the child's right to contact with both parents. Thus, it is incumbent on courts, wherever possible, to put in place measures which will ensure the continued contact of the child with both parents after return. This includes, for example, making return conditional on the discontinuation of criminal proceedings. Moreover, where there are no measures which can provide effective protection for the returning abductor, serious consideration has to be given to the impact on the child of the separation from that abductor.

The CRC's innovatory acknowledgment that children have a right to participate in the making of decisions which affect their lives has significant implications for Abduction Convention proceedings. Whilst the Abduction Convention is seen as providing only a first aid remedy, it has to be understood that return has a major impact on the life of the child, even though it is not a decision on the merits of the case. Thus, it is essential to allow sufficiently mature children to express their views about the decision, irrespective of how much weight is to be attached to those views. Whilst the CRC does not expressly mandate direct hearing by the decision-maker, the rationales behind the right to participate, supported by empirical research into the benefits of such participation, do require giving children the opportunity to talk directly to the judge.[3] Furthermore, whilst the CRC does not expressly recognise the child's right to be represented separately, the need to ensure that the child's voice is heard effectively and that his interests are properly presented does mean that separate representation is always desirable and often essential.[4]

At first sight, the statement in Article 12(1) of the CRC that appropriate weight should be given to the views of children in light of their age and maturity, confirms the approach taken to children's objections in Article 13(2) of the Abduction Convention. However, as seen in chapter 12, many courts have interpreted and applied this exception paternalistically, in a way which is inconsistent with the concept of the child's right to participate. Furthermore, the tendency of some courts to order return on the basis of the policy of the Convention, even where the exception is established, effectively makes the child's rights meaningless. In particular, as reiterated throughout the book, the policy of the Abduction Convention should be seen as including the policy behind the exceptions and not only that behind the return mechanism. Whilst the Abduction Convention predated the CRC, it is suggested that today the need to give effect to the rights of children should be seen as part of the policy of the Convention.

It is not clear that the inclusion of the best interests standard in the CRC has any major implications for the Abduction Convention because this standard had been adopted by developed countries many years previously. Indeed, one of the reasons why the Abduction Convention was necessary was that determining abduction cases according to the best interests principle provided an incentive for abductors to seek a forum which they per-

---

[1] See generally ch 6 at II.
[2] Arts 9 and 10 of the CRC.
[3] Chapter 14 at III A.
[4] See generally ch 15.

ceived would view the child's best interests in a way more favourable to them and to adopt delaying tactics which would influence the best interests determination. Thus, the drafters of the Convention were keenly aware of the tension between the need to protect the interests of children as a group on the one hand and individual children on the other, and they saw the mandatory return mechanism subject to the exceptions as the 'fragile compromise' between these competing objectives.[5] The criticism of this compromise, voiced over the years, was largely a reaction to the restrictive interpretation adopted by the courts to the grave risk exception combined with the change in the profile of the typical abductor, and not a response to the enactment of Article 3 of the CRC.[6] Nonetheless, the enactment of the best interests standard in this global human rights instrument may have increased the importance attached thereto. Moreover, the fact that the child's right to family life, which is recognised as a human right by the European Convention on Human Rights, is interpreted in light of the best interests principle, can be seen as upgrading the status of the standard.[7]

Finally, it should be remembered that the CRC contains a fundamental message about the centrality of children and their perspectives in matters affecting them, wider than the specific rights enacted therein. Thus, issues affecting the child have to be viewed through his eyes and not through those of adults. The implications of this perception mean that findings concerning children of all ages have to take into account the situation from the viewpoint of the child. Thus, in Abduction Convention proceedings, the court should take into account the child's perspective when determining where he was habitually resident and, where relevant, whether he has become settled in his new environment for the purposes of Article 12(2).

B Primary Carer Abductions

There are legal and sociological explanations for the fact that most abductions are carried out by primary carers[8] and not by non-custodial parents, as envisaged by the drafters of the Convention. In particular, the granting of joint legal custody and ne exeat orders, has become increasingly common in many jurisdictions. Accordingly, unilateral relocations by custodial parents were often lawful in 1980, but are usually unlawful abductions today. In addition, changes in social norms, such as the entry of more women into the labour market, have given mothers the confidence to take the initiative in breaking out of unhappy marriages and relocating with their children to another country in order to improve the quality of their own and their children's lives.[9] Furthermore, international travel is physically easier and less expensive.[10]

In the field of social science, there has been a great deal of research shedding light on the sociological and psychological aspects of child abduction.[11] The combination of empirical surveys which show that most abductions to which the Abduction Convention applies are carried out by primary carers, together with scientific evidence as to the irreversible harm

---

[5] Ch 11 at I A.
[6] Indeed, Art 3 can possibly be understood as having a collective focus, see ch 6 at II B.
[7] See *Neulinger v Switzerland* App no 41615/07 (ECHR, 6 July 2010) [134].
[8] Ch 3 at I A.
[9] Ch 4 at II A.
[10] *Re E (Children)* [2011] UKSC 27 [6].
[11] See generally in ch 3.

which may be caused, especially to young children, by separation from their primary carer, must raise questions as to the way in which the mandatory return mechanism should be applied to primary carer abductions of young children.

Some suggest that the solution to the problem is to restore the position intended by the drafters,[12] by redefining 'abduction' so that it only includes removal by a non-primary carer. This would mean that the Abduction Convention's return mechanism would not apply in the 40 per cent of cases in which the abductor was the sole primary carer. However, it is suggested that this proposal is inappropriate for two main reasons. Firstly, removals by primary carers still violate the child's right to contact with the other parent. Whilst in cases where the child's relationship with the left-behind parent was not significant or was damaging to him, his right to have contact with both parents may conflict with his other rights or interests, the balancing of rights should be carried out by the courts of the State of his habitual residence, unless the actual return will involve disproportionate violation of his rights, in which case one of the exceptions should be invoked. Secondly, the proposal is swimming against the tide of social and legal change in many countries, in which fathers are playing greater roles in the upbringing of their children and the traditional division between custodial parents and visiting parents is gradually being broken down.[13] Even where the child's primary residence is defined in a residence or similar order, he may well spend considerably more time with the other parent than was customary 30 years ago.

Nonetheless, the change in the profile of the typical abductor and the high incidence of cases involving domestic violence, together with current knowledge as to the harmful effects on children of being exposed to domestic violence, make it essential to ensure that the return of children does not in fact cause them harm, rather than protect them from harm as intended by the drafters of the Convention. As seen above, initiatives have been taken by courts in some countries and by the Hague Conference to find ways to protect returning children. In particular, in common law countries, wide use is made of undertakings or conditions to return. However, the evidence available suggests that these measures are by no means always effective.[14] Accordingly, courts must ensure that protective measures do indeed provide effective and enforceable protection for children and where this cannot be guaranteed, they have to refuse return.

In this respect, lessons might be learnt from the research on relocation which shows the importance of reality testing and not being satisfied with solutions which look good on paper. Furthermore, note might be taken of the attitude of many courts in relocation cases to the harm which will be caused to the child by preventing the primary carer mother from relocating, especially where she is socially isolated in the country where she is living.[15] Whilst of course it must be remembered that return ordered under the Abduction Convention is only a first aid measure and that this does not preclude the mother from requesting relocation, there are cases where even return in these circumstances is likely to cause considerable distress to the mother, which may cause a grave risk of harm to the child or place him in an intolerable situation within Article 13(1)(b).[16] Finally, consideration

---

[12] C Bruch, 'The Promises and Perils of a Protocol to the 1980 Convention on the Civil Aspects of International Child Abduction' (2011) 1 *Festschrift Fur Ingeborg Schwenzer* 237, 239–41.

[13] eg, in Israel, there is currently a proposal to abolish the concepts of custody and access and for course to approve or devise a parenting plan, which will define how much time the child will spend with each parent, Draft Parents and Children Law 2012.

[14] Ch 11 at III.

[15] Ch 4 at II Ai.

[16] ibid at III Bib.

should be given to ways in which relocation law might prevent some primary carer abductions.[17] Similarly, it should be borne in mind that effective methods of enforcing access might avoid some of the applications for return by non-primary carers.[18]

C The Call for a Protocol

The background to and failure of the attempt to secure consensus for drafting a Protocol is a relevant development, which needs to be taken into account in charting the way ahead. The idea of a Protocol to the Abduction Convention was first raised formally in 2000 at the General Affairs and Policy Meeting of the Hague Conference.[19] At first, the purpose of the proposed Protocol was limited to remedying the ineffective access provision in Article 21 of the Abduction Convention.[20] However, later on, Switzerland put forward a more general proposal for a Protocol, containing a variety of provisions designed to protect abducted children.[21] In 2010, the Permanent Bureau canvassed views from Member States and experts about the desirability and feasibility of a Protocol.[22] A preliminary report[23] summarising these views was published in May 2011 before the first part of the Sixth Special Commission Meeting, even though the discussion on a Protocol was scheduled for the second part of the meeting, due to take place in January 2012.[24]

However, in December 2011, the Permanent Bureau published a document[25] explaining that the focus of the second part of the Sixth Special Commission Meeting had changed and that the question of the desirability of a Protocol had been taken off the agenda. The background to this change was stated to be the fact that it had become clear, after further consultation, that it was not possible to achieve a consensus in relation to work on a Protocol document at that time. In particular, diverging views among States had become apparent and some States were intransigently opposed to a Protocol. The main reason for the opposition to the Protocol in general and to the inclusion of particular issues therein was the belief that most of the problems experienced with the operation of the Convention arose from a lack of compliance with the existing provisions and that efforts would be better directed to training of judicial and Central Authority personnel and promoting use of the Guides to Good Practice.[26]

The problems identified in this book with the operation of the Convention are broader than those discussed in relation to the Protocol proposals. Nonetheless, whilst not discounting the advantages of a binding Protocol, the current author tends to agree that most of the difficulties encountered in the application and operation of the Convention might

---

[17] ibid at III A.
[18] Ch 18 at III Biii.
[19] 'Consultations on the Desirability and Feasibility of a Protocol to the Hague Convention of 25 October 1980 on the Civil Aspects of International Child Abduction', Preliminary Document No 7 (2001), www.hcch.net/upload/wop/abduct2011pd07e.pdf, 4 et seq ('Consultations') (detailing the chronology of the discussions in relation to a Protocol),
[20] ibid.
[21] ibid, 5.
[22] ibid.
[23] ibid.
[24] ibid, 7.
[25] 'Guide to Part II of the Sixth Meeting of the Special Commission and Consideration of the Desirability and Feasibility of Further Work in Connection with the 1980 and 1996 Conventions', Preliminary Document No 13 (2011), www.hcch.net/upload/wop/abduct2012pd13_e.pdf ('Guide to Part II').
[26] ibid, Annex, xxiii.

be dealt with to a considerable extent by other 'soft law' means, which would reduce the disparities in the application and interpretation of the Convention. However, it has to be recognised that there are differences in legal culture and in some Contracting States it may be very difficult to bring about change without a binding legal instrument.[27]

The fact that there seems to be no likelihood of a Protocol to the Abduction Convention in the near future makes it more important to find solutions which can be implemented without such an instrument. Understandably, most of the excellent work of the Permanent Bureau, especially the Guides to Good Practice, is directed at encouraging the passing of appropriate national implementing legislation and improving Central Authority practice. However, many of the critical problems highlighted in this book arise from the way in which judges interpret and apply the Convention. It is the thesis of this book that these problems can be largely resolved by the proper interpretation and application of the Convention, in light of a correct understanding of its objectives. Accordingly, the author hopes that the insights gained from the discussion and analysis in this book together with her recommendations, summarised briefly below, will contribute to improving the way in which the Convention is applied and in particular to increasing uniformity in judicial interpretation and application.

III Conclusions

A Hierarchy of Objectives

As has been apparent in the analysis sections in the book, in certain situations there will be tension between the various different objectives of the Abduction Convention. In particular, it has been argued that the objective of protecting the child from the harmful effects of abduction includes protecting him from the harmful effects of return.[28] Where there are no protective measures which can prevent the harm which will result from return, the objective of protecting the child will require that he is not returned and this will conflict with the objectives of deterrence, justice between the parents and the rule of law. Sometimes it will also conflict with the objective of hearing the dispute in the *forum conveniens*. Indeed, the tension between the different objectives of the Abduction Convention lies at the heart of the challenges posed by primary carer abductions. Courts rarely address these tensions and usually simply recite laconically the objective(s) which appear to support the decision in the particular case, most often the need to combat the phenomenon of international child abduction and to ensure that disputes are determined in the home country. It is suggested that there is a need for more judicial awareness and transparency in relation to the conflicts inherent within the Convention scheme.

It is submitted that the objective of protecting children has to be seen as the primary focus of the Convention, which overrides the other objectives in case of conflict. The notion that the interests of an individual child may be sacrificed on the altar of the collective benefit of the whole community of children is morally indefensible and inconsistent

---

[27] 'Consultations' (n 19), 41.
[28] Ch 5 at II Ci.

with the Kantian principle that a person should always be treated as an end in himself and not only as a means to an end.[29] This claim is strengthened by the fact that the deterrence value of the Convention cannot be proven and there are indeed reasons to doubt whether the Convention has any substantial deterrent effect.[30]

However, it is possible to protect individual children without conducting a full blown best interests analysis. In order to do this, it is necessary to adopt appropriate expedited procedures for identifying risk of harm and for enabling children to express their views. It is only necessary to take more time to check things out thoroughly in cases where this preliminary investigation reveals that one of the defences might apply. This will not have any effect on the majority of cases, in which it can be ascertained relatively quickly that the defences do not apply and return can be ordered.

It is important not to see the Abduction Convention simply as a procedural venue-selecting mechanism for two reasons. Firstly, it has been shown that decisions as to forum may be outcome determinative.[31] Indeed in the abduction context, when return is refused, it is virtually inconceivable that in subsequent custody proceedings the left-behind parent will succeed in obtaining custody and permission to return to the country of origin. Even where return is ordered, the abductor may not be in a position to start proceedings in the requesting State.

Secondly, the decision under the Abduction Convention does not simply determine the forum for the dispute, but also where the child is going to be living pending the determination of the merits of the case. The implications of this fact are more far-reaching than the likely impact on the outcome of the final determination. Rather, return has colossal significance for the day-to-day life of the child pending the substantive proceedings. Accordingly, the objective of adjudicating disputes in the *forum conveniens* must be subsidiary to that of protecting children from harm. Of course, the conflict between these two objectives may be resolved by separating adjudication and return. As already seen, Brussels II bis does allow the requesting State to retain jurisdiction even where return is refused. It is too early to assess how well this mechanism is working. If it proves to be successful, then other Contracting States might want to take it on board in those cases where one of the exceptions is established, but the requesting State is clearly the *forum conveniens*. One way of achieving this result is to stay the return order until the requesting State has given a decision on the merits.[32] The possibility of such a solution might lead to less restrictive interpretation and application of the exceptions.[33]

Finally, as seen throughout the book, courts quite often invoke the private international law doctrine of comity to support their decision to order return. While comity, in all senses, is undoubtedly a worthy goal, it cannot justify harming children and there is no evidence to suggest that States that have a better return record are more likely to have their own abducted children returned.

---

[29] See ch 5 at II Ciic.
[30] ibid at II Ciib.
[31] DW Roberston, 'Forum Non Conveniens in American and England, Rather Fantastic Fiction' (1987) 103 *Law Quarterly Review* 398, 419–20.
[32] eg *F v M and N (Abduction: Acquiescence: Settlement)* [2008] EWHC 1525 (Fam); *JPC v SMW* [2007] EWHC 1349 (Fam).
[33] Ch 1 at II Civ.

B Recommendations in Relation to the Interpretation and Application of the Abduction Convention

In the chapters which discussed the provisions of the Convention, a view was expressed as to which of the possible approaches to interpreting and applying the various components of the particular provisions was most consistent with the parameters for analysis. It was thought that it would be helpful to repeat the main conclusions reached in each chapter here, even though these brief summaries cannot fully reflect the detailed discussion and insights offered there. The order in which the conclusions are listed matches the sequence of chapters in the book and does not imply any hierarchy of importance.

Whilst none of the recommendations require amendment to the Convention, which as seen above is unlikely to be a feasible option in the foreseeable future, some of them may require changes to be made to the national legislation in some Contracting States. Although many of the recommendations are based on the cumulative effect of various aspects of the analysis in each chapter, for reasons of convenience, the reader is referred to the section containing the main discussion of the issue.

i Wrongful Removal and Retention

(a) Anticipatory breach should be treated as a wrongful retention for the purposes of allowing the left-behind parent to submit a return application, but not for the purposes of the 12-month limitation period.[34]

(b) The concept of custody rights should be interpreted widely, in accordance with the child's right to maintain contact with both parents.[35]

(c) The requirement of the actual exercise of custody rights should be interpreted more stringently so as to exclude cases where there was no real contact between the child and the left-behind parent.[36]

(d) Removal or retention should be treated as wrongful, wherever there has been a breach of custody rights either under the domestic law or the choice of law rules of the State of habitual residence.[37]

ii Habitual Residence

(a) The Convention should apply to removals and retentions from a third country, provided that the child was habitually resident at the relevant time in a Contracting State.[38]

(b) It should be possible to order the return of the child to a third country, if this best fulfils the objectives of the Convention, where return to the habitual residence is not practicable or removal was from that third county.[39]

(c) In determining the child's habitual residence, the combined model should be adopted, according to which the factual situation is examined from the child's perspective with the settled intention of the parents being a very relevant but not necessarily decisive

---

[34] Ch 7 at II B and C.
[35] ibid at IV Cia.
[36] ibid at IV Cib.
[37] ibid at IV Gi.
[38] Ch 8 at II A.
[39] ibid.

factor.[40] It would be helpful if, in determining habitual residence, courts were to bear in mind that the Convention is designed to protect a child who has been removed 'from the social and family environment in which his life has developed'.[41]

iii Passage of Time and Settlement (Article 12(2))

(a) The determination as to whether a child has settled should take into account the child's perspective.[42]
(b) There should not be any discretion to order the return of the child where the exception in Article 12(2) has been established. If such a discretion is to exist, it should be exercised very sparingly with emphasis being placed on the interests of the child and not the wrongful behaviour of the abductor.[43]

iv Consent and Acquiescence (Article 13(1)(a))

(a) The consent and acquiescence defences should be interpreted purposively. Thus, for example, there is room for a wider approach where there has been reasonable reliance by the abductor.[44]
(b) Where the exception is established, in exercising the discretion to return, the most important consideration should be the interests of the child.[45]

v Grave Risk of Harm or Intolerable Situation (Article 13(1)(b))

(a) An overly restrictive approach to the Article 13(1)(b) exception will not adequately protect children. The fact that most abductors are primary carers necessarily means that the exception will be established more often than might have been anticipated. In particular, giving little or no weight to the consequences of such an abductor's inability or reasonable refusal to return with a child is not consistent with the rationale behind the exception. Similarly, failing to treat domestic violence against the abductor as a potential risk to the child ignores the clear evidence that being exposed to violence between adults is harmful to children. Furthermore, blaming the abductor for creating the situation where return will cause harm to the child does not provide protection from that harm.[46]
(b) In determining whether the grave risk exception exists, the court should focus on the immediate short-term interests of the child. In this way, it can give effect to the CRC's instruction to treat the best interests of the child as a primary consideration without undermining the scheme of the Convention, under which the child's long-term interests are to be determined by the courts of the place of his habitual residence prior to the abduction.[47]

---

[40] ibid at II C and V.
[41] Perez-Vera Report, Proceedings of the 14th Session of the Hague Conference Oct 1980, www.hcch.net/upload/expl28.pdf, para 11.
[42] Ch 9 at III E.
[43] ibid at III Ci.
[44] Ch 10 at VI.
[45] ibid at V E.
[46] Ch 11 at IV Ci.
[47] ibid at IV E.

(c) Whilst it is legitimate to put in place protective measures which will neutralise the risk of harm or make an intolerable situation tolerable, so that the child can be returned, courts have to make sure that any such measures will indeed be enforceable and effective. To this end, greater use should be made of mirror orders and other mechanisms which can ensure protection for the child. Nonetheless, it has to be recognised that all such mechanisms are limited and that there will be cases where it will not be possible to provide adequate protection for a returning child.[48]

vi Child's Objections (Article 13(2))

(a) The child objection exception should be applied in a way which gives effect to the child's right to participate. This requires not taking a paternalistic approach to the maturity and independence of the child's views. Similarly, it requires taking into account all clearly held views of the child, not only those which are expressed in the form of an objection and not only those which are of exceptional strength.[49]

(b) In exercising the discretion to return a child who objects, the emphasis should be on the interests of the child. In particular, it should be remembered that the main objective of the Convention is to protect children and thus so-called Convention objectives, such as comity and deterrence, should not override the interests of the individual child. Consideration should be given to the potential adverse effect on the relationship with the left-behind parent, which may result from returning the child against his will.[50]

vii Protection of Human Rights and Fundamental Freedoms (Article 20)

Article 20 should be interpreted restrictively, even in an era of increased recognition of human rights. It is preferable to use Article 13(1)(b) to cover situations where harm will be caused to the child as a result of the breach of the abductor's human rights.[51]

viii Ascertaining Children's Views

There are many advantages of hearing children directly.[52] Sufficiently mature abducted children should be given the opportunity to express their views directly to the judge, inter alia in order to give full effect to their right to participate.[53]

ix Separate Representation for Children

The advantages of separate representation for children in abduction cases[54] by far outweigh any disadvantages. Every abducted child should be separately represented, inter alia in order to ensure that his interests are presented properly and objectively. This is particularly important in certain types of cases, such as those in which the grave risk or child objection exceptions are raised.[55]

---

[48] ibid at V.
[49] Ch 12 at III E.
[50] Ibid at II Ci.
[51] Ch 13 at IV.
[52] Ch 14 at III A
[53] ibid at IV.
[54] Ch 15 at III B.
[55] ibid at IV.

x Mediation

(a) The effort to find solutions to the problems which currently hamper the use of mediation in Abduction Convention cases should be continued. In particular, ways need to be found to ensure that mediate agreements are enforceable in all relevant States.[56]
(b) It is important to ensure that children participate in mediation.[57]

xi Compensating the Left-Behind Parent

Greater use should be made of the power in Article 26(4) to compensate the left-behind parent for costs incurred as a result of the abduction. This power should be extended to cover cases where return is refused and to include wider compensation. However, compensation should not be ordered or should be reduced, where the behaviour of the left-behind parent makes a full award inappropriate, or where there is a grave risk that the award will expose the child to physical or psychological harm or otherwise place him in an intolerable situation.[58]

xii Access Rights

(a) Central Authorities should do everything in their power to assist foreign non-custodial parents to enforce their access rights. Courts should give great weight to previous access orders, unless this is clearly not in the best interests of the child because of the change in circumstances.[59]
(b) States should ensure that their courts have jurisdiction to make an interim access order in favour of the left-behind parent, where return proceedings are pending.[60]
(c) Where return is refused, the requested State should immediately have jurisdiction to make custody and access orders and these should be respected by other Contracting States, as part of the reciprocity inherent in the Abduction Convention.[61]

C Recommendations Concerning other Aspects of Implementation of the Abduction Convention

This book has only briefly addressed issues relating to the practical operation of the Convention, in order to provide a context for the main discussion of the judicial application of the Convention. Thus, the analysis in the book does not provide sufficient basis for making detailed recommendations as to how the operation of the Convention might be improved.[62] Accordingly, this section will be limited to the making of a few general recommendations on matters of principle.

---

[56] Ch 16 at III C.
[57] ibid at III D.
[58] Ch 17 at III.
[59] Ch 18 at IV.
[60] ibid at III Biii.
[61] ibid and Ch 6 at IV Ei.
[62] Many useful ideas can be found in the Guides to Good Practice, published by the Permanent Bureau, and referred to throughout the book.

i Expedition

The failure of many Contracting States to ensure that cases are dealt with speedily might be seen as the Achilles heel of the operation of the Convention. Expedition is absolutely essential in order to achieve the objectives of the Convention. In particular, the fundamental premise that return will protect the child from the harmful effects of abduction is only true where he is returned quickly. Furthermore, the objective of restoring the *status quo ante* may not be achievable after the passage of time. Indeed, some of the substantive problems highlighted in the book are caused by or exacerbated by the lack of speed. For example, in some cases the harm caused to the child upon return is a direct result of the fact that he has become settled in the State of refuge and lost all connection with the State of origin during the delay in processing the case. Similarly, in some cases the delay is the reason that the child now objects to returning or that his objections have become stronger. The determination of many courts that the left-behind parent should not be prejudiced by the delay, at least where it is not his fault, and that the abductor should not benefit from the delay, especially where she is partly responsible for it, means that children are frequently the victims of bureaucratic inefficiency and failure to manage cases in a firm and expeditious manner. It is suggested that if judges were to start to refuse return where the delay causes or increases the harm which will be caused to the child by return, rather than simply commenting on the undesirability of the delay,[63] this might provide an incentive to Central Authorities, court administrators and judges to ensure quicker and more efficient handling of these cases.

ii Article 15 Declarations

There is a need to improve the procedure for obtaining Article 15 declarations and in particular to ensure expedition.[64] Given the judicial nature of the declaration, it would be preferable if such declarations were made by judicial bodies. Whilst Article 15 does refer to administrative bodies, it is suggested that this should be understood to refer to those administrative authorities who have jurisdiction under local law to make return orders. Accordingly, since only courts can make return orders in the vast majority of, if not all, Contracting States, Article 15 declarations should also only be issued by courts. It would perhaps have been helpful to provide clarification about the use of Article 15, including the status of the declaration in a Protocol.[65] However, it is suggested that it should be possible to make some improvements in relation to Article 15 even without a Protocol, by means of recommendations of a future Special Commission or in a Good Practice Guide.

iii Enforcement

Whilst the Good Practice Guide to enforcement provides some helpful recommendations,[66] it does not give clear-cut solutions to all the problems and, in particular, to the critical question of whether coercion should be used. Some of the enforcement problems might be avoided if greater weight is attached to the child's objections. Whilst there is clearly great

---

[63] See eg per Justice Procaccia in RFamA 1855/08 (SC) *RB v VG* 8 April 2008 (Isr) http://elyon1.court.gov.il/files/08/550/018/r03/08018550.r03.pdf [INCADAT cite: HC/E/IL 923], [51].
[64] See generally ch 7 at III E.
[65] See discussion in 'Consultations' (n 19), 36.
[66] See generally ch 2 at III H.

importance in ensuring the rule of law, it is essential to ensure that enforcement is carried out in a way which protects the welfare of the child.

iv Research

The fact that nearly 30 years after the Convention came into force, we know so little about the aftermath of return is a matter of concern. Accordingly, developing mechanisms to collect follow-up information should be treated as a matter of priority.[67] This information should relate to the outcome of subsequent proceedings and the degree of contact between the child and both his parents following the return or non-return. Ideally, this information should be linked to relevant findings in the Abduction Convention proceedings, such as failure to establish the grave risk or child objection defences or exercise of discretion to order return despite the establishment of one of the defences. In addition, research into the effectiveness of various types of protective measures would be particularly helpful, as it would enable States to adopt measures which had been shown to be successful in other States. Furthermore, if this research were to identify the effectiveness of such measures in particular States, it would be of assistance to judges in deciding whether proposed protective measures would sufficiently neutralise the risk of the damage involved in return in a particular case.

---

[67] ibid at IV A.

APPENDIX

28. CONVENTION ON THE CIVIL ASPECTS OF INTERNATIONAL CHILD ABDUCTION[1]

(Concluded 25 October 1980)

The States signatory to the present Convention,
Firmly convinced that the interests of children are of paramount importance in matters relating to their custody,
Desiring to protect children internationally from the harmful effects of their wrongful removal or retention and to establish procedures to ensure their prompt return to the State of their habitual residence, as well as to secure protection for rights of access,
Have resolved to conclude a Convention to this effect, and have agreed upon the following provisions –

CHAPTER I – SCOPE OF THE CONVENTION

Article 1

The objects of the present Convention are –
a) to secure the prompt return of children wrongfully removed to or retained in any Contracting State; and
b) to ensure that rights of custody and of access under the law of one Contracting State are effectively respected in the other Contracting States.

Article 2

Contracting States shall take all appropriate measures to secure within their territories the implementation of the objects of the Convention. For this purpose they shall use the most expeditious procedures available.

Article 3

The removal or the retention of a child is to be considered wrongful where –
a) it is in breach of rights of custody attributed to a person, an institution or any other body, either jointly or alone, under the law of the State in which the child was habitually resident immediately before the removal or retention; and
b) at the time of removal or retention those rights were actually exercised, either jointly or alone, or would have been so exercised but for the removal or retention.

The rights of custody mentioned in sub-paragraph a) above, may arise in particular by operation of law or by reason of a judicial or administrative decision, or by reason of an agreement having legal effect under the law of that State.

---

[1] This Convention, including related materials, is accessible on the website of the Hague Conference on Private International Law (www.hcch.net), under "Conventions" or under the "Child Abduction Section". For the full history of the Convention, see Hague Conference on Private International Law, *Actes et documents de la Quatorzième session (1980)*, Tome III, *Child abduction* (ISBN 90 12 03616 X, 481 pp.).

Article 4

The Convention shall apply to any child who was habitually resident in a Contracting State immediately before any breach of custody or access rights. The Convention shall cease to apply when the child attains the age of 16 years.

Article 5

For the purposes of this Convention –
a) "rights of custody" shall include rights relating to the care of the person of the child and, in particular, the right to determine the child's place of residence;
b) "rights of access" shall include the right to take a child for a limited period of time to a place other than the child's habitual residence.

CHAPTER II – CENTRAL AUTHORITIES

Article 6

A Contracting State shall designate a Central Authority to discharge the duties which are imposed by the Convention upon such authorities.

Federal States, States with more than one system of law or States having autonomous territorial organisations shall be free to appoint more than one Central Authority and to specify the territorial extent of their powers. Where a State has appointed more than one Central Authority, it shall designate the Central Authority to which applications may be addressed for transmission to the appropriate Central Authority within that State.

Article 7

Central Authorities shall co-operate with each other and promote co-operation amongst the competent authorities in their respective States to secure the prompt return of children and to achieve the other objects of this Convention.

In particular, either directly or through any intermediary, they shall take all appropriate measures –
a) to discover the whereabouts of a child who has been wrongfully removed or retained;
b) to prevent further harm to the child or prejudice to interested parties by taking or causing to be taken provisional measures;
c) to secure the voluntary return of the child or to bring about an amicable resolution of the issues;
d) to exchange, where desirable, information relating to the social background of the child;
e) to provide information of a general character as to the law of their State in connection with the application of the Convention;
f) to initiate or facilitate the institution of judicial or administrative proceedings with a view to obtaining the return of the child and, in a proper case, to make arrangements for organising or securing the effective exercise of rights of access;
g) where the circumstances so require, to provide or facilitate the provision of legal aid and advice, including the participation of legal counsel and advisers;
h) to provide such administrative arrangements as may be necessary and appropriate to secure the safe return of the child;
i) to keep each other informed with respect to the operation of this Convention and, as far as possible, to eliminate any obstacles to its application.

CHAPTER III – RETURN OF CHILDREN

Article 8

Any person, institution or other body claiming that a child has been removed or retained in breach of custody rights may apply either to the Central Authority of the child's habitual residence or to the Central Authority of any other Contracting State for assistance in securing the return of the child.

The application shall contain –

a) information concerning the identity of the applicant, of the child and of the person alleged to have removed or retained the child;
b) where available, the date of birth of the child;
c) the grounds on which the applicant's claim for return of the child is based;
d) all available information relating to the whereabouts of the child and the identity of the person with whom the child is presumed to be.

The application may be accompanied or supplemented by –

e) an authenticated copy of any relevant decision or agreement;
f) a certificate or an affidavit emanating from a Central Authority, or other competent authority of the State of the child's habitual residence, or from a qualified person, concerning the relevant law of that State;
g) any other relevant document.

Article 9

If the Central Authority which receives an application referred to in Article 8 has reason to believe that the child is in another Contracting State, it shall directly and without delay transmit the application to the Central Authority of that Contracting State and inform the requesting Central Authority, or the applicant, as the case may be.

Article 10

The Central Authority of the State where the child is shall take or cause to be taken all appropriate measures in order to obtain the voluntary return of the child.

Article 11

The judicial or administrative authorities of Contracting States shall act expeditiously in proceedings for the return of children.

If the judicial or administrative authority concerned has not reached a decision within six weeks from the date of commencement of the proceedings, the applicant or the Central Authority of the requested State, on its own initiative or if asked by the Central Authority of the requesting State, shall have the right to request a statement of the reasons for the delay. If a reply is received by the Central Authority of the requested State, that Authority shall transmit the reply to the Central Authority of the requesting State, or to the applicant, as the case may be.

Article 12

Where a child has been wrongfully removed or retained in terms of Article 3 and, at the date of the commencement of the proceedings before the judicial or administrative authority of the Contracting State where the child is, a period of less than one year has elapsed from the date of the wrongful removal or retention, the authority concerned shall order the return of the child forthwith.

The judicial or administrative authority, even where the proceedings have been commenced after the expiration of the period of one year referred to in the preceding paragraph, shall also order the return of the child, unless it is demonstrated that the child is now settled in its new environment.

Where the judicial or administrative authority in the requested State has reason to believe that the child has been taken to another State, it may stay the proceedings or dismiss the application for the return of the child.

Article 13

Notwithstanding the provisions of the preceding Article, the judicial or administrative authority of the requested State is not bound to order the return of the child if the person, institution or other body which opposes its return establishes that –

a) the person, institution or other body having the care of the person of the child was not actually exercising the custody rights at the time of removal or retention, or had consented to or subsequently acquiesced in the removal or retention; or *b)*   there is a grave risk that his or her return would expose the child to physical or psychological harm or otherwise place the child in an intolerable situation.

The judicial or administrative authority may also refuse to order the return of the child if it finds that the child objects to being returned and has attained an age and degree of maturity at which it is appropriate to take account of its views.

In considering the circumstances referred to in this Article, the judicial and administrative authorities shall take into account the information relating to the social background of the child provided by the Central Authority or other competent authority of the child's habitual residence.

Article 14

In ascertaining whether there has been a wrongful removal or retention within the meaning of Article 3, the judicial or administrative authorities of the requested State may take notice directly of the law of, and of judicial or administrative decisions, formally recognised or not in the State of the habitual residence of the child, without recourse to the specific procedures for the proof of that law or for the recognition of foreign decisions which would otherwise be applicable.

Article 15

The judicial or administrative authorities of a Contracting State may, prior to the making of an order for the return of the child, request that the applicant obtain from the authorities of the State of the habitual residence of the child a decision or other determination that the removal or retention was wrongful within the meaning of Article 3 of the Convention, where such a decision or determination may be obtained in that State. The Central Authorities of the Contracting States shall so far as practicable assist applicants to obtain such a decision or determination.

Article 16

After receiving notice of a wrongful removal or retention of a child in the sense of Article 3, the judicial or administrative authorities of the Contracting State to which the child has been removed or in which it has been retained shall not decide on the merits of rights of custody until it has been determined that the child is not to be returned under this Convention or unless an application under this Convention is not lodged within a reasonable time following receipt of the notice.

Article 17

The sole fact that a decision relating to custody has been given in or is entitled to recognition in the requested State shall not be a ground for refusing to return a child under this Convention, but the judicial or administrative authorities of the requested State may take account of the reasons for that decision in applying this Convention.

Article 18

The provisions of this Chapter do not limit the power of a judicial or administrative authority to order the return of the child at any time.

Article 19

A decision under this Convention concerning the return of the child shall not be taken to be a determination on the merits of any custody issue.

Article 20

The return of the child under the provisions of Article 12 may be refused if this would not be permitted by the fundamental principles of the requested State relating to the protection of human rights and fundamental freedoms.

CHAPTER IV – RIGHTS OF ACCESS

Article 21

An application to make arrangements for organising or securing the effective exercise of rights of access may be presented to the Central Authorities of the Contracting States in the same way as an application for the return of a child.

The Central Authorities are bound by the obligations of co-operation which are set forth in Article 7 to promote the peaceful enjoyment of access rights and the fulfilment of any conditions to which the exercise of those rights may be subject. The Central Authorities shall take steps to remove, as far as possible, all obstacles to the exercise of such rights.

The Central Authorities, either directly or through intermediaries, may initiate or assist in the institution of proceedings with a view to organising or protecting these rights and securing respect for the conditions to which the exercise of these rights may be subject.

CHAPTER V – GENERAL PROVISIONS

Article 22

No security, bond or deposit, however described, shall be required to guarantee the payment of costs and expenses in the judicial or administrative proceedings falling within the scope of this Convention.

Article 23

No legalisation or similar formality may be required in the context of this Convention.

Article 24

Any application, communication or other document sent to the Central Authority of the requested State shall be in the original language, and shall be accompanied by a translation into the official language or one of the official languages of the requested State or, where that is not feasible, a translation into French or English.

However, a Contracting State may, by making a reservation in accordance with Article 42, object to the use of either French or English, but not both, in any application, communication or other document sent to its Central Authority.

Article 25

Nationals of the Contracting States and persons who are habitually resident within those States shall be entitled in matters concerned with the application of this Convention to legal aid and advice in any other Contracting State on the same conditions as if they themselves were nationals of and habitually resident in that State.

Article 26

Each Central Authority shall bear its own costs in applying this Convention.

Central Authorities and other public services of Contracting States shall not impose any charges in relation to applications submitted under this Convention. In particular, they may not require any payment from the applicant towards the costs and expenses of the proceedings or, where applicable, those arising from the participation of legal counsel or advisers. However, they may require the payment of the expenses incurred or to be incurred in implementing the return of the child.

However, a Contracting State may, by making a reservation in accordance with Article 42, declare that it shall not be bound to assume any costs referred to in the preceding paragraph resulting from the participation of legal counsel or advisers or from court proceedings, except insofar as those costs may be covered by its system of legal aid and advice.

Upon ordering the return of a child or issuing an order concerning rights of access under this Convention, the judicial or administrative authorities may, where appropriate, direct the person who removed or retained the child, or who prevented the exercise of rights of access, to pay necessary expenses incurred by or on behalf of the applicant, including travel expenses, any costs incurred or payments made for locating the child, the costs of legal representation of the applicant, and those of returning the child.

Article 27

When it is manifest that the requirements of this Convention are not fulfilled or that the application is otherwise not well founded, a Central Authority is not bound to accept the application. In that case, the Central Authority shall forthwith inform the applicant or the Central Authority through which the application was submitted, as the case may be, of its reasons.

Article 28

A Central Authority may require that the application be accompanied by a written authorisation empowering it to act on behalf of the applicant, or to designate a representative so to act.

Article 29

This Convention shall not preclude any person, institution or body who claims that there has been a breach of custody or access rights within the meaning of Article 3 or 21 from applying directly to the judicial or administrative authorities of a Contracting State, whether or not under the provisions of this Convention.

Article 30

Any application submitted to the Central Authorities or directly to the judicial or administrative authorities of a Contracting State in accordance with the terms of this Convention, together with documents and any other information appended thereto or provided by a Central Authority, shall be admissible in the courts or administrative authorities of the Contracting States.

Article 31

In relation to a State which in matters of custody of children has two or more systems of law applicable in different territorial units –

a) any reference to habitual residence in that State shall be construed as referring to habitual residence in a territorial unit of that State;

b) any reference to the law of the State of habitual residence shall be construed as referring to the law of the territorial unit in that State where the child habitually resides.

Article 32

In relation to a State which in matters of custody of children has two or more systems of law applicable to different categories of persons, any reference to the law of that State shall be construed as referring to the legal system specified by the law of that State.

Article 33

A State within which different territorial units have their own rules of law in respect of custody of children shall not be bound to apply this Convention where a State with a unified system of law would not be bound to do so.

Article 34

This Convention shall take priority in matters within its scope over the *Convention of 5 October 1961 concerning the powers of authorities and the law applicable in respect of the protection of minors*, as between Parties to both Conventions. Otherwise the present Convention shall not restrict the application of an international instrument in force between the State of origin and the State addressed or other law of the State addressed for the purposes of obtaining the return of a child who has been wrongfully removed or retained or of organising access rights.

Article 35

This Convention shall apply as between Contracting States only to wrongful removals or retentions occurring after its entry into force in those States.
Where a declaration has been made under Article 39 or 40, the reference in the preceding paragraph to a Contracting State shall be taken to refer to the territorial unit or units in relation to which this Convention applies.

Article 36

Nothing in this Convention shall prevent two or more Contracting States, in order to limit the restrictions to which the return of the child may be subject, from agreeing among themselves to derogate from any provisions of this Convention which may imply such a restriction.

CHAPTER VI – FINAL CLAUSES

Article 37

The Convention shall be open for signature by the States which were Members of the Hague Conference on Private International Law at the time of its Fourteenth Session.
It shall be ratified, accepted or approved and the instruments of ratification, acceptance or approval shall be deposited with the Ministry of Foreign Affairs of the Kingdom of the Netherlands.

Article 38

Any other State may accede to the Convention.
The instrument of accession shall be deposited with the Ministry of Foreign Affairs of the Kingdom of the Netherlands.
The Convention shall enter into force for a State acceding to it on the first day of the third calendar month after the deposit of its instrument of accession.

The accession will have effect only as regards the relations between the acceding State and such Contracting States as will have declared their acceptance of the accession. Such a declaration will also have to be made by any Member State ratifying, accepting or approving the Convention after an accession. Such declaration shall be deposited at the Ministry of Foreign Affairs of the Kingdom of the Netherlands; this Ministry shall forward, through diplomatic channels, a certified copy to each of the Contracting States.

The Convention will enter into force as between the acceding State and the State that has declared its acceptance of the accession on the first day of the third calendar month after the deposit of the declaration of acceptance.

Article 39

Any State may, at the time of signature, ratification, acceptance, approval or accession, declare that the Convention shall extend to all the territories for the international relations of which it is responsible, or to one or more of them. Such a declaration shall take effect at the time the Convention enters into force for that State.

Such declaration, as well as any subsequent extension, shall be notified to the Ministry of Foreign Affairs of the Kingdom of the Netherlands.

Article 40

If a Contracting State has two or more territorial units in which different systems of law are applicable in relation to matters dealt with in this Convention, it may at the time of signature, ratification, acceptance, approval or accession declare that this Convention shall extend to all its territorial units or only to one or more of them and may modify this declaration by submitting another declaration at any time.

Any such declaration shall be notified to the Ministry of Foreign Affairs of the Kingdom of the Netherlands and shall state expressly the territorial units to which the Convention applies.

Article 41

Where a Contracting State has a system of government under which executive, judicial and legislative powers are distributed between central and other authorities within that State, its signature or ratification, acceptance or approval of, or accession to this Convention, or its making of any declaration in terms of Article 40 shall carry no implication as to the internal distribution of powers within that State.

Article 42

Any State may, not later than the time of ratification, acceptance, approval or accession, or at the time of making a declaration in terms of Article 39 or 40, make one or both of the reservations provided for in Article 24 and Article 26, third paragraph. No other reservation shall be permitted.

Any State may at any time withdraw a reservation it has made. The withdrawal shall be notified to the Ministry of Foreign Affairs of the Kingdom of the Netherlands.

The reservation shall cease to have effect on the first day of the third calendar month after the notification referred to in the preceding paragraph.

Article 43

The Convention shall enter into force on the first day of the third calendar month after the deposit of the third instrument of ratification, acceptance, approval or accession referred to in Articles 37 and 38.

Thereafter the Convention shall enter into force –
(1) for each State ratifying, accepting, approving or acceding to it subsequently, on the first day of the third calendar month after the deposit of its instrument of ratification, acceptance, approval or accession;
(2) for any territory or territorial unit to which the Convention has been extended in conformity with Article 39 or 40, on the first day of the third calendar month after the notification referred to in that Article.

Article 44

The Convention shall remain in force for five years from the date of its entry into force in accordance with the first paragraph of Article 43 even for States which subsequently have ratified, accepted, approved it or acceded to it.
If there has been no denunciation, it shall be renewed tacitly every five years.
Any denunciation shall be notified to the Ministry of Foreign Affairs of the Kingdom of the Netherlands at least six months before the expiry of the five year period. It may be limited to certain of the territories or territorial units to which the Convention applies.
The denunciation shall have effect only as regards the State which has notified it. The Convention shall remain in force for the other Contracting States.

Article 45

The Ministry of Foreign Affairs of the Kingdom of the Netherlands shall notify the States Members of the Conference, and the States which have acceded in accordance with Article 38, of the following –
(1) the signatures and ratifications, acceptances and approvals referred to in Article 37;
(2) the accessions referred to in Article 38;
(3) the date on which the Convention enters into force in accordance with Article 43;
(4) the extensions referred to in Article 39;
(5) the declarations referred to in Articles 38 and 40;
(6) the reservations referred to in Article 24 and Article 26, third paragraph, and the withdrawals referred to in Article 42;
(7) the denunciations referred to in Article 44.

In witness whereof the undersigned, being duly authorised thereto, have signed this Convention.

Done at The Hague, on the 25th day of October, 1980, in the English and French languages, both texts being equally authentic, in a single copy which shall be deposited in the archives of the Government of the Kingdom of the Netherlands, and of which a certified copy shall be sent, through diplomatic channels, to each of the States Members of the Hague Conference on Private International Law at the date of its Fourteenth Session.

INDEX

Introductory Note

References such as '178–9' indicate (not necessarily continuous) discussion of a topic across a range of pages. Wherever possible in the case of topics with many references, these have either been divided into sub-topics or only the most significant discussions of the topic are listed. Because the entire work is about 'child abduction', the use of this term (and certain others which occur constantly throughout the book) as an entry point has been minimised. Information will be found under the corresponding detailed topics.

12-month period 29, 142, 144–5, 226–8, 287

abducting parents/abductors 26–9, 44–60, 65–70, 88–90, 105–6, 143, 158–62, 241, 247–53, 227–32, 280–4, 289–93, 302–4, 311–12, 341–2, 357–61, 400–2, 417–22, 445
   custodial 71, 105, 270–1
   fathers 52, 203, 231, 281, 331, 341
   mothers 27, 31, 51–2, 57–9, 87, 232, 251, 281, 291, 297, 330, 357, 402
   potential 96, 99–102, 221, 240, 303
   primary carer 4, 61–2, 280
   reasons for abduction 55–8
   who abducts 55–8
absolute obligations 133, 313–14
abuse 44, 57, 78, 83, 277–8, 282–3, 293, 298, 301–3, 314–15, 360, 369, 394, 418
   allegations of 32, 70, 278, 285
   emotional 277–8, 422
   of language 183, 217
   sexual 23, 273, 276–8, 314
access 3, 149, 239, 308, 363, 423–33, 441, 451–2; *see also* contact
   applications 423, 425–6, 430
   arrangements 154, 161, 165, 428
   exercise 423, 428, 430, 432, 456
      effective 423, 452, 455
   orders 19, 44, 293, 425–6, 430–3, 447
      foreign 426, 430, 432
   rights 10, 86, 126, 130, 146, 149–50, 153, 157–8, 160, 162–9 173–4, 301, 423–33, 447, 452, 456
      Art 21 of Abduction Convention 424–9
      Brussels II bis Regulation 431–2
      certainty v flexibility 429
      consistency with intention of drafters 427
      enforcement 3, 423–33
      European Convention on contact concerning children 431
      European Custody Convention 430
      Hague Convention on the Protection of Children 430–1
      internal coherence 426–7
      peaceful enjoyment 423, 455
      promotion of Convention objectives 428–9
      rights/interests of child 429
   visits 184, 346
accessions 12–14, 41, 361, 458–9
acclimatisation 163, 185, 190–1, 195–6, 199, 201, 203, 211
accommodation 44, 52, 210, 291, 293–4
   costs 421
acquiescence 11, 20, 245–69, 379, 428, 445
   actions for benefit of children 255
   alleged 247, 265
   certainty v flexibility 268
   compatibility with summary nature of Convention proceedings 265
   consistency with intention of drafters 262–3
   content 247–8
   and contract law 267–8
   exercise of discretion 257–61
   following initiation of proceedings 256–7
   ignorance of rights 249–50
   and inaction 256
   internal coherence 261–2
   irrevocability 251
   passive 248, 262
   and private international law principles 266–7
   promotion of Convention objectives 263–5
   pursuance of other remedies 255
   and reliance 250–1
   and rights/interests of child 265–6
   statements made during negotiations 252–3
   statements made in immediate aftermath of removal or retention 254–5
   subjective or objective test 248–9
   vitiating factors 252
actual exercise of custody rights 156, 158, 161, 163, 166, 174, 245, 444
actual residence 176, 195, 202
adequate protection 23, 274, 292, 297, 315, 446
adjudication 3, 23, 96, 102, 105, 110, 127, 165, 171, 209, 239–40, 264, 304, 316, 356, 364, 416, 443
adjustment 50, 63, 68, 229–30, 244
administrative authorities 10–11, 39, 112, 134, 172, 225, 228, 234, 271, 306, 317, 448, 453–4, 456

Index

administrative decisions 141, 169, 451, 454
administrative proceedings 11, 40, 45, 113, 452, 455
ADR, *see* alternative dispute resolution
adults 49, 70, 111–12, 114–16, 119, 174, 195, 213, 325–7, 349, 352–3, 364–5, 386–7, 395–6, 439, 445
advance consent 253–4
age 10, 36, 65, 83, 115–17, 232, 319–25, 344–6, 348, 350–2, 374, 377–9, 384–5, 395, 438–9, 452
  child's objection 323–4
  sufficient age and maturity 320, 324, 340, 373–5, 378, 454
airports 46–7, 275
alienated parents 70, 333
alternative dispute resolution (ADR) 110, 409, 411, 414
American Law Institute model 77
anxieties 87–8, 274
appeals 21, 74, 76, 180–1,
application to Central Authority 43
appropriate forum 102–4, 127, 167, 171, 210, 241, 259, 342; *see also* forum, *forum conveniens*
  most 103, 165, 171
Article 15 declarations 172, 448
  and custody rights 154–6
assurances 23, 291–2, 297–8
attachment 66, 230, 232, 242, 336, 392
attachment relationships
  primary 66–7
  secure 66
attachment theory 67
attempted reconciliations 215–16, 251, 307–8
Australia 14–15, 40, 45, 74, 76, 85–6, 103, 178, 206, 209, 238–9, 249, 259, 288–9, 293–4, 314–15, 327–8, 342–3, 421, 424–6
  courts 86, 133, 206, 209
Austria 39, 48–9, 192
automatic recognition of judgments 9, 130, 171
automatic return 9, 97
autonomy 113, 117, 218, 329, 331, 337, 343–4, 411, 415
  party 413–14

balance 13, 20, 81, 88, 108, 110, 125, 130, 137, 164, 174, 219, 226, 236, 272, 287, 302, 349, 356, 364
  fair 26, 49, 356
Balcolme approach 320–2
Belgium 15, 37, 40, 133, 182–4, 200, 202, 275, 302, 332
  courts 183, 275, 302
best interests 7, 26–8, 73, 75–7, 117–20, 238–42, 264–6, 306–11, 336–8, 355–61, 363–5, 367–8, 395–6, 438–9; *see also* child's interests
  analysis/assessment/examination 76, 258, 292, 299, 303, 309, 443
  and Art 3 of CRC 111–13
binary solutions 109
biological parents 123, 202
birth of Abduction Convention 7–14
blameworthiness 105–6, 419–20
Brussels II bis Regulation 19–25, 431–2; *see also* Table of Legislation

Canada 8, 16, 40, 45–8, 75, 81, 86, 128, 145, 189, 200–2, 204, 207, 210, 218, 231, 240, 336, 360, 377
  courts 86, 158, 200, 210, 335
care 118, 149–50, 152–4, 159, 404–5
  foster 44, 184, 277, 281, 339, 404
  mother's 202, 327, 333
  primary 56, 65–6, 77, 280
  shared 74, 76–7, 81, 88
carers
  non-primary 56–8, 61, 65, 67–8, 162, 440–1
  primary, *see* primary carers
Central Authorities (CAs) 10–11, 36–41, 43–7, 228, 421–30, 432, 452–6
  obligations re enforcement of access rights 426
certainty v flexibility 108, 136–7, 173, 182, 195, 214, 218–20, 227, 235, 352, 362, 394, 429
  access rights 429
  Art 12(2) 243–4
  child objection 349–50
  consent/acquiescence 268
  custody rights 173
  fundamental human rights and freedoms 368–9
  grave risk 314
  habitual residence 218–20
  retention 145–6
change of habitual residence 30, 189, 201, 205, 208, 214, 216, 248, 265, 425
chasing orders 9, 18, 153, 157, 292
child-centred model, *see* independent model
child-centric approach 237–8, 242–3, 276, 352–3, 395–6
child objection defence/exception 22, 69–70, 120, 205, 234, 266, 272, 275, 285, 302, 317–53, 373–4, 377, 383, 390, 397, 402, 405, 446, 449
  age 323–4
  certainty v flexibility 349–50
  consistency with intention of drafters 344–5
  and Convention policy in exercise of discretion 341–2
  dilemma 317–19
  form of objections 327–8
  independence of objections 329–34
  and internal coherence 343–4
  interpretation of Art 13(2) 323–43
  maturity 324–7
  and private international law principles 349
  promotion of Convention objectives 345–8
  and rights/interests of child 348–9
  scope of court discretion 319–22
  and siblings 338–41
  strength of objections 328–9
  validity of objections 334–5
  and welfare considerations
    against returning child 337–8
    in favour of returning child 336–7
child psychologists 376–7
child welfare 64, 113, 367–8
  professionals 385–6, 388
child's interests 17, 24, 27, 75, 80, 109, 112, 125, 184–5, 212, 241, 266, 306, 348–9, 393–4, 397, 401, 410; *see also* best interests

child's objections, *see* child objections defence/
    exception
child's participation 112, 114–17, 374–5, 379–80,
    382–4, 386, 389, 401, 414
  making participation meaningful 386–7
child's rights 2, 34, 108–11, 113, 115, 117–19, 122,
    242, 266, 311, 318, 329–30, 344, 351, 366, 380,
    394–5, 404, 438
  and Abduction Convention 109–11
  and access rights 429
  and Art 12(2) 242–3
  and child's objection defence/exception 348–9
  conflicts with parental rights 124–5
  and consent/acquiescence 265–6
  and custody rights 166–7
  developments since 1980 437–9
  and fundamental human rights 355–8, 365–6
  and grave risk 306–11
  habitual residence 212–13
child's views/wishes
  appropriate weight 113, 117, 238, 327–8, 330,
    332–3, 335, 348, 353, 438
  hearing by judges 380–6
  making participation meaningful 386–7
  methods of ascertaining 375–80
  requirement to ascertain 373–88
child's voice 49, 116, 371–406, 438
child's welfare 17–18, 44, 57, 68, 74, 87, 99, 101–2,
    117, 123, 130, 162, 233, 238–40, 257–9, 266–7,
    306–8, 336–7, 345, 394–6
Chile 150, 354
choice of law rules 108, 126–9, 132, 146, 160, 169–70,
    178, 444; *see also* forum
civil law 14, 17
  countries 48, 116
co-operation 8, 13, 25, 29–30, 38, 42, 47, 124, 290,
    394, 423, 430, 452, 455
coercive measures 26, 47–9
coherence, internal, *see* internal coherence
combined model 77, 189, 192–9, 201, 203, 208–10,
    212–13, 216, 219–21, 444
comity 108, 127, 129–30, 132–6, 172–3, 238, 243,
    266–7, 293, 295, 312–14, 349, 368–9, 443, 446
  refusal 31, 134
commencement of proceedings 8, 10–11, 45–6,
    111, 226, 228–9, 286, 299, 405, 453; *see also*
    institution of proceedings
common law 128–30, 150, 176
  countries/jurisdictions 29, 103, 128, 132, 176, 187,
    233, 291, 293, 364, 375, 424, 440
common settled purpose 207–8
Commonwealth jurisdictions 186, 193
communications, judicial, *see* judicial
    communications
compatibility with summary nature of Convention
    proceedings 94, 106–7
  Art 12(2) 242
  child's objection 348
  consent/acquiescence 265
  custody rights 165–6
  fundamental human rights and freedoms 365
  grave risk 305

habitual residence 211–12
compensation 25, 81, 99, 447
  left-behind parents 417–22, 447
    Abduction Convention model 420–2
    arguments against 418–19
    arguments in favour 417–18
    criminal model 419–20
    tort model 419
compliance 13, 21, 49, 131, 294, 374, 441
concealment 64, 227, 229–31, 239, 241–2, 244
conflict of interests 40, 391, 393–4
connecting factors 126, 128, 169, 175–8, 204, 206
consensual removals 262–3, 266
consensus 9, 73, 103–4, 110, 131, 146, 186, 202, 225,
    441
consent 11, 16, 71–2, 77, 86, 100, 108, 136, 141–2, 148,
    157–8, 164–5, 169–70, 245–69, 445, 453
  actions for benefit of children 255
  advance 253–4
  certainty v flexibility 268
  compatibility with summary nature of Convention
    proceedings 265
  consistency with intention of drafters 262–3
  content 247–8
  and contract law 267–8
  exercise of discretion 257–61
  ignorance of rights 249–50
  internal coherence 261–2
  irrevocability 251
  normative framework 247–51
  orders 151, 218
  and private international law principles 266–7
  promotion of Convention objectives 263–5
  pursuance of other remedies 255
  real 262, 264
  and reliance 250–1
  and rights/interests of child 265–6
  statements made during negotiations 252–3
  subjective or objective test 248–9
  vitiating factors 252
consistency with general legal doctrines 2, 93,
    108–37
consistency with intention of drafters 59, 94–5, 149,
    158, 174, 227, 237, 344–5, 369
  access rights 427
  Art 12(2) 237
  child's objection 344–5
  consent/acquiescence 262–3
  custody rights 159–61
  fundamental human rights and freedoms 362–3
  grave risk 300–1
  habitual residence 206–7
  retention 144
constitutional principles 15, 112
constitutional rights 122, 373
contact 52, 79–83, 118–25, 156–7, 173–4, 427–31
  arrangements 15, 78–9, 83, 85, 90, 276, 413
  cross-frontier 89, 424
  degree of 65, 232, 449
  direct 80, 83, 118–19, 124
  frequency of 61, 77
  loss of 64, 67, 305

464 Index

contact (*cont*):
  orders 19, 24, 30, 79, 82–3, 403, 431
    foreign 430–1
  presumption 119–20
  reduced 67–8, 77, 400, 417
  regular 52–3, 67–8, 75, 80, 156, 167, 264–6, 316, 429
  right to contact with parents 118–20
  trans-frontier, *see* cross-frontier contact
contract 108, 128, 143–4, 216, 267, 430
convenience 102, 104
Convention proceedings 35, 57, 106–7, 165, 211, 242, 249, 265, 305, 318, 344, 346, 358, 365, 373, 375, 413, 415
conversations 211–12, 378, 380, 382–3, 385
costs 11, 25, 40, 44, 48, 78, 81–3, 90, 131, 136, 233, 291, 305, 342, 398, 410, 417–22, 447, 456
  accommodation 421
  financial 90, 99
  legal 78, 81, 291, 417, 421–2
counselling 49, 53, 276
country of habitual residence 9–10, 12, 23, 29, 52, 57, 89, 104–5, 126–7, 146–7, 162, 164–5, 170–2, 183–5, 301, 304, 308–10, 330, 387, 413
country of origin 4, 7, 10, 21, 23–5, 27, 29–33, 4 85–7, 104–6, 121, 183, 198–9, 203, 210–11, 214–16, 226–7, 259-60, 288–9, 300–5, 331, 347, 404, 413, 448; *see also* requesting State
country of refuge 7–8, 10–12, 20–1, 23–4, 27–33, 43–4, 103–5, 134–5, 154–6, 181–3, 203–4, 225–8, 291–7, 299–302, 312–13, 356–9, 361–3, 411–13, 428–31, 453–5; *see also* requested State
court orders 16, 48, 133, 142, 145, 148, 150–1, 154, 168, 185, 200, 216–18, 292, 294, 297, 303, 338, 402, 419, 424; *see also individual order types*
court welfare officers/services 376, 381, 384, 401
courtesy, judicial 132, 134–6, 172, 243, 349
courts
  Australia 86, 133, 206, 209
  Belgium 183, 275, 302
  Canada 86, 158, 200, 210, 335
  discretion 89, 228, 251, 290, 319, 373, 396
  England and Wales 24, 123, 127, 143, 146, 151, 153, 173, 202, 206, 255, 291, 298, 304, 310, 335, 347, 359, 363, 430
  First instance 21, 39, 258
  France 23, 27, 168, 173, 260, 304, 347, 430
  Germany 323, 352, 373, 377
  of habitual residence 272, 301
  Hungary 156, 288
  Israel 31, 60, 133–5, 155–6, 193–4, 197–200, 211–12, 218–19, 227–8, 245, 247–8, 250, 252–4, 256, 260–1, 285–7, 294–5, 330–2, 341–3, 383–5
  Latvia 24, 28
  Netherlands 127, 155, 287–8
  New Zealand 17, 153–4, 157–8, 164, 193, 208, 228–9, 241, 281, 321, 346, 390, 426
  Norway 298
  Poland 239, 403
  Scotland 156, 293
  Sharia 359
  Spain 146, 357–8
  Sweden 201, 217, 278, 295
  Turkey 357–8
  United Kingdom 24, 123, 127, 142–3, 145–6, 148, 151, 153, 155, 173, 177, 187, 202, 235, 249–50, 304, 310, 359, 363, 402
  United States 135, 208, 227, 292, 294, 318, 359, 424
criminal law 15–17, 99, 101
criminal model 417, 419–20
criminal offences 15–17, 100, 419
criminal proceedings 17, 31, 43, 47, 99, 233, 275, 291, 294, 419, 422, 438
criminal sanctions 16–17, 99–101
cross-border mediation 409, 412–13
cross-frontier contact 89, 424, 431
cultural norms 355, 365–8
cultural pluralism 366–7, 369
culture 112, 121, 150, 185, 355, 366–8, 412
custodial abductors 71, 105, 270–1
custodial mother 84, 99, 101, 260
custodial parent 68, 71–2, 74–5, 81, 84–5, 168–9, 418
custody 8–10, 15–18, 145–74, 355–9, 451–2
  American Law Institute model 77
  arrangements 209, 418
  decisions 9, 12, 18–19, 24, 31–3, 130, 304
  disputes 12, 66, 73, 97, 102, 126–7, 185, 209–10, 240–1, 258, 274, 299, 304, 307, 310, 312, 328, 337–8, 384–5, 387
  joint 26, 77
  joint legal 72, 174, 439
  legal, *see* legal custody
  and *ne exeat* rights, *see* rights, to veto removal
  orders 7–9, 12, 18, 26, 31–2, 171, 204, 292, 399
  permanent 218, 249
  proceedings 46–7, 105, 239, 247, 289, 292, 443
  shuttle arrangements 200–1, 216–17
custody rights 10, 15, 26, 29, 94, 97, 118, 126–7, 141–3, 145–67, 169–74, 204, 245, 250–1, 258–9, 327–8, 337, 427–8, 444, 452–3
  actual exercise 156–8, 161, 163, 166, 174, 245, 444
  and Article 15 declarations 154–6
  breach and exercise of rights analysis 157–73
  certainty v flexibility 173
  compatibility with summary nature of Convention proceedings 165–6
  consistency with intention of drafters 159–61
  consistency with parental rights 167–9
  consistency with private international law principles 169–73
  consistency with rights and interests of child 166–7
  definition 147, 154, 173
  internal coherence 157–9
  local law v autonomous definition 147–8
  non-exercise 156, 158–9, 245
  promotion of Convention objectives 161–5
  and unmarried fathers 151–4

daily life 183, 192, 199, 210, 212, 214
damage 42, 49, 67, 69, 89, 110, 118, 145, 244, 283, 302, 325, 340, 342, 345, 347, 385, 392–5, 404, 410, 414, 421, 449; *see also* harm
  irreparable 70, 87

long-term 69, 283
real 393–4
date of removal 142, 181, 227
date of wrongful removal or retention 13, 111, 226
daughters 257, 278, 357
defences 9–11, 15–19, 22–4, 31–3, 88–9, 97–100, 157–9, 223–78, 282–90, 298–301, 303–8, 310–12, 314–19, 334–6, 343–7, 352–60, 362–4, 366–8, 438–40, 445
    acquiescence, *see* acquiescence
    Art 12(2) 225–44
        12-month period 29, 142, 144–5, 226–8, 287
        case law 226–36
        certainty v flexibility 243–4
        compatibility with summary nature of Convention proceedings 242
        consistency with intention of drafters 237
        discretion to order return 233–6
        internal coherence 236
        and private international law principles 243
        promotion of Convention objectives 237–42
        and rights/interests of child 242–3
        settlement/settled in new environment 228–34, 240, 343, 390, 394, 402
    child objection, *see* child's objection
    consent, *see* consent
    grave risk, *see* grave risk
    intolerable situation 11, 49, 66, 88–9, 165, 270–1, 274, 276–7, 283–6, 288–9, 300–3, 311, 315–16, 339, 343, 362, 378, 422, 440, 445–7
    public policy 32, 270, 354, 362
    violation of fundamental human rights and freedoms, *see* fundamental human rights and freedoms
deference 134–5, 173, 267, 313
degree of maturity 22, 117, 317, 321, 324–5, 340, 345, 374, 376, 454
degree of settled purpose 190, 193
delay 7, 11, 22, 26–8, 38, 40, 46, 67, 106, 145, 227, 229, 232, 256–8, 260, 271–2, 287–8, 397–8, 448, 453
    and mediation 412
    significant 48, 105, 397, 405, 412
delaying tactics 412, 439
denunciation 459
dependency model 186
deposits 11, 13, 294, 346, 431, 455, 457–9
detection 231
deterrence 86, 98–102, 164, 185, 208, 239–40, 263, 303, 309, 346, 364, 442, 446
    general 99, 240
    research 99–100
deterrent effect 85, 98–102, 145, 239–40, 303, 309, 346, 418, 443
    likely 54, 99
    real/actual 99
direct contact 80, 83, 118–19, 124
direct hearing of children 378–80, 382, 388, 401, 438
direct judicial communications 31, 42, 296–7
discretion 116–17, 233–9, 241–4, 257–66, 268–9, 318–20, 336–42, 347–9, 445–6
    approach 234–6, 241, 243
    consent/acquiescence 257–61

courts 82, 89, 135, 153, 228, 251, 290, 297, 319, 373, 396
exercise of 233–4, 243, 257, 262, 267–8, 285, 322, 328, 347, 352
wide 86, 137, 263, 267, 421, 426
discrimination 58, 60, 111, 167–8, 358–9, 366
distress, emotional 417, 419, 422
divorce 19, 63–4, 67–8, 76–7, 98, 114, 131, 175–6, 215, 231, 375, 384, 411, 414
    proceedings 32, 248, 289, 398
domestic abuse policy 314
domestic law 31, 72, 83, 113, 129, 137, 147, 151, 160, 166, 168, 170, 234, 425, 432, 444
domestic violence 4, 31, 33, 52, 54, 57–8, 61, 85, 87, 89, 167, 213, 272, 277, 281–4, 294, 300–3, 311, 314, 440
    allegations 78, 272, 282, 400, 415
    escape from 282, 290, 303–5, 311, 314
    history of 120, 315, 415
    and mediation 415–16
    victims 4, 31, 282, 284, 297
domicile 129, 131, 175–8, 191, 206–7
    of origin 178, 204, 207
Dominican Republic 38, 45, 181, 183–5
drafters 1, 55, 57–9, 66, 94–5, 97, 144, 158–61, 170–1, 174–5, 206–7, 237, 262, 270, 300–1, 318, 344–5, 362–3, 427, 439–40
dual habitual residence 178, 205
due process 122, 355, 358–60, 366, 368, 391–2
Duncan Report 423–4, 426–8
duties 38, 40, 118–19, 123–4, 151–2, 156, 206, 213, 215, 263, 272, 290, 295, 351–2, 373, 394–5, 400, 424, 426, 452
Dyer Report 8–9, 55–6, 98, 100

ECJ, *see* European Court of Justice
ECtHR, *see* European Court of Human Rights
education 43, 83, 98, 122, 124, 150, 187–8, 248
    religious 122, 124
effective exercise of rights of access 423, 452, 455
effective protection 54, 68, 438
effectiveness 38, 51, 99, 271, 315, 449
emotional abuse 277–8, 422
emotional distress 417, 419, 422
emotional environment 68, 161
emotional turmoil 101, 254, 264–5, 385
empirical research/studies 4, 35–6, 47, 50, 54, 65, 68, 71, 80, 83, 100, 114, 375, 383, 438
employment 31, 83, 187–8, 197, 215, 232, 256
enforceability 23, 82–3, 85, 89, 119, 294, 413
    mediation 413
enforcement 17–19, 29–31, 47–9, 119, 130–1, 176, 293, 412–13
    access rights 3, 423–33
    fast-track 23
    judgments 19, 103, 116, 131, 148, 176, 284, 347, 374, 412, 431
    problems 47–8, 410, 448
England and Wales 7, 12, 15, 19, 24, 37, 39, 74, 103–4, 130, 145–6, 152–3, 194, 197–8, 201–2, 207, 247–9, 323–4, 336–7, 341–2; *see also* United Kingdom

Index

England and Wales (*cont*):
  courts 24, 146, 148, 151, 153, 173, 180, 202, 206, 227, 229, 235, 238, 262, 298, 304, 327, 335, 337, 359
  law 146, 155, 170, 173, 178, 180, 220, 376
environment 27, 57, 68, 96, 162, 172, 196, 203, 208, 226, 229–30, 232, 241–2, 275, 286–8, 299–300, 302, 364
  family 110, 194–5, 208, 214, 220–1, 366, 445
  new 20–1, 29, 32–3, 111, 196, 220, 225–6, 228–32, 237–8, 242, 244, 276, 286, 299, 336, 348, 439, 453
  social 98, 191, 208, 331
  stable 64–6, 288
equitable tolling 227, 241
European Convention on Human Rights 25–9; *see also Table of Legislation*
European Court of Human Rights (ECtHR) 24–9, 47–9, 112, 119, 124–5, 153, 287–8, 292, 299, 306, 308–9, 355–6, 365
  Grand Chamber 25, 27–8, 124–5, 287, 292, 311, 356–7, 366
European Court of Justice (ECJ) 152, 173, 187, 194–5, 221
European Custody Convention 17–19, 430; *see also Table of Legislation*
everyday life, *see* daily life
evidence, expert 11, 146, 166, 280, 283, 305
exceptions, *see* defences
exclusive jurisdiction 9, 29, 126, 160
exemplary punishment 101–2
exercise
  of custody rights, *see* custody, exercise of rights analysis
  of discretion 233–4, 243, 257, 262, 267–8, 285, 322, 328, 347, 352
  of rights of access 423, 428, 430, 432, 456
expedited return 1, 9
expenses 12, 44–5, 79, 165, 243, 390, 397, 420–1, 455–6
  reimbursement 417, 419, 422
expert evidence/testimony 11, 146, 166, 280, 283, 305
expert opinions 70, 183–4, 379, 386
expert reports 106, 272, 278, 305, 377–8, 380, 382, 385
experts 62, 70, 81–2, 273, 287, 305, 324–6, 334, 350, 352, 358, 375–9, 381–2, 384–5, 394, 396, 401, 413, 441
extended families 64, 83, 99, 328, 331, 384

facts, objective 193, 203, 219, 265, 279
factual test 194
fair balance 26, 49, 356
fair trial 358–9, 392
fairness 59, 104, 128, 313, 358
family environment 110, 194–5, 208, 214, 220–1, 366, 445
family justice systems 14, 114, 245, 361, 382
family life 25, 27, 60, 74, 98, 112, 122, 124–5, 148, 167–8, 267, 286, 308, 311–12, 355–7, 359, 439
  right to 148, 167
family members 44, 56, 58, 62, 70, 80–1, 83, 108–9, 329, 339
family relationships 109–10
fast-track enforcement 23
fathers 55–62, 77–82, 150–4, 167–70, 181–5, 196–202, 238–42, 249–57, 283–7, 293–4, 330–3
  abducting 52, 203, 231, 281, 331, 341
  left-behind 59, 90, 286, 313, 357, 419
  unmarried 126, 147, 151–4, 157, 162, 167–8, 171, 174, 204
fees 11, 420–1
financial costs 90, 99
financial support 259, 288, 292, 418
first instance courts/judges 21, 75, 235, 242–3, 258, 272, 275, 323, 327–9, 331, 336–7, 340, 357, 376, 383, 385
fixed-term relocations 197–8, 209–10, 214, 219
flexibility, *see* certainty v flexibility
forced marriage 367
foreign contact orders 430–1
foreign courts 131, 133–5, 155, 166, 260, 293–6, 308, 313, 359, 419, 426
foreign judgments, recognition 108, 126, 129–32, 169
foreign law 11, 129, 131, 133, 135, 146–7, 165–6, 174, 243, 364
former habitual residence 20, 30, 161, 183, 188–9, 191, 207–9
forum 23, 41, 103, 129–32, 135, 170–2, 177, 260, 364, 438, 443
  appropriate, *see* appropriate forum
  forum conveniens 23, 86–7, 96, 102–5, 127, 149, 165, 171, 184–5, 201, 208–10, 221, 239–41, 259, 264, 304, 342, 346–7, 364–5, 442–3
  forum non conveniens 103, 364
forum-shopping 105, 130, 177, 208
  natural 131, 364
foster care 44, 184, 277, 281, 339, 404
France 14, 25–6, 47, 75, 90, 151, 168, 181, 183–5, 196, 199–200, 211–12, 227, 259–60, 272, 275, 278, 281, 285, 287
  courts 23, 27, 168, 173, 260, 304, 347, 430
freedoms 25, 49, 99, 111, 122–4, 214, 343, 360–1, 366
  fundamental, *see* fundamental human rights and freedoms
  of movement 121, 168, 311, 349, 355, 360–1, 366
fundamental human rights and freedoms 11, 15, 22, 24, 109, 119, 354–69, 446, 455
  and parental rights 366–8
  and private international law principles 368
  and rights/interests of child 355–8, 365–6
  case law 355–61
  certainty v flexibility 368–9
  compatibility with summary nature of Convention proceedings 365
  consistency with intention of drafters 362–3
  freedom of movement 360–1
  internal coherence 361–2
  lack of due process in requesting State 358–60
  promotion of Convention objectives 363–5
fundamental principles 13, 15, 21, 250, 306, 354–6, 359, 361–4, 455

gender 36, 55, 58–61, 73, 109, 125, 359, 410, 417
  bias 59–60

preference rule 364, 368
general deterrence 99, 240
general legal doctrines 2, 93, 108, 110, 112, 114, 116, 118, 120, 122, 124, 126, 128, 130, 132, 134, 136, 220
general principles 37, 111–12, 267, 296, 429, 431
Germany 24, 45–6, 48, 124–5, 143, 189–90, 192, 196–7, 199, 209, 216, 281, 319, 323, 328, 336, 377, 419
  courts 323, 352, 373, 377
girls 122, 191, 199, 231, 256–7, 288, 324, 329, 335–6, 379, 383, 385
good faith 16, 77, 94, 422
grandparents 58, 151–3, 182, 196, 218, 330, 335
grave risk 11, 33, 62, 66–7, 69, 87–9, 102, 133–5, 163, 258–9, 266, 270–317, 338–9, 343, 354, 361–2, 365, 397, 439–40, 445–7
  action to ensure enforceability of undertakings/conditions 294–5
  certainty v flexibility 314
  compatibility with summary nature of Convention proceedings 305
  consistency with intention of drafters 300–1
  dilemma 270–1
  and domestic abuse policy 314
  internal coherence 298–300
  interpretation and application 273–89
  judicial liaison 296–8
  and parental rights 311–12
  and private international law principles 312–14
  promotion of Convention objectives 301–5
  protective measures 289–98
  of psychological harm 273, 280, 285
  and rights/interests of child 306–11
  scope of investigation 271–3
  undertakings 291–4
grave risk of harm, see grave risk
guardians 16, 147, 154, 331, 394–5, 400
  legal 118, 148
guidance 48, 74, 117, 180, 247, 271, 296, 386
guilt 341–2, 347, 401–2

habitual residence 8–12, 29–33, 104–6, 126–7, 156–60, 165–7, 169–222, 451–4
  and applicability of Convention 180–2
  certainty v flexibility 218–20
  change of 30, 189, 201, 205, 208, 214, 216, 248, 265, 425
  combined model 189, 192–9, 201, 203, 208–10, 212–13, 216, 219–21, 444
  as connecting factor 137, 176, 209, 221
  consistency with intention of drafters 206–7
  and contract law 216–18
  court of 272, 301
  definition 176, 221
  determination of 59, 104, 177, 179–80, 191, 200, 204, 208, 216, 218, 220–1, 406, 445
  dual 178, 205
  factual nature of 177–8, 200, 217, 222
  and fixed-term relocations 197–8, 209–10, 214, 219
  former 20, 30, 161, 183, 188–9, 191, 207–9
  independent model 190–201, 203, 208, 210, 212–13, 219
  internal coherence 204–6
  law of 126, 160, 169, 171–2, 204
  and matrimonial law 215–16
  models 186–95
  nature of determination 179–80
  new 20, 178, 188, 195, 215–16
  newborn children 201–3
  origin of concept 175–6
  parental intention approach/model 186, 189–97, 199–201, 203–9, 211–14, 216, 219, 221
  and parental rights 213–14
  and permanent relocations 195–7, 199
  and place to where child is returned 182–5
  previous 188–9, 195–6, 209
  promotion of Convention objectives 207–11
  and relocation for an indefinite period 198–200
  and rights/interests of child 212–13
  role in Abduction Convention 180–5
  and shuttle custody arrangements 200–1, 216–17
  single at all times or not 178–9
  use in relation to children 176–7
  and wrongfulness of removal or retention 182
Hague Child Protection Convention 1996 29–33, 430–1; *see also Table of Legislation*
Hague Conference on Private International Law 1, 3, 7–9, 12, 14, 41, 82–3, 95, 98, 108, 111, 126, 129, 144, 160, 175, 179–80, 221, 440–1, 451
harm 2, 7, 44, 49–50, 61–2, 64–6, 68–70, 74–5, 88–9, 96–8, 102, 110, 167, 208, 238–9, 345, 362, 366–9, 379, 385–6, 393–4, 398–9, 402–6, 437, 439–40, 442–3; *see also* damage; grave risk; harmful effects
  grave risk of, *see* grave risk
  long-term 66, 275
  physical 135, 274, 278, 293, 312
  potential 115, 239, 273–4, 276, 404
  psychological 29, 49, 270–2, 274–6, 280, 284–6, 328, 336, 340–1, 385, 422, 447
  real 98, 106, 162, 281, 302, 307, 368
  risk of 17, 115, 276, 279, 283, 301–2, 315, 365, 385, 446
  significant 62, 367–8
harmful effects 1, 9, 27, 66, 96–8, 161–2, 164, 174, 263, 303, 364, 368, 428, 440, 442, 448, 451
harmony 170, 337, 343
health 25, 43, 122, 248
  mental 69, 75, 87–9, 281, 284
hearing 21–2, 103, 106, 114–16, 228–9, 242–3, 265, 305, 341–2, 347, 376–88 414–15
  direct hearing of children 379–80, 382, 388, 401, 438
  indirect hearing of children 380–1, 397
hierarchy
  legal 362–3
  of objectives 442–3
home country/State 22, 53–4, 56–7, 65, 81, 101, 209, 261, 267, 271, 310, 442; *see also* country of origin

human rights 2, 13, 24–5, 28, 49, 108, 112, 122, 124, 168, 286, 299, 306, 311, 354–6, 358–62, 364–9, 389, 439, 446
  basic 25, 89
  fundamental 11, 15, 22, 24, 109, 119, 354, 360–2, 446, 455
  protection 15, 354, 362, 455
Hungary 40, 46, 50
  courts 156, 288
hybrid model, *see* combined model

identity 55, 64, 66, 80, 110–11, 150, 162, 242, 359, 453
  right to 121, 213
immediate mandatory return 299, 356
immigration
  restrictions 289, 312, 315
  status 230, 289
impartiality 297, 383
inaction 247, 264
  and consent 256
incentives 7–8, 20, 33, 45, 76, 84, 129, 438, 448
inchoate rights 151–2, 157, 163, 165–6, 173–4
incitement 69, 120, 331–4, 347
inconsistency 21, 112, 142, 147, 152, 283, 308–9, 311, 323, 351, 355–6, 359, 362, 365, 368
  internal 159, 179
  logical 312
  potential 33, 306–7, 311
independence of views/ objections 302, 322, 329, 331, 333–4, 346, 351–2, 384, 446
independent model 190–201, 203, 208, 210, 212–13, 219
indirect hearing 380–1, 397
influence, undue 332, 334–5, 401
information 35–8, 41–4, 50–3, 296–8, 386–7, 394–6
  obtaining of 50–1, 305, 365
  partial 298, 386
  post-return 50–1
  relevant 36, 38, 191, 296, 384, 386, 394, 397, 400, 406
  surveys 51–3
injustice 231, 238, 241, 264, 282, 364
institutions 38–42, 56, 112–113, 141, 159, 172, 192, 245, 396
institution of proceedings 45, 423, 451–3, 456; *see also* commencement of proceedings
integration 194, 196, 212, 237, 244, 286–8
intentions
  of drafters, *see* consistency with intention of drafters
  mutual 204, 208
  parental 186, 189–97, 199–201, 203–9, 211–14, 216, 219, 221
  requisite 187, 189–90
  settled 188, 191, 193, 199, 444
  shared 200, 202
  subjective 212, 248–9, 255, 269
inter-relationships 2, 7, 59, 71, 127, 142, 146–7, 161, 262, 299, 306
  between relocation and abduction 84–90
  with Brussels II bis Regulation 19–25
  with domestic proceedings 12
  with European Convention on Human Rights 25–9
  with European Custody Convention 17–19
  with national legislation 14–17
  with other legal instruments 14–34
  with United Nations Convention on the Rights of the Child 1989 33–4
interests
  best, *see* best interests
  child's 17, 24, 27, 75, 80, 109, 112, 125, 184–5, 212, 241, 266, 306, 348–9, 393–4, 397, 401, 410; *see also* child's rights
  conflict of 40, 391, 393–4
  long-term 239, 309–11, 315, 356, 445
  primary 301, 311
  short-term 303, 309–11, 356, 445
interference 25, 27, 110, 122, 124–5, 162, 286
internal coherence 94, 220
  access rights 426–7
  Art 12(2) 236
  child's objection 343–4
  consent/acquiescence 261–2
  custody rights 157–9
  fundamental human rights and freedoms 361–2
  grave risk 298–300
  habitual residence 204–6
  retention 144
internal inconsistency 159, 179
international comity, *see* comity
international relocation *see* relocation

interpretation 24–6, 93, 95–7, 120–1, 272–4, 362–3
  literal 158, 322, 373
  narrow 98–9, 135, 163, 236, 241, 244, 266, 298, 312, 343, 345, 362, 427
  recommendations 444–7
  restrictive 273, 306, 313, 354, 364, 368–9, 439
  wide 10, 134, 157, 164–6, 239, 263–4, 266, 268, 298–9, 346, 351, 355, 364
interviews 36, 63, 116, 293, 362, 375–6, 380, 383
  judicial 377–8
intolerable situation defence/exception 88–9, 165, 270–1, 274, 276–7, 284–5, 288–9, 300 315–16, 445–7; *see also* grave risk of harm
Ireland 22, 135, 152–3, 162, 168, 247, 335, 337, 341, 347
irreparable damage 70, 87
Israel 13, 45–6, 60, 84–6, 122–3, 133–4, 183–4, 189–91, 197–200, 202–3, 218, 226–8, 252–61, 274–5, 279–81, 288–92, 329–32, 336–8, 357–9, 402–4
  courts/judges 31, 60, 133–5, 155–6, 193–4, 197–200, 211–12, 218–19, 227–8, 245, 247–8, 250, 252–4, 256, 260–1, 275, 285–7, 294–5, 330–2, 383–5
Italy 17, 24, 134, 227, 288, 325, 331–2, 377, 384, 430

joint legal custody 72, 174, 439
joint primary carers 56, 60, 65
judgments, recognition and enforcement 19, 103, 116, 129–32, 148, 169, 171, 176, 284, 347, 374, 412, 431
judicial communications 42, 296–8, 413

direct 31, 42, 296–7
judicial courtesy 132, 134–6, 172, 243, 349
judicial discretion, *see* discretion, courts
judicial interviews 377–8
judicial liaison 42, 296–8, 315; *see also* liaison judges
jurisdiction rules 103, 108, 126–7, 130–1

language 3, 12, 103, 133, 150, 159, 183, 185, 191, 196, 198, 217, 232, 235
  abuse of 183, 217
Latvia, courts 24, 28
lawful removal 71, 142, 145, 157
lawyers 39–40, 45, 50–1, 297–8, 390–2, 394–6, 399–400
Lebanon 359
left-behind parents 26, 51–4, 64–7, 69–70, 143–7, 161–7, 183–5, 245–56, 260–9, 290–4, 347–8, 417–22, 446–8
  agreement 245, 252–3
  compensation 417–22, 447
  decisions 90
  fathers 59, 90, 286, 313, 357, 419
  mothers 231, 419
legal aid 28, 30, 39–40, 61, 104, 233, 297, 398, 404, 426, 432, 452, 455–6
legal basis 291, 296, 354
legal costs 78, 81, 291, 417, 421–2
legal custody 160, 251, 419
  joint 72, 174, 439
legal effect 141, 151, 154, 451
legal guardians 118, 148
legal hierarchy 362–3
legal proceedings, *see* proceedings
legal representation, *see* representation
legal systems 7, 13–14, 58, 71, 82, 99, 112, 115, 127, 135–7, 167, 176, 204, 233, 243, 295, 303, 313, 364–6, 418–19
liaison, judicial 42, 296, 298, 315
liaison judges 39, 166, 296–7, 365, 402
literal interpretation 158, 322, 373
living conditions 75, 198, 288
local law 146–7, 151, 155, 173, 355–6, 360, 426, 428, 432, 448
location of child 43–4
logical inconsistency 312
long-term damage 69, 283
long-term harm 66, 275
long-term interests 239, 309–11, 315, 356, 445
long-term settled position 229–30
long-term welfare 77, 90, 310
loss of contact 64, 67, 305

macro level 71, 84–6
maintenance 52, 292–3
mandatory return 3–4
  automatic 14
  defences, *see* defences
  immediate 299, 356
  mechanism 3, 11, 86, 139, 141, 160, 172–3, 204, 225, 244, 261–2, 268, 306, 417–18, 421, 425, 439–40
  policy 263, 322

marriage 1, 19, 57, 72 197, 215–16,
  forced 367
maternal grandmothers 151, 153, 182
maturation 66–8
mature children 11, 75, 85, 111, 120, 167, 321, 325, 335, 338, 340, 344–5, 348–9, 351, 353, 373, 379, 395, 402, 416
maturity 22, 27, 83, 113, 115, 117, 226, 302, 317, 319–26, 331, 333, 335, 339–41, 345–6, 348–52, 373–6, 378–9, 385, 438
  child's objection 324–7
  degree of 22, 117, 317, 321, 324–5, 340, 345, 374, 376, 454
  tests of 324–5
mediated agreements 410, 413, 415
mediation 3, 14, 35, 45, 88, 133, 253, 409–16, 430, 447
  advantages 410–11
  crossborder 409, 412–13
  and delay 412
  and domestic violence 415–16
  enforceability 413
  international nature 412
  problems and solutions 412–16
  and voice of child 414–15
mediators 409–12, 414–16
meetings
  Special Commission, see Special Commissions
  with judges 115–16, 376–9, 382–6, 401–2
mental health 69, 75, 281, 284
  primary carers 87–8
Mexico 56, 199, 207
micro level 71, 84–5, 89
Millett approach 321–2
mirror orders 47, 75, 82, 85–6, 88, 135, 278, 289, 294–8, 301, 313, 413, 433, 446
mobility, residential 61, 63, 76–7
money 80–1, 130, 211–12, 341
mothers 54–61, 78–81, 85–90, 150–3, 195–202, 209–14, 283–4, 286–9, 329–33
  abducting 27, 31, 51–2, 57–9, 87, 232, 251, 281, 291, 297, 330, 357, 402
  care 202, 327, 333
  custodial 84, 99, 101, 260
  left-behind 231, 419
  primary carer 2, 59, 303, 410, 440
motivation 9, 54, 56, 73, 78, 82, 90, 101, 318, 396, 427
moving, psychological impact 63
mutual intentions 204, 208
mutual trust 24, 42, 131, 134, 313

narrow approach 155, 168, 229, 235, 240–1, 250, 257, 260, 330–2, 343, 346, 348, 351, 399, 424
narrow interpretation 98–9, 135, 163, 236, 241, 244, 266, 298, 312, 343, 345, 362, 427
national legislation 14–15, 444
national security 25, 122
nationality 18, 36, 56, 146, 170, 177, 194, 360, 364, 412
natural forum 131, 364
natural justice 14, 21, 130
ne exeat rights, *see* rights, to veto removal
negotiations 9, 45, 86, 228, 246, 252–3, 264, 269, 411

Netherlands 7, 12, 40, 45–6, 119, 165, 287–8, 323, 377, 457–9
  courts 127, 155, 287–8
new environment 20–1, 29, 32–3, 111, 196, 220, 225–6, 228–32, 237–8, 242, 244, 276, 286, 299, 336, 348, 439, 453
new habitual residence 20, 178, 188, 195, 215–16
New Zealand 76, 78–9, 81, 88, 151–2, 154, 157, 173, 186, 193, 210, 239, 259, 270, 283, 297, 342, 352, 378, 425
  courts 17, 153–4, 157–8, 164, 193, 208, 228–9, 241, 281, 321, 346, 390, 426
newborn children 201–3
no-discretion approach 233–4, 236, 238–9, 243
non-consensual removals 261
non-contractual obligations 128, 176
non-custodial parents 55–6, 68, 81, 88–9, 148–50, 164, 427–9
non-exercise of custody rights 156, 158–9, 245
non-molestation undertakings 52–3, 88
non-primary carers 56–8, 61, 65, 162, 440–1
  psychological impact of move away from 67–9
non-recognition 21, 32, 154
  partial 171
non-relocating parent 73–5, 85
non-residential parents 79, 125
normative framework 247, 249, 251, 268
Northern Ireland 12, 336
Norway 56, 125, 297
  courts 298

objections, see child's objection
objective approach 190, 352
objective connections 197, 212–13
objective facts 193, 203, 219, 265, 279
objective tests 248–9, 269, 276
objectives 93–4, 96–8, 144–7, 172–4, 183–5; see also promotion of Convention objectives
  hierarchy of 442–3
  of justice 105–6
  private international law 170–1
objectivity 41, 350, 384
operation of Convention 35–53
  institutions and other actors 38–42
  sources of information and statistics 35–8
operation of law 30, 141, 148, 451
origin, country/State of, see country of origin
  domicile of 178, 204, 207

paramountcy 26, 113, 307–8, 310–11, 355–6, 363, 367
parental agreement 217–18, 220
Parental Alienation Syndrome (PAS) 69–70, 276, 332–4, 352, 382
parental intention approach/model 186, 189–97, 199–201, 203–9, 211–14, 216, 219, 221
  United Kingdom 187
  United States 188–9
parental responsibility 2, 19–23, 29–30, 103, 116, 131, 146, 148, 152, 166, 170, 176, 194, 284, 297, 347, 374, 410, 412–13, 431
parental rights 16, 97, 121–5, 132, 156, 174, 204, 206, 211–13, 429
  conflicts with children's rights 124–5
  and custody rights 167–9
  and fundamental human rights and freedoms 366–8
  and grave risk 311–12
  and habitual residence 213–14
  model 186, 207
  scope 123–4
  status 122–3
parental separation 61, 77, 123
parenting 60, 68, 77
  abilities 71, 277
  agreements 201, 218
  plans 154, 440
  shared 76, 119
parents
  abducting, see abducting parents/abductors
  biological 123, 202
  non-residential 79, 125
  relocating 72–6, 78–80, 85, 87–8, 90, 164, 264
  returning 47, 118, 135, 288–9, 291–2, 297, 316
  rights, see parental rights
  taking, see abducting parents/abductors
  unmarried 146, 167, 169
partial information 298, 386
partial non-recognition 171
participation
  child 112, 114–17, 374–5, 379–80, 382–4, 386, 389, 401, 414
  rights 124, 324, 386, 404
  and Art 12 of CRC 113–17
party autonomy 413–14
party status 389–90
PAS, see Parental Alienation Syndrome
passage of time 11, 18, 28, 190, 193, 199, 225, 244, 341, 343, 445, 448
passive acquiescence 248, 262
passports 86, 200
paternalistic approach 325–6, 331, 446
payments 81–2, 90, 413, 417–18, 420, 456
perceptions 54, 57, 75–6, 80, 111, 121, 194, 272, 324, 326, 332, 335, 345, 401, 410, 439
  child's 194, 199, 242, 381
Perez-Vera Report 11, 13, 95–8, 126, 144, 158, 160–1, 163–4, 173, 179, 182, 234–5, 237, 262–3, 273, 300–1, 344–5, 354, 362–3, 421
Permanent Bureau 9, 40–2, 47, 134, 282, 284, 296, 362, 409, 416, 424, 441–2, 447
permanent custody 218, 249
permanent relocations 195–7, 199
permanent separation 17, 285
permission 84–5, 89, 148, 150, 159, 164–5, 200, 249, 275, 288–9, 292, 302, 311, 383, 400, 430, 443
personal relationships 119, 423, 429
personal status 130–1, 169, 216, 366
philosophy 205, 212, 236, 260–1, 299, 343, 361, 369
physical harm 135, 274, 278, 293, 312
Piagetian theory 350
pluralism, cultural 366–7, 369
Poland 212, 214, 239, 241, 397
  courts 239, 403
police 17, 38–40, 43, 47, 211, 297

policy 84–7, 97, 130, 167, 213–18, 235–6, 260–1, 301–2, 314, 320–2, 341–2, 351, 438
  deterrent 239–40
  general 253, 321, 345
possession 15–16, 153–4, 166, 401
potential abductors 96, 99–102, 221, 240, 303
potential harm 115, 239, 273–4, 276, 404
potential inconsistency 33, 306–7, 311
precedence 15, 19, 106, 132, 171–2, 194, 302, 314, 316, 341, 348, 351, 367
predictability 75, 136–7
pressure 58, 252, 331, 333, 378, 384–6
presumptions 74–5, 79–80, 205–7, 321–2
  against relocation 75
  in favour of relocation 74, 77
  rebuttable 137
previous habitual residence 188–9, 195–6, 209
primary attachment relationship 66–7
primary care 56, 65–6, 77, 280
  versus shared care 88
primary carers 56, 58–62, 65–8, 87–8, 98–9, 439–40; see also non-primary carers
  abductors 4, 61–2, 280
  developments since 1980 439–41
  joint 56, 60, 65
  mental health 87–8
  mothers 2, 59, 303, 410, 440
  psychological impact of move away from 65–7
principles
  fundamental 13, 15, 21, 250, 306, 354–6, 359, 361–4, 455
  general 37, 111–12, 267, 296, 429, 431
  private international law, see private international law principles
private international law principles 126–36
  and Art 12(2) 243
  and child's objection 349
  choice of law rules 108, 126–9, 132, 146, 160, 169–70, 178, 444
  and consent/acquiescence 266–7
  and custody rights 169–73
  and fundamental human rights and freedoms 368
  and grave risk 312–14
  jurisdiction rules 103, 108, 126–7, 130–1
privileged conversations 250
proceedings, see also compatibility with summary nature of Convention proceedings
  Abduction Convention, 26, 31, 50–1, 53, 69, 104–6, 116, 132, 171, 271, 285, 377, 389, 391, 398, 402–3, 412, 421–2, 438–9
  commencement 8, 10–11, 111, 226, 228–9, 286, 299, 405, 453
  criminal 17, 31, 43, 47, 99, 233, 275, 291, 294, 419, 422, 438
  custody 46–7, 105, 239, 247, 289, 292, 443
  divorce 32, 248, 289, 398
  duration 36–7
  substantive 259–60, 443
  summary 166, 397
promotion of Convention objectives 96–106
  access rights 428–9
  Art 12(2) 237–42

child's objection 345–8
consent/acquiescence 263–5
custody rights 161–5
fundamental human rights and freedoms 363–5
grave risk 301–5
habitual residence 207–11
retention 144–5
prompt return 9–10, 38, 45, 62, 96–7, 181–2, 299, 301, 343, 423, 451–2
proportionality 25, 311, 356, 359–60, 364, 366
prosecution 16–17, 291–2
protection
  adequate 23, 274, 292, 297, 315, 446
  of child 44, 61, 145, 161, 163, 225, 238–9, 268, 302, 442
  effective 54, 68, 438
protective measures 22, 24, 30–1, 51, 62, 87, 271–2, 278, 281, 283–4, 289–303, 305, 313–14, 396, 411, 440, 442, 446, 449
Protocol, call for 441–2
provisional measures 44, 298, 315–16, 452
psychiatrists 297, 375, 384, 388
psychological aspects of abduction 61–70
psychological harm 29, 49, 270–2, 274–6, 280, 284–6, 328, 336, 340–1, 385, 422, 447
  grave risk of 273, 280, 285
psychological impact
  of abduction 64–5
  of move away from non-primary carer 67–9
  of move away from primary carer 65–7
  of moving 63
psychological research 61, 162
public policy 21, 30, 32, 103, 135, 146, 170, 217, 430
  defence/exception 32, 270, 354, 362
punishment 15, 99, 102
  exemplary 101–2
purpose, settled, see settled purpose
purpose of Convention 9–10

ratifications 12–14, 41, 54, 83, 110, 130, 438, 457–9
re-abduction 44, 211, 262
  and habitual residence 203–4
real consent 262, 264
real harm 98, 106, 162, 281, 302, 307, 368
reality testing 77–82, 88–90, 440
reasons for abduction 55–8
reciprocal recognition 9, 18
reciprocity 129–30, 132–4, 136, 172, 217, 243, 267, 290, 312, 349, 361, 447
recognition
  judgments 9, 19, 103, 116, 130–1, 148, 171, 176, 284, 347, 374, 412, 431
  reciprocal 9, 18
  rules 129, 131–2, 135, 171–2
reconciliation(s) 117, 187, 215, 254, 256, 262, 308–9
  attempted 215–16, 251, 307–8
reduced contact 67–8, 77, 400, 417
reforms 21–2, 76, 120
refuge, country/State of, see country of refuge
register/registration 18–19, 43, 151, 168, 255, 285, 413

regular contact 52–3, 67–8, 75, 80, 156, 167, 264–6, 316, 429
reimbursement of expenses 417, 419, 422
relational rights 61, 73, 80, 109, 119
  model 109
relationships 59–61, 70, 76, 109–10, 118–20, 161–5, 403–4
  parent-child 109, 212
  personal 119, 423, 429
  social 192, 194, 231
relevant factors 85, 89, 235, 242, 257–8, 269, 287, 290, 342, 347, 367
relevant information 36, 38, 191, 296, 384, 386, 394, 397, 400, 406
reliance 24, 62, 118, 126, 136, 159, 254, 257, 265, 269, 279, 305, 313, 319, 331, 346, 357–8, 365, 397, 426
  and consent/acquiescence 250–1
  reasonable 269, 445
religious education 122, 124
relocating parent 72–6, 78–80, 85, 87–8, 90, 164, 264
relocation 63, 71–90, 194–9, 207–11, 361, 402
  decisions 72, 78–9, 84–6
  disputes 61, 67, 72–3, 77–8, 81–2, 89, 136, 400
  fixed-term 197–8, 209–10, 214, 219
  for an indefinite period 198–200
  inter-relationship between relocation and abduction 84–90
  law 59, 68, 71–3, 75–9, 81, 83–9, 441
    approaches 72–7
    empirical evidence 77–9
    implications for abduction law 86–90
    implications of abduction law for 84–6
    international harmonisation initiatives 82–4
    scholarly analysis 79–82
  permanent 195–7, 199
  research 77–9
  temporary 214, 216, 218
removal
  consensual 262–3, 266
  date of 142, 181, 227
  lawful 71, 142, 145, 157
  right to veto 58–9, 72, 94, 146, 150, 157, 164
  unilateral 1, 145, 161–2, 164, 172, 174, 187, 236, 301
  unlawful 71, 299, 438
  wrongful, see wrongful removal or retention
renvoi 127, 129, 146, 160, 166, 169–70
reports, expert 106, 272, 278, 305, 377–8, 380, 382, 385
representation 39–40, 45, 104, 267, 269, 289, 374, 420, 426, 456
  separate 49, 116, 243, 335, 375, 388–401, 404–5, 438, 446
requested State 4, 10, 12, 15, 23–4, 43––4, 134–5, 155–6, 172–3, 278, 294–7, 299–301, 313, 356–63, 428, 453–5; see also country of refuge
requesting State, 4, 13, 30–1, 43, 46–7, 51–2, 134–56, 155–6, 278–9, 283–4, 288–9, 291–7, 303, 312–14, 355–68, 443, 453; see also country of origin
requirement to ascertain child's views, see child's views, requirement to ascertain
requisite intention 187, 189–90

research 62–3, 65–8, 76–8, 84–7, 449
  psychological 61, 162
  relocation 88–9
  social science 62, 67–8, 72, 333
  studies 47–8, 62–4, 70, 73, 77–8, 293
reservations 11–12, 18, 40, 266, 296–7, 411, 418, 432, 455–6, 458–9
residence
  actual 176, 195, 202
  habitual, see habitual residence
  orders 143, 148, 195, 403
residential mobility 61, 63, 76–7
responsibility 115, 190, 248, 329, 336, 360, 382, 386–7, 396, 409
  parental 2, 19–23, 29–30, 103, 116, 131, 146, 148, 152, 166, 170, 176, 194, 284, 297, 347, 374, 410, 412–13, 431
restrictive interpretation 273, 306, 313, 354, 364, 368–9, 439
retention
  consistency with intentions of drafters 144
  internal coherence 144
  promotion of Convention objectives 144–5
  unlawful , see unlawful retention
  wrongful, see wrongful removal or retention
return
  applications 1, 26, 36, 39, 45, 56, 161, 404, 412, 423, 425–9, 444
    by child 403–5
  automatic 9, 97
  decisions 71, 85, 116, 284, 383, 431, 433
  expedited 1, 9
  mandatory, see mandatory return
  mechanism 12, 97–9, 122, 310, 438, 440
  orders 10, 21, 23–9, 90, 134, 136, 143–4, 160, 164, 168–9, 256–7, 259–60, 285, 301, 304, 347, 359–61, 365, 388–9, 402–3
    enforcement 47–50
  prompt 9–10, 38, 45, 62, 96–7, 181–2, 299, 301, 343, 423, 451–2
  safe 46–7, 295, 452
  speedy 97, 234, 236, 239, 243, 260, 267, 271
  summary, see summary return
  voluntary 37, 44–5, 252–3, 413, 452–3
returning parent 47, 118, 135, 288–9, 291–2, 297, 316
Reunite Outcomes Study 36–7, 40, 50–3, 57–8, 65, 281, 293
rights
  access, see access, rights
  child's, see child's rights
  to contact with parents 118–20
  custody, see custody rights
  to family life 148, 167
  human, see human rights
  to identity 121, 213
  inchoate 151–2, 157, 163, 165–6, 173–4
  ne exeat 94, 148–9, 158, 160–1, 163–4, 173
  parental, see parental rights
  participation, see participation, rights
  to protection and to survival and development 118
  relational, see relational rights

to veto removal 58–9, 72, 94, 146, 148–50, 157–8, 160–1, 163–4, 173
Romania 26, 45, 48–9, 279, 287–8
Rotlevy Representation Sub-Committee 392–6, 398
rule of law 105, 165, 241, 264, 304
Russia 13

safe harbour orders 294, 301
safe return 295, 452
  measures to ensure 46–7
safeguards 23, 290, 356, 405, 416, 431
safety 44, 46, 57, 213, 282, 295, 299–300, 304, 311–15, 334
schools 65, 193–4, 198–9, 231, 238, 255, 279, 330, 332, 334
Scotland 37, 44–7, 56, 153, 156, 178, 197, 199, 229, 231–2, 249, 281, 285, 293, 327, 335, 337, 339, 376, 424; *see also* United Kingdom
  courts 156, 293
security 63, 86, 162, 229–30, 431, 455
  national 25, 122
  situation 279–80, 284
separate representation 49, 116, 243, 335, 375, 388–405, 438, 446
  arguments against 396–9
  arguments in favour 399–403
  scope of right 392–6
  source of right 391–2
separation 17, 53, 61–2, 65–7, 118, 201, 239, 275, 280–1, 285–6, 302, 312, 325, 331, 339–40, 438, 440
  parental 61, 64, 77, 123
  permanent 17, 285
  potential 286, 302
  of siblings 53, 285–6, 302, 400
settled children 235–6, 238–9, 241–4
settled intention 188, 191, 193, 199, 444
settled purpose 187–9, 192–3, 196–9, 201, 207, 216, 219–20
settlement 11, 24, 105, 189, 203, 212, 225–6, 238–41, 243–4, 262, 299, 341, 343, 402, 405, 443, 445
  defence/exception 228–34, 240, 343, 390, 394, 402
  definition 229–30
  degree of 229–30
  emotional element 231, 242
sexual abuse 23, 273, 276–8, 314
shared care 74, 76–7, 81
  versus primary care 88
shared intention 200, 202
shared parenting 76, 119
Sharia courts 359
short-term interests 303, 309–11, 356, 445
shuttle custody arrangements 200–1, 216–17
siblings 53, 65, 302, 304, 336, 389, 397, 400
  and child's objection 338–41
  non-mature 338, 340
  younger 285–6, 336, 338–9
significant delay 48, 105, 397, 405, 412
significant harm 62, 367–8
social background 44, 257, 271, 375, 452, 454
social environment 98, 191, 208, 331
social relationships 192, 194, 231

social science research 62, 67–8, 72, 333
social workers 46, 218, 350, 375, 377, 379–80, 386, 394
sociological issues 54–61
solitary event 142, 144–5
solutions, agreed 110, 410–11, 430
South Africa 14, 38, 45, 74, 112, 133, 182, 247, 272, 277, 281, 293, 310–11, 331, 342, 355–6, 389, 395, 405
Spain 146, 170, 198, 254, 331, 333, 358
  courts 146, 357–8
Special Commissions 1, 9, 35, 38, 40–2, 45–6, 55–6, 82–3, 87, , 217, 253, 282, 295–6, , 315, 413, 441, 424, 448
stability 77, 102, 130, 161–2, 167, 229–30, 232, 242, 306
stable environment 64–6, 288
stalemate 32, 129
State of habitual residence, *see* country of habitual residence
State of origin, *see* country of origin
State of refuge, *see* country of refuge
statements 10–11, 27, 46, 74, 113, 150, 156, 160, 182, 196, 211, 230, 235, 246–9, 252, 254–5, 264–5, 267, 298, 308
statistics 35–8, 52, 59–60, 133, 425
status 55–6, 95, 122, 130–1, 133, 148, 198, 367, 389, 439, 448
  of child in Abduction Convention proceedings 389–406
  immigration 230, 289
  personal 130–1, 169, 216, 366
status quo 86–7, 96–8, 106, 126, 184–5, 225, 237, 245, 248, 251, 253, 270, 292, 302, 304, 387, 417–18, 427, 448
structure of Abduction Convention 9–12
subjective approach 249–50, 254, 264
subjective intentions 212, 248–9, 255, 269
subjective tests 249–50, 256, 265, 269
substantive proceedings 259–60, 443
sufficient age and maturity 320, 324, 340, 373–5, 378
summary proceedings, *see* compatibility with summary nature of Convention proceedings
summary return 225, 233, 235–6, 238–9, 242–4, 248–9, 251, 255, 257, 263, 309–10, 361
  mechanism 9–10, 28, 236, 365, 367
support financial 259, 288, 292, 418
surveys 51–3, 55–60, 318, 425, 439
Sweden 99, 198, 201, 210, 217–18, 278, 377
  courts 201, 217, 278, 295
Switzerland 27–8, 47–9, 124–5, 153, 184, 192, 277, 281, 287, 315, 331, 341, 356, 360, 389, 405, 409, 441

taking parents, *see* abducting parents/abductors
temporary accommodation 192
temporary relocation 214, 216, 218
territorial units 12, 15, 36–7, 456–9
terrorist attacks 279–80
tests 128, 137, 151, 156–7, 184, 191–4, 230, 263, 269, 276, 285, 322, 328, 348–50, 390, 397–8
  factual 194
  of maturity 324–5

tests (cont):
  objective 248–9, 269, 276
  subjective 249–50, 256, 265, 269
third countries 178–9, 182–5, 202, 205, 444
third parties 112, 123, 156, 383, 404–5
threshold conditions/requirements 159, 163–4, 206, 320, 322, 328, 411, 425
tort law 128, 137, 417, 419–20, 422
tort model 417, 419
trans-frontier contact, *see* cross-frontier contact
transfer of custody 79, 162, 165
transparency 221, 297, 442
trial, fair 358–9, 392
trial periods 189, 198–9, 212
trust, mutual 24, 42, 131, 134, 313
Turkey, courts 357–8

uncertainty 33, 75–6, 137, 145–6, 173, 219–21, 243, 314, 421–2
undertakings 17, 23, 31, 47, 52–3, 59, 87–8, 99, 162, 252, 259, 276–8, 281, 283, 295–6, 298–302, 312–13, 315, 396–7, 402
  action to ensure enforceability 294–5
  enforcement 292, 313
  grave risk 291–4
  non-molestation 52–3, 88
  unenforceable 293, 410
undue influence 332, 334–5, 401
unenforceable undertakings 293, 410
unexecuted agreements 253, 267
unexpressed reservations 191, 193, 195, 197
unilateral removal 1, 145, 161–2, 164, 172, 174, 187, 236, 301
United Kingdom 15, 19, 21, 45, 60, 74, 123, 148, 151, 176–7, 187–90, 202, 206–7, 209–10, 238–9, 260, 310, 339, 394–5, 397–8; *see also* England and Wales; Scotland
  courts 24, 123, 127, 142–3, 145–6, 148, 151, 153, 155, 173, 177, 187, 202, 235, 249–50, 304, 310, 359, 363, 402
  House of Lords/Supreme Court 21, 27–8, 50, 88–9, 98, 105, 123, 135, 142, 145, 147–8, 153, 233, 235, 249–50, 273–4, 310, 359, 390, 402
  parental intention model 187
United Nations Convention on the Rights of the Child 1989 33–4; *see also* Table of Legislation
United States 8–9, 15–16, 33, 63, 122, 132–3, 135–6, 180–2, 188–93, 195–203, 206–8, 216–17, 254, 257–9, 322–4, 327–31, 336–8, 351, 358, 419–21
  courts 95, 135, 148, 156, 164, 173, 186, 201, 208, 212, 221, 227, 292, 294–5, 313, 318, 338, 351, 359–60, 424
  parental intention model 188–9
  State Department 57, 133, 150, 277, 292, 313, 354
unlawful removal 71, 299, 438; *see also* wrongful removal or retention

unlawful retention 157, 206, 218; *see also* wrongful removal or retention
unmarried parents 146, 167, 169
  fathers 126, 147, 157, 162, 167–8, 171, 174, 204
  and custody rights 151–4

very young children 68, 191, 229, 231–2, 319, 346
violence 57, 61–2, 68, 78, 87–8, 101, 136, 162, 183, 239, 266, 273, 275, 280, 282–3, 292–3, 303–4, 314, 415–16, 418
  allegations 273, 282
  domestic, *see* domestic violence
  serious 283, 314
visitation 8, 67–8, 90, 119, 217, 292, 423
voice of child 49, 116, 371–406, 438
  and mediation 414–15
voluntary return 37, 44–5, 252–3, 413, 452–3

waivers 120, 248–50, 255, 261, 266–7, 418–19
war zones 274, 279
welfare
  child's 17–18, 44, 57, 68, 74, 87, 99, 101–2, 117, 123, 130, 162, 233, 238–40, 257–9, 266–7, 306–8, 336–7, 345, 394–6
  considerations 238, 258, 336–7, 405, 426
  long-term 77, 90, 310
  officers 116, 375–6, 381, 383–5, 401, 403
  principle 111–12, 123, 125, 308, 336–7
whereabouts 20, 29, 32, 43, 228, 239, 241, 417, 452–3
wide discretion 86, 137, 263, 267, 421, 426
wide interpretation 10, 134, 157, 164–6, 239, 263–4, 266, 268, 298–9, 346, 351, 355, 364
witnesses 103, 106, 210–11, 265, 315, 359
women 4, 54, 59–60, 78, 213, 282, 314, 359, 411, 415, 439
wrongful removal or retention 3–4, 9–10, 12–13, 15, 20, 23, 29, 31, 141–74, 182–3, 226–7, 236–7, 242–5, 261, 263–4, 427–8, 444, 451, 451–57; *see also* unlawful removal and unlawful retention
  date of 13, 111, 226
  identification 142–4
  and habitual residence 182
  relationship between concepts 142

young children 62, 67–8, 194–6, 232, 280, 324, 345–6, 395, 440
  very 68, 191, 232, 319, 346
younger siblings 285–6, 336, 338–9

Zimbabwe 14, 135, 233–40, 243, 246, 257–8, 260–1, 266–7, 321–2, 336–7, 341, 343, 347, 352, 390, 397, 399, 401–2, 405